The O'Leary Series

Microsoft® Office Excel 2003

Introductory Edition

Timothy J. O'Leary
Arizona State University

Linda I. O'Leary

McGraw-Hill Technology Education

Boston Burr Ridge, IL Dubuque, IA Madison, WI New York San Francisco St. Louis
Bangkok Bogotá Caracas Kuala Lumpur Lisbon London Madrid Mexico City
Milan Montreal New Delhi Santiago Seoul Singapore Sydney Taipei Toronto

Technology Education

MICROSOFT® OFFICE EXCEL 2003, INTRODUCTORY EDITION
Published by McGraw-Hill Technology Education, an imprint of the McGraw-Hill Companies, Inc. 1221 Avenue of the Americas, New York, NY, 10020.

Some ancillaries, including electronic and print components, may not be available to customers outside the United States.

This book is printed on acid-free paper.

2 3 4 5 6 7 8 9 0 QPD/QPD 0 9 8 7 6 5

ISBN 0-07-283568-0

Editor-in-Chief: *Bob Woodbury*
Sponsoring editor: *Don Hull*
Developmental editor: *Jennie Yates*
Marketing manager: *Andy Bernier*
Media producer: *Elizabeth Mavetz*
Project manager: *Jim Labeots*
Manager, new book production: *Heather D. Burbridge*
Coordinator freelance design: *Artemio Ortiz Jr.*
Photo research coordinator: *Ira C. Roberts*
Supplement producer: *Matthew Perry*
Senior digital content specialist: *Brian Nacik*
Cover design: *Asylum Studios*
Interior design: *Artemio Ortiz Jr.*
Typeface: *10.5/13 New Aster*
Compositor: *Rogondino & Associates/Cecelia G. Morales*
Printer: *Quebecor World Dubuque Inc.*

Library of Congress Control Number 2003111994

www.mhhe.com

Technology Education

McGraw-Hill Technology Education

At McGraw-Hill Technology Education, we publish instructional materials for the technology education market—in particular, for computer instruction in post secondary education that ranges from introductory courses in traditional four-year universities to continuing education and proprietary schools. McGraw-Hill Technology Education presents a broad range of innovative products—texts, lab manuals, study guides, testing materials, and technology-based training and assessment tools.

We realize that technology has created and will continue to create new mediums for professors and students to use in managing resources and communicating information to one another. McGraw-Hill Technology Education provides the most flexible and complete teaching and learning tools available and offers solutions to the changing needs of the classroom. McGraw-Hill Technology Education is dedicated to providing the tools for today's instructors and students, which will enable them to successfully navigate the world of Information Technology.

- McGraw-Hill/Osborne—This division of The McGraw-Hill Companies is known for its best-selling Internet titles, Harley Hahn's *Internet & Web Yellow Pages* and the *Internet Complete Reference*. For more information, visit Osborne at www.osborne.com.
- Digital Solutions—Whether you want to teach a class online or just post your "bricks-n-mortar" class syllabus, McGraw-Hill Technology Education is committed to publishing digital solutions. Taking your course online doesn't have to be a solitary adventure, nor does it have to be a difficult one. We offer several solutions that will allow you to enjoy all the benefits of having your course material online.
- Packaging Options—For more information about our discount options, contact your McGraw-Hill Sales representative at 1-800-338-3987 or visit our website at **www.mhhe.com/it**.

McGraw-Hill Technology Education is dedicated to providing
the tools for today's instructors and students.

What does this logo mean?

It means this courseware has been approved by the Microsoft® Office Specialist Program to be among the finest available for learning _Microsoft Office Word 2003, Microsoft Office Excel 2003, Microsoft Office Access 2003_, and _Microsoft Office PowerPoint 2003_. It also means that upon completion of this courseware, you may be prepared to take an exam for Microsoft Office Specialist qualification.

What is a Microsoft Office Specialist?

A Microsoft Office Specialist is an individual who has passed exams for certifying his or her skills in one or more of the Microsoft Office desktop applications such as Microsoft Word, Microsoft Excel, Microsoft PowerPoint, Microsoft Outlook, Microsoft Access, or Microsoft Project. The Microsoft Office Specialist Program typically offers certification exams at the "Specialist" and "Expert" skill levels.* The Microsoft Office Specialist Program is the only program in the world approved by Microsoft for testing proficiency in Microsoft Office desktop applications and Microsoft Project. This testing program can be a valuable asset in any job search or career advancement.

More Information:

To learn more about becoming a Microsoft Office Specialist, visit www.microsoft.com/officespecialist

To learn about other Microsoft Office Specialist approved courseware from McGraw-Hill Technology Education, visit http://www.mhhe.com/catalogs/irwin/it/mous/index.mhtml

---

* The availability of Microsoft Office Specialist certification exams varies by application, application version and language. Visit www.microsoft.com/officespecialist for exam availability.

Who benefits from Microsoft Office Specialist certification?

Employers
Microsoft Office Specialist certification helps satisfy employers' needs for qualitative assessments of employees' skills. Training, coupled with Microsoft Office Specialist certification, offers organizations of every size the ability to enhance productivity and efficiency by enabling their employees to unlock many advanced and laborsaving features in Microsoft Office applications. Microsoft Office Specialist certification can ultimately improve the bottom line.

Employees
Microsoft Office Specialist certification demonstrates employees' productivity and competence in Microsoft Office applications, the most popular business applications in the world. Achieving Microsoft Office Specialist certification verifies that employees have the confidence and ability to use Microsoft Office applications in meeting and exceeding their work challenges.

Instructors
Microsoft Office Specialist certification validates instructors' knowledge and skill in using Microsoft Office applications. It serves as a valuable credential, demonstrating their potential to teach students these essential applications. The Microsoft Office Specialist Authorized Instructor program is also available to those who wish to further demonstrate their instructional capabilities.

Students
Microsoft Office Specialist certification distinguishes students from their peers. It demonstrates their efficiency in completing assignments and projects, leaving more time for other studies. Improved confidence toward meeting new challenges and obstacles is yet another benefit. Achieving Microsoft Office Specialist certification gives students the marketable skills necessary to set them apart in the competitive job market.

To learn more about becoming a Microsoft Office Specialist, visit www.microsoft.com/officespecialist

To purchase a Microsoft Office Specialist certification exam, visit www.DesktopIQ.com

---

Brief Contents

Labs

Detailed Contents

Acknowledgments

The new edition of The O'Leary Series has been made possible only through the enthusiasm and dedication of a great team of people. Because the team spans the country, literally from coast to coast, we have utilized every means of working together including conference calls, FAX, e-mail, and document collaboration. We have truly tested the team approach and it works!

Leading the team from McGraw-Hill are Don Hull, Sponsoring Editor, and Jennie Yates, Developmental Editor. Their renewed commitment, direction, and support have infused the team with the excitement of a new project.

The production staff is headed by James Labeots, Project Manager, whose planning and attention to detail has made it possible for us to successfully meet a very challenging schedule. Members of the production team include: Artemio Ortiz, Designer; Pat Rogondino and Cecelia Morales, Compositors; Susan Defosset, Copy Editor; Heather Burbridge, Production Supervisor; Matthew Perry, Supplement Coordinator; and Elizabeth Mavetz, Media Producer. We would particularly like to thank Pat, Cecelia, and Susan—team members for many past editions whom we can always depend on to do a great job.

Finally, we are particularly grateful to a small but very dedicated group of people who helped us develop the manuscript. Colleen Hayes, Susan Demar, and Kathy Duggan have helped on the last several editions and continue to provide excellent developmental support. To Steve Willis, Carol Cooper, and Sarah Martin who provide technical expertise, youthful perspective, and enthusiasm, our thanks for helping get the manuscripts out the door and meeting the deadlines.

Preface

Introduction

The 20th century not only brought the dawn of the Information Age, but also rapid changes in information technology. There is no indication that this rapid rate of change will be slowing—it may even be increasing. As we begin the 21st century, computer literacy will undoubtedly become prerequisite for whatever career a student chooses. The goal of the O'Leary Series is to assist students in attaining the necessary skills to efficiently use these applications. Equally important is the goal to provide a foundation for students to readily and easily learn to use future versions of this software. This series does this by providing detailed step-by-step instructions combined with careful selection and presentation of essential concepts.

About the Authors

Tim and Linda O'Leary live in the American Southwest and spend much of their time engaging instructors and students in conversation about learning. In fact, they have been talking about learning for more than 25 years. Something in those early conversations convinced them to write a book, to bring their interest in the learning process to the printed page. Today, they are as concerned as ever about learning, about technology, and about the challenges of presenting material in new ways, both in terms of content and the method of delivery.

A powerful and creative team, Tim combines his years of classroom teaching experience with Linda's background as a consultant and corporate trainer. Tim has taught courses at Stark Technical College in Canton, Ohio, Rochester Institute of Technology in upper New York state, and is currently a professor at Arizona State University in Tempe, Arizona. Tim and Linda have talked to and taught students from ages 8 to 80, all of them with a desire to learn something about computers and the applications that make their lives easier, more interesting, and more productive.

About the Book

Times are changing, technology is changing, and this text is changing, too. Do you think the students of today are different from yesterday? There is no doubt about it—they are. On the positive side, it is amazing how much effort students will put toward things they are convinced are relevant to them. Their effort directed at learning application programs and exploring the Web seems at times limitless. On the other hand, students can often be shortsighted, thinking that learning the skills to use the application is the only objective. The mission of the series is to build upon and extend this interest by not only teaching the specific application skills but by introducing the concepts that are common to all applications, providing students with the confidence, knowledge, and ability to easily learn the next generation of applications.

Same Great Features as the Office XP Edition with some new additions!

- **Introduction to Computer Essentials**—A brief introduction to the basics of computer hardware and software (appears in Office Volume I only).
- New **Introduction to Outlook**—A lab devoted to Microsoft Office Outlook 2003 basics (appears in Office Volume I only).
- **Introduction to Microsoft Office 2003**—Presents an overview to the Microsoft Office 2003 components: Office Word, Excel, Access, PowerPoint, and Outlook. Includes a hands-on section that introduces the features that are common to all Office 2003 applications, including using menus, task panes, and the Office Help system.
- **Lab Organization**—The lab text is organized to include main and subtopic heads by grouping related tasks. For example, tasks such as changing fonts and applying character effects appear under the "Formatting" topic head. This results in a slightly more reference-like approach, making it easier for students to refer back to the text to review. This has been done without losing the logical and realistic development of the case.
- **Relevant Cases**—Four separate running cases demonstrate the features in each application. Topics are of interest to students—At Arizona State University, over 600 students were surveyed to find out what topics are of interest to them.
- **Focus on Concepts**—Each lab focuses on the concepts behind the application. Students learn the concepts, so they can succeed regardless of the software package they might be using. The concepts are previewed at the beginning of each lab and summarized at the end of each lab.
- All **Numbered Steps** and bullets appear in left margin space making it easy not to miss a step.
- **Clarified Marginal Notes**—Marginal notes have been enhanced by more clearly identifying the note content with box heads and the use of different colors.

  Additional Information—Brief asides with expanded discussion of features.

  Having Trouble?—Procedural tips advising students of possible problems and how to overcome them.

  Another Method—Alternative methods of performing a procedure.

- **Focus on Careers**—A new feature, appearing at the end of each lab, which provides an example of how the material covered may be applied in the "real world."
- A **Microsoft Office Specialist Skills** table, appearing at the end of each lab, contains page references to Microsoft Office Specialist skills learned in the lab.
- **End-of-Chapter Material**
    - Screen Identification (appears in the first lab of each application)
    - Matching
    - Multiple Choice
    - Fill-In
    - True/False

    Hands-On Practice Exercises—Students apply the skills and concepts they learned to solve case-based exercises. Many cases in the practice exercises tie to a running case used in another application lab. This helps to demonstrate the use of the four applications across a common case setting. For example, the Adventure Travel Tours case used in the Word labs is continued in practice exercises in Excel, Access, and PowerPoint.

    - Step-by-Step
    - On Your Own
- **Rating System**—The 3-star rating system identifies the difficulty level of each practice exercise in the end-of-lab materials.

rating system
★ Easy
★★ Moderate
★★★ Difficult

- **Continuing Exercises**—A continuing exercise icon identifies exercises that build off of exercises completed in earlier labs.
- **Working Together Labs**—At the completion of the brief and introductory texts, a final lab demonstrates the integration of the MS Office applications.
- **References**

    Command Summary—Provides a table of all commands used in the labs.

    Glossary of Key Terms—Includes definitions for all bolded terms used in the labs and included in the Key Terms list at the end of each lab.

    Data File List—Helps organize all data and solution files.

    Microsoft Office Specialist Certification Guide—Links all Microsoft Office Specialist objectives to text content and end-of-chapter exercises.

Instructor's Guide

We understand that, in today's teaching environment, offering a textbook alone is not sufficient to meet the needs of the many instructors who use our books. To teach effectively, instructors must have a full complement of supplemental resources to assist them in every facet of teaching from preparing for class, to conducting a lecture, to assessing students' comprehension. ***The O'Leary Series*** offers a fully-integrated supplements package and Web site, as described below.

Instructor's Resource Kit

The **Instructor's Resource Kit** contains a computerized Test Bank, an Instructor's Manual, and PowerPoint Presentation Slides. Features of the Instructor's Resource Kit are described below.

- **Instructor's Manual** The Instructor's Manual contains lab objectives, concepts, outlines, lecture notes, and command summaries. Also included are answers to all end-of chapter material, tips for covering difficult materials, additional exercises, and a schedule showing how much time is required to cover text material.
- **Computerized Test Bank** The test bank contains over 1,300 multiple choice, true/false, and discussion questions. Each question will be accompanied by the correct answer, the level of learning difficulty, and corresponding page references. Our flexible Diploma software allows you to easily generate custom exams.
- **PowerPoint Presentation Slides** The presentation slides will include lab objectives, concepts, outlines, text figures, and speaker's notes. Also included are bullets to illustrate key terms and FAQs.

Online Learning Center/Web Site

Found at **www.mhhe.com/oleary**, this site provides additional learning and instructional tools to enhance the comprehension of the text. The OLC/Web Site is divided into these three areas:

- **Information Center** Contains core information about the text, supplements, and the authors.
- **Instructor Center** Offers instructional materials, downloads, and other relevant links for professors.
- **Student Center** Contains data files, chapter competencies, chapter concepts, self-quizzes, flashcards, additional Web links, and more.

Skills Assessment

SimNet (Simulated Network Assessment Product) provides a way for you to test students' software skills in a simulated environment.

- Pre-testing options
- Post-testing options
- Course placement testing
- Diagnostic capabilities to reinforce skills
- Proficiency testing to measure skills
- Web or LAN delivery of tests.
- Computer-based training tutorials

For more information on skills assessment software, please contact your local sales representative, or visit us at **www.mhhe.com/it**.

Digital Solutions to Help You Manage Your Course

PageOut is our Course Web Site Development Center that offers a syllabus page, URL, McGraw-Hill Online Learning Center content, online exercises and quizzes, gradebook, discussion board, and an area for student Web pages.

Available free with any McGraw-Hill Technology Education product, PageOut requires no prior knowledge of HTML, no long hours of coding, and a way for course coordinators and professors to provide a full-course Web site. PageOut offers a series of templates—simply fill them with your course information and click on one of 16 designs. The process takes under an hour and leaves you with a professionally designed Web site. We'll even get you started with sample Web sites, or enter your syllabus for you! PageOut is so straightforward and intuitive, it's little wonder why over 12,000 college professors are using it. For more information, visit the PageOut Web site at www.pageout.net.

Online courses are also available. Online Learning Centers (OLCs) are your perfect solutions for Internet-based content. Simply put, these Centers are "digital cartridges" that contain a book's pedagogy and supplements. As students read the book, they can go online and take self-grading quizzes or work through interactive exercises. These also provide students appropriate access to lecture materials and other key supplements.

Online Learning Centers can be delivered through any of these platforms:

- Blackboard.com
- WebCT (a product of Universal Learning Technology)

McGraw-Hill has partnerships with WebCT and Blackboard to make it even easier to take your course online. Now you can have McGraw-Hill content delivered through the leading Internet-based learning tool for higher education.

Computing Concepts

Computing Essentials 2004 and ***Computing Today*** offer a unique, visual orientation that gives students a basic understanding of computing concepts. *Computing Essentials* and *Computing Today* are some of the few books on the market that are written by a professor who still teaches the courses every semester and loves it. The books encourage "active" learning with their exercises, explorations, visual illustrations, and inclusion of screen shots and numbered steps. While combining the "active" learning style with current topics and technology, these texts provide an accurate snapshot of computing trends. When bundled with software application lab manuals, students are given a complete representation of the fundamental issues surrounding the personal computing environment.

Select features of these texts include:

- **Using Technology**—Engaging coverage of hot, high-interest topics, such as phone calls via the Internet, using the Internet remotely with a Personal Digital Assistant (PDA), and Client and Server operating systems. These Web-related projects direct the student to explore current popular uses of technology.
- **Expanding Your Knowledge**—Geared for those who want to go into greater depth on a specific topic introduced within the chapter. These projects meet the needs of instructors wanting more technical depth of coverage.
- **Building Your Portfolio**—Develops critical thinking and writing skills while students examine security, privacy, and ethical issues in technology. By completing these exercises, students will be able to walk away from the class with something to show prospective employers.
- **Making IT Work for You**—Based on student surveys, *Computing Essentials* identified several special interest topics and devoted a two-page section on each in the corresponding chapter. Making IT Work for You sections engage students by presenting high interest topics that directly relate to the concepts presented in the chapter. Topics include downloading music from the Internet, creating personal Web sites, and using the Internet to make long-distance phone calls. Many of these are supported by short video presentations that will be available via CD and the Web.
- **On the Web Explorations**—Appear throughout the margins of the text and encourage students to go to the Web to visit several informative and established sites in order to learn more about the chapter's featured topic.
- **A Look to the Future Sections**—Provide insightful information about the future impact of technology and forecasts of how upcoming enhancements in the world of computing will play an important and powerful role in society.
- **End-of-Chapter Material**—A variety of material including objective questions (key terms, matching, multiple choice, and short answer completion) and critical thinking activities. This will help to reinforce the information just learned.

STUDENT'S GUIDE

As you begin each lab, take a few moments to read the **Case Study** and the Concept Preview. The case study introduces a real-life setting that is interwoven throughout the entire lab, providing the basis for understanding the use of the application. Also, notice the Additional Information, Having Trouble?, and Another Method boxes scattered throughout the book. These tips provide more information about related topics, help get you out of trouble if you are having problems, and offer suggestions on other ways to perform the same task. Finally, read the text between the steps. You will find the few minutes more it takes you is well worth the time when you are completing the practice exercises.

Many learning aids are built into the text to ensure your success with the material and to make the process of learning rewarding. The pages that follow call your attention to the key features in the text.

Objectives

Appear at the beginning of the lab and identify the main features you will be learning.

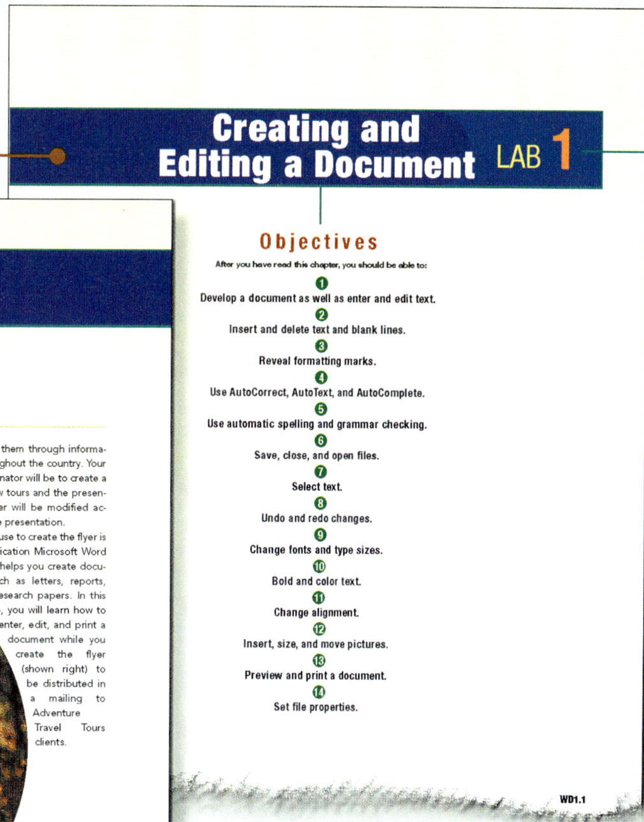
Creating and Editing a Document LAB 1

Objectives

After you have read this chapter, you should be able to:

1. Develop a document as well as enter and edit text.
2. Insert and delete text and blank lines.
3. Reveal formatting marks.
4. Use AutoCorrect, AutoText, and AutoComplete.
5. Use automatic spelling and grammar checking.
6. Save, close, and open files.
7. Select text.
8. Undo and redo changes.
9. Change fonts and type sizes.
10. Bold and color text.
11. Change alignment.
12. Insert, size, and move pictures.
13. Preview and print a document.
14. Set file properties.

WD1.1

Case Study

Introduces a real-life setting that is interwoven throughout the lab, providing the basis for understanding the use of the application.

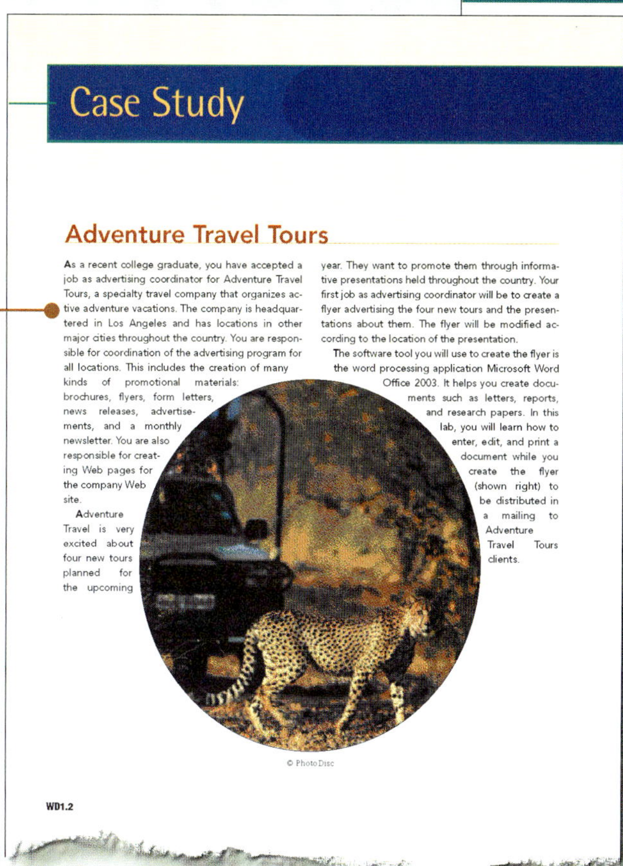
Case Study

Adventure Travel Tours

As a recent college graduate, you have accepted a job as advertising coordinator for Adventure Travel Tours, a specialty travel company that organizes active adventure vacations. The company is headquartered in Los Angeles and has locations in other major cities throughout the country. You are responsible for coordination of the advertising program for all locations. This includes the creation of many kinds of promotional materials: brochures, flyers, form letters, news releases, advertisements, and a monthly newsletter. You are also responsible for creating Web pages for the company Web site.

Adventure Travel is very excited about four new tours planned for the upcoming year. They want to promote them through informative presentations held throughout the country. Your first job as advertising coordinator will be to create a flyer advertising the four new tours and the presentations about them. The flyer will be modified according to the location of the presentation.

The software tool you will use to create the flyer is the word processing application Microsoft Word Office 2003. It helps you create documents such as letters, reports, and research papers. In this lab, you will learn how to enter, edit, and print a document while you create the flyer (shown right) to be distributed in a mailing to Adventure Travel Tours clients.

© PhotoDisc

WD1.2

• Objectives, Case Study
• Concept Preview, Another Method, Having Trouble?

Concept Preview
Provides an overview to the concepts that will be presented throughout the lab.

Another Method
Offers additional ways to perform a procedure.

Having Trouble?
Helps resolve potential problems as you work through each lab.

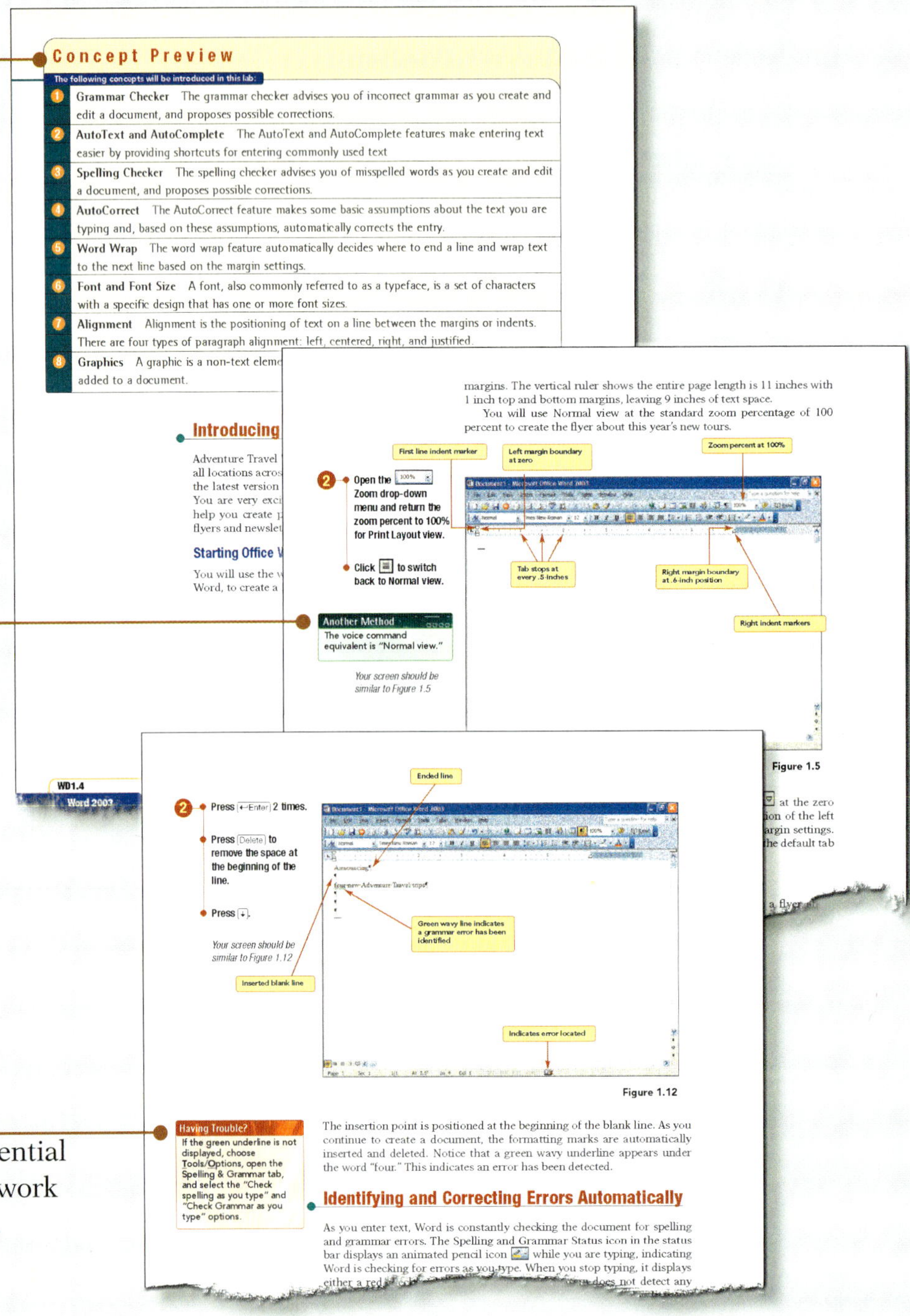

• Numbered and Bulleted Steps, Additional Information

Numbered and Bulleted Steps

Provide clear Step-by-Step Instructions on how to complete a task, or series of tasks.

Additional Information

Offers brief asides with expanded coverage of content.

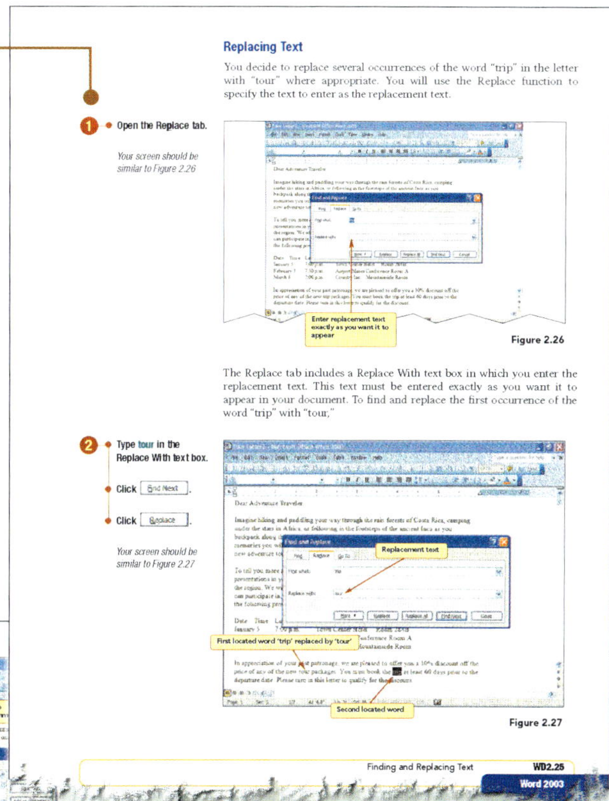

Replacing Text

You decide to replace several occurrences of the word "trip" in the letter with "tour" where appropriate. You will use the Replace function to specify the text to enter as the replacement text.

1 • Open the Replace tab.

Your screen should be similar to Figure 2.26

Figure 2.26

The Replace tab includes a Replace With text box in which you enter the replacement text. This text must be entered exactly as you want it to appear in your document. To find and replace the first occurrence of the word "trip" with "tour,"

2 • Type tour in the Replace With text box.

• Click Find Next.

• Click Replace.

Your screen should be similar to Figure 2.27

Figure 2.27

Finding and Replacing Text WD2.25

Word 2003

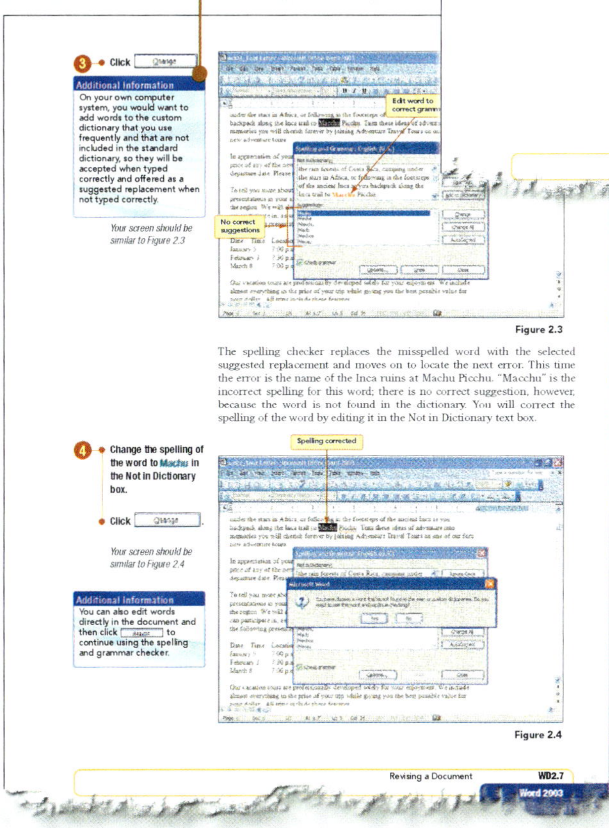

3 • Click Change.

Additional Information

On your own computer system, you would want to add words to the custom dictionary that you use frequently and that are not included in the standard dictionary, so they will be accepted when typed correctly and offered as a suggested replacement when not typed correctly.

Your screen should be similar to Figure 2.3

Figure 2.3

The spelling checker replaces the misspelled word with the selected suggested replacement and moves on to locate the next error. This time the error is the name of the Inca ruins at Machu Picchu. "Macchu" is the incorrect spelling for this word; there is no correct suggestion, however, because the word is not found in the dictionary. You will correct the spelling of the word by editing it in the Not in Dictionary text box.

4 • Change the spelling of the word to Machu in the Not in Dictionary box.

• Click Change.

Your screen should be similar to Figure 2.4

Additional Information

You can also edit words directly in the document and then click Resume to continue using the spelling and grammar checker.

Figure 2.4

Revising a Document WD2.7

Word 2003

Figures and Callouts, Tables

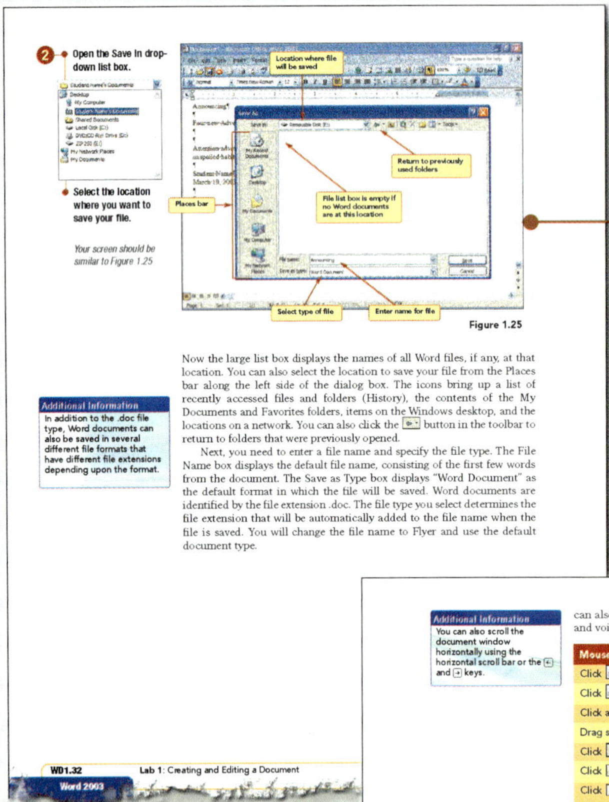

2 Open the Save In drop-down list box.

Select the location where you want to save your file.

Your screen should be similar to Figure 1.25

Figure 1.25

Additional Information
In addition to the .doc file type, Word documents can also be saved in several different file formats that have different file extensions depending upon the format.

Now the large list box displays the names of all Word files, if any, at that location. You can also select the location to save your file from the Places bar along the left side of the dialog box. The icons bring up a list of recently accessed files and folders (History), the contents of the My Documents and Favorites folders, items on the Windows desktop, and the locations on a network. You can also click the button in the toolbar to return to folders that were previously opened.

Next, you need to enter a file name and specify the file type. The File Name box displays the default file name, consisting of the first few words from the document. The Save as Type box displays "Word Document" as the default format in which the file will be saved. Word documents are identified by the file extension .doc. The file type you select determines the file extension that will be automatically added to the file name when the file is saved. You will change the file name to Flyer and use the default document type.

WD1.32 Word 2003 Lab 1: Creating and Editing a Document

Figures and Callouts

Show how your screen should look at the completion of a step with callouts identifying the important changes.

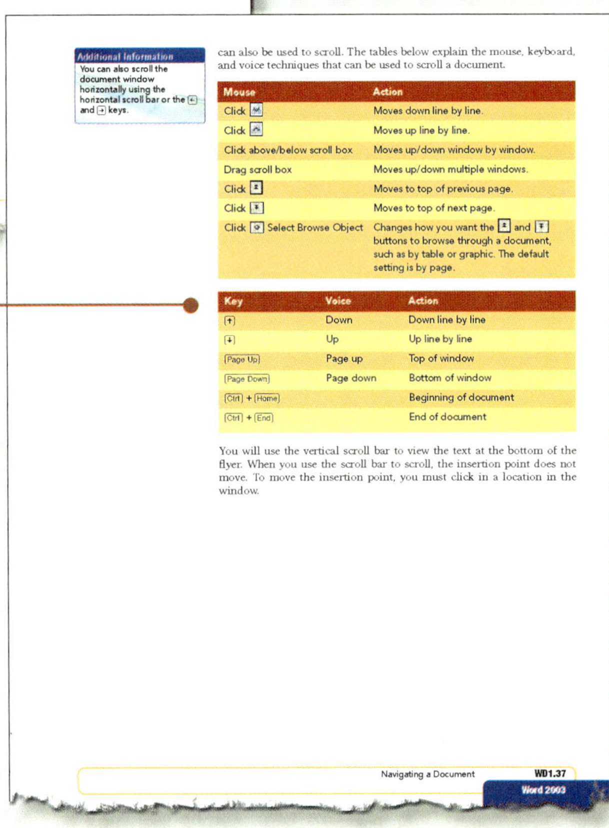

Additional Information
You can also scroll the document window horizontally using the horizontal scroll bar or the ← and → keys.

can also be used to scroll. The tables below explain the mouse, keyboard, and voice techniques that can be used to scroll a document.

Mouse	Action
Click	Moves down line by line.
Click	Moves up line by line.
Click above/below scroll box	Moves up/down window by window.
Drag scroll box	Moves up/down multiple windows.
Click	Moves to top of previous page.
Click	Moves to top of next page.
Click Select Browse Object	Changes how you want the and buttons to browse through a document, such as by table or graphic. The default setting is by page.

Key	Voice	Action
↑	Down	Down line by line
↓	Up	Up line by line
Page Up	Page up	Top of window
Page Down	Page down	Bottom of window
Ctrl + Home		Beginning of document
Ctrl + End		End of document

You will use the vertical scroll bar to view the text at the bottom of the flyer. When you use the scroll bar to scroll, the insertion point does not move. To move the insertion point, you must click in a location in the window.

Navigating a Document WD1.37 Word 2003

Tables

Provide quick summaries of toolbar buttons, key terms, and procedures for specific tasks.

Focus on Careers, Concept Summary

You have completed adding the properties to the document. Not until the file is saved are the new properties you added saved with the file. Because you have finished working on the flyer for now, you will exit the application and save the file at the same time.

4 Click OK.

Exiting Word

The Exit command in the File menu is used to quit the Word program. Alternatively, you can click the Close button in the application window title bar. If you attempt to close the application without first saving your document, Word displays a warning asking if you want to save your work. If you do not save your work and you exit the application, any changes you made since last saving it are lost.

1 Click Close.

Click Yes to save the changes you made to the file.

The Windows desktop is visible again.

Focus on Careers

EXPLORE YOUR CAREER OPTIONS

Food Service Manager

Have you noticed flyers around your campus advertising job positions? Many of these jobs are in the food service industry. Food service managers are traditionally responsible for overseeing the kitchen and dining room. However, these positions increasingly involve administrative tasks, including recruiting new employees. As a food service manager your position would likely include creating newspaper notices and flyers to attract new staff. These flyers should be eye-catching and be error free. The typical salary range of a food service manager is $24,000 to $41,000. Demand for skilled food service managers is expected to increase through 2010.

Exiting Word

Concept Summary

Offers a visual summary of the concepts presented throughout the lab.

Focus on Careers

Provides an example of how the material covered may be applied in the "real world."

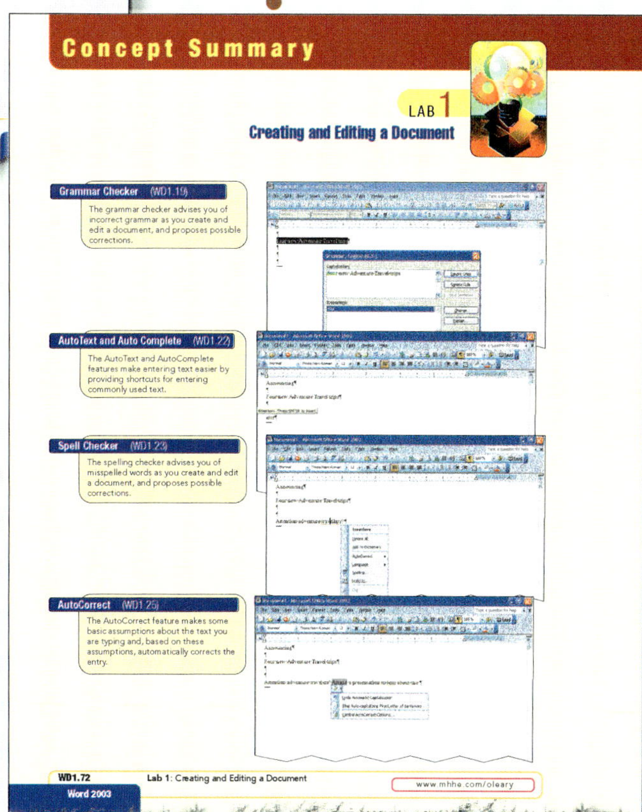
Concept Summary

LAB 1

Creating and Editing a Document

Grammar Checker (WD1.19)

The grammar checker advises you of incorrect grammar as you create and edit a document, and proposes possible corrections.

AutoText and Auto Complete (WD1.22)

The AutoText and AutoComplete features make entering text easier by providing shortcuts for entering commonly used text.

Spell Checker (WD1.23)

The spelling checker advises you of misspelled words as you create and edit a document, and proposes possible corrections.

AutoCorrect (WD1.25)

The AutoCorrect feature makes some basic assumptions about the text you are typing and, based on these assumptions, automatically corrects the entry.

WD1.72 Word 2003 Lab 1: Creating and Editing a Document www.mhhe.com/oleary

• Key Terms and Microsoft Office Specialist Skills, Command Summary

Key Terms and Microsoft Office Specialist Skills

Includes a list of all bolded terms with page references and a table showing the Microsoft Office Specialist certification skills that were covered in the lab.

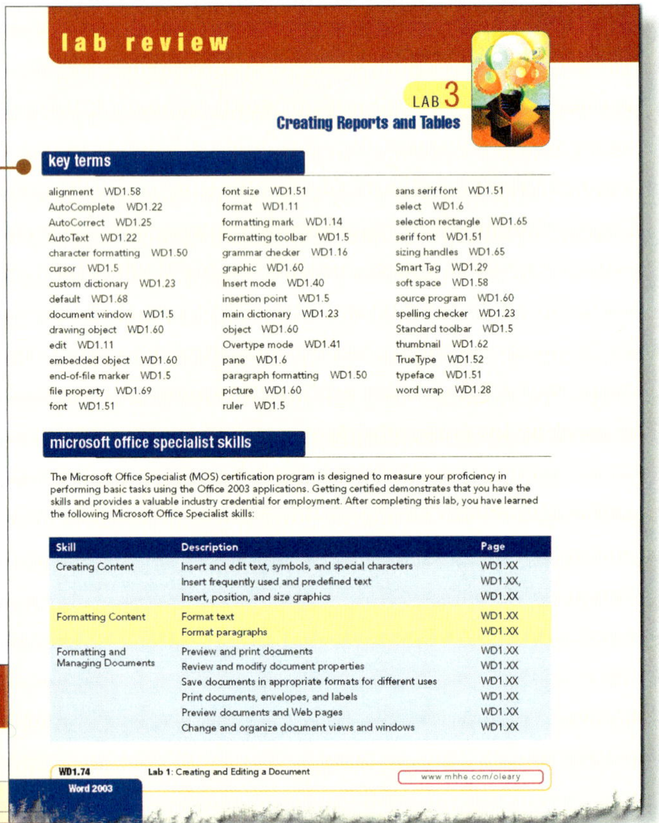

lab review

LAB 3

Creating Reports and Tables

key terms

alignment WD1.58
AutoComplete WD1.22
AutoCorrect WD1.25
AutoText WD1.22
character formatting WD1.50
cursor WD1.5
custom dictionary WD1.23
default WD1.68
document window WD1.5
drawing object WD1.60
edit WD1.11
embedded object WD1.60
end-of-file marker WD1.5
file property WD1.69
font WD1.51
font size WD1.51
format WD1.11
formatting mark WD1.14
Formatting toolbar WD1.5
grammar checker WD1.16
graphic WD1.60
Insert mode WD1.40
insertion point WD1.5
main dictionary WD1.23
object WD1.60
Overtype mode WD1.41
pane WD1.6
paragraph formatting WD1.50
picture WD1.60
ruler WD1.5
sans serif font WD1.51
select WD1.6
selection rectangle WD1.65
serif font WD1.51
sizing handles WD1.65
Smart Tag WD1.29
soft space WD1.58
source program WD1.60
spelling checker WD1.23
Standard toolbar WD1.5
thumbnail WD1.62
TrueType WD1.52
typeface WD1.51
word wrap WD1.28

microsoft office specialist skills

The Microsoft Office Specialist (MOS) certification program is designed to measure your proficiency in performing basic tasks using the Office 2003 applications. Getting certified demonstrates that you have the skills and provides a valuable industry credential for employment. After completing this lab, you have learned the following Microsoft Office Specialist skills:

Skill	Description	Page
Creating Content	Insert and edit text, symbols, and special characters	WD1.XX
	Insert frequently used and predefined text	WD1.XX,
	Insert, position, and size graphics	WD1.XX
Formatting Content	Format text	WD1.XX
	Format paragraphs	WD1.XX
Formatting and Managing Documents	Preview and print documents	WD1.XX
	Review and modify document properties	WD1.XX
	Save documents in appropriate formats for different uses	WD1.XX
	Print documents, envelopes, and labels	WD1.XX
	Preview documents and Web pages	WD1.XX
	Change and organize document views and windows	WD1.XX

WD1.74 Word 2003 Lab 1: Creating and Editing a Document www.mhhe.com/oleary

Command Summary

Provides a table of commands and keyboard and toolbar shortcuts for all commands used in the lab.

command summary

Command	Shortrtcut Key	Button	Voice	Action
File/Page Setup				Changes layout of page including margins, paper size, and paper source
File/Versions				Saves, opens, and deletes document versions
Edit/Cut	Ctrl + X		Cut	Cuts selection to Clipboard
Edit/Copy	Ctrl + C		Copy	Copies selection to Clipboard
Edit/Paste	Ctrl + V		Paste	Pastes item from Clipboard
Edit/Find	Ctrl + F			Locates specified text
Edit/Replace	Ctrl + H			Locates and replaces specified text
Insert/Break/Page break	Ctrl + ←Enter			Inserts hard page break
Insert/Date and Time				Inserts current date or time, maintained by computer system, in selected format
Insert/AutoText				Enters predefined text
Insert/AutoText/AutoText				Create new AutoText entries
Insert/Picture/AutoShapes		AutoShapes		Inserts selected AutoShape
Format/Font/Font/Underline style/Single	Ctrl + U			Underlines selected text with a single line
Format/Paragraph/Indents and Spacing/Special/First Line				Indents first line of paragraph from left margin
Format/Paragraph/Indents and Spacing/Line Spacing	Ctrl + #			Changes amount of white space between lines
Format/Bullets and Numbering				Creates a bulleted or numbered list
Format /Tabs				Specifies types and position of tab stops
Format/Styles and Formatting				Displays the Styles and Formatting Task pane

Lab Review WD2.71 Word 2003

• Lab Exercises: Screen Identification, Matching, Multiple Choice, True/False, Fill-in

Lab Exercises

Reinforce the terminology and concepts presented in the lab through Screen Identification, Matching, Multiple Choice, True/False, and Fill-in questions.

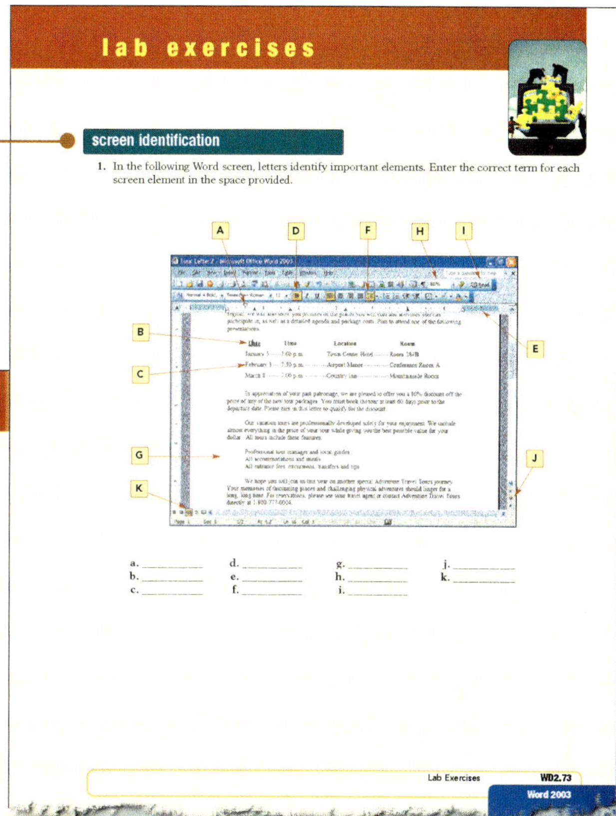

lab exercises

screen identification

1. In the following Word screen, letters identify important elements. Enter the correct term for each screen element in the space provided.

A D F H I B C E G J K

a. __________ d. __________ g. __________ j. __________
b. __________ e. __________ h. __________ k. __________
c. __________ f. __________ i. __________

Lab Exercises WD2.73
Word 2003

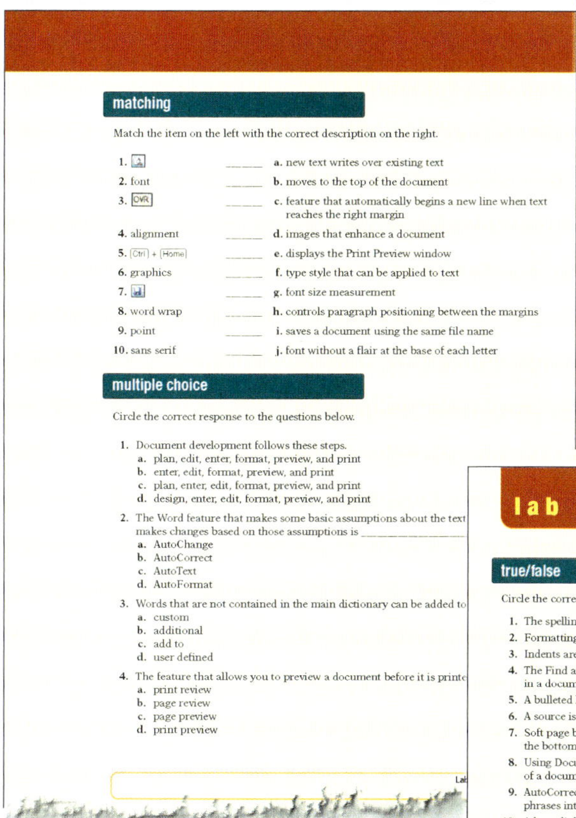

matching

Match the item on the left with the correct description on the right.

1. [button] ______ a. new text writes over existing text
2. font ______ b. moves to the top of the document
3. OVR ______ c. feature that automatically begins a new line when text reaches the right margin
4. alignment ______ d. images that enhance a document
5. Ctrl + Home ______ e. displays the Print Preview window
6. graphics ______ f. type style that can be applied to text
7. [button] ______ g. font size measurement
8. word wrap ______ h. controls paragraph positioning between the margins
9. point ______ i. saves a document using the same file name
10. sans serif ______ j. font without a flair at the base of each letter

multiple choice

Circle the correct response to the questions below.

1. Document development follows these steps.
   a. plan, edit, enter, format, preview, and print
   b. enter, edit, format, preview, and print
   c. plan, enter, edit, format, preview, and print
   d. design, enter, edit, format, preview, and print
2. The Word feature that makes some basic assumptions about the text makes changes based on those assumptions is ____________
   a. AutoChange
   b. AutoCorrect
   c. AutoText
   d. AutoFormat
3. Words that are not contained in the main dictionary can be added to
   a. custom
   b. additional
   c. add to
   d. user defined
4. The feature that allows you to preview a document before it is printe
   a. print review
   b. page review
   c. page preview
   d. print preview

Lab

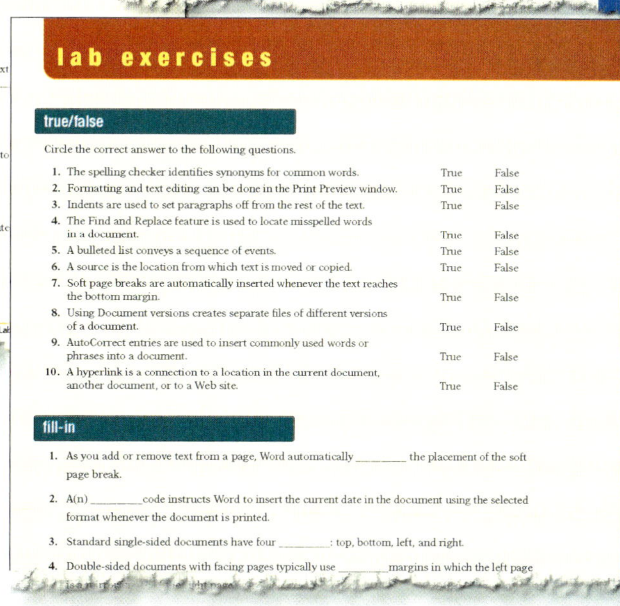

lab exercises

true/false

Circle the correct answer to the following questions.

1. The spelling checker identifies synonyms for common words. True False
2. Formatting and text editing can be done in the Print Preview window. True False
3. Indents are used to set paragraphs off from the rest of the text. True False
4. The Find and Replace feature is used to locate misspelled words in a document. True False
5. A bulleted list conveys a sequence of events. True False
6. A source is the location from which text is moved or copied. True False
7. Soft page breaks are automatically inserted whenever the text reaches the bottom margin. True False
8. Using Document versions creates separate files of different versions of a document. True False
9. AutoCorrect entries are used to insert commonly used words or phrases into a document. True False
10. A hyperlink is a connection to a location in the current document, another document, or to a Web site. True False

fill-in

1. As you add or remove text from a page, Word automatically ________ the placement of the soft page break.
2. A(n) ________code instructs Word to insert the current date in the document using the selected format whenever the document is printed.
3. Standard single-sided documents have four ________: top, bottom, left, and right.
4. Double-sided documents with facing pages typically use ________margins in which the left page

Lab Exercises: Step-by-Step, On Your Own

Lab Exercises

Provide hands-on practice and develop critical thinking skills through step-by-step and on-your-own practice exercises. These exercises have a rating system from easy to difficult and test your ability to apply the knowledge you have gained in each lab. Exercises that build off of previous exercises are noted with a Continuing Exercise icon.

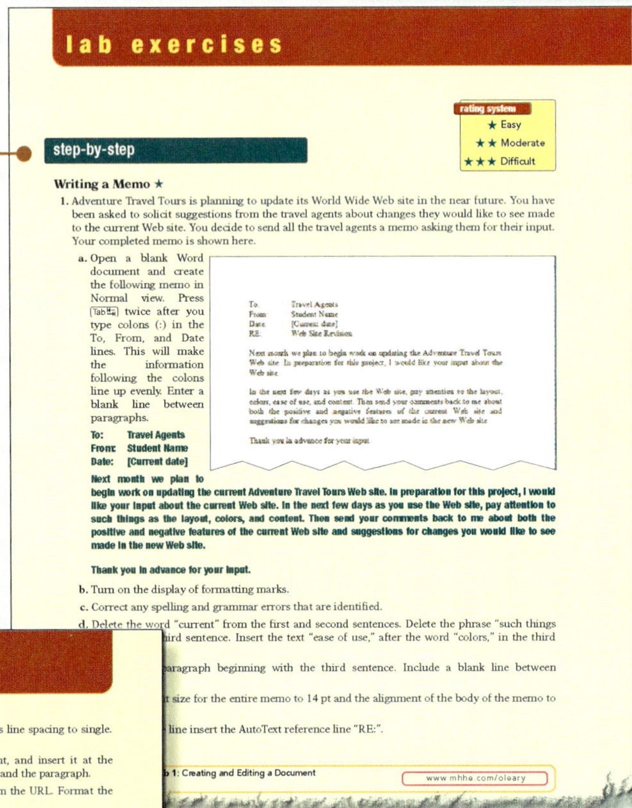

lab exercises

rating system
★ Easy
★★ Moderate
★★★ Difficult

step-by-step

Writing a Memo ★

1. Adventure Travel Tours is planning to update its World Wide Web site in the near future. You have been asked to solicit suggestions from the travel agents about changes they would like to see made to the current Web site. You decide to send all the travel agents a memo asking them for their input. Your completed memo is shown here.

a. Open a blank Word document and create the following memo in Normal view. Press Tab twice after you type colons (:) in the To, From, and Date lines. This will make the information following the colons line up evenly. Enter a blank line between paragraphs.

To: Travel Agents
From: Student Name
Date: [Current date]

Next month we plan to begin work on updating the current Adventure Travel Tours Web site. In preparation for this project, I would like your input about the current Web site. In the next few days as you use the Web site, pay attention to such things as the layout, colors, and content. Then send your comments back to me about both the positive and negative features of the current Web site and suggestions for changes you would like to see made in the new Web site.

Thank you in advance for your input.

b. Turn on the display of formatting marks.

c. Correct any spelling and grammar errors that are identified.

d. Delete the word "current" from the first and second sentences. Delete the phrase "such things ... ird sentence. Insert the text "ease of use," after the word "colors," in the third

... aragraph beginning with the third sentence. Include a blank line between

... t size for the entire memo to 14 pt and the alignment of the body of the memo to

... line insert the AutoText reference line "RE:".

... 1: Creating and Editing a Document www.mhhe.com/oleary

On Your Own

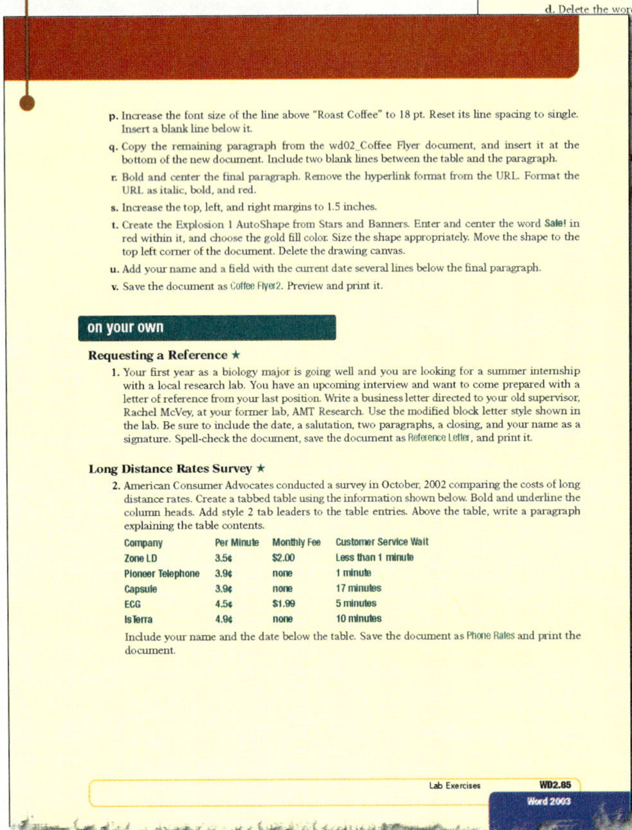

p. Increase the font size of the line above "Roast Coffee" to 18 pt. Reset its line spacing to single. Insert a blank line below it.

q. Copy the remaining paragraph from the wd02_Coffee Flyer document, and insert it at the bottom of the new document. Include two blank lines between the table and the paragraph.

r. Bold and center the final paragraph. Remove the hyperlink format from the URL. Format the URL as italic, bold, and red.

s. Increase the top, left, and right margins to 1.5 inches.

t. Create the Explosion 1 AutoShape from Stars and Banners. Enter and center the word Sale! in red within it, and choose the gold fill color. Size the shape appropriately. Move the shape to the top left corner of the document. Delete the drawing canvas.

u. Add your name and a field with the current date several lines below the final paragraph.

v. Save the document as Coffee Flyer2. Preview and print it.

on your own

Requesting a Reference ★

1. Your first year as a biology major is going well and you are looking for a summer internship with a local research lab. You have an upcoming interview and want to come prepared with a letter of reference from your last position. Write a business letter directed to your old supervisor, Rachel McVey, at your former lab, AMT Research. Use the modified block letter style shown in the lab. Be sure to include the date, a salutation, two paragraphs, a closing, and your name as a signature. Spell-check the document, save the document as Reference Letter, and print it.

Long Distance Rates Survey ★

2. American Consumer Advocates conducted a survey in October, 2002 comparing the costs of long distance rates. Create a tabbed table using the information shown below. Bold and underline the column heads. Add style 2 tab leaders to the table entries. Above the table, write a paragraph explaining the table contents.

Company	Per Minute	Monthly Fee	Customer Service Wait
Zone LD	3.5¢	$2.00	Less than 1 minute
Pioneer Telephone	3.9¢	none	1 minute
Capsule	3.9¢	none	17 minutes
ECG	4.5¢	$1.99	5 minutes
IsTerra	4.9¢	none	10 minutes

Include your name and the date below the table. Save the document as Phone Rates and print the document.

Lab Exercises WD2.85
Word 2003

The O'Leary Series

Microsoft® Office Excel 2003

Introductory Edition

Introduction to Microsoft Office 2003

Objectives

After completing the Introduction to Microsoft Office 2003, you should be able to:

1. Describe Office System 2003.
2. Describe the Office 2003 applications.
3. Start an Office 2003 application.
4. Recognize the basic application window features.
5. Use menus, shortcut menus, and shortcut keys.
6. Use toolbars and task panes.
7. Use Office Help.
8. Exit an Office 2003 application.

What Is Microsoft Office System 2003?

Microsoft Office System 2003 is a comprehensive, integrated system of programs, servers and services designed to solve a wide array of business needs. Although the programs can be used individually, they are designed to work together seamlessly making it easy to connect people and organizations to information, business processes and each other. The applications include tools used to create, discuss, communicate, and manage projects. If you share a lot of documents with other people, these features facilitate access to common documents. This version has expanded and refined the communication and collaboration features and integration with the World Wide Web. In addition, several new interface features are designed to make it easier to perform tasks and help users take advantage of all the features in the applications.

The Microsoft Office System 2003 is packaged in different combinations of components. The major components and a brief description are provided in the following table.

Component	Description
Microsoft Office 2003	
Office Word 2003	Word Processor
Office Excel 2003	Spreadsheet
Office Access 2003	Database manager
Office PowerPoint 2003	Presentation graphics
Office Outlook 2003	Desktop information manager
Office FrontPage 2003	Web site creation and management
Office InfoPath 2003	Creates XML forms and documents
Office OneNote 2003	Note-taking
Office Publisher 2003	Desktop publishing
Office Visio 2003	Drawing and diagramming
Office SharePoint Portal Server v2.0 and Services	

The five components of Microsoft Office 2003—Word, Excel, Access, PowerPoint, and Outlook—are the applications you will learn about in this series of labs. They are described in more detail in the following sections.

Office Word 2003

Office Word 2003 is a word processing software application whose purpose is to help you create text-based documents. Word processors are one of the most flexible and widely used application software programs. A word processor can be used to manipulate text data to produce a letter, a report, a memo, an e-mail message, or any other type of correspondence.

Two documents you will produce in the first two Word labs, a letter and flyer, are shown here.

March 25, 2005

Dear Adventure Traveler:

Imagine hiking and paddling your way through the rain forests of Costa Rica, camping under the stars in Africa, or following in the footsteps of the ancient Inca as you backpack along the Inca trail to Machu Picchu. Turn these dreams of adventure into memories you will cherish forever by joining Adventure Travel Tours on one of our four new adventure tours.

To tell you more about these exciting new adventures, we are offering several presentations in your area. These presentations will focus on the features and cultures of the region. We will also show you pictures of the places you will visit and activities you can participate in, as well as a detailed agenda and package costs. Plan to attend one of the following presentations:

Date	Time
January 5 -----	7:00 p.m. --------
February 3 ----	7:30 p.m. --------
March 8 -------	7:00 p.m. --------

In appreciation of your past patr
price of any of the new tour packages. Y
departure date. Please turn in this letter t

Our vacation tours are professior
almost everything in the price of your to
dollar. All tours include these features:

- **Professional tour manager and**
- **All accommodations and meals**
- **All entrance fees, excursions, t**

We hope you will join us this ye
Your memories of fascinating places an
long, long time. For reservations, please
directly at 1-800-777-0004.

A letter containing a tabbed table, indented paragraphs, and text enhancements is quickly created using basic Word features.

Announcing

New Adventure Travel Tours

Attention adventure travelers! Attend an Adventure Travel presentation to learn about some of the earth's greatest unspoiled habitats and find out how you can experience the adventure of a lifetime. This year we are introducing four new tours and offering you a unique opportunity to combine many different outdoor activities while exploring the world.

India Wildlife Adventure
Inca Trail to Machu Picchu
Safari in Tanzania
Costa Rica Rivers and Rain Forests

Presentation dates and times are January 5 at 7:00 p.m., February 3 at 7:30 p.m., and March 8 at 7:00 p.m. All presentations are held at convenient hotel locations. The hotels are located in downtown Los Angeles, in Santa Clara, and at the airport.

Call 1-800-777-0004 for presentation locations, a full color brochure, and itinerary information, costs, and trip dates.

Visit our Web site at www.AdventureTravelTours.com

A flyer incorporating many visual enhancements such as colored text, varied text styles, and graphic elements is both eye-catching and informative.

The beauty of a word processor is that you can make changes or corrections as you are typing. Want to change a report from single spacing to double spacing? Alter the width of the margins? Delete some paragraphs and add others from yet another document? A word processor allows you to do all these things with ease.

Word 2003 includes many group collaboration features to help streamline how documents are developed and changed by group members. You can also create and send e-mail messages directly from within Word using all its features to create and edit the message. In addition, you can send an entire document as your e-mail message, allowing the recipient to edit the document directly without having to open or save an attachment.

Word 2003 is closely integrated with the World Wide Web, detecting when you type a Web address and automatically converting it to a hyperlink. You can also create your own hyperlinks to locations within documents, or to other documents, including those at external locations such as a Web site or file server. Its many Web-editing features, including a Web Page Wizard that guides you step by step, help you quickly create a Web page.

Office Excel 2003

Office Excel 2003 is an electronic worksheet that is used to organize, manipulate, and graph numeric data. Once used almost exclusively by accountants, worksheets are now widely used by nearly every profession. Marketing professionals record and evaluate sales trends. Teachers record grades and calculate final grades. Personal trainers record the progress of their clients.

Excel includes many features that not only help you create a well-designed worksheet, but one that produces accurate results. Formatting features include visual enhancements such as varied text styles, colors, and graphics. Other features help you enter complex formulas and identify and correct formula errors. You can also produce a visual display of data in the form of graphs or charts. As the values in the worksheet change, charts referencing those values automatically adjust to reflect the changes.

Excel also includes many advanced features and tools that help you perform what-if analysis and create different scenarios. And like all Office 2003 applications, it is easy to incorporate data created in one application into another. Two worksheets you will produce in Labs 2 and 3 of Excel are shown on the next page.

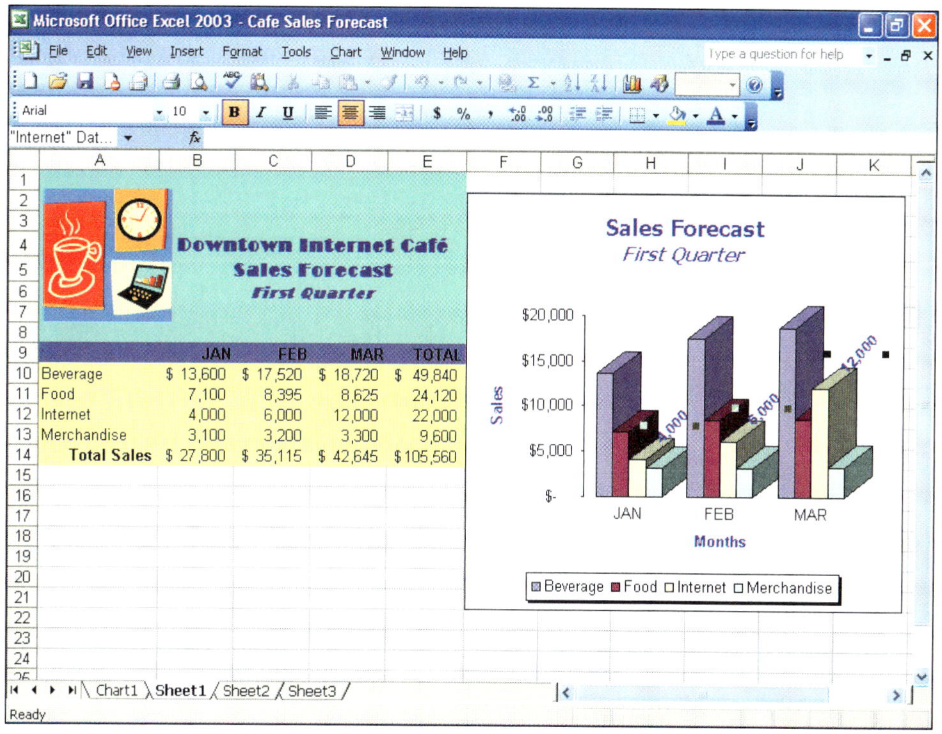

A worksheet showing the quarterly sales forecast containing a graphic, text enhancements, and a chart of the data is quickly created using basic Excel features.

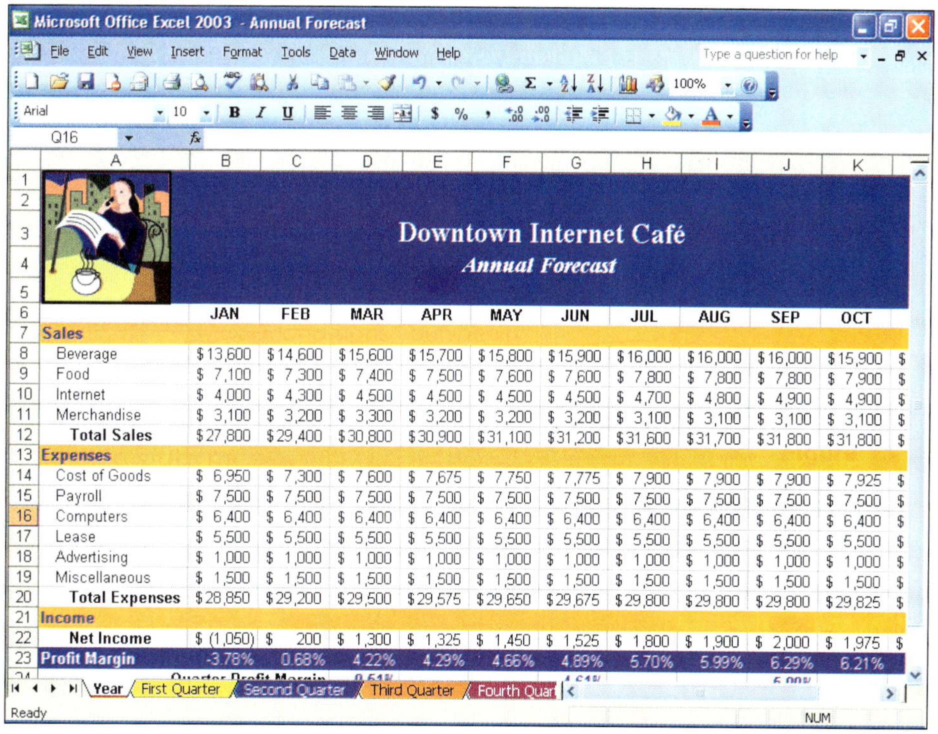

A large worksheet incorporating more complex formulas, visual enhancements such as colored text, varied text styles, and graphic elements is both informative and attractive.

You will see how easy it is to analyze data and make projections using what-if analysis and what-if graphing in Lab 3 and to incorporate Excel data in a Word document as shown in the following figures.

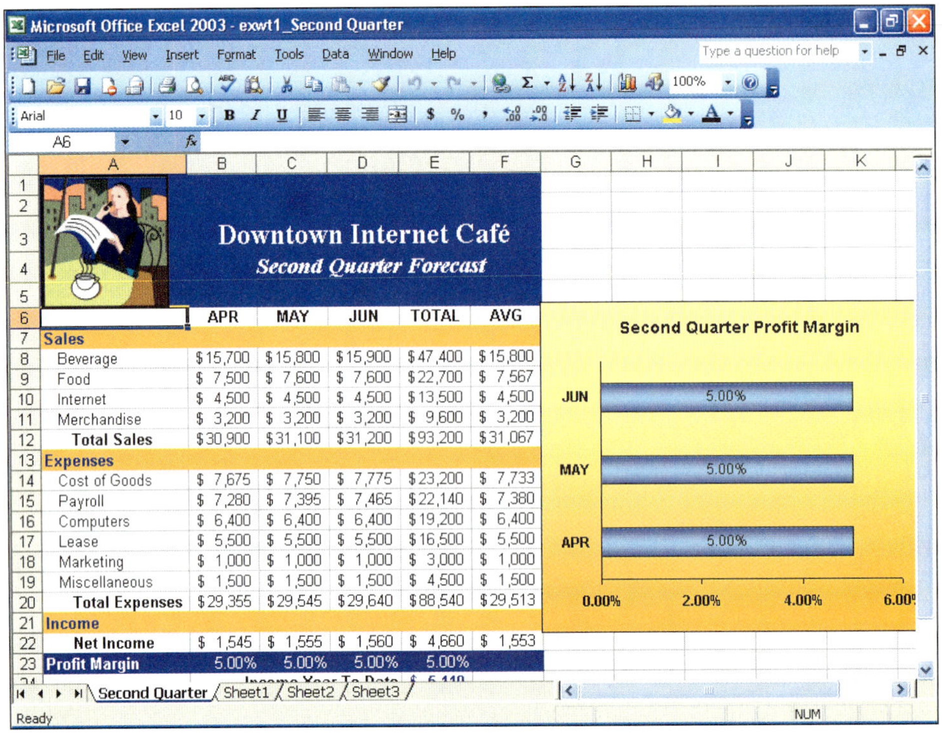

Changes you make in worksheet data while performing what-if analysis are automatically reflected in charts that reference that data.

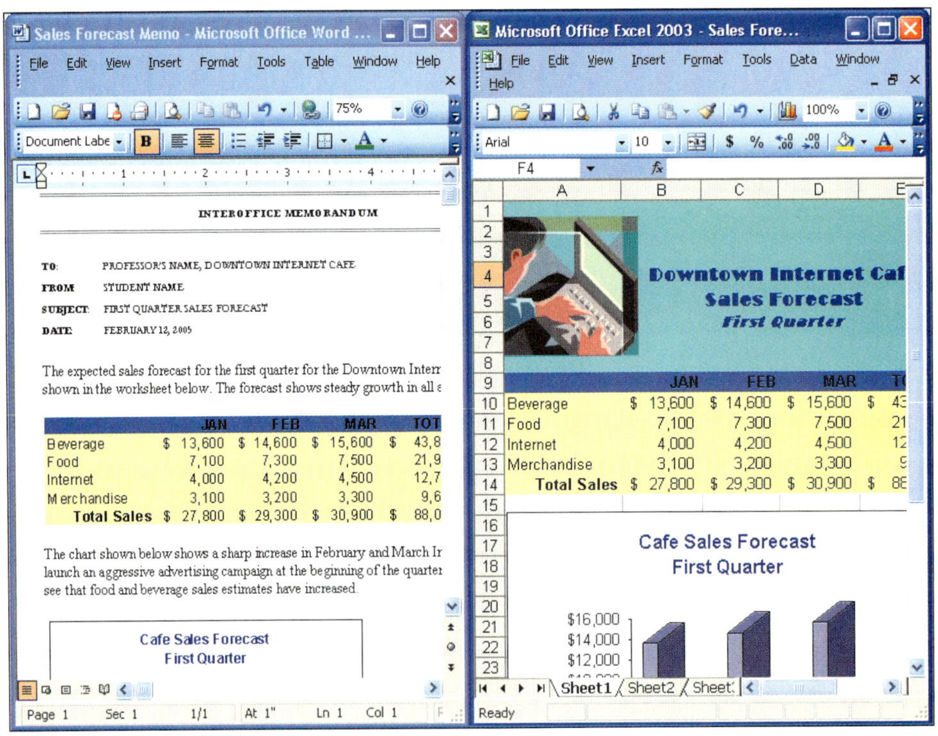

Worksheet data and charts can be copied and linked to other Office documents such as a Word document.

Office Access 2003

Office Access 2003 is a relational database management application that is used to create and analyze a database. A database is a collection of related data. In a relational database, the most widely used database structure, data is organized in linked tables. Tables consist of columns (called fields) and rows (called records). The tables are related or linked to one another by a common field. Relational databases allow you to create smaller and more manageable database tables, since you can combine and extract data between tables.

The program provides tools to enter, edit, and retrieve data from the database as well as to analyze the database and produce reports of the output. One of the main advantages of a computerized database is the ability to quickly add, delete, and locate specific records. Records can also be easily rearranged or sorted according to different fields of data, resulting in multiple table arrangements that provide more meaningful information for different purposes. Creation of forms makes it easier to enter and edit data as well. In the Access labs you will create and organize the database table shown below.

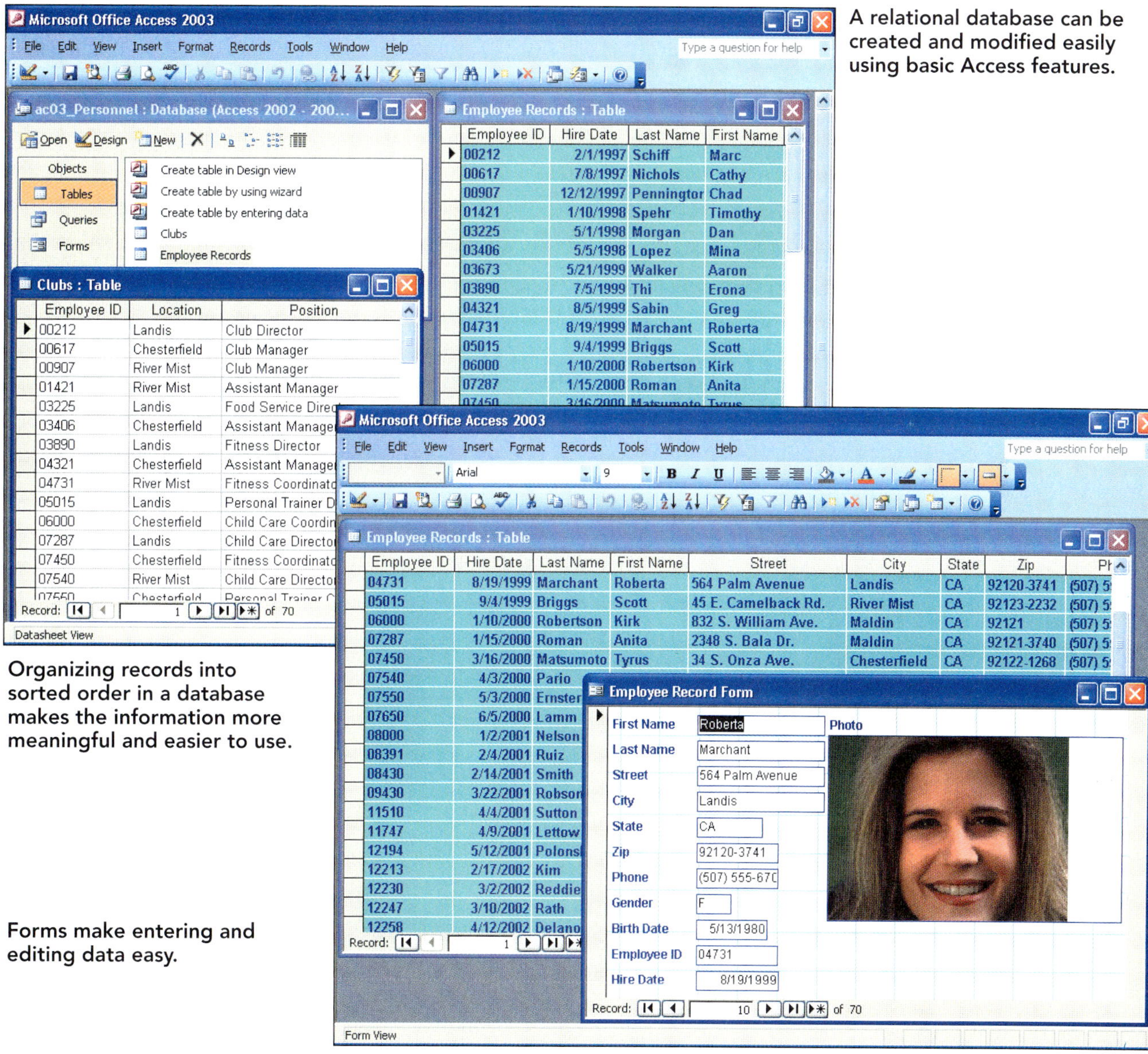

A relational database can be created and modified easily using basic Access features.

Organizing records into sorted order in a database makes the information more meaningful and easier to use.

Forms make entering and editing data easy.

Another feature is the ability to analyze the data in a table and perform calculations on different fields of data. Additionally, you can ask questions or query the table to find only certain records that meet specific conditions to be used in the analysis. Information that was once costly and time-consuming to get is now quickly and readily available. This information can then be quickly printed out in the form of reports ranging from simple listings to complex, professional-looking reports in different layout styles, or with titles, headings, subtotals, or totals.

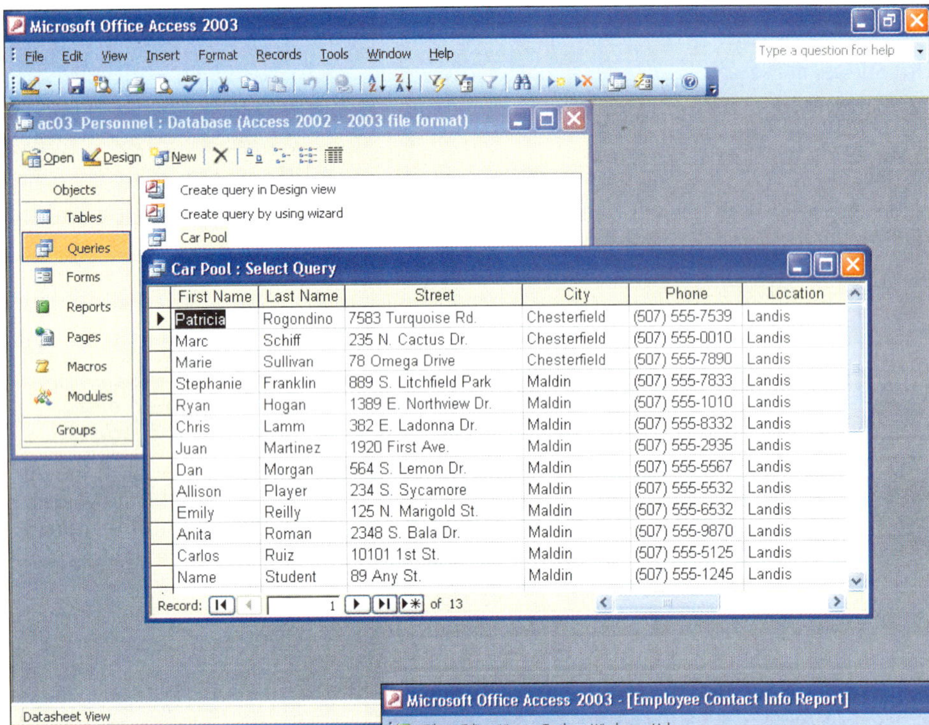

A database can be queried to locate and display only specified information.

A professional-looking report can be quickly generated from information contained in a database.

Office PowerPoint 2003

Office PowerPoint 2003 is a graphics presentation program designed to help you produce a high-quality presentation that is both interesting to the audience and effective in its ability to convey your message. A presentation can be as simple as overhead transparencies or as sophisticated as an on-screen electronic display. In the first two PowerPoint labs you will create and organize the presentation shown on the next page.

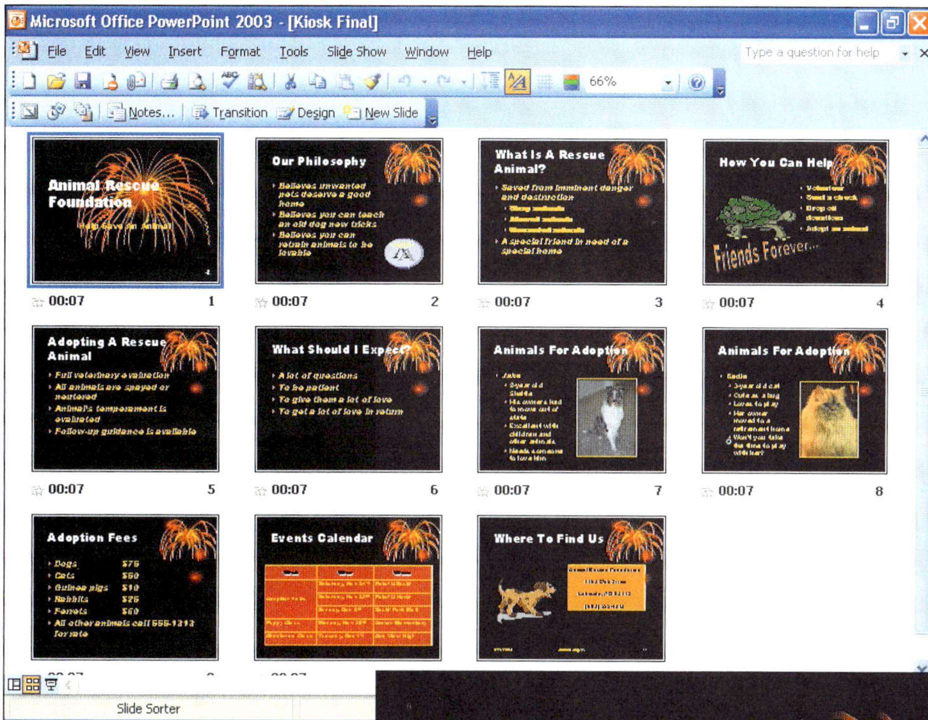

A presentation consists of a series of pages or "slides" presenting the information you want to convey in an organized and attractive manner.

When running an onscreen presentation, each slide of the presentation is displayed full-screen on your computer monitor or projected onto a screen.

Office Outlook 2003

Office Outlook 2003 is a personal information manager (PIM) program that is designed to get you organized and keep you organized. PIMs, also known as desktop managers, are designed to maximize your personal productivity by making it efficient and easy to perform everyday tasks such as scheduling meetings, recording contact information, and communicating with others, to name a few. Outlook 2003 includes an integrated e-mail program, a calendar, and contact and task management features.

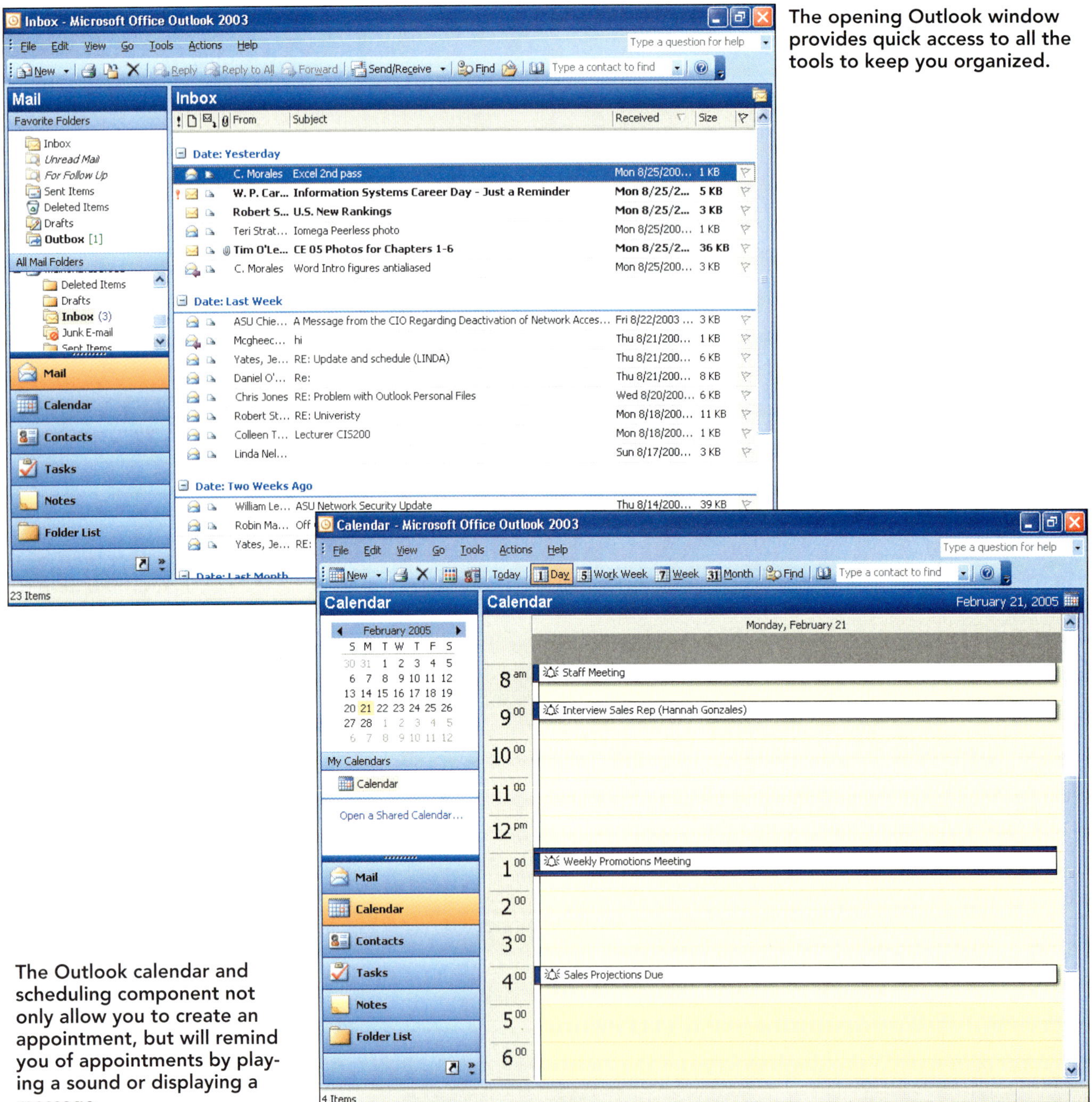

The opening Outlook window provides quick access to all the tools to keep you organized.

The Outlook calendar and scheduling component not only allow you to create an appointment, but will remind you of appointments by playing a sound or displaying a message.

Common Office 2003 Features

Additional Information

Please read the Before You Begin and Instructional Conventions sections in the Overview to Office Excel 2003 (EXO.3) before starting this section.

Additional Information

It is assumed that you are already familiar with basic Windows operating system features. To review these features, refer to your Windows text or if available, the O'Leary Series *Introduction to Windows* text.

Now that you know a little about each of the applications in Microsoft Office 2003, we will take a look at some of the features that are common to all Office 2003 applications. This is a hands-on section that will introduce you to the features and allow you to get a feel for how Office 2003 works. Although Word 2003 will be used to demonstrate how the features work, only common features will be addressed. These features include using menus, Office Help, task panes, toolbars, and starting and exiting an application. The features that are specific to each application will be introduced individually in each application text.

Starting an Office 2003 Application

There are several ways to start an Office 2003 application. The two most common methods are by using the Start menu or by clicking a desktop shortcut for the program if it is available. If you use the Start menu, the steps will vary slightly depending on the version of Windows you are using.

1 • **Click start to display the Start menu.**

• **Select All Programs.**

Having Trouble?

If you are using Windows 2002 or earlier, select Programs.

• **Select** Microsoft Office.

• **Choose** Microsoft Office Word 2003.

OR

1 • **Double-click the** Microsoft Office Word 2003 **shortcut on the desktop.**

2 • **If necessary, click Maximize in the title bar to maximize the window.**

Additional Information

Your window may appear with olive green or silver colors, depending upon the Windows settings on your computer.

Your screen should be similar to Figure 1

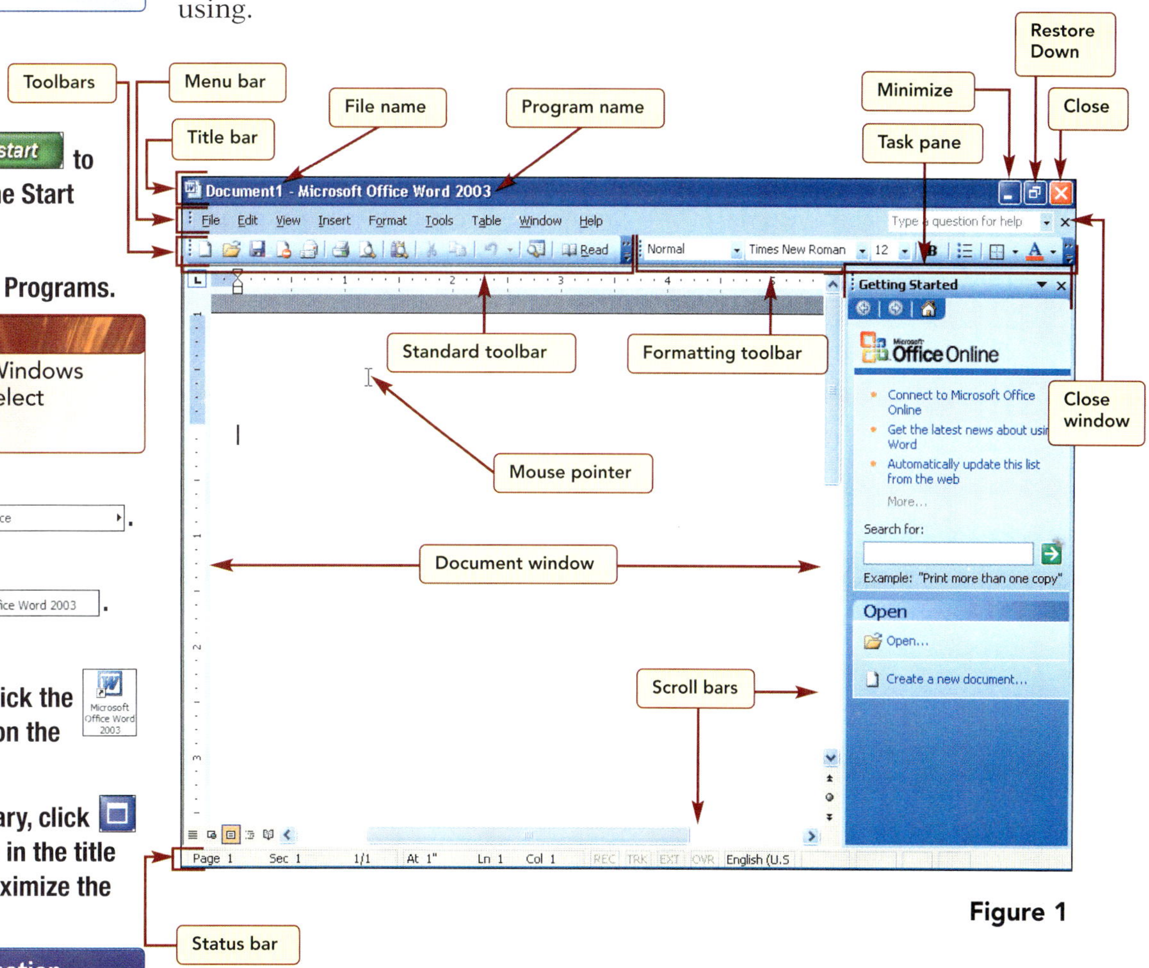

Figure 1

Additional Information

Application windows can be sized, moved, and otherwise manipulated like any other windows on the desktop.

The Word program is started and displayed in a window on the desktop. The left end of the application window title bar displays the file name followed by the program name, Microsoft Office Word 2003. The right end of the title bar displays the Minimize, Restore Down, and Close buttons. They perform the same functions and operate in the same way as all Windows versions.

The **menu bar** below the title bar displays the application's program menu. The right end displays the document window's Close Window button. As you use the Office applications, you will see that the menu bar contains many of the same menus, such as File, Edit, and Help. You will also see several menus that are specific to each application.

The **toolbars** located below the menu bar contain buttons that are mouse shortcuts for many of the menu items. Commonly, the Office applications will display two toolbars when the application is first opened: Standard and Formatting. They may appear together on one row (as in Figure 1), or on separate rows.

The large center area of the program window is the **document window** where open application files are displayed. Currently, there is a blank Word document open. In Word, the mouse pointer appears as when positioned in the document window and as a when it can be used to select items. The **task pane** is displayed on the right side of the document window. Task panes provide quick access to features as you are using the application. As you perform certain actions, different task panes automatically open. In this case, since you just started an application, the Getting Started task pane is automatically displayed, providing different ways to create a new document or open an existing document.

Additional Information

Use Tools/Options and select Startup task pane to display the Getting Started task pane when starting the application.

The **status bar** at the bottom of the window displays location information and the status of different settings as they are used. Different information is displayed in the status bar for different applications.

On the right and bottom of the document window, are vertical and horizontal scroll bars. A **scroll bar** is used with a mouse to bring additional lines of information into view in a window. The vertical scroll bar is used to move up or down, and the horizontal scroll bar moves side to side in the window.

As you can see, many of the features in the Word window are the same as in other Windows applications. The common user interface makes learning and using new applications much easier.

Using Menus

Additional Information

Use Tools/Customize/Options and check or clear the "Always show full menus" option to change how your menus operate.

A menu is one of many methods you can use to accomplish a task in a program. When opened, a menu displays a list of commands. When an Office program menu is first opened, it may display a short version of commands. The short menu is a personalized version of the menu that displays basic and frequently used commands and hides those used less often. An expanded version will display automatically after the menu is open for a few seconds.

1 **Click File to open the File menu.**

Point to each menu in the menu bar to see the full menu for each.

Additional Information

Once one menu is expanded, others expand automatically until you choose a command or perform another action.

Point to the View menu.

Your screen should be similar to Figure 2

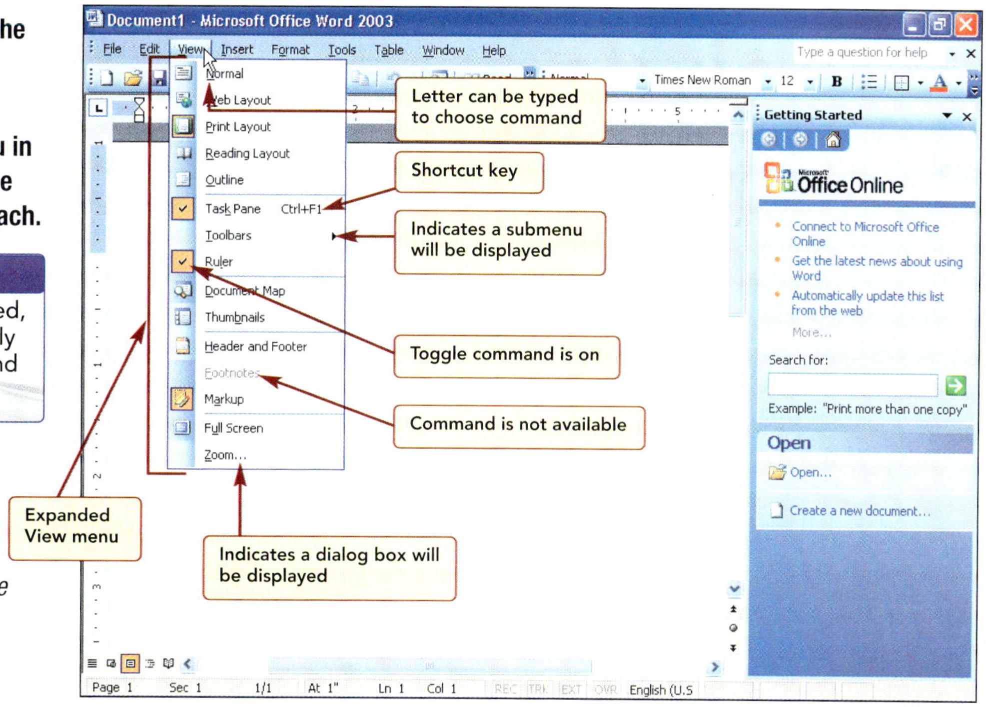

Figure 2

Additional Information

If you do not want to wait for the expanded menu to appear, you can click [⌄] at the bottom of the menu or double-click the menu name to display the full menu immediately.

Many commands have images next to them so you can quickly associate the command with the image. The same image appears on the toolbar button for that feature. Menus may include the following features (not all menus include all features):

Feature	Meaning
Ellipsis (…)	Indicates a dialog box will be displayed.
▸	Indicates a submenu will be displayed.
Dimmed	Indicates the command is not available for selection until certain other conditions are met.
Shortcut key	A key or key combination that can be used to execute a command without using the menu.
Checkmark	Indicates a toggle type of command. Selecting it turns the feature on or off. A checkmark indicates the feature is on.
Underlined letter	Indicates the letter you can type to choose the command.

Additional Information

If underlined command letters are not displayed, this feature is not active on your system.

On the View menu, two options, Task Pane and Ruler, are checked, indicating these features are on. The Task Pane option also displays the shortcut key combination, Ctrl + F1, after the option. This indicates the command can be chosen by pressing the keys instead of using the menu. The Footnotes option is dimmed because it is not currently available. The Toolbars option will display a submenu when selected, and the Zoom command a dialog box of additional options.

Once a menu is open, you can select a command from the menu by pointing to it. A colored highlight bar, called the **selection cursor**, appears over the selected command.

2 **Point to the Toolbars command to select it and display the submenu.**

Your screen should be similar to Figure 3

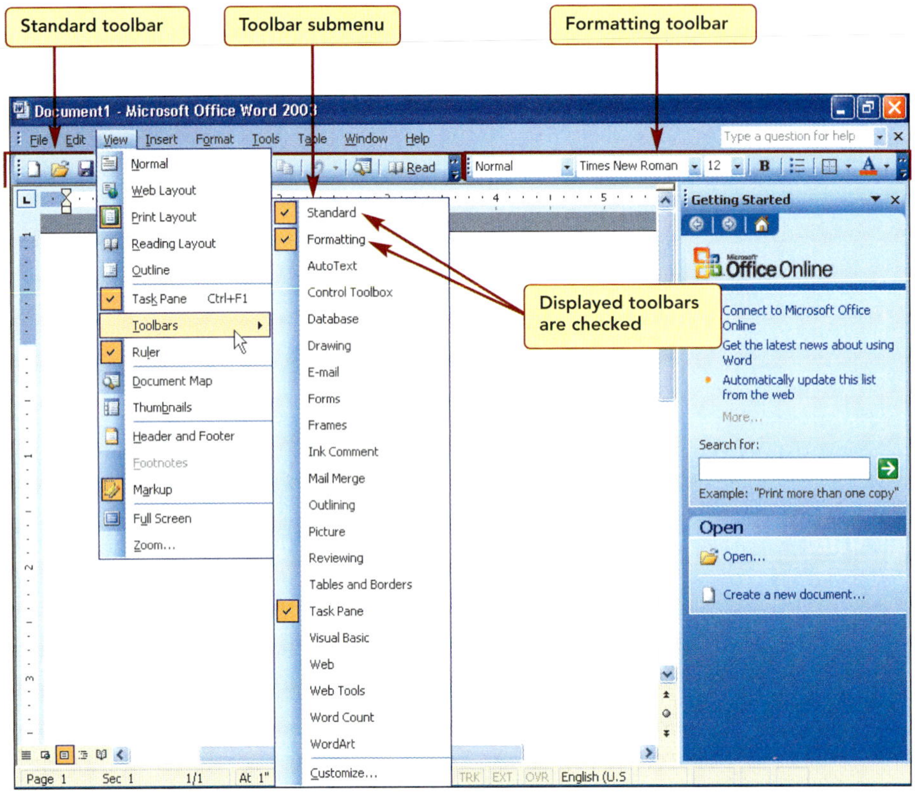

Figure 3

Currently there are three selected (checked) Toolbar options: Standard, Formatting, and although not technically a toolbar, the Task Pane. If other toolbars are selected in your menu, this is because once a toolbar has been turned on, it remains on until turned off.

To choose a command, you click on it. When the command is chosen, the associated action is performed. You will close the task pane and any other open toolbars and display the Drawing toolbar.

3 Click on Task Pane to turn off this feature.

- Open the View menu again, select Toolbars, and if it is not already selected, click on the Drawing toolbar option to turn it on.

- If necessary, choose **V**iew/**T**oolbars again and deselect any other toolbar options (there should be 3 selected toolbar options).

Your screen should be similar to Figure 4

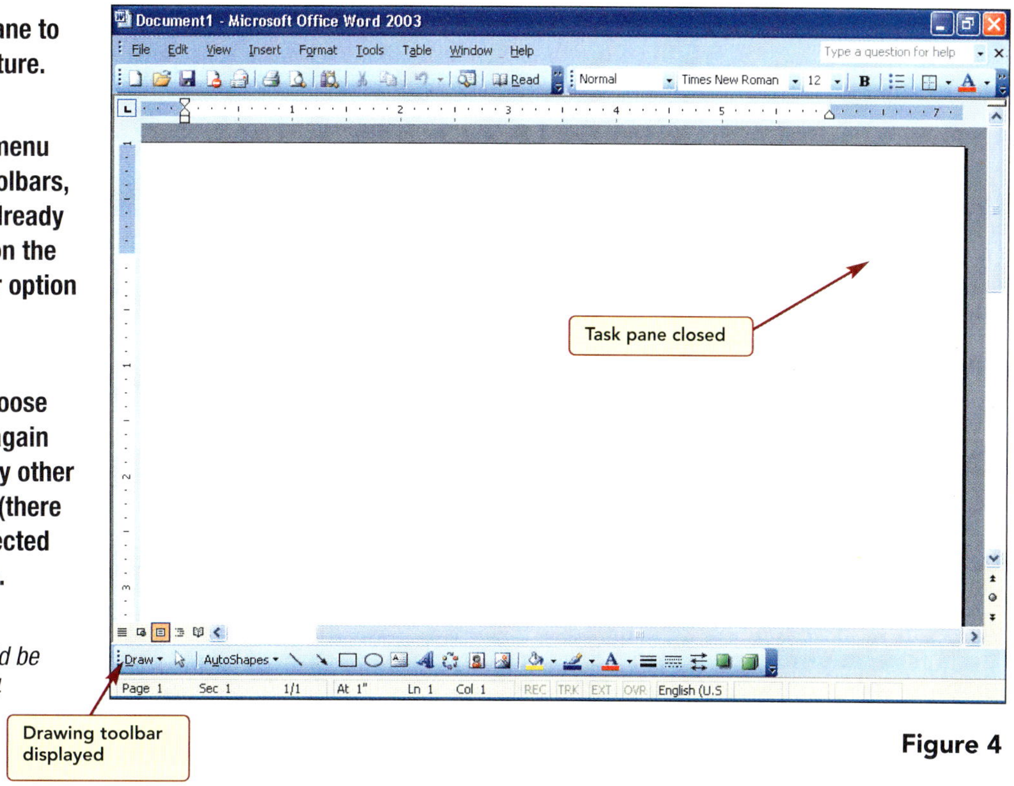

Figure 4

Additional Information

If you have a microphone and have installed and trained the Speech Recognition feature, you can speak the command sequences to open menus and choose commands. For example, to open a toolbar, you would say "View Toolbars."

Additional Information

Using voice commands, saying "Right click" will open the shortcut menu for the selected item.

The task pane is closed and the Drawing toolbar is displayed above the status bar. Any other toolbars that were open which you deselected are closed.

Using Shortcut Menus

Another way to access menu options is to use the **shortcut menu**. The shortcut menu is opened by right-clicking on an item on the screen. This menu displays only those options associated with the item. For example, right-clicking on any toolbar will display the toolbar menu options only. You will use this method to hide the Drawing toolbar again.

1 **Point to the Drawing toolbar and right-click.**

Your screen should be similar to Figure 5

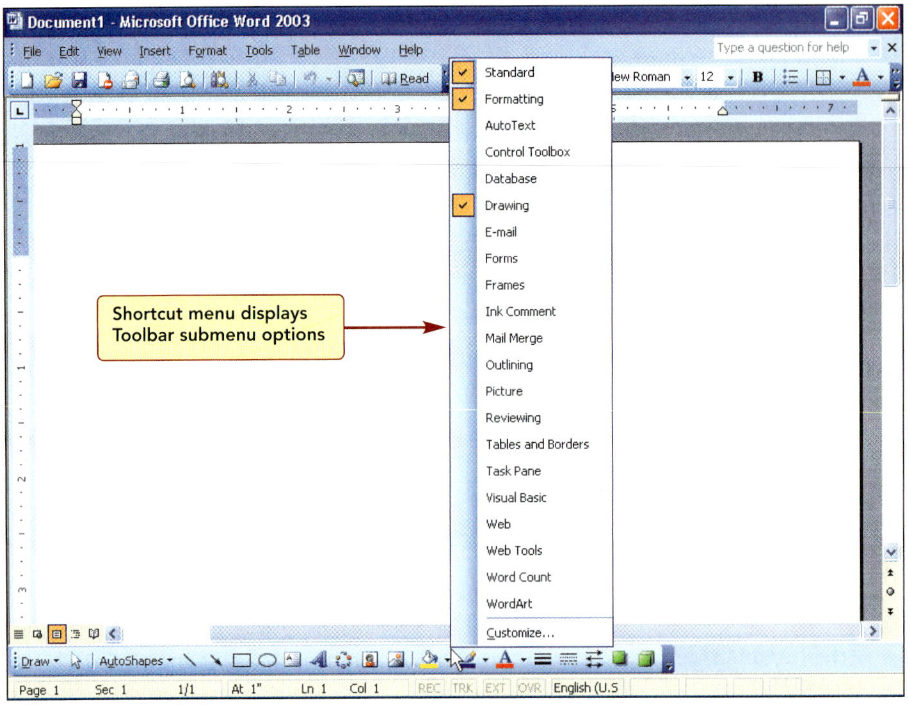

Figure 5

Additional Information

The Customize option can be used to change features of toolbars and menus.

The shortcut menu displays only the Toolbar submenu options on the View menu. Using a shortcut menu saves time over selecting the main menu command sequence.

2 **Choose Drawing to turn off this feature.**

Your screen should be similar to Figure 6

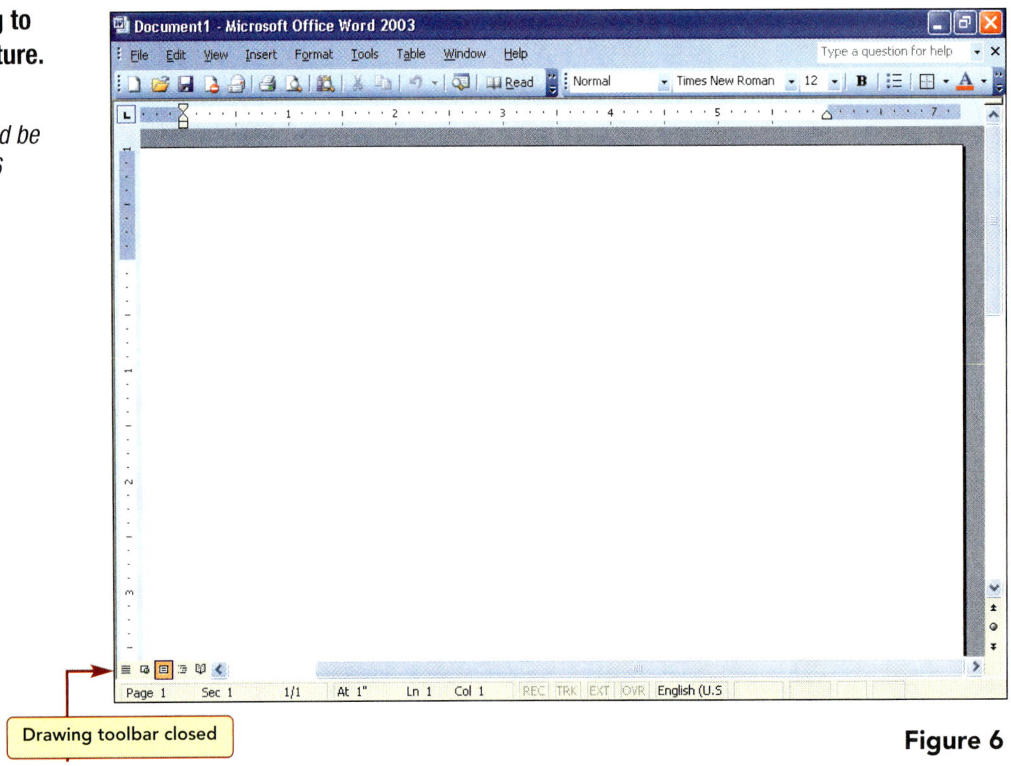

Figure 6

The Drawing toolbar is no longer displayed.

Using Shortcut Keys

A third way to perform a command is to use the shortcut key or key combination associated with a particular command. If you will recall, the shortcut key associated with the View/Task Pane command is Ctrl + F1. To use the key combination, you hold down the first key while pressing the second.

Additional Information

Not all commands have shortcut keys.

1 **Hold down Ctrl and press the F1 function key.**

Having Trouble?

Function keys are located above the numeric keys on the keyboard.

Your screen should be similar to Figure 7

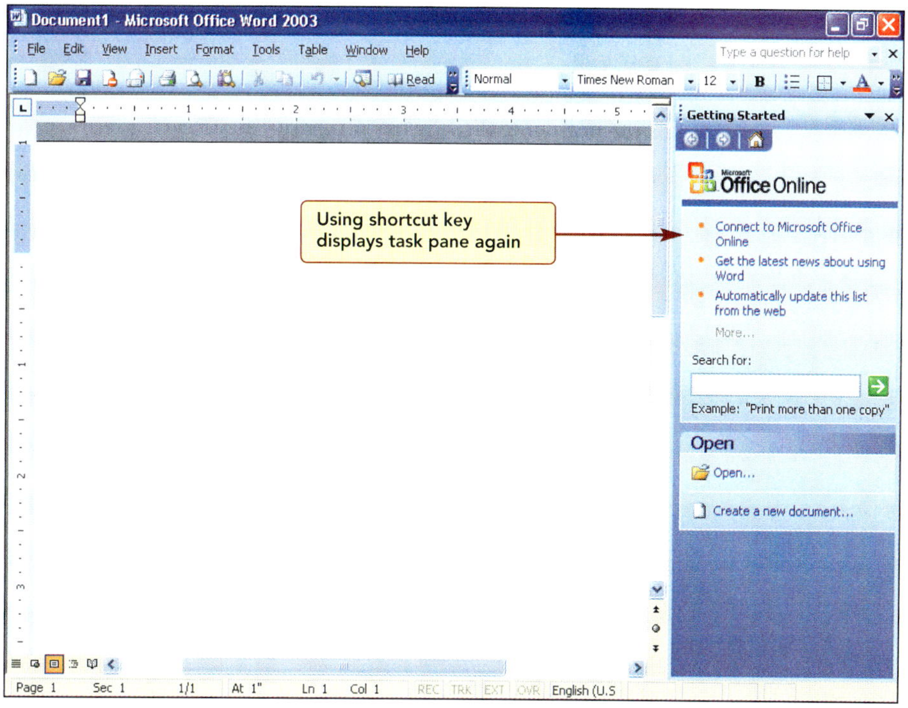

Figure 7

Additional Information

Using the Speech Recognition feature, you can also use voice shortcuts for many commands. For example, to show the task pane, you would say "show task pane." Many voice commands also have several different words you can say to initiate the command. You could also say "task pane" or "view task pane."

The task pane is displayed again. Using shortcut keys is the quickest way to perform many actions; however, you need to remember the key combination in order to use it.

Using Toolbars

Initially, Word displays two toolbars, Standard and Formatting, below the menu bar (see Figure 3). The **Standard toolbar** contains buttons that are used to complete the most frequently used menu commands. The **Formatting toolbar** contains buttons that are used to change the appearance or format of the document. There are many features that can be used to make working with toolbars easier.

Displaying Toolbars on Separate Rows

The default toolbar arrangement is to display both toolbars on one row. Because there is not enough space to display all the buttons on both toolbars on a single row, many buttons are hidden. The Toolbar Options button located at the end of a toolbar displays a drop-down button list of those buttons that are not displayed. Toolbars initially display the basic buttons. Like menus, they are personalized automatically, displaying those buttons you use frequently and hiding others. When you use a button from this list, it then is moved to the toolbar, and a button that has not been used recently is moved to the Toolbar Options list. It also contains an option to display the toolbars on separate rows. You will use this option to quickly see all the toolbar buttons.

1 **Click Toolbar Options.**

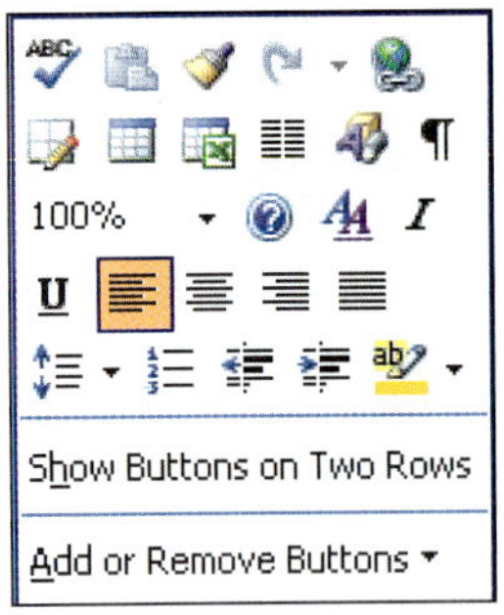

Choose Show Buttons on Two Rows.

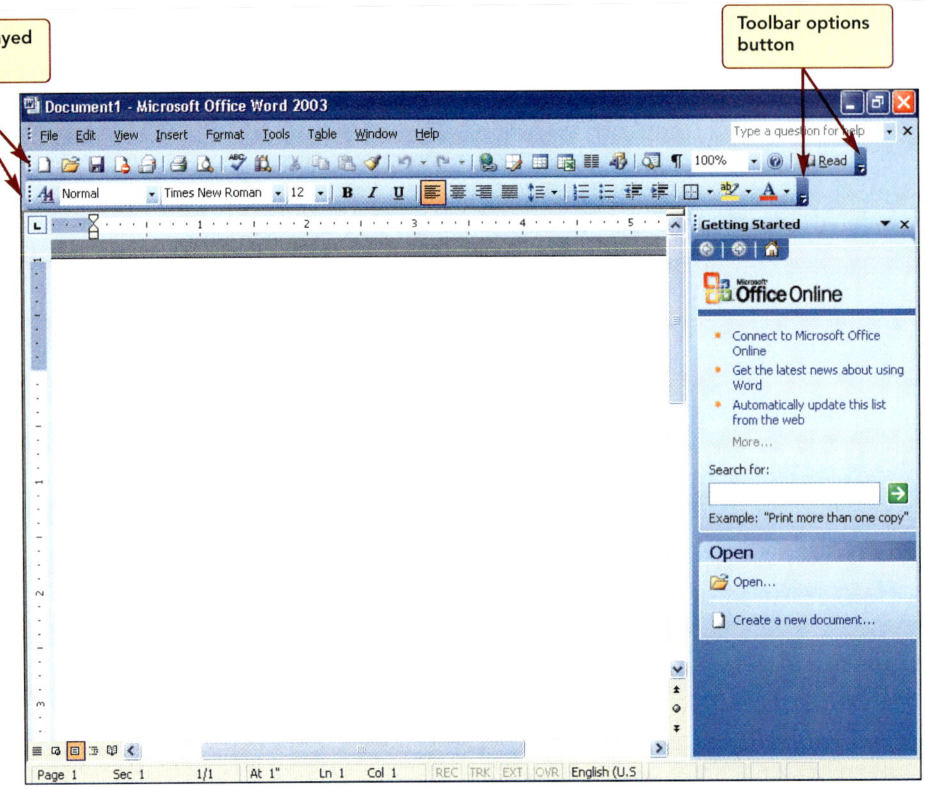

Figure 8

Another Method

You can also use Tools/Customize/Options, or choose Customize/Options from the toolbar shortcut menu and select "Show Standard and Formatting toolbars on two rows."

Your screen should be similar to Figure 8

Additional Information

The Add or Remove Buttons option allows you to customize existing toolbars by selecting those buttons you want to display and by creating your own customized toolbars.

The two toolbars now occupy separate rows, providing enough space for all the buttons to be displayed. Now using Toolbar Options is no longer necessary, and when selected only displays the options to return the toolbars display to one row and the Add or Remove Buttons option.

When a toolbar is open, it may appear docked or floating. A **docked toolbar** is fixed to an edge of the window and displays a vertical bar, called the move handle, on the left edge of the toolbar. Dragging this bar up or down allows you to move the toolbar. If multiple toolbars share the same row, dragging the bar left or right adjusts the size of the toolbar. If docked, a toolbar can occupy a row by itself, or several can be on a row together. A **floating toolbar** appears in a separate window and can be moved anywhere on the desktop.

2 • **Point to the move handle of the Standard toolbar and, when the mouse pointer appears as ✥, drag the toolbar into the document window.**

Your screen should be similar to Figure 9

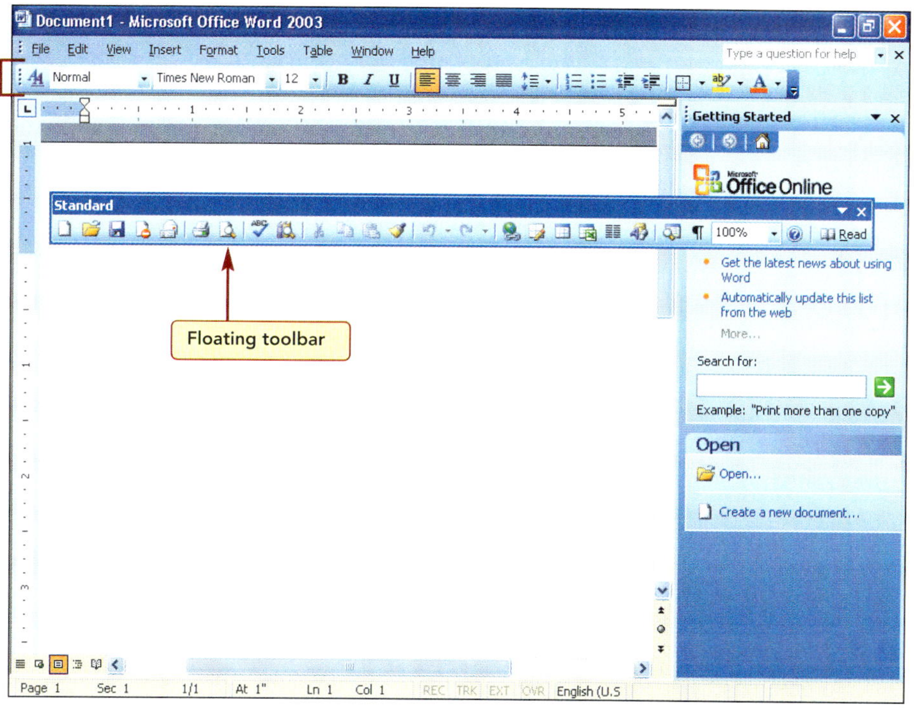

Figure 9

The Standard toolbar is now a floating toolbar and can be moved to any location in the window by dragging the title bar. If you move a floating toolbar to the edge of the window, it will attach to that location and become a docked toolbar. A floating toolbar can also be sized by dragging the edge of the toolbar.

3 • **Drag the title bar of the floating toolbar (the mouse pointer appears as ✥) to move the toolbar to the row below the Formatting toolbar.**

• **Move the Formatting toolbar below the Standard toolbar.**

• **Align both toolbars with the left edge of the window by dragging the move handle horizontally.**

Your screen should be similar to Figure 10

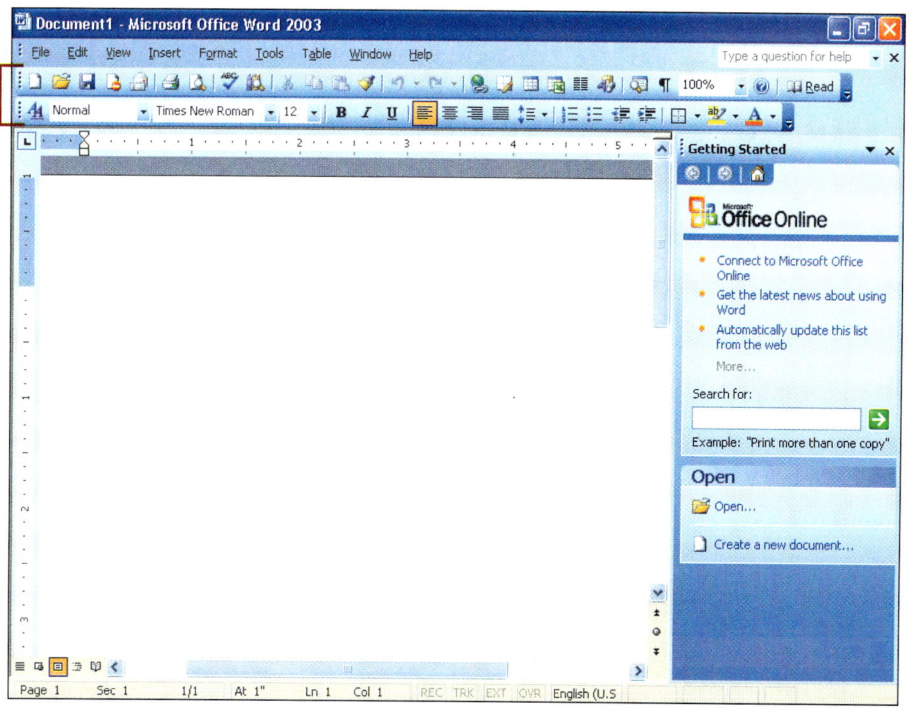

Figure 10

The two toolbars again occupy two rows. To quickly identify the toolbar buttons, you can display the button name by pointing to the button.

4 **Point to any button on the Standard toolbar.**

Your screen should be similar to Figure 11

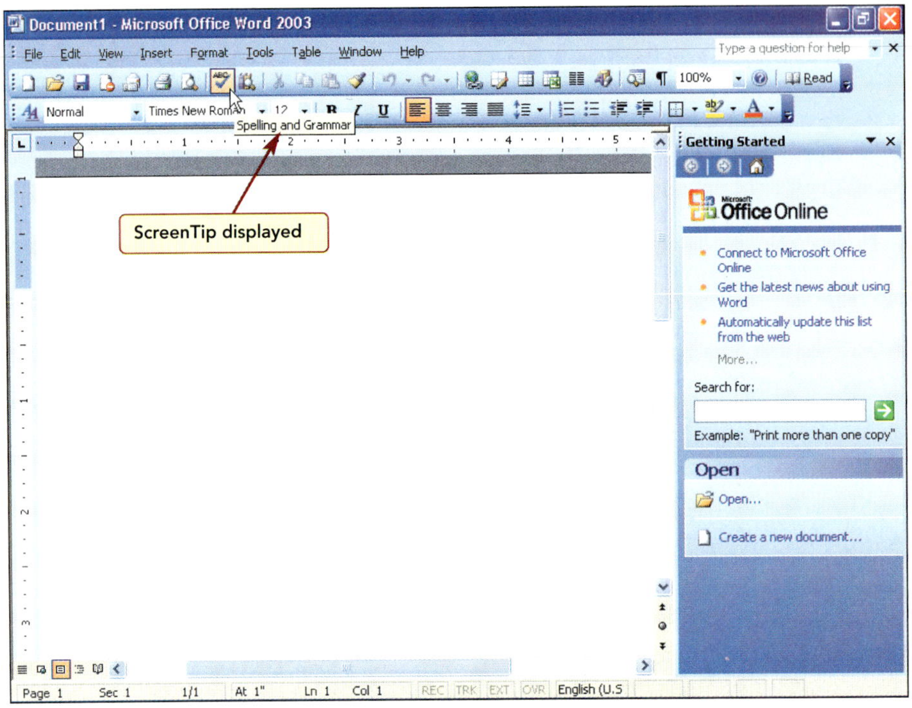

Figure 11

A ScreenTip containing the button name appears next to the mouse pointer. Clicking on a button will perform the associated action. You will use the Help button to access Microsoft Word Help.

5 **Click Microsoft Office Word Help.**

Another Method

You can also choose Help/Microsoft Office Word Help, or press F1 to access Help.

Your screen should be similar to Figure 12

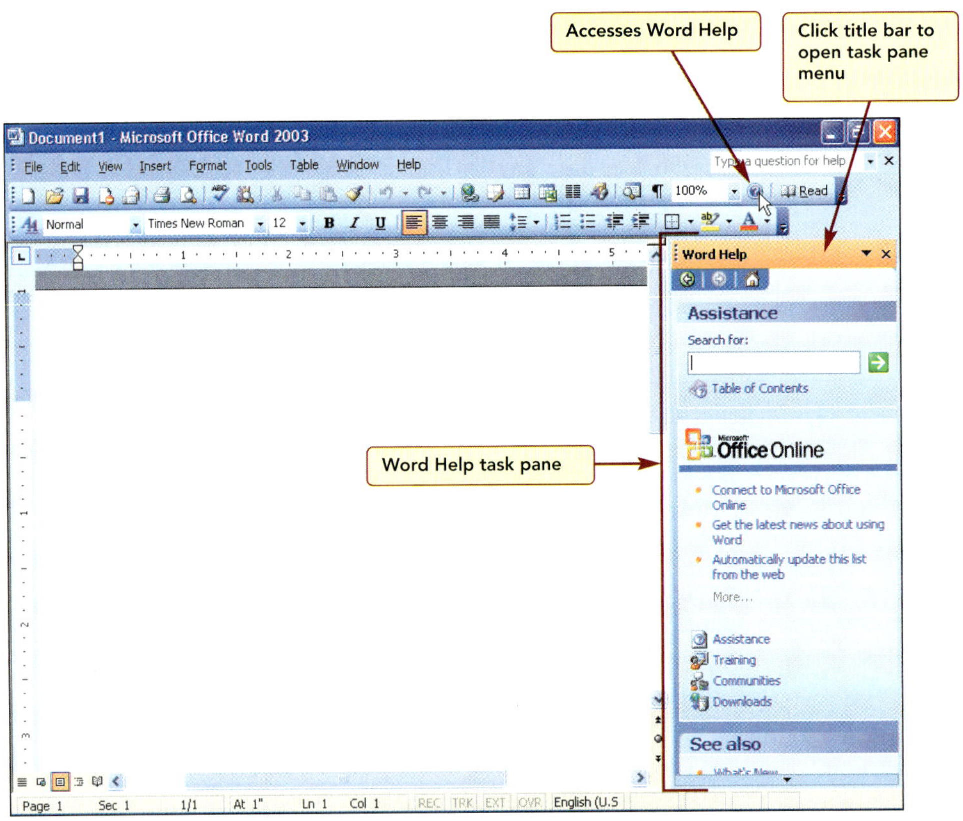

Figure 12

The Getting Started task pane is replaced by the Microsoft Word Help task pane. The name of the task pane appears in the task pane title bar.

Using Task Panes

Additional Information

You can drag the pane divider line to adjust the width of the pane. When there is more information in the pane than can be displayed, [scroll up] and [scroll down] appear to scroll the information into view.

Task panes appear automatically when certain features are used. They can also be opened manually from the task pane menu. Clicking the task pane title bar displays a drop-down menu of other task panes you can select. In Word there are 14 different task panes. You will redisplay the Getting Started task pane. Then you will quickly return to the previously displayed task pane using the [Back] Back toolbar button in the task pane.

1

- **Click on the task pane title bar.**

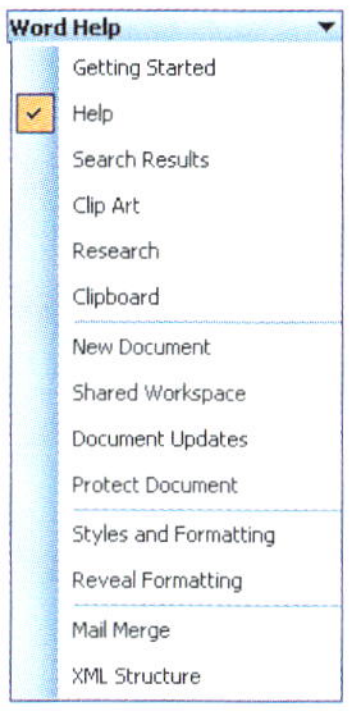

- **Choose Getting Started.**

Another Method

You can also click the [Home] Home button to quickly display the Getting Started task pane.

- **Click [Back] Back.**

Your screen should be similar to Figure 13

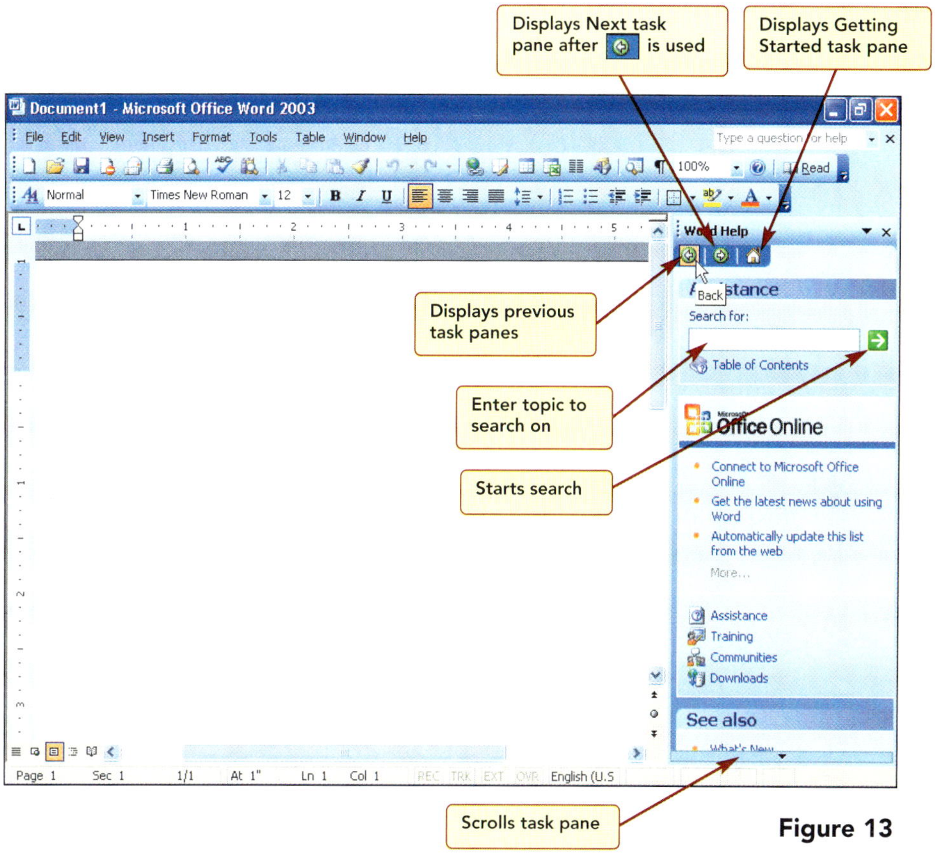

Figure 13

The Help task pane is displayed again. Likewise, clicking the [Forward] Forward button will display the task pane that was viewed before using [Back] Back.

Using Office Help

Additional Information

Although you can also simply enter a word or phrase in the Search box, the best results occur when you type a complete sentence or question.

There are several ways you can get help. One method is to conduct a search of the available help information by entering a sentence or question you want help on in the Search text box of the Help task pane. Notice the insertion point is positioned in the Search text box. This indicates it is ready for you to type an entry. You will use this method to learn about getting Help while you work.

1 **Type How do I get help? in the Search box.**

Having Trouble?

If the insertion point is not displayed in the Search box, simply click in the box to activate it.

Click [Start Searching icon] Start Searching.

Your screen should be similar to Figure 14

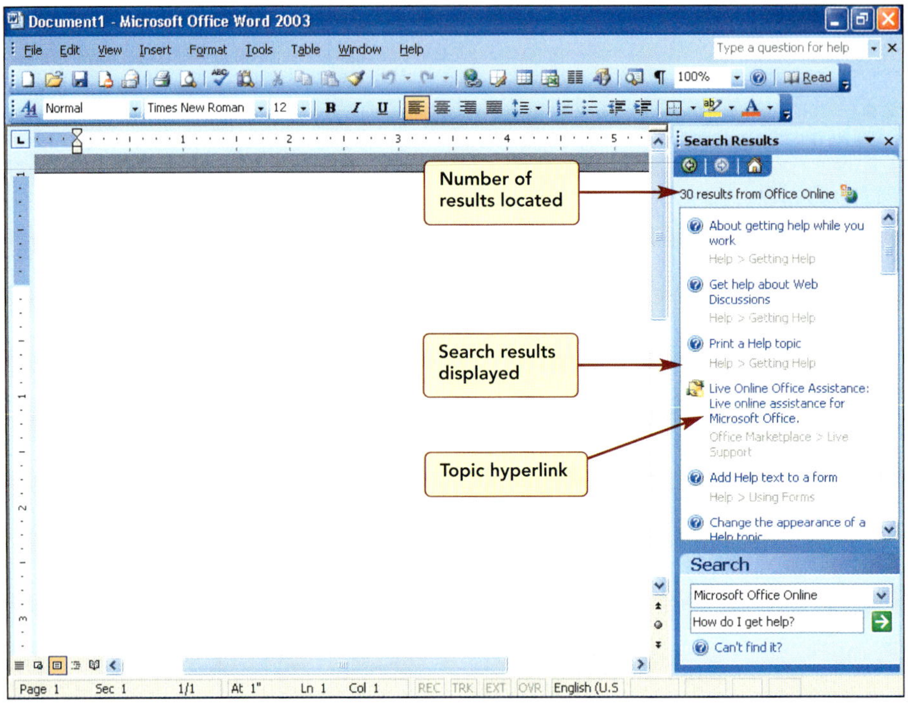

Figure 14

Additional Information

In addition to being connected to the Internet, the Online Content settings must be selected. Click Online Content Settings in the Help task pane and select all the options to turn on these features.

Additional Information

The number of results located and where they were found is displayed at the top of the list.

If you are connected to the Internet, the Microsoft Office Online Web site is searched and the results are displayed in the Search Results task pane. If you are not connected, the offline help information that is provided with the application and stored on your computer is searched. Generally the search results are similar, but fewer in number.

The Search Results pane displays a list of located results. The results are shown in order of relevance, with the most likely matches at the top of the list. Each result is a **hyperlink** or connection to the information located on the Online site or in Help on your computer. Clicking the hyperlink accesses and displays the information associated with the hyperlink.

You want to read the information in the topic "About getting help while you work."

2 **From the Search Results list click the "About getting help while you work" hyperlink.**

Additional Information

When you point to the hyperlink, it appears underlined and the mouse pointer appears as .

Your screen should be similar to Figure 15

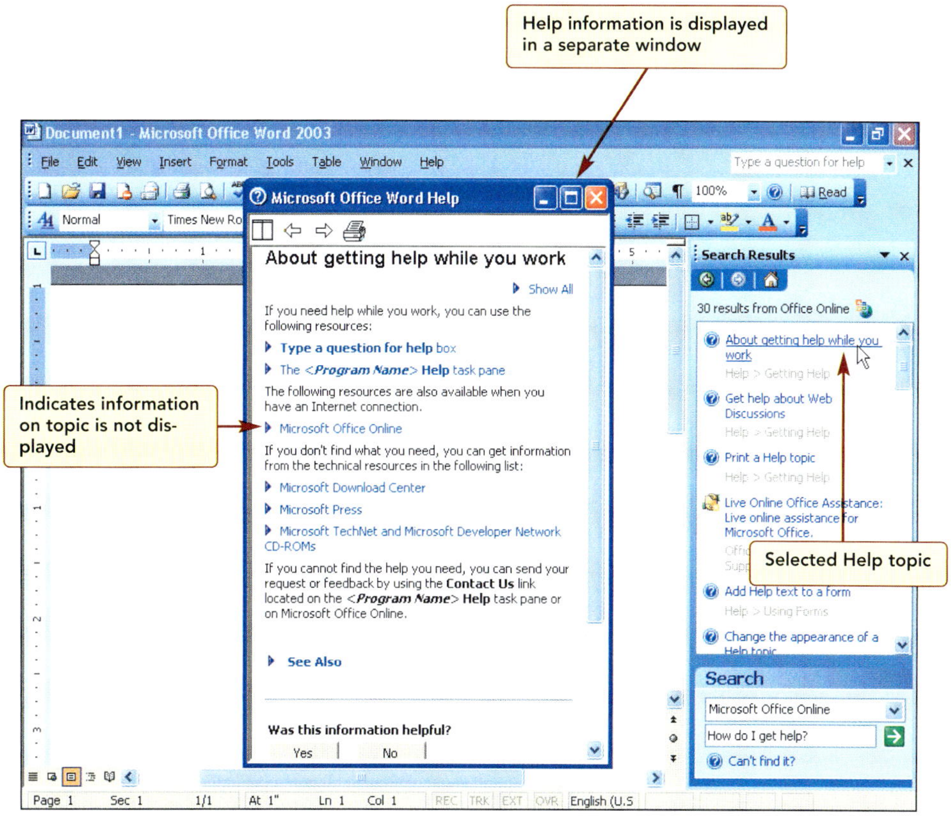

Figure 15

The information on the selected topic is displayed in a separate Help window. The Help window on your screen will probably be a different size and arrangement than in Figure 15. Depending on the size of your Help window, you may need to scroll the window to see all the Help information provided. As you are reading the help topic, you will see many subtopics preceded with ▶. This indicates the information in the subtopic is not displayed. Clicking on the subtopic heading displays the information about the topic.

3 If necessary, use the scroll bar to scroll the Help window to see the information on this topic.

- **Scroll back up to the top of the window.**

Additional Information

Clicking the scroll arrows scrolls the text in the window line by line, and dragging the scroll bar up or down moves to a general location within the window area.

- **Click the "Type a question for help box" subtopic.**
- **Click the "The <Program name> Help task pane" subtopic.**
- **Read the information on both subtopics.**

Your screen should be similar to Figure 16

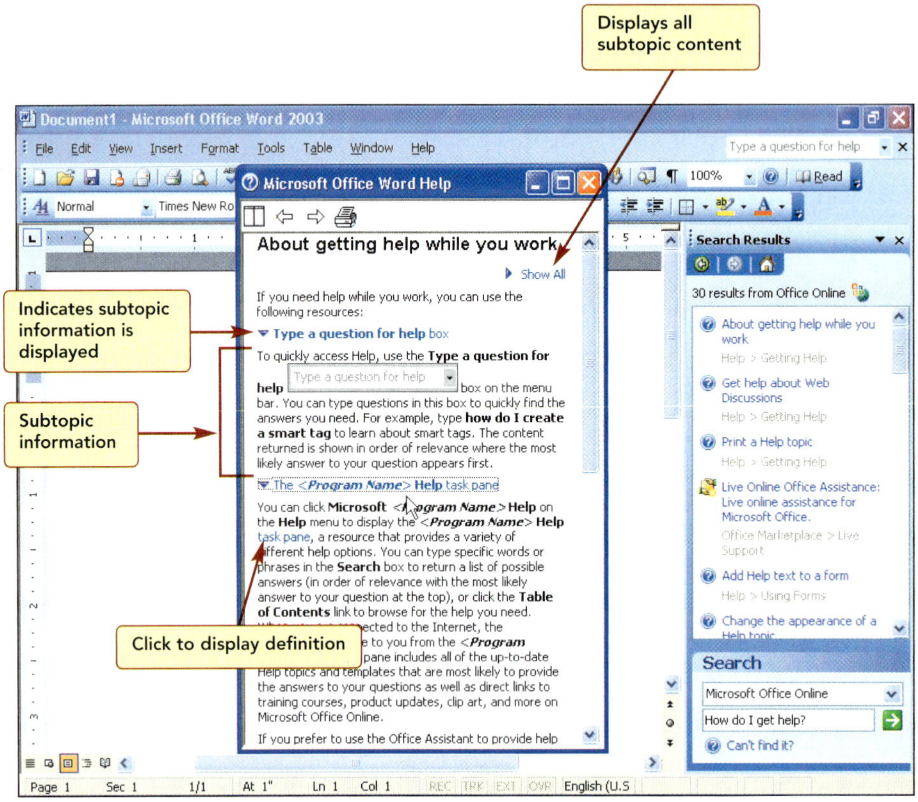

Figure 16

The ▸ preceding the subtopic has changed to ▾ indicating the subtopic content is displayed. The selected subtopics provide information about accessing Help using the "Type a question for help" box and the Help task pane. Notice the blue words "task pane" within the subtopic content. This indicates that clicking on the text will display a definition of the term. You can continue to click on the subtopic headings to display the information about each topic individually, or you can click Show All to display all the available topic information.

4

- **Click "task pane" to see the definition.**
- **Click Show All at the top of the Help window.**
- **Scroll the window to see the Microsoft Office Online subtopic.**
- **Read the information on this subtopic.**

Your screen should be similar to Figure 17

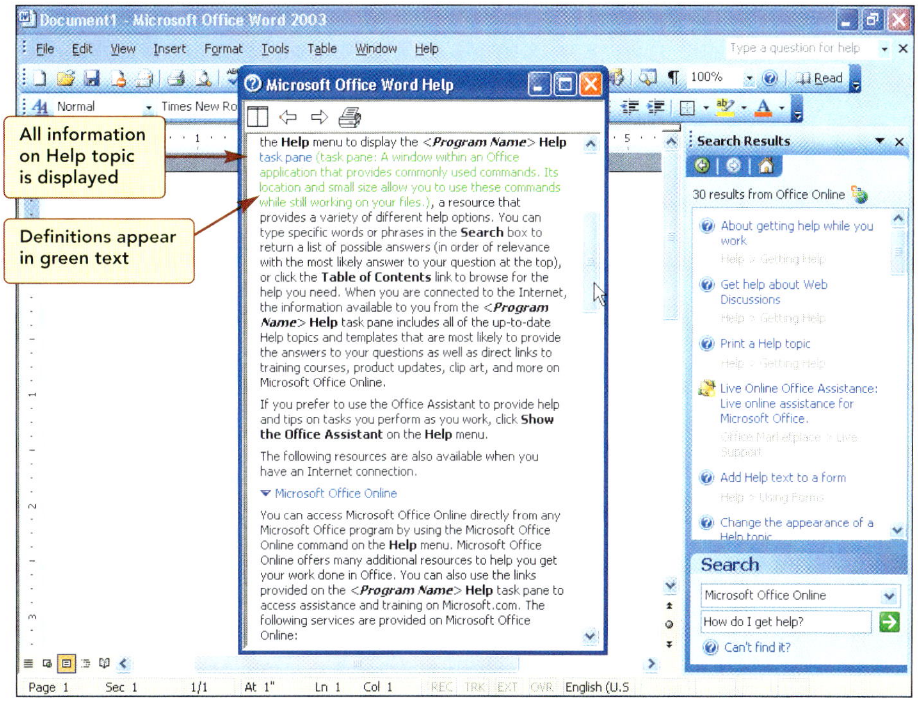

Figure 17

The information under all the subtopics is fully displayed, including definitions.

Using the Help Table of Contents

Another source of help is to use the Help table of contents. Using this method allows you to browse the Help topics to locate topics of interest to you.

1

- **Click Close in the Help window title bar to close the Help window.**
- **Click Back in the task pane.**
- **Click Table of Contents (below the Search box).**

Your screen should be similar to Figure 18

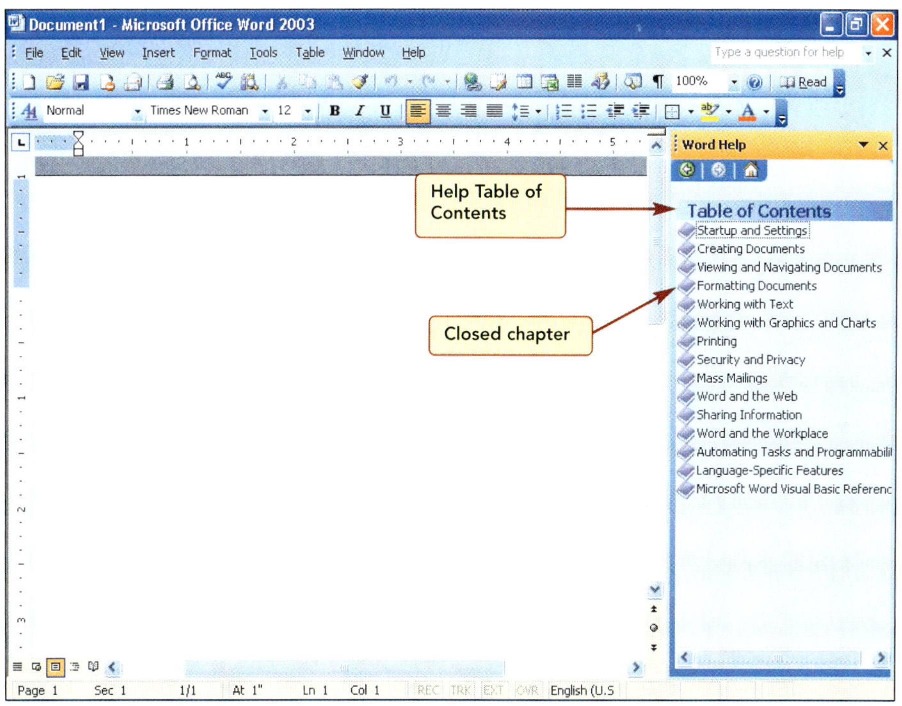

Figure 18

The entire Word Help Table of Contents is displayed in the Help task pane. Clicking on an item preceded with a Closed Book icon opens a chapter, which expands to display additional chapters or topics. The Open Book icon identifies those chapters that are open. Clicking on an item preceded with displays the specific Help information.

2 **Click "Startup and Settings" to open this chapter.**

Click "Getting Help."

Click "About getting help while you work."

Additional Information

Pointing to an item in the Table of Contents that is not entirely visible in the pane displays a ScreenTip of the entire topic heading.

Your screen should be similar to Figure 19

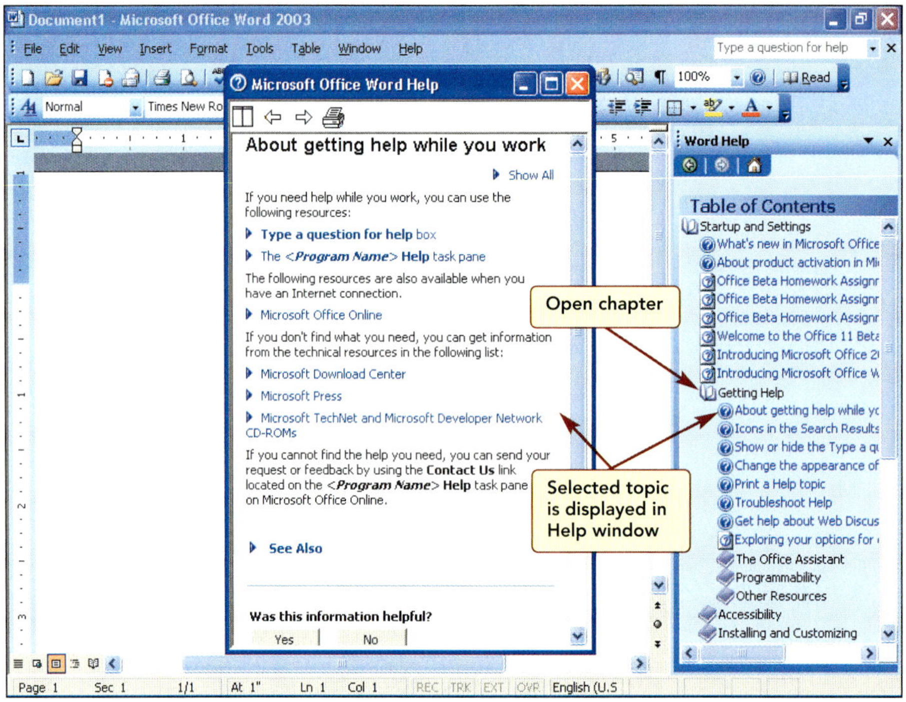

Figure 19

The Help window opens again and displays the information on the selected topic. To close a chapter, click the icon.

Exiting an Office 2003 Application

Now you are ready to close the Help window and exit the Word program. The Exit command on the File menu can be used to quit most Windows programs. Alternatively, you can click the Close button in the program window title bar.

1 **Click Close in the Help window title bar to close the Help window.**

Click Close in the Task pane title bar to close the task pane.

Another Method

You could also use Ctrl + F1 to close a task pane.

Click Close in the Word window title bar to exit Word.

The program window is closed and the desktop is visible again.

Introduction to Microsoft Office 2003

key terms

docked toolbar I.18
document window I.12
floating toolbar I.18
Formatting toolbar I.17
hyperlink I.22
menu bar I.12
scroll bar I.12
selection cursor I.14
shortcut menu I.15
Standard toolbar I.17
status bar I.12
task pane I.12
toolbar I.12

command summary

Command	Shortcut Key	Button	Voice	Action
start/All Programs				Opens program menu
File/Exit	Alt + F4			Exits Office program
View/Toolbars			View toolbars	Hides or displays toolbars
View/Task Pane	Ctrl + F1		Task pane Show task pane View task pane Hide task pane	Hides or displays task pane
Tools/Customize/Options				Changes settings associated with toolbars and menus
Help/Microsoft Word Help	F1			Opens Help window

lab exercises

rating system

★ Easy

★★ Moderate

★★★ Difficult

step-by-step

Using an Office Application ★

1. All Office 2003 applications have a common user interface. You will explore the Excel 2003 application and use many of the same features you learned about while using Word 2003 in this lab.

   a. Use the Start menu or a shortcut icon on your desktop to start Office Excel 2003. Close the Getting Started Task Pane.
   b. What shape is the mouse pointer when positioned in the document window area? ________
   c. Excel also has nine menus. Which menu is not the same as in Word? ________ Open the Tools Menu. How many commands in the Tools menu will display a submenu when selected? ______ How many commands are listed in the Formula Auditing submenu? __________
   d. Click on a blank space near the Formatting toolbar to open the toolbar shortcut menu. How many toolbars are available in Excel? ________
   e. Display the Chart toolbar. Dock the Chart toolbar above the Status bar. Change it to a floating toolbar. Close the Chart toolbar.
   f. Use the shortcut key combination to display the Task Pane. How many Task Panes are available? ___________
   g. Display the Help Task Pane and search for help information on "worksheet." How many search results were returned? ______ Read the "About viewing workbooks and worksheets" topic. What is the definition of a worksheet? ____
   ____
   h. Close the Help window. Close the Excel window to exit the program.

on your own

Exploring Microsoft Help ★

1. In addition to the Help information you used in this lab, Office 2003 Online Help also includes many interactive tutorials. Selecting a Help topic that starts a tutorial will open the browser program on your computer. Both audio and written instructions are provided. You will use one of these tutorials to learn more about using Office 2003. Start Word 2003 and search for Help on "shortcut keys." Then select the "Work with the Keyboard in Office" topic. Follow the directions in the tutorial to learn about this feature. When you are done, close the browser window and the Word window.

Overview of Microsoft Office Excel 2003

What Is an Electronic Spreadsheet?

The electronic spreadsheet, or worksheet, is an automated version of the accountant's ledger. Like the accountant's ledger, it consists of rows and columns of numerical data. Unlike the accountant's ledger, which is created on paper using a pencil and a calculator, the electronic spreadsheet is created by a computer system running spreadsheet application software.

In contrast to word processing software which manipulates text, spreadsheet programs manipulate numerical data. The first spreadsheet program, VisiCalc, was introduced in 1979. Since then spreadsheets have evolved into a powerful business tool that has revolutionized the business world.

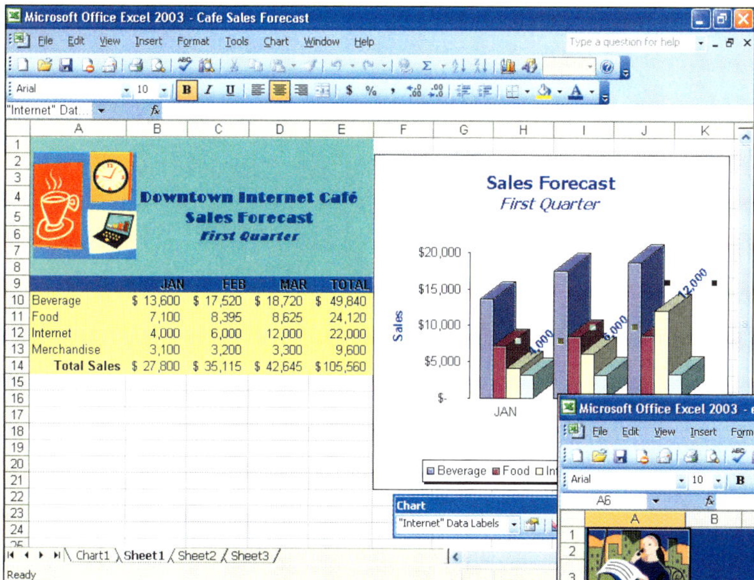

A chart of the first quarter sales visually shows sales trends

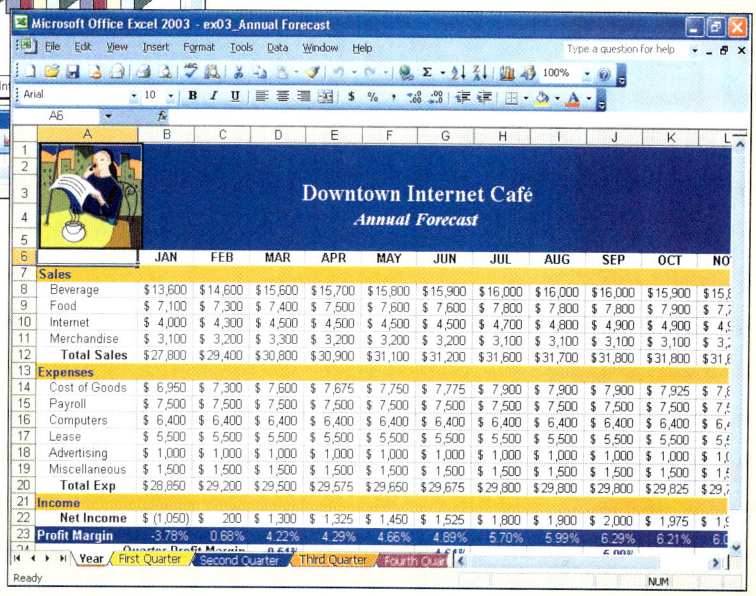

A worksheet for the Downtown Internet Café Annual Forecast

The electronic spreadsheet eliminates the paper, pencil, and eraser. With a few keystrokes, the user can quickly change, correct, and update the data. Even more impressive is the spreadsheet's ability to perform calculations from very simple sums to the most complex financial and mathematical formulas. The calculator is replaced by the electronic spreadsheet. Analysis of data in the spreadsheet has become a routine business procedure. Once requiring hours of labor and/or costly accountants' fees, data analysis is now available almost instantly using electronic spreadsheets.

Nearly any job that uses rows and columns of numbers can be performed using an electronic spreadsheet. Typical uses include the creation of budgets and financial planning for both business and personal situations.

Excel 2003 Features

Spreadsheet applications help you create well-designed spreadsheets that produce accurate results. These programs not only make it faster to create spreadsheets, they also produce professional-appearing results. Their advantages include the ability to quickly edit and format data, perform calculations, create charts, and print the spreadsheet.

The Microsoft Office Excel 2003 spreadsheet program uses a workbook file that contains one or more worksheets. Each worksheet can be used to organize different types of related information. Numeric or text data is entered into the worksheet in a location called a cell. These entries can then be erased, moved, copied, or edited. Formulas can be entered that perform calculations using data contained in specified cells. The results of the calculations are displayed in the cell containing the formula.

The design and appearance of the worksheet can be enhanced in many ways. There are several commands that control the format or display of a cell. For instance, numeric entries can be displayed with dollar signs or with a set number of decimal places. Text or label entries can be displayed centered, left-, or right-aligned to improve the spreadsheet's appearance. You can further enhance the appearance of the worksheet by changing the type style and size and by adding special effects such as bold, italic, borders, boxes, drop shadows, and shading to selected cells. Columns and rows can be inserted and deleted. The cell width can be changed to accommodate entries of varying lengths.

You can change the values in selected cells and observe their effect on related cells in the worksheet. This is called what-if or sensitivity analysis. Questions that once were too expensive to ask or took too long to answer can now be answered almost instantly and with little cost. Planning that was once partially based on instinct has been replaced to a great extent with facts. However, any financial planning resulting from the data in a worksheet is only as accurate as that data and the logic behind the calculations.

You can also produce a visual display of data in the form of graphs or charts. As the values in the worksheet change, charts referencing those values automatically adjust to reflect the changes. You can also enhance the appearance of a graph by using different type styles and sizes, adding three-dimensional effects, and including text and objects such as lines and arrows.

Case Study for Office Excel 2003 Labs

The Downtown Internet Café is a new concept in coffeehouses, combining the delicious aromas of a genuine coffeehouse with the fun of using the Internet. You are the new manager for the coffeehouse and are working with the owner, Evan, to develop a financial plan for the next year.

Lab 1: Your first project is to develop a forecast for the Cafe showing the estimated sales and expenses for the first quarter. You will learn to enter numbers, perform calculations, copy data, label rows and columns, and format entries in a spreadsheet using Office Excel 2003.

Lab 2: After creating the first quarter forecast, you decide to chart the sales data to make it easier to see the trends and growth patterns. You also want to see what effect a strong advertising promotion of the new Cafe features will have on the forecasted sales data.

Lab 3: You have been asked to revise the workbook to include forecasts for the second, third, and fourth quarters. Additionally, the owner wants you to create a composite worksheet that shows the entire year's forecast and to change the data to achieve a 5 percent profit margin in the second quarter.

Working Together: Your analysis of sales data for the first quarter has shown a steady increase in total sales. Evan, the Cafe owner, has asked you for a copy of the forecast that shows the growth in Internet sales if a strong sales promotion is mounted. You will include the worksheet and chart data in a Word memo that you will e-mail to the owner.

Before You Begin

To the Student

The following assumptions have been made:

- Microsoft Office Excel 2003 has been properly installed on your computer system.
- You have the data files needed to complete the series of Excel 2003 labs and practice exercises. These may be supplied by your instructor and are also available at the online learning center Web site found at **www.mhhe.com/oleary**.
- You are already familiar with how to use Microsoft Windows and a mouse.

To the Instructor

A complete installation of Microsoft Office 2003 is required in which all components are installed and are available to students while completing the labs.

Please be aware that the following settings are assumed to be in effect for the Office Excel 2003 program. These assumptions are necessary so that the screens and directions in the labs are accurate.

- The Getting Started task pane is displayed when Excel is started (use Tools/Options/View/Startup Task Pane).
- The horizontal and vertical scroll bars are displayed (use Tools/Options/View).
- The status bar is displayed (use Tools/Options/View).
- The fill handle is displayed (use Tools/Options/Edit/Allow all drag and drop).
- The Paste Options and Show Insert Options buttons are displayed (use Tools/Options/Edit).
- The fill handle is displayed (use Tools/Options/Edit/Allow cell drag and drop).
- The Standard and Formatting toolbars are displayed on separate rows (use Tools/Customize/Options).
- Full menus are always displayed (use Tools/Customize/Options).
- The ScreenTips feature is active (use Tools/Customize/Options/Show ScreenTips on toolbar).
- The Normal view is on; zoom is 100 percent (use View/Normal; View/Zoom/100%).
- The Office Clipboard is not displayed automatically (click Options on the Clipboard task pane and clear the Show Office Clipboard Automatically option).
- The feature to access Online Help is on (choose Online Content Settings from the Help task pane and select the Show content and links from Microsoft Office Online option).
- The Office Assistant feature is not on (right-click on the Assistant character, choose Options, and clear the Use the Office Assistant option).
- All default settings for a new workbook are in effect.

In addition, all figures in the labs reflect the use of a standard VGA display monitor set at 800 by 600. The 800 by 600 setting displays rows 1 through 27 and columns A through L. If another monitor setting is used, there may be more or fewer rows and columns displayed in the window than in the figures. The Windows appearance setting is Windows XP style. These settings can be changed using The Display Properties dialog box.

Microsoft Office Language Bar

The Microsoft Office Language bar (shown below) may also be displayed when you start the application. Commonly, it will appear in the title bar; however, it may appear in other locations depending upon your setup. The Language bar provides buttons to access and use the Speech Recognition and Handwriting recognition features of Office.

Instructional Conventions

Hands-on instructions you are to perform appear as a sequence of numbered black steps. Within each step, a series of bullets identifies the specific actions that must be performed. Step numbering begins over within each main topic heading throughout the lab.

Command sequences you are to issue appear following the word "Choose." Each menu command selection is separated by a /. If the menu command can be selected by typing a letter of the command, the letter will appear underlined and bold. Items that need to be selected will follow the word "Select" and will appear in black text. You can select items with the mouse or directional keys. (See Example A.)

Example A

1
- **Choose File/Page Setup.**
- **Select Portrait.**

Commands that can be initiated using a button and the mouse appear following the word "Click." The icon (and the icon name if the icon does not include text) is displayed following "Click." The menu equivalent, keyboard shortcut, and/or voice command appear in an Another Method margin note when the action is first introduced. (See Example B.)

Example B

1
- **Click**  **Open.**

Another Method

The menu equivalent is **F**ile/**O**pen and the keyboard shortcut is Ctrl + O.

Plain blue text identifies file names you need to select or enter. Information you are asked to type appears in blue and bold. (See Example C.)

Example C

1. Choose **File/Open**.

   Select ex01_Forecast1.

2. Move to B3.

   Type **Sales Forecast**.

Creating and Editing a Worksheet

LAB 1

Objectives

After completing this lab, you will know how to:

1. Enter, edit, and clear cell entries.
2. Adjust column widths.
3. Save, close, and open workbooks.
4. Spell-check a worksheet.
5. Use the thesaurus.
6. Copy and move cell entries.
7. Specify ranges.
8. Enter formulas and functions.
9. Insert rows.
10. Change cell alignment.
11. Format cells.
12. Enter and format a date.
13. Preview and print a worksheet.

Case Study

Downtown Internet Café

You are excited about your new position as manager and financial planner for a local coffeehouse. Evan, the owner, has hired you as part of a larger effort to increase business at the former Downtown Café. Evan began this effort by completely renovating his coffeehouse, installing Internet hookups and outlets for laptops, and changing its name to the Downtown Internet Café. You and Evan expect to increase sales by attracting Internet-savvy cafe-goers, who, you hope, will use the Downtown Internet Café as a place to meet, study, or just relax.

Evan wants to create a forecast estimating sales and expenses for the first quarter. As part of a good business plan, you and Evan need a realistic set of financial estimates and goals.

In this lab, you will help with the first quarter forecast by using Microsoft Office Excel 2003, a spreadsheet application that can store, manipulate, and display numeric data. You will learn to enter numbers, perform calculations, copy data, and label rows and columns as you create the basic structure of a worksheet for the Downtown Internet Café. You will then learn how to enhance the worksheet using formatting features and by adding color as shown here.

© Corbis

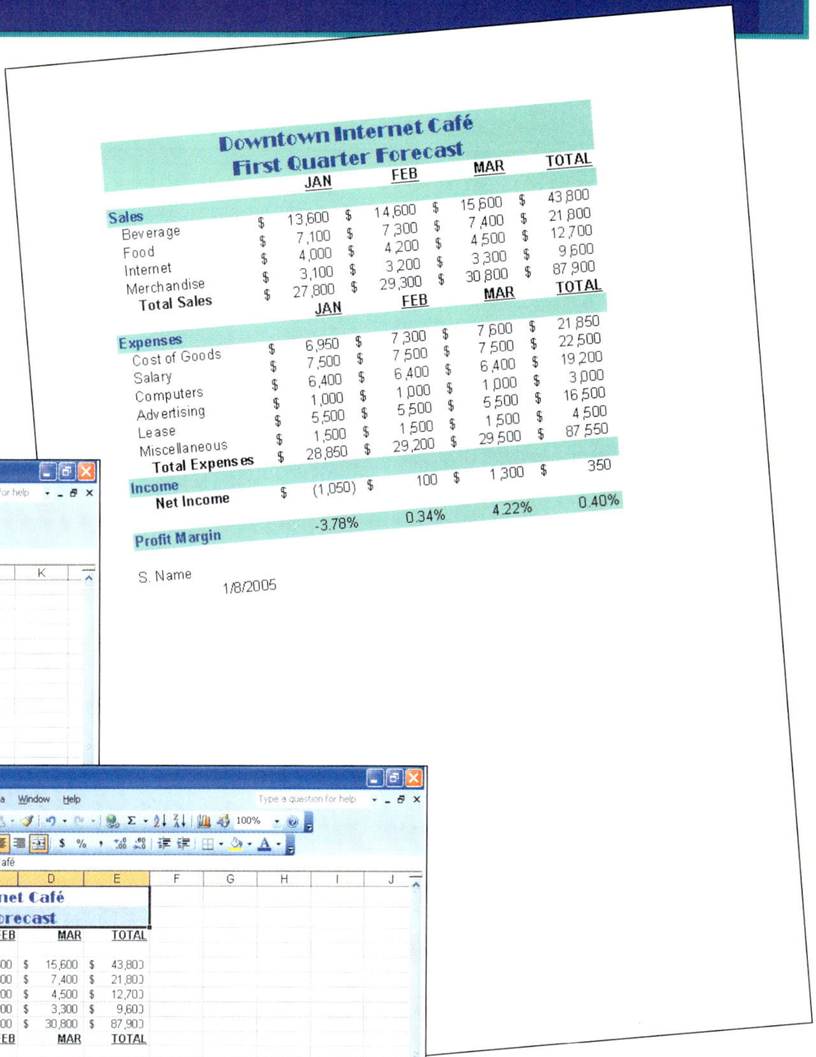

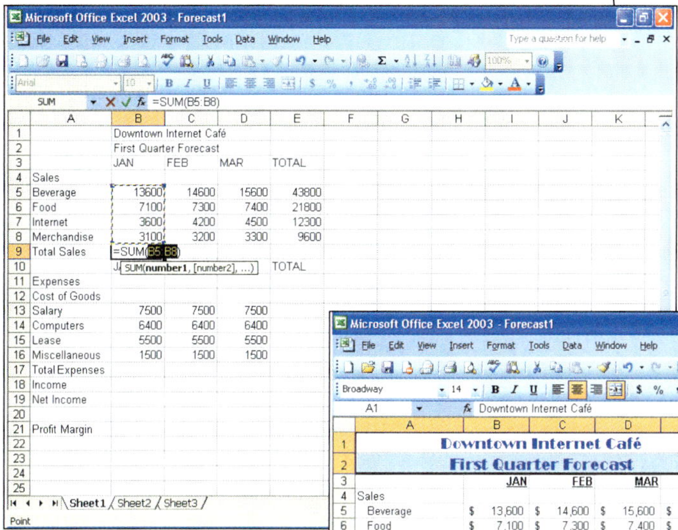

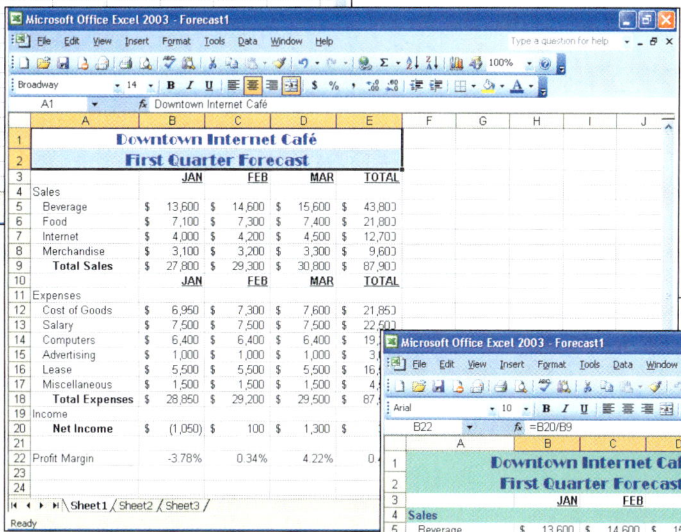

Enter labels, numbers, and formulas to create the basic structure of a worksheet.

Basic formatting, such as alignment, indents, and numeric styles quickly improve the appearance of the worksheet.

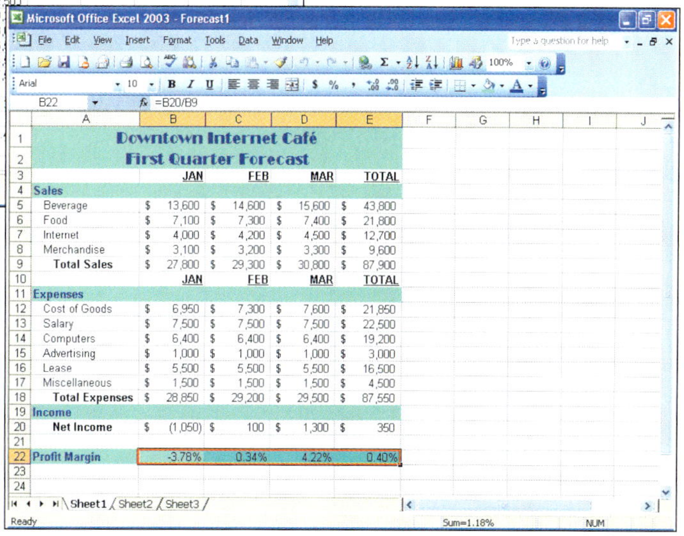

Adding color text and background fill further enhances the appearance of the worksheet.

Concept Preview

The following concepts will be introduced in this lab:

1. **Text and Numeric Entries** The information or data you enter in a cell can be text, numbers, or formulas.
2. **AutoCorrect** The AutoCorrect feature makes some basic assumptions about the text you are typing and, based on these assumptions, automatically corrects the entry.
3. **Column Width** The size or width of a column controls the amount of information that can be displayed in a cell.
4. **Spelling Checker** The spelling checker locates misspelled words, duplicate words, and capitalization irregularities in the active worksheet and proposes the correct spelling.
5. **Thesaurus** The thesaurus is a reference tool that provides synonyms, antonyms, and related words for a selected word or phrase.
6. **Copy and Move** The contents of worksheet cells can be duplicated (copied) or moved to other locations in the worksheet or between worksheets, saving you time by not having to retype the same information.
7. **Range** A selection consisting of two or more cells on a worksheet is a range.
8. **Formula** A formula is an equation that performs a calculation on data contained in a worksheet.
9. **Relative Reference** A relative reference is a cell or range reference in a formula whose location is interpreted in relation to the position of the cell that contains the formula.
10. **Function** A function is a prewritten formula that performs certain types of calculations automatically.
11. **Recalculation** When a number in a referenced cell in a formula changes, Excel automatically recalculates all formulas that are dependent upon the changed value.
12. **Alignment** Alignment settings allow you to change the horizontal and vertical placement and the orientation of an entry in a cell.
13. **Fonts** A font, also commonly referred to as a typeface, is a set of characters with a specific design.
14. **Number Formats** Number formats affect the appearance of numbers onscreen and when printed.

Introducing Office Excel 2003

As part of the renovation of the Downtown Internet Café, new computers and the most current versions of software programs were installed, including the latest version of the Microsoft Office System suite of applications, Office 2003. You are very excited to see how this new and powerful application can help you create professional budgets and financial forecasts.

Starting Office Excel 2003

You will use the spreadsheet application Excel 2003 included in the Microsoft Office System 2003 suite to create the first quarter forecast for the cafe.

1

- **Start Office Excel 2003.**
- **If necessary, maximize the Excel application window.**

Additional Information

See "Common Office 2003 Features" page I.11 for information on how to start the application and for a discussion of features common to all Office 2003 applications.

Your screen should be similar to Figure 1.1

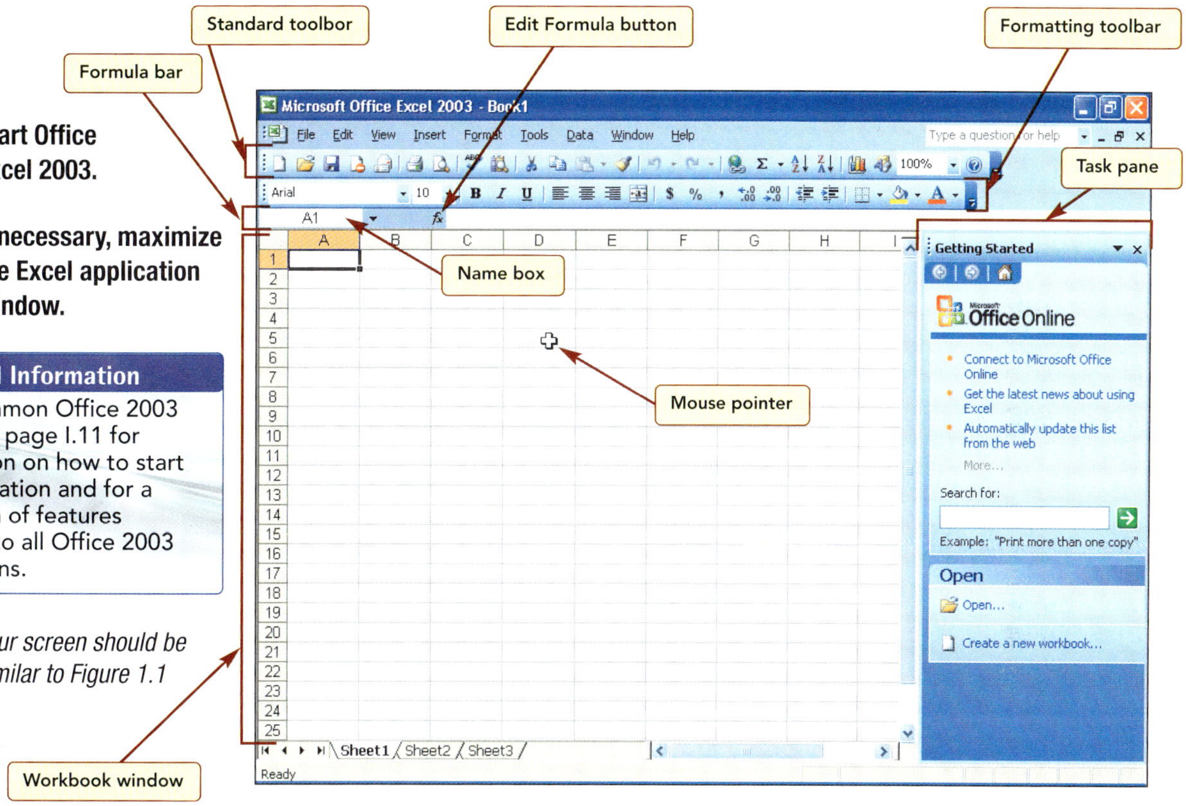

Figure 1.1

Additional Information

Because Excel remembers settings that were on when the program was last closed, your screen might look slightly different.

After a few moments, the Excel application window is displayed.

Exploring the Excel Window

The Excel window title bar displays the program name followed by Book1, the name of the open file. The menu bar below the title bar displays the Excel program menu. It consists of nine menus that provide access to the commands and features you will use to create and modify a worksheet.

The toolbars, normally located below the menu bar, contain buttons that are mouse shortcuts for many of the menu items. The **Standard toolbar** contains buttons that are used to complete the most frequently used menu commands. The **Formatting toolbar** contains buttons that are

Having Trouble?

If necessary, use View/Toolbars and select or deselect the appropriate toolbar to display or hide it.

Additional Information

If you have a microphone and have installed and trained the Speech Recognition feature, you can speak the command sequences to open menus and choose commands. For example, to select a toolbar, you would say "View Toolbars."

Having Trouble?

If the Standard and Formatting toolbars are on a single row, use Tools/Customize/Options/Show Standard and Formatting toolbars on two rows.

Having Trouble?

If your task pane is not displayed, choose View/Task Pane.

used to change the appearance or format of the document. Excel includes 21 different toolbars. Many of the toolbars appear automatically as you use different features. Your screen may display other toolbars if they were on when the program was last exited.

Below the toolbars is the formula bar. The **formula bar** displays entries as they are made and edited in the workbook window. The **Name box**, located at the left end of the formula bar, provides information about the selected item. The Edit Formula button is used to create or edit a formula.

The task pane is displayed on the right side of the window. There are 12 different task panes that display depending on the task being performed. Because you just started Excel, the Getting Started task pane is automatically displayed, providing different ways to create a new workbook or open an existing workbook.

The large area to the left of the task pane is the **workbook window**. A **workbook** is an Excel file that stores the information you enter using the program in worksheets. You will learn about the different parts of the workbook window and worksheets shortly.

The mouse pointer can appear as many different shapes. The mouse pointer changes shape depending upon the task you are performing or where the pointer is located on the window. Most commonly it appears as a ↖ or ✥. When it appears as a ✥, it is used to move to different locations in the workbook window and when it appears as a ↖, it is used to select items.

1 **Move the mouse pointer into the center of the workbook window to see it appear as ✥.**

Move the mouse pointer to the menu bar to see it appear as ↖.

Your screen should be similar to Figure 1.2

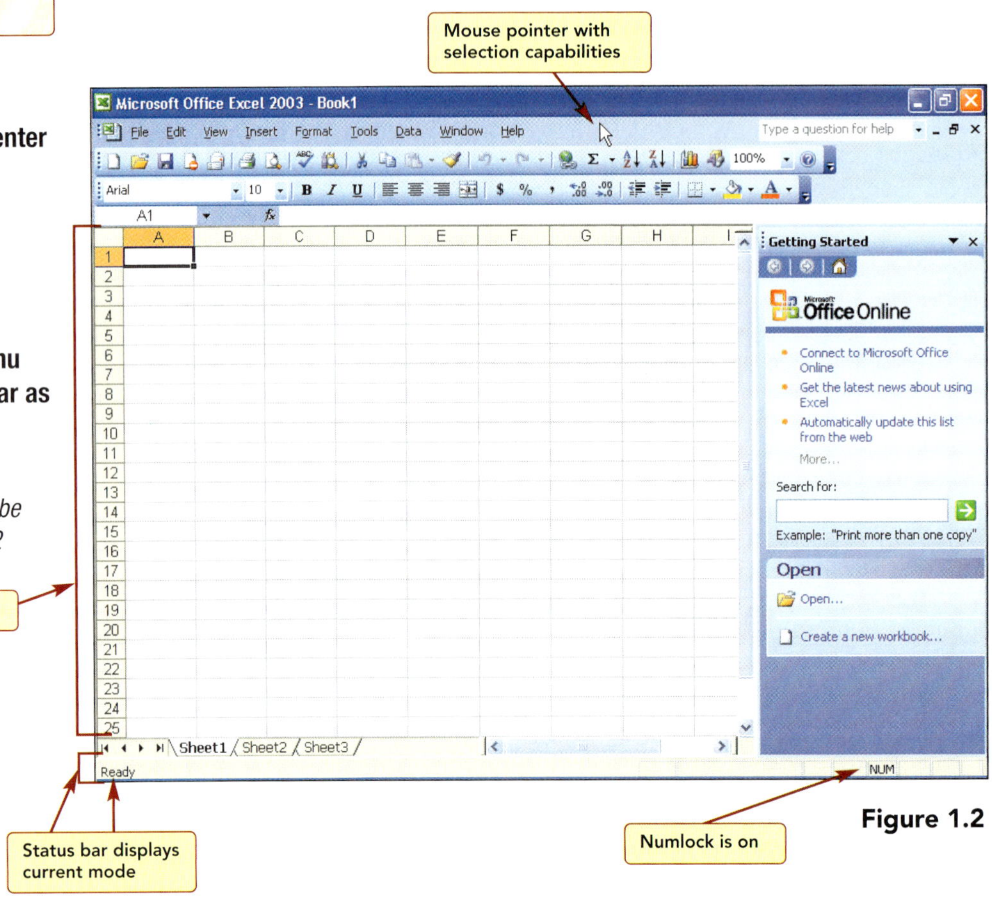

Figure 1.2

The status bar at the bottom of the Excel window displays information about various Excel settings. The left side of the status bar displays the current mode or state of operation of the program, in this case, Ready. When Ready is displayed, you can move around the workbook, enter data, use the function keys, or choose a command. As you use the program, the status bar displays the current mode. The modes will be discussed as they appear throughout the labs. If your status bar displays NUM, this is a keyboard indicator that tells you the NumLock key is on. When on, using the numeric keypad enters numbers. When off, it moves the cell selector. Pressing Num Lock on your keyboard toggles between these settings.

Exploring the Workbook Window

The workbook window displays a new blank workbook file containing three blank sheets. A **sheet** is used to display different types of information, such as financial data or charts. Whenever you open a new workbook, it displays a worksheet. A **worksheet**, also commonly referred to as a **spreadsheet**, is a rectangular grid of **rows** and **columns** used to enter data. It is always part of a workbook and is the primary type of sheet you will use in Excel. The worksheet is much larger than the part you are viewing in the window. The worksheet actually extends 256 columns to the right and 65,536 rows down.

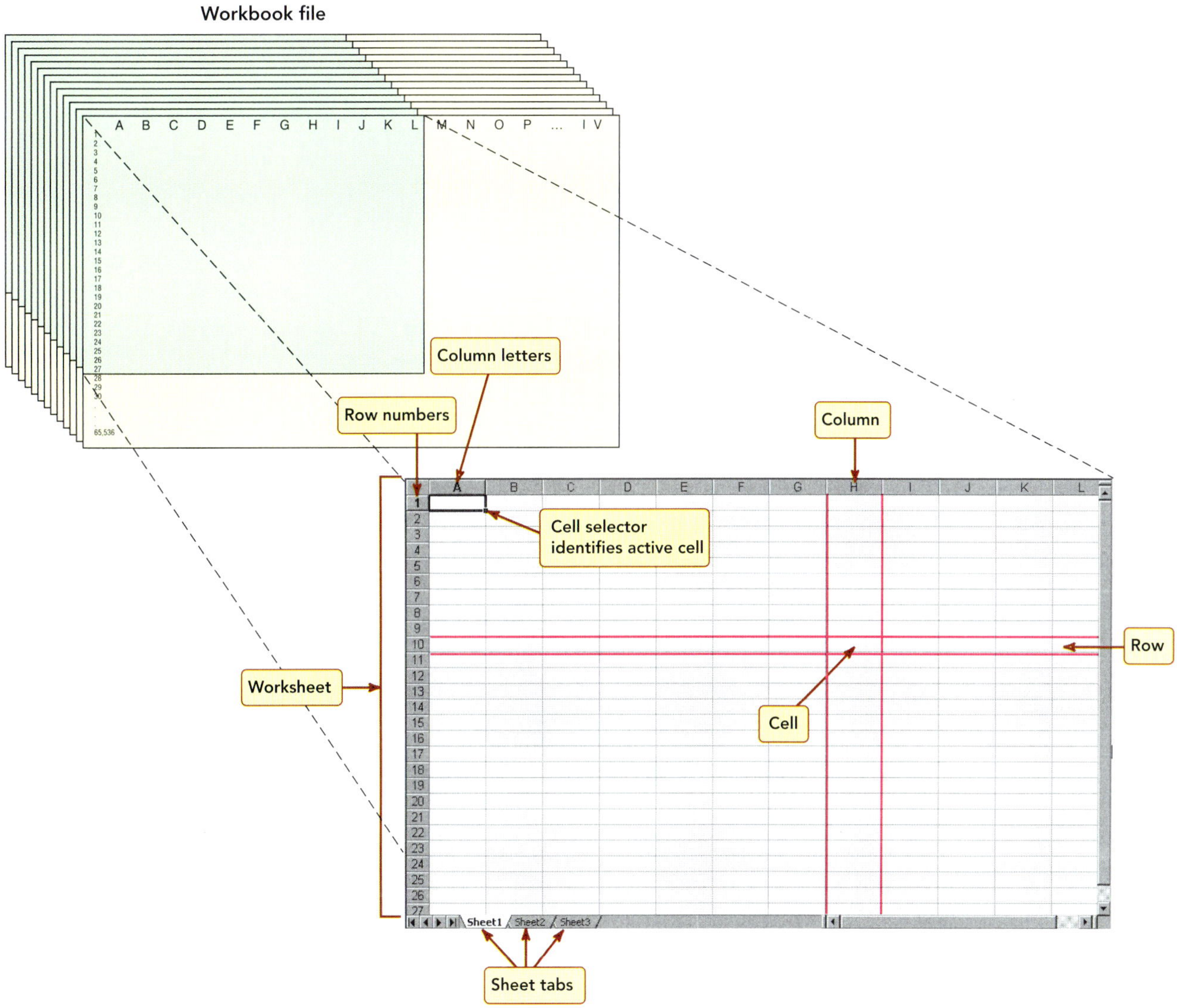

The **row numbers** along the left side and the **column letters** across the top of the workbook window identify each worksheet row and column. The intersection of a row and column creates a cell. Notice the heavy border, called the **cell selector**, surrounding the cell located at the intersection of column A and row 1. The cell selector identifies the **active cell**, which is the cell your next entry or procedure affects. Additionally, the Name box in the formula bar displays the **cell reference**, consisting of the column letter and row number of the active cell. The reference of the active cell is A1.

Each sheet in a workbook is named. Initially, the sheets are named Sheet1, Sheet2, and so on, displayed on **sheet tabs** at the bottom of the workbook window. The name of the **active sheet**, which is the sheet you can work in, appears bold. The currently displayed worksheet in the workbook window, Sheet1, is the active sheet.

1 Click the Sheet2 tab.

Another Method

You can also press Ctrl + Page Down to move to the next sheet and Ctrl + Page Up to move to the previous sheet.

Your screen should be similar to Figure 1.3

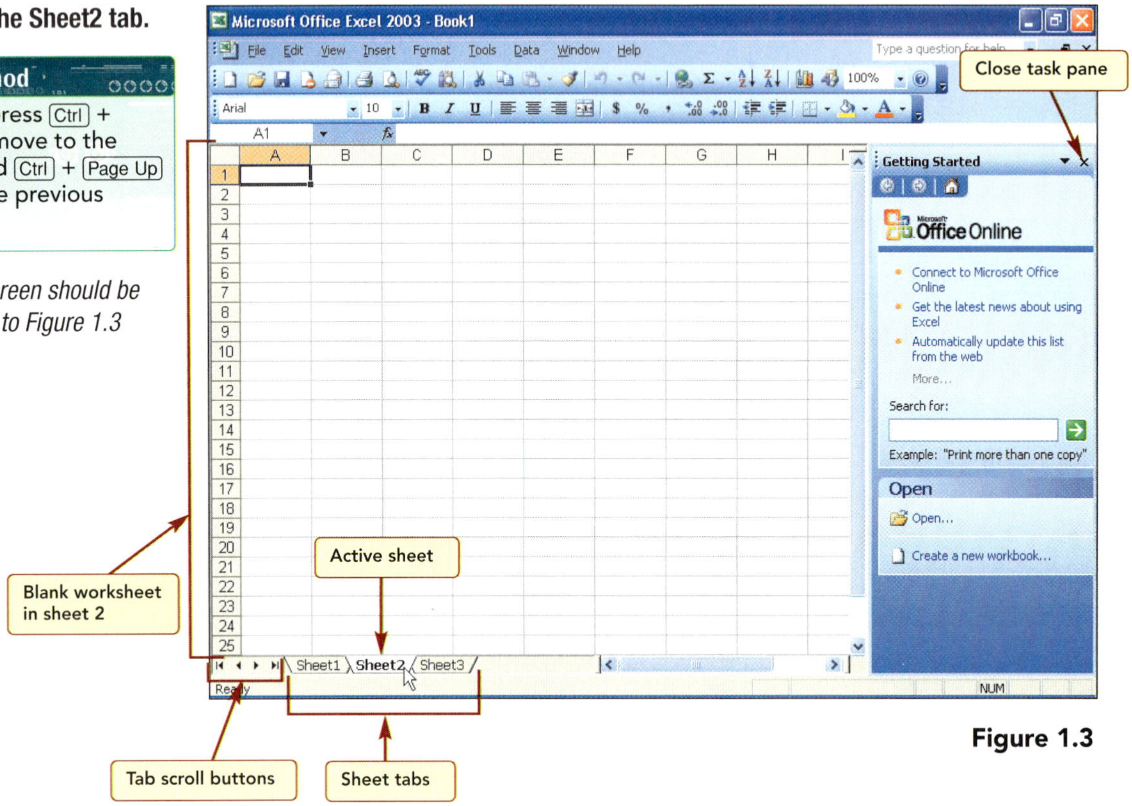

Figure 1.3

An identical blank worksheet is displayed in the window. The Sheet2 tab letters are bold, the background is highlighted, and it appears in front of the other sheet tabs to show it is the active sheet.

The sheet tab area also contains **tab scroll buttons**, which are used to scroll tabs right or left when there are more worksheet tabs than can be seen. You will learn about these features throughout the labs.

2 • **Click the Sheet1 tab to make it the active sheet again.**

• **Click ✕ Close in the task pane title bar to close the task pane.**

Another Method

The View/Task Pane command can also be used to hide the task pane.

Your screen should be similar to Figure 1.4

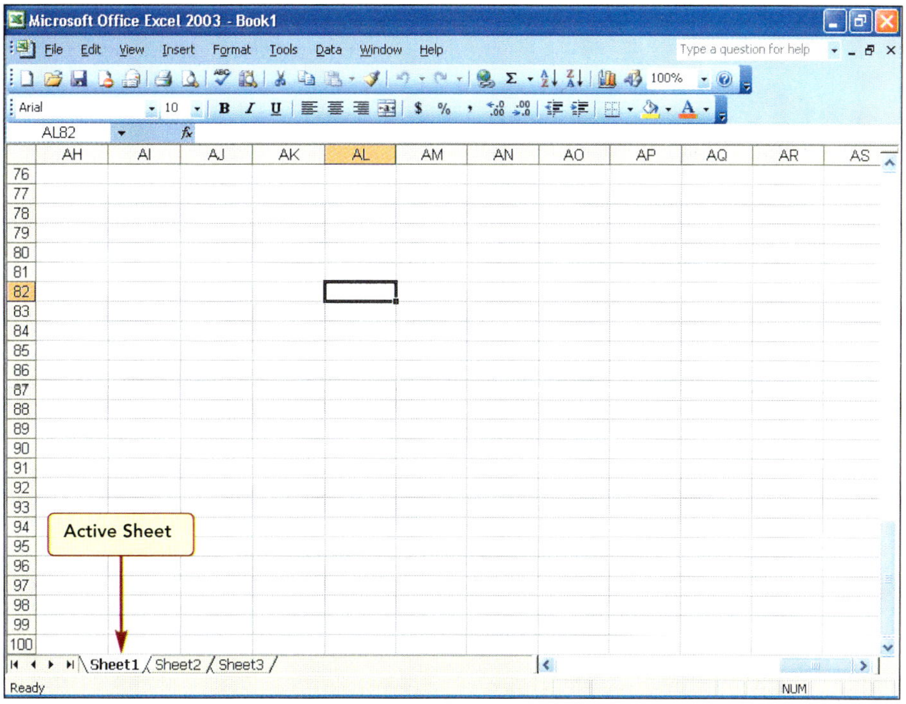

Figure 1.4

Additional Information

Do not be concerned if your workbook window displays more or fewer column letters and row numbers than shown here. This is a function of your computer monitor settings.

With the task pane closed, the workbook window is now the full width of the application window space, allowing much more of the worksheet to be displayed.

Moving Around the Worksheet

The mouse, keyboard or voice commands can be used to move the cell selector from one cell to another in the worksheet. To move using a mouse, simply point to the cell you want to move to and click the mouse button. Depending upon what you are doing, using the mouse to move may not be as convenient as using the keyboard, in which case the directional keys can be used. You will use the mouse, then the keyboard to move the cell selector.

Additional Information

Using voice commands requires that the Speech Recognition feature be installed and the use of a microphone. Voice command equivalents will be identified in tables and marginal notes.

Additional Information

You can use the directional keys in the numeric keypad (with NumLock off) or, if you have an extended keyboard, you can use the separate directional keypad area.

1 Click cell B3.

Press → (3 times).

Press ↓ (4 times).

Another Method

The voice commands are "Down," "Right," "Up," or "Left."

Your screen should be similar to Figure 1.5

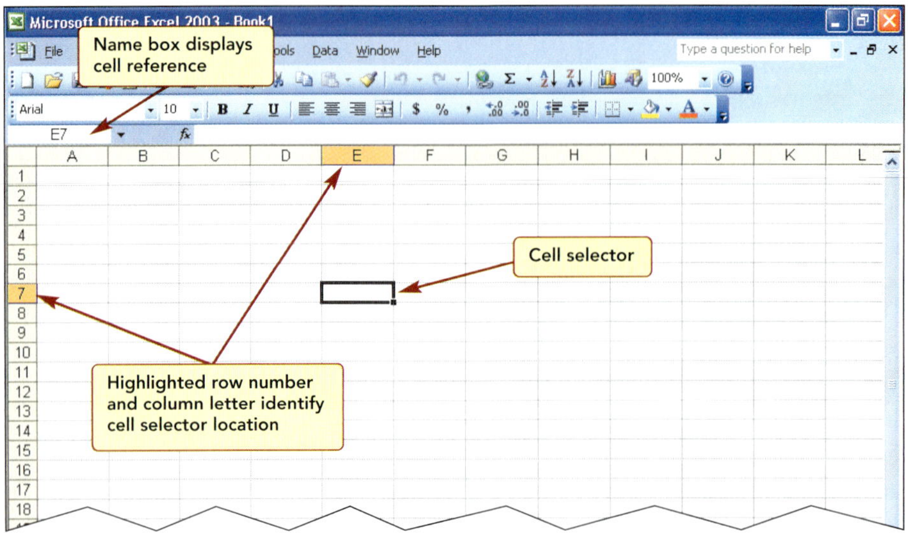

Figure 1.5

The cell selector is now in cell E7, making this cell the active cell. The Name box displays the cell reference. In addition, the row number and column letter are gold to further identify the location of the active cell.

As you have learned, the worksheet is much larger than the part you are viewing in the window. To see an area of the worksheet that is not currently in view, you need to scroll the window. Either the keyboard or the mouse can be used to quickly scroll a worksheet. Again, both methods are useful depending upon what you are doing. The keyboard, voice, and mouse procedures shown in the tables that follow can be used to move around the worksheet.

Having Trouble?

If your row number and column letter are highlighted, this is a function of your Windows settings.

Additional Information

Keys joined with a + indicate that you need to hold down the first key while pressing the second.

Keyboard	Voice	Action
Page Down	Page down	Moves cell selector down one full window
Page Up	Page up	Moves cell selector up one full window
Alt + Page Down		Moves cell selector right one full window
Alt + Page Up		Moves cell selector left one full window
Ctrl + Home	Home	Moves cell selector to upper-left corner cell of worksheet
Ctrl + End		Moves cell selector to last used cell of worksheet
Home		Moves cell selector to beginning of row
End →		End Moves cell selector to last-used cell in row
End ↓		Moves cell selector to last-used cell in column

Mouse	Action
Click scroll arrow	Scrolls worksheet one row/column in direction of arrow
Click above/below scroll box	Scrolls worksheet one full window up/down
Click right/left of scroll box	Scrolls worksheet one full window right/left
Drag scroll box	Scrolls worksheet multiple windows up/down or right/left

In addition, if you hold down the arrow keys, the Alt + Page Up or Alt + Page Down keys, or the Page Up or Page Down keys, you can quickly scroll through the worksheet. When you use the scroll bar, however, the cell selector does not move until you click on a cell that is visible in the window.

You will scroll the worksheet to see the rows below row 25 and the columns to the right of column L.

2

- **Press Page Down (3 times).**
- **Press Alt + Page Down (3 times).**

Your screen should be similar to Figure 1.6

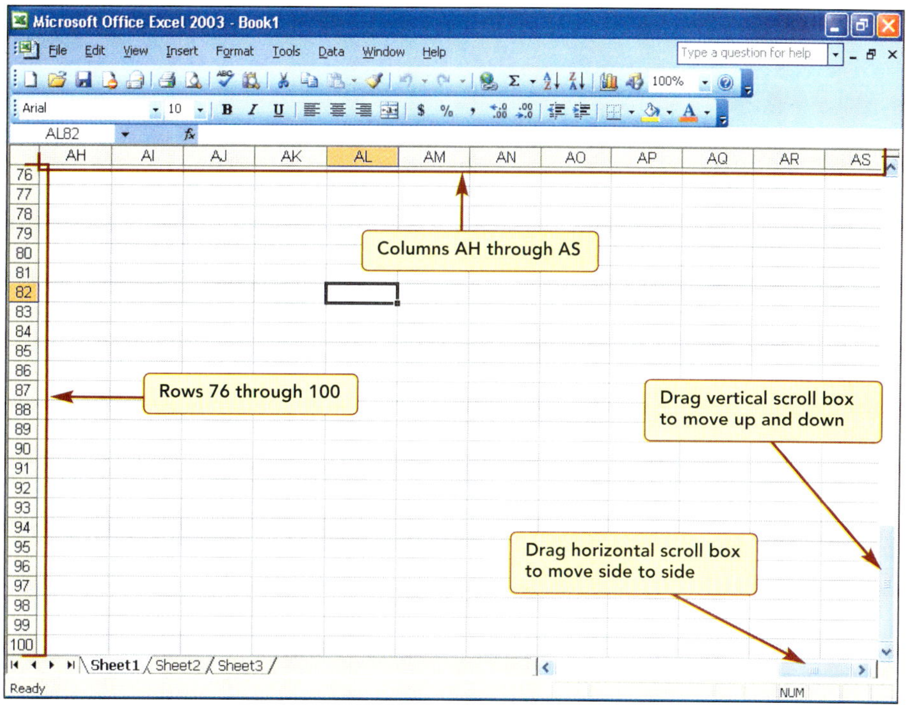

Figure 1.6

Having Trouble?

Your screen may display more or fewer rows and columns and the cell selector may be in a different cell. This is a function of your screen and system settings.

The worksheet scrolled downward and left three full windows, and the window displays rows 76 through 100 and columns AH through AS of the worksheet. The cell selector is in cell AL82. As you scroll the worksheet using the keyboard, the cell selector also moves.

It is even more efficient to use the scroll bar to move long distances.

3

- **Slowly drag the vertical scroll box up the scroll bar until row 1 is displayed.**
- **Slowly drag the horizontal scroll box left along the scroll bar until column A is displayed.**

Additional Information

The position of the scroll box indicates the relative location of the area you are viewing within the worksheet, and the size of the scroll box indicates the proportional amount of the used area.

Your screen should be similar to Figure 1.7

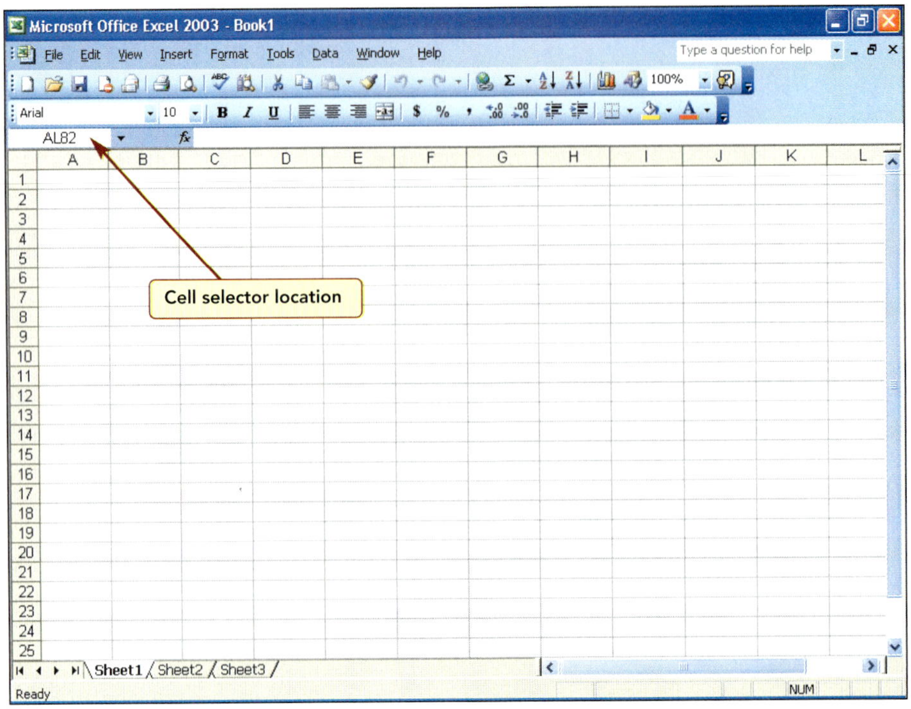

Figure 1.7

Notice that the Name box displays the cell selector location as AL82. When you use the scroll bar to scroll the worksheet, the cell selector does not move.

4

- **Practice moving the cell selector around the worksheet using each of the keys presented in the table on page EX1.10.**
- **Press Ctrl + Home to move to cell A1.**

Another Method

You can also type a cell address in the Name box to move to that location.

Your screen should be similar to Figure 1.8

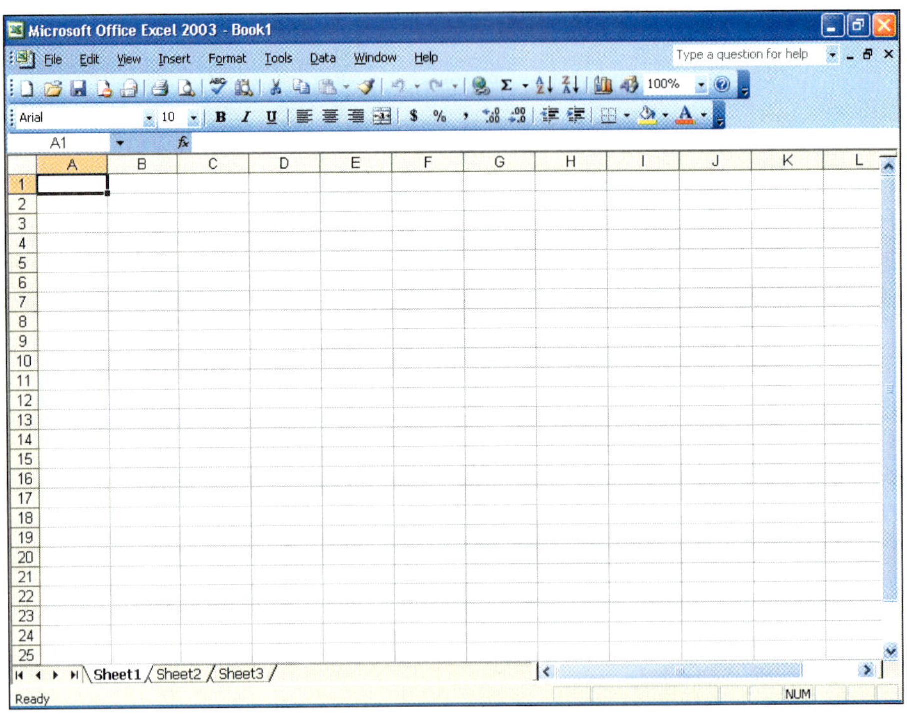

Figure 1.8

You can use the mouse or the keyboard with most of the exercises in these labs. As you use both the mouse and the keyboard, you will find that it is more efficient to use one or the other in specific situations.

Creating New Worksheets

Now that you are familiar with the parts of the workbook and with moving around the worksheet, you are ready to create a worksheet showing the forecast for the first three months of operation for the Downtown Internet Cafe. As you create a new worksheet, the development progresses through several stages.

Developing a Worksheet

Worksheet development consists of four steps: planning, entering and editing, testing, and formatting. The objective is to create well-designed worksheets that produce accurate results and are clearly understood, adaptable, and efficient.

Step	Description
1. Plan	Specify the purpose of the worksheet and how it should be organized. This means clearly identifying the data that will be input, the calculations that are needed to achieve the results, and the output that is desired. As part of the planning step, it is helpful to sketch out a design of the worksheet to organize the worksheet's structure. The design should include the worksheet title and row and column headings that identify the input and output. Additionally, sample data can be used to help determine the formulas needed to produce the output.
2. Enter and edit	Create the structure of the worksheet using Excel by entering the worksheet labels, data, and formulas. As you enter information, you are likely to make errors that need to be corrected or edited, or you will need to revise the content of what you have entered to clarify it or to add or delete information.
3. Test	Test the worksheet for errors. Use several sets of real or sample data as the input, and verify the resulting output. The input data should include a full range of possible values for each data item to ensure the worksheet can function successfully under all possible conditions.
4. Format	Enhance the appearance of the worksheet to make it more readable or attractive. This step is usually performed when the worksheet is near completion. It includes many features such as boldface text, italic, and color.

As the complexity of the worksheet increases, the importance of following the design process increases. Even for simple worksheets like the one you will create in this lab, the design process is important. You will find that you will generally follow these steps in the order listed above for your first draft of a worksheet. However, you will probably retrace steps such as editing and formatting as the final worksheet is developed.

During the planning phase, you have spoken with the Cafe manager regarding the purpose of the worksheet and the content in general. The primary purpose is to develop a forecast for sales and expenses for the next year. First, Evan wants you to develop a worksheet for the first quarter forecast and then extend it by quarters for the year. After reviewing past budgets and consulting with Evan, you have designed the basic layout for the first quarter forecast for the Cafe, as shown below.

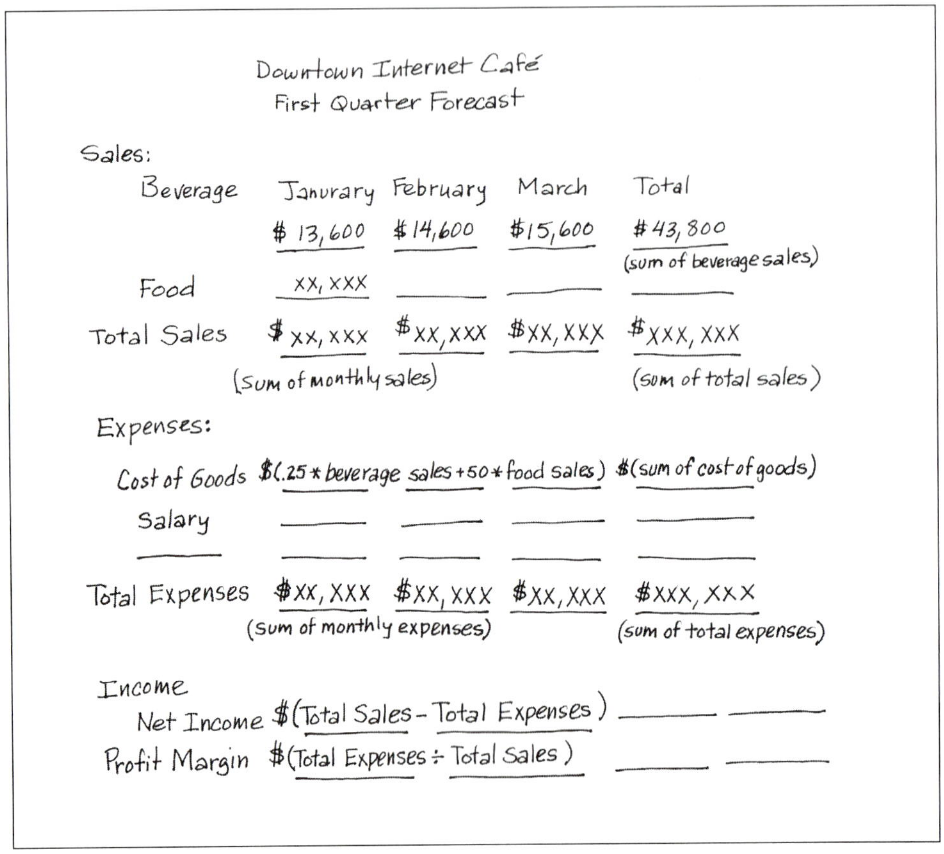

Entering and Editing Data

Additional Information

You can also enter data in Dictation mode using the Speech Recognition feature.

Now that you understand the purpose of the worksheet and have a general idea of the content, you are ready to begin entering the data. When you first start Office Excel, a new blank Excel workbook file is opened containing three blank worksheets. Each worksheet is like a blank piece of paper that already has many predefined settings. These settings, called **default** settings, are generally the most commonly used settings. You will use the blank worksheet with the default settings to create the worksheet for the Cafe.

As you can see, the budget you designed above contains both descriptive text entries and numeric data. These are two types of entries you can make in a worksheet.

Concept 1

Text and Numeric Entries

1 The information or data you enter in a cell can be text, numbers, or formulas. **Text** entries can contain any combination of letters, numbers, spaces, and any other special characters. **Number** entries can include only the digits 0 to 9 and any of the special characters, + – ( ) , . / $ % ? =. Number entries can be used in calculations. The third type of entry is a formula. Formulas perform calculations on values in the worksheet. You will learn about formula entries later in the lab.

Entering Text

You enter data into a worksheet by moving to the cell where you want the data displayed and typing the entry using the keyboard. First, you will enter the worksheet headings. Row and column **headings** are entries that are used to create the structure of the worksheet and describe other worksheet entries. Generally, headings are text entries. The column headings in this worksheet consist of the three months (January through March) and a total (sum of entries over three months) located in columns B through E. To enter data in a worksheet, you must first select the cell where you want the entry displayed. The column heading for January will be entered in cell B2.

1 ● **Move to B2.**

● **Type January.**

Having Trouble?

Do not be concerned if you made a typing error. You will learn how to correct it shortly.

Your screen should be similar to Figure 1.9

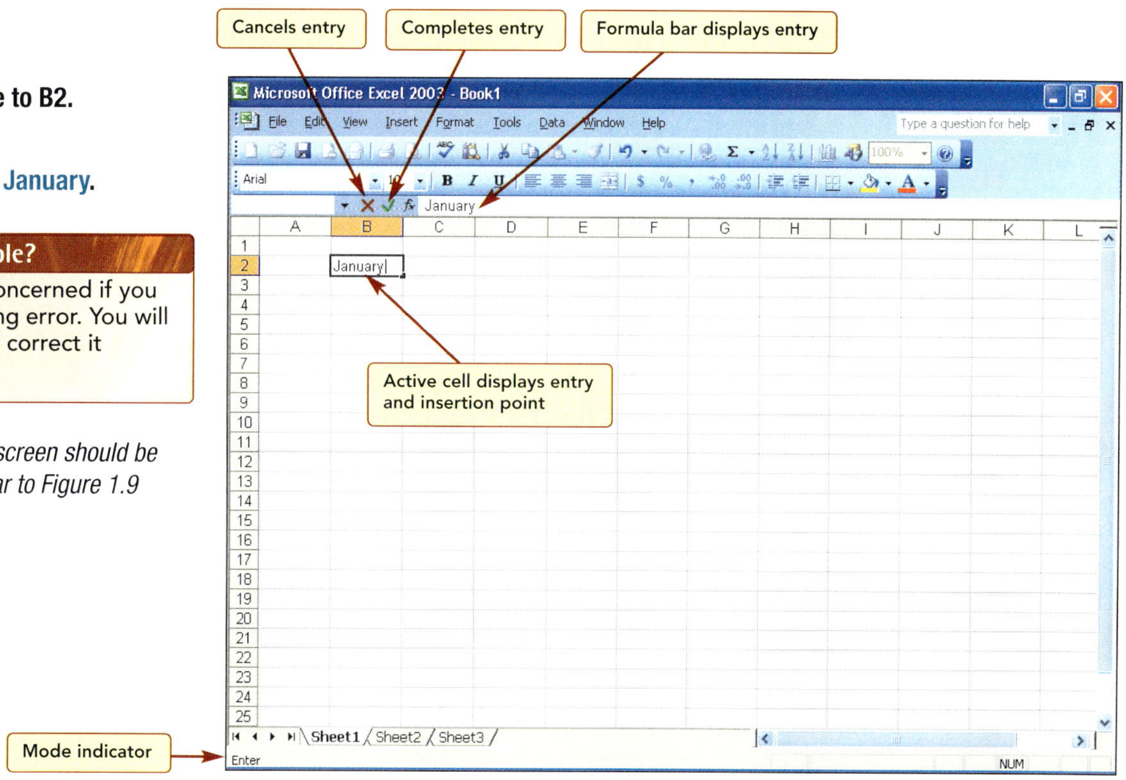

Figure 1.9

Several changes have occurred in the window. As you type, the entry is displayed both in the active cell and in the formula bar. An insertion point appears in the active cell and marks your location in the entry. Two new buttons, ✕ and ✓, appear in the formula bar. They can be used with a mouse to cancel your entry or complete it.

Notice also that the mode displayed in the status bar has changed from Ready to Enter. This notifies you that the current mode of operation in the worksheet is entering data.

Although the entry is displayed in both the active cell and the formula bar, you need to press the ←Enter key or click ✓ to complete your entry. If you press Esc or click ✕, the entry is cleared and nothing appears in the cell. Since your hands are already on the keyboard, it is quicker to press ←Enter than it is to use the mouse to click ✓.

2 Press ←Enter.

Your screen should be similar to Figure 1.10

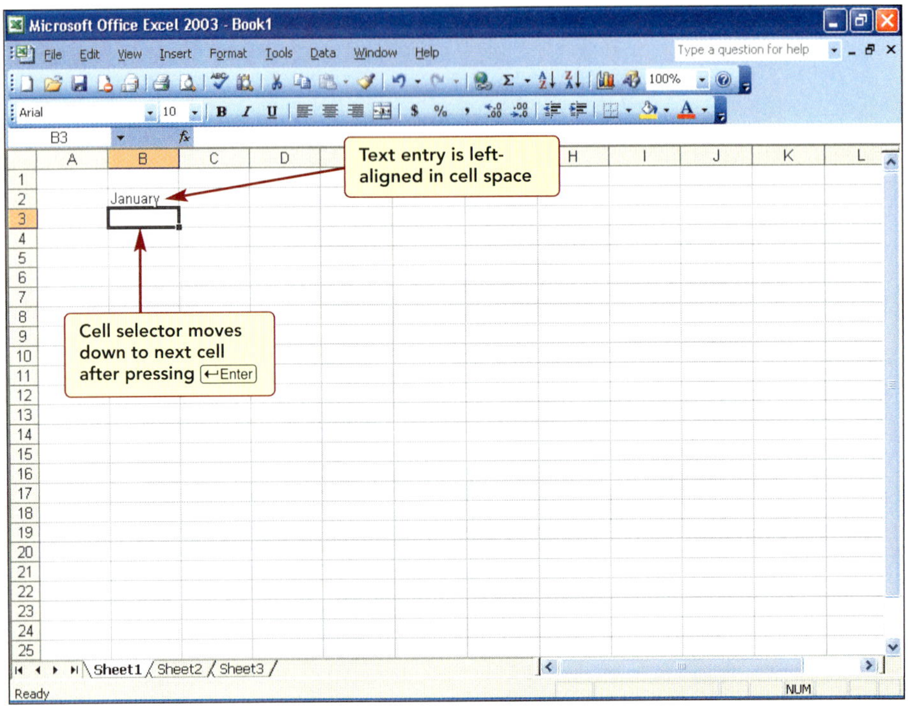

Figure 1.10

Additional Information

Pressing ⇧Shift + ←Enter to complete an entry moves the cell selector up a cell, and Ctrl + ←Enter completes the entry without moving the cell selector.

The entry January is displayed in cell B2, and the mode has returned to Ready. In addition, the cell selector has moved to cell B3. Whenever you use the ←Enter key to complete an entry, the cell selector moves down one cell.

Notice that the entry is positioned to the left side of the cell space. This is one of the worksheet default settings.

Clearing an Entry

After looking at the entry, you decide you want the column headings to be in row 3 rather than in row 2. This will leave more space above the column headings for a worksheet title. The Delete key can be used to clear the contents from a cell. You will remove the entry from cell B2 and enter it in cell B3.

1 • **Move to B2.**

• **Press** Delete.

Another Method

The menu equivalent is Edit/Clear/Contents and the voice command is "Delete." Clear Contents is also an option on the shortcut menu.

• **Move to B3.**

• **Type January.**

• **Click** ✓.

Your screen should be similar to Figure 1.11

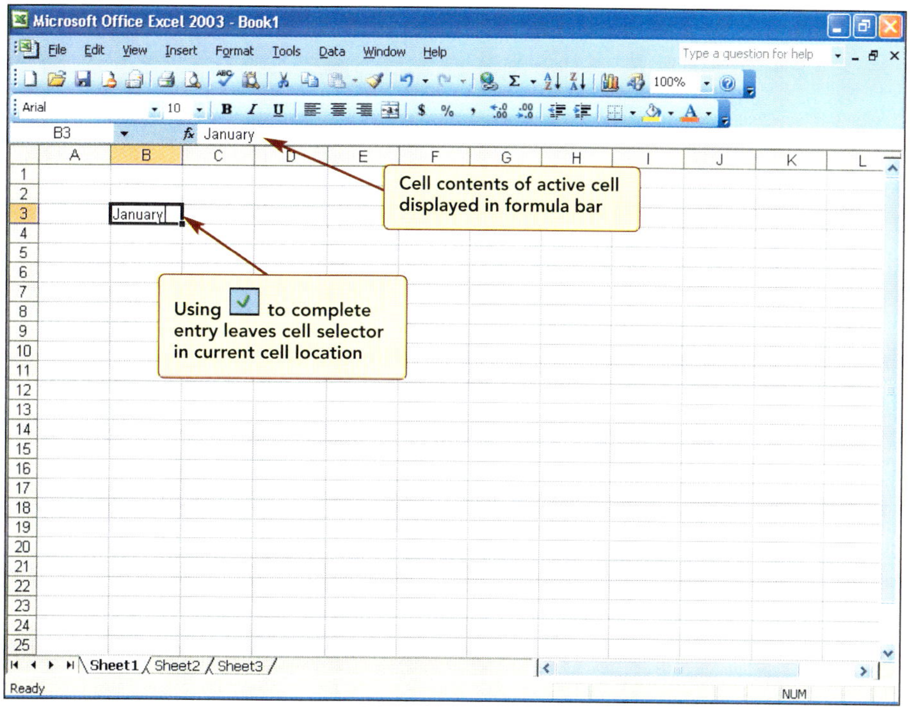

Figure 1.11

The cell selector remains in the active cell when you use ✓ to complete an entry. Because the cell selector is positioned on a cell containing an entry, the contents of the cell are displayed in the formula bar.

Editing an Entry

Next, you decide to change the heading from January to JAN. An entry in a cell can be entirely changed in the Ready mode or partially changed or edited in the Edit mode. To use the Ready mode, you move the cell selector to the cell you want to change and retype the entry the way you want it to appear. As soon as a new character is entered, the existing entry is cleared.

Generally, however, if you need to change only part of an entry, using the Edit mode is quicker. To change to Edit mode, double-click on the cell whose contents you want to edit.

1 Double-click B3.

Having Trouble?

The mouse pointer must be ✥ when you double-click on the cell.

Another Method

Pressing the F2 key will also change to Edit mode. The insertion point is positioned at the end of the entry.

Your screen should be similar to Figure 1.12

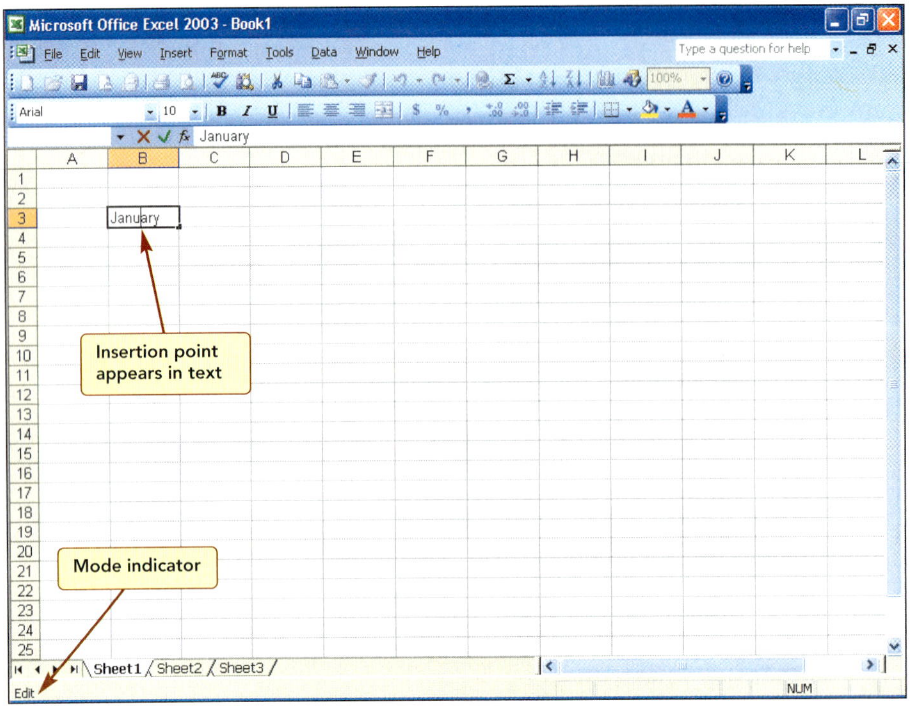

Figure 1.12

The status bar shows that the new mode of operation is Edit. The insertion point appears in the entry, and the mouse pointer changes to an I-beam when positioned on the cell. The mouse pointer can now be used to move the insertion point in the entry by positioning the I-beam and clicking. You can also use the arrow keys located on the numeric keypad or the directional keypad to move the insertion point. The keyboard directional keys and voice commands used to move within text are described in the following table.

Key	Voice	Movement
→	Right	One character to right
←	Left	One character to left
↑	Up	One line up
↓	Down	One line down
Ctrl + →	Next word	One word to right
Ctrl + ←	Back word	One word to left
Home	Home	Left end of line
End	Go end	Right end of line

Holding down a directional key or key combination moves quickly in the direction indicated, saving multiple presses of the key. Many of the insertion point movement keys can be held down to execute multiple moves.

Another Method

Using voice commands, you can say "Delete" or "Backspace."

Additional Information

You can also use Ctrl + Delete to delete everything to the right of the insertion point.

After the insertion point is appropriately positioned, you can edit the entry by removing the incorrect characters and typing the correct characters. The Delete key erases characters to the right of the insertion point, and the Backspace key erases characters to the left of the insertion point. You will change this entry to JAN.

2

- **If necessary, move the insertion point to the end of the entry.**
- **Press Backspace (4 times).**
- **Press Home.**
- **Press →.**
- **Press Caps Lock.**
- **Press Insert.**

Additional Information

The status bar displays CAPS and OVR to let you know these features are on.

- **Type AN.**
- **Press ←Enter.**

Your screen should be similar to Figure 1.13

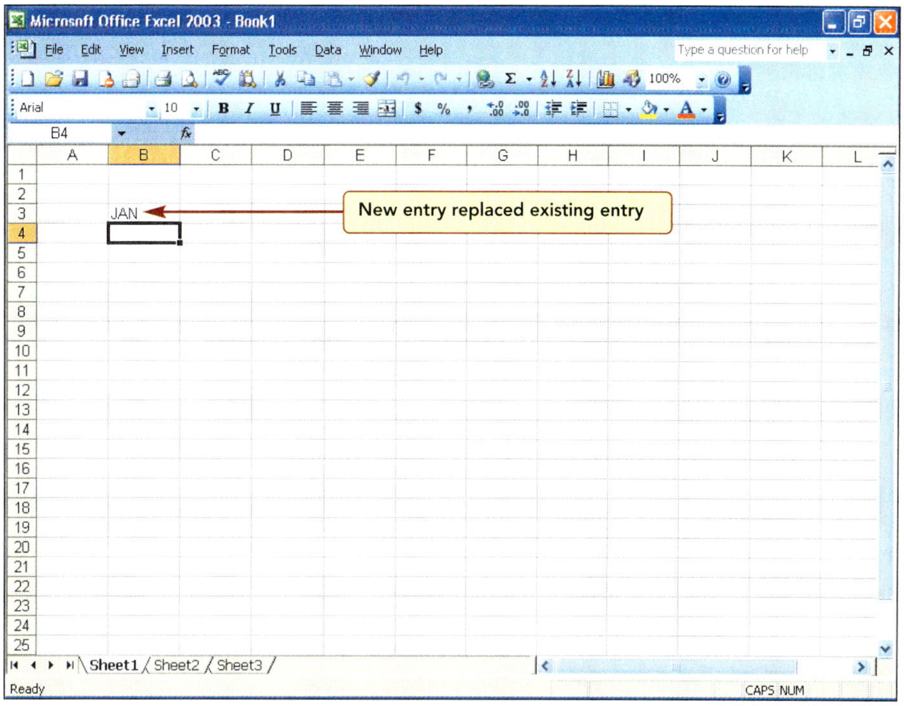

Figure 1.13

Additional Information

The Caps Lock indicator light on your keyboard is lit when this feature is on.

Additional Information

Overwrite is automatically turned off when you leave Edit mode or if you press Insert again.

The four characters at the end of the entry were deleted using Backspace. Turning on the Caps Lock feature produced an uppercase letters AN without having to hold down ⇧Shift. Finally, by pressing Insert the program switched from inserting text to overwriting text as you typed. The insertion point changed to a highlight to show that the character will be replaced.

The new heading JAN is entered into cell B3, replacing January. As you can see, editing will be particularly useful with long or complicated entries.

Next, you will enter the remaining three headings in row 3. You can also complete an entry by moving to any other worksheet cell.

3

- Move to C3.
- Type **FEB**.
- Press → or Tab or click D3.
- Complete the column headings by entering **MAR** in cell D3 and **TOTAL** in cell E3.

Having Trouble?

Remember to press ←Enter or an arrow key to complete each entry.

- When you are done, turn off Caps Lock.

Your screen should be similar to Figure 1.14

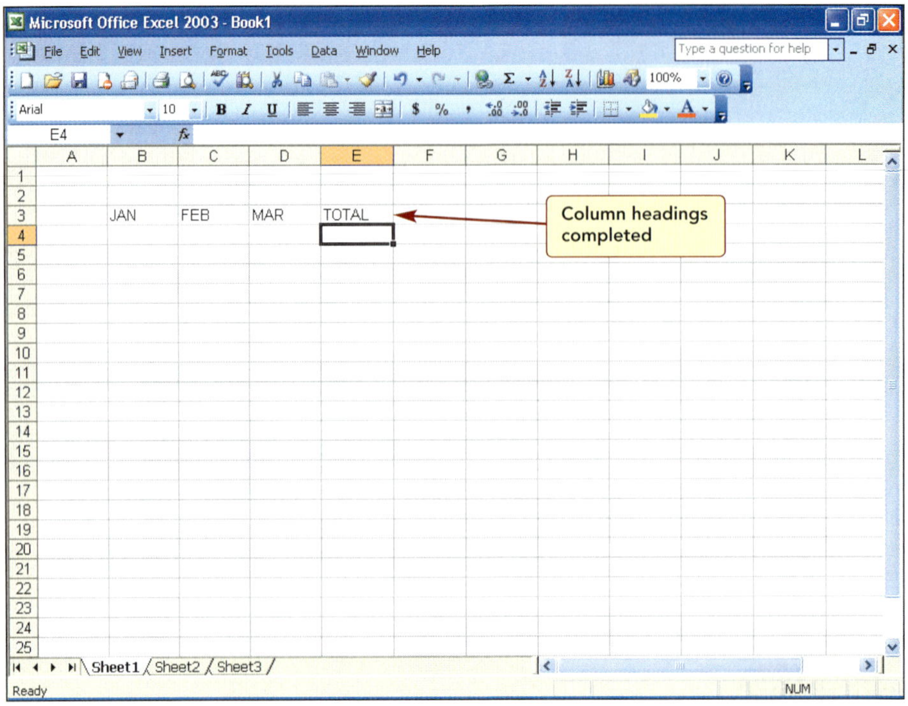

Figure 1.14

The column headings are now complete for the first quarter.

Using AutoCorrect

As soon as you complete an entry in a cell, Excel checks the entry for accuracy. This is part of the automatic correcting feature of Office Excel.

Concept 2

AutoCorrect

2 The **AutoCorrect** feature makes some basic assumptions about the text you are typing and, based on these assumptions, automatically corrects the entry. The AutoCorrect feature automatically inserts proper capitalization at the beginning of sentences and in the names of days of the week. It will also change to lowercase letters any words that were incorrectly capitalized because of the accidental use of the Caps Lock key. In addition, it also corrects many common typing and spelling errors automatically.

One way the program automatically makes corrections is by looking for certain types of errors. For example, if two capital letters appear at the beginning of a word, the second capital letter is changed to a lowercase letter. If a lowercase letter appears at the beginning of a sentence, the first letter of the first word is capitalized. If the name of a day begins with a lowercase letter, the first letter is capitalized.

Another way the program makes corrections is by checking all entries against a built-in list of words that are commonly spelled incorrectly or typed incorrectly. If it finds the entry on the list, the program automatically replaces the error with the correction. For example, the typing error "aboutthe" is automatically changed to "about the" because the error is on the AutoCorrect list. You can also add words that you want to be automatically corrected to the AutoCorrect list. Words you add are added to the list on the computer you are using and will be available to anyone who uses the machine later.

Above the column headings, in rows 1 and 2, you want to enter a title for the worksheet. While entering the title, you will intentionally misspell two words to demonstrate how the AutoCorrect feature works.

1. **Move to B1.**
   - **Type Downtown Internet Cafe.**
   - **Press ←Enter.**
   - **Type Firts Quater Forecast.**
   - **Press ←Enter.**

Your screen should be similar to Figure 1.15

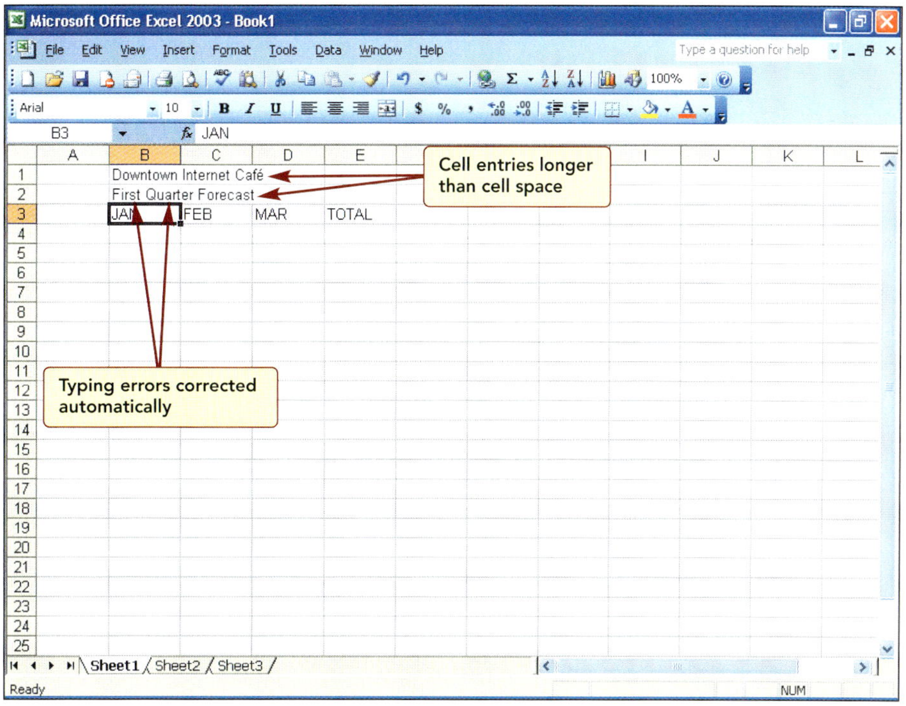

Figure 1.15

Additional Information

Excel automatically adds an accent over the e in Café if the feature to recognize French words is enabled.

The two typing errors were automatically corrected when you completed the entry. When a text entry is longer than the cell's column width, Excel will display as much of the entry as it can. If the cell to the right is empty, the whole entry will be displayed. If the cell to the right contains an entry, the overlapping part of the entry is not displayed.

Next, the row headings need to be entered into column A of the worksheet. The row headings and what they represent are shown on the next page.

Heading	Represents
Sales	
Drink	Income from sales of drinks (espresso, gourmet coffee, cold drinks)
Food	Income from sales of sandwiches and salads
Internet	Income from Internet connection time charges
Merchandise	Income from sales of Cafe tee shirts, mugs, etc.
Total Sales	Sum of all sales
Expenses	
Cost of Goods	Cost of beverage and food items sold
Salary	Personnel expenses
Computers	Monthly payment for computer hardware
Lease	Monthly lease expense
Miscellaneous	Monthly expenses for T1 line, phone, electricity, water, trash removal, etc.
Income	
Net Income	Total sales minus total expenses
Profit Margin	Net income divided by total sales

2 **Complete the row headings for the Sales portion of the worksheet by entering the following headings in the indicated cells:**

Cell	Heading
A4	Sales
A5	Drink
A6	Food
A7	Internet
A8	Merchandise
A9	Total Sales

Having Trouble?

Remember to press ←Enter or an arrow key to complete each entry.

Your screen should be similar to Figure 1.16

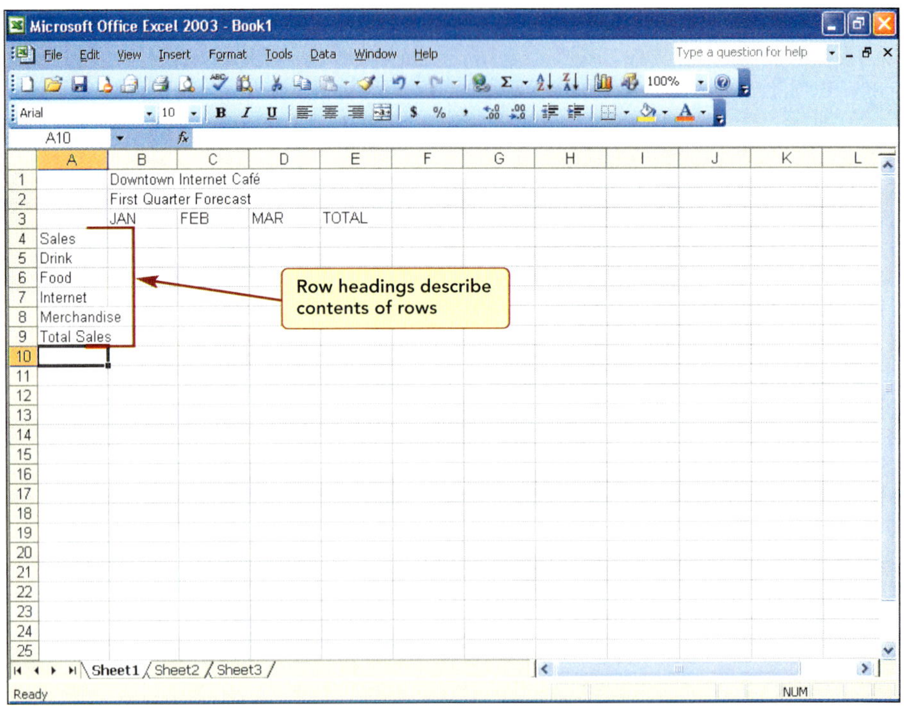

Figure 1.16

Entering Numbers

Next, you will enter the expected beverage sales numbers for January through March into cells B5 through D5. As you learned earlier, number entries can include the digits 0 to 9 and any of these special characters: + – ( ), . / $ % ? =. When entering numbers, it is not necessary to type the comma to separate thousands or the currency ($) symbol. You will learn about adding these symbols shortly.

You will enter the expected beverage sales for January first. Unlike text entries, Excel displays number entries right-aligned in the cell space by default.

1

- **Move to B5.**
- **Type 13600.**
- **Press ↵Enter.**

Additional Information

You can use the number keys above the alphabetic keys or the numeric keypad area to enter numbers. If you use the numeric keypad, the Num Lock key must be on.

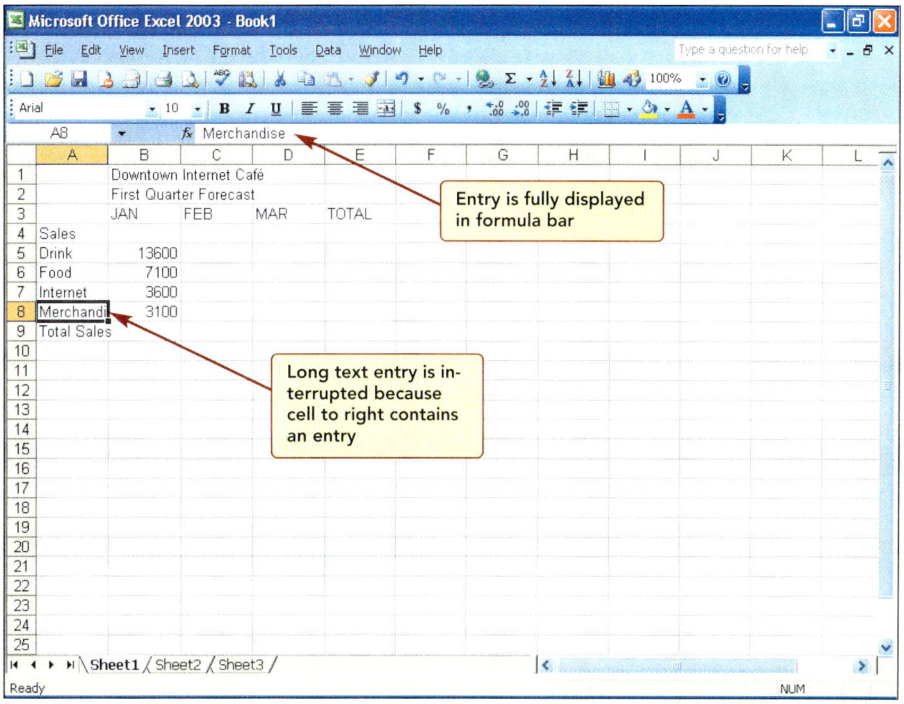

Figure 1.17

- **In the same manner, enter the January sales numbers for the remaining items using the values shown below.**

Cell	Number
B6	7100
B7	3600
B8	3100

- **Move to A8.**

Your screen should be similar to Figure 1.17

After entering the numbers for January in column B, any long headings in column A were cut off or interrupted. Notice that the entry in cell A8 is no longer completely displayed. It is a long text entry and because the cell to the right (B8) now contains an entry, the overlapping part of the entry is shortened. However, the entire entry is fully displayed in the formula bar. Only the display of the entry in the cell has been shortened.

Changing Column Widths

To allow the long text entries in column A to be fully displayed, you can increase the column's width.

Concept 3

Column Width

3 The size or width of a column controls the amount of information that can be displayed in a cell. A text entry that is larger than the column width will be fully displayed only if the cells to the right are blank. If the cells to the right contain data, the text is interrupted. On the other hand, when numbers are entered in a cell, the column width is automatically increased to fully display the entry.

The default column width setting is 8.43. The number represents the average number of digits that can be displayed in a cell using the standard type style. The column width can be any number from 1 to 255.

When the worksheet is printed, it appears as it does currently on the screen. Therefore, you want to increase the column width to display the largest entry. Likewise, you can decrease the column width when the entries in a column are short.

Additional Information

ScreenTips are displayed next to the mouse pointer and give you additional information about the feature you are using.

Additional Information

You can also adjust the size of any row by dragging the row divider line or by using Format/Row/Height.

Dragging the Column Boundary

The column width can be quickly adjusted by dragging the boundary line located to the right of the column letter. Dragging it to the left decreases the column width, while dragging it to the right increases the width. As you drag, a temporary column reference line shows where the new column will appear and a ScreenTip displays the width of the column.

1 • Point to the boundary line to the right of the column letter A, then click and drag the mouse pointer to the right.

Having Trouble?

Make sure the mouse pointer changes to ✛ before you drag the column boundary line to size the column.

• When the ScreenTip displays 15.00, release the mouse button.

Another Method

The menu equivalent is Format/Column/Width.

Your screen should be similar to Figure 1.18

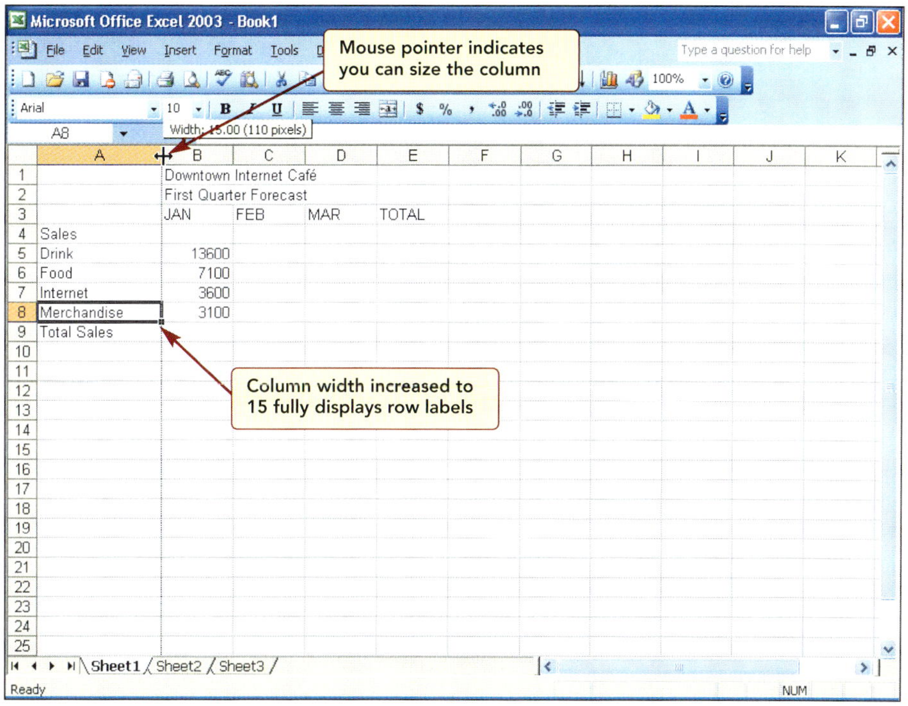

Figure 1.18

Now, however, the column width is wider than needed.

Using AutoFit

Another way to change the column width is to use the **AutoFit** feature to automatically adjust the width to fit the column contents.

1 • Double-click the right A column boundary line.

Having Trouble?

Make sure the mouse pointer changes to ✛ before you double-click on the column boundary line.

Another Method

The menu equivalent is Format/Column/AutoFit Selection.

Your screen should be similar to Figure 1.19

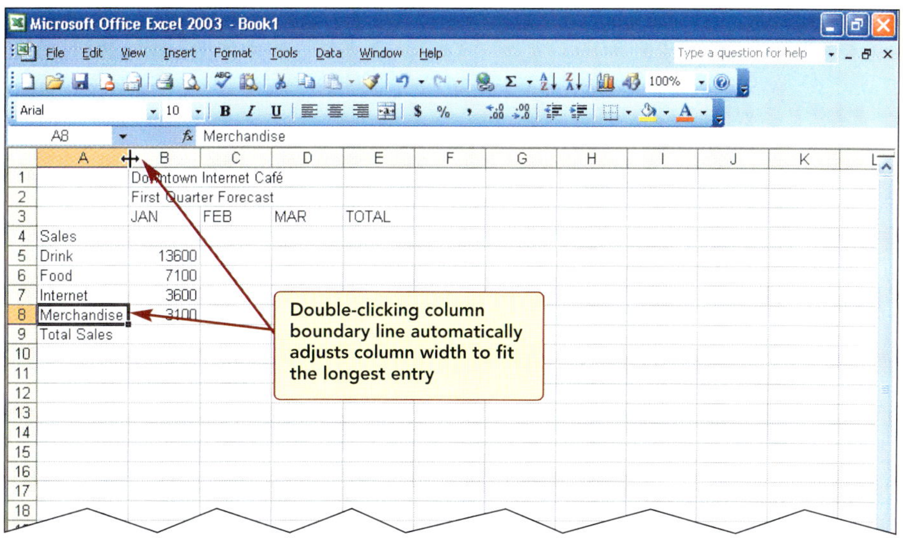

Figure 1.19

The column width is sized to just slightly larger than the longest cell contents. When using AutoFit, double-click the boundary to the right of the column heading of the column you want to fit to contents.

Saving, Closing, and Opening Workbooks

You have a meeting you need to attend shortly, so you want to save your work to a file and close the file. As you enter and edit data to create a new workbook, the changes you make are immediately displayed onscreen and are stored in your computer's memory. However, they are not permanently stored until you save your work to a file on a disk. After a workbook is saved as a file, it can be closed and opened again at a later time to be further edited.

As a backup against the accidental loss of work because of power failure or other mishap, Office 2003 applications include an AutoRecover feature. When this feature is on, as you work you may see a pulsing disk icon briefly appear in the status bar. This icon indicates that the program is saving your work to a temporary recovery file. The time interval between automatic saving can be set to any period you specify; the default is every 10 minutes. When you start up again, the recovery file is automatically opened containing all changes you made up to the last time it was saved by AutoRecover. You then need to save the recovery file. If you do not save it, it is deleted when closed. While AutoRecover is a great feature for recovering lost work, it should not be used in place of regularly saving your work.

Saving a New Workbook

You will save the work you have completed so far on the workbook. The Save or Save As commands on the File menu are used to save files. The Save command or the Save button will save the active file using the same file name by replacing the contents of the existing file with the document as it appears on your screen. The Save As command is used to save a file with a new file name or to a new location. This action leaves the original file unchanged.

When a workbook is saved for the first time, either command can be used. It is especially important to save a new file very soon after you create it as the AutoRecovery feature does not work until a file name has been specified.

1 **Choose File/Save As.**

Another Method

The voice command is "Save."

Your screen should be similar to Figure 1.20

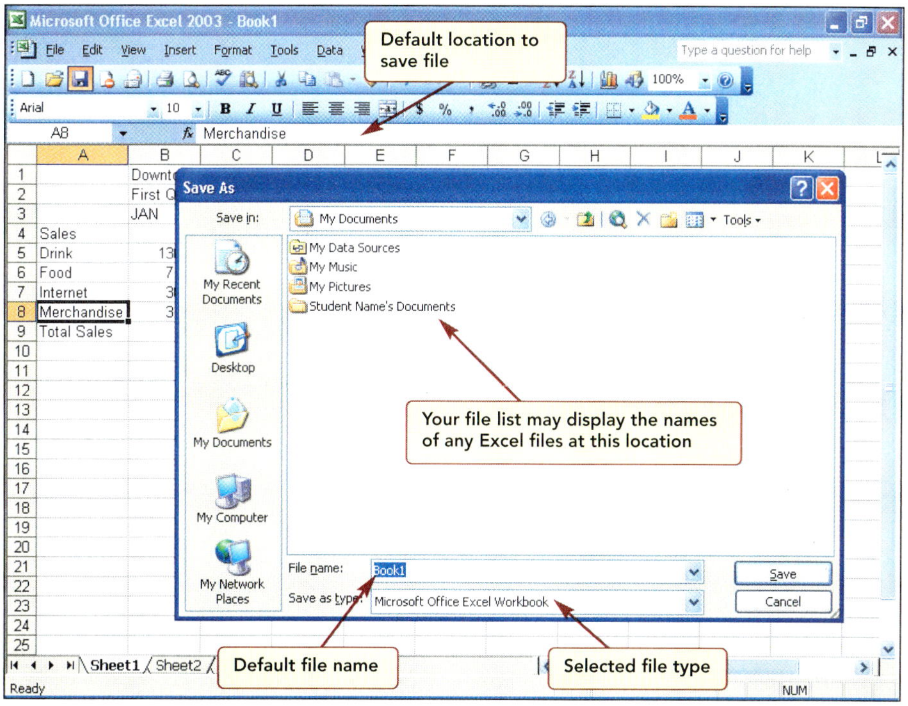

Figure 1.20

Additional Information

Depending on the dialog box view, the files may be displayed differently and may display file details, such as the size, type, and date modified.

This Save As dialog box is used to specify the location to save the file and the file name. The Save In drop-down list box displays the default folder as the location where the file will be saved, and the File Name text box displays the proposed file name. The file list box displays the names of any Excel workbook files in the default location. Only Excel workbook files are listed, because the selected file type in the Save As Type list box is Excel Workbook. First you need to change the location where the file will be saved.

2 • **Open the Save In drop-down list box.**

• **Select the appropriate location to save the file.**

> **Having Trouble?**
>
> If you are saving to a floppy disk and an error message is displayed, check that your disk is properly inserted in the drive and click OK.

Your screen should be similar to Figure 1.21

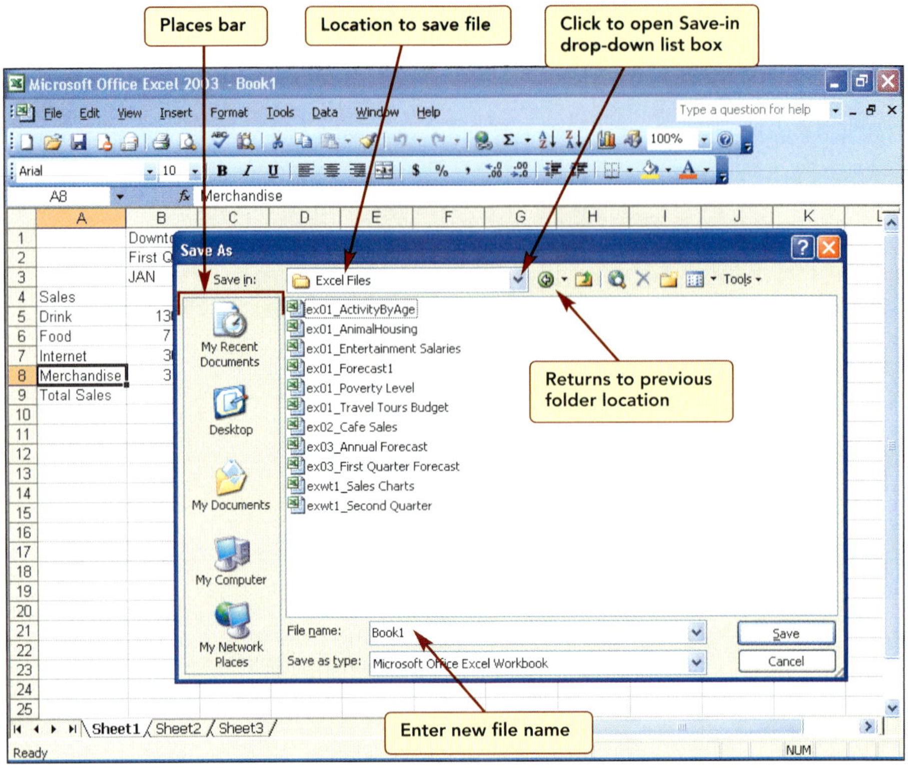

Figure 1.21

> **Additional Information**
>
> If your system uses Windows NT, My Network Places is Network Neighborhood.

If the location you are saving to does not contain other Excel files, your file list will be empty as shown here. Otherwise, your file list may display Excel file names. You can also select the location to save your file from the Places bar along the left side of the dialog box. The icons bring up a list of recently accessed files and folders, the contents of the My Documents and Favorites folder, the Windows desktop, and folders that reside on a network or Web through My Network Places. Selecting a folder from one of these lists changes to that location. You can also click the ⇦ button in the toolbar to return to folders that were previously opened.

> **Additional Information**
>
> Windows documents can have up to 256 characters in the file name. Names can contain letters, numbers, and spaces; the symbols /, \, ?, :, *, ", < and > cannot be used.

Next, you need to enter a file name and specify the file type. The File Name box displays the default file name, Book1. The Save as Type box displays Microsoft Excel Workbook as the default format in which the file will be saved. Workbooks are identified by the file extension .xls. The file type you select determines the file extension that will be automatically added to the file name when the file is saved. Your Save As dialog box may or may not display file extensions depending upon your Windows setup.

> **Additional Information**
>
> In addition to the .xls file type, Excel workbooks can also be saved in several different file formats that have different file extensions depending upon the format.

You will change the file name to Forecast and use the default file type setting.

3 • **Double-click in the File Name text box to highlight the file name.**

• **Type Forecast.**

• **Click Save or press ←Enter.**

Additional Information

The file name can be entered in either uppercase or lowercase letters and will appear exactly as you type it.

Your screen should be similar to Figure 1.22

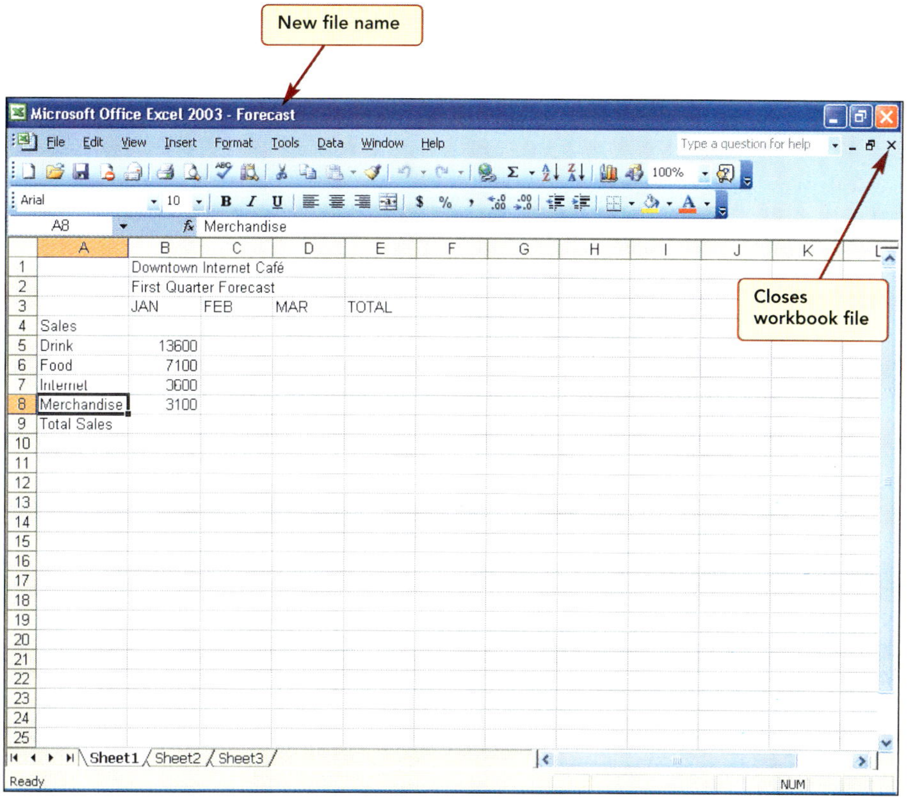

Figure 1.22

Additional Information

The file name in the title bar may display the workbook file extension, .xls.

The new file name is displayed in the application window title bar. The worksheet data that was on your screen and in the computer's memory is now saved at the location you specified in a new file called Forecast.

Closing a Workbook

You are now ready to close the workbook file.

1 • **Click ✕ Close Window (in the menu bar).**

Having Trouble?

The menu equivalent is File/Close and the voice command is "Close worksheet."

Because you did not make any changes to the document since saving it, the document window is closed immediately and the Excel window displays an empty workspace. If you had made additional changes, Excel would ask if you wanted to save the file before closing it. This question prevents the accidental closing of a file that has not been saved first.

Note: If you are running short on lab time, this is an appropriate place to end your session.

Opening an Existing Workbook

After attending your meeting, you continued working on the Café forecast. To see what has been done so far, you will open the workbook file named ex01_Forecast1.

Additional Information

You can also quickly open a recently used file by selecting it from the list of file names displayed at the bottom of the File menu and at the top of the New Workbook task pane.

1

- **Choose View/Task Pane.**
- **Click More… (in the task pane).**

Another Method

The menu equivalent is File/Open, the keyboard shortcut is Ctrl + O, and the voice command is "Open." You can also click Open in the Standard toolbar.

Your screen should be similar to Figure 1.23

Additional Information

Clicking or Blank Workbook on the New Workbook task pane opens a blank new workbook. The voice command is "New file."

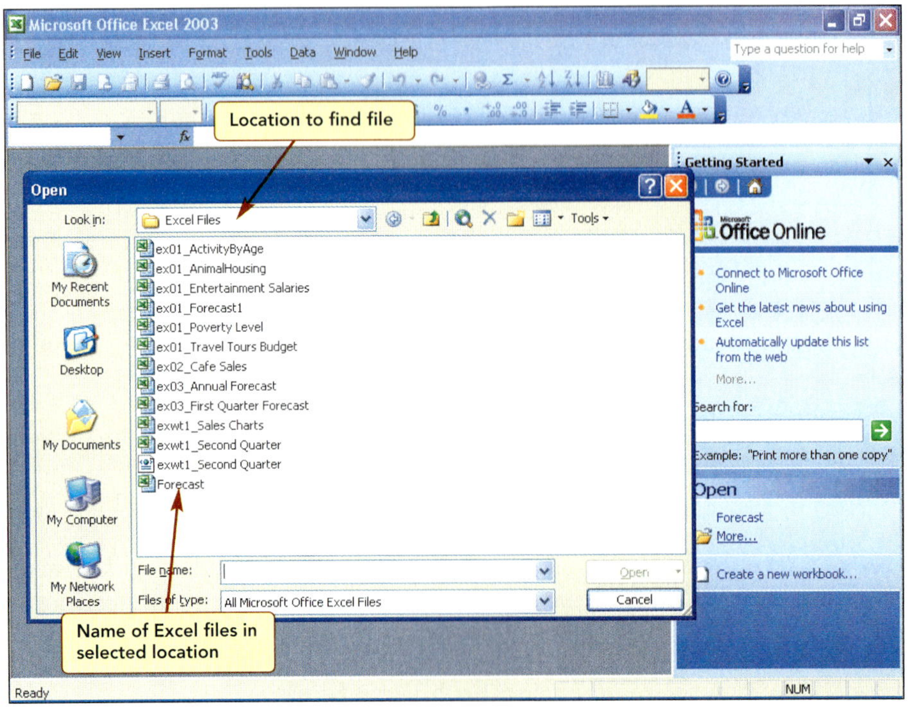

Figure 1.23

In the Open dialog box, you specify the location and name of the file you want to open. The Look In drop-down list box displays the last specified location, in this case the location where you saved the Forecast workbook. The large list box displays the names of all Excel workbooks with the file extensions displayed in the Files of Type box. As in the Save As dialog box, the Places bar can be used to quickly access recently used files. When selecting a file to open, it is sometimes helpful to see a preview of the file first. To do this, you can change the dialog box view.

2 • **If necessary, select the location containing your data files from the Look In drop-down list box.**

• **Open the Views drop-down list.**

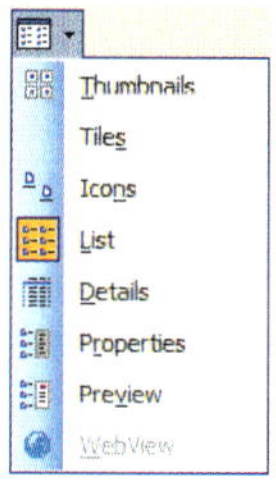

• **Choose Preview.**

• **Select ex01_Forecast1.**

Your screen should be similar to Figure 1.24

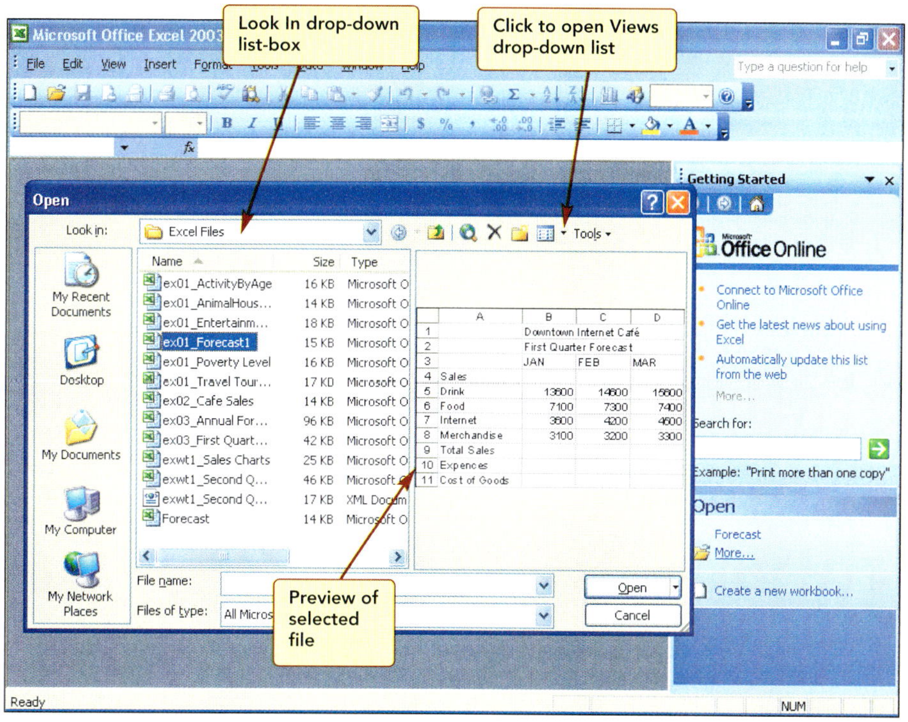

Figure 1.24

Additional Information

To see a preview, the workbook must be saved with the Save Preview Picture option selected under File/Properties. You will learn about this feature in Lab 2.

A preview of the selected file is displayed in the right pane of the dialog box. You will return the view to the list of file names and open this file.

3

- **Open the Views drop-down list.**
- **Choose List.**
- **Select ex01_Forecast1.**
- **Click Open.**

Another Method

You could also double-click the file name to both select it and choose Open.

Your screen should be similar to Figure 1.25

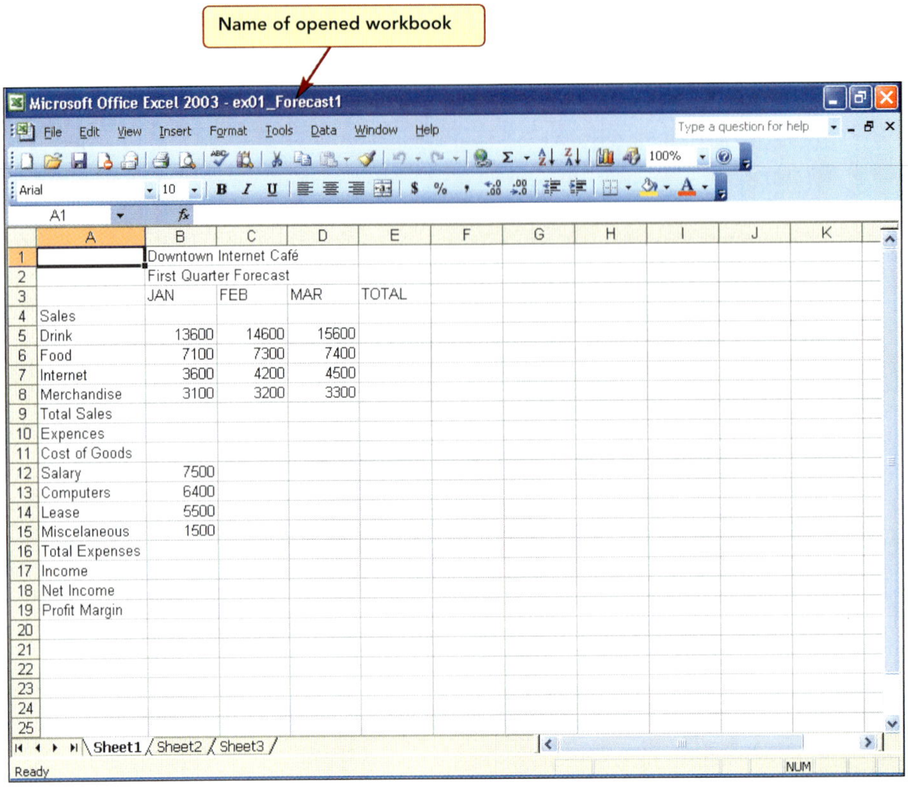

Figure 1.25

The workbook is opened and displayed in the workbook window. The workbook contains the additional sales values for February and March, the expense row headings, and several of the expense values for the month of January.

Using Language Tools

When entering information into a worksheet, you are likely to make spelling and typing errors. To help locate and correct these errors, the spelling checker feature can be used. Additionally, you may find that the descriptive headings you have entered may not be exactly the word you want. The thesaurus can suggest better words to clarify the meaning of the worksheet.

Checking Spelling

In your rush to get the row headings entered you realize you misspelled a few words. For example, the Expenses label is spelled "Expences." Just to make sure there are no other spelling errors, you will check the spelling of all text entries in this worksheet.

Concept 4

Spelling Checker

4 The **spelling checker** locates misspelled words, duplicate words, and capitalization irregularities in the active worksheet and proposes the correct spelling. This feature works by comparing each word to a dictionary of words, called the **main dictionary**, that is supplied with the program. You can also create a **custom dictionary** to hold words you commonly use but that are not included in the main dictionary. If the word does not appear in the main dictionary or in a custom dictionary, it is identified as misspelled.

When you check spelling, the contents of all cell entries in the entire active worksheet are checked. If you are in Edit mode when you check spelling, only the contents of the text in the cell are checked. The Spell Checker does not check spelling in formulas or in text that results from formulas.

Excel begins checking all worksheet entries from the active cell forward. You will check the spelling in the worksheet next.

1 **Click Spelling.**

Another Method

The menu equivalent is **T**ools/**S**pelling, the keyboard shortcut is F7, and the voice command is "Spelling."

Your screen should be similar to Figure 1.26

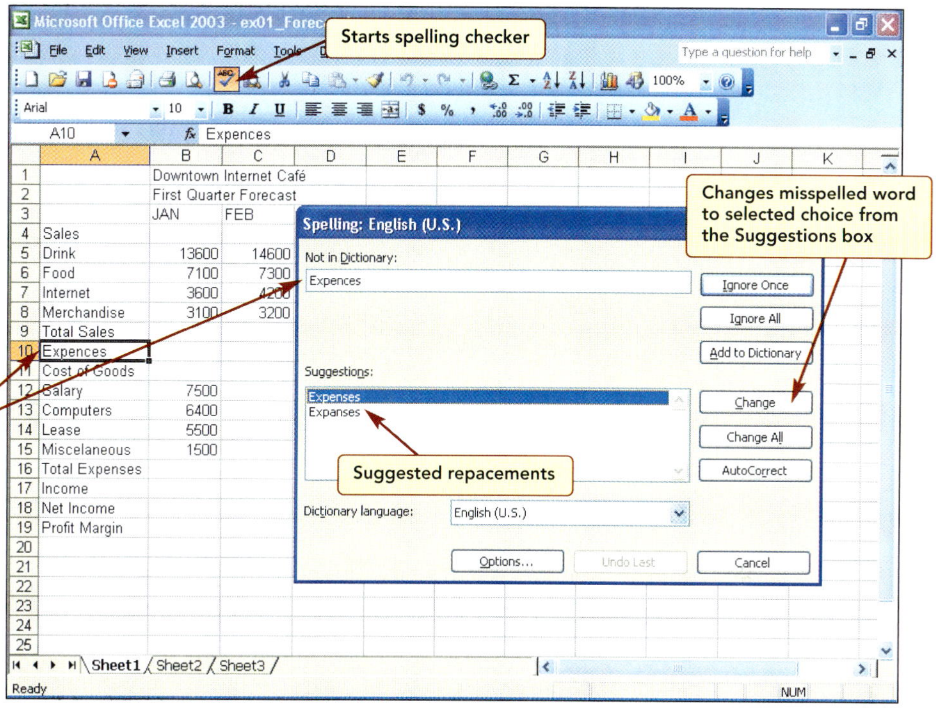

Figure 1.26

Additional Information

Spell checking operates the same way in all Office 2003 programs. The dictionaries are shared between Office applications.

The spelling checker immediately begins checking the worksheet for words that it cannot locate in its main dictionary. The cell selector moves to the first cell containing a misspelled word, in this case Expences, and the Spelling dialog box is displayed. The word it cannot locate in the dictionary is displayed in the Not in Dictionary text box. The Suggestions text box displays a list of possible replacements. If the selected replacement is not correct, you can select another choice from the suggestions list or type the correct word in the Not in Dictionary text box.

The option buttons shown in the table below have the following effects:

Option	Effect
Ignore Once	Leaves selected word unchanged
Ignore All	Leaves this word and all identical words in worksheet unchanged
Add to Dictionary	Adds selected word to a custom dictionary so Excel will not question this word during subsequent spell checks
Change	Changes selected word to word highlighted in Suggestions box
Change All	Changes this word and all identical words in worksheet to word highlighted in Suggestions box
AutoCorrect	Adds a word to the AutoCorrect list so the word will be corrected as you type

You want to accept the suggested replacement, Expenses.

2 **Click** Change.

Your screen should be similar to Figure 1.27

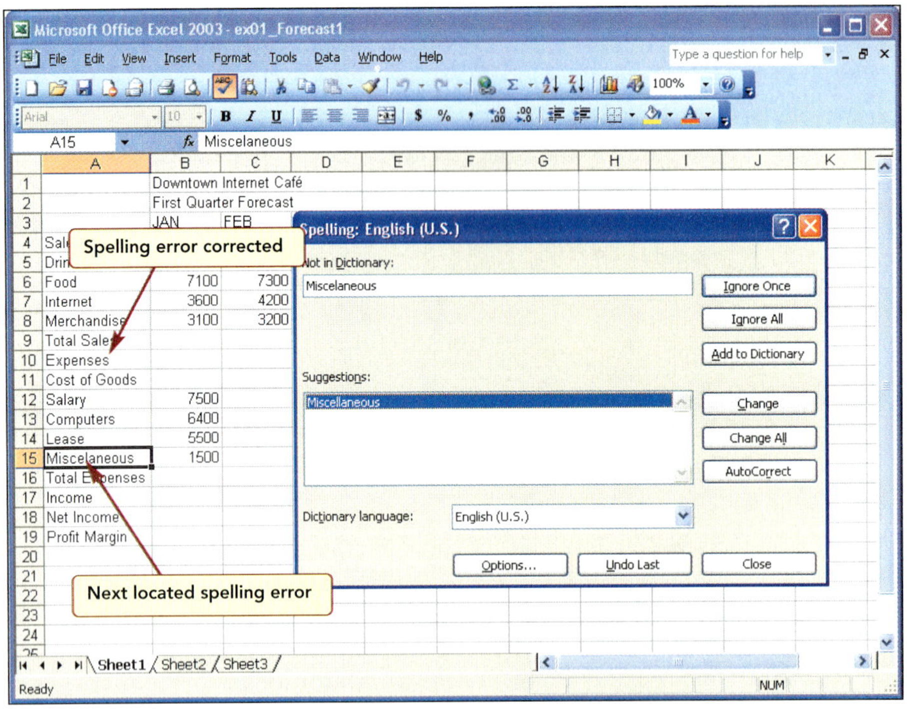

Figure 1.27

The correction is made in the worksheet, and the program continues checking the worksheet and locates another error, Miscelaneous. You will make this correction. When no other errors are located, a dialog box is displayed, informing you that the entire worksheet has been checked.

3
- **Change this word to Miscellaneous.**
- **Click [OK] to end spell checking.**

The worksheet is now free of spelling errors.

Using the Thesaurus

The next text change you want to make is to find a better word for "Drink" in cell A5. To help find a similar word, you will use the thesaurus tool.

Concept 5
Thesaurus

5 The **thesaurus** is a reference tool that provides synonyms, antonyms, and related words for a selected word or phrase. **Synonyms** are words with a similar meaning, such as "cheerful" and "happy." **Antonyms** are words with an opposite meaning, such as "cheerful" and "sad." Related words are words that are variations of the same word, such as "cheerful" and "cheer." The Thesaurus can help to liven up your documents by adding interest and variety to your text.

To access the thesaurus, you hold down [Alt] while clicking on the cell containing the word you want looked up.

1
- **Hold down [Alt] and click on cell A5.**
- **If necessary scroll the task pane and click on the Thesaurus: English (U.S.) reference tool.**

Another Method

Moving to the cell and clicking [Research] Research opens the Research task pane and enters the word in the Search For box, but does not start the search.

Your screen should be similar to Figure 1.28

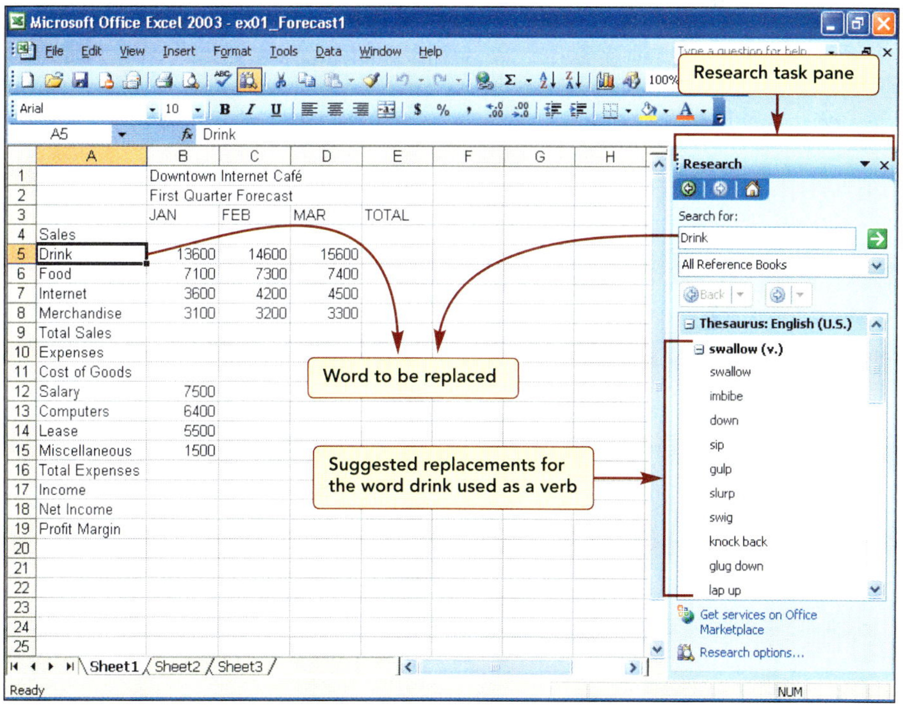

Figure 1.28

The Research task pane opens and the word you clicked on is entered in the Search For text box. The first section of the list box displays words that have similar meanings for the word "drink" used as a verb. The first word in the list is the closest in meaning and appears both in bold as the category heading and as the first word in the list. Notice the ⊟ symbol before the word "swallow." This indicates the list of synonyms is displayed. Clicking the word will close the section and hide the list of words.

2 Click "swallow."

Your screen should be similar to Figure 1.29

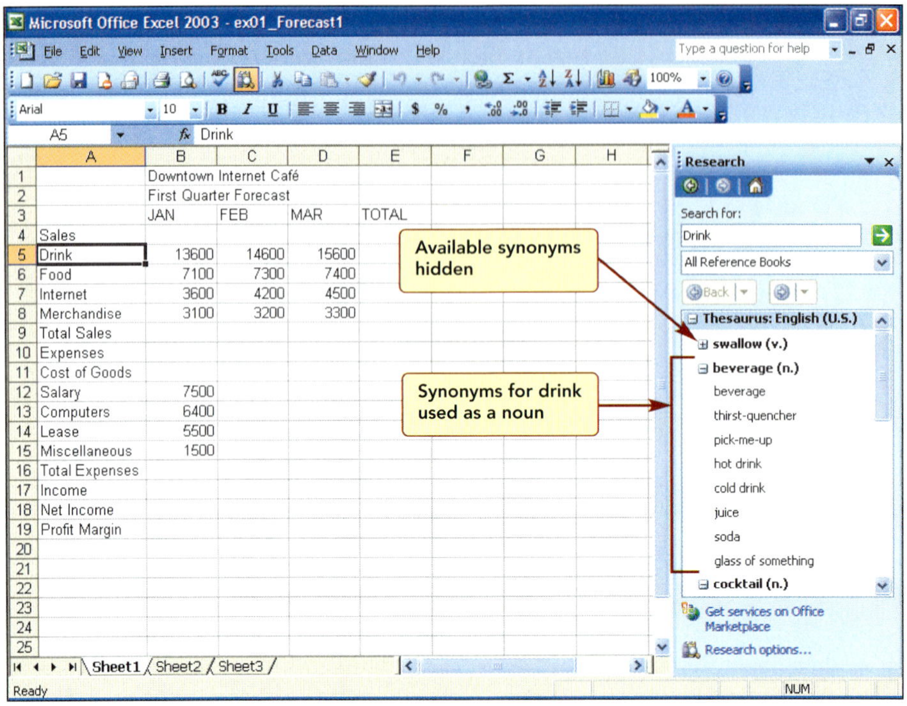

Figure 1.29

Now a ⊞ symbol appears before the category heading, indicating all available words are hidden. You want to find a synonym for "drink" used as a noun. "Beverage" is the closest in meaning and is the category heading.

Additional Information
You will learn about Copy and Paste in the next section.

When you point to a word in the list, the button appears. Clicking opens a menu of three options: Insert, Copy, and Lookup. The Insert option inserts the word into the active cell. The Copy option is used to copy and then paste the word into any worksheet cell. The Lookup option displays a definition and additional related words for the current word. You decide to use the word "beverage" and will insert the word into cell A5 in place of "Drink."

3

- **Click to display the menu for the word "beverage."**
- **Choose Insert.**
- **Close the Research task pane.**

Additional Information
If you click on a word in the list, a definition and additional related words for that word will be displayed. This is because Lookup is the default setting.

Your screen should be similar to Figure 1.30

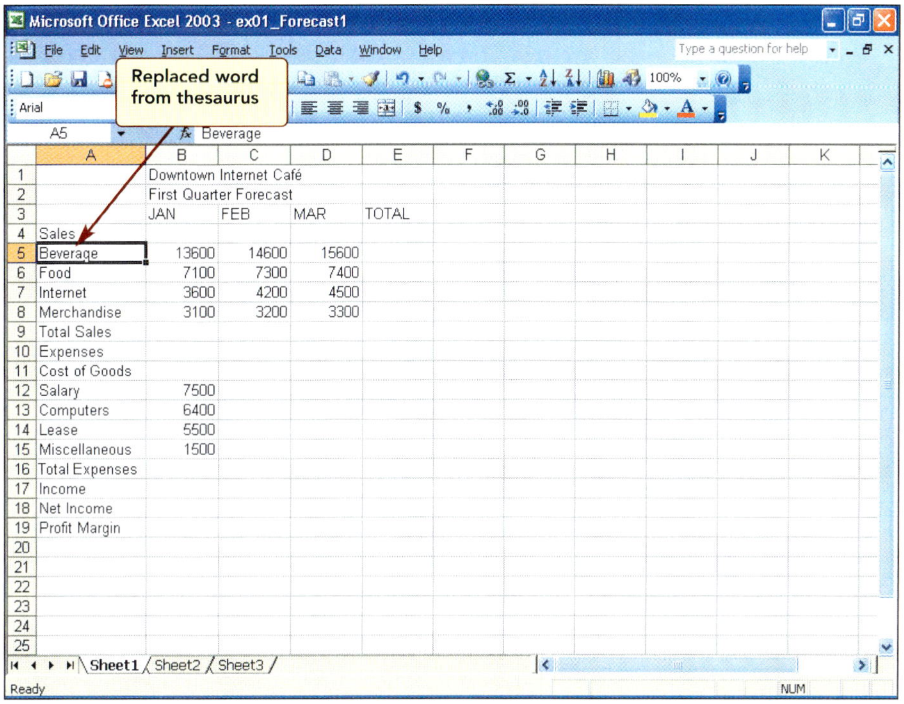

Figure 1.30

The word "Drink" is replaced with the selected word from the thesaurus. Notice the replacement word is capitalized correctly. This is because the replacement text follows the same capitalization as the word it replaces.

Duplicating Cell Contents

Next, you want to enter the estimated expenses for salary, computers, lease, and miscellaneous for February and March. They are the same as the January expense numbers. Because these values are the same, instead of entering the same number repeatedly into each cell you can quickly copy the contents of one cell to another. You also want to move information from one location in the worksheet to another.

Concept 6

Copy and Move

6 The contents of worksheet cells can be duplicated (copied) or moved to other locations in the worksheet or between worksheets, saving you time by not having to retype the same information. An entry that is copied leaves the original, called the **source** or **copy area**, and inserts a duplicate at a new location, called the **destination** or **paste area**. A selection that is moved is removed or cut from the original location in the source and inserted at the destination.

When a selection is cut or copied, the selection is stored in the system Clipboard, a temporary Windows storage area in memory. The system Clipboard contents are then inserted at the new location specified by the location of the insertion point.

Office 2003 also includes an Office Clipboard that can store up to 24 items that have been cut or copied. This allows you to insert multiple items from various Office files and paste all or part of the collection of items into another file.

Using Copy and Paste

When using Copy and Paste, you first use the Copy command to copy the cell contents to the system Clipboard. Then you move to the new location where you want the contents copied and use the Paste command to insert the system Clipboard contents into the selected cells. Be careful when pasting to the new location because any existing entries are replaced.

To use the Copy command, you first must select the cell or cells in the source containing the data to be copied. You will copy the value in cell B12 into cells C12 and D12.

1 Move to B12.

Click Copy.

Another Method

The menu equivalent is Edit/Copy, the shortcut key is Ctrl + C and the voice command is "Copy." Copy is also available on the shortcut menu.

Your screen should be similar to Figure 1.31

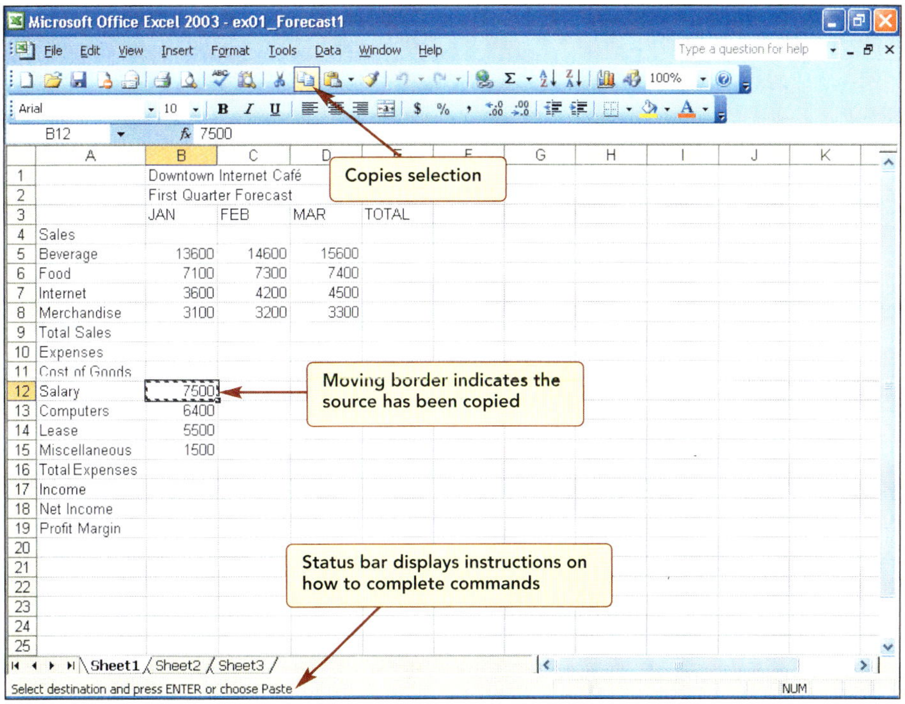

Figure 1.31

A moving border identifies the source and indicates that the contents have been copied to the system Clipboard. The instructions displayed in the status bar tell you to select the destination where you want the contents copied. You will copy it to cell C12.

2 Move to C12.

Click Paste.

Another Method

The menu equivalent is Edit/Paste, the shortcut key is Ctrl + V, and the voice command is "Paste." Paste is also available on the shortcut menu.

Your screen should be similar to Figure 1.32

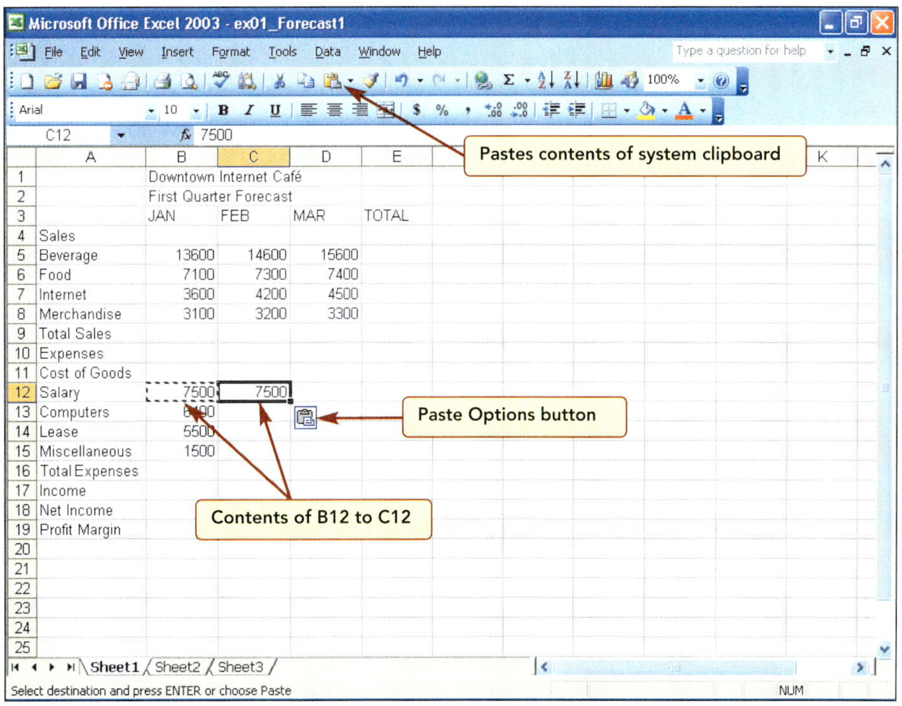

Figure 1.32

The contents of the system Clipboard are inserted at the specified destination location. Each time the paste command is used, the Paste

Options button is available. Clicking on the button opens the Paste Options menu that allows you to control how the information you are pasting is inserted. The default option, Keep Source Formatting, will insert the copy exactly as it appears in the source and is appropriate for this and most situations.

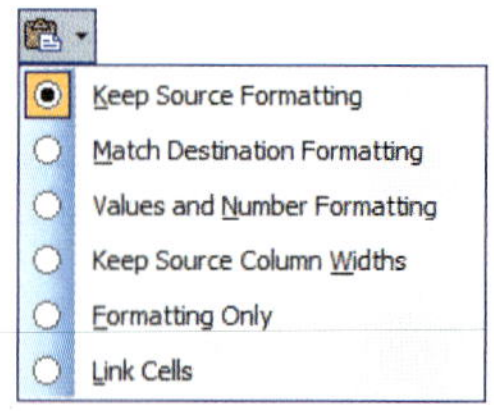

The moving border is still displayed, indicating the system Clipboard still contains the copied entry. Now you can complete the data for the Salary row by pasting the value again from the system Clipboard into cell D12. While the moving border is still displayed, you can also simply press ←Enter to paste. However, as this method clears the contents of the system Clipboard immediately, it can only be used once.

3 **Move to D12.**

Press ←Enter.

Your screen should be similar to Figure 1.33

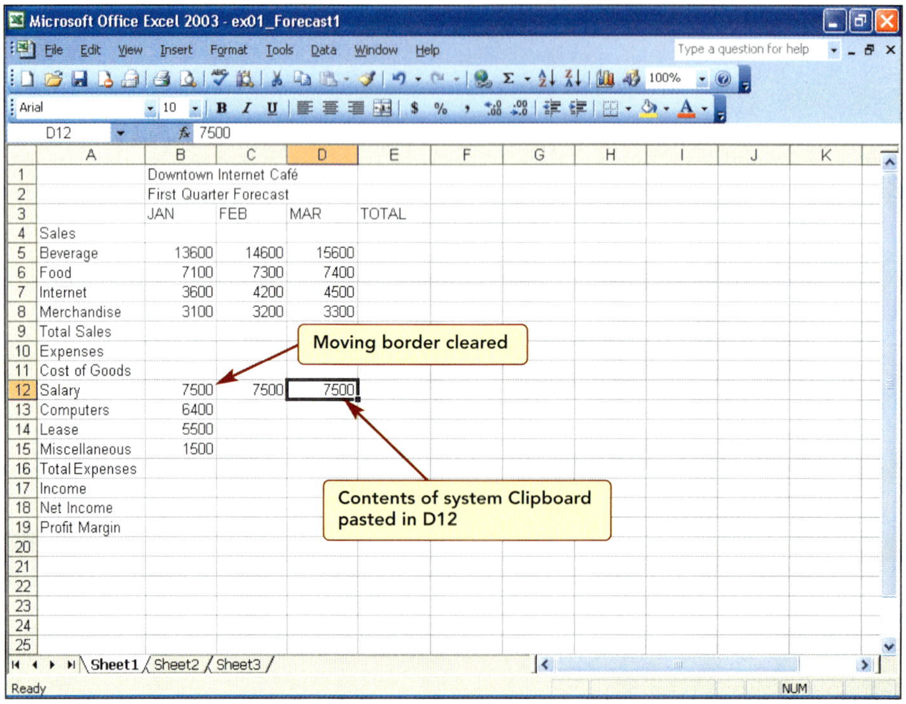

Figure 1.33

The contents of the system Clipboard are inserted at the specified destination location and the moving border is cleared, indicating the system Clipboard is empty.

Selecting a Range

Now you need to copy the Computers value in cell B13 to February and March. You could copy and paste the contents individually into each cell as you did with the Salary values. A quicker method, however, is to select a paste area that consists of multiple cells, called a range, and paste the contents to all cells in the selection at once.

Concept 7

Range

7 A selection consisting of two or more cells on a worksheet is a **range.** The cells in a range can be adjacent or nonadjacent. An **adjacent range** is a rectangular block of adjoining cells. A **nonadjacent range** consists of two or more selected cells or ranges that are not adjoining. In the example shown below, the shaded areas show valid adjacent and nonadjacent ranges. A **range reference** identifies the cells in a range. A colon is used to separate the first and last cells of an adjacent range reference. For example, A2:C4 indicates the range consists of cells A2 through C4. Commas separate the cell references of a nonadjacent range. For example, A10,B12,C14 indicates the range consists of cells A10, B12, and C14 of a nonadjacent range.

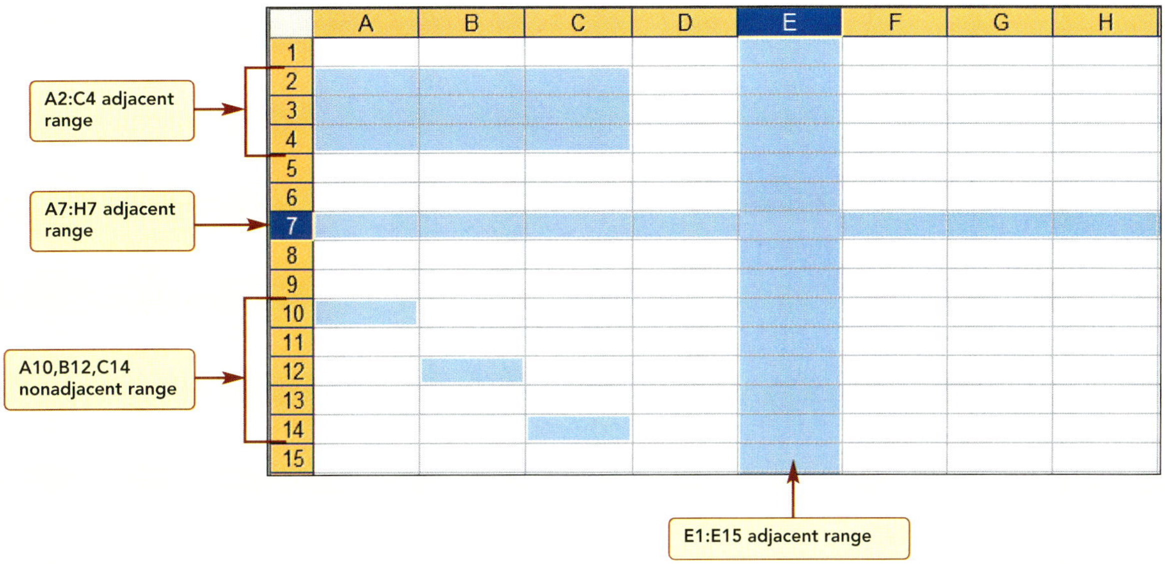

You can select a range using the mouse, keyboard, or voice commands shown in the following table. Several of these features use the F8 key to turn on and off Extend mode. When this mode is on, EXT appears in the status bar and navigation keys select cells rather than move to cells.

To Select	Mouse	Keyboard	Voice
A range	Click first cell of range and drag to the last cell.	Move to first cell of range, hold down ⇧Shift, and move to the last cell using the directional keys or press F8 and use the navigation keys to expand the highlight.	Press F8 and say the navigation voice commands to expand the highlight.
A large range	Click first cell of range, hold down ⇧Shift, and click last cell of range.		
All cells on worksheet	Click the ☐ All button located at the intersection of the row and column headings.		
Nonadjacent cells or ranges	Select first cell or range, hold down Ctrl while selecting the other cell or range.		
Entire row or column	Click the row or column heading.		Current column: Hold down Ctrl and say "Spacebar." Current row: Hold down ⇧Shift and say "Spacebar."
Adjacent rows or columns	Drag across the row or column headings.		
Nonadjacent rows or columns	Select first row or column, hold down Ctrl, and select the other rows or columns.		

To complete the data for the Computer row, you want to copy the value in cell B13 to the system Clipboard and then copy the system Clipboard contents to the adjacent range of cells C13 through D13.

1 Move to B13.

Click Copy.

Drag to select the range of cells C13:D13.

Click Paste.

Your screen should be similar to Figure 1.34

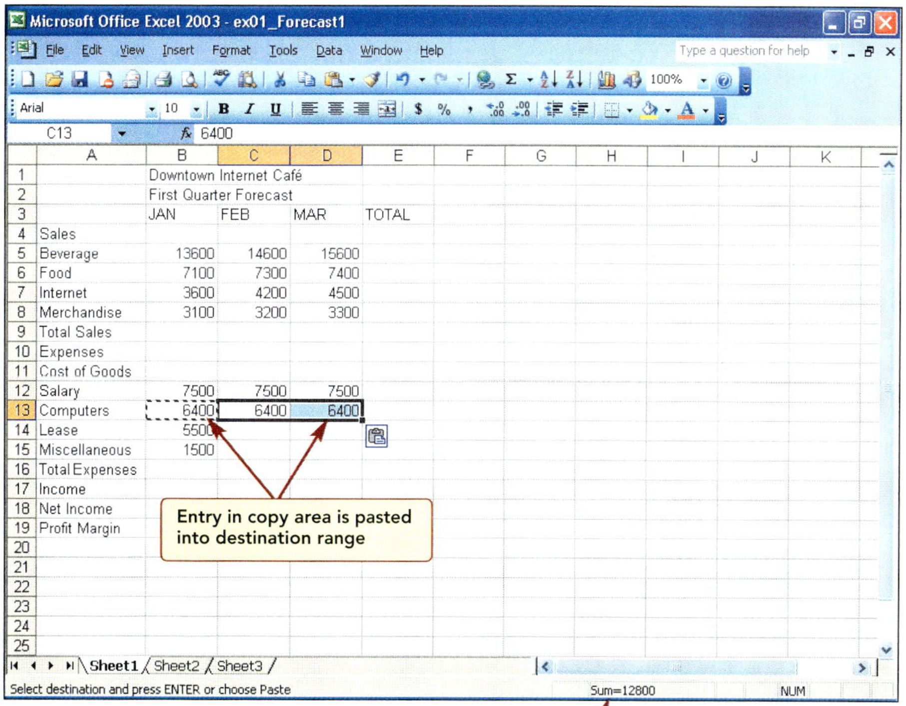

Figure 1.34

Additional Information
The paste area does not have to be adjacent to the copy area.

Additional Information
Right-clicking the Auto-Calculate button displays the Shortcut menu.

The destination range is highlighted and identified by a dark border surrounding the selected cells. The entry copied from cell B13 was pasted into the selected destination range. Also notice the AutoCalculate button in the status bar is now active. This button displays the sum of values in a selected range of cells. It can also display the average, count, minimum, or maximum values in a range by selecting the appropriate option from the button's shortcut menu.

Using the Fill Handle

Next, you will copy the January Lease expenses to cells C14 through D14 and Miscellaneous expenses to cells C15 through D15. You can copy both values at the same time across the row by first specifying a range as the source. Another way to copy is to drag the **fill handle**, the black box in the lower-right corner of the selection.

1 Drag to select cells B14:B15.

- Point to the fill handle and when the mouse pointer is a +, drag the mouse to extend the selection to cells D14:D15.

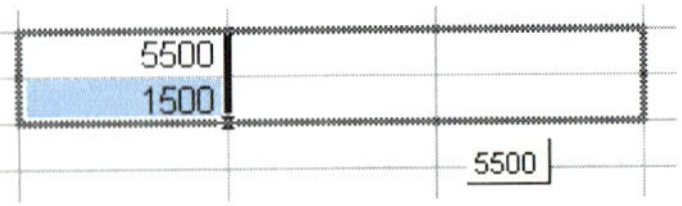

- Release the mouse button.

Another Method

The menu equivalent is Edit/Fill/Right and the shortcut key is Ctrl + R.

Your screen should be similar to Figure 1.35

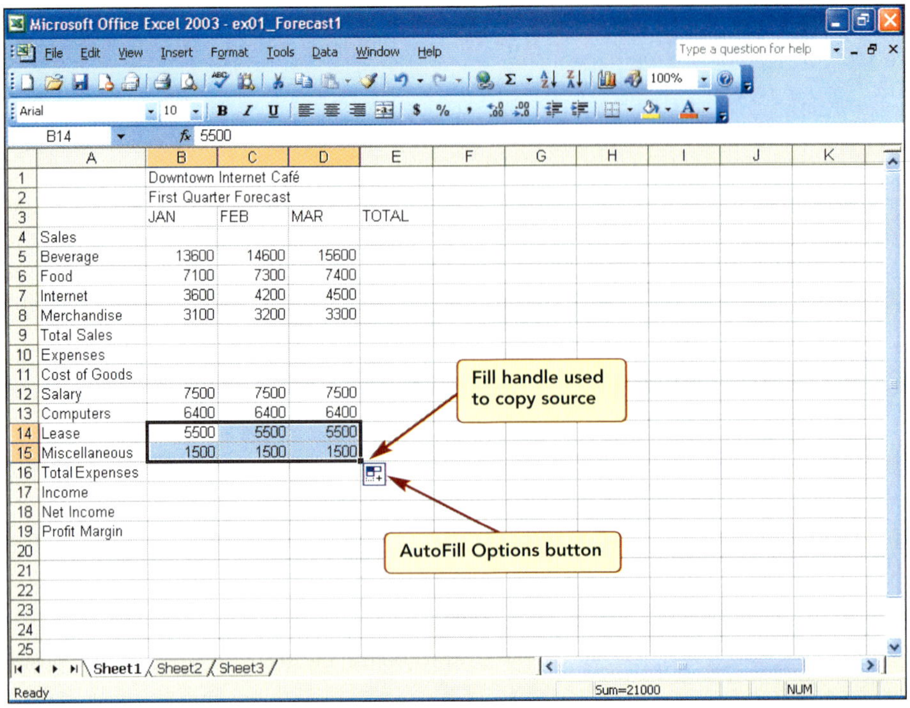

Figure 1.35

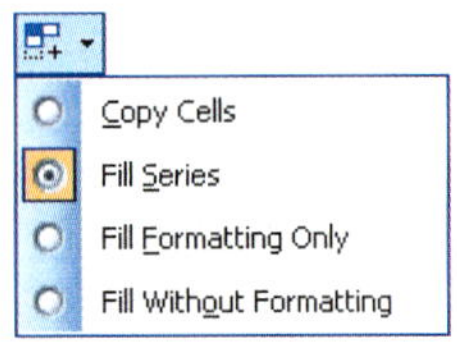

The range of cells to the right of the source is filled with the same value as in the source cell. The Fill command does not copy the source to the system Clipboard and therefore you cannot paste the source multiple times. When you copy by dragging the fill handle, the AutoFill Options button appears. Its menu commands are used to modify how the fill operation was performed.

Inserting Copied Cells

You also decide to include another row of month headings above the expense columns to make the worksheet data easier to read. To do this quickly, you can insert copied data between existing data. To indicate where to place the copied text, you move the cell selector to the upper-left cell of the area where you want the selection inserted and specify the direction you want to shift the surrounding cells.

1 Copy the contents of cells A3:E3.

- **Move to A10.**
- **Choose Insert/Copied Cells.**
- **If necessary, select Shift Cells Down from the Insert Paste dialog box.**

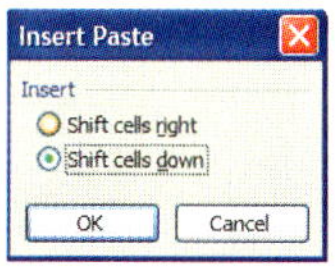

- **Click OK.**
- **Press Esc to clear the moving border.**

Another Method

The voice command is "Escape."

Your screen should be similar to Figure 1.36

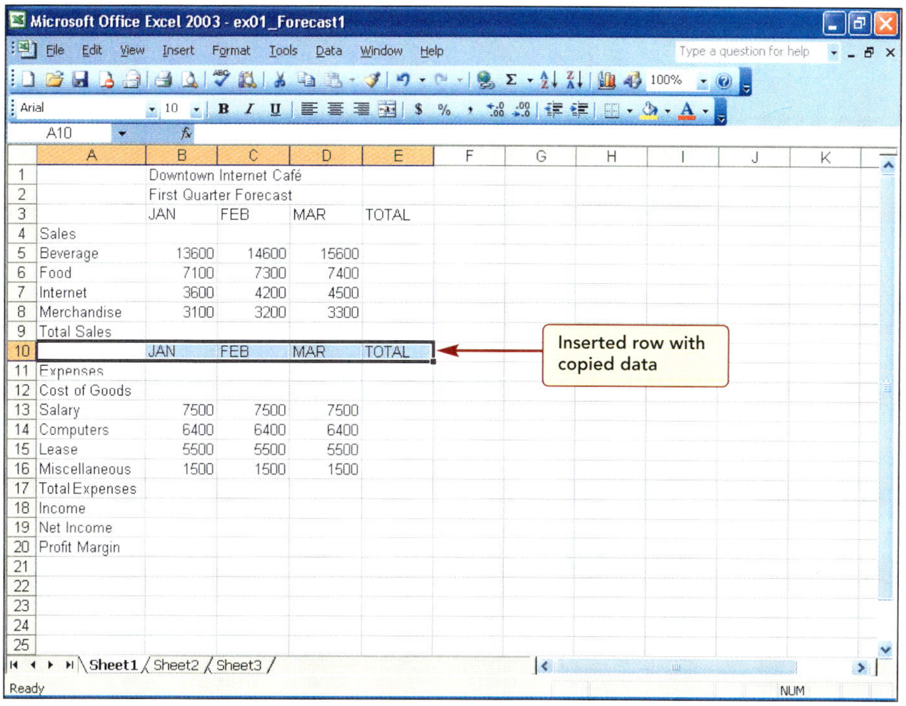

Figure 1.36

Additional Information

You can also insert cut selections between existing cells by choosing Cut Cells from the Insert menu.

Another Method

The Cut command shortcuts are [cut button] or Ctrl + X. The voice command is "Cut."

Additional Information

Holding down Ctrl while dragging a selection copies it to the new location.

The copied data is inserted into the existing row (10) and all entries below are moved down one row.

Moving Entries

You also decide the Profit Margin row of data would stand out more if a blank row separated it from the Net Income row. You could remove the cell contents using Edit/Cut and then paste the contents from the system Clipboard into the new location. Alternatively, you can use drag and drop editing to move the cell contents. This method is quickest and most useful when the distance between cells is short and they are visible within the window, whereas Cut and Paste is best for long-distance moves.

1 Move to cell A20.

Point to the border of the selection and when the mouse pointer shape is ✥, drag the selection down one row to cell A21 and release the mouse button.

Additional Information

As you drag, an outline of the cell selection appears and the mouse pointer displays the cell reference to show its new location in the worksheet.

Choose **File/Save As** and save the changes you have made to the workbook as Forecast1 to your data file location.

Your screen should be similar to Figure 1.37

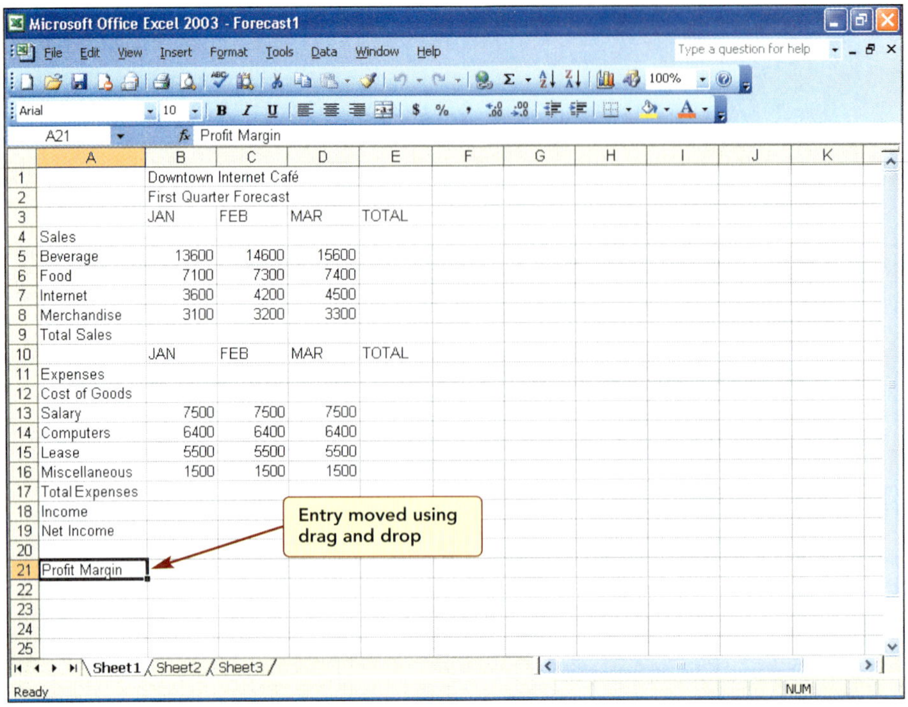

Figure 1.37

The cell contents were moved into cell A21 and cleared from the original cell.

Review of Copying and Moving Methods

To review, you have learned three methods to copy or move an entry:

1. Use the Copy, Cut, and Paste commands: **Edit/Copy** (Ctrl + C) or [Copy button], **Edit/Cut** (Ctrl + X) or [Cut button], and **Edit/Paste** (Ctrl + V) or [Paste button].
2. Use the **Edit/Fill** command: Right, Left, Up, or Down or drag the fill handle.
3. Drag the cell border of the selection to move. Hold down Ctrl while dragging a selection to copy.

When you use the Copy and Cut commands, the contents are copied to the system Clipboard and can be copied to any location in the worksheet, another workbook, or another application multiple times. When you use Edit/Fill or drag the fill handle, the destination must be in the same row or column as the source, and the source is not copied to the system Clipboard. Dragging the cell border to move or copy also does not copy the source to the system Clipboard.

Working with Formulas

The remaining entries that need to be made in the worksheet are formula entries.

Concept 8

Formula

8 A **formula** is an equation that performs a calculation on data contained in a worksheet. The resulting value from formulas is a **variable** value because it can change if the data it depends on changes. In contrast, a number entry is a **constant** value. It does not begin with an equal sign and does not change unless you change it directly by typing in another entry. A formula always begins with an equal sign (=) and uses arithmetic operators. An **operator** is a symbol that specifies the type of numeric operation to perform. Excel includes the following operators: + (addition), – (subtraction), / (division), * (multiplication), % (percent), ^ (exponentiation).

In a formula that contains more than one operator, Excel calculates the formula from left to right and performs the calculation in the following order: percent, exponentiation, multiplication and division, and addition and subtraction (see Example A). This is called the **order of precedence.** If a formula contains operators with the same precedence (for example, addition and subtraction), they are again evaluated from left to right. The order of precedence can be overridden by enclosing the operation you want performed first in parentheses (see Example B). When there are multiple sets of parentheses, Excel evaluates them working from the innermost set of parentheses out.

Example A:	=5*4–3	Result is 17 (5 times 4 to get 20, and then subtract 3 for a total of 17)
Example B:	=5*(4–3)	Result is 5 (4 minus 3 to get 1, and then 1 times 5 for a total of 5)

The values on which a numeric formula performs a calculation are called **operands.** Numbers or cell references can be operands in a formula. Usually cell references are used, and when the numeric entries in the referenced cell(s) change, the result of the formula is automatically recalculated.

Entering Formulas

The first formula you will enter will calculate the total Beverage sales for January through March (cell E5) by summing the numbers in cells B5 through D5. You will use cell references in the formula as the operands and the + arithmetic operator to specify addition. A formula is entered in the cell where you want the calculated value to be displayed. As you enter the formula, Excel helps you keep track of the cell references by identifying the referenced cell with a colored border and using the same color for the cell reference in the formula.

1 Move to E5.

Type **=b5+c5+d5**.

Additional Information

Cell references can be typed in either uppercase or lowercase letters. Spaces between parts of the formula are optional.

Press Ctrl + ←Enter or click ✓.

Your screen should be similar to Figure 1.38

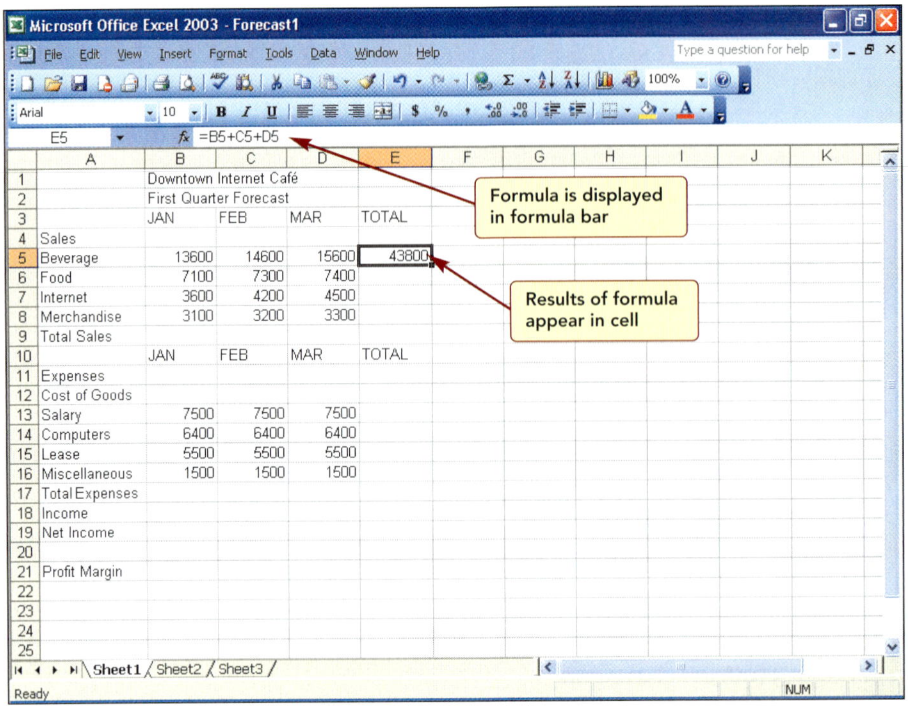

Figure 1.38

The number 43800 is displayed in cell E5, and the formula that calculates this value is displayed in the formula bar.

Copying Formulas

The formulas to calculate the total sales for rows 5 through 8 can be entered next. Just as you can with text and numeric entries, you can copy formulas from one cell to another.

1 Copy the formula in cell E5 to cells E6 through E8 using any of the copying methods.

Move to E6.

If necessary, press Esc to clear the moving border.

Your screen should be similar to Figure 1.39

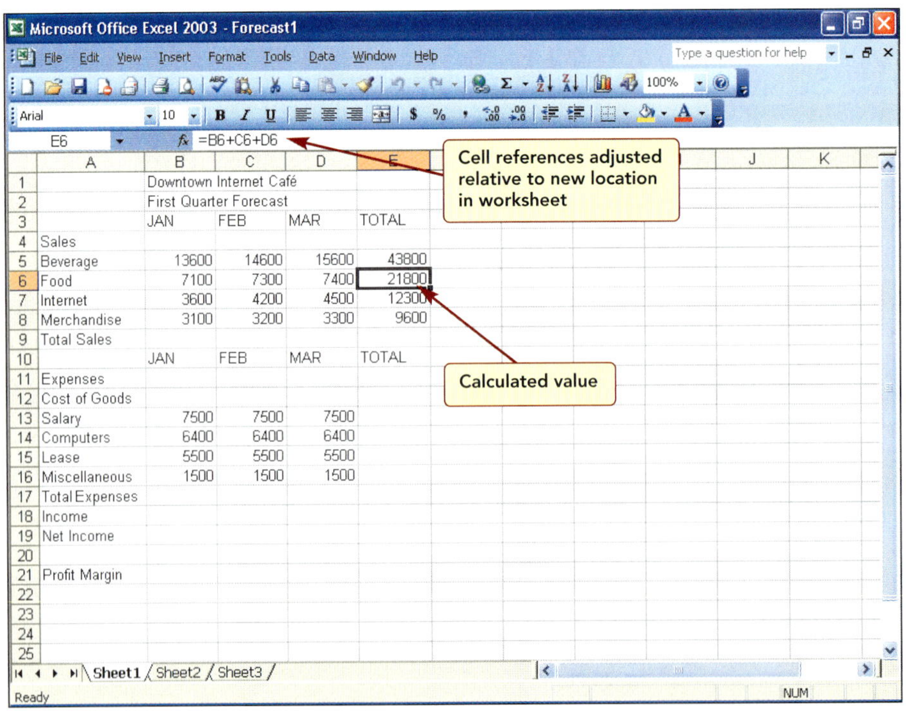

Figure 1.39

The calculated result, 21800, is displayed in the cell. The formula displayed in the formula bar is =B6+C6+D6. The formula to calculate the Food total sales is not an exact duplicate of the formula used to calculate the Beverage total sales (=B5+C5+D5). Instead, the cells referenced in the formula have been changed to reflect the new location of the formula in row 6. This is because the references in the formula are relative references.

Concept 9

Relative Reference

9 A **relative reference** is a cell or range reference in a formula whose location is interpreted by Excel in relation to the position of the cell that contains the formula. When a formula is copied, the referenced cells in the formula automatically adjust to reflect the new worksheet location. The relative relationship between the referenced cell and the new location is maintained. Because relative references automatically adjust for the new location, the relative references in a copied formula refer to different cells than the references in the original formula. The relationship between cells in both the copied and pasted formula is the same although the cell references are different.

For example, in the figure here, cell A1 references the value in cell A4 (in this case, 10). If the formula in A1 is copied to B2, the reference for B2 is adjusted to the value in cell B5 (in this case, 20).

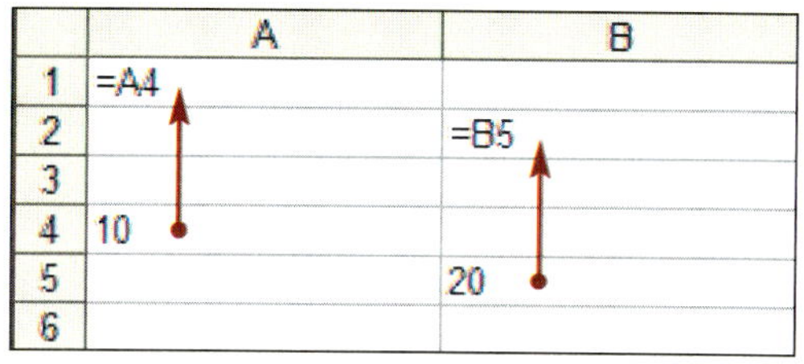

2 **Move to cell E7 and then to cell E8.**

Your screen should be similar to Figure 1.40

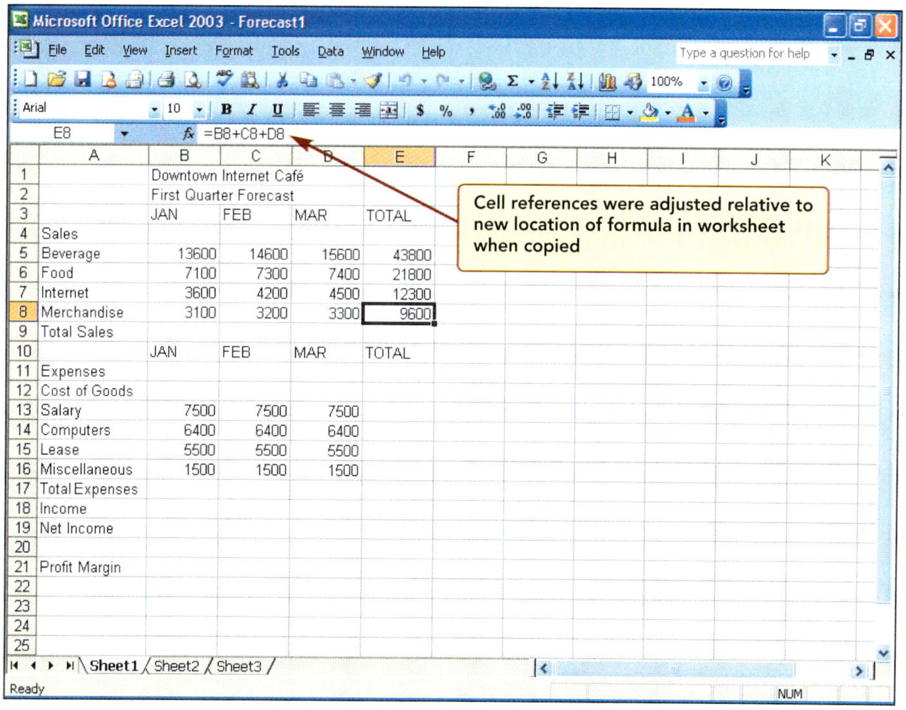

Figure 1.40

The formulas in these cells have also changed to reflect the new row location and to appropriately calculate the total based on the sales.

Entering Functions

Next, you will calculate the monthly total sales. The formula to calculate the total sales for January needs to be entered in cell B9 and copied across the row. You could use a formula similar to the formula used to calculate the category sales in column E. The formula would be =B5+B6+B7+B8. However, it is faster and more accurate to use a function.

Concept 10

Function

10 A **function** is a prewritten formula that performs certain types of calculations automatically. The **syntax** or rules of structure for entering all functions is:

=Function name (argument1, argument2,...)

The function name identifies the type of calculation to be performed. Most functions require that you enter one or more arguments following the function name. An **argument** is the data the function uses to perform the calculation. The type of data the function requires depends upon the type of calculation being performed. Most commonly, the argument consists of numbers or references to cells that contain numbers. The argument is enclosed in parentheses, and commas separate multiple arguments. Some functions, such as several of the date and time functions, do not require an argument. However, you still need to enter the opening and closing parentheses, for example =NOW(). If a function starts the formula, enter an equal sign before the function name; for example, =SUM(D5:F5)/25.

Additional Information

Use Help for detailed explanations of every function.

Excel includes several hundred functions divided into nine categories. Some common functions and the results they calculate are shown in the following table.

Category	Function	Calculates
Financial	PMT	Calculates the payment for a loan based on constant payments and a constant interest rate
	PV	Returns the present value of an investment—the total amount that a series of future payments is worth now
	FV	Returns the future value of an investment—the total amount that a series of payments will be worth
Time & Date	TODAY	Returns the serial number that represents today's date
	DATE	Returns the serial number of a particular date
	NOW	Returns the serial number of the current date and time
Math & Trig	SUM	Adds all the numbers in a range of cells
	ABS	Returns the absolute value of a number (a number without its sign)
Statistical	AVERAGE	Returns the average (arithmetic mean) of its arguments
	MAX	Returns the largest value in a set of values; ignores logical values and text
	MIN	Returns the smallest value in a set of values; ignores logical values and text
Lookup & Reference	COLUMNS	Returns the number of columns in an array or reference
	CHOOSE	Chooses a value or action to perform from a list of values, based on an index number
Database	DSUM	Adds the numbers in the field (column) or records in the database that match the conditions you specify
	DAVERAGE	Averages the values in a column in a list or database that match conditions you specify
Text	DOLLAR	Converts a number to text, using currency format
	UPPER	Converts text to uppercase
Logical	IF	Returns one value if a condition you specify evaluates to True and another value if it evaluates to False
	AND	Returns True if all its arguments are True; returns False if any arguments are False
	OR	Returns True if any arguments are True; returns False if all arguments are False
Information	ISLOGICAL	Returns True if value is a logical value, either True or False
	ISREF	Returns True if value is a reference

You will use the SUM function to calculate the total sales for January. Because the SUM function is the most commonly used function, it has its own toolbar button.

1 Move to B9.

Click AutoSum.

Another Method

Pressing Alt + = is the keyboard shortcut for AutoSum.

Your screen should be similar to Figure 1.41

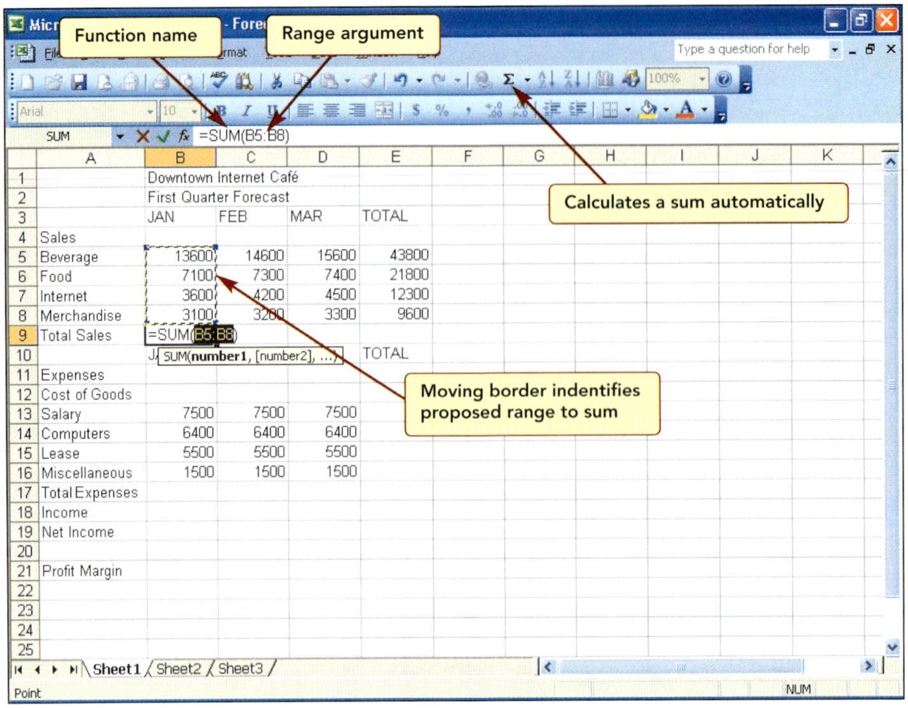

Figure 1.41

Additional Information

The AutoSum button can also calculate a grand total if the worksheet contains subtotals. Select a cell below or to the right of a cell that contains a subtotal and then click AutoSum.

Excel automatically proposes a range based upon the data above or to the left of the active cell. The formula bar displays the name of the function followed by the range argument enclosed in parentheses. You will accept the proposed range and enter the function.

2 Click Enter.

Your screen should be similar to Figure 1.42

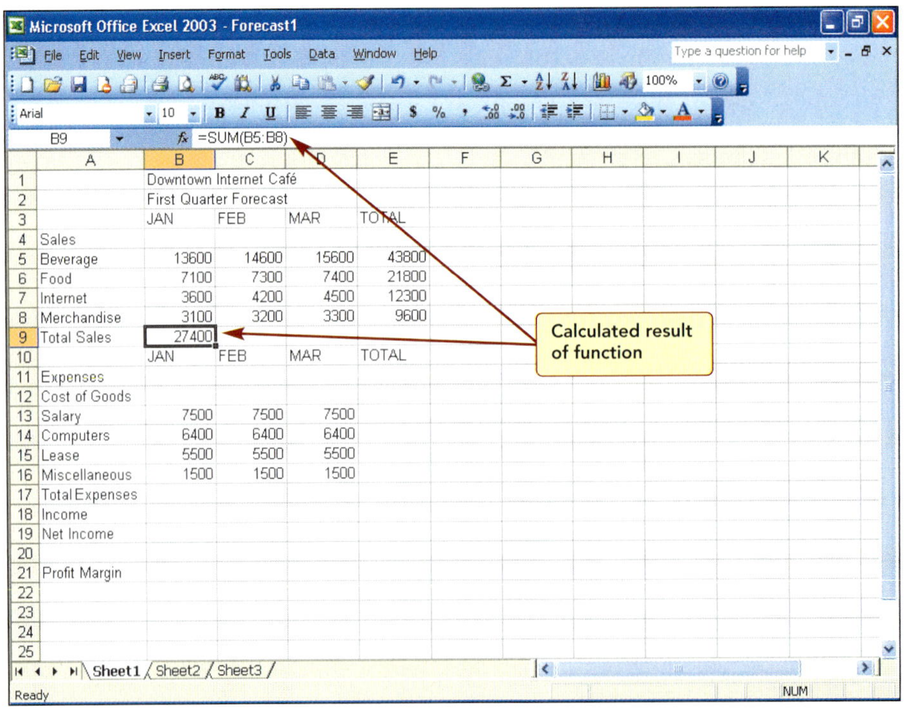

Figure 1.42

The result, 27400, calculated by the SUM function is displayed in cell B9. Next you need to calculate the total sales for February and March and the Total column.

3 **Copy the function from cell B9 to cells C9 through E9.**

Move to C9.

Your screen should be similar to Figure 1.43

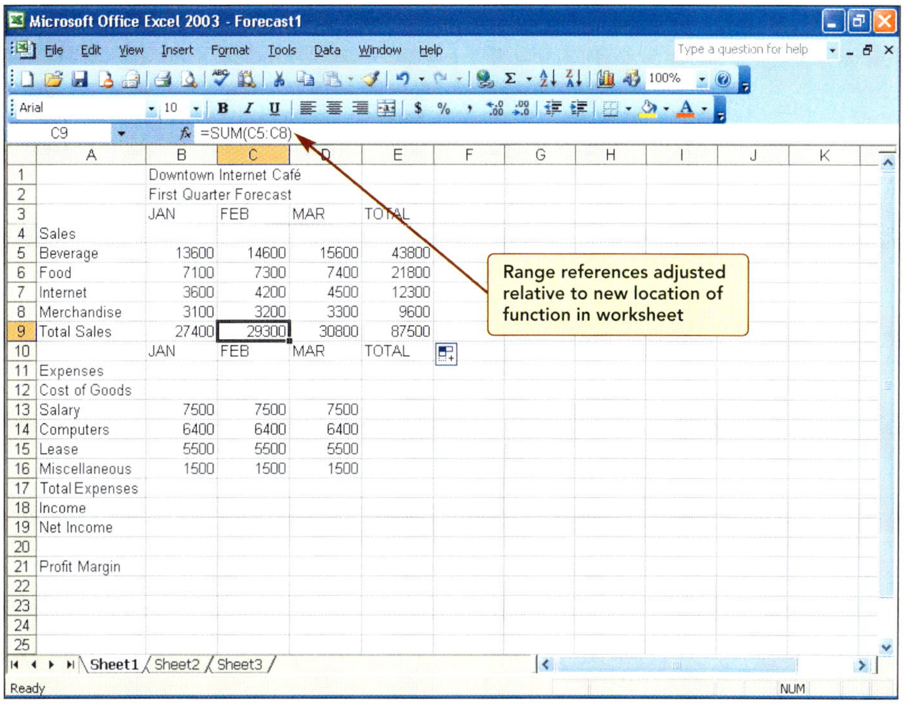

Figure 1.43

The result calculated by the function, 29300, is displayed in cell C9 and the copied function is displayed in the formula bar. The range reference in the function adjusted relative to its new cell location because it is a relative reference.

Using Pointing to Enter a Formula

Next, you will enter the formula to calculate the cost of goods sold. These numbers are estimated by using a formula to calculate the number as a percent of sales. Evan suggested using estimated percents for this worksheet so he could get an idea of what to expect from the first three months after the remodel. He wants you to calculate beverage expenses at 25 percent of beverage sales and food expenses at 50 percent of food sales.

Rather than typing in the cell references for the formula, you will enter them by selecting the worksheet cells. In addition, to simplify the process of entering and copying entries, you can enter data into the first cell of a range and have it copied to all other cells in the range at the same time by using Ctrl + ←Enter to complete the entry. You will use this feature to enter the formulas to calculate the beverage expenses for January through March. This formula needs to calculate the beverage cost of goods at 25 percent first and add it to the food cost of goods calculated at 50 percent.

1 Select B12:D12.

Type **=**.

Click cell B5.

Additional Information

Even when a range is selected, you can still point to specify cells in the formula. You can also use the direction keys to move to the cell.

Your screen should be similar to Figure 1.44

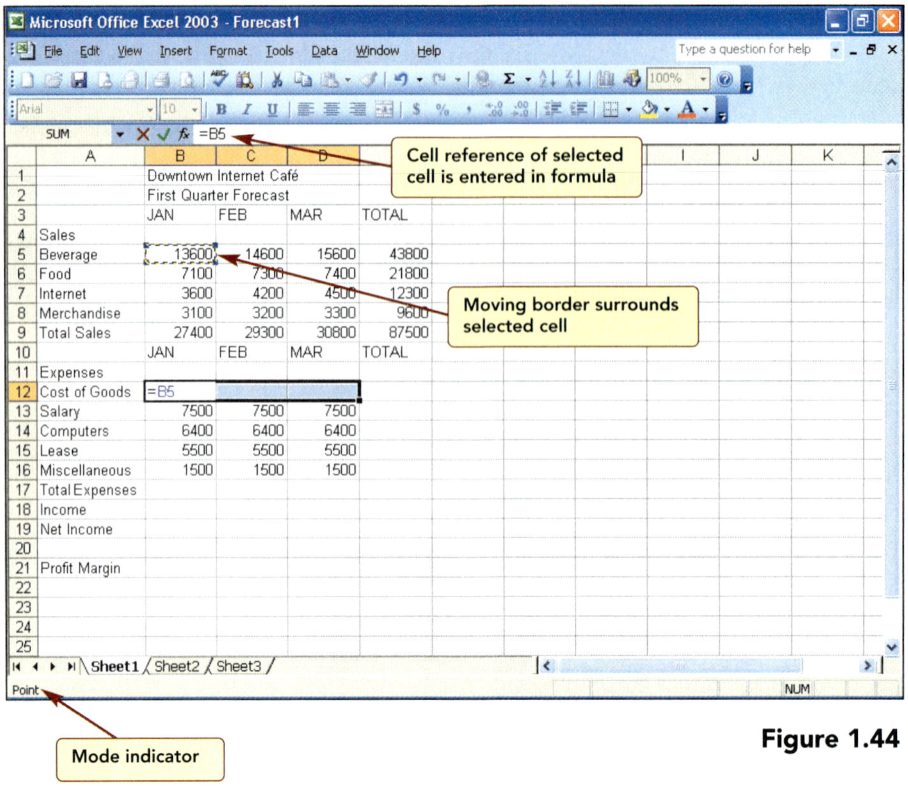

Figure 1.44

Notice that the status bar displays the current mode as Point. This tells you that the program is allowing you to select cells by highlighting them. The cell reference, B5, is entered following the = sign. You will complete the formula by entering the percentage value to multiply by and adding the Food percentage to the formula.

2 Type ***25%**.

Type **+**.

Click on B6.

Type ***50%**.

Press Ctrl + ←Enter.

Your screen should be similar to Figure 1.45

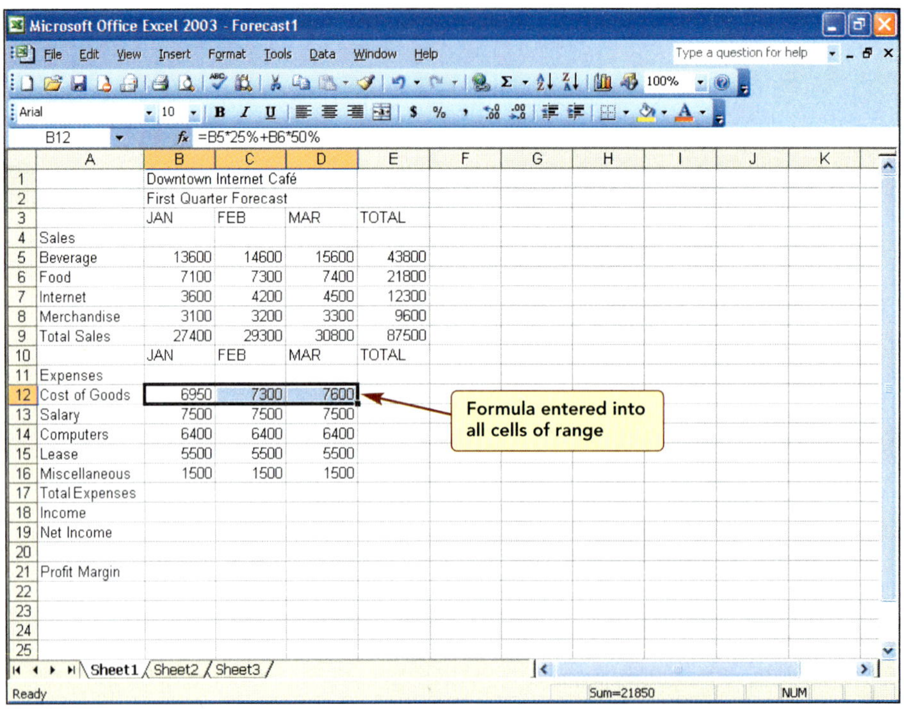

Figure 1.45

The formula to calculate the January cost of goods expense was entered in cell B12 and copied to all cells of the selected range. You can now calculate the total expenses in row 17 and column E. To do this quickly, you will preselect the range and use the Σ AutoSum button. Then you will enter the formula to calculate the net income. Net income is calculated by subtracting total expenses from total sales.

3

- **Select B12 through E17.**
- **Click Σ AutoSum.**
- **Select B19 through E19.**
- **Enter the formula =B9-B17.**
- **Press Ctrl + ←Enter.**

Your screen should be similar to Figure 1.46

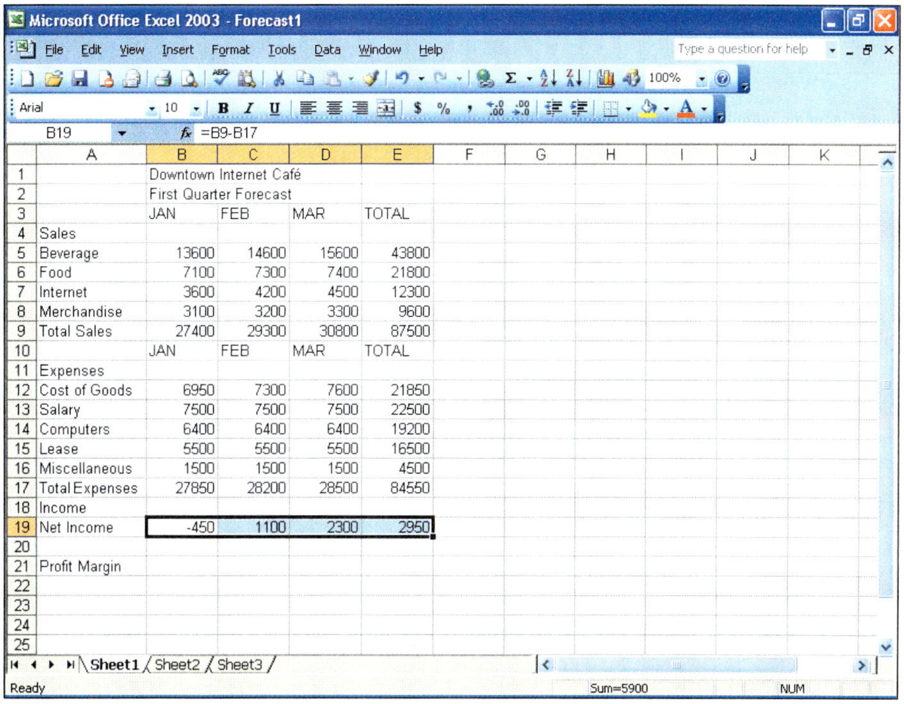

Figure 1.46

The formula is quickly entered into all cells of the range. The final formula you need to enter is to calculate the profit margin.

4 **Select B21 through E21.**

Enter the formula =B19/B9.

Press Ctrl + ←Enter.

Your screen should be similar to Figure 1.47

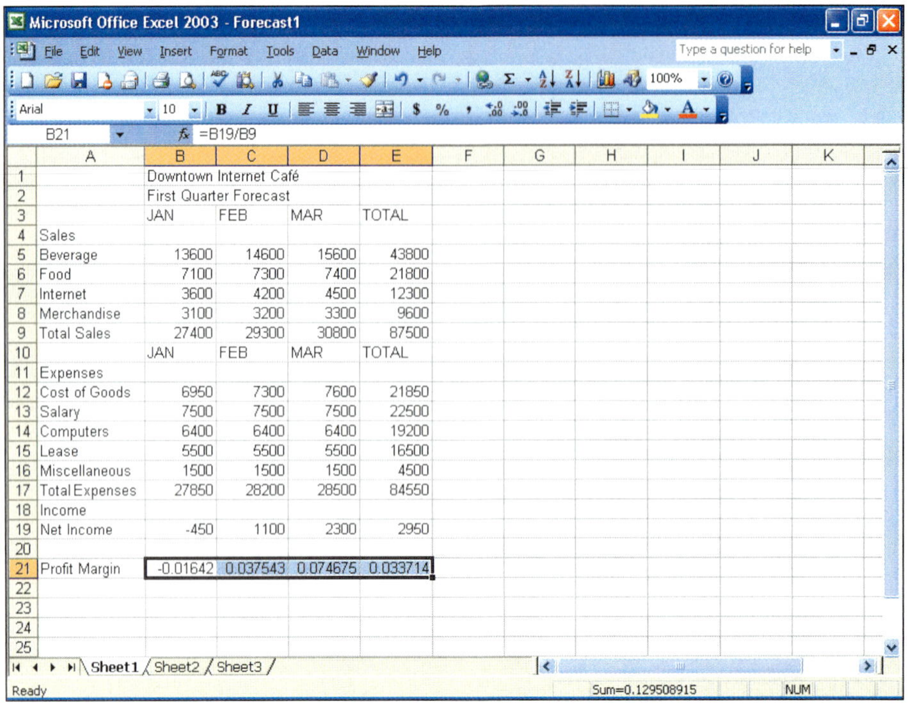

Figure 1.47

The profit margins are calculated and displayed in cells B21 through E21.

Recalculating the Worksheet

Now that you have created the worksheet structure and entered some sample data for the forecasted sales for the first quarter, you want to test the formulas to verify that they are operating correctly. A simple way to do this is to use a calculator to verify that the correct result is displayed. You can then further test the worksheet by changing values and verifying that all cells containing formulas that reference the value are appropriately recalculated.

Concept 11

Recalculation

11 When a number in a referenced cell in a formula changes, Excel automatically **recalculates** all formulas that are dependent upon the changed value. Because only those formulas directly affected by a change in the data are recalculated, the time it takes to recalculate the workbook is reduced. Without this feature, in large worksheets it could take several minutes to recalculate all formulas each time a number is changed in the worksheet. Recalculation is one of the most powerful features of electronic worksheets.

After considering the sales estimates for the three months, you decide that the estimated Internet sales for January are too low and you want to increase this number from 3600 to 4000.

1 Change the entry in cell B7 to 4000.

Press Ctrl + ←Enter to complete the edit.

Your screen should be similar to Figure 1.48

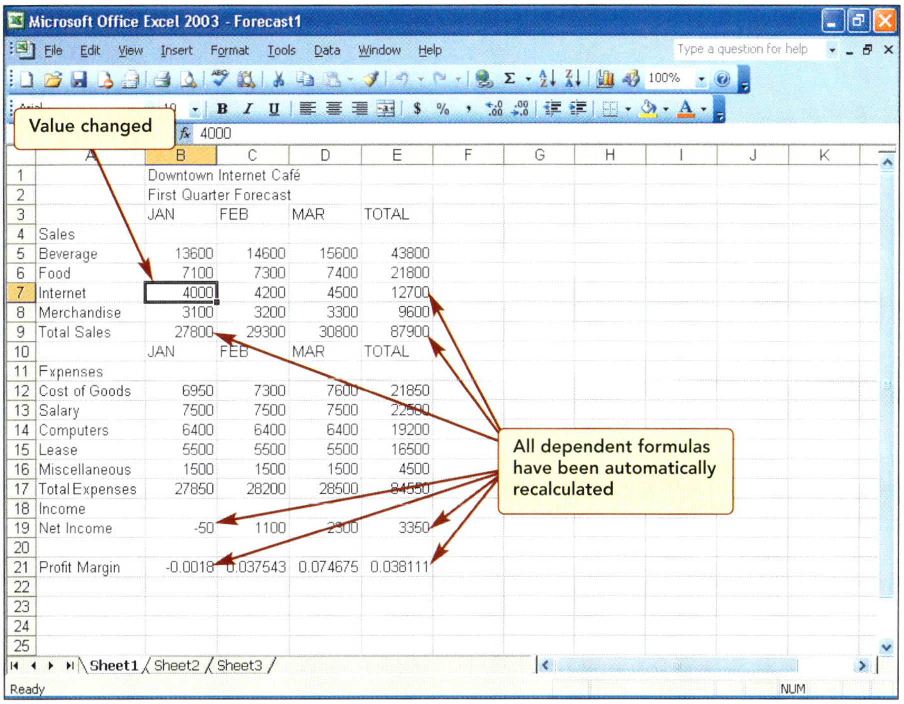

Figure 1.48

The Internet total in cell E7 has been automatically recalculated. The number displayed is now 12700. Likewise, the January total in cell B9 and the grand total in cell E9 have increased by 400 to reflect the change in cell B7. Finally, the Net Income and Profit Margin values have also adjusted appropriately.

The formulas in the worksheet are correctly calculating the desired result. The Sales portion of the worksheet is now complete.

Inserting Rows

Finally, you realize that you forgot to include a row for the Advertising expenses. To add this data, you will insert a blank row below the Lease row. To indicate where you want to insert a single blank row, move the cell pointer to the row immediately below the row where you want the new row inserted and use **I**nsert/**R**ows. If you want to insert multiple rows, select a range of rows and Excel inserts the same number of rows you selected in the range. In a similar manner, you can insert blank columns by moving the cell pointer to the right of the column where you want to insert the new column and use **I**nsert/**C**olumns.

1 Move to A15.

- Choose Insert/Rows.
- Enter the heading Advertising in cell A15 and the value 1000 in cells B15 through D15.
- Copy the function from cell E14 to E15 to calculate the total advertising expense.
- Move to cell B18.
- Click Save to save the worksheet using the same file name.

Your screen should be similar to Figure 1.49

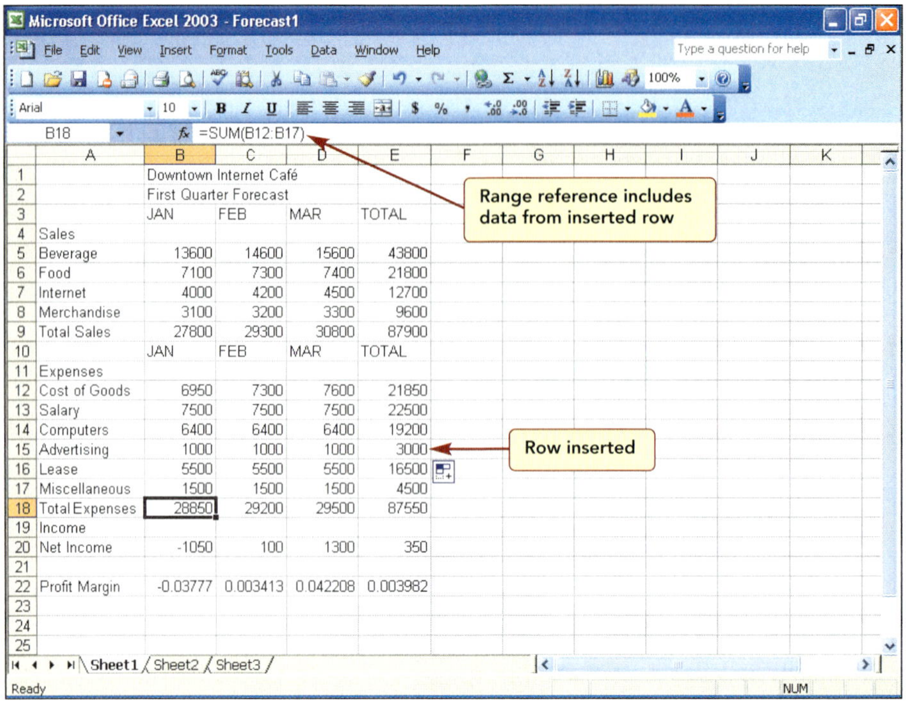

Figure 1.49

Additional Information

To delete a row or column, move to it and choose Edit/Delete/Entire Row or Entire Column. The entire row or column and all its contents are removed.

The range in the formula to calculate monthly total expenses in row 18 has been revised to include the data in the inserted row. Additionally, the net income in row 20 and profit margin in row 22 have been recalculated to reflect the change in data.

Formatting the Worksheet

Now that many of the worksheet values are entered, you want to improve the appearance of the worksheet by changing the format of the headings. **Format** controls how entries are displayed in a cell and includes such features as the position of data in a cell, text font, color, patterns, borders, and number formats such as commas and dollar signs. Applying different formats greatly improves both the appearance and readability of the data in a worksheet.

Changing Cell Alignment

You decide the column headings would look better if they were right-aligned in their cell spaces, so that they would appear over the numbers in the column. Alignment is a basic format setting that is used in most worksheets.

Concept 12

Alignment

12 **Alignment** settings allow you to change the horizontal and vertical placement and the orientation of an entry in a cell.

Horizontal placement allows you to left-, right-, or center-align text and number entries in the cell space. Entries can also be indented within the cell space, centered across a selection, or justified. You can also fill a cell horizontally with a repeated entry.

Vertical placement allows you to specify whether the cell contents are displayed at the top, the bottom, or the center of the vertical cell space or justified vertically.

You can also change the angle of text in a cell by varying the degrees of rotation.

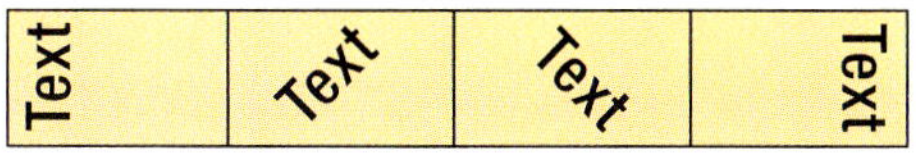

First you will change the column heading in cell B3 to right-aligned.

1 • **Move to cell B3.**

• **Choose Format/Cells.**

Another Method

The shortcut key is Ctrl + 1. Format Cells is also an option on the shortcut menu.

• **Open the Alignment tab.**

Your screen should be similar to Figure 1.50

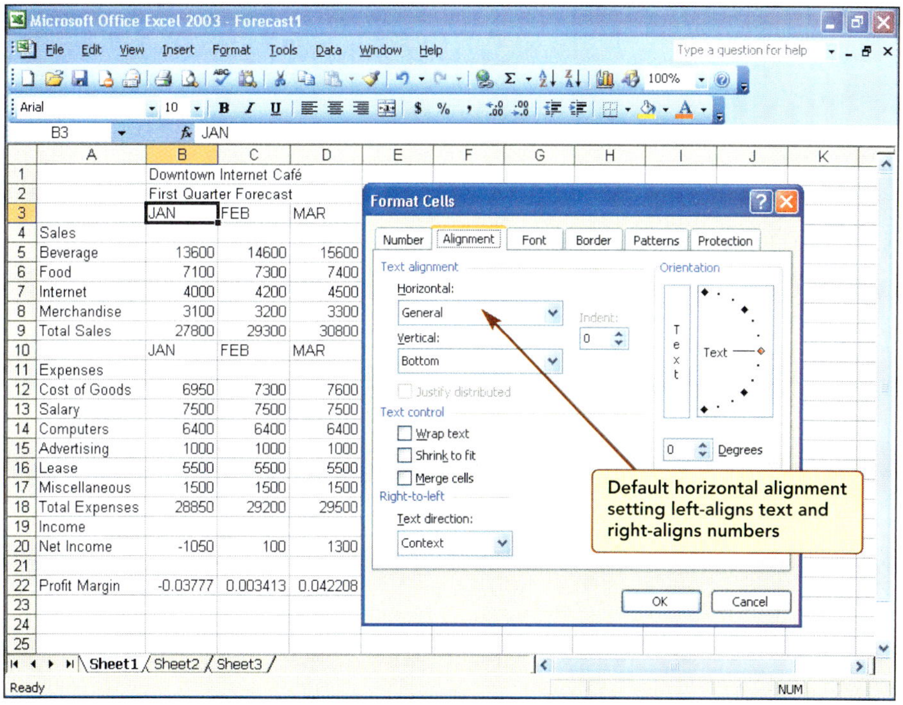

Figure 1.50

The Alignment tab shows the default workbook alignment settings. The horizontal alignment setting is General. This setting left-aligns text entries and right-aligns number entries. The vertical alignment is set to Bottom for both types of entries, and the orientation is set to zero degrees rotation from the horizontal position. You want to change the horizontal alignment of the entry to right-aligned.

2 **Open the Horizontal drop-down list box.**

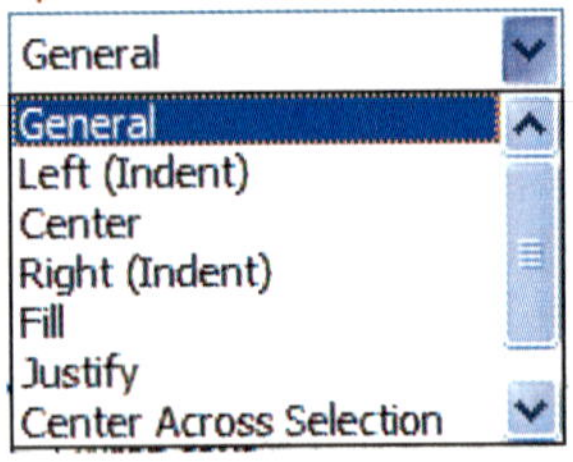

- **Select Right (Indent).**
- **Click OK.**

Your screen should be similar to Figure 1.51

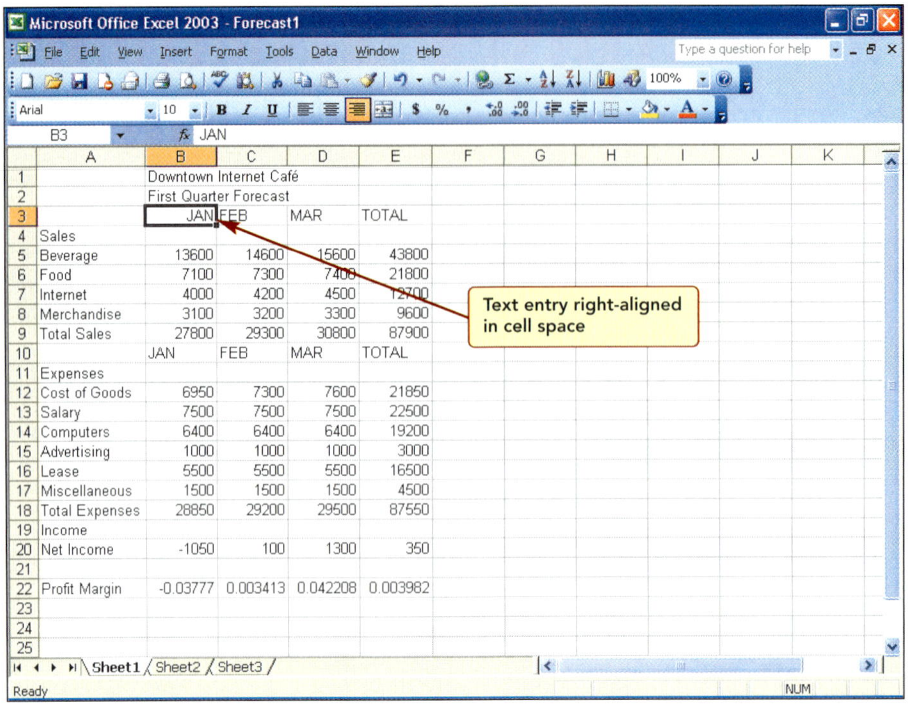

Figure 1.51

A quicker way to change the alignment is to use the Formatting toolbar, or voice command shortcuts shown in the following table.

Formatting toolbar	Voice	Action
	Align left	Left-aligns entry
	Center	Centers entry
	Align right	Right-aligns entry

Additional Information

If you do not hold down ⇧Shift while double-clicking on a border, the cell selector moves to the last-used cell in the direction indicated.

You can quickly align a range of cells by selecting the range and then using the command or button. A quick way to select a range of filled cells is to hold down ⇧Shift and double-click on the edge of the active cell in the direction in which you want the range expanded. For example, to select the range to the right of the active cell, you would double-click the right border. You will use this method to select and right-align the remaining column entries.

3 — Move to cell C3.

- Hold down ⇧Shift and double-click the right cell border of cell C3.

Having Trouble?

The mouse pointer must be ✥ when you click the cell border.

- Click Align Right.
- In a similar manner, right-align the entries in row 10.

Your screen should be similar to Figure 1.52

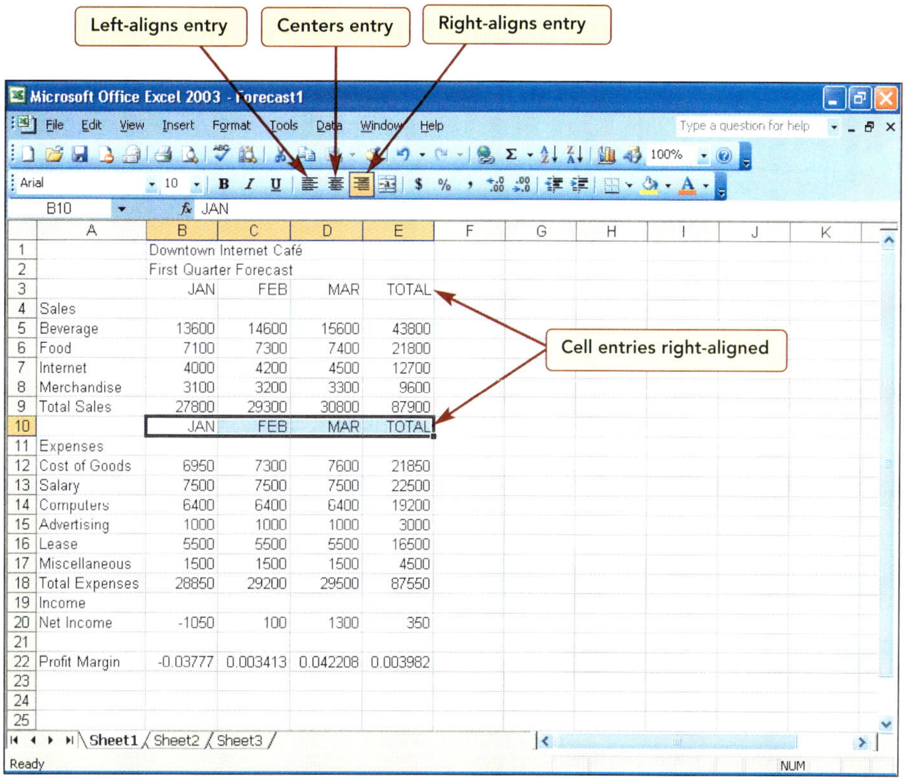

Figure 1.52

The entries in the selected range are right-aligned in their cell spaces.

Indenting Entries

Additional Information

You can also select entire nonadjacent rows or columns by holding down Ctrl while selecting the rows or columns.

Next, you would like to indent the row headings in cells A5 through A8 and A12 through A17 from the left edge of the cell. You want to indent the headings in both ranges at the same time. To select nonadjacent cells or cell ranges, after selecting the first cell or range hold down Ctrl while selecting each additional cell or range. You will select the cells and indent their contents.

1 — Select A5 through A8.

- Hold down Ctrl.
- Select A12 through A17.
- Release Ctrl.
- Click Increase Indent.

Another Method

The menu equivalent is Format/Cells/Alignment/Horizontal/Left(Indent)/1.

Your screen should be similar to Figure 1.53

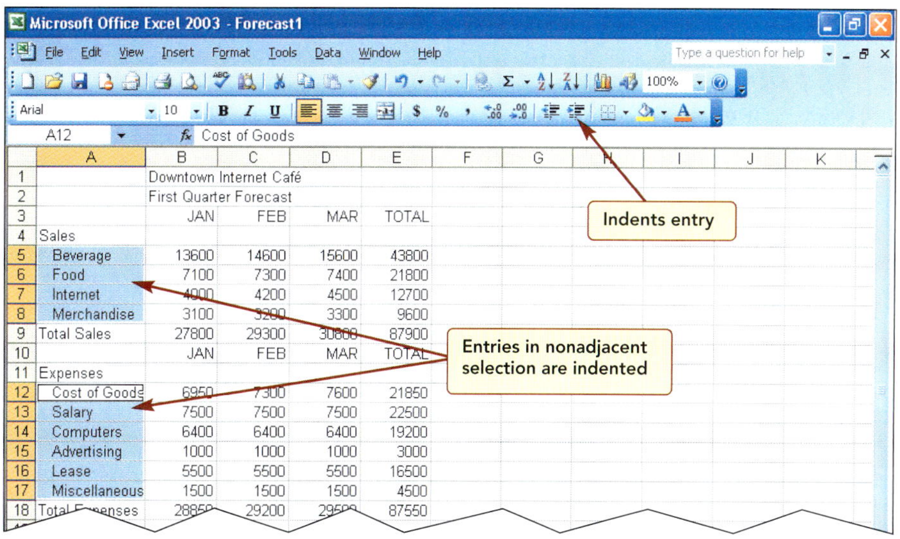

Figure 1.53

Each entry in the selected range is indented two spaces from the left edge of the cell. You would also like to indent the Total Sales, Total Expenses, and Net Income headings four spaces.

2 **Select A9, A18, and A20.**

Click Increase Indent twice.

Your screen should be similar to Figure 1.54

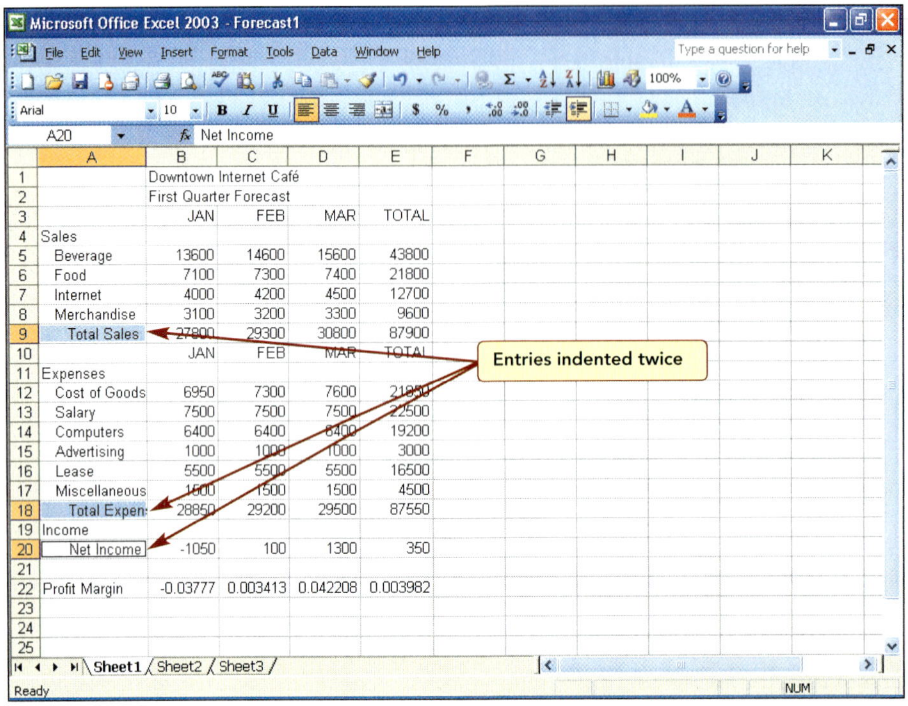

Figure 1.54

Centering Across a Selection

Next, you want to center the worksheet titles across columns A through E so they are centered over the worksheet data.

1 **Select A1 through E1.**

Click Merge and Center.

Another Method

The menu equivalent is Format/Cells/Alignment/Horizontal/Center Across Selection/Merge cells.

Your screen should be similar to Figure 1.55

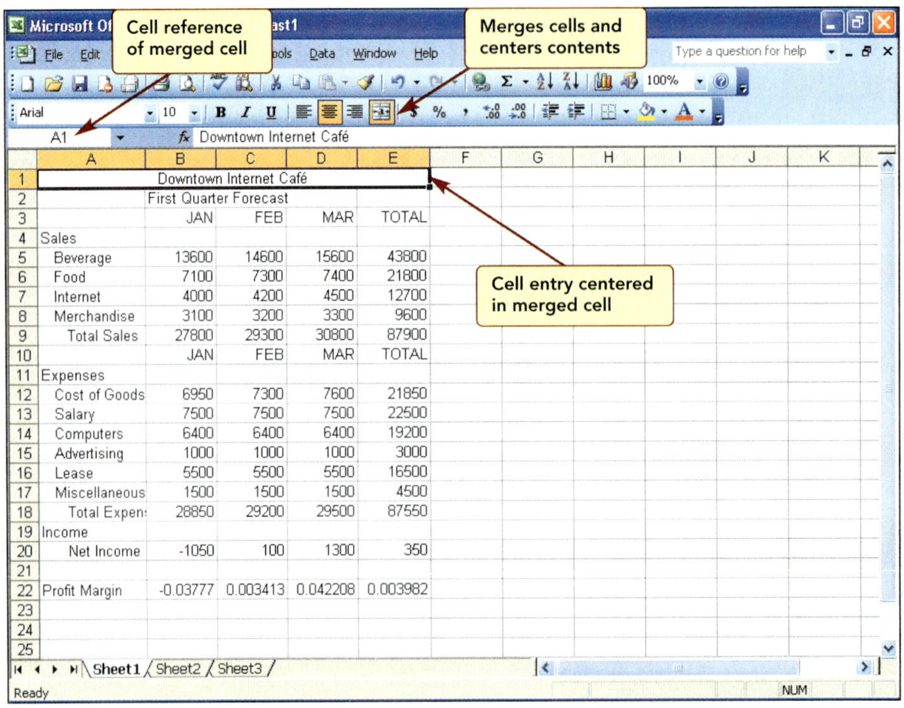

Figure 1.55

Another Method

You could also use Format/Cells/Alignment/Horizontal/Center Across Selection to center the contents across a range. The cells, however, are not merged and the cell contents to be centered must be in the leftmost cell of the selected range.

The contents of the range are centered in the range. Additionally, the five cells in the selection have been combined into a single large **merged cell**. The cell reference for a merged cell is the upper-left cell in the original selected range, in this case A1. When creating a merged cell and centering the contents, only the contents of the upper-leftmost data in the selected range are centered. If other cells in the range contained data, it would be deleted.

2 ● **Merge and center and the second title line.**

Your screen should be similar to Figure 1.56

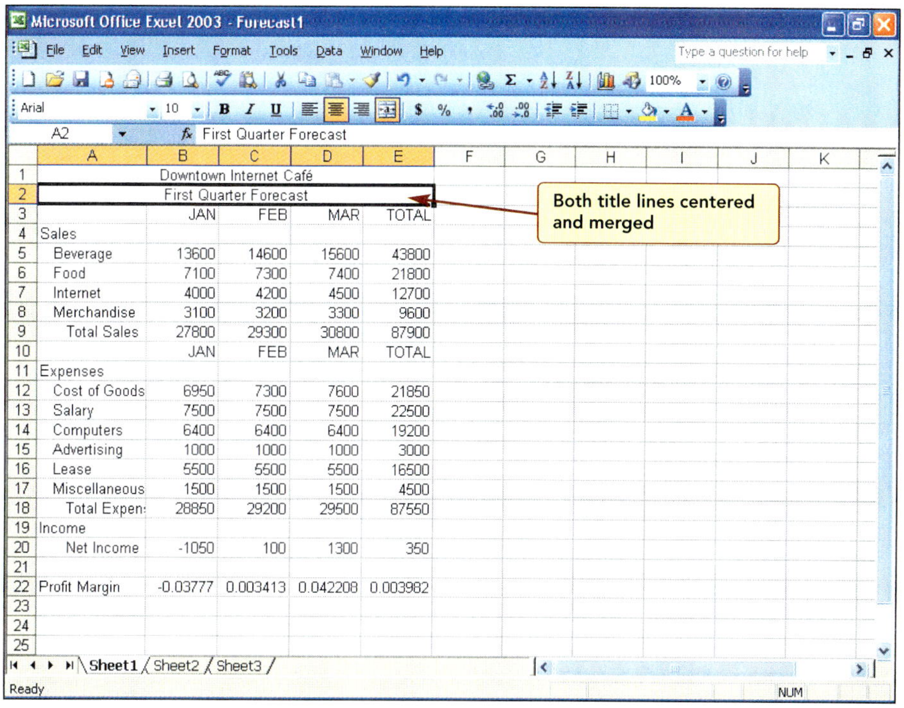

Figure 1.56

After cells have been merged, you can split them back into their original cells by selecting the merged cell and clicking to unmerge the cells.

Changing Fonts and Font Sizes

Additional Information

The Font settings are common to all Office 2003 programs.

Finally, you want to improve the worksheet appearance by enhancing the appearance of the title. One way to do this is to change the font and font size used in the title.

Concept 13

Font

13 A font, also commonly referred to as a **typeface**, is a set of characters with a specific design. The designs have names such as Times New Roman and Courier. Using fonts as a design element can add interest to your document and give readers visual cues to help them find information quickly.

There are two basic types of fonts, serif and sans serif. **Serif** fonts have a flair at the base of each letter that visually leads the reader to the next letter. Two common serif fonts are Roman and Times New Roman. Serif fonts generally are used in paragraphs. **Sans serif** fonts do not have a flair at the base of each letter. Arial and Helvetica are two common sans serif fonts. Because sans serif fonts have a clean look, they are often used for headings in documents. It is good practice to use only two types of fonts in a worksheet, one for text and one for headings. Too many styles can make your document look cluttered and unprofessional.

Each font has one or more sizes. **Size** is the height and width of the character and is commonly measured in points, abbreviated pt. One **point** equals about 1/72 inch, and text in most worksheets is 10 pt or 12 pt.

Here are several examples of the same text in various fonts and sizes.

Typeface	Font Size (12 pt/18 pt)
Arial (Sans Serif)	This is 12 pt. This is 18 pt.
Courier New (Serif)	This is 12 pt. This is 18 pt.
Times New Roman (Serif)	This is 12 pt. This is 18 pt.

1 **Select A1 and A2.**

Open the Arial Font drop-down list box.

Another Method

The menu equivalent is Format/Cells/Font/Font and the voice command is "Font."

Your screen should be similar to Figure 1.57

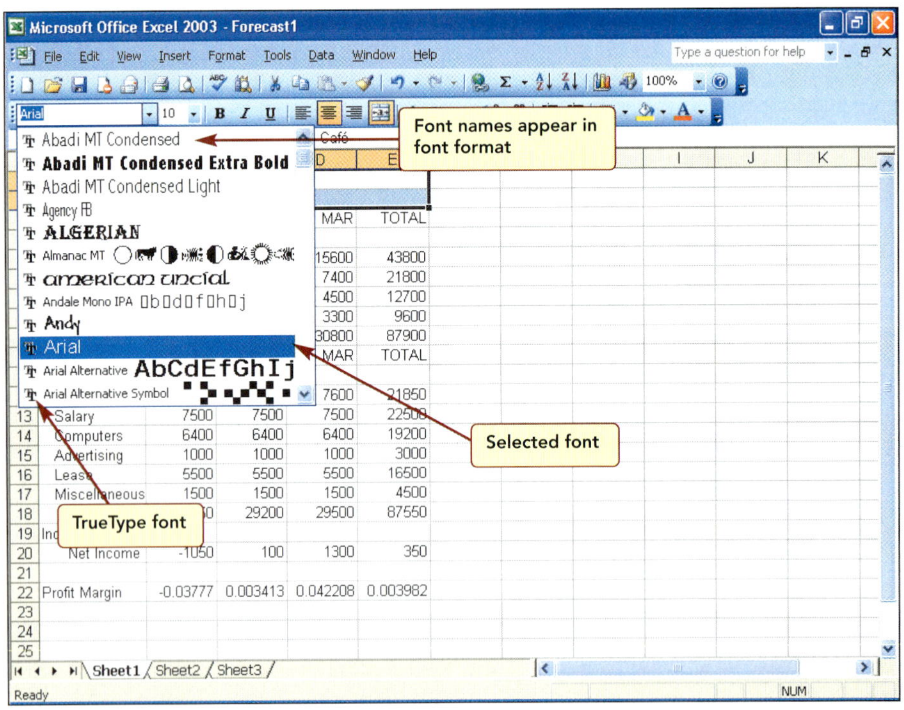

Figure 1.57

The Font drop-down menu displays examples of the available fonts on your system in alphabetical order. The default worksheet font, Arial, is highlighted. Notice the preceding the font name. This indicates the font is a TrueType font. TrueType fonts appear onscreen as they will appear when printed. They are installed when Windows is installed. Fonts that are preceded with a blank space or are printer fonts. These fonts are supported by your printer and are displayed as closely as possible to how they will appear onscreen, but may not match exactly when printed. You will change the font and increase the font size to 14.

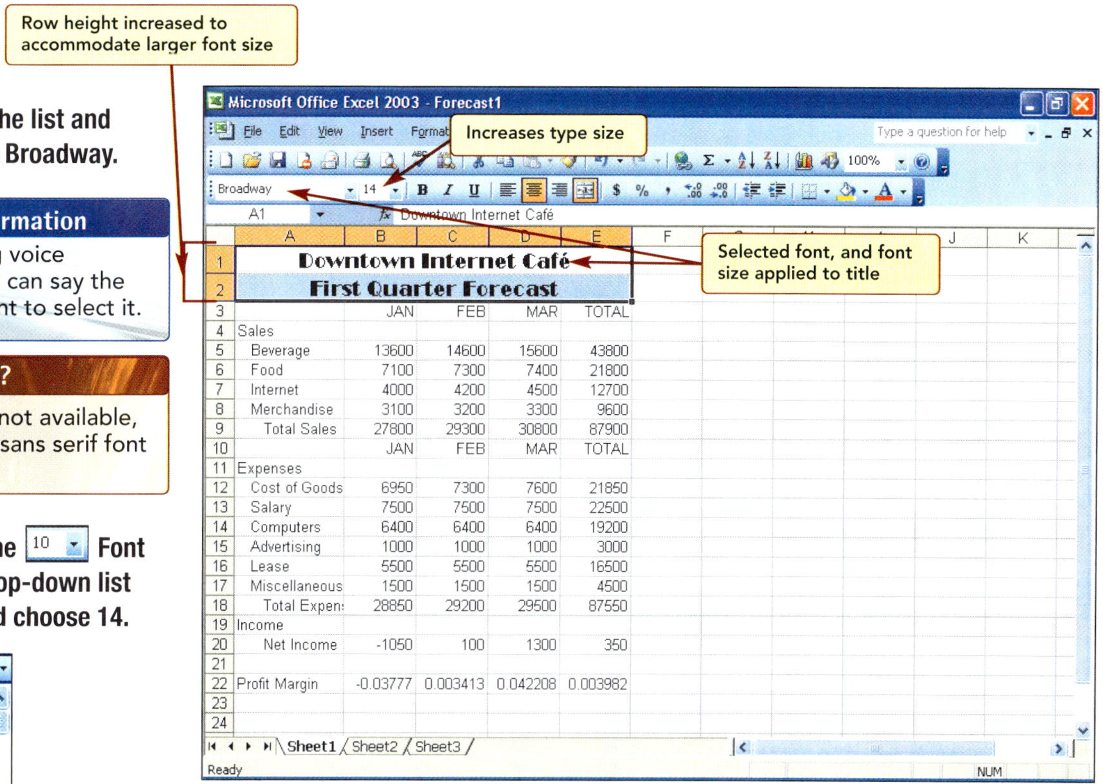

2 • **Scroll the list and choose Broadway.**

Additional Information

If you are using voice commands you can say the name of the font to select it.

Having Trouble?

If Broadway is not available, select another sans serif font of your choice.

• **Open the 10 Font Size drop-down list box and choose 14.**

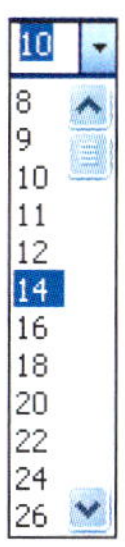

Your screen should be similar to Figure 1.58

Figure 1.58

Another Method

The menu equivalent is Format/Cells/Font/Size and the voice command is "Font size" followed by the size number.

The title appears in the selected typeface and size and the Font and Size buttons display the name of the font and size used in the active cell. Notice that the height of the row has increased to accommodate the larger font size of the heading.

Applying Character Effects

In addition to changing font and font size, you can apply different **character effects** to enhance the appearance of text. The table below describes some of the effects and their uses.

Format	Example	Use
Bold	**Bold**	Adds emphasis
Italic	*Italic*	Adds emphasis
Underline	<u>Underline</u>	Adds emphasis
Strikethrough	~~Strikethrough~~	Indicates words to be deleted
Superscript	"To be or not to be."[1]	Used in footnotes and formulas
Subscript	H_2O	Used in formulas
Color	Color Color Color	Adds interest

You want to add bold, italic, and underlines to several worksheet entries.

1

- **Select B3 through E3.**
- **Click B Bold.**

Another Method

The menu equivalent is Format/Cells/Font/Font Style/Bold, the keyboard shortcut is Ctrl + B, and the voice command is "Bold."

- **Click U Underline.**
- **Select A5 through A8.**
- **Click B Bold.**
- **Click I Italic.**

Another Method

The menu equivalent for underline is Format/Cells/Font/Underline/Single or Ctrl + U, and for italic is Format/Cells/Font/Font Style/Italic or Ctrl + I. The voice commands are "Underline" or "Italic."

Your screen should be similar to Figure 1.59

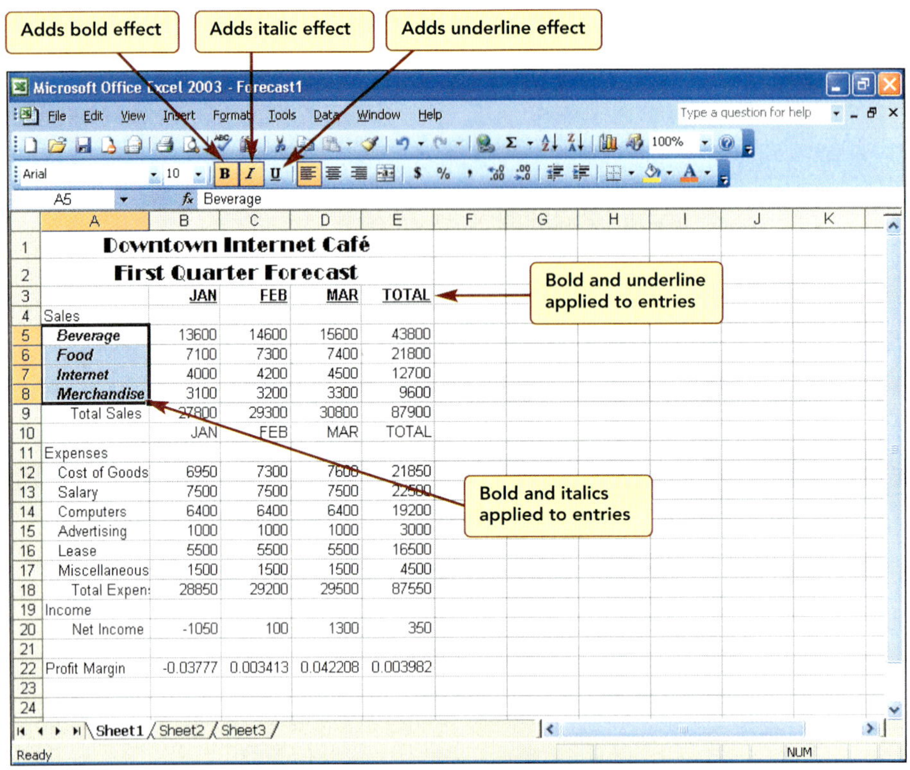

Figure 1.59

Using Undo

Sometimes formatting changes you make do not have the expected result. In this case, you feel that the sales category names would look better without the formatting. You will quickly undo the last two actions you performed.

1

- **Open the Undo drop-down list.**
- **Move the mouse pointer down the list to highlight the Italic and Bold actions.**
- **Click on the highlighted selection.**

Another Method

The menu equivalent is **E**dit/**U**ndo and the keyboard shortcut is Ctrl + Z. You can also click or say "Undo" repeatedly to undo the actions in the list one by one.

Your screen should be similar to Figure 1.60

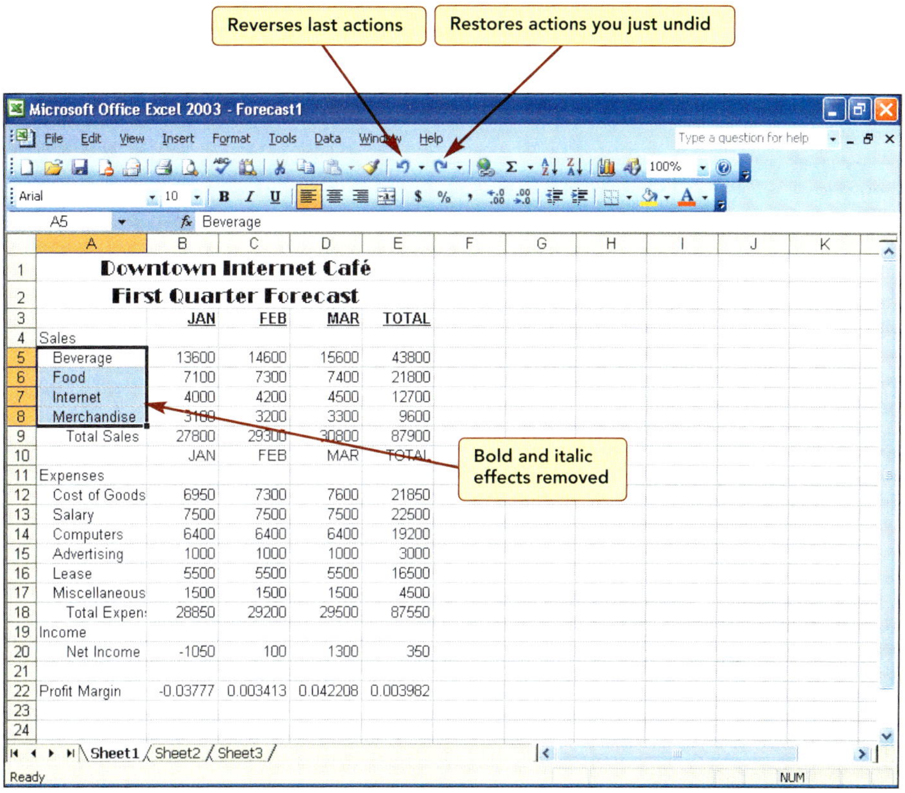

Figure 1.60

Additional Information

The menu equivalent is **E**dit/**R**edo, the keyboard shortcut is Ctrl + Y, and the voice command is "Redo."

The two actions you selected are undone. Undo reverses the selected actions regardless of the current cell pointer location. If you change your mind after you Undo an action, the Redo button is available so that you can restore the action you just undid.

Using Format Painter

You do think, however, that the Total Sales, Total Expenses, and Net Income headings would look good in bold. You will bold the entry in cell A9 and then copy the format from A9 to the other cells using **Format Painter**. This feature applies the formats associated with the current selection to new selections. To turn on the feature, move the insertion point to the cell whose formats you want to copy and click the Format Painter button. Then you select the cell to which you want the formats applied. The format is automatically applied to the entire cell contents simply by clicking on the cell. If you double-click the Format Painter button, you can apply the format multiple times. You will also format the headings in row 10.

1 **Apply bold to cell A9.**

With cell A9 selected, double-click Format Painter.

Additional Information

When Format Painter is on, the mouse pointer appears as ✚🖌.

Click A18.

Click A20.

Click Format Painter to turn it off.

Another Method

You also can also press Esc to turn off Format Painter.

Use Format Painter to copy the format from cell B3 to cells B10 through E10.

Double-click the A column boundary line to fit the contents.

Your screen should be similar to Figure 1.61

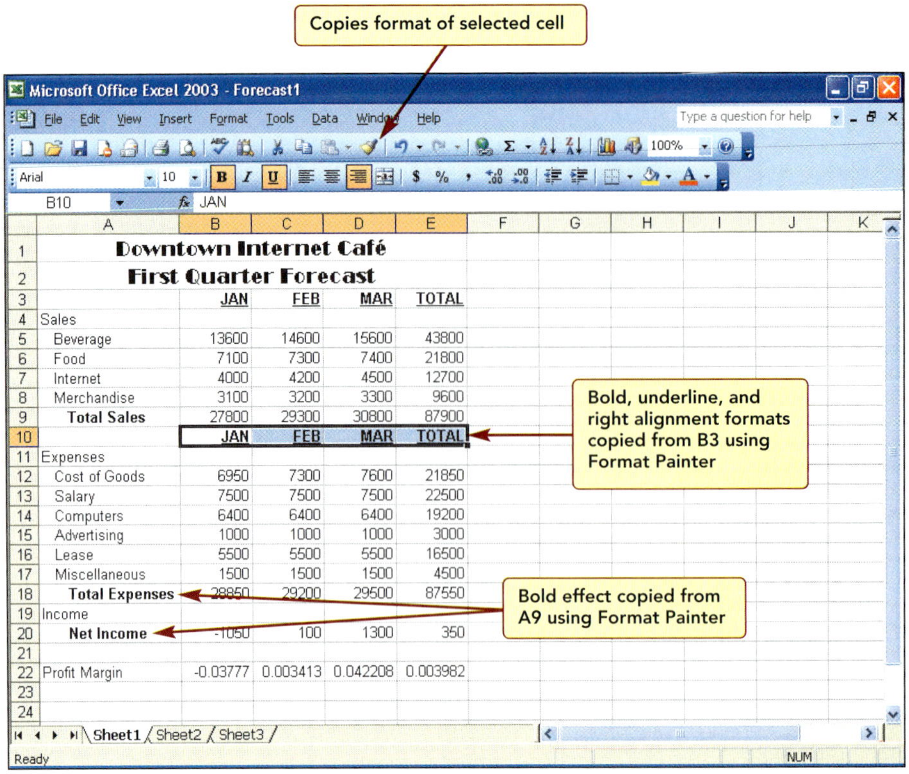

Figure 1.61

The formatting was quickly added to each cell as it was selected.

Formatting Numbers

You also want to improve the appearance of the numbers in the worksheet by changing their format.

Concept 14

Number Format

14

Number formats change the appearance of numbers onscreen and when printed, without changing the way the number is stored or used in calculations. When a number is formatted, the formatting appears in the cell while the value without the formatting is displayed in the formula bar.

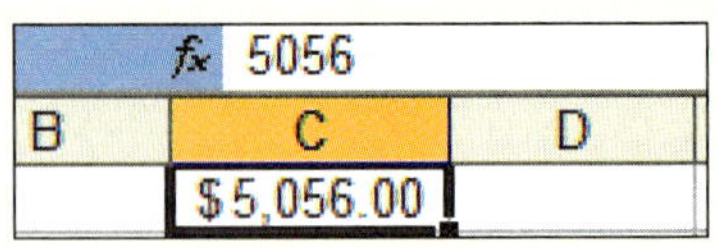

The default number format setting in a worksheet is General. General format, in most cases, displays numbers just as you enter them, unformatted. Unformatted numbers are displayed without a thousands separator such as a comma, with negative values preceded by a – (minus sign), and with as many decimal place settings as cell space allows. If a number is too long to be fully displayed in the cell, the General format will round numbers with decimals and use scientific notation for large numbers.

First, you will change the number format of cells B5 through E9 to display as currency with dollar signs, commas, and decimal places. The Currency format category includes options that allow you to specify the number of decimal places, the way that negative numbers will appear, and whether a currency symbol such as a dollar sign will be displayed.

1

- **Select cells B5 through E9.**
- **Choose Format/Cells.**

Another Method

The keyboard shortcut is Ctrl + 1.

- **If necessary, open the Number tab.**
- **From the Category list box, select Currency.**
- **Click OK to use the default Currency format settings.**

Your screen should be similar to Figure 1.62

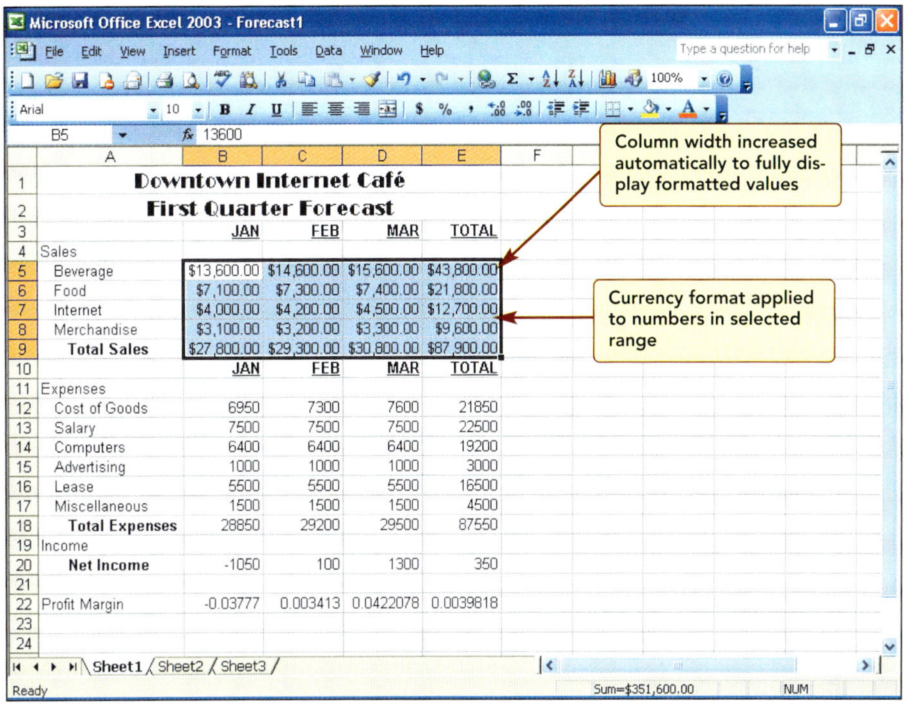

Figure 1.62

Additional Information

Excel will also automatically apply a format to a cell based on the symbols you use when entering the number. For example, entering 10,000 in a cell formats the cell to Comma format, and entering $102.20 formats the cell to Currency with two decimal places.

The number entries in the selected range appear with a currency symbol, comma, and two decimal places. The column widths increased automatically to fully display the formatted values.

A second format category that displays numbers as currency is Accounting. You will try this format next on the same range. Additionally, you will specify zero as the number of decimal places because all the values are whole values.

2 Choose **Format/Cells**

- **From the Category list box, select Accounting.**
- **Reduce the decimal places to 0.**
- **Click OK.**

Your screen should be similar to Figure 1.63

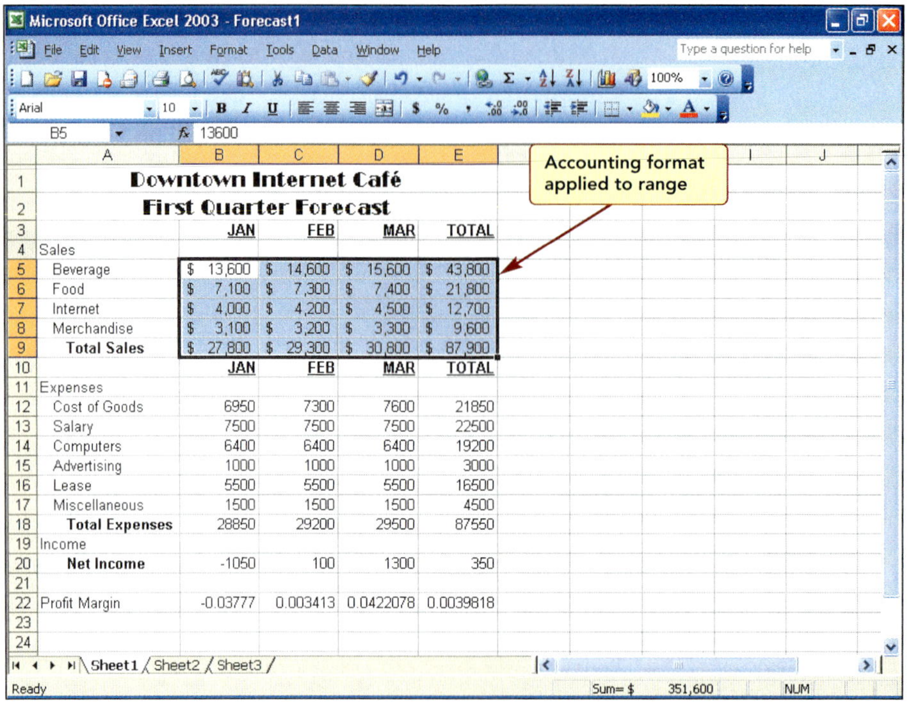

	A	B	C	D	E
1	Downtown Internet Café				
2	First Quarter Forecast				
3		JAN	FEB	MAR	TOTAL
4	Sales				
5	Beverage	$ 13,600	$ 14,600	$ 15,600	$ 43,800
6	Food	$ 7,100	$ 7,300	$ 7,400	$ 21,800
7	Internet	$ 4,000	$ 4,200	$ 4,500	$ 12,700
8	Merchandise	$ 3,100	$ 3,200	$ 3,300	$ 9,600
9	Total Sales	$ 27,800	$ 29,300	$ 30,800	$ 87,900
10		JAN	FEB	MAR	TOTAL
11	Expenses				
12	Cost of Goods	6950	7300	7600	21850
13	Salary	7500	7500	7500	22500
14	Computers	6400	6400	6400	19200
15	Advertising	1000	1000	1000	3000
16	Lease	5500	5500	5500	16500
17	Miscellaneous	1500	1500	1500	4500
18	Total Expenses	28850	29200	29500	87550
19	Income				
20	Net Income	-1050	100	1300	350
21					
22	Profit Margin	-0.03777	0.003413	0.0422078	0.0039818

Figure 1.63

The numbers now appear in Accounting format. The primary difference between the Accounting and the Currency formats is that the Accounting format aligns numbers at the decimal place and places the dollar sign in a column at the left edge of the cell space. In addition, it does not allow you to select different ways of displaying negative numbers but displays them in black in parentheses.

You decide the Accounting format will make it easier to read the numbers in a column and you will use this format for the rest of the worksheet. An easier way to apply the Accounting format is to use the $ Currency button on the Formatting toolbar.

Another Method

The voice command is "Currency style."

3 Select the range B12 through E20.

- Click **Currency Style.**
- Click **Decrease Decimal twice.**

Your screen should be similar to Figure 1.64

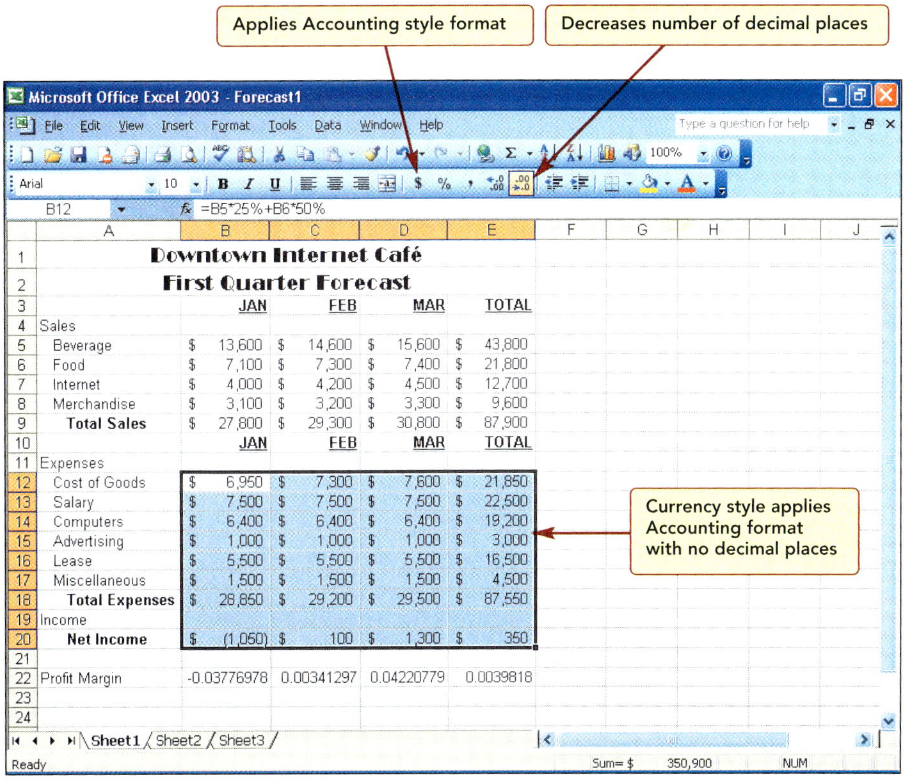

Figure 1.64

Finally, you want the Profit Margin values to be displayed as percentages with two decimal places.

4 Select B22 through E22.

- Click **Percent Style.**

> **Another Method**
>
> The menu equivalent is Format/Style/Percent and the voice command is "Percent style."

- Click **Increase Decimal twice.**

> **Another Method**
>
> You could also use Format/Cells/Number/Percentage/Decimal Places/2. The voice command is "Increase decimal."

Your screen should be similar to Figure 1.65

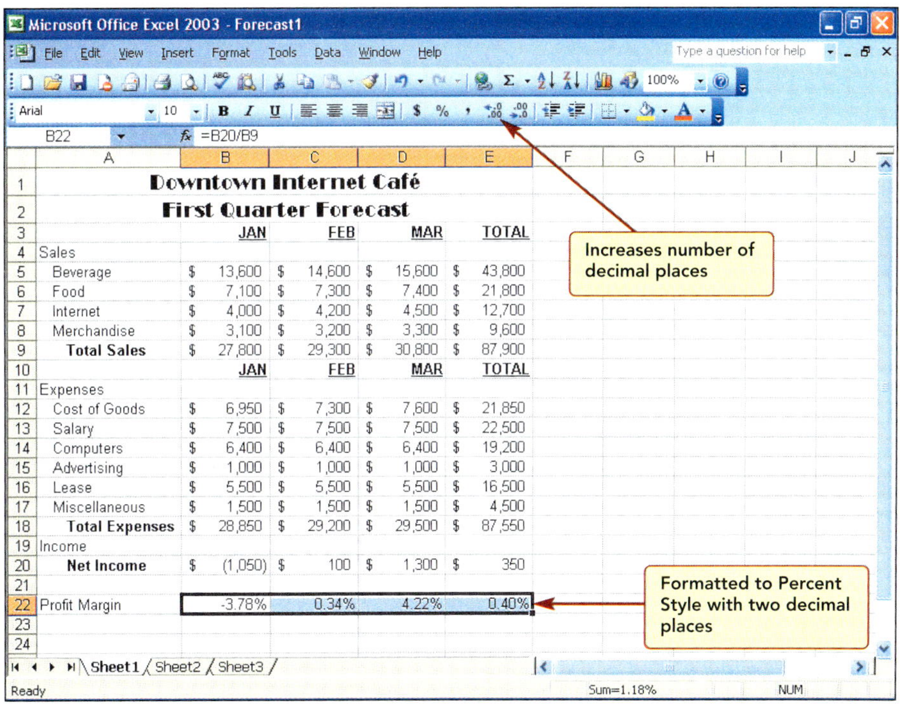

Figure 1.65

Adding Color

The last formatting change you would like to make to the worksheet is to add color to the text and to the background of selected cells. First you will change the color of the text.

1

- **Select A1 through A2.**
- **Open the Font Color palette.**

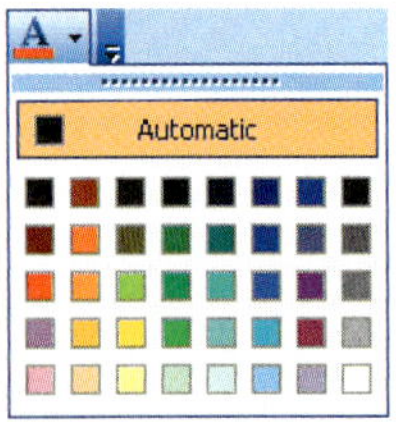

- **Select a color of your choice.**

Another Method

The menu equivalent is Format/Cells/Font/Color and the voice command is "Font color" followed by the color name.

Additional Information

A ScreenTip displays the name of the color as you point to it.

Your screen should be similar to Figure 1.66

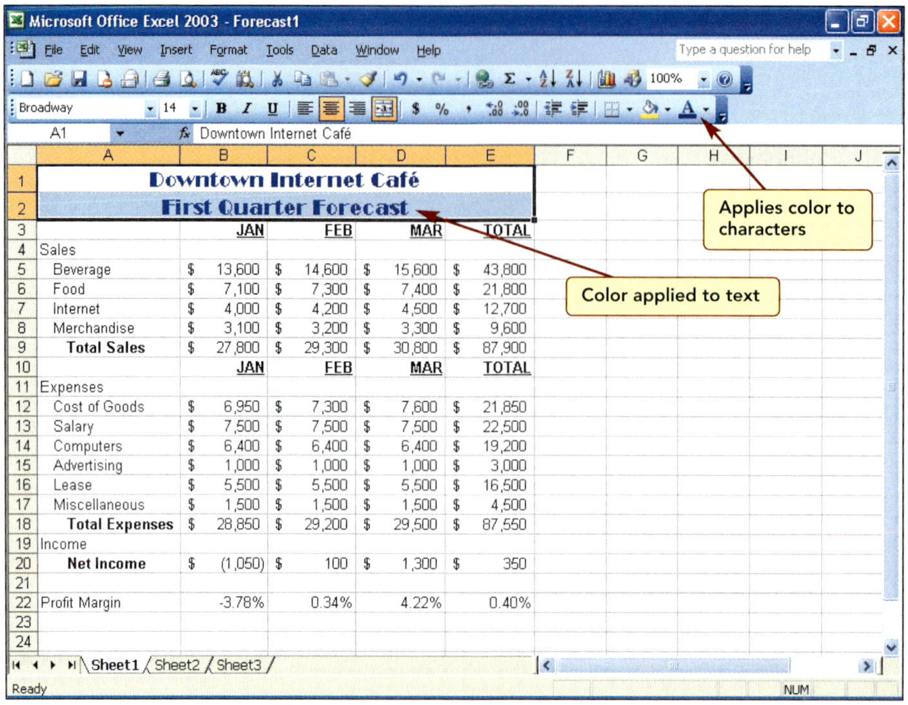

Figure 1.66

Additional Information

This text uses the font color of blue and the cell fill color of turquoise.

The selected color appears in the button and can be applied again simply by clicking the button. Next, you will change the cell background color, also called the fill color. Generally, when adding color to a worksheet, use a dark font color with a light fill color or a light font color with a dark fill color.

2 Open the Fill Color palette.

- Select a fill color of your choice.

Another Method

The menu equivalent is Format/Cells/Patterns/Color.

- Apply the same font color, fill color, and bold to cell A4.

- Use Format Painter to quickly copy the format from cell A4 to cells A11, A19, and A22.

- Select cells B4 through E4 and click Fill Color to apply the last selected fill color.

- Apply the same fill color to B11 through E11, B19 through E19, and B22 through E22.

- Click Save to save the worksheet changes.

Your screen should be similar to Figure 1.67

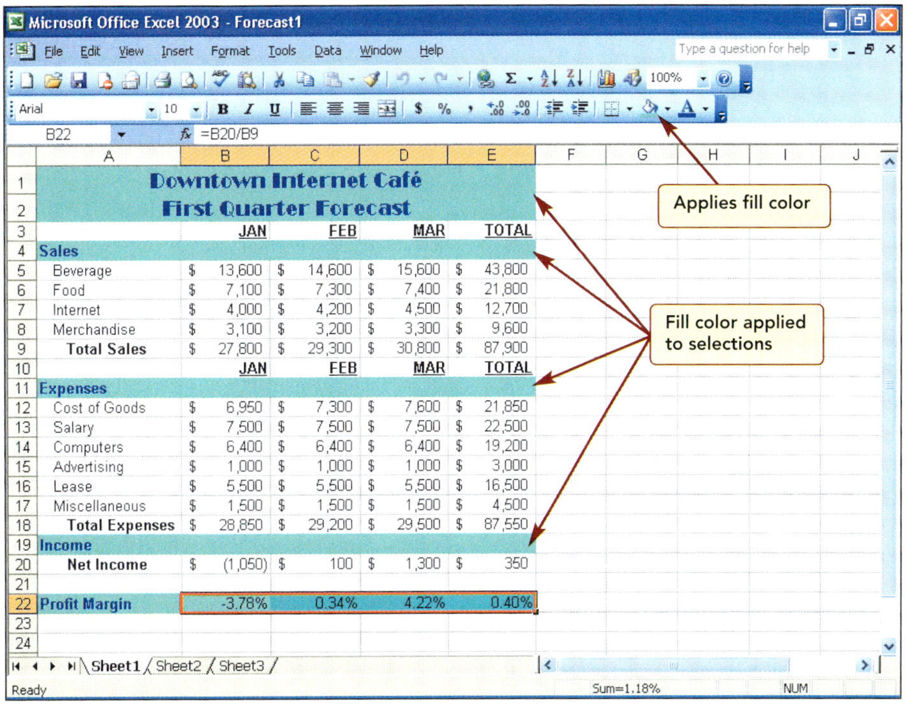

Figure 1.67

Entering the Date

Now that the worksheet is complete, you want to include your name and the date in the worksheet as documentation. There are many ways to enter the date. For example, you could type the date using the format mm/dd/yy or as month dd,yyyy. When a date is entered as text, Excel converts the entry to a numeric entry that allows dates to be used in calculations. Excel stores all dates as **serial values** with each day numbered from the beginning of the 20th century. The date serial values are consecutively assigned beginning with 1, which corresponds to the date January 1, 1900, and ending with 2958465 which is December 31, 9999. You can also enter the date using one of Excel's date and time functions. You will use the Today function to enter the date.

1 Enter your first initial and last name in cell A24.

• Enter **=Today()** in cell A25.

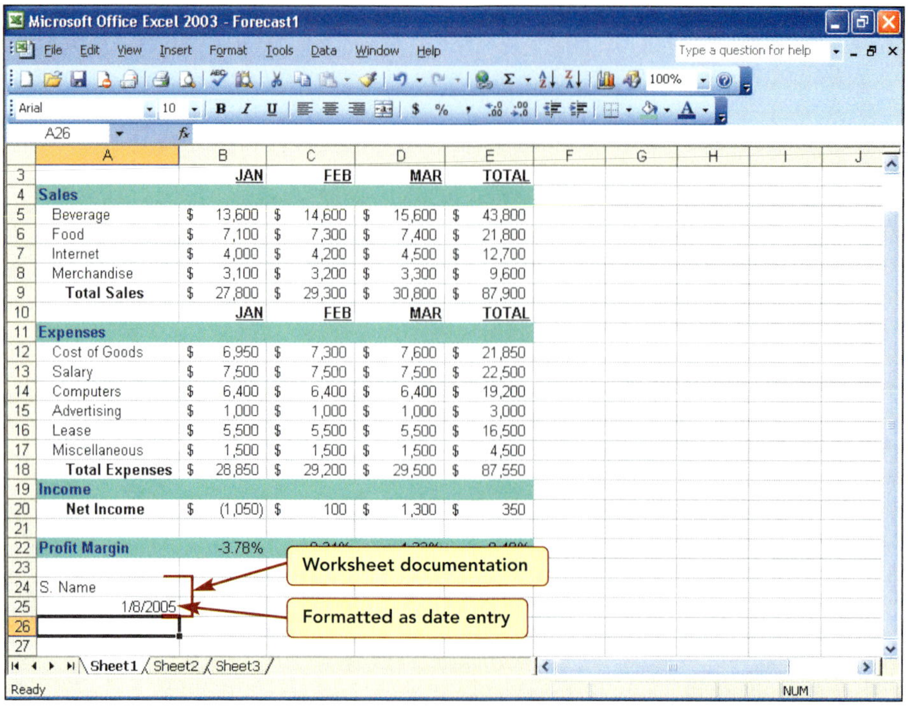

Figure 1.68

Additional Information

The Today function does not require arguments; however, you still need to enter the opening and closing parentheses.

Another Method

You can quickly insert the current date using Ctrl + ;.

Your screen should be similar to Figure 1.68

Additional Information

Dates, like other numeric entries, can be formatted to display in many different ways. Use Format/Cells/Number/Date to change the date format.

The Today function displays the date using the default date format mm/dd/yyyy. It is right-aligned in the cell because it is a numeric entry.

Previewing and Printing a Worksheet

Although you still plan to make more changes to the worksheet, you want to print a copy of the estimated first quarter forecast for the owner to get feedback regarding the content and layout. While creating this worksheet, you have been using Normal view, which is designed for on-screen viewing and working. Another view, Print Preview, shows you how the worksheet will appear on the printed page. To save time and unnecessary printing and paper waste, it is always a good idea to first preview onscreen how your worksheet will appear when printed.

Previewing the Worksheet

Previewing a worksheet allows you to look over each page and make necessary adjustments before printing it.

1 Click Print Preview.

Another Method

The menu equivalent is File/Print Preview and the voice command is "Print Preview."

Your screen should be similar to Figure 1.69

Additional Information

If you have a monochrome printer, the preview appears in shades of gray, as it will appear when printed.

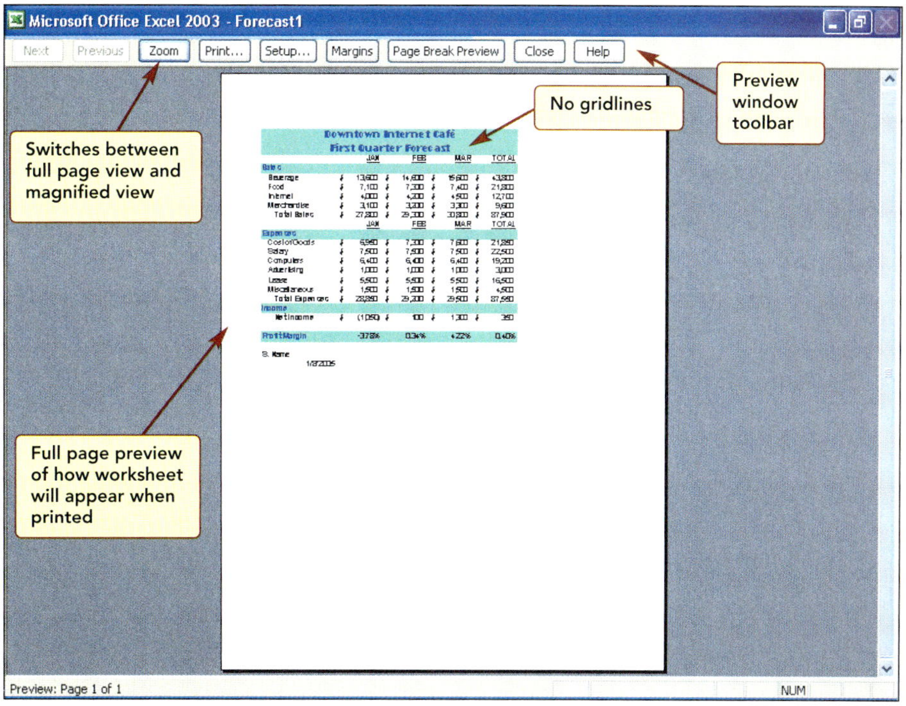

Figure 1.69

The print preview window displays the worksheet as it will appear on the printed page. Notice that the row and column lines are not displayed and will not print. This is one of the default print settings. Your worksheet may appear slightly different from that shown in Figure 1.69. This is because the way pages appear in the preview window depends on the available fonts, the resolution of the printer, and the available colors.

The preview window also includes its own toolbar. While previewing, you can change from full-page view to a magnified view using Zoom or by clicking on the preview page.

2 Click the worksheet title.

Additional Information

The area you click on is the area that will display in the preview window.

Your screen should be similar to Figure 1.70

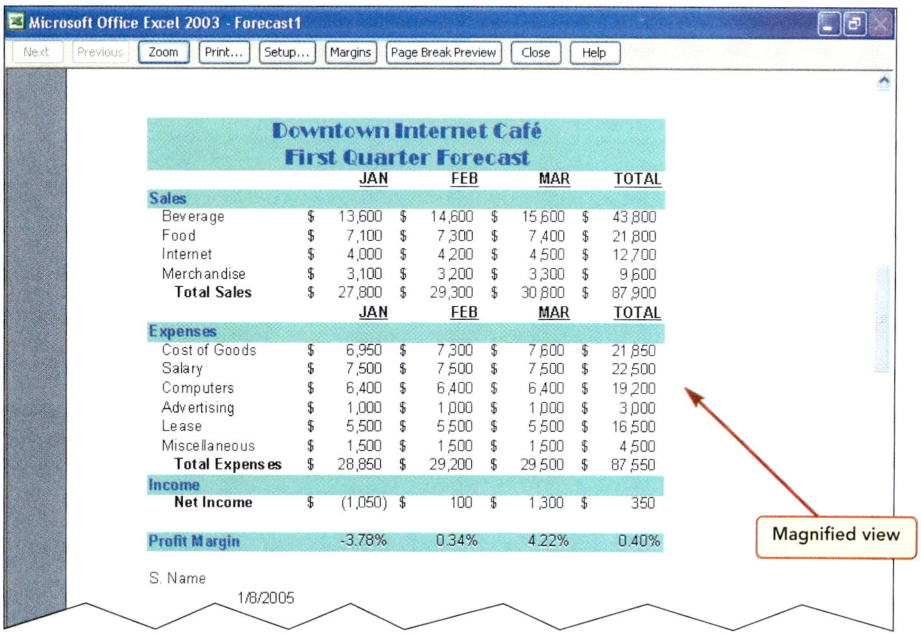

Figure 1.70

The worksheet is displayed in the actual size it will appear when printed.

Printing the Worksheet

The worksheet looks good and does not appear to need any further modifications immediately.

Now you are ready to print the worksheet.

1 **Click on the worksheet again to return to full-page view.**

Click Print...

Your screen should be similar to Figure 1.71

Another Method

You can also use File/Print or the keyboard shortcut Ctrl + P from the worksheet window. Clicking Print on the Standard toolbar or saying "Print" will send the workbook directly to the printer.

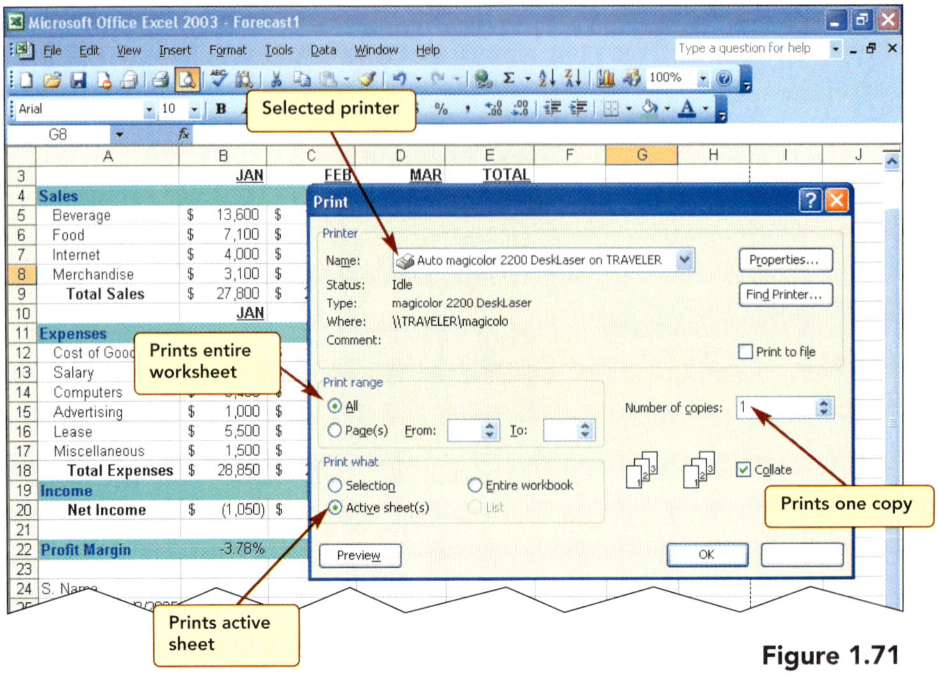

Figure 1.71

Note: Please consult your instructor for printing procedures that may differ from the following directions.

From the Print dialog box, you need to specify the printer you will be using and the document settings. The printer that is currently selected is displayed in the Name drop-down list box in the Printer section of the dialog box.

The Print Range area lets you specify how much of the worksheet you want printed. The range options are described in the following table:

Option	Action
All	Prints the entire worksheet
Pages	Prints pages you specify by typing page numbers in the text box
Selection	Prints selected range only
Active Sheet	Prints the active worksheet
Entire Workbook	Prints all worksheets in the workbook

The default settings of All and Active sheet are correct. In the Copies section, the default setting of one copy of the worksheet is acceptable.

2
- **If necessary, make sure your printer is on and ready to print.**
- **If you need to change the selected printer to another printer, open the Name drop-down list box and select the appropriate printer.**
- **Click OK.**

> **Additional Information**
> If you do not have a color printer, the colors appear as shades of gray.

The printed copy should be similar to the document shown in the Case Study at the beginning of the lab.

Exiting Office Excel 2003

The Exit command in the File menu is used to quit the Excel program. Alternatively, you can click the × Close button in the application window title bar. If you attempt to close the application without first saving the workbook, Excel displays a warning asking whether you want to save your work. If you do not save your work and you exit the application, all changes you made from the last time you saved are lost.

1
- **Move to cell A1.**
- **Click × (in the application window title bar).**
- **Click Yes to resave the worksheet.**

> **Additional Information**
> Excel saves the file with the cell selector in the same cell location it is in at the time it is saved.

Because you added the date since last saving the worksheet, you were prompted to save it again before closing it.

Focus on Careers

EXPLORE YOUR CAREER OPTIONS

Fan Coordinator

Did you know that 40 percent of the advertised positions in sports are for marketing and promotion? A marketing graduate hired as a basketball fan coordinator would use Excel to keep track of the income and expenses for coordinated half-time activities at professional sporting events. These worksheets would provide valuable information for promoting sponsors' products and services at games. A fan coordinator might start out as an unpaid intern, but after graduation could expect to earn from $25,000 to $32,000.

concept summary

LAB 1

Creating and Editing a Worksheet

Text and Numeric Entries (EX1.15)

The information or data you enter in a cell can be text, numbers, or formulas.

AutoCorrect (EX1.20)

The AutoCorrect feature makes some basic assumptions about the text you are typing and, based on these assumptions, automatically corrects the entry.

Column Width (EX1.24)

The size or width of a column controls the amount of information that can be displayed in a cell.

Spelling Checker (EX1.33)

The spelling checker feature locates all misspelled words, duplicate words, and capitalization irregularities in the active worksheet and proposes the correct spelling.

Thesaurus (EX1.35)

The thesaurus is a reference tool that provides synonyms, antonyms, and related words for a selected word or phrase.

Copy and Move (EX1.38)

The contents of worksheet cells can be duplicated (copied) or moved to other locations in the worksheet or between worksheets, saving you time by not having to retype the same information.

Range (EX1.41)

A selection consisting of two or more cells on a worksheet is a range.

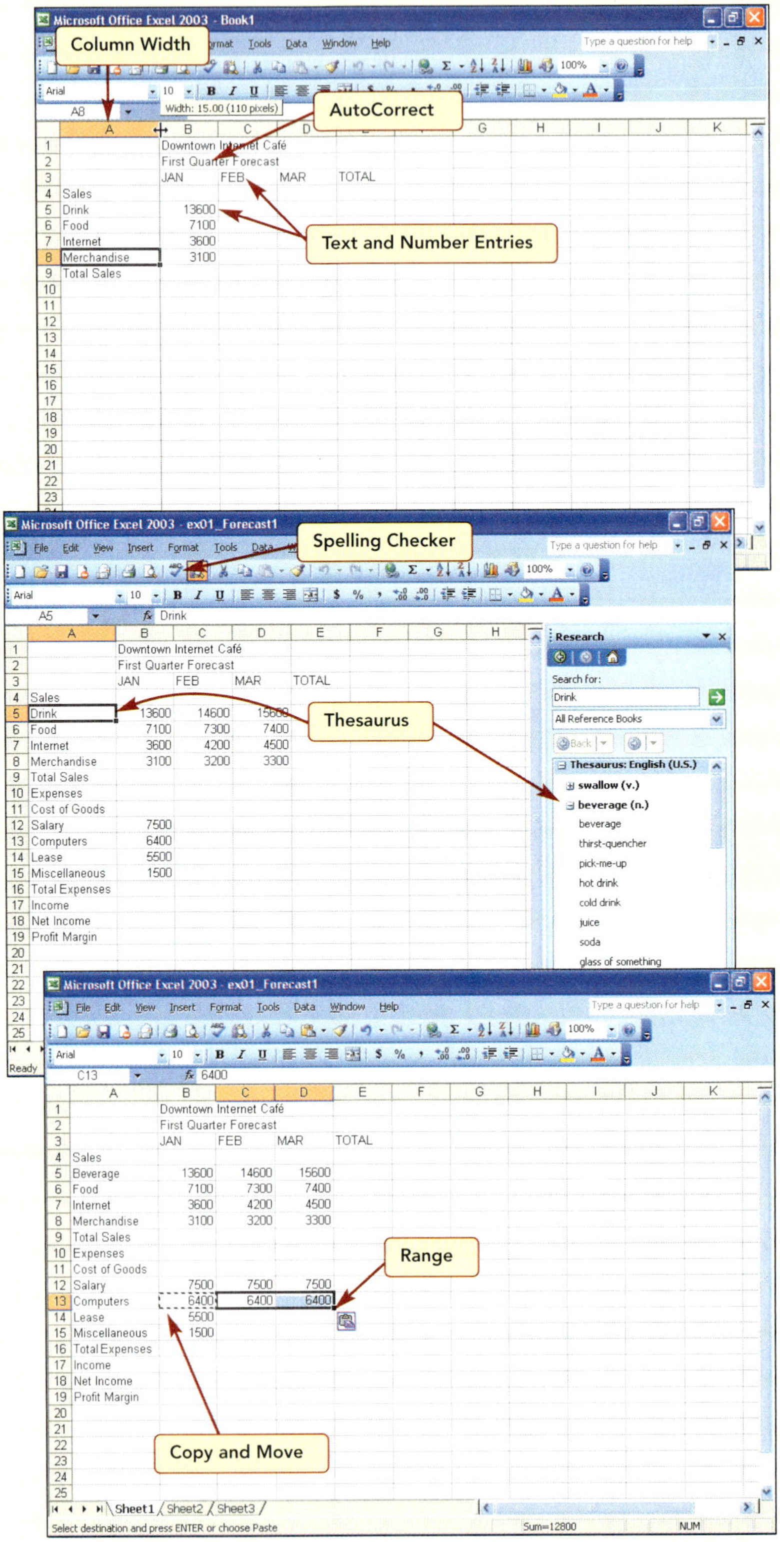

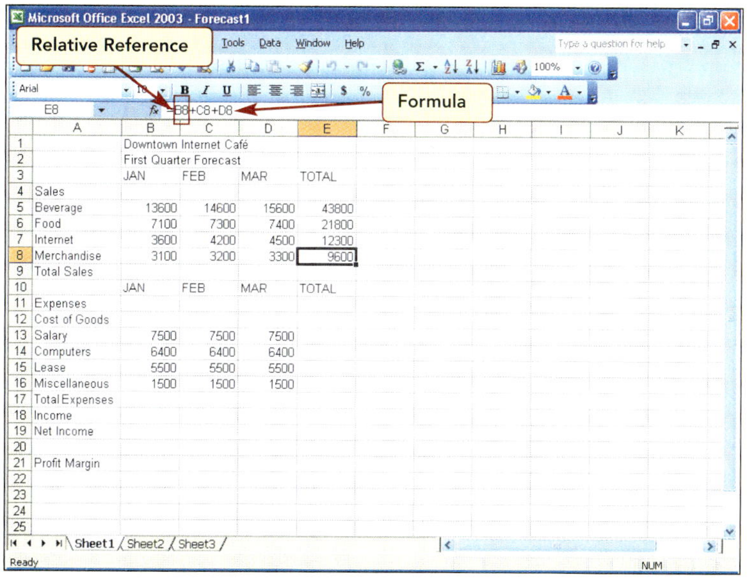

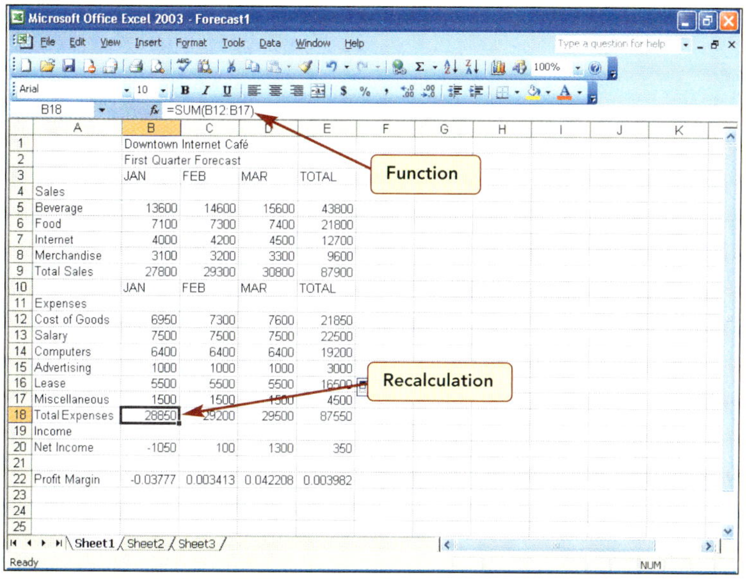

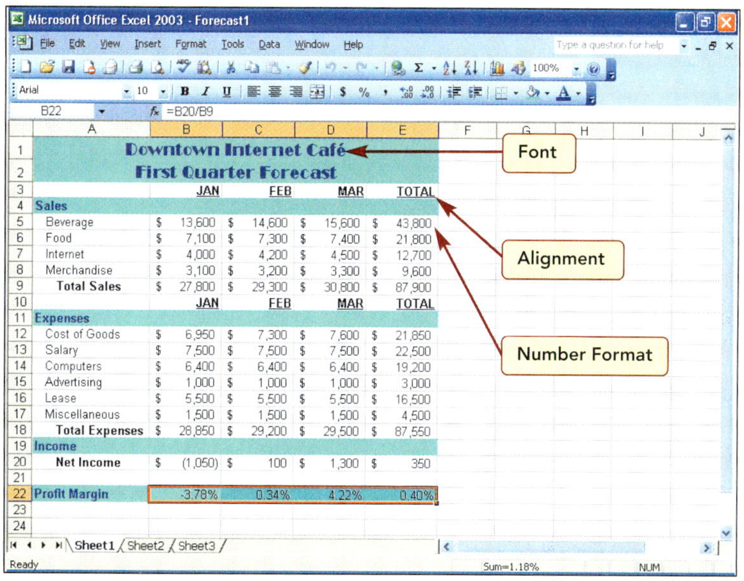

Formula (EX1.47)

A formula is an equation that performs a calculation on data contained in a worksheet.

Relative Reference (EX1.49)

A relative reference is a cell or range reference in a formula whose location is interpreted by Excel in relation to the position of the cell that contains the formula.

Function (EX1.50)

A function is a prewritten formula that performs certain types of calculations automatically.

Recalculation (EX1.57)

Excel automatically recalculates formulas whenever a change occurs in a referenced cell.

Alignment (EX1.59)

Alignment settings allow you to change the horizontal and vertical placement and the orientation of an entry in a cell.

Font (EX1.64)

Fonts consist of typefaces, point sizes, and styles that can be applied to characters to improve their appearance.

Number Format (EX1.68)

Number formats affect the appearance of numbers onscreen and when printed.

lab review

LAB 1

Creating and Editing a Worksheet

key terms

active cell EX1.8
active sheet EX1.8
adjacent range EX1.41
alignment EX1.59
antonym EX1.35
argument EX1.50
AutoCorrect EX1.20
AutoFit EX1.25
cell EX1.8
cell reference EX1.8
cell selector EX1.8
character effect EX1.66
column EX1.7
column letter EX1.8
constant EX1.47
copy area EX1.38
custom dictionary EX1.33
default EX1.14
destination EX1.38
fill handle EX1.43
font EX1.64
format EX1.58
Format Painter EX1.67
Formatting toolbar EX1.5
formula EX1.47
formula bar EX1.6
function EX1.50
heading EX1.15
main dictionary EX1.33
merged cell EX1.63
Name box EX1.6
nonadjacent range EX1.41
number EX1.15
number format EX1.68
operand EX1.47
operator EX1.47
order of precedence EX1.47
paste area EX1.38
point EX1.64
range EX1.41
range reference EX1.41
recalculation EX1.57
relative reference EX1.49
row EX1.7
row number EX1.8
sans serif EX1.64
serial value EX1.73
serif EX1.64
sheet EX1.7
sheet tab EX1.8
size EX1.64
source EX1.38
spelling checker EX1.33
spreadsheet EX1.7
Standard toolbar EX1.5
synonym EX1.35
syntax EX1.50
tab scroll buttons EX1.8
text EX1.15
thesaurus EX1.35
typeface EX1.64
variable EX1.47
workbook EX1.6
workbook window EX1.6
worksheet EX1.7

microsoft office specialist skills

The Microsoft Office Specialist certification program is designed to measure your proficiency in performing basic tasks using the Office 2003 applications. Certification demonstrates that you have the skills and provides a valuable industry credential for employment. After completing this lab, you have learned the following Microsoft Office Excel 2003 Specialist skills:

Skill Sets	Skill Standards	Page
Creating Data and Content	Enter and edit cell content	EX1.14
	Locate, select, and insert supporting information	EX1.35
Analyzing Data	Insert and modify formulas	EX1.47
	Use statistical, date and time, financial, and logical functions	EX1.73
Formatting Data and Content	Apply and modify cell formats	EX1.68
	Modify row and column formats	EX1.24,1.58
Managing Workbooks	Insert, delete, and move cells	EX1.45,1.57
	Preview data in other views	EX1.74
	Print data	EX1.76

command summary

Command	Shortcut Key	Button	Voice	Action
File/New	Ctrl + N		New file	Opens a new blank workbook
File/Open <file name>	Ctrl + O		Open	Opens an existing workbook file
File/Close			Close worksheet	Closes open workbook file
File/Save			Save	Saves file using same file name
File/Save As <file name>				Saves file using a new file name
File/Print Preview			Print preview	Displays worksheet as it will appear when printed
File/Print	Ctrl + P		Print	Prints a worksheet
File/Exit	Alt + F4			Exits Excel program

lab review

command summary

Command	Shortcut Key	Button	Voice	Action
Edit/Undo	Ctrl + Z		Undo	Reverses last editing or formatting change
Edit/Redo	Ctrl + Y		Redo	Restores changes after using Undo
Edit/Cut	Ctrl + X		Cut	Cuts selected data from the worksheet
Edit/Copy	Ctrl + C		Copy	Copies selected data to System Clipboard
Edit/Paste	Ctrl + V		Paste	Pastes selections stored in System Clipboard
Edit/Fill				Fills selected cells with contents of source cell
Edit/Clear/Contents	Delete		Delete	Clears cell contents
Edit/Delete/Entire Row				Deletes selected rows
Edit/Delete/Entire Column				Deletes selected columns
Insert/Cut Cells				Inserts row of cuts text into the table
Insert/Copied Cells				Inserts row and copies text from Clipboard
Insert/Rows				Inserts a blank row
Insert/Columns				Inserts a blank column
Format/Cells	Ctrl + 1			Changes font and attributes of cells
Format/Cells/Number/Category/Accounting			Currency style	Applies Accounting format to selection
Format/Cells/Number/Category/Date				Applies Date format to selection
Format/Cells/Number/Category/Percent			Percent style	Applies Percent format to selection
Format/Cells/Number/Category/Decimal places			Increase decimal	Increase decimal
			Decrease decimal	Increases or decreases number of decimal places associated with a number value

command summary

Command	Shortcut Key	Button	Voice	Action
Format/Cells/Alignment/Horizontal/Left (Indent)			Left	Left-aligns entry in cell space
Format/Cells/Alignment/Horizontal/Center			Center	Center-aligns entry in cell space
Format/Cells/Alignment/Horizontal/Right			Right	Right-aligns entry in cell space
Format/Cells/Alignment/Indent				Indents cell entry
Format/Cells/Alignment/Horizontal/Center Across Selection/Merge Cells				Centers cell contents across selected cells and combines cells
Format/Cells/Font/Font			Font	Changes text font
Format/Cells/Font/Size			Font size	Changes text size
Format/Cells/Font/Font Style/Bold	Ctrl + B	B	Bold	Bolds selected text
Format/Cells/Font/Font Style/Italic	Ctrl + I	I	Italic	Italicizes selected text
Format/Cells/Font/Underline/Single	Ctrl + U	U	Underline	Underlines selected text
Format/Cells/Font/Color			Font color	Adds color to text
Format/Cells/Patterns/Color			Fill color	Adds color to cell background
Format/Row/Height				Changes height of selected row
Format/Column/Width				Changes width of column
Format/Column/AutoFit Selection				Changes column width to match widest cell entry
Format/Style/Percent		%	Percent style	Changes number to percentage
Tools/Spelling	F7		Spelling	Spell-checks worksheet
Tools/Customize/Options/Show Standard and Formatting Toolbars on two rows				Shows the Standard toolbar and the Formatting toolbar in two rows

screen identification

In the following worksheet, several items are identified by letters. Enter the correct term for each item in the space provided.

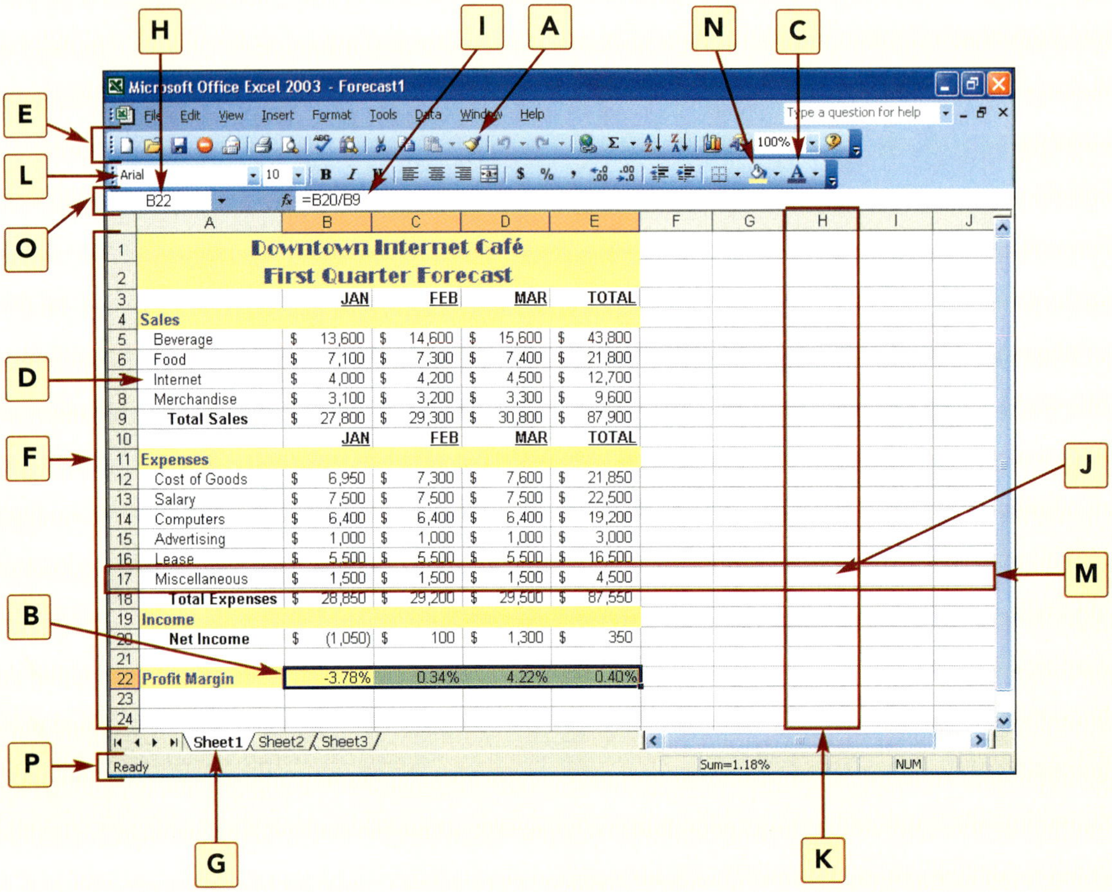

Possible answers for the screen identification are:

Standard toolbar	Row
Column	Column labels
Status bar	Workbook window
Font color	Cell
Numeric entry	Formula bar
Fill color	Active sheet
Font	Text label
Range	Cell reference
Formula	Format painter

A. ____________________ **I.** ____________________

B. ____________________ **J.** ____________________

C. ____________________ **K.** ____________________

D. ____________________ **L.** ____________________

E. ____________________ **M.** ____________________

F. ____________________ **N.** ____________________

G. ____________________ **O.** ____________________

H. ____________________ **P.** ____________________

matching

Match the lettered item on the right with the numbered item on the left.

1. source ______ **a.** undoes last action

2. * ______ **b.** a set of characters with a specific design

3.  ______ **c.** the cell you copy from

4. font ______ **d.** two or more worksheet cells

5. .xls ______ **e.** a cell reference

6.  ______ **f.** enters a SUM function

7. =C19+A21 ______ **g.** an arithmetic operator

8.  ______ **h.** merges cells and centers entry

9. D11 ______ **i.** a formula summing two cells

10.  ______ **j.** Excel workbook file name extension

11. range

true/false

Circle the correct answer to the following questions.

1.	When a selection is cut, it is stored in the system Clipboard.	True	False
2.	The default column width setting in Excel is 8.43.	True	False
3.	An adjacent range is two or more selected cells or ranges that are adjoining.	True	False
4.	A function is a prewritten formula that performs a calculation.	True	False
5.	The spell checker can only find misspelled words if they are entered in the main dictionary.	True	False
6.	When a formula containing relative references is copied, the cell references in the copied formula refer to the same cells that are referenced in the original formula.	True	False
7.	A colon is used to separate cell references in nonadjacent ranges.	True	False
8.	Recalculation is one of the most powerful features of electronic worksheets.	True	False
9.	Cell alignment allows you to change the horizontal and vertical placement and the orientation of an entry in a cell.	True	False
10.	Number formats affect the way that numbers are used in calculations.	True	False

lab exercises

fill-in

Complete the following statements by filling in the blanks with the correct key terms.

1. The ________________ displays the cell selector and will be affected by the next entry or procedure.
2. ________________ are integers assigned to the days from January 1, 1900, through December 31, 2099, that allow dates to be used in calculations.
3. Cells or ranges that are included in the same selection but are not located next to each other are part of a ____________________________.
4. The _______________ is the location that receives the data from the copy area.
5. A(n) _____________ window is used to display an open workbook file.
6. The ______________ dictionary holds words the user enters that are not included in the main dictionary.
7. A(n) ___________________ cell is a cell made up of several selected cells combined into one.
8. A(n) ________________ is a rectangular grid of rows and columns.
9. A(n) _____________ entry is used to perform a calculation.
10. _____________ fonts have a flare at the base of each letter to lead the reader to the next character.

multiple choice

Circle the correct response to the questions below.

1. _________________ entries can contain any combination of letters, numbers, spaces, and any other special characters.
   a. Number
   b. Variable
   c. Constant
   d. Text
2. ______________ consist of typefaces and sizes that can be applied to characters to improve their appearance.
   a. cells
   b. headings
   c. objects
   d. fonts

3. The ________________ is the place to which a selection is moved or copied.
   a. destination area
   b. source area
   c. copy area
   d. source

4. The ________________ feature in Excel automatically inserts proper capitalization at the beginning of sentences and in the names of days of the week.
   a. AutoName
   b. AutoCorrect
   c. CorrectWords
   d. Word Wrap

5. The amount of information that is displayed in a cell is determined by the ________________.
   a. column size
   b. row size
   c. column width
   d. row height

6. Whenever a formula containing ________ references is copied, the referenced cells are automatically adjusted.
   a. relative
   b. automatic
   c. fixed
   d. variable

7. Which of the following is not a valid Excel formula?
   a. =(5 + 8) (2 + 1)
   b. 5 + 8 * 2 + 1
   c. = 5 + 8 (2 + 1)
   d. =(5 + 8) * (2 + 1)

8. When a number in a referenced cell is changed, all the formulas that use the cell reference are ________________.
   a. recalculated
   b. reformatted
   c. redefined
   d. left unchanged

9. The Currency number format can display ________________.
   a. dollar signs
   b. commas
   c. decimal places
   d. all the above

10. The ________________ is a reference tool that provides synonyms and related words for a selected word.
   a. synonymn locator
   b. thesaurus
   c. spelling checker
   d. research book

rating system

★ Easy

★★ Moderate

★★★ Difficult

step-by-step

Animal Rescue Foundation Adoption Analysis ★

1. Edward Corwin works for the Animal Rescue Foundation. One of his responsibilities is to collect and analyze data on the animals that enter the shelters. He has compiled a list of the cost of housing animals by the local shelters for four different years. Follow the directions below to complete the worksheet shown here.

Animal Angels Housing Analysis
Years 2005 through 2008

Shelter	2005	2006	2007	2008
Nobody's Pets	$127,000	$154,200	$ 137,600	$ 152,800
Pets Unlimited	154,500	251,000	202,500	220,300
FOCAS	13,600	18,900	15,500	14,700
Wood Green Animal Shelter	2,300	2,500	1,800	2,100
PetWhere Shelter	1,200	1,500	1,400	1,600
ASPCA	129,100	154,300	128,500	133,400
New River Animal Shelter	10,300	14,200	11,500	10,200
NewPet Shelter	19,300	19,900	18,900	22,300
City of Dogs Shelter	10,200	11,500	12,600	12,500
Humane World	29,100	12,500	25,700	28,900
Total	$496,600	$640,500	$556,000	$598,800

Student Name
4/22/2005

a. Open the workbook ex01_Animal Housing.

b. Spell check the worksheet.

c. Modify the title in cell B2 so the first letter of each word is capitalized. Increase the font size to 14 point. Merge and center both title lines across columns A through E.

d. Bold and center the headings in row 5.

e. Adjust the column widths so all the data is fully displayed.

f. In row 16, enter a function to total the 2005 and 2006 columns.

g. Format the numbers in rows 6 and 16 using the Currency style with zero decimal places, and the numbers in rows 7 through 15 using the Comma style with zero decimal places.

h. Edward has just received the information for the last two years. Enter the following data in the cells indicated.

Row	Col D	Col E
5	2007	2008
6	137600	152800
7	202500	220300
8	15500	14700
9	1800	2100
10	1400	1600
11	128500	133400
12	11500	10200
13	18900	22300
14	12600	12500
15	25700	28900

i. If necessary, format the data to match the style of the corresponding information in columns B and C.

j. Copy the Total function to calculate the total for the new years.

k. Insert a blank row above the Total row.

l. Add font and fill colors to the worksheet, as you like.

m. Enter your name and the current date on separate rows just below the worksheet.

n. Move to cell A1. Save the workbook as Animal Housing Analysis. Preview and print the worksheet.

Lifestyle Fitness Analysis Worksheet ★

2. Mary Ellen is a manager at the Lifestyle Fitness Club. One of her responsibilities is to collect and analyze data on trends in fitness for the club. She has compiled a list of the activities that are done by teens 12–19 and adults 20 and older. Follow the directions below to complete the worksheet shown here.

a. Open the workbook ex01_Activity By Age.

b. Modify the title in cell B2 so the first letter of each word is capitalized. Merge and center the titles across columns A through D. Increase the font size to 14 point.

c. Spell check the worksheet and correct any misspelled words.

d. Enter the formula **=(C6-B6)/100** in cell D6. Copy the formula down column D for the rest of the activities. Format the numbers in column D as a percent. Center the data in cells B6 through D25.

e. Insert a new row below row 3 and a new row below row 6.

f. Bold and center the titles in rows 5 and 6. Underline the titles in row 6. Adjust the column widths so all the data is fully displayed.

g. Add font and fill colors to the worksheet as you like.

h. Enter your name and the current date on separate rows just below the worksheet.

Lifestyle Fitness Club
Percent of Activity by Age

Activity	Children 12 - 19	Adults +20	Percent Change
Walking for exercise	60	69	9%
Bicycling	48	24	-24%
Swimming	46	24	-22%
Jogging, running	44	12	-32%
Basketball	37	4	-33%
Social dancing	37	22	-15%
Home exercise	36	29	-7%
Gardening, yard work	28	48	20%
In-line skating	28	6	-22%
Volleyball	26	3	-23%
Weight training	25	11	-14%
Bowling	20	8	-12%
Baseball, softball	17	7	-10%
Skating	14	5	-9%
Exercise classes, aerobics	14	7	-7%
Fishing	13	11	-2%
Golf	13	13	0%
Ice hockey	13	4	-9%
Tennis	11	4	-7%
Alpine skiing	7	3	-4%

Student Name
4/12/2005

i. Move to cell A1. Save the workbook as Activity By Age2. Preview and print the worksheet.

Comparative U.S. Families at Poverty Level ★ ★

3. Terrence Lewis works for an agency that provides help to families in poverty. He has been doing some research on the percent of families that fall into this category. He has started a worksheet with data from the years 1997–2006. Follow the directions below to complete the worksheet shown here:

a. Open the workbook ex01_Poverty Level.

b. Spell check the worksheet and correct any misspelled words.

c. Edit the title in cell D2 so the first letter of each word is uppercase except the words "of" and "or." Merge and center the title across columns A through J. Increase the font size to 14, and bold and apply a font color of your choice to the title.

d. Center-align and underline the column headings in row 4. Left-align cells A5 through A14.

e. Calculate the average for the Official percentage in cell B15 using the Average function =Average(B5:B14). Format the cell as a percentage with two decimal places. Copy the formula to cells C15 through J15.

f. Next, you would like to calculate the percent of change from 1997 to 2006. Enter the heading **Percent Change** in cell A16. Enter the formula **=(B14-B5)/B15** in cell B16. Format the cell as a percentage with two decimal places. Copy the formula to cells C16 through J16.

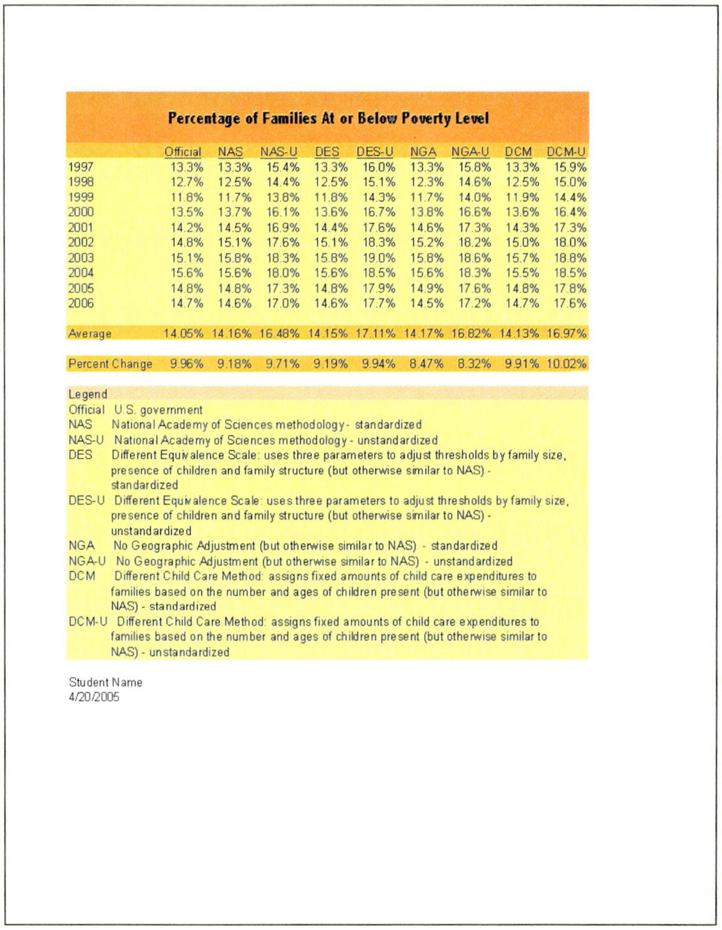

Percentage of Families At or Below Poverty Level

	Official	NAS	NAS-U	DES	DES-U	NGA	NGA-U	DCM	DCM-U
1997	13.3%	13.3%	15.4%	13.3%	16.0%	13.3%	15.8%	13.3%	15.9%
1998	12.7%	12.5%	14.4%	12.5%	15.1%	12.3%	14.6%	12.5%	15.0%
1999	11.8%	11.7%	13.8%	11.8%	14.3%	11.7%	14.0%	11.9%	14.4%
2000	13.5%	13.7%	16.1%	13.6%	16.7%	13.8%	16.6%	13.6%	16.4%
2001	14.2%	14.5%	16.9%	14.4%	17.6%	14.6%	17.3%	14.3%	17.3%
2002	14.8%	15.1%	17.6%	15.1%	18.3%	15.2%	18.2%	15.0%	18.0%
2003	15.1%	15.8%	18.3%	15.8%	19.0%	15.8%	18.6%	15.7%	18.8%
2004	15.6%	15.6%	18.0%	15.6%	18.5%	15.6%	18.3%	15.5%	18.5%
2005	14.8%	14.8%	17.3%	14.8%	17.9%	14.9%	17.6%	14.8%	17.8%
2006	14.7%	14.6%	17.0%	14.6%	17.7%	14.5%	17.2%	14.7%	17.6%
Average	14.05%	14.16%	16.48%	14.15%	17.11%	14.17%	16.82%	14.13%	16.97%
Percent Change	9.96%	9.18%	9.71%	9.19%	9.94%	8.47%	8.32%	9.91%	10.02%

Legend

Official	U.S. government
NAS	National Academy of Sciences methodology - standardized
NAS-U	National Academy of Sciences methodology - unstandardized
DES	Different Equivalence Scale: uses three parameters to adjust thresholds by family size, presence of children and family structure (but otherwise similar to NAS) - standardized
DES-U	Different Equivalence Scale: uses three parameters to adjust thresholds by family size, presence of children and family structure (but otherwise similar to NAS) - unstandardized
NGA	No Geographic Adjustment (but otherwise similar to NAS) - standardized
NGA-U	No Geographic Adjustment (but otherwise similar to NAS) - unstandardized
DCM	Different Child Care Method: assigns fixed amounts of child care expenditures to families based on the number and ages of children present (but otherwise similar to NAS) - standardized
DCM-U	Different Child Care Method: assigns fixed amounts of child care expenditures to families based on the number and ages of children present (but otherwise similar to NAS) - unstandardized

Student Name
4/20/2005

g. Format the data in cells B5 through J14 as a percentage with one decimal place. AutoFit columns B through J.

h. Adjust the width of column A to fully display the labels.

i. Insert a blank row between rows 14 and 15 and another between rows 16 and 17.

j. Add fill colors to the worksheet as you like.

k. Enter your name and the current date on separate rows just below the legend.

l. Move to cell A1. Save and replace the workbook as Poverty Level2. Preview and print the worksheet.

Entertainment Industry Salary Analysis ★ ★

4. Enrico Torres is a writer for a local newspaper. The paper is planning a series about myths in the entertainment industry. In his research on this topic, he has found some interesting data on salaries for jobs in entertainment. He has entered this data into a worksheet but still needs to format the data and perform some analysis of the information. Follow the directions below to complete the worksheet shown here:

Entertainment Industry Salary Analysis

	Employment	Median Hourly	Mean Hourly	Deviation	Mean Annual
Entertainment/Media Occupations	1,513,420	$15.76	$18.58	($2.82)	$38,640.00
Art Directors	20,560	$27.35	$30.30	($2.95)	$63,020.00
Fine Artists	11,930	$15.00	$17.20	($2.20)	$35,770.00
Multi-Media Artists	31,120	$19.77	$21.47	($1.70)	$44,650.00
Commercial/Industrial Designers	33,910	$23.45	$24.55	($1.10)	$51,060.00
Fashion Designers	10,460	$23.33	$27.04	($3.71)	$56,240.00
Floral Designers	71,280	$8.83	$9.29	($0.46)	$19,330.00
Graphic Designers	133,630	$16.62	$18.25	($1.63)	$37,970.00
Interior Designers	30,680	$17.57	$19.55	($1.98)	$40,670.00
Merchandise Displayers	51,240	$10.06	$11.19	($1.13)	$23,280.00
Set and Exhibit Designers	8,470	$15.11	$16.26	($1.15)	$33,810.00
Actors	63,500				$41,570.00
Producers and Directors	46,750				$48,740.00
Athletes	9,920				$62,960.00
Sports Officials	76,740				$28,375.00
Dancers	20,900	$10.80	$13.44	($2.64)	$27,950.00
Choreographers	10,860	$12.99	$15.42	($2.43)	$32,080.00
Music Directors and Composers	6,660				$36,900.00
Musicians and Singers	52,180				$44,520.00
Announcers	49,770	$9.52	$13.13	($3.61)	$27,320.00
News Correspondents	65,930	$14.00	$18.04	($4.04)	$37,510.00
PR Specialists	128,570	$19.03	$21.01	($1.98)	$43,700.00
Editors	104,210	$18.93	$21.32	($2.39)	$44,350.00
Technical Writers	50,700	$22.98	$24.07	($1.09)	$50,060.00
Writers and Authors	41,410	$20.32	$22.81	($2.49)	$47,440.00
Interpreters and Translators	16,780	$14.95	$16.13	($1.18)	$33,550.00
AV Equipment Technicians	34,110	$14.57	$17.72	($3.15)	$36,860.00
Broadcast Technicians	33,560	$12.96	$15.89	($2.93)	$33,060.00
Sound Engineering Technicians	10,380	$18.98	$25.56	($6.58)	$53,170.00
Photographers	65,360	$10.72	$13.18	($2.46)	$27,420.00
Camera Operators	20,970	$13.40	$16.28	($2.88)	$33,860.00
Film and Video Editors	10,990	$16.42	$19.81	($3.39)	$41,200.00
Average		$16.29	$18.75	($2.46)	$39,907.34

Rates for occupations where workers typically work fewer than 2,080 hours per year are not available.

Student Name
4/30/2005

a. Open the workbook ex01_Entertainment Salaries. Spell check the worksheet.

b. Adjust the width of column A to 29.00.

c. Merge and center the title in row 1 over columns A through E. Format the title in row 1 to Tahoma 14 point, apply a font color of your choice. Add fill color of your choice to the text in rows 1 and 2.

d. Bold and center the column labels in row 3. Change the font size of cells A3 through F38 to 8. Adjust the column widths of columns B through E to fully display the column headings.

e. Format the data in column B using the Comma style and no decimal places. Format the data in columns C through D to Currency with two decimal places. Format the data in column E to Currency with no decimal places.

f. Enter and right-align the row heading **Average** in row 36.

g. Use the Average function to average the data in column C. (Hint: Type **=AVERAGE(C4:C35)**.)

h. Copy the function to columns D and E.

i. Insert a new column between D and E. Label the new column **Deviation**. Center and top align the label. Calculate the deviation from the Median and Mean Hourly rate. (Hint: =C4–D4)

j. Copy the formula down the column. Delete the zero values for the rows that do not have an hourly rate. Format the column to currency with two decimal places.

k. Apply a fill color of your choice to rows 4 through 36 of the worksheet. Add additional fill color and font colors of your choice to the worksheet. Adjust the column widths as needed.

l. Enter your name and the current date on separate rows below the worksheet.

m. Move to cell A1. Save and replace the workbook file as Entertainment Salaries2. Preview and print the worksheet.

Pecan Groves Homeowners Association ★ ★ ★

5. The Pecan Groves Homeowners Association is planning a large building project and wants to project how much there is likely to be in the cash budget after expenses. Using last year's final budget numbers, you will create a projected budget for 2005. Follow the directions below to complete the worksheet shown here.

a. Open the workbook file ex01_Pecan Groves Budget. Adjust the width of column A to fully display the headings.

b. Spell check the worksheet and correct any misspelled words. Use the Thesaurus to find another word for Lawyer in cell A19.

c. In column C, calculate a 6 percent increase for all the income numbers for the year 2005. (Hint: =B6*1.06)

d. Calculate totals for 2004 and 2005 using the SUM function for Total Receipts (B6:B7 and B9:B11), Total Administrative (B16:B20), Total Maintenance (B23:B26), and Total Miscellaneous. Calculate the Total Expenditures using a formula. Calculate the Total Cash Balance by subtracting Total Expenditures from Total Receipts.

e. Calculate a 12 percent increase in Administrative and Maintenance expenditures, and a 15 percent increase in Miscellaneous expenditures.

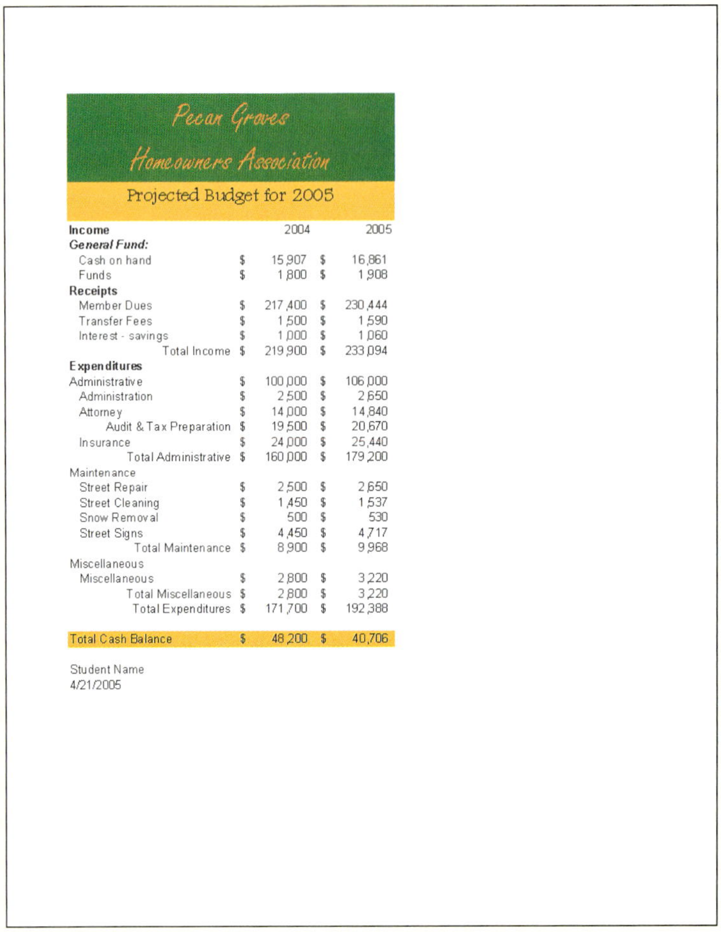
Pecan Groves
Homeowners Association
Projected Budget for 2005

Income		2004		2005
General Fund:				
Cash on hand	$	15,907	$	16,861
Funds	$	1,800	$	1,908
Receipts				
Member Dues	$	217,400	$	230,444
Transfer Fees	$	1,500	$	1,590
Interest - savings	$	1,000	$	1,060
Total Income	$	219,900	$	233,094
Expenditures				
Administrative	$	100,000	$	106,000
Administration	$	2,500	$	2,650
Attorney	$	14,000	$	14,840
Audit & Tax Preparation	$	19,500	$	20,670
Insurance	$	24,000	$	25,440
Total Administrative	$	160,000	$	179,200
Maintenance				
Street Repair	$	2,500	$	2,650
Street Cleaning	$	1,450	$	1,537
Snow Removal	$	500	$	530
Street Signs	$	4,450	$	4,717
Total Maintenance	$	8,900	$	9,968
Miscellaneous				
Miscellaneous	$	2,800	$	3,220
Total Miscellaneous	$	2,800	$	3,220
Total Expenditures	$	171,700	$	192,388
Total Cash Balance	$	48,200	$	40,706

Student Name
4/21/2005

f. Format the data with the Accounting number format with zero decimal places.

g. In the Income section, indent the row subheads. Right-align the total headings except for the Total Cash Balance.

h. Delete rows 13 and 14.

i. Change the font type, size, and color of the worksheet title lines to a format of your choice. Merge and center the titles across columns A through C.

j. Apply character effects and colors of your choice to the worksheet.

k. Enter your name and the current date on separate rows just below the worksheet.

l. Move to cell A1. Save the workbook file as Pecan Groves Budget2. Preview and print the worksheet.

on your own

Tracking Your Grades ★

1. A worksheet can be used to track your grades in a class or for each semester. Design and create a worksheet to record your grades in any class. The worksheet should include grades for at least four test scores, showing the number of points you earned on each test and the number of possible points. Include an appropriate title, row and column headings, and formulas to calculate your total points earned and total possible points. Include a formula to calculate your percent. Format the worksheet appropriately using features presented in this lab. Enter real or sample data for the four tests. Include your name and date above the worksheet. Spell check the worksheet. Save the workbook as Class Grades and print the worksheet.

Creating a Personal Budget ★

2. Create a personal three-month budget using a worksheet. Enter an appropriate title and use descriptive labels for your monthly expenses (food, rent, car payments, insurance, credit card payments, etc.). Spell check your worksheet. Enter your monthly expenses (or, if you prefer, any reasonable sample data). Use formulas to calculate total expenses for each month and to calculate the average monthly expenditures for each expense item. Enhance the worksheet using features you learned in this lab. Enter your name and the current date on separate rows just below the worksheet. Save the workbook as Personal Budget. Preview and print the worksheet.

Tracking Employee Hours ★ ★

3. Julie Bradley is the office assistant for a small publishing company. She has four part-time employees (Anthony, Mel, Latisha, and Betty). Using the steps in the planning process, plan and create a worksheet for Julie that can be used to record and analyze the hours each employee works per day during the month. Hours-worked data for each employee will be entered into the worksheet. Using that data, the worksheet will calculate the total number of hours for each person. Additionally, it will calculate the total weekly hours for the company. Write a short paragraph describing how you used each of the planning steps. Enter sample data in a worksheet. Include your name and the current date on separate rows just below the worksheet. Spell check the worksheet. Save the workbook as Weekly Hours. Preview and print the worksheet.

Cell Phone Analysis ★ ★ ★

4. Use the library and/or the Web to locate information on cell phone usage trends. Create a worksheet to display information relating to the increasing usage by country, age group, or any other trend you locate. Calculate totals or averages based on your data. Enhance the worksheet using features you learned in this lab. Enter your name and the current date on separate rows just below the worksheet. Spell check the worksheet. Save the workbook as Phone Analysis. Preview and print the worksheet.

Home Sales Analysis ★ ★ ★

5. A national home seller network wants to analyze the trend in home sales for the past three years. Design and create a worksheet to record the median price for homes in eight states for three years in the two categories: Resale and New Construction. Include an appropriate title, row and column headings, and formulas to calculate average price by category and by year. Include a formula to calculate the percent growth over the three years. Format the worksheet appropriately using features presented in this tutorial. Enter sample data for the three years. Include your name and date above the worksheet. Spell check the worksheet. Save the workbook as Home Sales Analysis and print the worksheet.

Charting Worksheet Data

LAB 2

Objectives

After completing this lab, you will know how to:

1. Use styles.
2. Insert and size a graphic.
3. Create a chart using the Chart Wizard.
4. Move, size, and format a chart.
5. Change the type of chart.
6. Create, explode, and rotate a pie chart.
7. Apply patterns and color to a chart.
8. Document a workbook.
9. Size and align a sheet on a page.
10. Add predefined headers and footers

Case Study

Downtown Internet Café

Evan is impressed with how quickly you were able to create the first quarter sales forecast for the Downtown Internet Café. He made several suggestions to improve the appearance of the worksheet, including applying different formats and adding a graphic. Evan also expressed concern that the sales values seem a little low and has asked you to contact several other Internet cafes to inquire about their startup experiences.

While speaking with other Internet cafe managers, you heard many exciting success stories. Internet connections attract more customers, and the typical customer stays longer at an Internet cafe than at a regular cafe. As a result, they spend more money. In your discussions you have found that Internet connection sales are responsible for approximately 25 percent of their total sales.

© Corbis

You would like to launch an aggressive advertising campaign to promote the new Internet aspect of the Downtown Internet Café. You believe that the campaign will lead to an increase in sales not only in Internet connection time but also in food and beverage sales. To convince Evan, you need an effective way to illustrate the sales growth you are forecasting. You will use Excel 2003's chart-creating and formatting features to produce several different charts of your sales estimates, as shown on the following page.

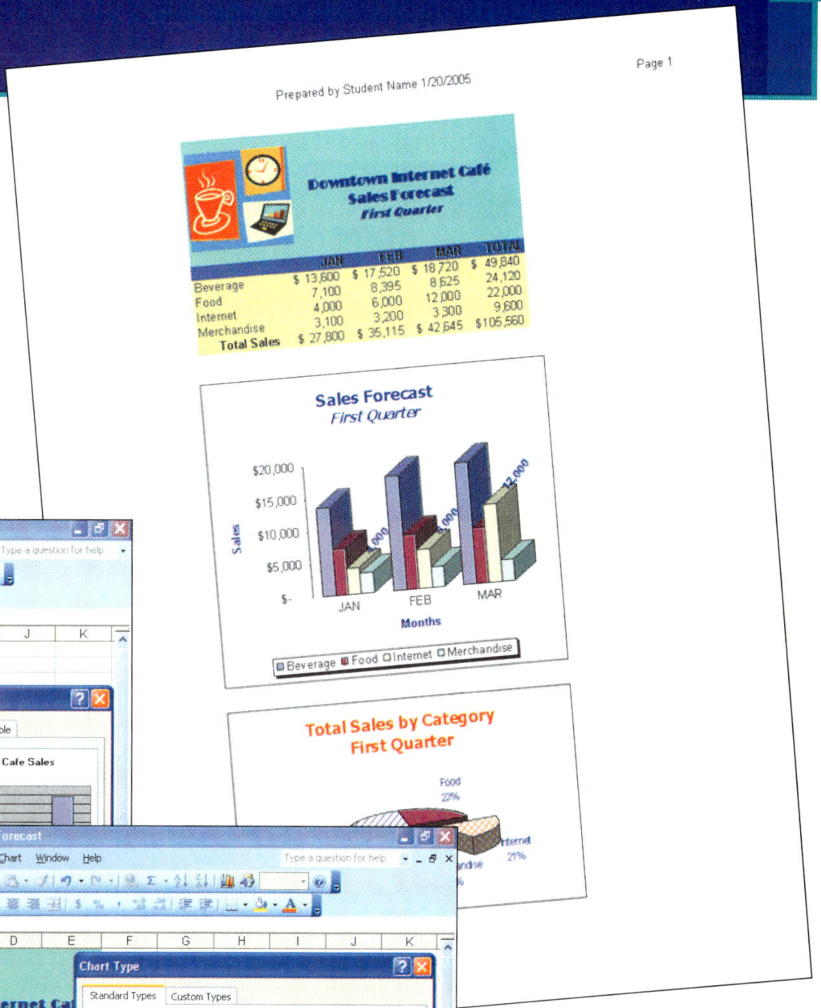

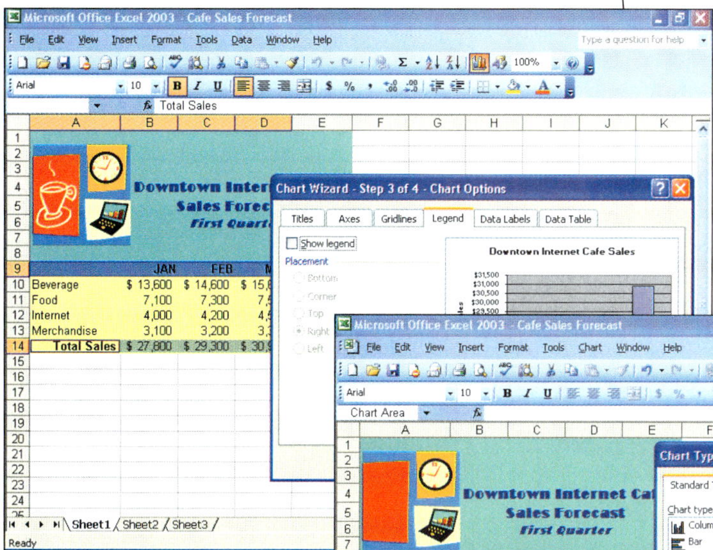

The Chart Wizard makes it easy to create a chart from data in a worksheet.

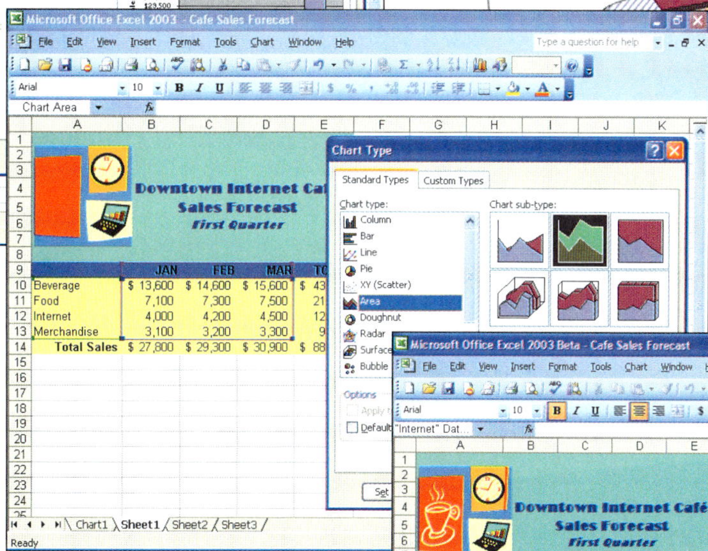

Many different types of charts can be created and modified to visually represent worksheet data.

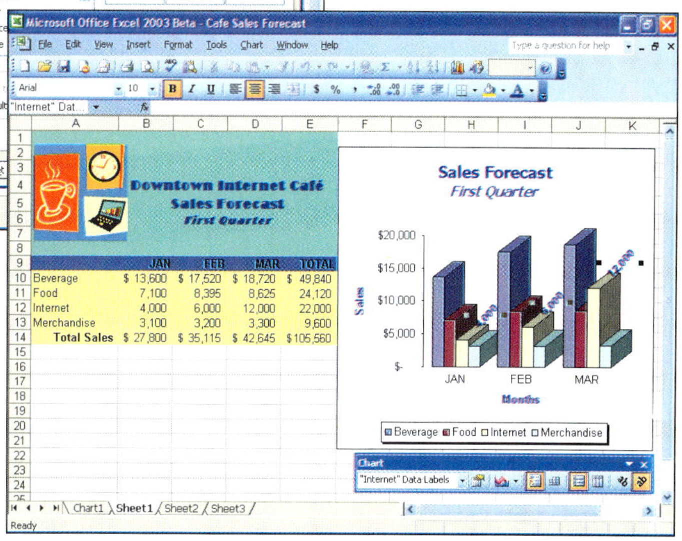

The addition of features such as data labels, color, and patterns add emphasis to the chart.

Concept Preview

The following concepts will be introduced in this lab:

1. **Style** A style consists of a combination of formats that have been named and that can be quickly applied to a selection.
2. **Graphics** A graphic is a non-text element or object, such as a drawing or picture, that can be added to a document.
3. **Chart** A chart is a visual representation of data that is used to convey information in an easy-to-understand and attractive manner. Different types of charts are used to represent data in different ways.
4. **Chart Elements** A chart consists of a number of elements that are used to graphically display the worksheet data.
5. **Chart Object** A chart object is a graphic object that is created using charting features included in Excel. A chart object can be inserted into a worksheet or into a special chart sheet.
6. **Group** A group is two or more objects that behave as a single object when moved or sized.
7. **Data Label** Data labels provide additional information about a data marker.
8. **Headers and Footers** Headers and footers provide information that typically appears at the top and bottom of each page and commonly include information such as the date and page number.

Improving the Appearance of the Worksheet

To focus Evan's attention solely on the sales values for the Downtown Internet Cafe, you created a new worksheet containing only those values. You have added some formatting to it already, but want to improve its appearance by changing the format of the sales values and adding a graphic. Then you will create the charts to see the sales trends better.

Using Styles

You saved the sales portion of the worksheet in a new file.

1 **Start Office Excel 2003.**

Open the file ex02_Cafe Sales.

Your screen should be similar to Figure 2.1

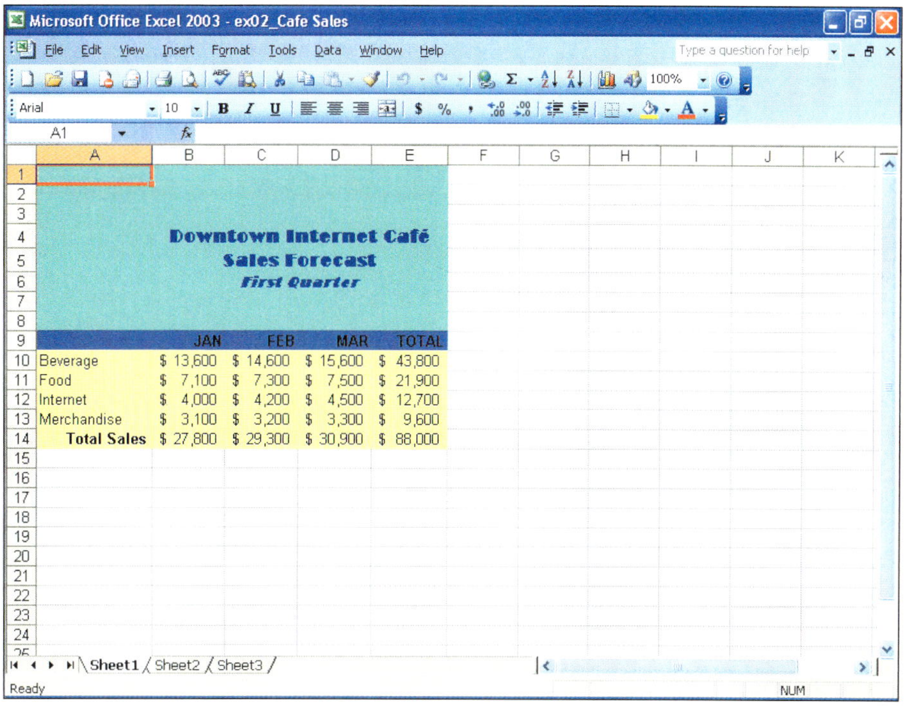

Figure 2.1

You first want to change the format of the Food, Internet, and Merchandise values to display commas only, without dollar signs. Another way to apply number formats is to select a predefined format style.

Concept 1

Style

1 A **style** consists of a combination of formats that have been named and that can be quickly applied to a selection. Excel includes six predefined styles, or you can create your own custom styles. The default worksheet style is Normal. It sets the number format to General and controls other format settings that are applied to all entries, including font type, font size, alignment, and indentation. Examples of the six predefined styles are shown below.

Style	Example
Normal	89522
Comma	89,522.00
Comma [0]	89,522
Currency	$ 89,522.00
Currency [0]	$ 89,522
Percent	89.52200%

Currently the worksheet values are formatted using the Accounting style with zero decimal places displayed. This format is the same as the Currency [0] style. You will use the Comma [0] style for the three rows you want to change.

2 • **Select the range B11 through E13.**

• **Choose Format/Style.**

Your screen should be similar to Figure 2.2

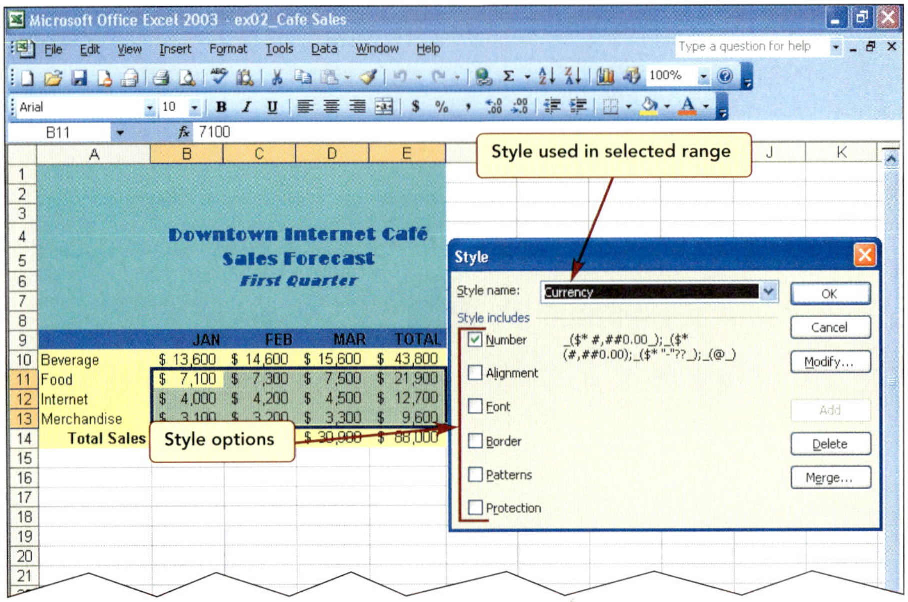

Figure 2.2

The Style dialog box displays the name of the style used in the selected range, Currency, in the Style Name list box. The check boxes in the Style Includes area of the dialog box show the options that are included in this style followed by a description or sample. You want to use the Comma [0] style.

3 • **Open the Style Name drop-down list box.**

• **Select Comma [0].**

• **Click OK.**

Additional Information

Using Comma Style on the Formatting toolbar or the voice command "Comma style" applies the Comma number format with two decimal places.

Your screen should be similar to Figure 2.3

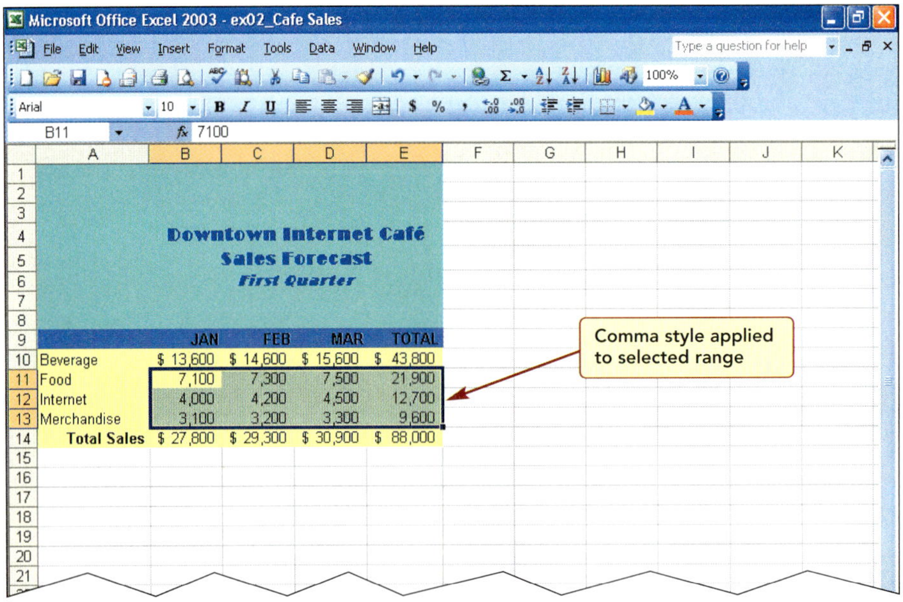

Figure 2.3

The Comma [0] style applies the comma number format with zero decimal places. Using a style applies many formats in one easy step making it quicker to apply formats to cells.

Working with Graphics

Now you want to add a graphic next to the worksheet title to add interest.

Concept 2

Graphics

2 A **graphic** is a non-text element or object, such as a drawing or picture, that can be added to a document. An **object** is an item that can be sized, moved, and manipulated.

A graphic can be a simple drawing object consisting of shapes, such as lines and boxes, that can be created using features on the Drawing toolbar. A **drawing object** is part of the Excel workbook. A **picture** is an illustration such as a scanned photograph. Pictures are graphics that were created from another program and inserted in the worksheet as embedded objects. An **embedded object** becomes part of the Excel workbook and can be opened and edited using the **source program**, the program in which it was created.

drawing object

graphic illustration

photograph

Add graphics to your worksheets to help the reader understand concepts, to add interest, and to make your worksheet stand out from others.

Inserting a Graphic

You want to insert a graphic to the left of the title in the worksheet. Graphic files can be obtained from a variety of sources. Many simple drawings called **clip art** are found in the Clip Organizer that comes with Office 2003 as well as in Microsoft's Clip Art and Media Web site. You can also create graphic files using a scanner to convert any printed document, including photographs, to an electronic format. Most images that are scanned are stored as Windows bitmap files (.bmp). All types of graphics, including clip art, photographs, and other types of images, can be found on the Internet. These files are commonly stored as .jpg or .pcx files. Keep in mind that any images you locate on the Internet may be protected by copyright and should be used only with permission. You can also purchase CDs containing graphics for your use.

You decide to use the Clip Organizer to find a suitable graphic.

1

- Move to cell A1.
- Click to display the Drawing toolbar.
- Click Insert Clip Art on the Drawing toolbar.

Another Method

The menu equivalent is Insert/Picture/Clip Art. You could also display the Getting Started task pane and select Clip Art from the task pane menu. The voice command is "Insert clip art."

Your screen should be similar to Figure 2.4

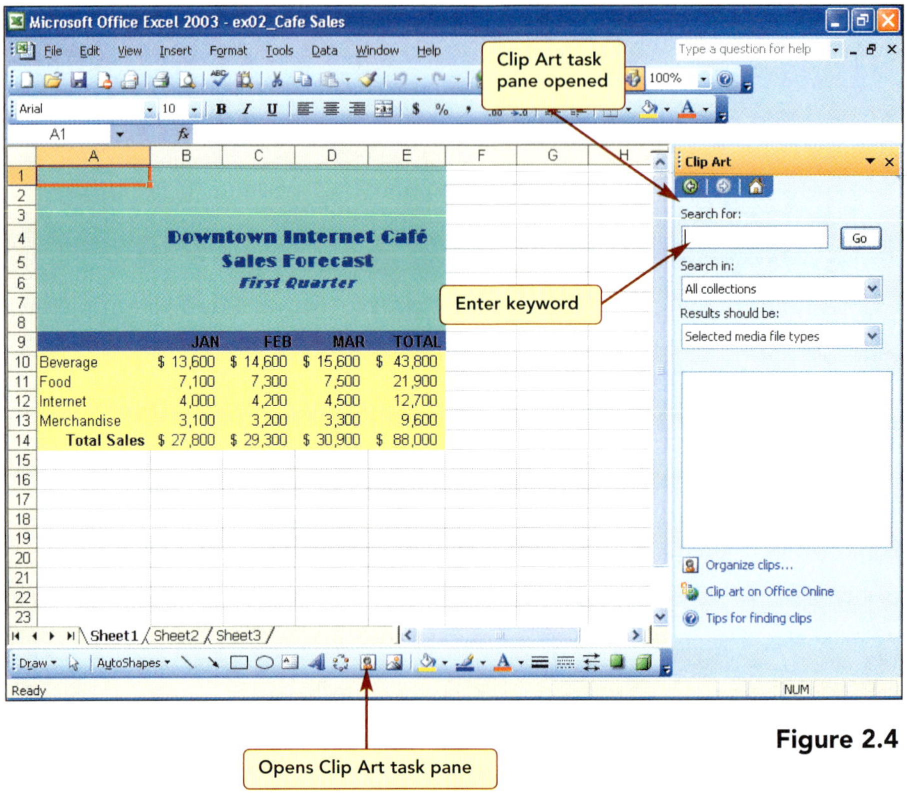

Figure 2.4

Additional Information

You can also insert graphics directly from files on your computer using Insert/Picture/From File or Insert Picture from file. The voice command is "Insert picture from file."

The Clip Art task pane appears. In the Search For text box, you can enter a **keyword**, a word or phrase that is descriptive of the type of graphic you want to locate. The graphics in the Clip Organizer are organized by topic and are identified with several keywords that describe the graphic. You can also specify the locations to search and the type of media files, such as clip art, movies, photographs, or sound, that you want displayed in the search results. You want to find clip art and photographs of computers.

2 In the Search text box, type **computer**.

Having Trouble?
If the Search text box already contains text, highlight the existing text before typing the new keyword.

- If All Collections is not displayed in the Search In text box, select Everywhere from the drop-down list.

Having Trouble?
Click the box next to an option to select or deselect it (clear the checkmark).

- Open the Results Should Be drop-down list, select Photographs and Clip Art and deselect all other options.
- Click Go.

Your screen should be similar to Figure 2.5

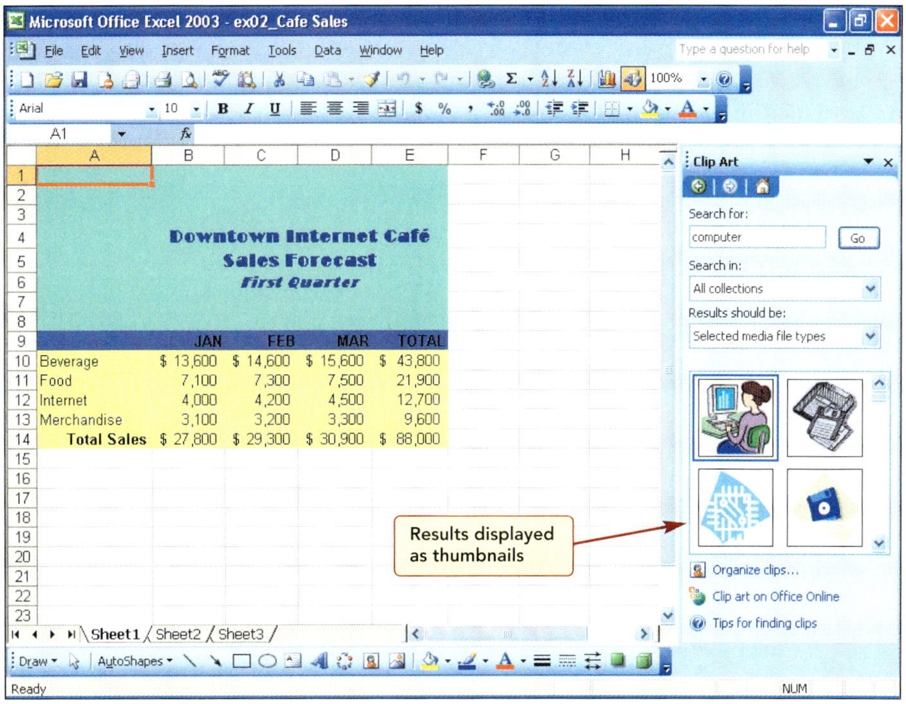

Figure 2.5

Having Trouble?
If your thumbnails appear in a single column, increase the width of your task pane by dragging the left edge of the pane until two columns are displayed.

The program searches all locations on your computer and, if you have an Internet connection established, Microsoft's Clip Art and Media Web site for clip art and graphics that match your search term. The Results area displays **thumbnails**, miniature representations of pictures, of all located graphics. Pointing to a thumbnail displays a ScreenTip containing the keywords associated with the picture and information about the picture properties. It also displays a drop-down list bar that accesses the item's shortcut menu.

Additionally, because it is sometimes difficult to see the graphic in the thumbnail, you can preview it in a larger size.

3 **Point to any thumbnail to see a ScreenTip.**

Click ⌄ next to any graphic to open the shortcut menu.

Additional Information

The shortcut menu commands are used to work with and manage the items in the Clip Organizer.

Choose Preview/Properties.

Your screen should be similar to Figure 2.6

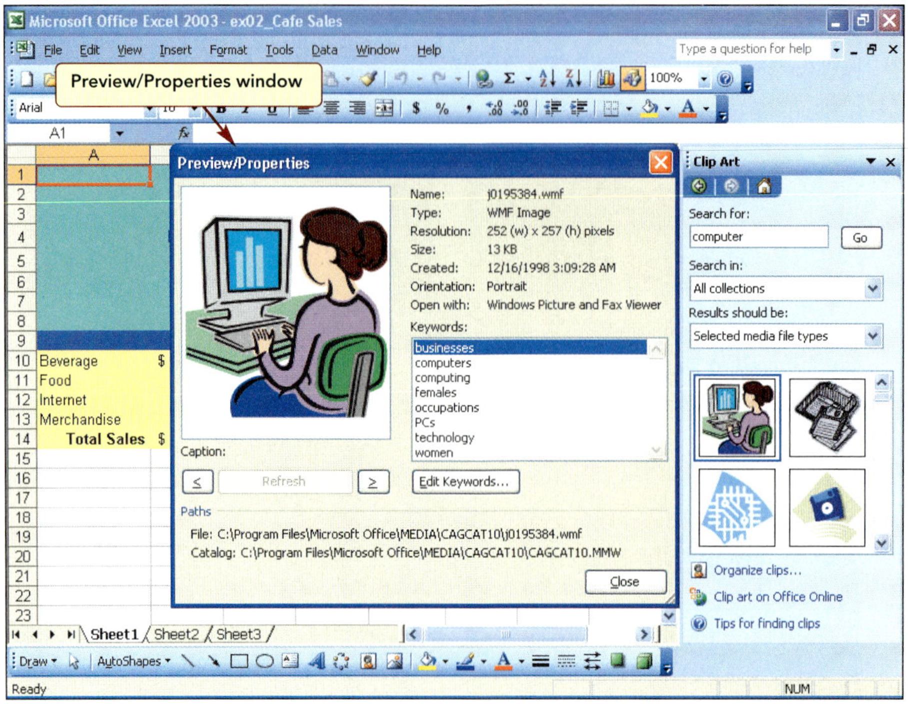

Figure 2.6

Having Trouble?

Your Preview/Properties dialog box will display information about the graphic you selected.

Additional Information

Entering keywords separated with a comma will expand the search to any graphics associated with either keyword.

The Preview/Properties dialog box displays the selected graphic larger so it is easier to see. It also displays more information about the properties associated with the graphic.

Because so many pictures were located, you decide to narrow your search to display only pictures of computers and coffee. Adding a second word to your search will narrow the number of graphics located. This is because it requires that both words be associated with the graphic in order for it to appear in the results.

4. Click **Close** to close the Preview dialog box.

- Add the word **coffee** to the Search For text box.
- Click **Go**.
- If necessary, scroll the results area to locate the graphic of a coffee cup, clock, and computer. 

Your screen should be similar to Figure 2.7

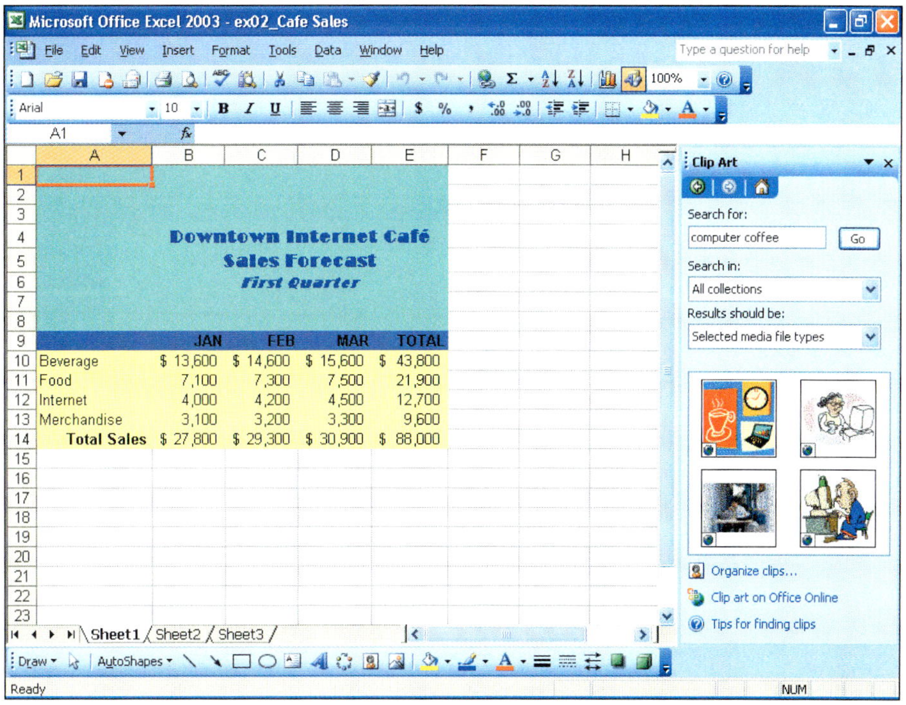

Figure 2.7

Having Trouble?

If this graphic is not available close the Clip Art task pane, choose Insert/Picture/From File or click and choose ex02_computer.bmp from your data file location. Skip to the next section, Sizing Graphics.

Because the search term is more specific, fewer results are displayed. You believe this is a good choice and will insert it into the document.

5 **Click on the graphic to insert it in the document.**

Another Method

You could also choose Insert from the thumbnail's shortcut menu.

Click ☒ in the task pane title bar to close it.

Your screen should be similar to Figure 2.8

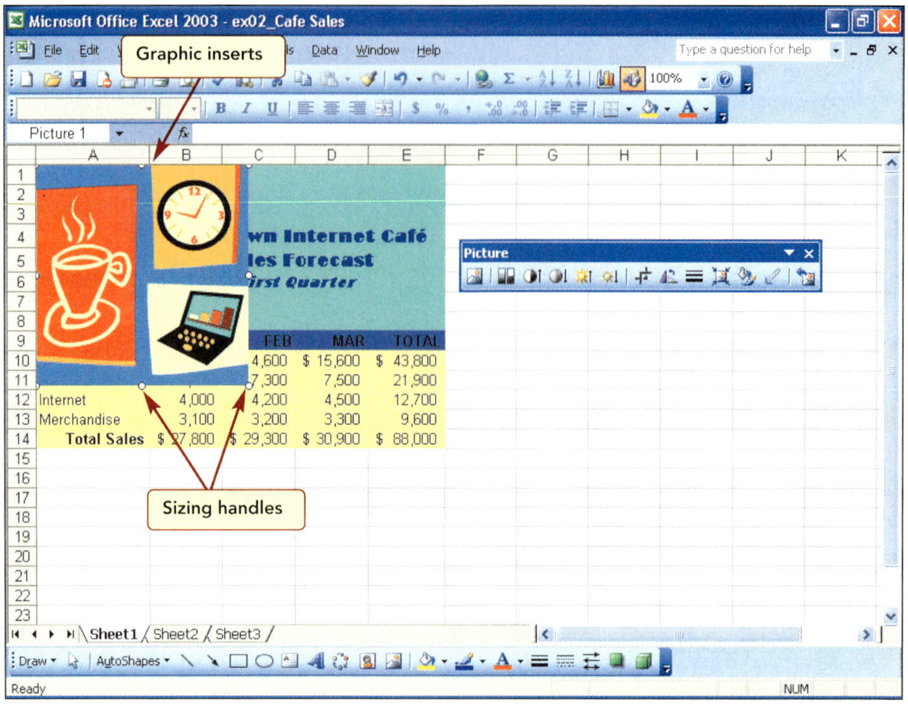

Figure 2.8

Sizing Graphics

The ClipArt image is inserted in the worksheet, but it is much too large. When a graphic object is inserted into the workbook, it can be manipulated in many ways. You can change its size, add borders or shading, or move it to another location, including the margin, headers and footers, or on top of or below other objects.

You want to reduce the size of the graphic and position it next to the title. The picture is surrounded by eight small circles, called **sizing handles**, indicating that it is a selected object and can now be sized and moved anywhere in the document. The handles are used to size the object. The mouse pointer changes to ↔ when pointing to a handle. The direction of the arrow indicates the direction in which you can drag to size the graphic. When you hold down the mouse button and drag to size the graphic the mouse pointer shape changes to a +. A graphic object is moved by dragging it to the new location. The mouse pointer changes to ✥ when you can move the graphic.

The Picture toolbar is also automatically displayed. Its buttons are used to modify the selected picture object. Your Picture toolbar may be floating or docked along an edge of the window, depending on its location when last used.

Additional Information

A selected graphic object can be deleted by pressing Delete.

Having Trouble?

If the Picture toolbar is not displayed, right-click on any toolbar to open the shortcut menu and select Picture, or use View/Toolbars/Picture.

1

- Point to the lower-right corner sizing handle.

- With the pointer as a ↘, drag the mouse inward to reduce the size of the graphic until the bottom of the graphic is even with row 6.

Additional Information

Dragging a corner handle maintains the original proportions of the pictures.

- Point to the center of the graphic, and when the mouse pointer is ✥, drag the graphic to position it as in Figure 2.9.

- Click outside the graphic to deselect the object.

- Turn off the Drawing toolbar.

- Save the revised worksheet as Café Sales Forecast to your data file location.

Your screen should be similar to Figure 2.9

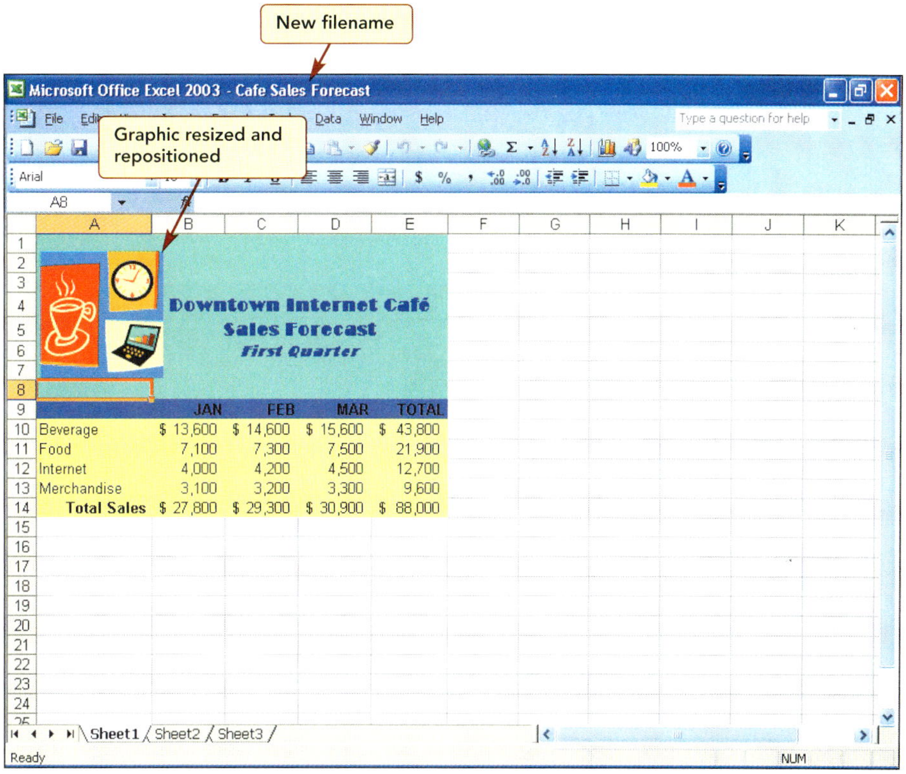

Figure 2.9

The addition of a graphic adds a nice touch to the worksheet title.

Working with Charts

Although the worksheet shows the sales data for each category, it is difficult to see how the different categories change over time. To make it easier to see the sales trends, you decide to create a chart of this data.

Concept 3

Charts

3 A **chart** is a visual representation of data that is used to convey information in an easy-to-understand and attractive manner. Different types of charts are used to represent data in different ways. The type of chart you create depends on the type of data you are charting and the emphasis you want the chart to impart.

Excel 2003 can produce 14 standard types of graphs or charts, with many different sub-types for each standard type. In addition, Excel includes professionally designed, built-in custom charts that include additional formatting and chart refinements. The basic chart types and how they represent data are described in the following table.

Type	Description
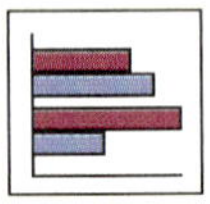	Area charts show the magnitude of change over time by emphasizing the area under the curve created by each data series.
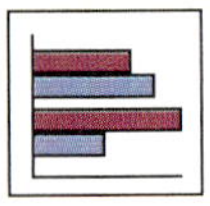	Bar charts display data as evenly spaced bars. The categories are displayed along the Y axis and the values are displayed horizontally, placing more emphasis on comparisons and less on time.
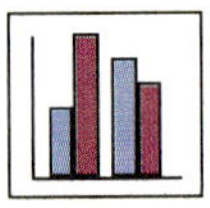	Column charts display data as evenly spaced bars. They are similar to bar charts, except that categories are organized horizontally and values vertically to emphasize variation over time.
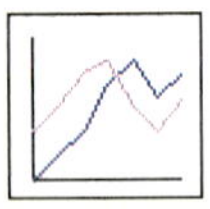	Line charts display data along a line. They are used to show changes in data over time, emphasizing time and rate of change rather than the amount of change.
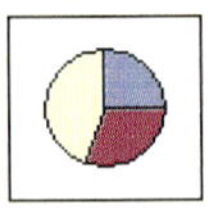	Pie charts display data as slices of a circle or pie. They show the relationship of each value in a data series to the series as a whole. Each slice of the pie represents a single value in the series.
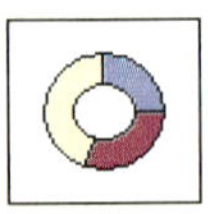	Doughnut charts are similar to pie charts except that they can show more than one data series.
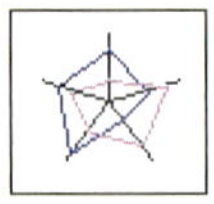	Radar charts display a line or area chart wrapped around a central point. Each axis represents a set of data points.
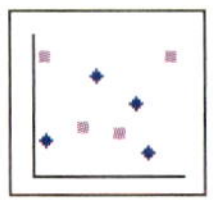	XY (scatter) charts are used to show the relationship between two ranges of numeric data.
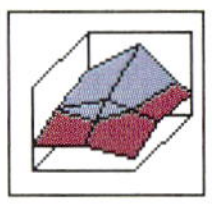	Surface charts display values in a form similar to a rubber sheet stretched over a 3-D column chart. These are useful for finding the best combination between sets of data.
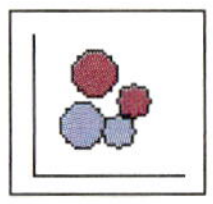	Bubble charts compare sets of three values. They are similar to a scatter chart with the third value displayed as the size of bubble markers.
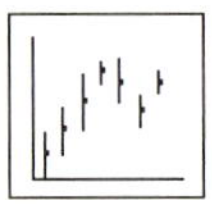	Stock charts are high-low-close charts. They require three series of values in this order.
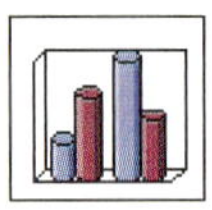	Cylinder charts display values with a cylindrical shape.
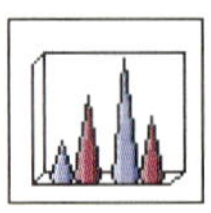	Cone charts display values with a conical shape.
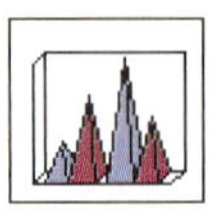	Pyramid charts display values with a pyramid shape.

Creating a Single Data Series Chart

All charts are drawn from data contained in a worksheet. To create a new chart, you select the worksheet range containing the data you want displayed as a chart plus any row or column headings you want used in the chart. Excel then translates the selected data into a chart based upon the shape and contents of the worksheet selection.

A chart consists of a number of parts or elements that are important to understand so that you can identify the appropriate data to select in the worksheet.

Concept 4

Chart Elements

4 A chart consists of a number of elements that are used to graphically display the worksheet data. In a two-dimensional chart, the selected worksheet data is visually displayed within the X- and Y-axis boundaries. The **X axis**, also called the category axis, is the bottom boundary line of the chart and is used to label the data being charted. The left boundary line of the chart is the **Y axis**, also called the **value axis**. This axis is a numbered scale whose numbers are determined by the data used in the chart. Typically, the X-axis line is the horizontal line and the Y-axis line is the vertical line. In 3-D charts there can also be an additional axis, called the **Z axis**, which allows you to compare data within a series more easily. This axis is the vertical axis, while the X and Y axes depict the horizontal surface of the chart.

Other basic elements of a two-dimensional chart are:

Element	Description
Category names	Labels that correspond to the headings for the worksheet data that is plotted along the X axis
Plot area	The area within the X- and Y-axis boundaries where the chart appears
Data series	Related data points that are distinguished by different colors or patterns
Data marker	A bar, dot, or other symbol that represents one number from the worksheet
Chart gridlines	Lines extending from the axis line across the plot area that make it easier to read the chart data
Legend	A box that identifies the chart data series and data markers
Chart title	A descriptive label displayed above the charted data that explains the contents of the chart
Category-axis title	A descriptive label displayed along the X axis
Value-axis title	A descriptive label displayed along the Y axis

(continued)

Concept 4 (continued)

Chart Elements

4 The basic parts of a two-dimensional chart are shown in the figure below.

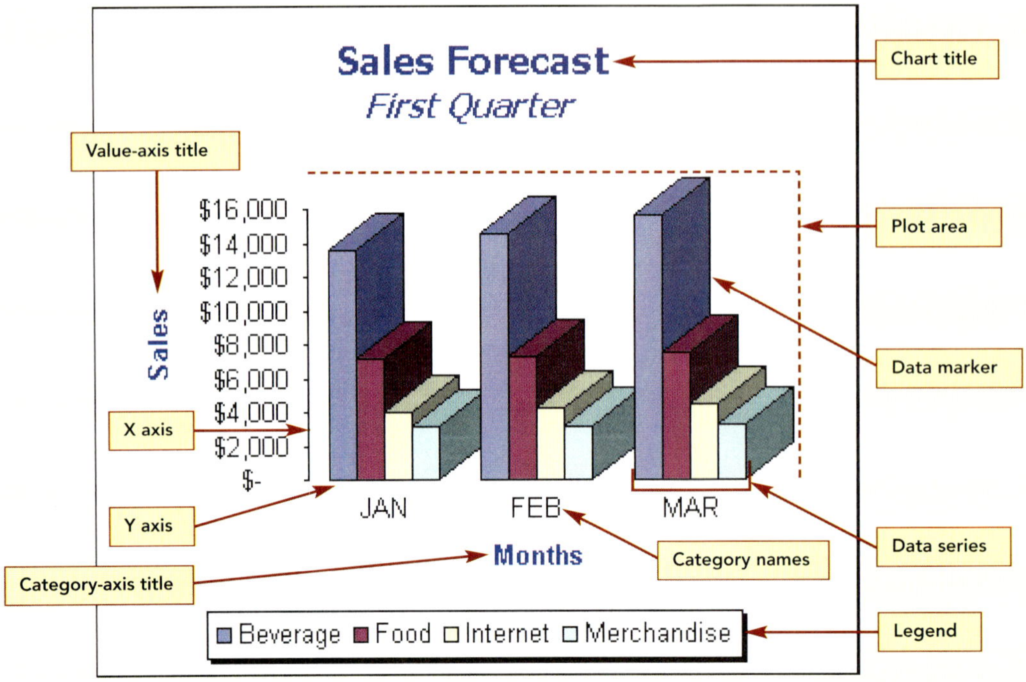

Selecting the Data to Chart

The first chart you want to create will show the total sales pattern over the three months. This chart will use the month headings in cells B9 through D9 to label the X axis. The numbers to be charted are in cells B14 through D14. In addition, the heading Total Sales in cell A14 will be used as the chart legend, making the entire range A14 through D14.

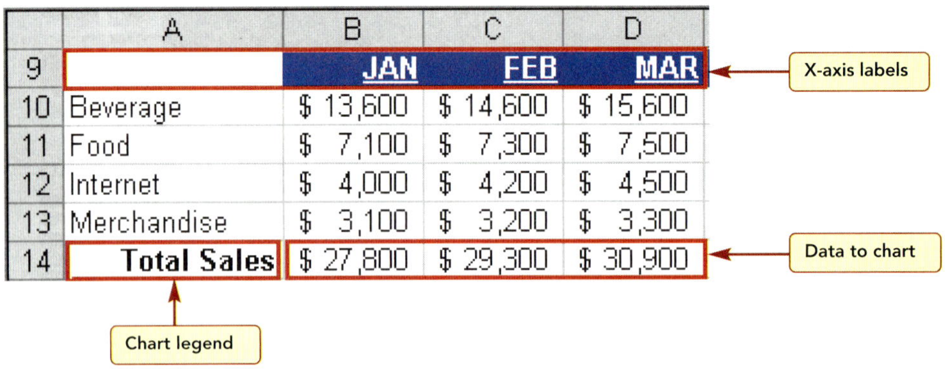

	A	B	C	D
9		JAN	FEB	MAR
10	Beverage	$ 13,600	$ 14,600	$ 15,600
11	Food	$ 7,100	$ 7,300	$ 7,500
12	Internet	$ 4,000	$ 4,200	$ 4,500
13	Merchandise	$ 3,100	$ 3,200	$ 3,300
14	Total Sales	$ 27,800	$ 29,300	$ 30,900

Notice that the two ranges, B9 through D9 and A14 through D14, are not adjacent and are not the same size. When plotting nonadjacent ranges in a chart, the selections must form a rectangular shape. To do this, you will include the blank cell, A9, in the selection. You will specify the range and create the chart.

1. **Select A9 through D9.**

   Hold down Ctrl.

   Select A14 through D14.

Your screen should be similar to Figure 2.10

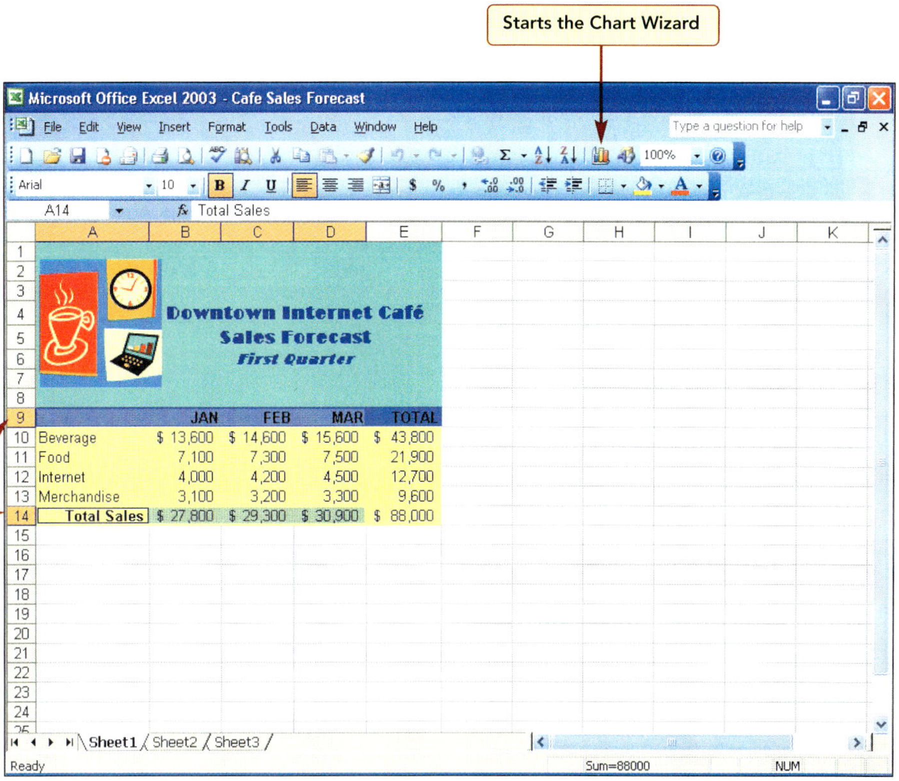

Figure 2.10

Using the Chart Wizard

Next you will use the Chart Wizard to help you create the chart. A **wizard** is an interactive program that guides you through the steps to help you quickly perform many complicated tasks, in this case create a chart, by asking you questions and creating the item based on your responses.

Additional Information

Wizards are available in all Office 2003 applications.

1. **Click** Chart **Wizard.**

Another Method

The menu equivalent is Insert/Chart and the voice command is "Chart Wizard."

   Move the Chart Wizard dialog box to the right to see as much of the worksheet as possible.

Having Trouble?

Drag the title bar of the dialog box to move it.

Your screen should be similar to Figure 2.11

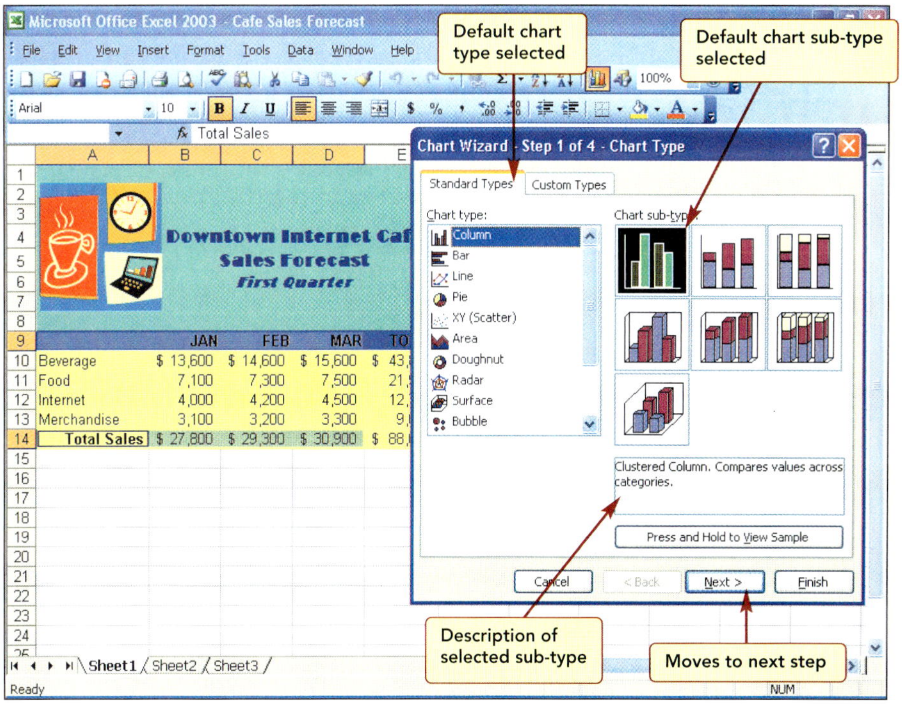

Figure 2.11

The first step is to select the chart type from the Chart Type list box. The default chart type is a column chart. Each type of chart includes many variations. The variations associated with the column chart type are displayed as buttons in the Chart Sub-type section of the dialog box. The default column sub-type is a clustered column. A description of the selected sub-type is displayed in the area below the sub-type buttons. You will use the default column chart type and move to the next step.

2 Click Next >.

Another Method

You can also press ←Enter or say "Next" to move to the next step.

Your screen should be similar to Figure 2.12

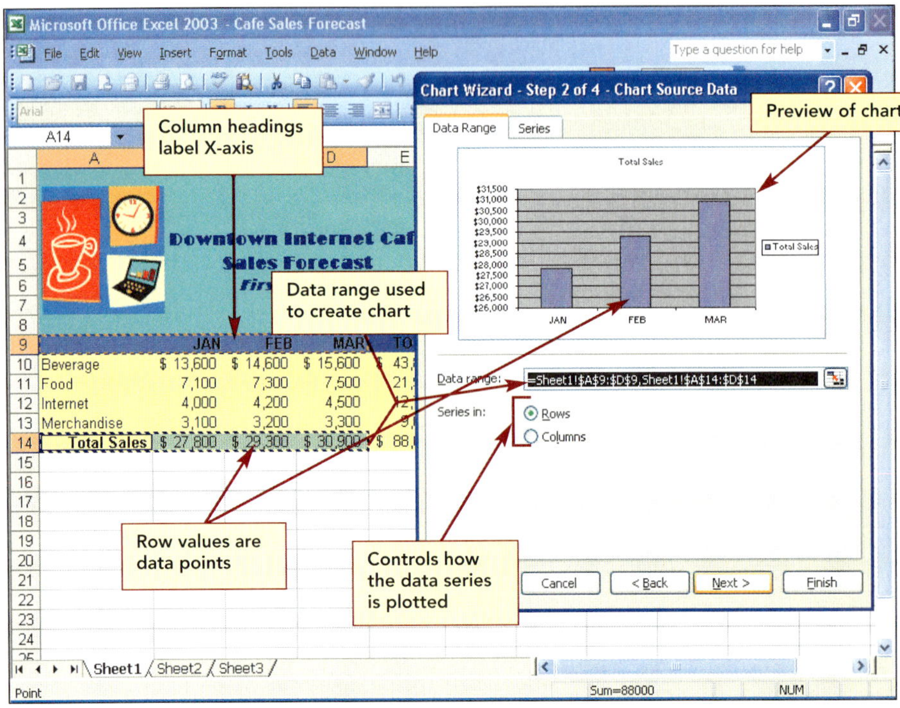

Figure 2.12

In the second Chart Wizard dialog box, you specify the data range on the worksheet you want to plot. Because you selected the data range before starting the Chart Wizard, the range is correctly displayed in the Data Range text box. In addition, the data range is identified with a moving border in the worksheet. The dialog box also displays a preview of the chart that will be created using the specified data and selected chart type.

The two Series In options change the way that Excel plots the data series from the rows or columns in the selected data range. The orientation Excel uses by default varies depending upon the type of chart selected and the number of rows and columns defined in a series. The worksheet data range that has the greater number of rows or columns appears along the X axis and the smaller number is charted as the data series. When the data series is an equal number of rows and columns, as it is in this case, the default is to plot the rows. The first row defines the X-axis category labels and the second row the plotted data. The content of the first cell in the second row is used as the legend text. You will accept the default settings and continue to the next step.

3 Click Next >.

- If necessary, open the Titles tab.

Your screen should be similar to Figure 2.13

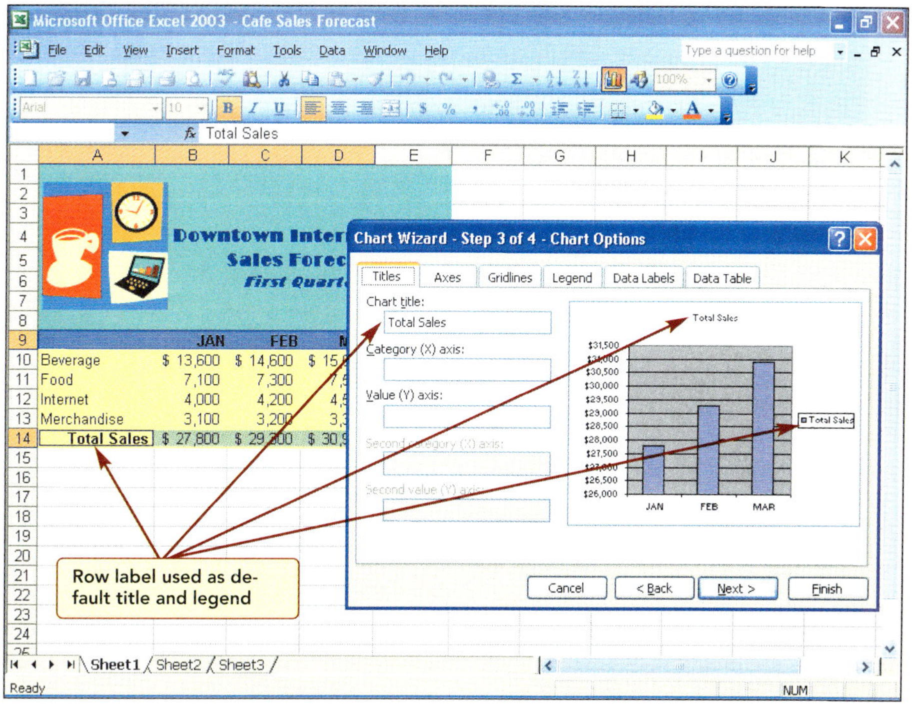

Figure 2.13

In the step 3 dialog box, you can turn some standard options on and off and change the appearance of chart elements such as a legend and titles. To clarify the data in the chart, you will add a more descriptive chart title as well as titles along the X and Y axes. As you add the titles, the preview chart will update to display the new settings.

4 In the Chart Title text box, replace the existing text with **Downtown Internet Cafe Sales**.

- Press Tab.

Having Trouble?

Do not use ←Enter after typing the title text as this is the same as clicking Next >. Click < Back if needed to return to the previous Wizard step.

- In the Category (X) Axis text box, enter **Months**.

- In the Value (Y) Axis text box, enter **Total Sales**.

Your screen should be similar to Figure 2.14

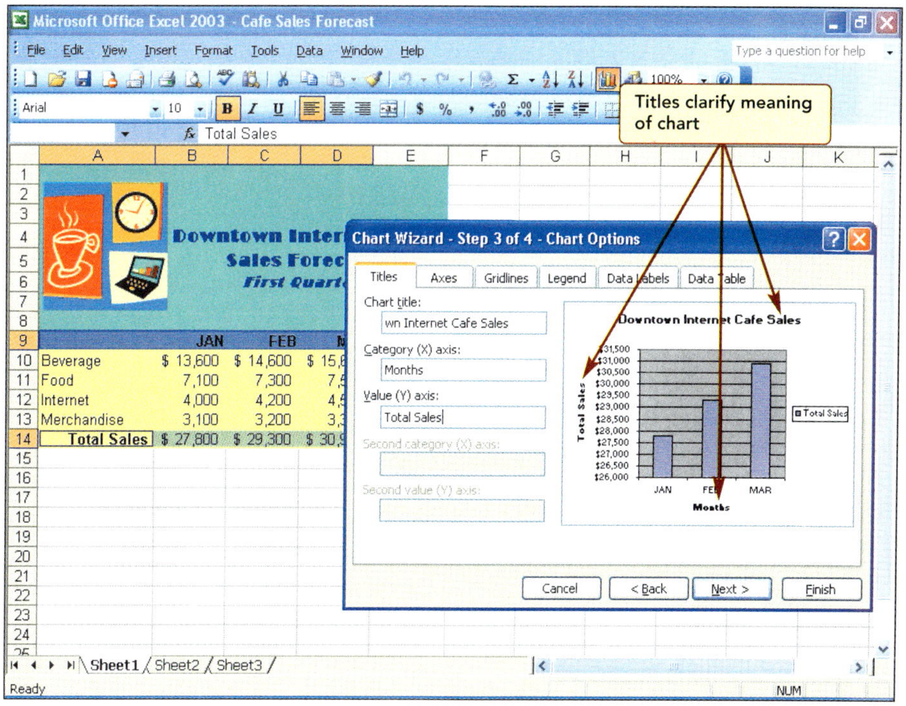

Figure 2.14

The titles clearly describe the information displayed in the chart. Now, because there is only one data range, and the category title fully explains this data, you decide to clear the display of the legend.

5 **Open the Legend tab.**

Click Show Legend to clear the checkmark.

Your screen should be similar to Figure 2.15

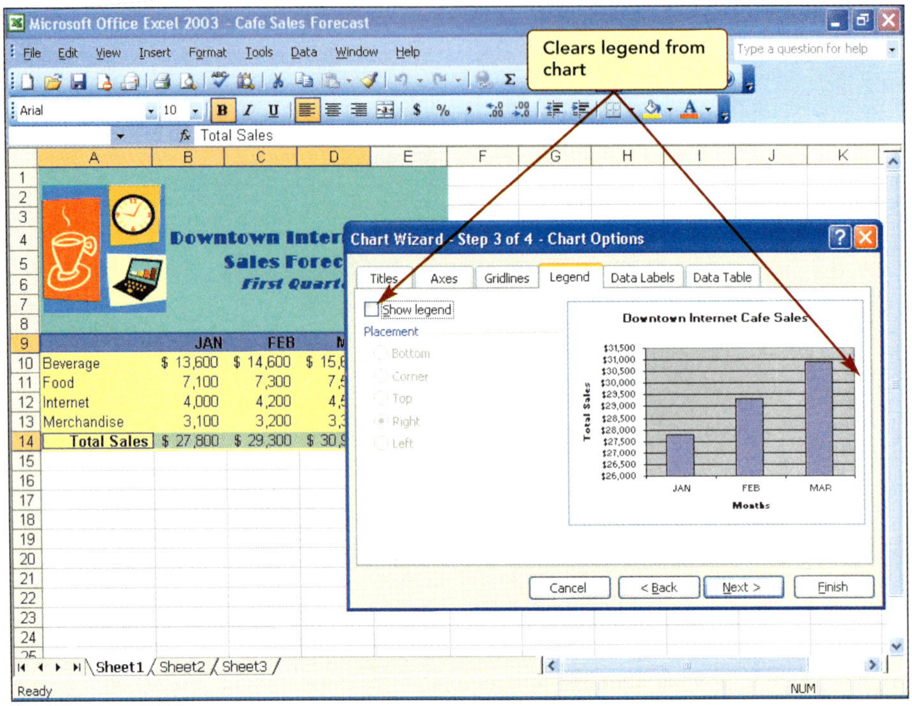

Figure 2.15

The legend is removed and the chart area resized to occupy the extra space.

6 **Click** Next >.

Your screen should be similar to Figure 2.16

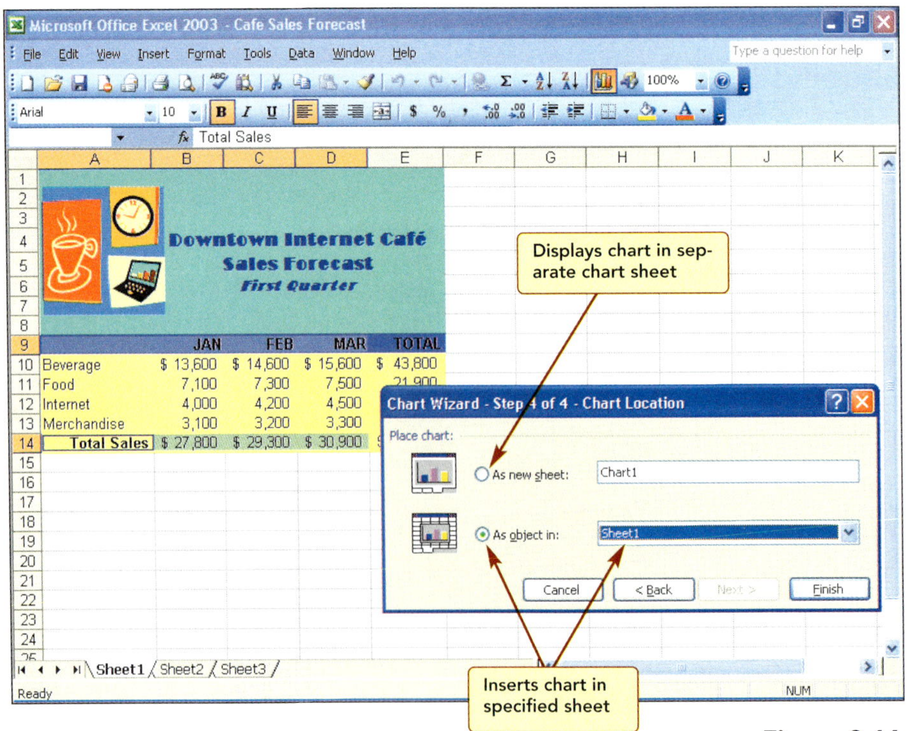

Figure 2.16

In the last step, you specify where you want the chart displayed in the worksheet. A chart can be displayed in a separate chart sheet or as an object in an existing sheet.

Concept 5

Chart Object

5 A **chart object** is a graphic object that is created using charting features included in Excel. A chart object can be inserted into a worksheet or into a special chart sheet.

Charts that are inserted into a worksheet are embedded objects. An **embedded chart** becomes part of the sheet in which it is inserted and is saved as part of the worksheet when you save the workbook file. Like all graphic objects, an embedded chart object can be sized and moved in a worksheet. A worksheet can contain multiple charts.

A chart that is inserted into a separate chart sheet is also saved with the workbook file. Only one chart can be added to a chart sheet and it cannot be sized and moved.

You would like this chart displayed as an object in the Sales Forecast worksheet. This is the default selection. You have provided all the information needed by the Wizard to create the chart.

7 **Click** Finish.

- **If necessary, move the Chart toolbar to the bottom-right corner of the window.**

Having Trouble?

If your Chart toolbar is not automatically displayed, open it by selecting it from the toolbar shortcut menu. Move toolbars by dragging the title bar of a floating toolbar or the move handle of a docked toolbar.

Your screen should be similar to Figure 2.17

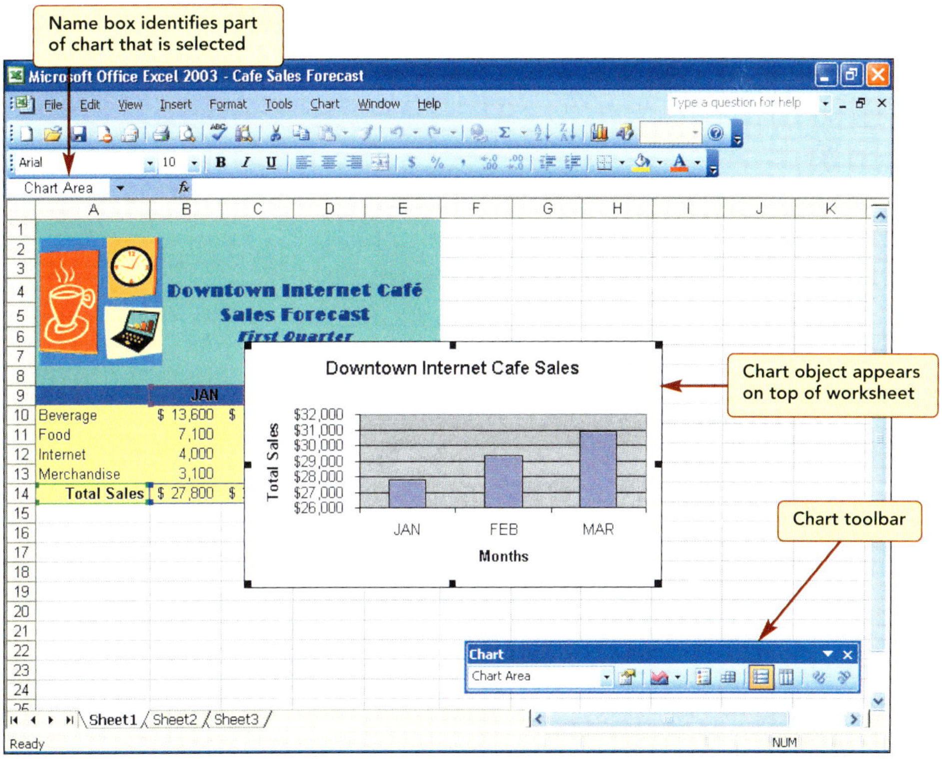

Figure 2.17

The chart with the settings you specified using the Chart Wizard is displayed in the worksheet. It covers some of the worksheet data because it is a separate chart object that can be moved and sized within the worksheet.

Notice that the Name box displays "Chart Area." The Name box identifies the part of the chart that is selected, in this case the entire chart and all its contents.

Also notice that the Chart toolbar is automatically displayed whenever a chart is selected. The Chart toolbar contains buttons for the most frequently used chart editing and formatting features. These buttons are identified below.

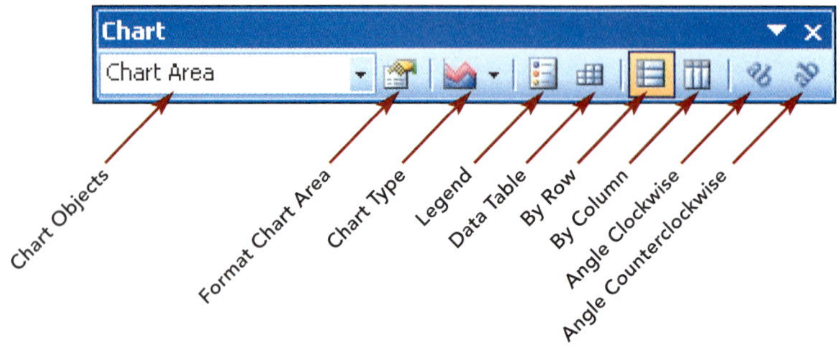

Moving and Sizing a Chart

You want to move the chart so that it is displayed to the right of the worksheet data. In addition, you want to increase the size of the chart. A selected chart object is moved by pointing to it and dragging it to a new location. When you move the mouse pointer into the selected chart object, it will display a chart ScreenTip to advise you about the chart element that will be affected by your action. When moving the entire chart, the chart ScreenTip must display "Chart Area." Then you will increase the size of the chart by dragging a sizing handle. This is the same as sizing a graphic object. If you hold down Alt while dragging to move and size a chart object, the chart automatically snaps into position or aligns with the closest worksheet cell when you release the mouse button. Release the mouse button before you release Alt.

1 **Move the mouse pointer to different elements within the chart and note the different chart ScreenTips that appear.**

With the chart ScreenTip displaying "Chart Area," drag the chart object so the upper-left corner is in cell F4.

Additional Information

The mouse pointer changes to a ✥ while dragging to move an object.

Point to the bottom-center sizing handle, hold down Alt, and drag the chart border line down until it is even with the bottom of row 20.

Your screen should be similar to Figure 2.18

Additional Information

Your chart may display different value intervals.

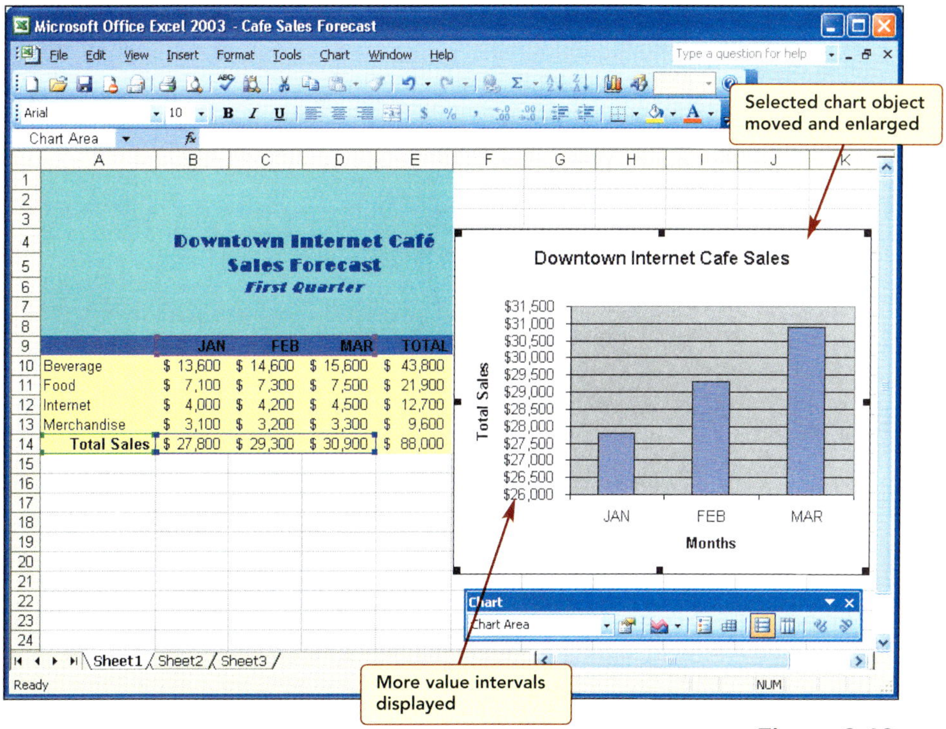

Figure 2.18

As you enlarge the chart, more value intervals are displayed along the Y axis, making the data in the chart easier to read. Additionally, the fonts in the chart change proportionally as you resize the chart. The chart includes standard formats that are applied to the selected chart sub-type, such as a shaded background in the plot area and blue columns.

It is now easy to see how the worksheet data you selected is represented in the chart. Each column represents the total sales for that month in row 14. The month labels in row 9 have been used to label the X-axis category labels. The range or scale of values along the Y axis is determined from the data in the worksheet. The upper limit is the maximum value in the worksheet rounded upward to the next highest interval.

Changing the Chart Location

Although this chart compares the total sales for the three months, you decide you are more interested in seeing a comparison for the sales categories. You could delete this chart simply by pressing Delete while the chart is selected. Instead, however, you will move it to a separate worksheet in case you want to refer to it again.

When a chart is selected, the Chart menu replaces the Data menu on the menu bar. In addition, many of the commands under the other menus change to commands that apply to charts only. The Chart menu contains commands that can be used to modify the chart.

1

- **Choose Chart/Location.**
- **Select As new sheet.**
- **Click OK.**
- **Save the workbook.**

Your screen should be similar to Figure 2.19

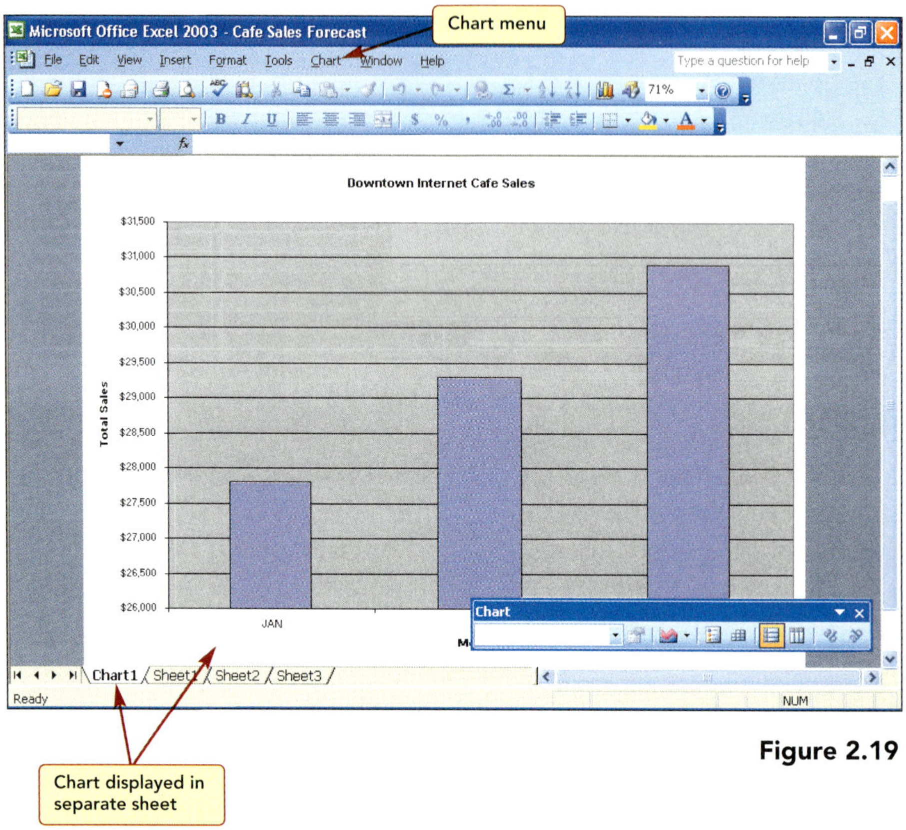

Figure 2.19

The column chart is now an object displayed in a separate chart sheet. Generally, you display a chart in a chart sheet when you want the chart displayed separately from the associated worksheet data. The chart is still automatically linked to the worksheet data from which it was created. The new chart sheet, named Chart1, was inserted to the left of the worksheet, Sheet1. The chart sheet is the active sheet, or the sheet in which you are currently working.

Creating a Multiple Data Series Chart

Now you are ready to continue your analysis of sales trends. You want to create a second chart to display the sales data for each category for the three months. You could create a separate chart for each category and then compare the charts; however, to make the comparisons between the categories easier, you will display all the categories on a single chart.

The data for the three months for the four categories is in cells B10 through D13. The month headings (X-axis data series) are in cells B9 through D9 and the legend text is in the range A10 through A13.

1

- **Click the Sheet1 tab.**
- **Select A9 through D13.**
- **Click Chart Wizard.**
- **Click Next >.**

Your screen should be similar to Figure 2.20

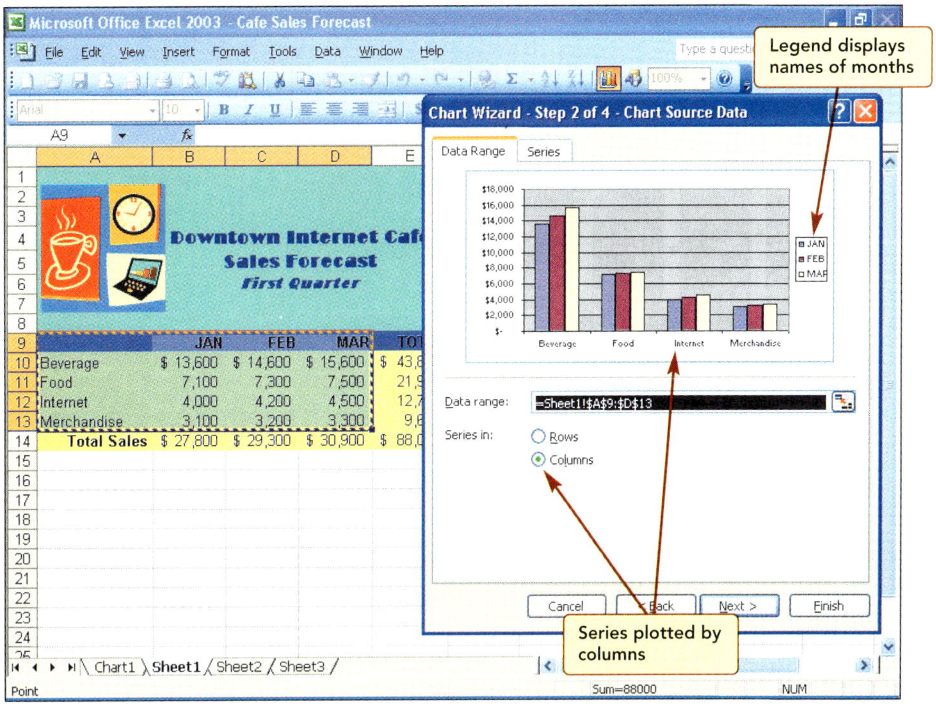

Figure 2.20

Additional Information

If you want to change the series orientation of an existing chart, you can use By Row or By Column in the Chart toolbar. The voice commands are "By row" or "By column."

When plotting the data for this chart, the Chart Wizard selected Columns as the data series orientation because the data range has fewer columns than rows. This time, however, you want to change the data series to Rows so that the months are along the X axis.

2 — **Select Rows.**

Your screen should be similar to Figure 2.21

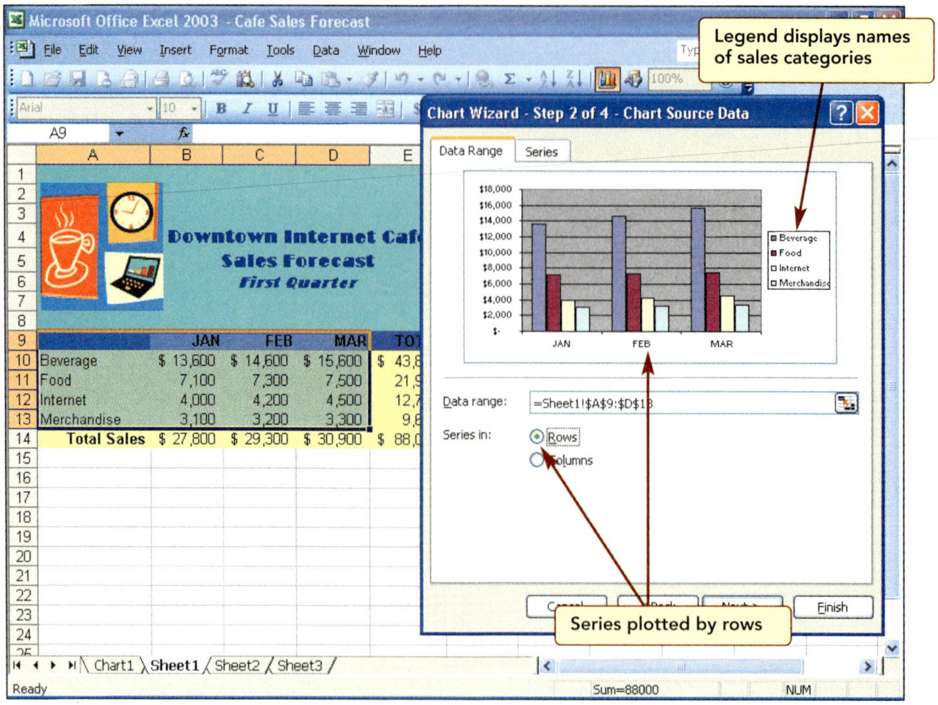

Figure 2.21

The sample chart is redrawn with the new orientation. The column chart now compares the sales by month rather than by category. The legend displays the names of the sales categories. Next, you will specify the chart titles and finish the chart.

Additional Information

You can finish the chart at any time while running the Chart Wizard, which accepts the default settings for the remaining steps.

3 Click Next >.

- **Open the Titles tab and enter the titles shown below:**

Title	**Entry**
Chart title	Sales Forecast
Category	Months
Value	Sales

- **Click Finish.**
- **Move and size the chart until it covers cells F2 through K22.**

Your screen should be similar to Figure 2.22

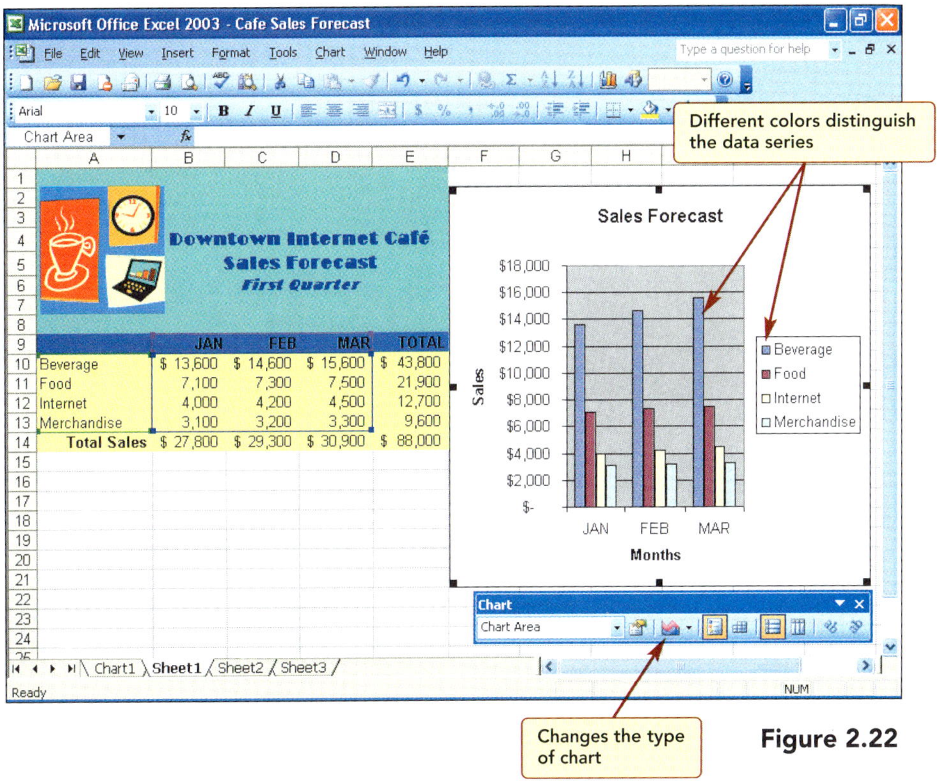

Figure 2.22

A different column color identifies each data series, and the legend identifies the categories. The column chart shows that sales in all categories are increasing, with the greatest increase occurring in beverage sales.

Changing the Chart Type

Next, you would like to see how the same data displayed in the column chart would look as a line chart. A line chart displays data as a line and is commonly used to show trends over time. You can change the chart type easily using the Chart Type button on the Chart toolbar.

1 Open the Chart Type drop-down list.

Another Method

The menu equivalent is Chart/Chart Type and the voice command is "Chart type" followed by the chart type name.

Click Line Chart.

Your screen should be similar to Figure 2.23

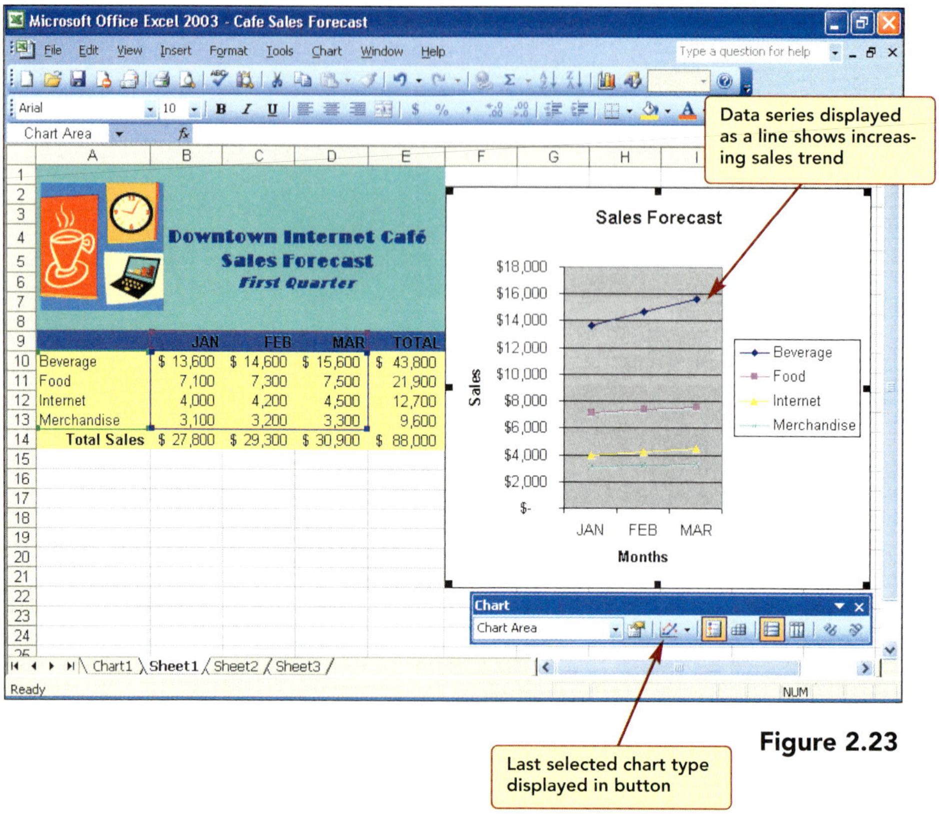

Figure 2.23

The line chart shows the increasing sales trend from month to month. Notice that the Chart Type button displays a line chart, reflecting the last-selected chart type. You do not find this chart very interesting, so you will change it to a 3-D bar chart next.

2 **Open the Chart Type drop-down list.**

Click 3-D Bar Chart.

Your screen should be similar to Figure 2.24

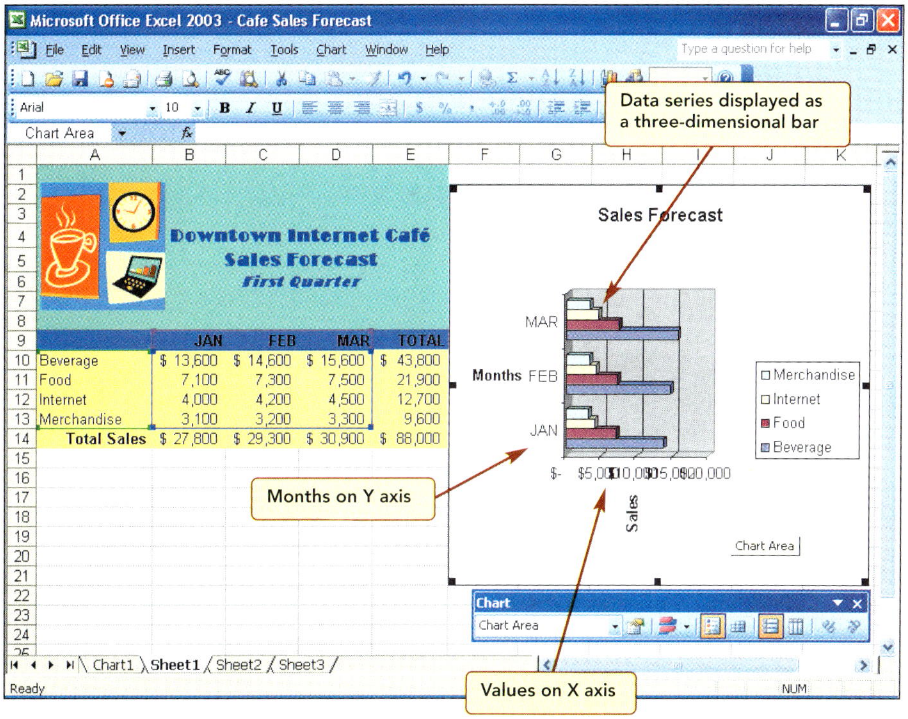

Figure 2.24

The 3-D bar chart reverses the X and Y axes and displays the data series as a three-dimensional bar. As you can see, it is very easy to change the chart type and format after the data series are specified. The same data can be displayed in many different ways. Depending upon the emphasis you want the chart to make, a different chart style can be selected.

Although the 3-D bar chart shows the sales trends for the three months for the sales categories, again it does not look very interesting. You decide to look at several other chart types to see whether you can improve the appearance. First you would like to see the data represented as an area chart. An area chart represents data the same as a line chart, but, in addition, it shades the area below each line to emphasize the degree of change.

3 • **Open the Chart Type drop-down list.**

• **Click Area Chart.**

Your screen should be similar to Figure 2.25

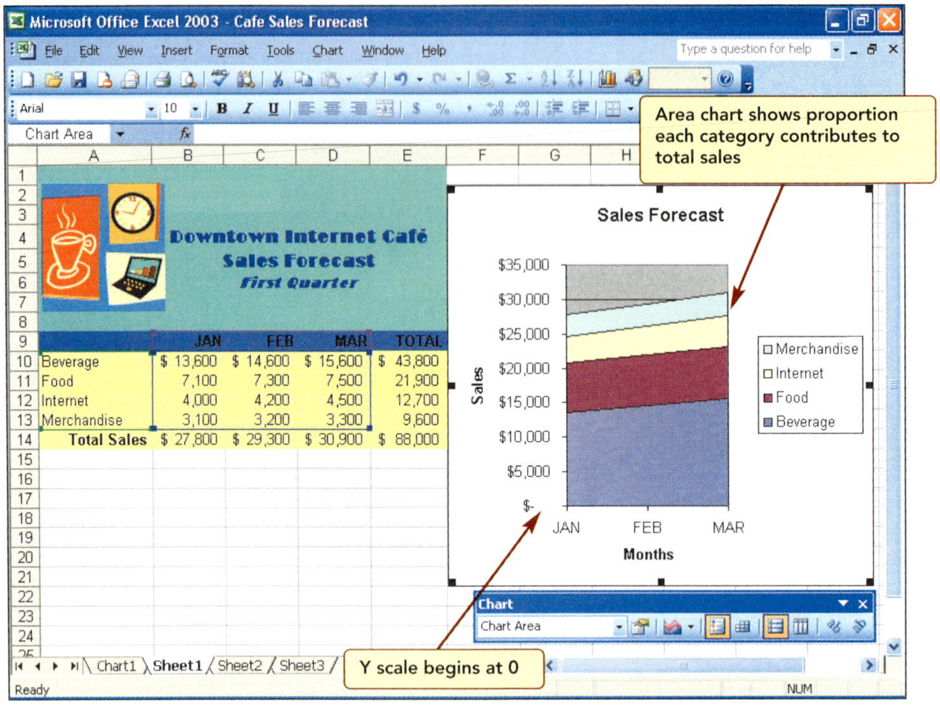

Figure 2.25

The Y-axis scale has changed to reflect the new range of data. The new Y-axis range is the sum of the four categories or the same as the total number in the worksheet. Using this chart type, you can see the magnitude of change that each category contributes to the total sales in each month.

Again, you decide that this is not the emphasis you want to show and will continue looking at other types of charts. Because all chart types are not available from the Chart Type drop-down list, you will use the Chart Type menu option in the Chart menu instead.

4 **Choose Chart/Chart Type.**

Your screen should be similar to Figure 2.26

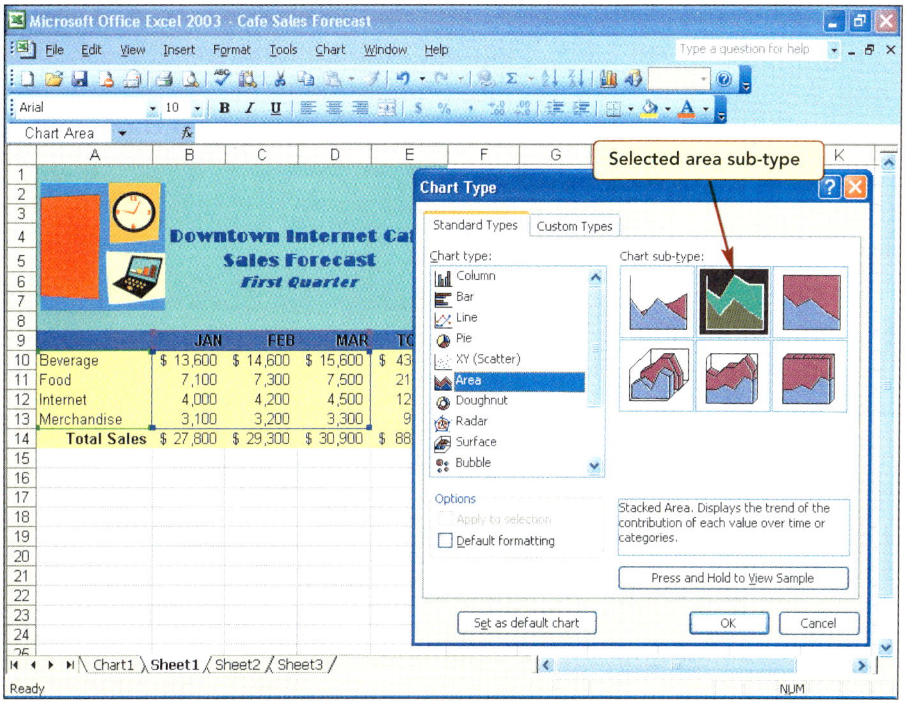

Figure 2.26

The Chart Type dialog box contains the same options as the Chart Wizard—Step 1 dialog box. The current chart type, Area, is the selected option. You want to see how this data will look as a stacked-column chart.

5 **Select Column.**

Select Stacked column with a 3-D visual effect.

Click and hold Press and Hold to View Sample.

Your screen should be similar to Figure 2.27

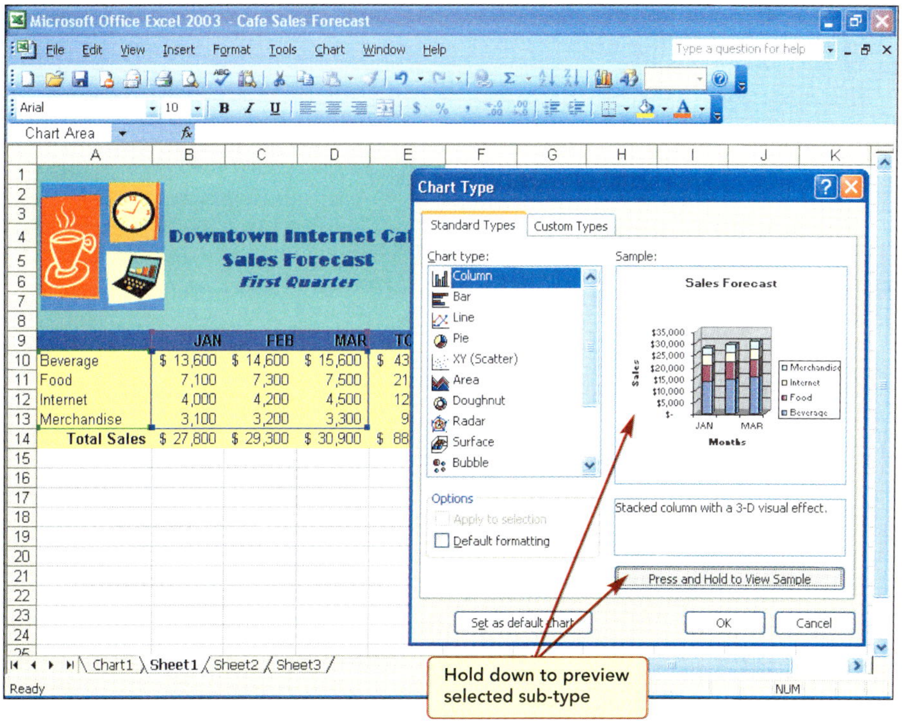

Figure 2.27

The sample chart is redrawn showing the data as a **stacked-column chart**. This type of chart also shows the proportion of each sales category to the total sales. You want to see the other types of charts that are available.

6 **Open the Custom Types tab.**

Click Area Blocks.

Your screen should be similar to Figure 2.28

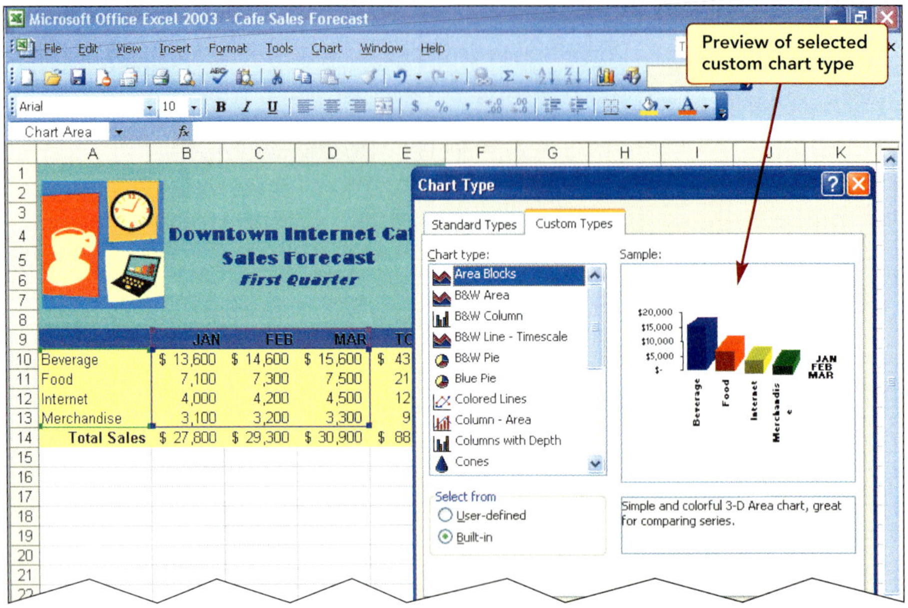

Figure 2.28

The Sample area shows how the data you selected for the chart will appear in this style. Custom charts are based upon standard types that are enhanced with additional display settings and custom formatting. Although this chart is interesting, you feel that the data is difficult to read.

7 **Select several other custom chart types to see how the data appears in the Sample area.**

Select Columns with Depth.

Your screen should be similar to Figure 2.29

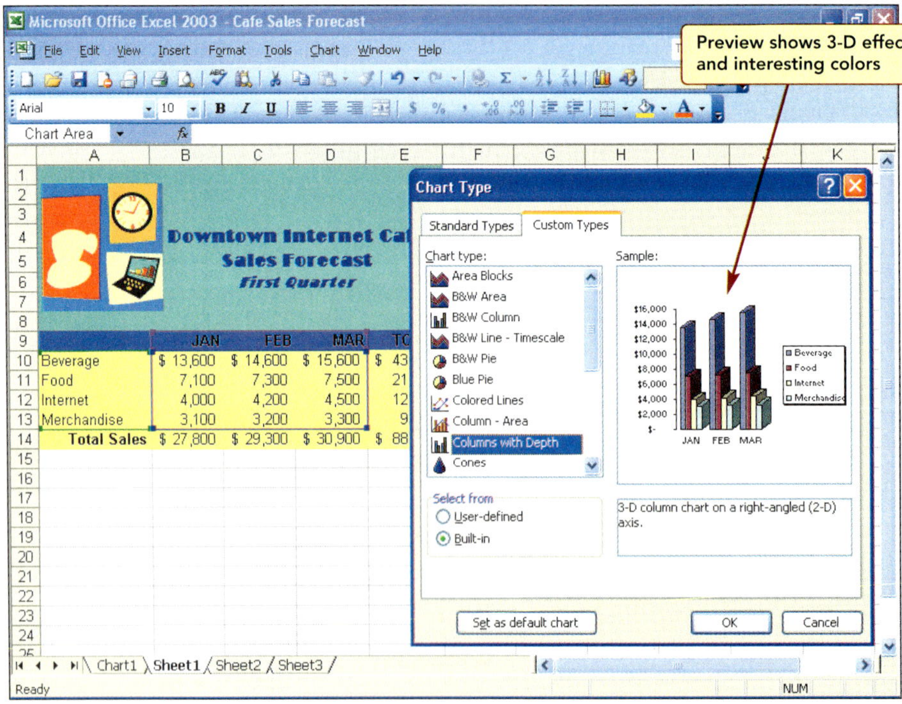

Figure 2.29

This chart shows the sales for each category for each month with more interesting colors and three-dimensional depth.

8 Click **OK**.

Your screen should be similar to Figure 2.30

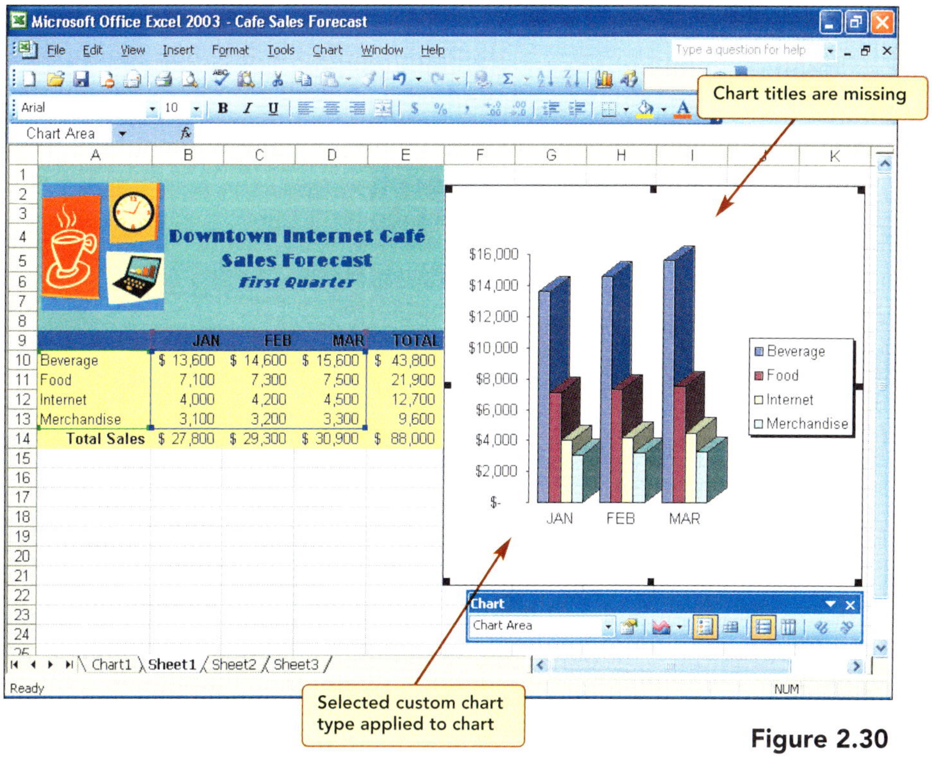

Figure 2.30

In a column chart that includes a 3-D visual effect, the front part of the column identifies the plotted value.

Adding Chart Titles

Unfortunately, when applying a custom chart type, the chart titles are deleted and you need to add them again.

1 Choose **Chart/Chart Options.**

In the Titles tab, enter the following titles:

Title	**Entry**
Chart title	**Sales Forecast**
Category	**Months**
Value (Z) axis	**Sales**

Your screen should be similar to Figure 2.31

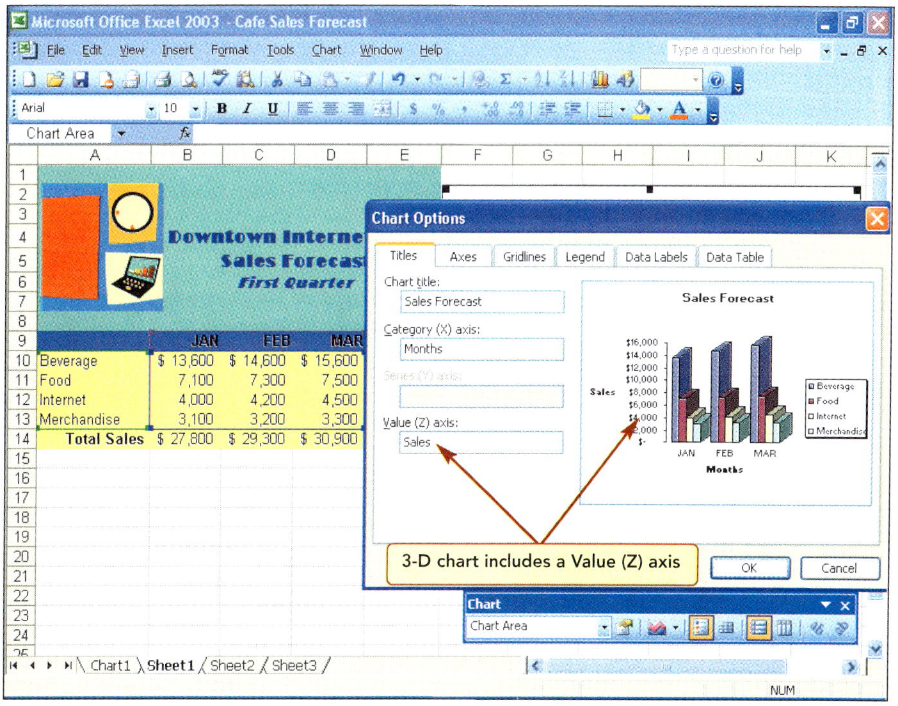

Figure 2.31

Notice that this time instead of entering the value-axis data in the Y axis, you entered it in the Z axis. This is because the Y axis is used as a series axis on a three-dimensional chart. This three-dimensional chart has only one series of data so the Y axis is not used.

Moving the Legend

While looking at the preview chart, you decide to move the legend below the X axis.

1
- **Open the Legend tab.**
- **Select Bottom.**
- **Click OK.**

Your screen should be similar to Figure 2.32

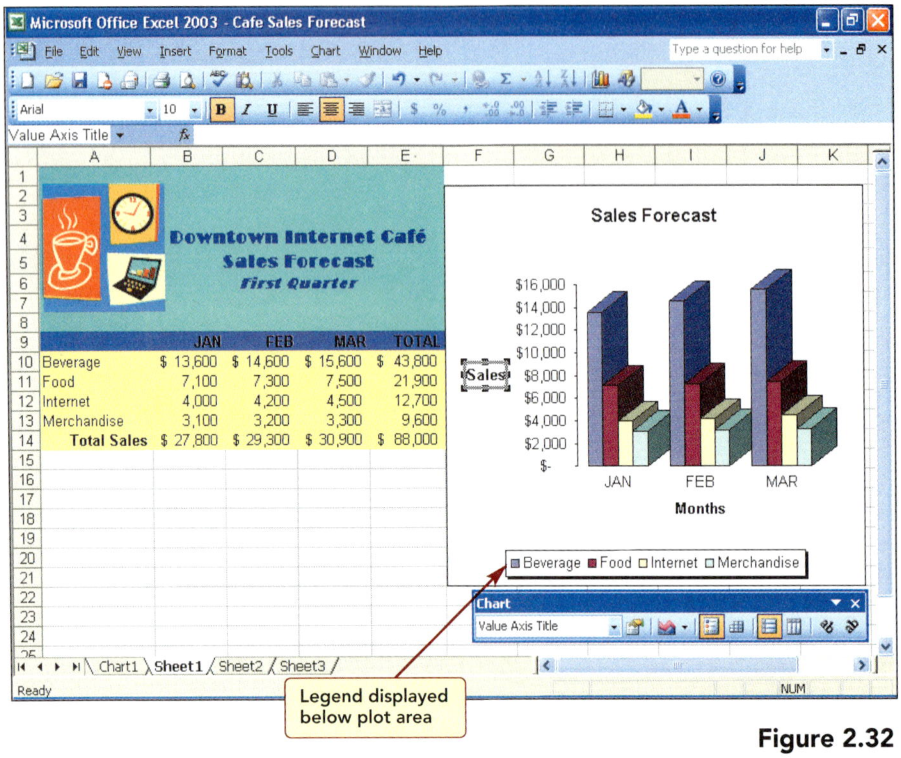

Figure 2.32

The legend is centered below the plot area of the chart and resized to fit the space.

Formatting Chart Elements

Next, you want to improve the appearance of the chart by applying formatting to the different chart parts. All the different parts of a chart are separate objects. Because a chart consists of many separate objects, it is a group.

Concept 6

Group

6 A **group** is two or more objects that behave as a single object when moved or sized. A chart consists of many separate objects. For example, the chart title is a single object within the chart object. Some of the objects in a chart are also groups that consist of other objects. For example, the legend is a group object consisting of separate items, each identifying a different data series.

Other objects in a chart are the axis lines, a data series, a data marker, the entire plot area, or the entire chart.

The first formatting change you want to make is to improve the appearance of the chart title. An entire group or each object in a group can be individually selected and then formatted or edited. By selecting the entire group, you can format all objects within the group at once. Alternatively, you can select an object within a group and format it individually.

1 Click on the chart title to select it.

Your screen should be similar to Figure 2.33

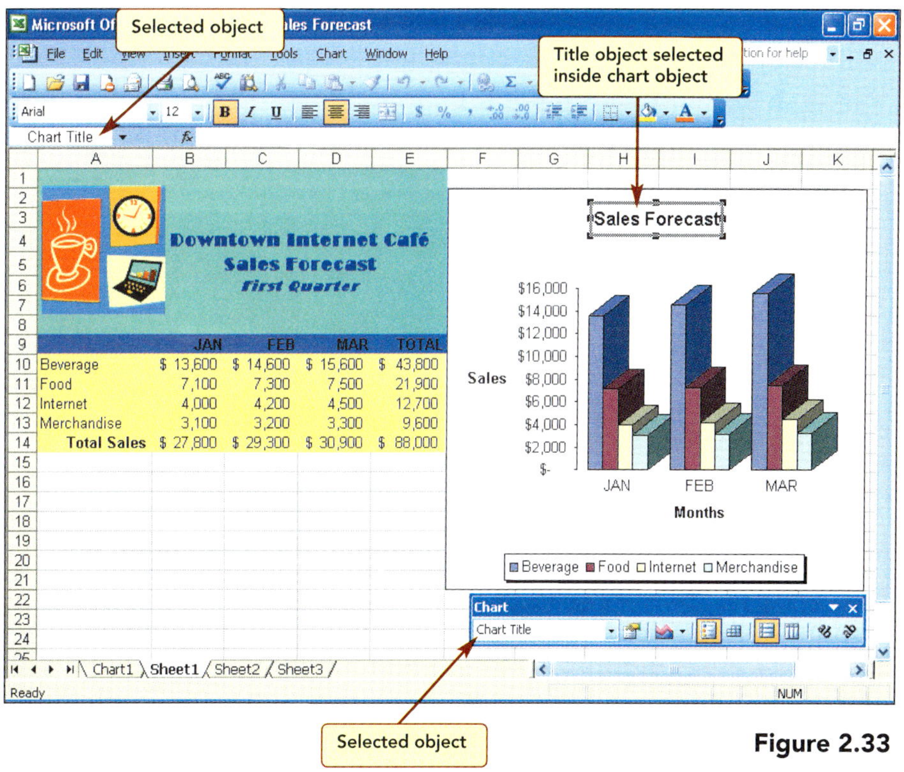

Figure 2.33

The title object is surrounded by a dotted border, indicating that it is a selected object and that the text inside it can be modified. In addition, the Name box and Chart Objects button display "Chart Title" as the selected chart object.

As different objects in the chart are selected, the commands on the Format menu change to commands that can be used on the selected object. In addition, the Format Object button on the Chart toolbar can be used to format the selected object.

2 Click Format Chart Title.

Another Method

The menu equivalent is Format/Selected Chart Title and the shortcut is Ctrl + 1.

- Open the Font tab.
- Scroll the Font list and select Tahoma.
- Scroll the Size list and select 14.
- Open the Color list and select blue.
- Click OK.

Your screen should be similar to Figure 2.34

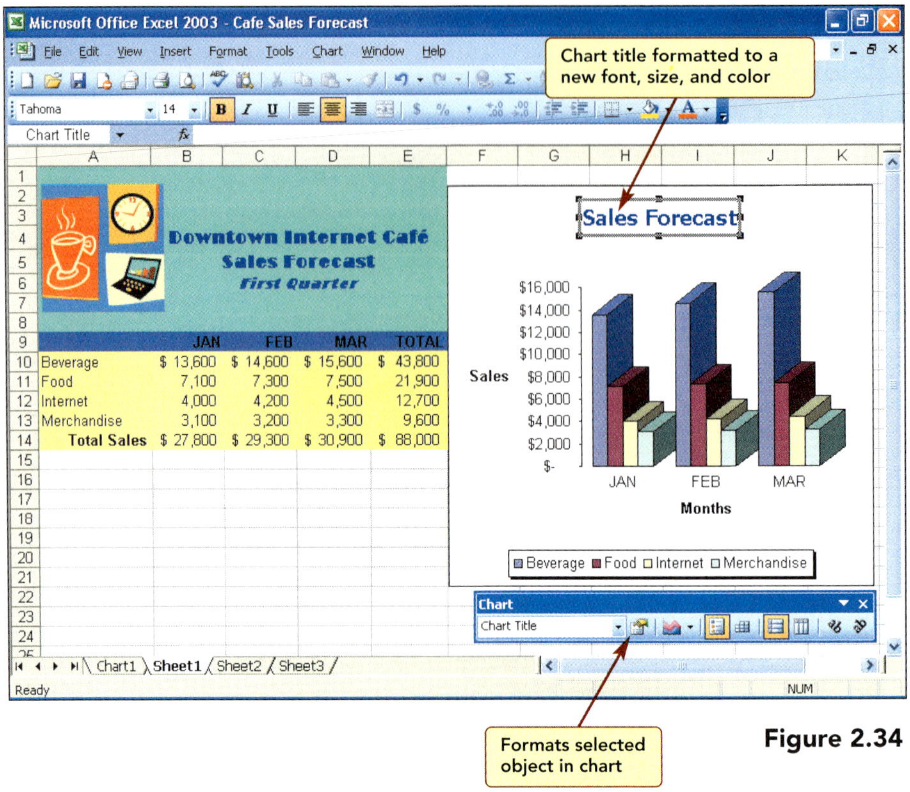

Figure 2.34

Next, you want to change the color of the axis titles. A quicker way to make many formatting changes is to use the Formatting toolbar buttons.

3 Click the category-axis title Months.

- Open the Font Color palette and change the color to blue.
- Change the color of the Sales title to blue in the same manner.
- Click outside the title to deselect it.

Your screen should be similar to Figure 2.35

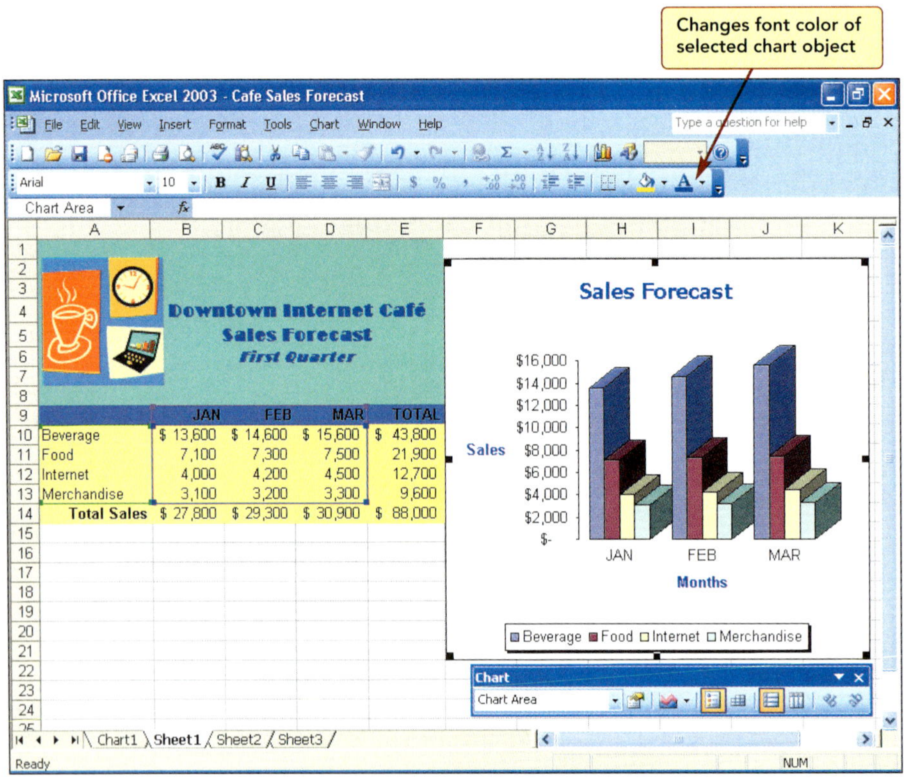

Figure 2.35

Changing Title Orientation

You also want to change the orientation of the Sales title along the axis so that it is parallel with the axis line. To do this, you will rotate the label 90 degrees. You can quickly select a chart object and open the related Format dialog box by double-clicking the object.

1 **Double-click the Sales title to open the Format Axis Title dialog box.**

Open the Alignment tab.

Drag the Orientation indicator line upward to rotate the text 90 degrees.

Your screen should be similar to Figure 2.36

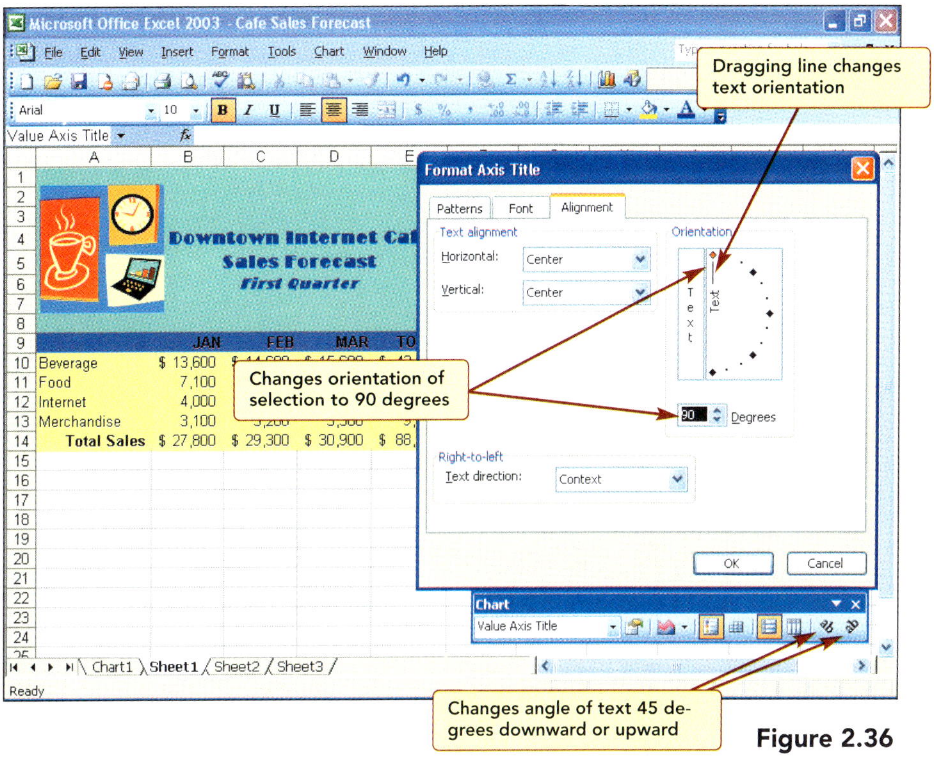

Figure 2.36

You could also enter a positive number in the Degrees box to rotate the selection from lower left to upper right or a negative number to rotate text in the opposite direction. Alternatively, you can use the Degrees scroll buttons to increase and decrease the degrees.

2 **Click** OK.

Your screen should be similar to Figure 2.37

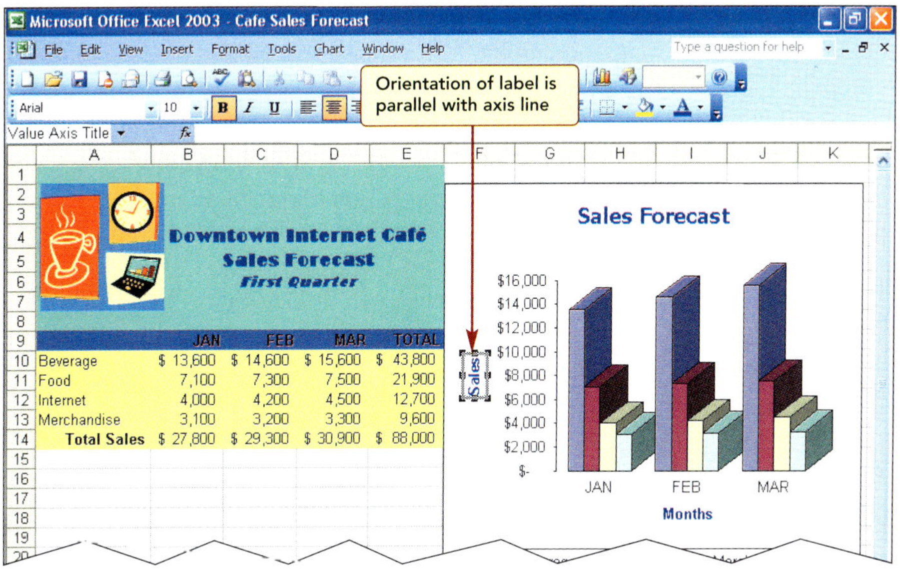

Figure 2.37

The Sales label is now displayed parallel with the Y-axis line.

Finally, you want to add a second line to the chart title. You want the subtitle to be in a smaller font size and italicized. You can select individual sections of text in an object and apply formatting to them just as you would format any other text entry.

3

- **Select the chart title.**
- **Click at the end of the title to place the insertion point.**
- **Press ←Enter.**
- **Type First Quarter.**
- **Drag to select the words "First Quarter."**
- **Click *I* Italic.**
- **Change the font size to 12.**
- **Click in the title to deselect it.**
- **Save the workbook.**

Your screen should be similar to Figure 2.38

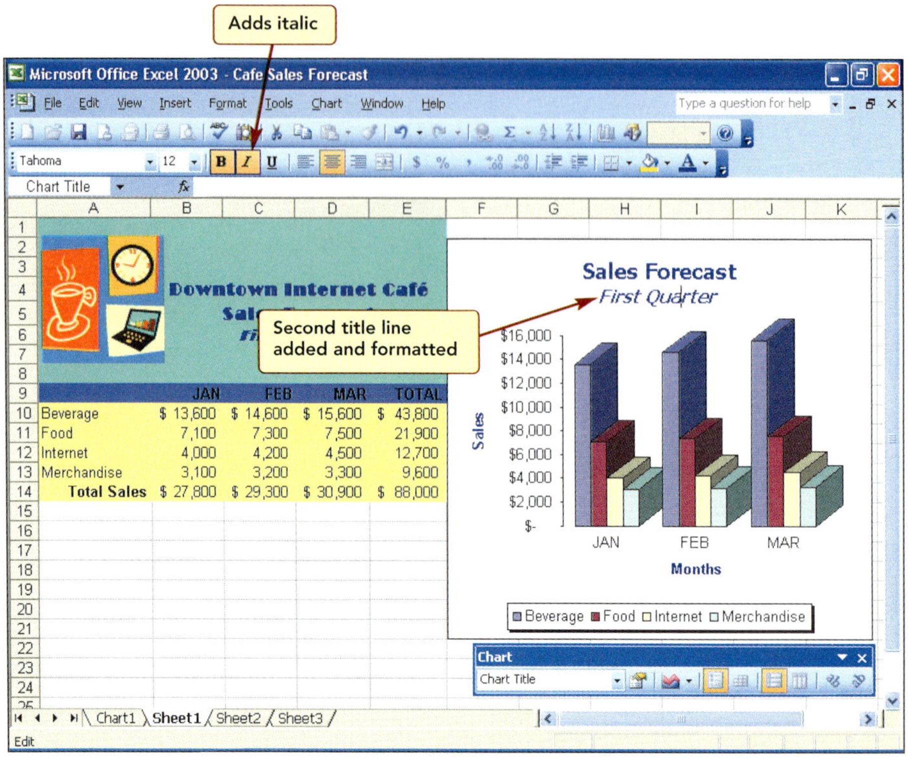

Figure 2.38

Changing Worksheet Data

So far, the charts you have created reflect your original sales estimates for the quarter. You are planning to heavily promote the Internet aspect of the Cafe, and anticipate that Internet usage will increase dramatically in February and March and then level off in the following months. You also expect to see an increase in the food and beverage sales. You want to change the worksheet to reflect these increases.

1 **Change the February Internet sales value to 6000.**

Change the March Internet sales value to 12000.

Increase the February and March Beverage sales by 20%.

Increase the February and March Food sales by 15%.

Having Trouble?

Change the entry to a formula and multiply the existing value by 1.20 or 1.15.

Your screen should be similar to Figure 2.39

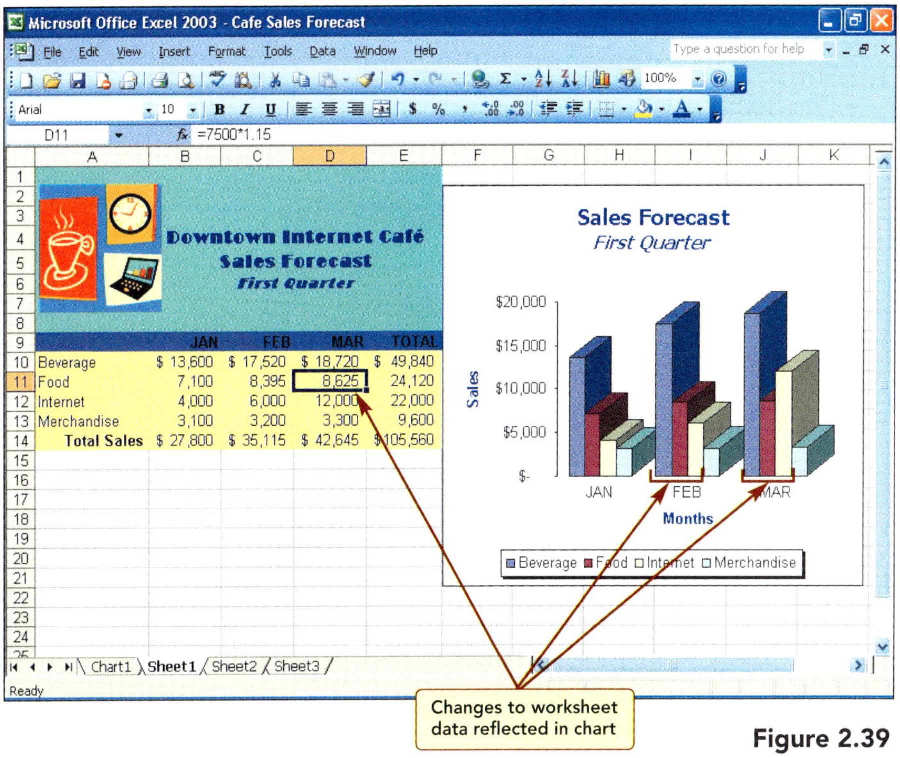

Figure 2.39

The worksheet has been recalculated, and the chart columns that reference those worksheet cells have been redrawn to reflect the change in the sales data. Because the chart is linked to the source data, changes to the source data are automatically reflected in the chart.

Adding Data Labels

Finally, to make sure that Evan sees your projected increase in Internet sales, you will include data labels containing the actual numbers plotted for the Internet sales on the column chart.

Concept 7

Data Labels

7 **Data labels** provide additional information about a data marker. They can consist of the value of the marker, the name of the data series or category, a percent value, or a bubble size. The different types of data labels that are available depend on the type of chart and the data that is plotted.

Value data labels are helpful when the values are large and you want to know the exact value for one data series. Data labels that display a name are helpful when the size of the chart is large and when the data point does not clearly identify the value. The percent data label is used when you want to display the percent of each series on charts that show parts of the whole. Bubble size is used on bubble charts to help the reader quickly see how the different bubbles vary in size.

1 Click on any Internet data column series to select the Internet data series.

Having Trouble?

The Screen tip will display "Series Internet" Point.

Another Method

Choose "Series Internet" from the Chart Objects list.

- Click Format Data Series.
- Open the Data Labels tab.

Another Method

The menu equivalent is Format/Selected Data Series/Data Labels.

Your screen should be similar to Figure 2.40

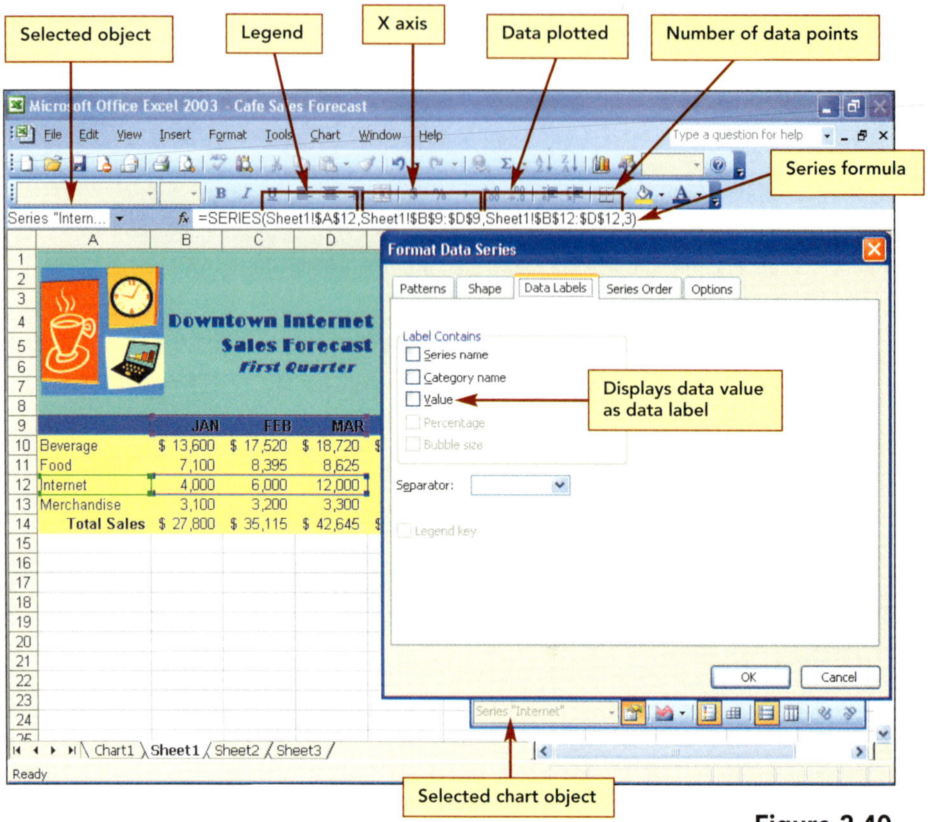

Figure 2.40

Notice that the formula bar displays a series formula. A **series formula** links the chart object to the source worksheet, in this case, Sheet1. The formula contains four arguments: a reference to the cell that includes the data series name (used in the legend), references to the cells that contain the categories (X-axis numbers), references to the numbers plotted, and an integer that specifies the number of data series plotted.

You want to display the Internet values as the data labels for the data series.

2 **Select Value.**

- **Click OK.**
- **Click on any data label to select the series.**
- **Click Angle Counterclockwise (on the Chart toolbar).**
- **Click B Bold.**
- **Change the font color of the data labels to blue.**
- **Select each data label and drag it to position the labels as in Figure 2.41.**
- **Save the workbook.**

Your screen should be similar to Figure 2.41

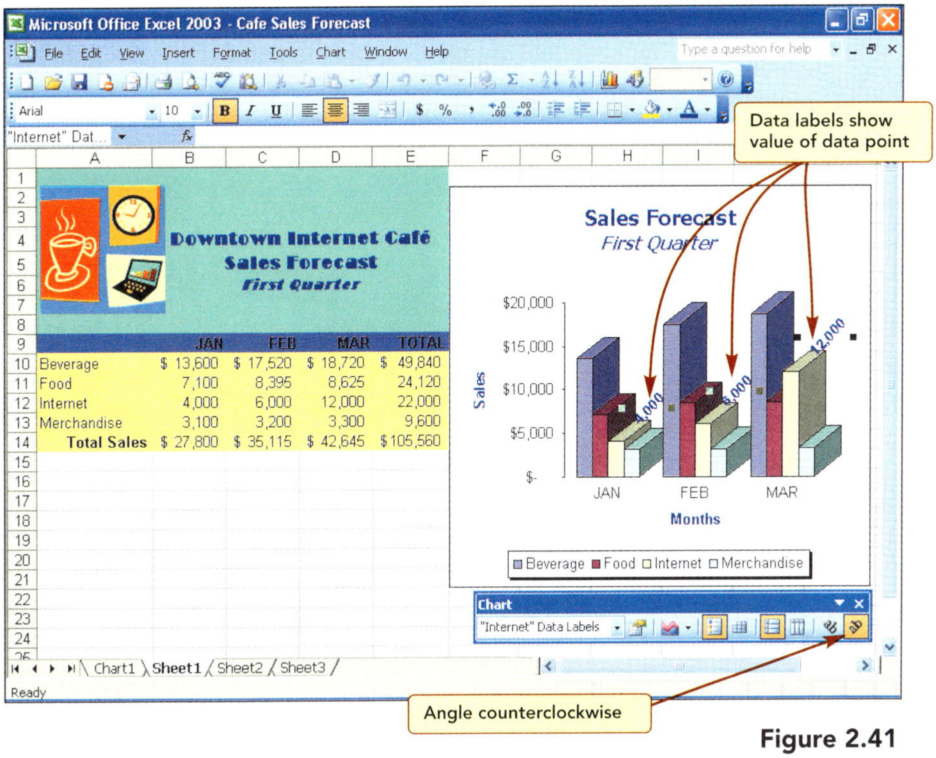

Figure 2.41

Additional Information

Use Angle Clockwise to rotate labels 45 degrees clockwise. The voice commands are "Angle clockwise" or "Angle counterclockwise."

Data labels containing the actual values for total sales are displayed above the Internet sales columns on the chart. Using Angle Counterclockwise quickly changed the angle of a label to 45 degrees in a counterclockwise direction.

Creating and Formatting a Pie Chart

The last chart you will make will use the Total worksheet data in column E. You want to see what proportion each type of sales is of total sales for the quarter. The best chart for this purpose is a pie chart.

A pie chart compares parts to the whole in a similar manner to a stacked-column chart. However pie charts have no axes. Instead, the worksheet data that is charted is displayed as slices in a circle or pie. Each slice is displayed as a percentage of the total.

Selecting the Pie Chart Data

The use of X (category) and data series settings in a pie chart is different from their use in a column or line chart. The X series labels the slices of the pie rather than the X axis. The data series is used to create the slices in the pie. Only one data series can be specified in a pie chart.

The row labels in column A will label the slices, and the total values in column E will be used as the data series.

In addition to creating a chart using the Wizard, you can create a chart by selecting the chart type from the Chart Type toolbar button after the data series has been selected.

Additional Information

You can also create a chart using the default chart type (column) in a new chart sheet by selecting the data range and pressing F11.

1 Select A10:A13 and E10:E13.

Having Trouble?

Hold down Ctrl while selecting nonadjacent ranges.

- Display the Chart toolbar.
- Open the Chart Type drop-down menu and choose 3-D Pie Chart.

Your screen should be similar to Figure 2.42

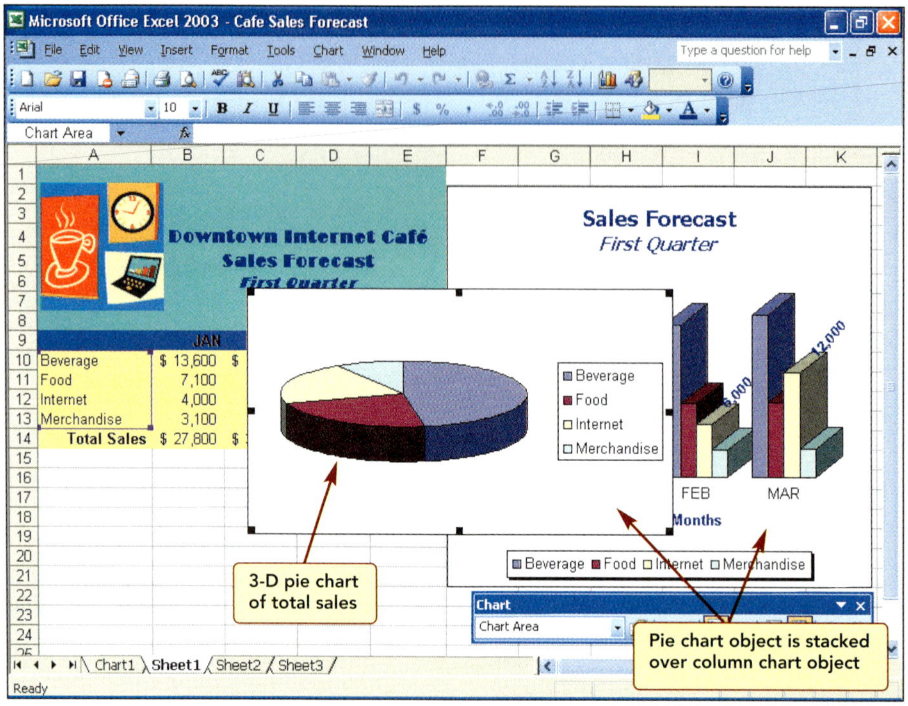

Figure 2.42

A three-dimensional pie chart is drawn in the worksheet. Each value in the data series is displayed as a slice of the pie chart. The size of the slice represents the proportion of total sales that each sales category represents.

As objects are added to the worksheet, they automatically **stack** in individual layers. The stacking order is apparent when objects overlap. Stacking allows you to create different effects by overlapping objects. Because you can rearrange the stacking order, you do not have to add or create the objects in the order in which you want them to appear.

2 Move the column chart to top-align with cell A17 below the worksheet data.

Additional Information

Hold down Alt while moving to snap the chart to the cells.

- Move and size the pie chart to be displayed over cells F1 through K14.

Your screen should be similar to Figure 2.43

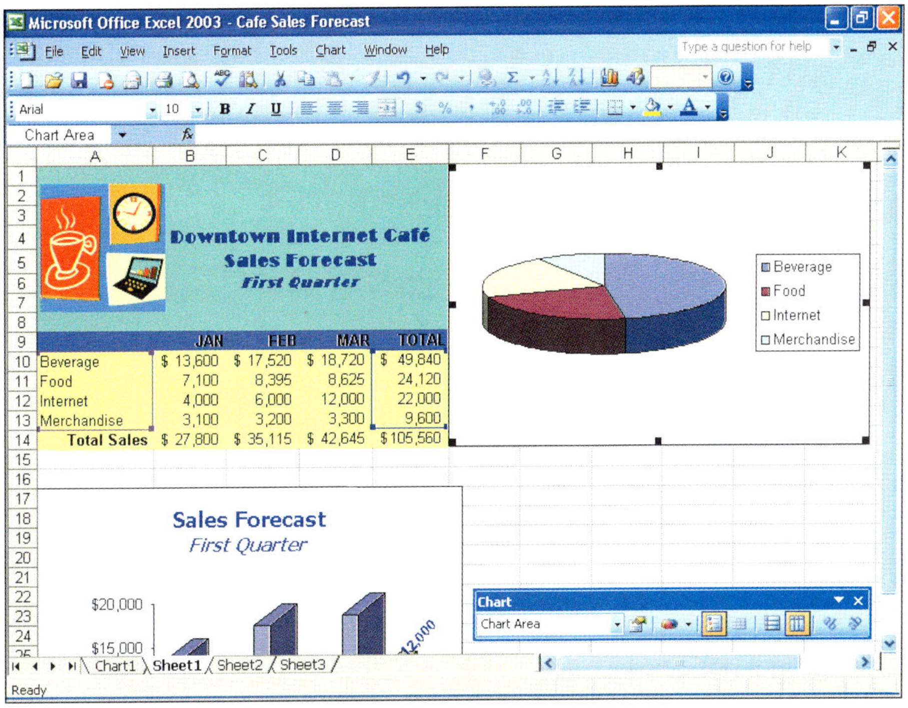

Figure 2.43

Formatting the Pie Chart

To clarify the meaning of the chart, you need to add a chart title. In addition, you want to turn off the legend and display data labels to label the slices of the pie.

1 Choose Chart/Chart Options.

- Open the Titles tab.
- In the Chart Title text box, type **Total Sales by Category**.
- Open the Legend tab and clear the Show Legend option.

Another Method

You can also click Legend to turn on/off the display of the legend. The voice command is "Legend."

- Open the Data Labels tab and select the Category name and Percentage options.
- Click OK.

Your screen should be similar to Figure 2.44

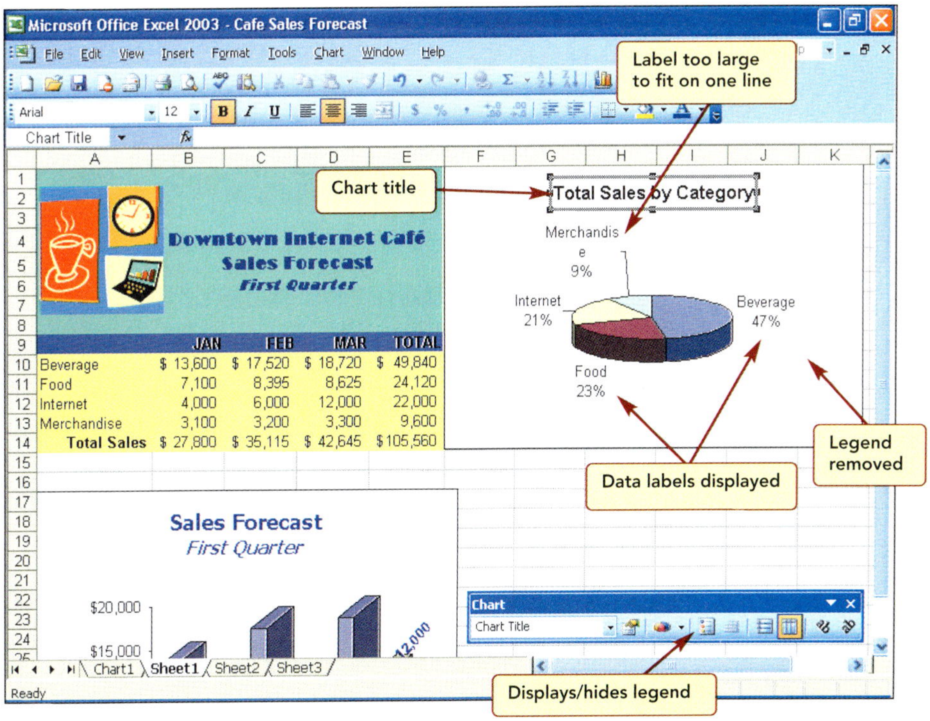

Figure 2.44

The pie chart is redrawn to show the data labels and percents. The data label size is based on the size of the chart and the text is appropriately sized. Because the default size of data labels is a little too large, the entire Merchandise label does not appear on one line. To fix this, you will change the font of the data label text. You also want to enhance the appearance of the data labels and title.

2 Add the subtitle First Quarter.

- Change both title lines to Tahoma, 14 pt and red.
- Select the data labels.
- Change the font to Arial Narrow and blue.

Your screen should be similar to Figure 2.45

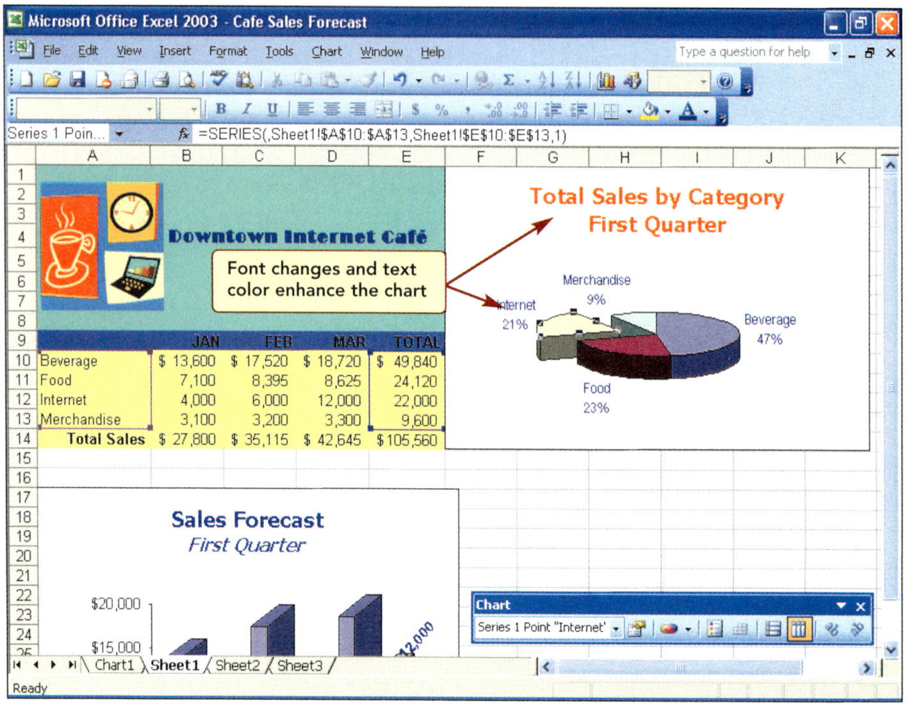

Figure 2.45

Exploding and Rotating the Pie

Next, you want to separate slightly or **explode** the Internet slice of the pie to emphasize the data in that category. The Internet slice is an object within the pie chart group. To select an object within a group, first select the group and then select the object within the group. Sizing handles surround the selected object.

1

- Click on the pie chart to select the group.
- Click on the Internet slice.
- Drag the selected slice away from the pie.

Your screen should be similar to Figure 2.46

Additional Information

If all slices on the pie are selected, dragging one slice explodes all slices at the same time.

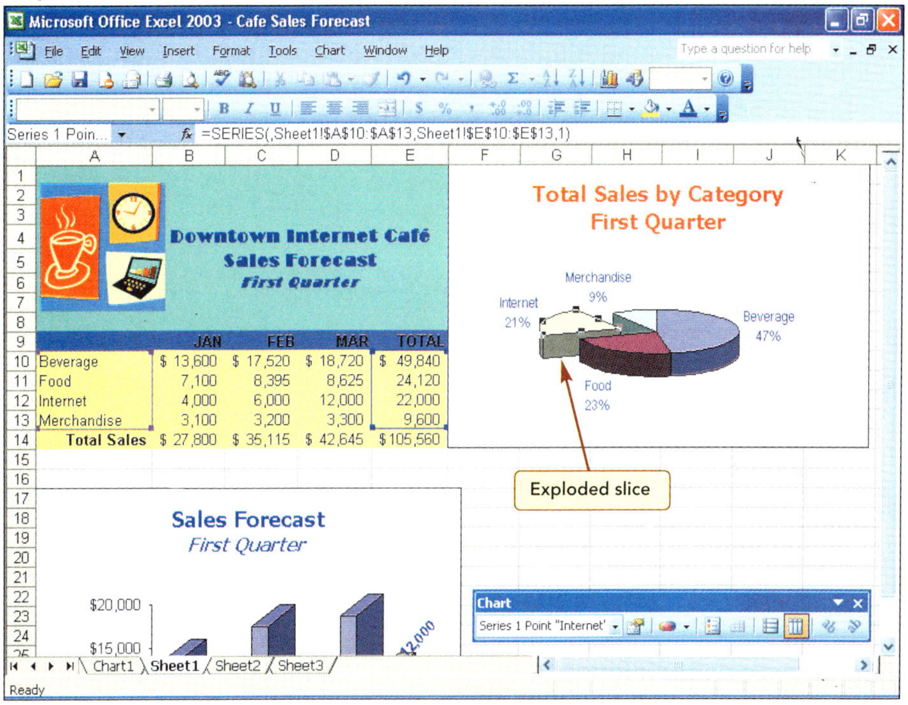

Figure 2.46

The slice is separated from the rest of the pie chart. You also want to change the position of the Internet slice so that it is toward the front of the pie. When a pie chart is created, the first data point is placed to the right of the middle at the top of the chart. The rest of the data points are placed in order to the right until the circle is complete. To change the order in which the slices are displayed, you can rotate the pie chart.

2

- Double-click the Internet data series slice.
- Open the Options tab.
- Change the Angle of first slice setting to 180 degrees.
- Click OK.

Your screen should be similar to Figure 2.47

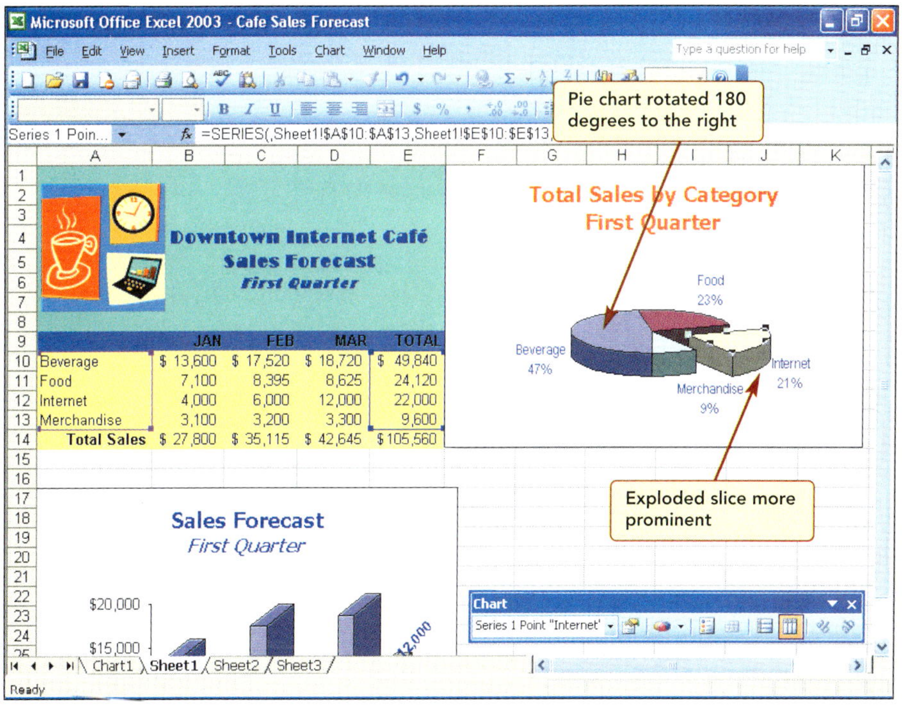

Figure 2.47

The entire pie chart has rotated 180 degrees to the right and now the Internet data slice appears toward the front of the chart.

Applying Patterns and Color

The last change you would like to make is to add patterns to the pie chart data points. As you have seen, when Excel creates a chart each data series (or data point in the case of a pie chart) is automatically displayed in a different color. Although the data series are easy to distinguish from one another onscreen, if you do not have a color printer the colors are printed as shades of gray and may be difficult to distinguish. To make the data series more distinguishable on a black-and-white printer, you can apply a different pattern to each data series object.

1 **Double-click the Beverage data series slice.**

Open the Patterns tab.

Your screen should be similar to Figure 2.48

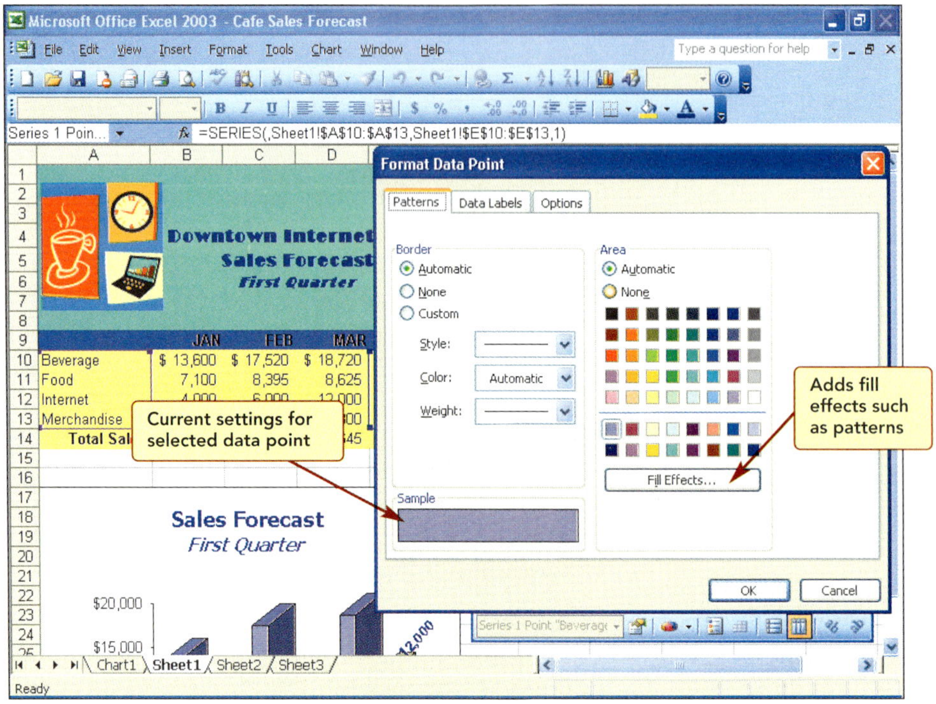

Figure 2.48

The options available in the Patterns tab vary depending upon the type of data point that is selected. In this case, because the selected data point is a pie slice, the options let you change the border and the background area. The current setting for the selcted data point is displayed in the sample area. This consists of a black border with a fill color of periwinkle blue. You will add a pattern.

2 **Click** Fill Effects... **.**

- **Open the Pattern tab.**

Your screen should be similar to Figure 2.49

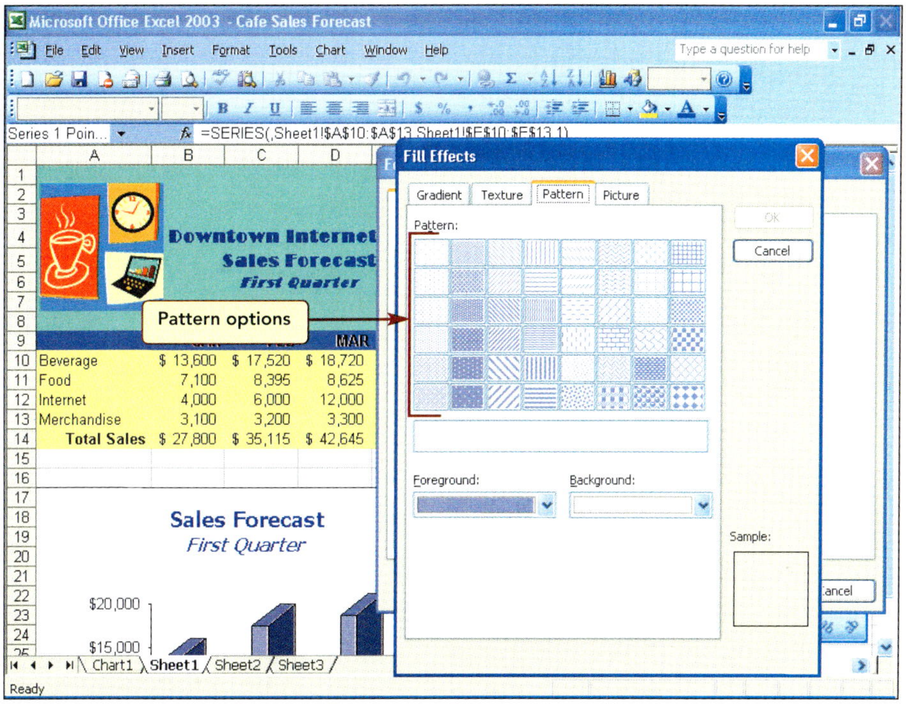

Figure 2.49

From the Fill Effects dialog box, you can change options for gradients, textures, patterns, and pictures used in formatting the selected object. You will add a pattern to the existing fill.

3 **From the Pattern palette, select the Wide upward diagonal pattern.**

Additional Information

The name of the selected pattern appears in the text box below the Pattern options box.

- **Click** OK **(twice) to close both dialog boxes.**

Your screen should be similar to Figure 2.50

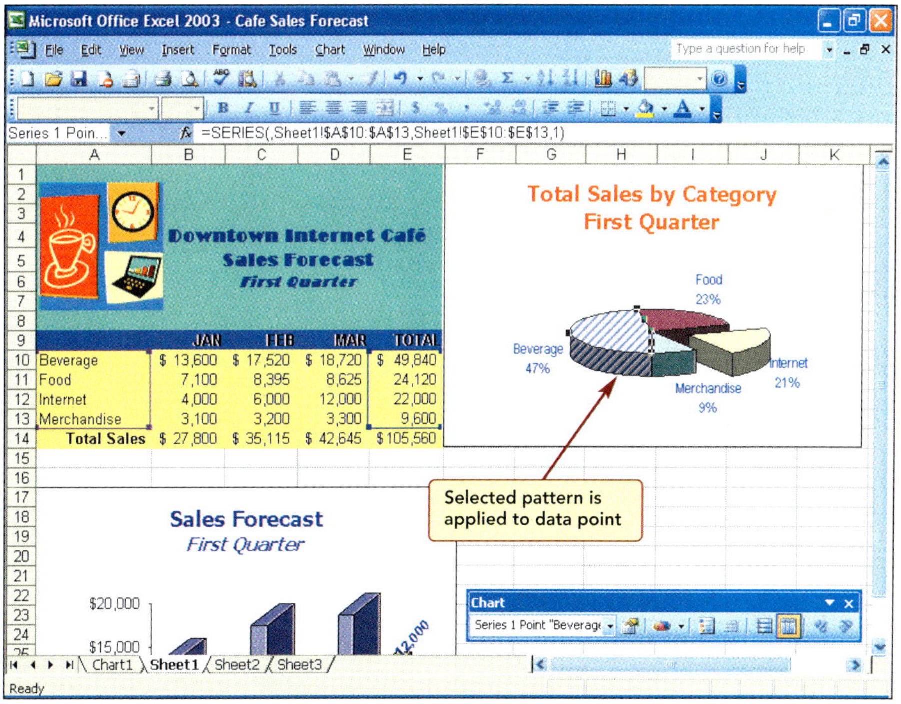

Figure 2.50

The pattern is applied to the selected data point. Next, you will add a pattern to the Internet data series slice.

4 Double-click the Internet data series slice.

- Click Fill Effects... .
- Open the Pattern tab.

Your screen should be similar to Figure 2.51

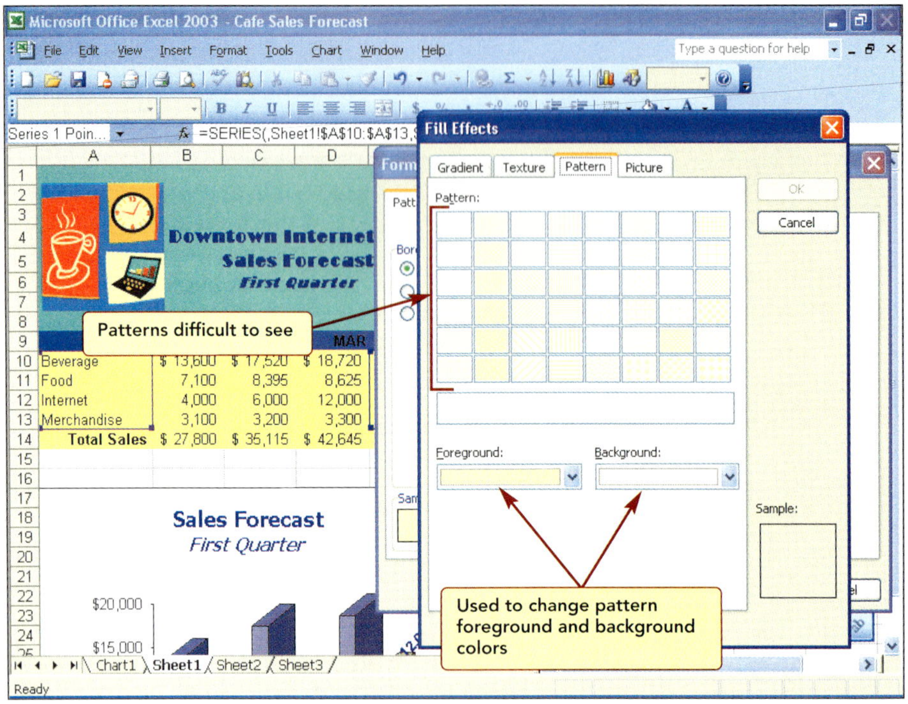

Figure 2.51

Because yellow is a light color, it is difficult to see the patterns in the Fill Effects dialog box. A pattern consists of a foreground color and a background color. The default foreground color is the same as the fill color and the background color is white. To increase the contrast, you can change the color selection of either.

5 From the Foreground color drop-down list, select the red color.

- Select the Outlined diamond pattern.
- Click OK (twice).

Your screen should be similar to Figure 2.52

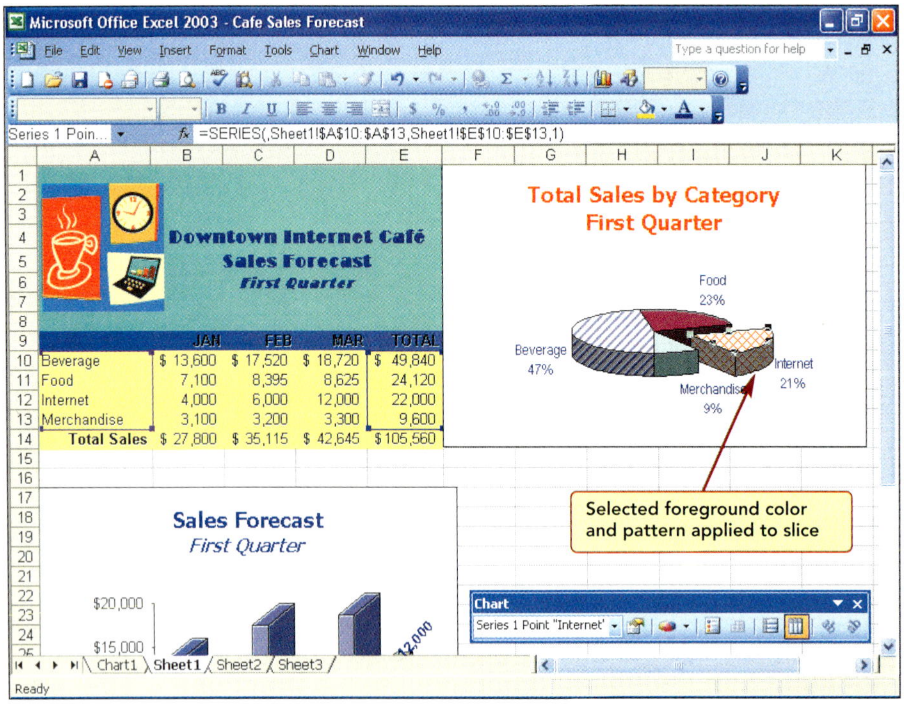

Figure 2.52

You will leave the other two data points without patterns. Now that you have finished working on the pie chart, you will move it below the column chart.

6

- **Select the pie chart and move it below the column chart to top-align with cell A39.**
- **Deselect the chart.**
- **Close the Chart toolbar.**
- **Save the workbook.**

Your screen should be similar to Figure 2.53

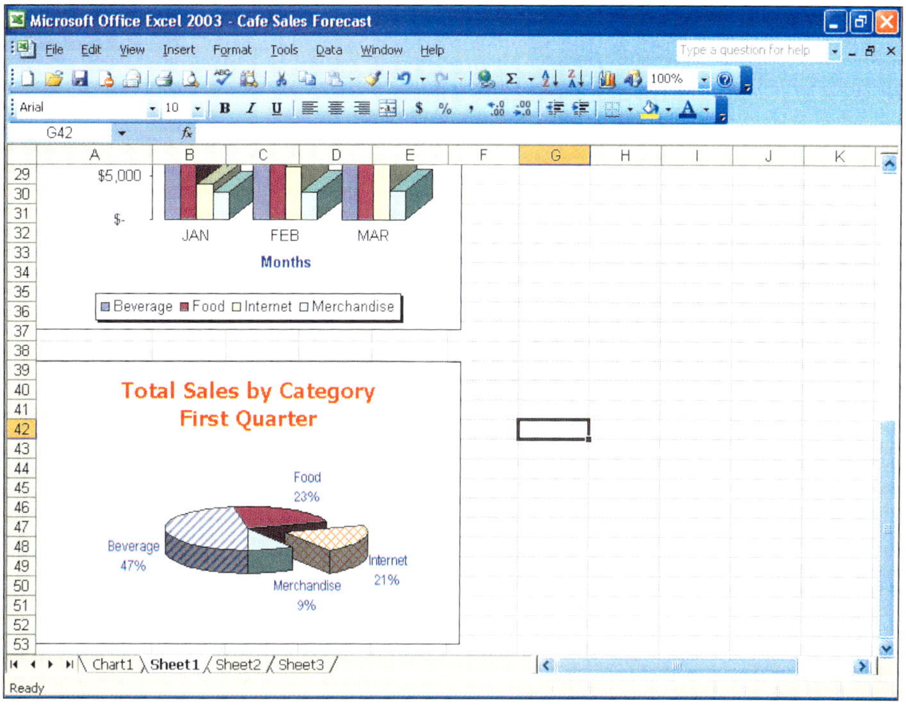

Figure 2.53

Setting File Properties

You have finished working on the worksheet for now and want to save the changes you have made to the file. Along with the content of the file, each file can include additional **file properties** or settings that are associated with the file. Some of these properties are automatically generated. These include statistics such as the date the file was created and last modified. Others, such as the author of the file, are properties that you can add to the file.

Documenting a Workbook

The information you can associate with the file includes a title, subject, author, keywords, and comments about the workbook file. Additionally, you can specify that a picture of the first page of the file should be saved for previewing in the Open dialog box. This information helps you locate the workbook file you want to use and helps indicate the objectives and use of the workbook. You will look at the file properties and add documentation to identify you as the author and to specify a title for the document.

1 Choose File/Properties.

- Select each tab in the Properties dialog box and look at the recorded information.
- Open the Summary tab.
- Enter the following information in the Summary tab.

Title	Downtown Internet Cafe
Subject	Sales Forecast
Author	your name

Additional Information

The Author text box may be blank or may show your school or some other name. Clear the existing contents first if necessary.

- Select the Save preview picture option.

Additional Information

Saving a preview picture with your file increases the file size.

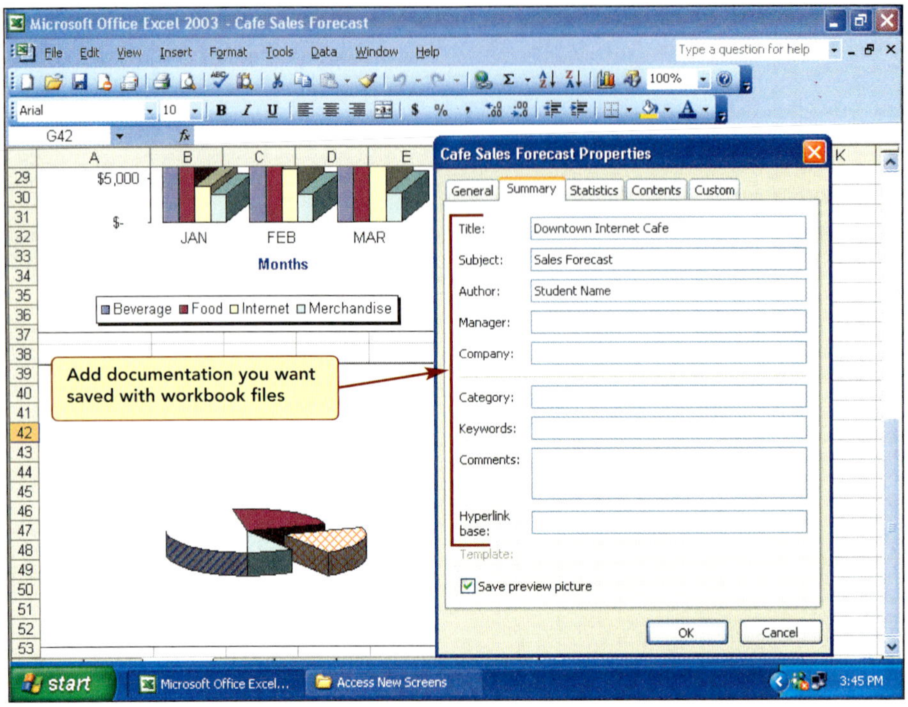

Figure 2.54

Your screen should be similar to Figure 2.54

You have completed adding the properties to the document. Not until the file is saved are the new properties you added saved with the file.

2 Click OK to close the Properties dialog box.

- Save the workbook.

Preparing the Worksheet and Charts for Printing

Now you are ready to preview and print the worksheet and chart sheet. It is very important before printing charts to preview how they will appear when printed. Formats that look good onscreen may not produce good printed results.

Before printing, you can change the layout of the worksheet and charts to improve the appearance of the printed output. The size and alignment of the worksheet can be changed to make it more attractive on the paper. Additionally, you can include information in a header on each page.

Previewing the Entire Workbook

Your workbook file includes a new chart sheet and a worksheet. You will preview the entire workbook. To preview them all at once, you first need to change the print setting to print the entire workbook.

1. **Choose File/Print/Entire workbook.**
   - **If necessary, select the printer you will use from the Name list box.**
   - **Click Preview.**
   - **If necessary, reduce the zoom to see the full page.**

Your screen should be similar to Figure 2.55

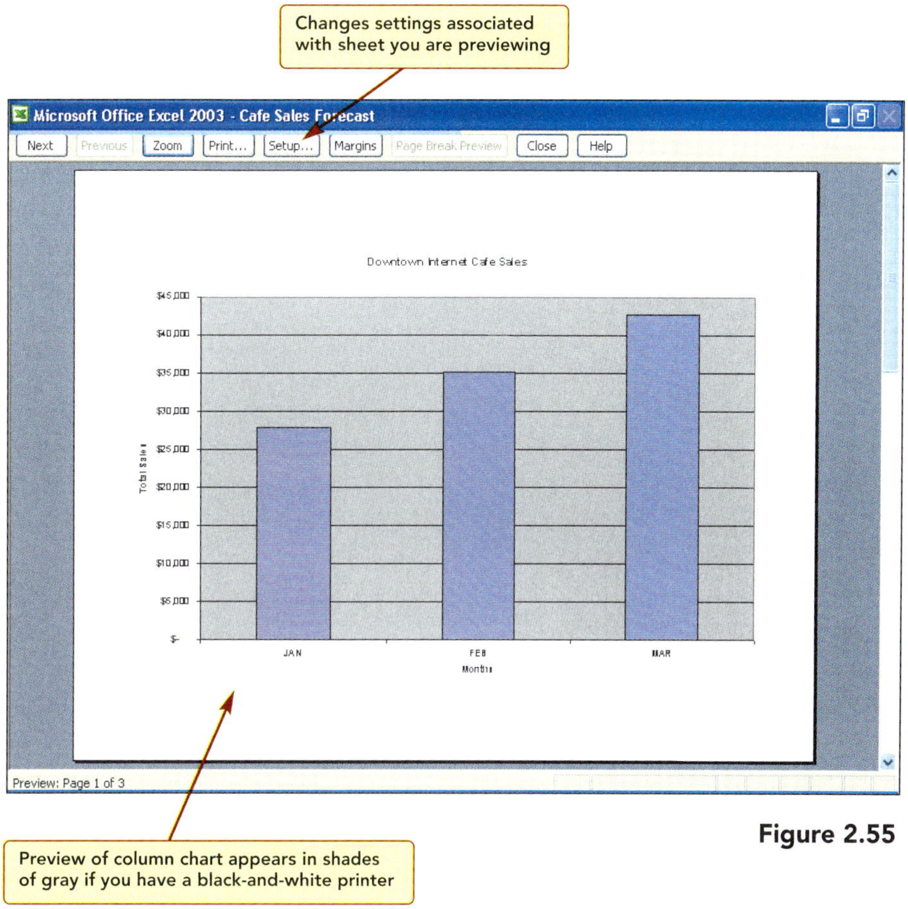

Figure 2.55

Because the column chart is on a separate chart sheet, it is displayed on a page by itself. In addition, if you are not using a color printer, the preview displays the chart colors in shades of gray as they will appear when printed on a black-and-white printer. The Print Preview toolbar buttons are used to access many print and page layout changes while you are previewing a document.

2 Click [Next] to see the worksheet and charts in Sheet1.

Your screen should be similar to Figure 2.56

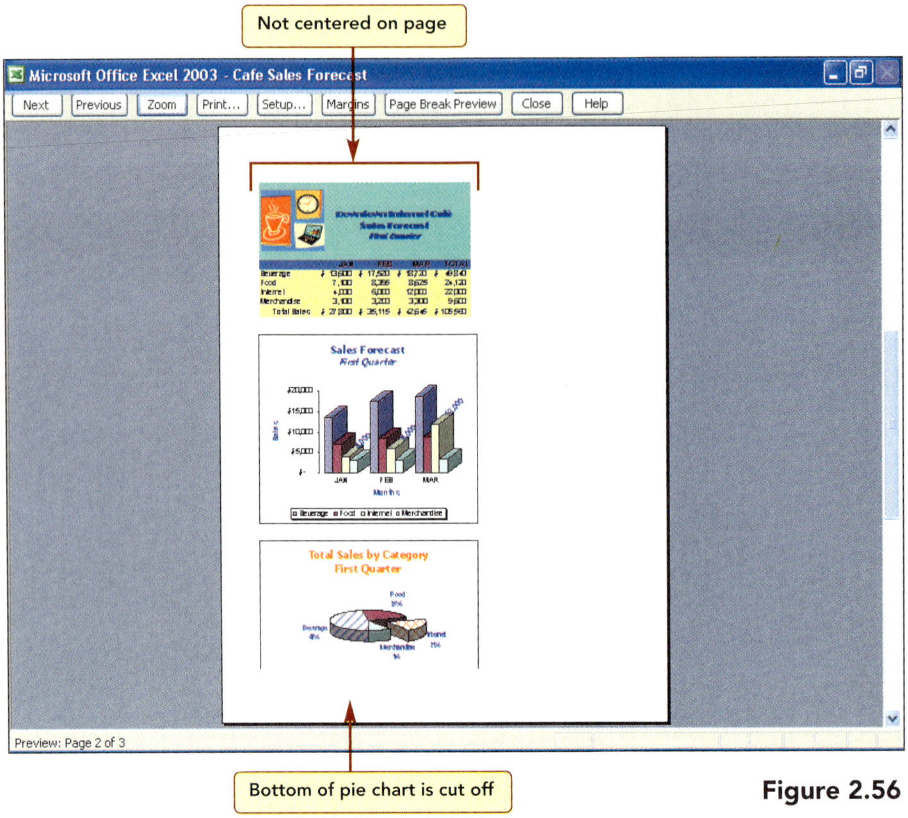

Figure 2.56

> **Having Trouble?**
>
> Depending upon the printer, your chart may not exceed the margins. If this is the case, skip the next section.

You can now see that the bottom of the pie chart is cut off and will not print on the page. You can also see that the worksheet and charts are not centered on the page. You will make several changes to the layout of the page to correct these problems.

Sizing the Worksheet to Fit the Page

First you will reduce the worksheet and chart sizes so they will fit on one page. Although you could resize the charts in the worksheet, a quicker way is to use the scaling feature to reduce or enlarge the worksheet contents by a percentage or to fit it to a specific number of pages. You want to have the program scale the worksheet to fit on one page.

1 Click Setup... .

- If necessary, open the Page tab.
- Select Fit to.
- Click OK .

Another Method

The menu equivalent is File/Page Setup/Page/Fit to.

Your screen should be similar to Figure 2.57

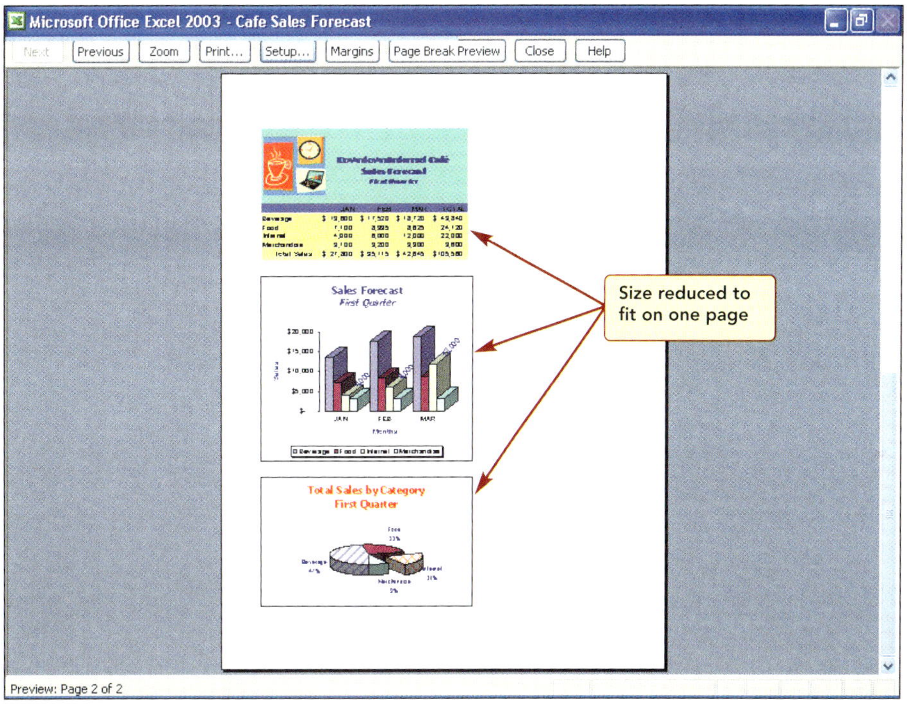

Figure 2.57

The size of the worksheet and charts has been reduced and they now fit on a single page.

Aligning a Sheet on a Page

Additional Information

The margins can be changed individually by adjusting the size of the settings.

You would also like to center the worksheet horizontally on the page. The default worksheet margin settings include 1-inch top and bottom margins and .75-inch right and left margins. The **margins** are the blank space outside the printing area around the edges of the paper. The worksheet contents appear in the printable area inside the margins. You want to center the worksheet data horizontally within the existing margins.

1 Click Setup... .

- Open the Margins tab.
- Select Horizontally.

Your screen should be similar to Figure 2.58

Another Method

The menu equivalent is File/Page Setup/Margins/Horizontally.

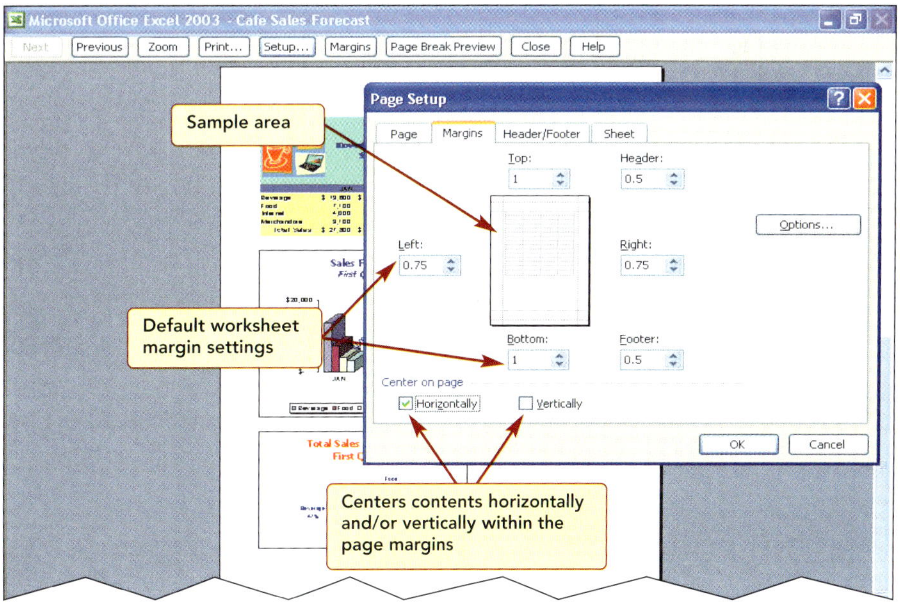

Figure 2.58

The sample area shows the effect of this change on the page layout.

Adding Predefined Headers and Footers

Finally, you want to include your name and the date in a header.

Concept 8

Headers and Footers

8 Headers and footers provide information that typically appears at the top and bottom of each page and commonly include information such as the date and page number. A **header** is a line or several lines of text that appears at the top of a page just above the top margin line. The header usually contains the file name or worksheet title. A **footer** is a line or several lines of text that appears at the bottom of a page just below the bottom margin line. The footer usually contains the page number and perhaps the date. Headers and footers can also contain graphics, such as a company logo. Each worksheet in a workbook can have a different header and footer.

You can select from predefined header and footer text or enter your own custom text. The information contained in the predefined header and footer text is obtained from the file properties associated with the workbook and from the program and system settings.

Header and footer text can be formatted like any other text. In addition, you can control the placement of the header and footer text by specifying where it should appear: left-aligned, centered, or right-aligned in the header or footer space.

You will add a predefined header to the worksheet that displays your name, the date, and page number.

1

- **Open the Header/Footer tab in the Page Setup dialog box.**
- **Open the Header drop-down list box and select the Prepared By [your name] [date], Page 2 option.**

Another Method

The menu equivalent is File/Page Setup/Header/Footer.

Your screen should be similar to Figure 2.59

Additional Information

Predefined footers can be added by selecting the footer option from the Footer drop-down list.

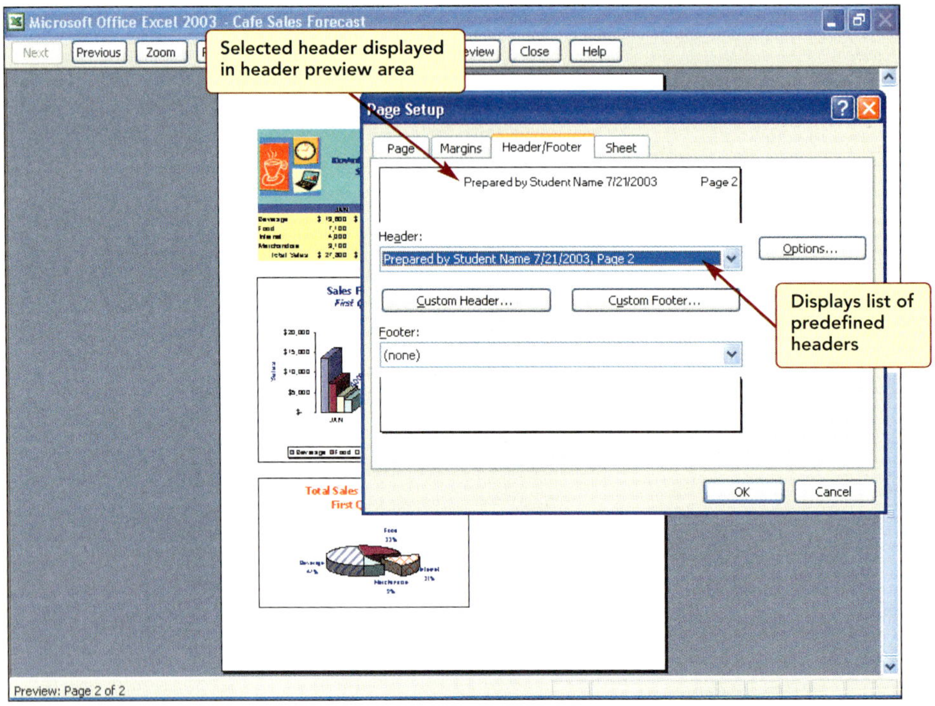

Figure 2.59

The selected header is displayed in the header area of the dialog box. It could then be edited or formatted to meet your needs.

2 Click OK.

Your screen should be similar to Figure 2.60

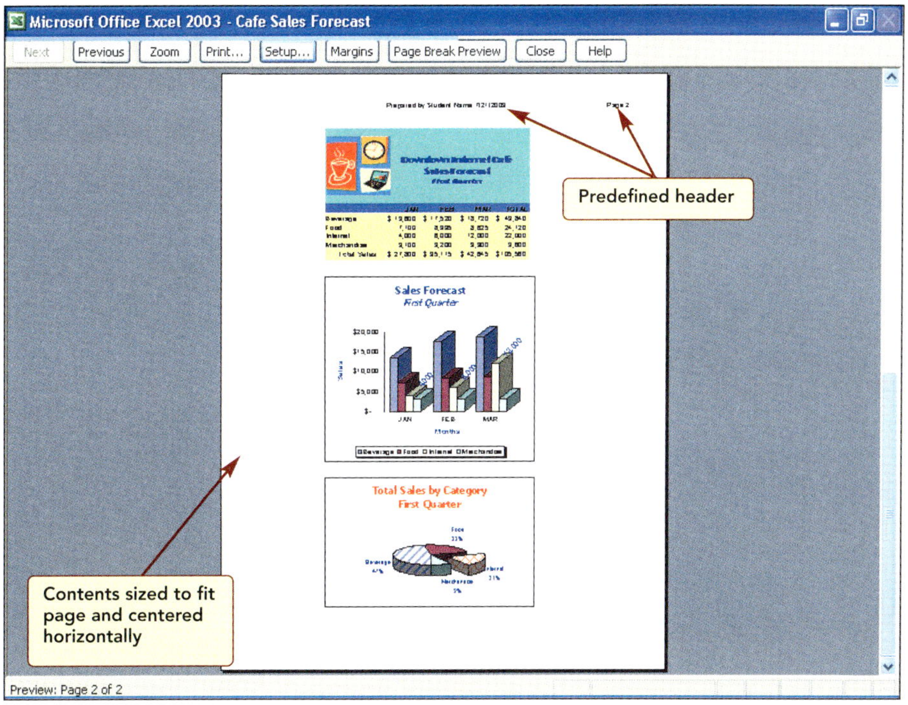

Figure 2.60

The preview window displays the worksheet centered horizontally between the right and left margins. The header you selected is displayed above the top margin line. It now appears the way you want it to look when printed. Next, you will add a footer to the Chart sheet. Each sheet has its own header and footer definitions.

3 Click Previous to see the Chart1 sheet.

Click Setup... .

Add a predefined footer to the chart sheet that displays your name, page number, and date.

Click OK to close the Page Setup dialog box.

Your screen should be similar to Figure 2.61

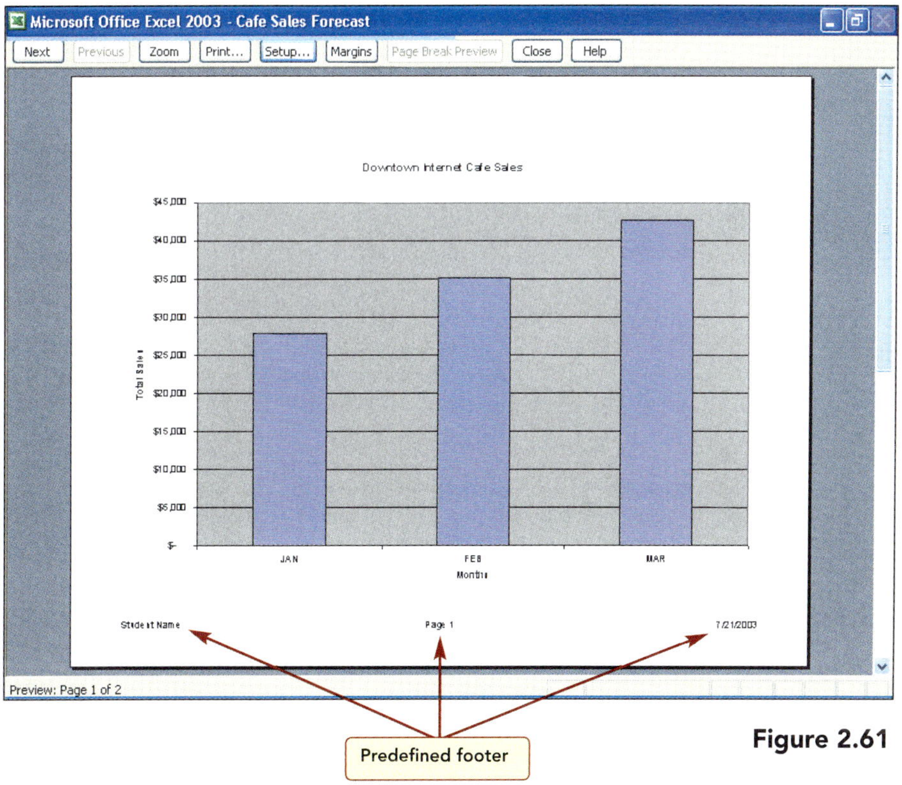

Figure 2.61

Now that the workbook is set up the way you want it for printing, you will print a copy of the worksheet and chart from the print preview window. Because you previewed the workbook from the Print dialog box, the worksheets will print immediately using the specified print settings. Then you will exit the application and save the file at the same time.

4
- **Click Print... .**
- **Move to cell A9 of Sheet1.**
- **If necessary, close the Chart toolbar.**
- **Exit Excel, saving the workbook again.**

The workbook documentation and page layout settings you specified have been saved with the workbook file.

Your printed output should be similar to that shown here.

Focus on Careers

EXPLORE YOUR CAREER OPTIONS

Financial Advisor

With the stock market fluctuations in the last few years, investors are demanding more from their financial advisors than ever before. An advisor needs to promote the company's potential and growth in order to get investors to buy stock. One way to do this is to create a worksheet of vital information and to chart that information so the investor can see why the stock is a good investment. The position of Financial Advisor usually requires a college degree and commands salaries from $24,000 to $50,000, depending on experience.

LAB 2

Charting Worksheet Data

Style (EX2.5)

A style consists of a combination of formats that have been named and that can be quickly applied to a selection.

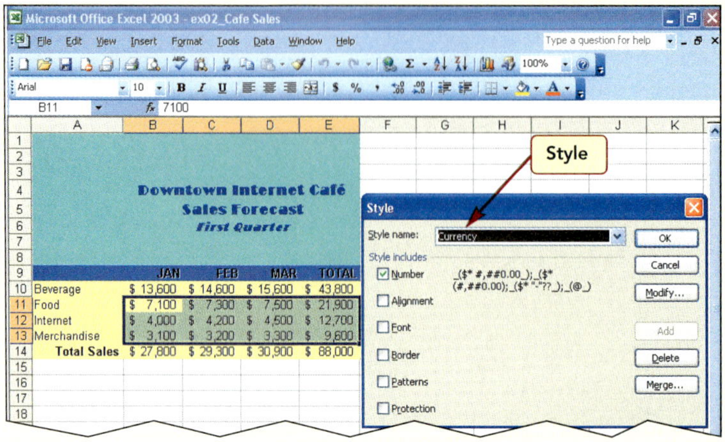

Graphics (EX2.7)

A graphic is a non-text element or object, such as a drawing or picture, that can be added to a document.

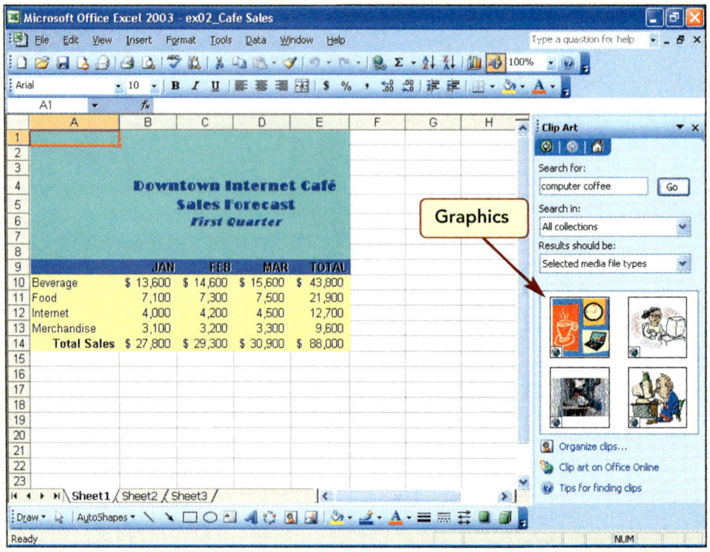

Chart (EX2.14)

A chart is visual representation of data that is used to convey information in an easy-to-understand and attractive manner. Different types of charts are used to represent data in different ways.

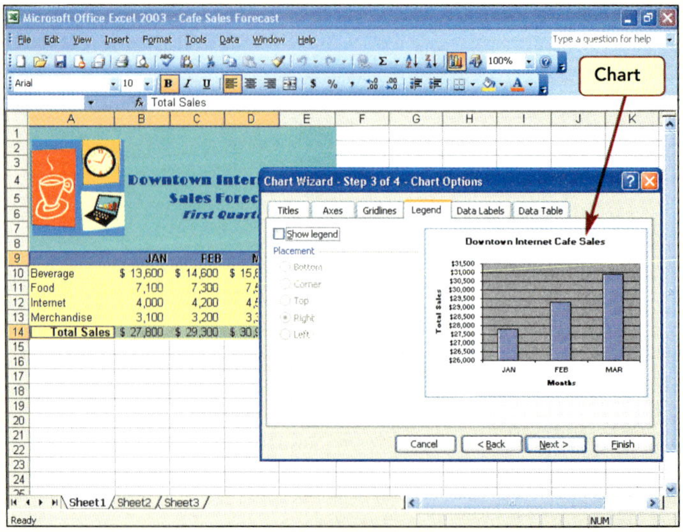

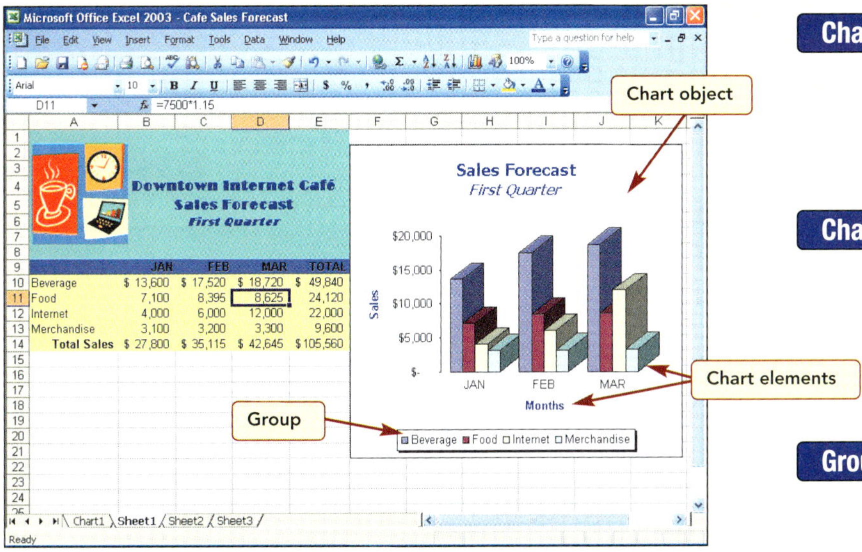

Chart Elements (EX2.15)

A chart consists of a number of elements that are used to graphically display the worksheet data.

Chart Object (EX2.21)

A chart object is a graphic object that is created using charting features included in Excel. A chart object can be inserted into a worksheet or into a special chart sheet.

Group (EX2.35)

A group is two or more objects that behave as a single object when moved or sized.

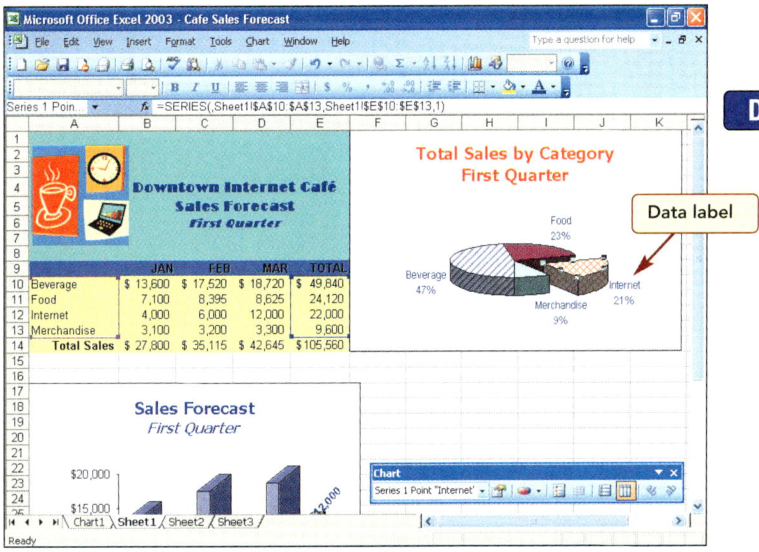

Data Labels (EX2.39)

Data labels provide additional information about a data marker.

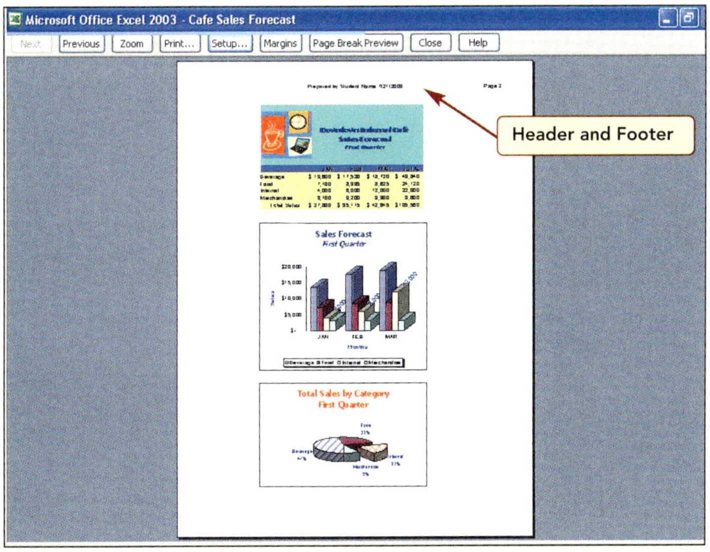

Headers and Footers (EX2.54)

Headers and footers provide information that typically appears at the top and bottom of each page and commonly include information such as the date and page number.

lab review

LAB 2

Charting Worksheet Data

key terms

area chart EX2.14
bar chart EX2.14
category axis EX2.15
category-axis title EX2.15
category name EX2.15
chart EX2.14
chart gridlines EX2.15
chart object EX2.21
chart title EX2.15
clip art EX2.7
column chart EX2.14
data label EX2.39
data marker EX2.15
data series EX2.15
drawing object EX2.7
embedded chart EX2.21
embedded object EX2.7
explode EX2.44
file property EX2.49
footer EX2.54
graphic EX2.7
group EX2.35
header EX2.54
keyword EX2.8
legend EX2.15
line chart EX2.14
margin EX2.53
object EX2.7
picture EX2.7
pie chart EX2.14
plot area EX2.15
series formula EX2.40
sizing handle EX2.12
source program EX2.7
stack EX2.42
stacked-column chart EX2.31
style EX2.5
thumbnail EX2.9
value axis EX2.15
value-axis title EX2.15
wizard EX2.17
X axis EX2.15
Y axis EX2.15
Z axis EX2.15

microsoft office specialist skills

The Microsoft Office Specialist certification program is designed to measure your proficiency in performing basic tasks using the Office 2003 applications. Certification demonstrates that you have the skills and provides a valuable industry credential for employment. After completing this lab, you have learned the following Microsoft Office Excel 2003 Specialist skills:

Skill Sets	Skill Standards	Page
Creating Data and Content	Insert, position, and size graphics	EX2.7
Analyzing Data	Create, modify, and position diagrams and charts based on worksheet data	EX2.15
Managing Workbooks	Setup pages for printing	EX2.53
	Print data	EX2.51

command summary

Command	Shortcut Key	Button	Voice	Action
File/Page Setup/Header/Footer				Adds header and/or footer
File/Page Setup/Margins/ Horizontally				Horizontally centers contents between margins
File/Page Setup/Page/Fit to				Sizes print area to fit on a specified number of pages
File/Print/Entire Workbook				Prints all sheets in a workbook
File/Properties/Summary				Specifies information to document a file
View/Toolbar/Picture				Shows the picture toolbar
Insert/Chart			Chart Wizard	Starts the Chart Wizard
Insert/Picture/Clip Art			Insert clip art	Inserts selected graphic from Clip Organizer and Microsoft's Clip Art and Media Web site
Insert/Picture/From File			Insert picture from file	Inserts a picture from a file
Format/Style				Applies selected style to cells
Format/Selected Chart Title	Ctrl + 1			Changes format of selected chart title
Format/Selected Data Series	Ctrl + 1			Changes format of selected data series
Chart/Chart Type			Chart type	Changes type of chart
Chart/Chart Options				Changes titles, legends, and other chart options
Chart/Location				Places chart in selected worksheet or chart sheet

lab exercises

matching

Match the lettered item on the right with the numbered item on the left.

1.  _____ **a.** numbered scale along the left boundary line of the chart
2. data marker _____ **b.** bottom boundary line of the chart
3.  _____ **c.** identifies each number represented in a data series
4. X axis _____ **d.** area of chart bounded by X and Y axes
5. explode _____ **e.** changes the type of chart
6. plot area _____ **f.** identifies the chart data series and data markers
7. column chart _____ **g.** a chart that displays data as vertical columns
8. Value axis _____ **h.** starts the Chart Wizard
9.  _____ **i.** to separate a slice slightly from other slices of the pie
10. category ranges _____ **j.** identify the data along the X axis
11. legend

true/false

Circle the correct answer to the following questions.

1. A drawing object is created using a special drawing program that is included with Excel. True False
2. The chart title is visually displayed within the X- and Y-axis boundaries. True False
3. A line chart displays data commonly used to show trends over time. True False
4. The X-axis title line is called the category-axis title. True False
5. An entire group can be selected and then formatted or edited. True False
6. A data series links the chart object to the source worksheet. True False
7. A pie chart is best suited for data that compares parts to the whole. True False
8. Exploding a slice of a pie chart emphasizes the data. True False
9. To make a slice of a pie chart easier to read, patterns can be added to it. True False
10. A header is a line or several lines of text that appears at the top of each page just below the top margin. True False

fill-in

Complete the following statements by filling in the blanks with the correct key terms.

1. The small circles that surround a selected object are called ______________________.
2. ______________ is a collection of graphics that is usually bundled with a software application.
3. The X axis of a chart is also called the _____________ axis.
4. A(n) _____________ is a named combination of formats.
5. A(n) _______________ is an object that contains other objects.
6. The ____________ is the part of the chart that gives a description of the symbols used in a chart.
7. A(n) _____________ formula is a formula that links a chart object to the source worksheet.
8. The axis of the chart that usually contains numerical values is called the _____________ or _______________.
9. ___________________ provide additional informaion about a data marker.
10. A(n) ______________ is text displayed at the top of each page.

multiple choice

Circle the correct response to the questions below.

1. A visual representation of data in an easy-to-understand and attractive manner is called a(n) _______________.
   a. object
   b. picture
   c. chart
   d. drawing
2. 3-D charts have an additional axis called the _________________.
   a. W axis
   b. X axis
   c. Y axis
   d. Z axis
3. A chart consists of a number of _________________________ that are used to graphically display the worksheet data.
   a. elements
   b. groups
   c. gridlines
   d. titles

4. A chart that is inserted in a worksheet is an ______________ object and becomes part of the worksheet.
   a. attached
   b. enabled
   c. embedded
   d. inserted

5. A group is one or more ________________ that behave as one when moved or sized.
   a. objects
   b. lines
   c. data markers
   d. symbols

6. _______________ provide additional information about information displayed in the chart.
   a. data masks
   b. data labels
   c. headers
   d. chart titles

7. The _______________ of a chart usually displays a number scale determined by the data in the worksheet.
   a. Z axis
   b. value axis
   c. X axis
   d. category axis

8. A(n) _____________ describes the symbols used within the chart to identify different data series.
   a. X axis
   b. legend
   c. Y axis
   d. chart title

9. A ______________ chart show the relationship of each value in a data series to the series as a whole.
   a. line
   b. bar
   c. pie
   d. bubble

10. A _________________ is a line of text that appears at the bottom of a page just below the bottom margin line.
    a. footer
    b. header
    c. footing
    d. heading

rating system

★ Easy

★★ Moderate

★★★ Difficult

step-by-step

Teens and Money Management ★

1. Max's economics paper is on teens and money. He has some data saved in a worksheet on where teens say they learn about money management. He has asked you to help him chart the data and make the worksheet look more attractive. The completed worksheet with charts is shown here.

   a. Open the workbook ex02_Money Data.

   b. Format the data in column C to Percent style with no decimal places.

   c. Insert a graphic of your choice to the left of the worksheet title, or use ex02_money, size as needed. Save the workbook as Teens and Money.

   d. Use the Chart Wizard to create a column chart of the data in cells B7 through C11. Preview the chart in the dialog box. Plot the data series by columns.

   e. Enter the chart title **Where Teens Learn Money Management**. Turn off the display of the legend. Embed the chart in the worksheet.

   f. Size the chart over cells A16 through F37. Change the chart type to 3-D Bar Chart.

   g. Change the chart title color to green. Change the color for the Parents data series to green.

   h. Document the workbook; include your name as the author.

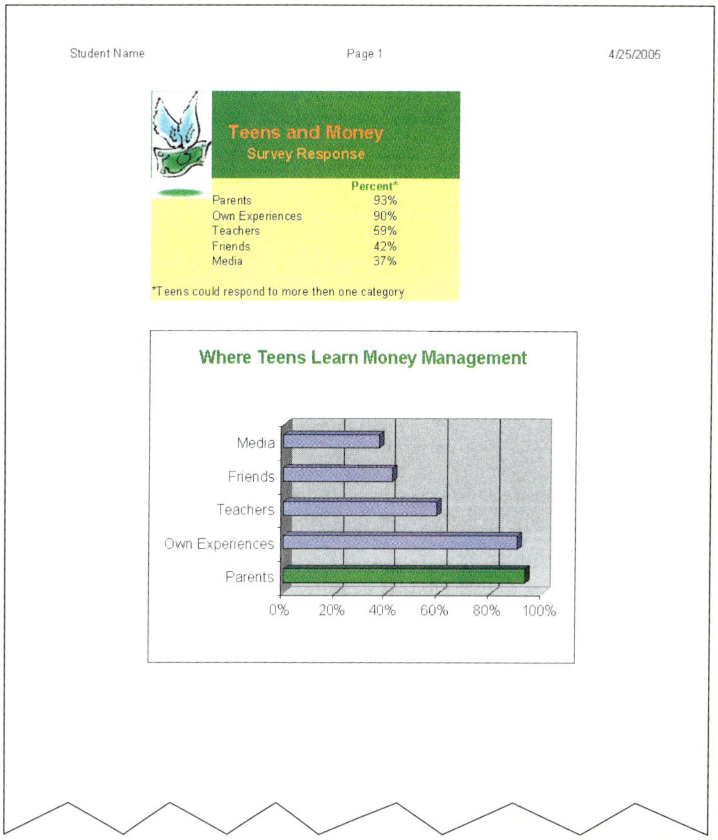

   i. Preview the worksheet. Add a predefined header to the worksheet that displays your name, page number, and date. Center the worksheet horizontally on the page.

   j. Print the worksheet on one page.

   k. Save the workbook again.

Student E-mail Analysis ★★

2. Amit Yoshi works for a university newspaper and has been collecting information on the number of students who e-mail their professors. Amit wants to graph some of the data in a worksheet for his upcoming article. The completed worksheet with charts is shown here.

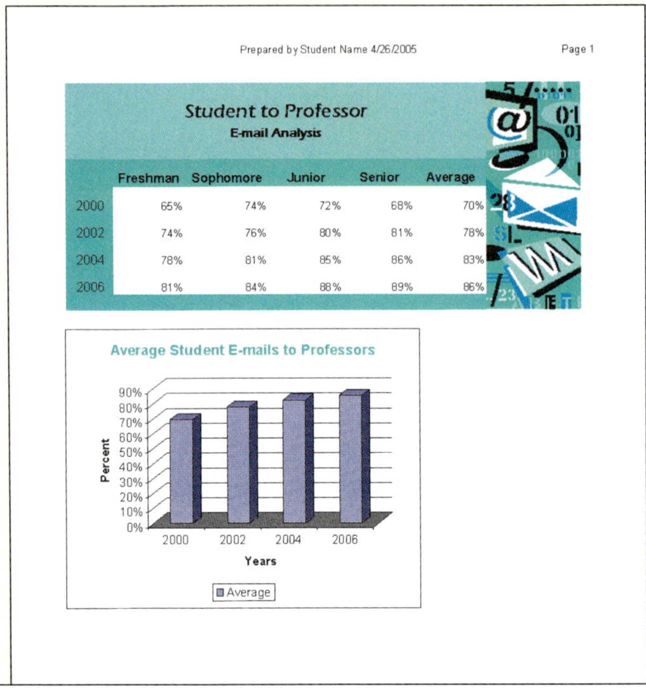

   a. Open the workbook file ex02_Email Analysis.
   b. Insert a clip art image of your choice to the right of the data. Size the image as necessary. If you do not have an image, you can use ex02_Email.
   c. Create a line chart on a separate sheet using the data in cells A5 through E9. Title the chart appropriately.
   d. Change the chart type to Bar chart. Increase the size of the chart title and add a text color of your choice. Save the workbook as Email Analysis.
   e. Create a 3-D column chart in the worksheet showing the average percentage for the four grade levels for the four years (column F). Title the chart appropriately. Change the orientation of the Y-axis title to vertical. Move the legend to the bottom of the chart.
   f. Position the chart below the worksheet data and size it appropriately. Increase the size of the chart title and add color.
   g. While reviewing the charts, Amit realized that the Sophomore and Senior columns of data were transposed. Correct the data using the table below.

	Sophomore	Senior
2000	74	68
2002	76	81
2004	81	86
2006	84	89

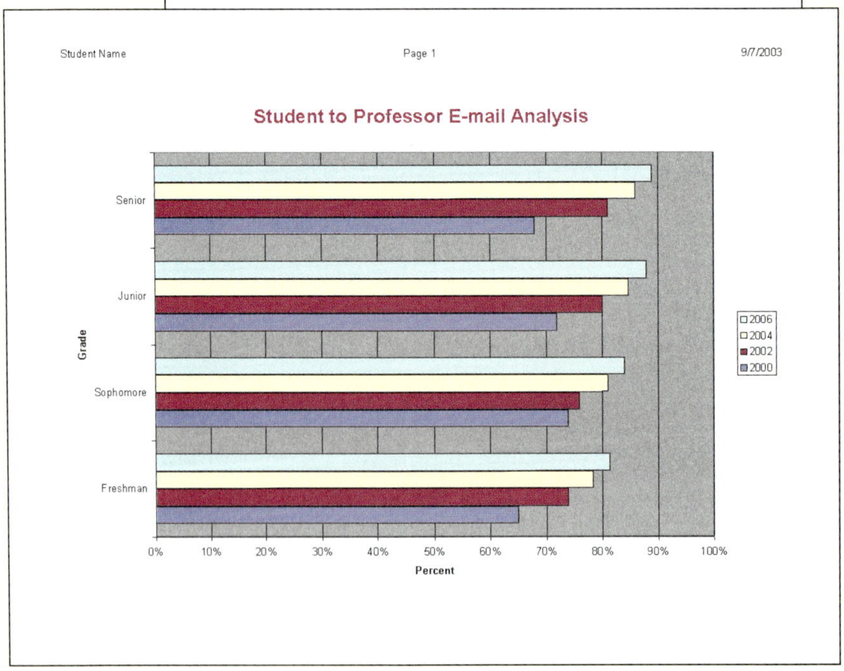

   h. Document the workbook file by adding your name as author and include a preview picture.
   i. Preview the workbook. Add a predefined header to the worksheet and chart sheet that displays your name, page number, and date. Center the worksheet horizontally on the page. Print the worksheet. Print the chart sheet.
   j. Save the workbook again.

Tracking Animal Adoptions ★ ★

3. Richard Phillipe volunteers for Animal Angels, an agency that places animals for adoption. He has compiled a worksheet of the number of adoptions in the downtown shelter for the last year. He would like to create a chart that shows how the adoptions differ by month and a chart that shows the total number of adoptions this year. The completed worksheet with charts is shown here.

a. Open the file ex02_Adoptions.

b. Insert a clip art image of your choice in the top left corner of the worksheet. Size and position the image as necessary. If you don't have an image, use ex02_Pets.

c. Save the workbook as Adoption Tracking.

d. Chart the monthly data for the three animal categories as a column chart. Set the series to be displayed in Rows.

e. Enter the chart title **Adoptions by Month**, and the Value (Y) axis title of **Number of Animals**. Display the legend below the chart. Insert the chart in the worksheet.

f. Position the chart over cells A16 through N31.

g. Change the chart type to line.

h. Create a 3-D pie chart of the data in columns A11:A13 and N11:N13. Title the chart **Total Adoptions**. Turn off the legend and use the category name and percentage to label the data labels. Insert the chart in the worksheet.

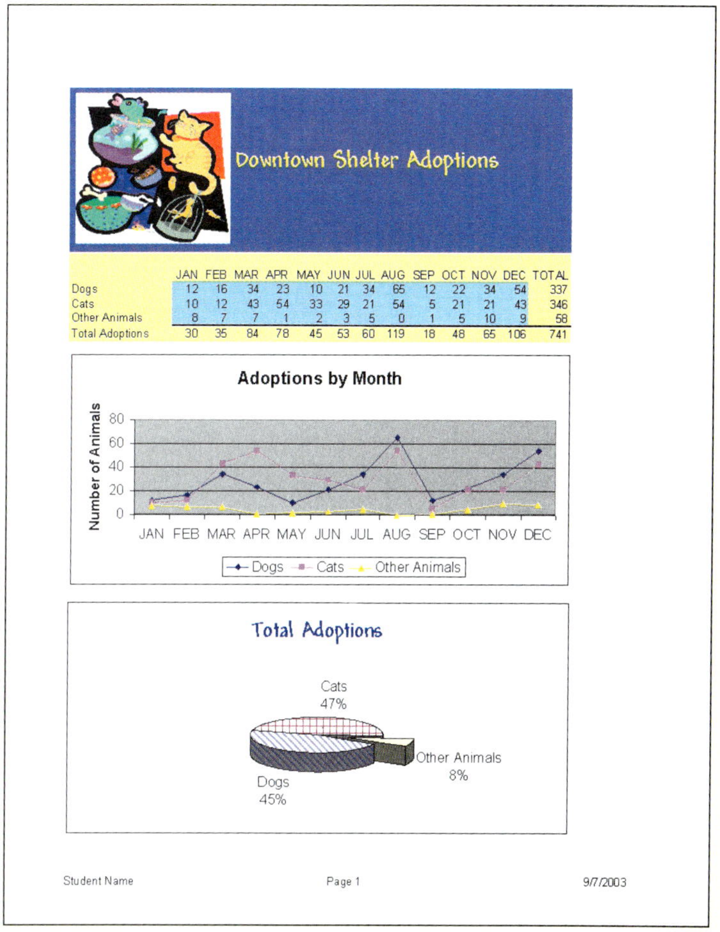

i. Position the chart over cells A33 through N48. Add color and font refinements to the chart title as you like. Rotate the chart 120 degrees so the Dogs slice is at the front of the chart. Explode the Other Animals slice. Add patterns and colors of your choice to the pie chart.

j. Richard found an error in the data. Change the value of Other Animals in June to **3** and Dogs to **22** in October.

k. Document the workbook file by adding your name as author and include a preview picture.

l. Save the workbook.

m. Preview the worksheet. Add a predefined footer to the worksheet that displays your name, page number, and date. Center the worksheet horizontally on the page. Print the worksheet.

n. Save the workbook file again.

Children's Sports Participation ★★★

4. Mary Ellen is the program coordinator for Lifestyle Fitness, a physical conditioning and health center. She is proposing to management that they increase their emphasis on child fitness. To reinforce the need for this type of investment, she has found some recent data about growth in the number of children (in millions) participating in sports. She wants to create several charts of this data to emphasize the demand.

   a. Create a worksheet of the following data.

	2000	2002	2004
Baseball	3421	3694	3876
Basketball	6200	7420	7543
In-line Skating	7110	8176	8211
Running/Jogging	3429	3257	3432
Slow-pitch Softball	3946	4261	4644
Soccer	2674	3510	3864
Touch Football	4040	4363	4547
Volleyball	3941	4295	4754

   b. Add an appropriate title over the data and format the numbers to show commas with no decimal places. Calculate the percent change from 2000 to 2004 in column E ((2004 value – 2000 value)/2000 value). Add a column heading for the percent

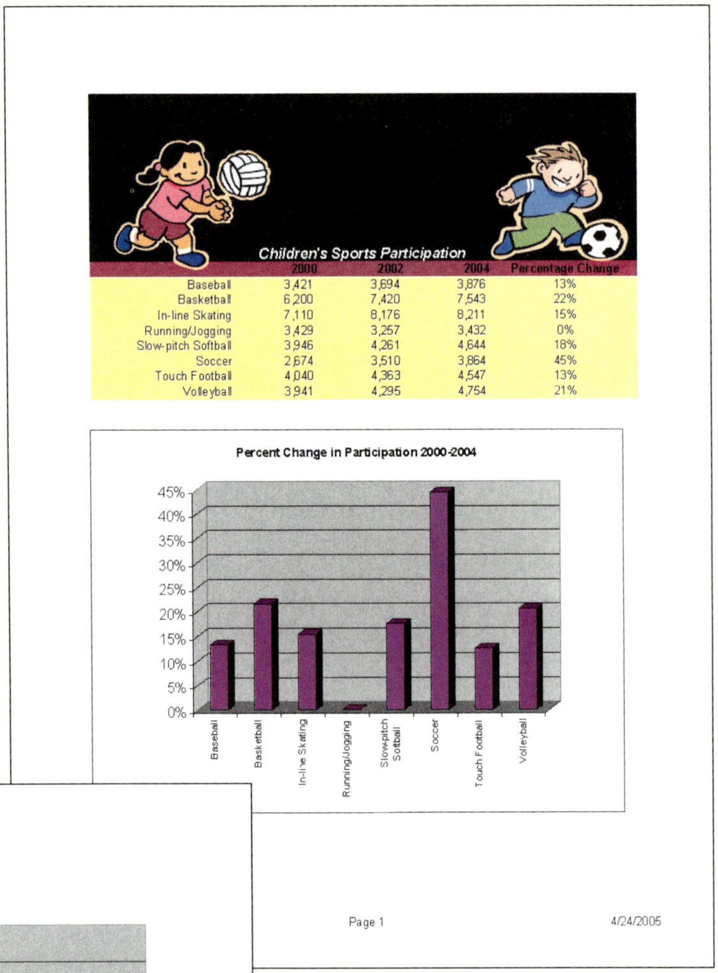
Children's Sports Participation

	2000	2002	2004	Percentage Change
Baseball	3,421	3,694	3,876	13%
Basketball	6,200	7,420	7,543	22%
In-line Skating	7,110	8,176	8,211	15%
Running/Jogging	3,429	3,257	3,432	0%
Slow-pitch Softball	3,946	4,261	4,644	18%
Soccer	2,674	3,510	3,864	45%
Touch Football	4,040	4,363	4,547	13%
Volleyball	3,941	4,295	4,754	21%

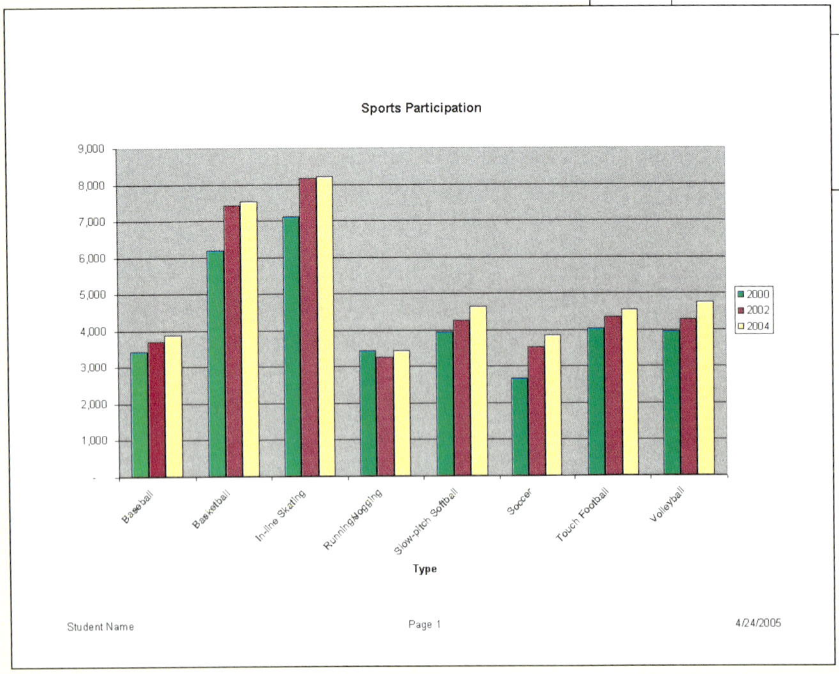

change column. Change the cell formatting of column E to percentage with no decimal places. Enhance the worksheet as you like to improve its appearance with font and fill colors and clip art (you can use ex02_Soccer and ex02_Volleyball.) Save the workbook as Youth Sports Data.

c. Create a column chart of the worksheet data in columns A through D as a new sheet. Enter a chart title and Y-axis title. Enhance the chart using features presented in the lab.

d. Create an embedded 3-D column chart in the worksheet showing the Gain/Loss data for the sports. Include the title **Percent Change in Participation 2000-2004**. Remove the legend and format the Y-axis title to a font size of 12 and no decimal places. Format the X-axis title to display the labels at a 90-degree angle.

e. Move the chart below the worksheet and resize it appropriately.

f. Enhance the chart using features presented in the lab.

g. Document the workbook by adding your name as author. Save the workbook with a picture preview.

h. Preview the workbook. Add a predefined footer to the worksheet that displays your name, page number, and date on both sheets. Center the worksheet horizontally on the page. Print the worksheet and the column chart.

i. Save the workbook again.

Internet Experience ★★★

5. Wendy Murray's class is studying Internet technology. She has discovered some intriguing research that compares how long men and women have been using the Internet. She would like to share this information with her students.

   a. Create a worksheet of the data in the table below. Total the rows. Add an appropriate heading for the totaled row.

Years on Internet

	Female	Male
Less than 6 months	135	138
6–12 months	182	198
1–3 years	690	1059
4–6 years	509	1352
Over 7 years	182	590

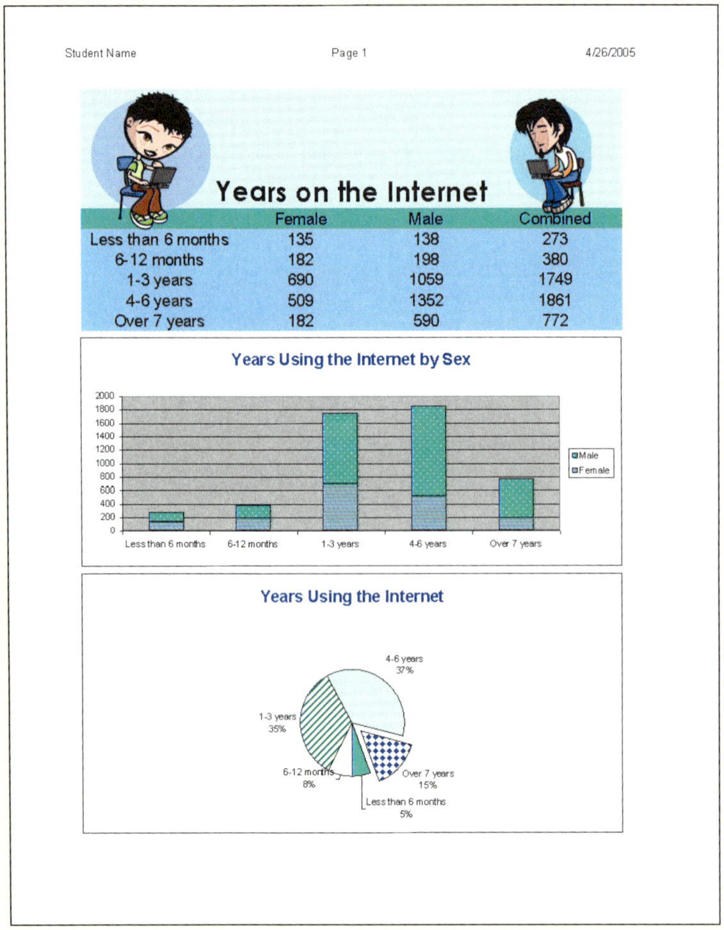

   b. Format the worksheet using the features you have learned. Add fill color behind the data. Insert clip art graphics of your choice, or use ex02_Computer Girl and ex02_Computer Boy.

   c. Save the workbook as Internet Use Comparison.

   d. Create an embedded stacked-column chart for the five time periods for both female and male users. Move the legend to the bottom of the chart. Include an appropriate chart title.

   e. Display the chart below the worksheet. Change the color of the chart to colors that match the worksheet. Add patterns to the columns.

   f. Create a pie chart of the total data. Include an appropriate title. Remove the legend and display data labels for the category name and percentage. Embed the chart in the worksheet and move it below the first chart. Format the chart to be similar to your previous chart. Explode a slice of the pie. Rotate the pie to display the exploded slice at the front.

   g. Document the workbook file by adding your name as author. Include a preview picture.

   h. Preview the worksheet. Add a predefined header to the worksheet that displays your name, page number, and date. Center the worksheet horizontally on the page. Print the worksheet.

   i. Save the workbook file again.

on your own

Job Market Seminar ★

1. Nancy Fernandez is preparing for an upcoming job market seminar she is presenting. She has collected data comparing the average hourly pay rate for several professional jobs in the state to the U.S. average rates. Open the workbook ex02_ Job Market. Calculate the percent difference between the New Jersey and U.S. average in column D. Add appropriate fill and font colors to the worksheet. Add a graphic to the top left corner of the worksheet. Nancy thinks the information would be much more meaningful and have greater impact if it were presented in a chart. Create an appropriate chart of the data for General Managers/Top Exec., Engineering, Math and Natural Sciences Managers, and Industrial Production Managers on a separate chart sheet. Include appropriate chart titles. Add a pattern to the data series and change the plot area fill color. Enhance the chart in other ways using different font sizes and font colors. Position the legend at the bottom of the chart. Add a predefined header to the chart sheet that displays your name, page number, and date. Save the workbook as Seminar and print the chart.

Grade Tracking ★

2. Create a worksheet that tracks your grades. It can be a record of the test scores you received this semester, or it can be a record of your GPA each semester. Create an embedded chart that best represents your grade trends. Use the formatting techniques you have learned to change the appearance of the worksheet and the chart. Save the workbook as Grades. Include a header or footer that displays your name and the current date in the worksheet. Print the worksheet with the chart.

Stock Market Workbook ★ ★

3. You are interested in the stock market. Use Help to learn more about the Stock chart type. Pick four related stocks and enter data about their performance over a period of time. Create an embedded stock chart of the data. Save the worksheet with the chart as Stocks. Include a header or footer that displays your name and the current date in the worksheet. Print the worksheet and the chart.

Graduate School Data ★ ★ ★

4. Ashmit Agrawal is considering graduate school and has gathered some data to present to his parents to make a case for paying part of his tuition and fees. Open the file ex02_Graduate School. Using what you learned in the lab, create two embedded charts from the data on the Earnings worksheet. One chart should represent the unemployment rate of people based on their level of education and the other should represent median earning by level. Create a pie chart on the Payback worksheet to represent the number of years after graduation that it will take to earn back what he paid for the higher education. Use the difference in Salary as the data labels. Use the features you have learned to enhance the appearance of the worksheets and charts. Include a header on both worksheets that displays your name and the current date. Save the worksheet as Graduate School2. Print the worksheet with the charts.

Insurance Comparisons ★ ★ ★

5. Roberto Sanchez is thinking about purchasing a new home. However, he is concerned about the insurance rates. Before purchasing, he wants to find out the insurance rates on the home he is evaluating. Select three different comparable insurance companies, then use the Web or visit several insurance agents to get the insurance premium cost information for different amounts of coverage (minimum required). Use your own personal information as the basis for the insurance quotes. Create a worksheet that contains the cost of minimum coverage, cost of optional coverage, deductibles available, and insurance premium quotes. Create an embedded chart of the data that shows the coverage and premiums. Enhance the chart appropriately. Include a header or footer that displays your name and the current date in the worksheet. Save the workbook as Insurance. Print the worksheet and chart.

Managing and Analyzing a Workbook

LAB 3

Objectives

After completing this lab, you will know how to:

1. Correct worksheet errors.
2. Use absolute references.
3. Copy, move, name, and delete sheets.
4. Use AutoFill.
5. Reference multiple sheets.
6. Use Find and Replace.
7. Zoom the worksheet.
8. Split windows and freeze panes.
9. Use What-If analysis and Goal Seek.
10. Control page breaks.
11. Change page orientation.
12. Add custom headers and footers.
13. Print selected sheets and areas.

Case Study

Downtown Internet Café

You presented your new, more optimistic, first quarter sales forecast for the Downtown Internet Café to Evan. He was impressed with the charts and projected increase in sales if an aggressive advertising promotion is launched. However, because the Café's funds are low due to the cost of the recent renovations, he has decided to wait on the launching the advertising campaign.

Evan wants you to continue working on the Café forecast using the original, more conservative projected sales values for the first quarter. In addition, he asks you to include an Average calculation and to extend the forecast for the next three quarters.

After discussing the future sales, you agree that the Café will likely lose money during the first month of operations. Then the Café should show increasing profitability. Evan stresses that the monthly profit margin should reach 5 per cent in the second quarter.

As you develop the Café's financial forecast, the worksheet grows in size and complexity. You will learn about features of Office Excel 2003 that help you manage a large workbook efficiently. You will also learn how you can manipulate the data in a worksheet to reach a goal using the what-if analysis capabilities of Excel. The completed annual forecast is shown here.

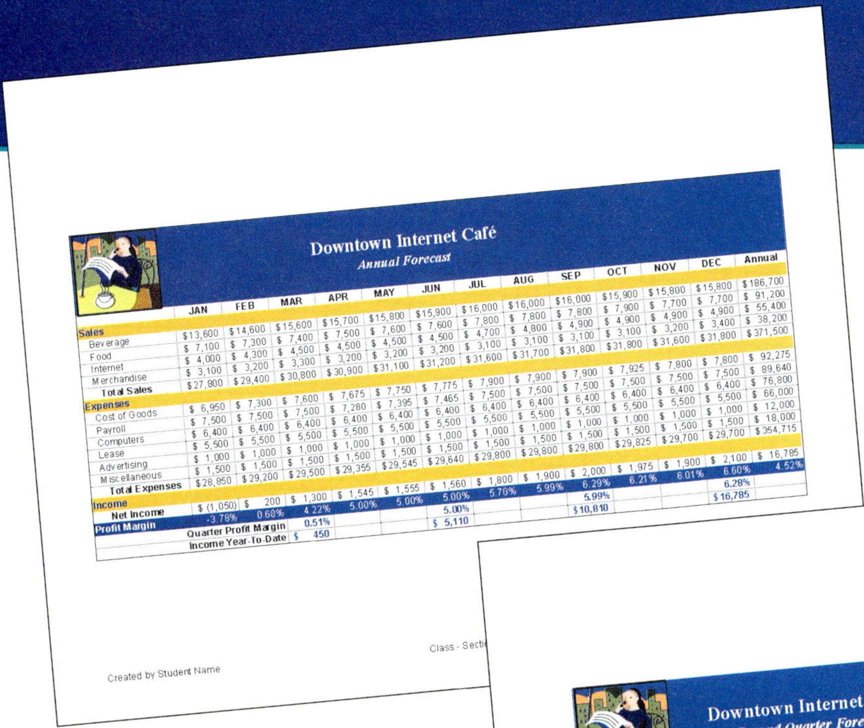

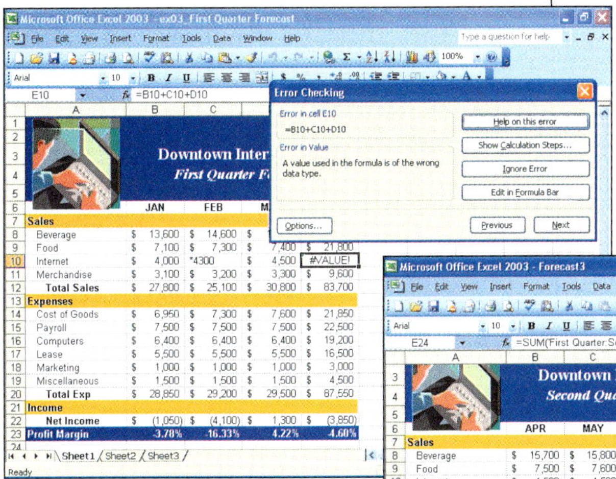

Formula errors are identified and easily corrected using the Error Checking feature.

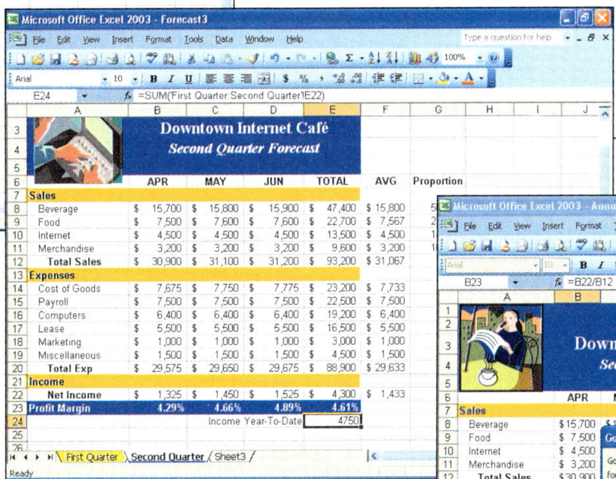

Multiple sheets in a workbook make it easy to edit several sheets simultaneously and to perform calculations based on data from multiple sheets.

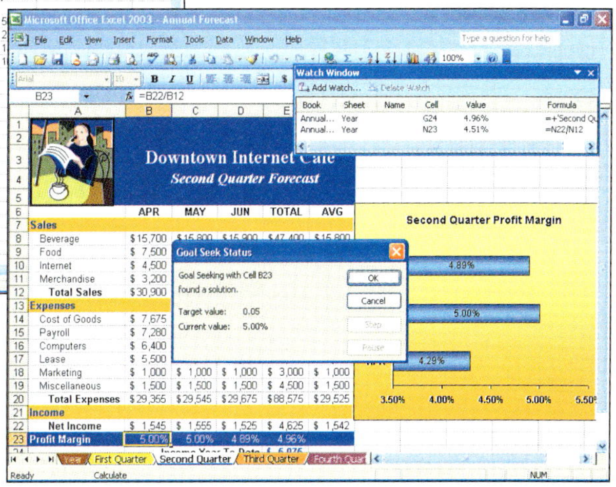

Forecasting values using Goal Seek to help perform what-if analysis is a powerful feature of Excel.

Concept Preview

The following concepts will be introduced in this lab:

1. **Absolute Reference** An absolute reference is a cell or range reference in a formula whose location does not change when the formula is copied.
2. **Sheet Name** Each sheet in a workbook can be assigned a descriptive sheet name to help identify the contents of the sheet.
3. **AutoFill** The AutoFill feature makes entering a series of headings easier by logically repeating and extending the series.
4. **Sheet and 3-D References** A formula that contains references to cells in other sheets of a workbook allows you to use data from multiple sheets and to calculate new values based on this data.
5. **Find and Replace** The Find and Replace feature helps you quickly find specific information and automatically replace it with new information.
6. **Split Windows** The split window feature allows you to divide a worksheet window into sections, making it easier to view different parts of the worksheet at the same time.
7. **Freeze Panes** Freezing panes prevents the data in the panes from scrolling as you move to different areas in the worksheet.
8. **What-If Analysis** What-if analysis is a technique used to evaluate the effects of changing selected factors in a worksheet.
9. **Goal Seek** The Goal Seek tool is used to find the value needed in one cell to attain a result you want in another cell.

Correcting Worksheet Errors

After talking with Evan, the owner of the Café, about the first quarter forecast, you are ready to begin making the changes he suggested. Evan returned the workbook file to you containing several changes he made to the format of the worksheet.

1. **Start Office Excel 2003.**

   Open the workbook ex03_First Quarter Forecast.

   Your screen should be similar to Figure 3.1

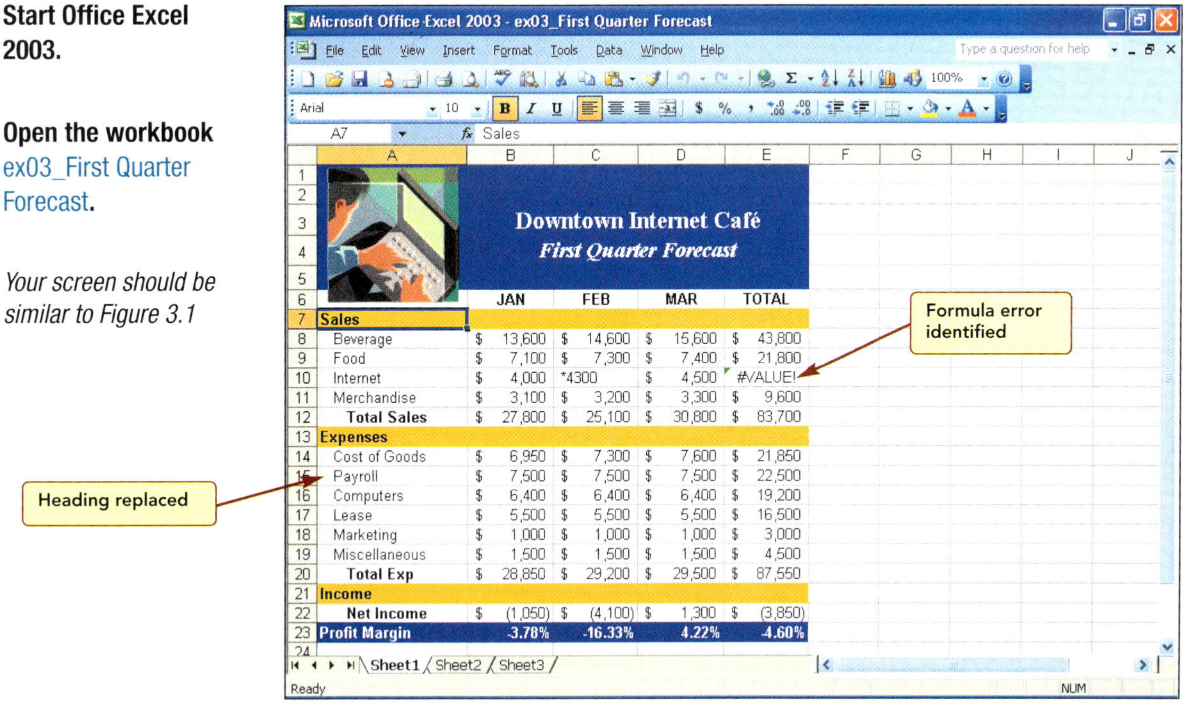

Figure 3.1

As you can see, Evan made several formatting changes to the worksheet. He changed the fill and text colors and made several changes to the row headings. For example, the Salary heading has been replaced with Payroll. Evan also decided to increase the February Internet sales value to $4,300. He included an asterisk (*) in the cell entry to make sure you saw the change. However, this has resulted in a formula error.

Excel 2003 includes several tools to help you find and correct errors in formula entries. These tools provide the capability to display the relationships between formulas and cells and to identify and suggest corrections to potential problems in formulas.

Using the Formula Error Checker

As you check the worksheet, you notice a problem in cell E10. When a formula cannot properly calculate a result, an error value is displayed and a green triangle appears in the top-left corner of the cell. Each type of error value has a different cause, as described in the following table.

Error Value	Cause
#####	Column not wide enough to display result, or negative date or time is used
#VALUE!	Wrong type of argument or operand is used
#DIV/0!	Number is divided by zero
#NAME?	Text in formula not recognized
#N/A	Value not available
#REF!	Cell reference is not valid
#NUM!	Invalid number values
#NULL!	Intersection operator is not valid

You can correct each identified error individually or use Excel's formula error checker tool to check them all, one at a time. The formula error checker is similar to the spelling checker in that it goes to each location in the worksheet containing a formula error, identifies the problem, and suggests corrections. You will use the formula error checker to correct this error and check the entire worksheet for others.

1

- **Choose Tools/Error Checking.**
- **If necessary, move the dialog box to see the located formula error.**

Your screen should be similar to Figure 3.2

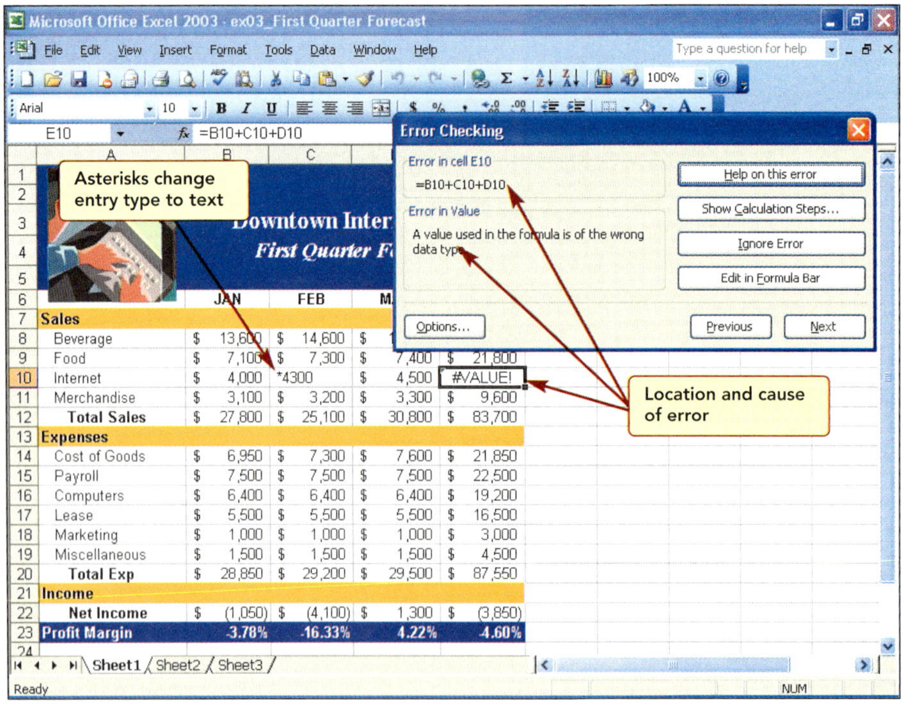

Figure 3.2

The Error Checking dialog box identifies the location and cause of the error. In this case, when Evan changed the February Internet sales values, he included an asterisk in the cell entry to make sure you noticed the change. This caused Excel to interpret the entry as a text entry, which cannot be used in this formula. To correct the problem, you need to enter the value correctly.

2 **Edit the entry in cell C10 to 4300.**

Press ←Enter to complete the edit.

Your screen should be similar to Figure 3.3

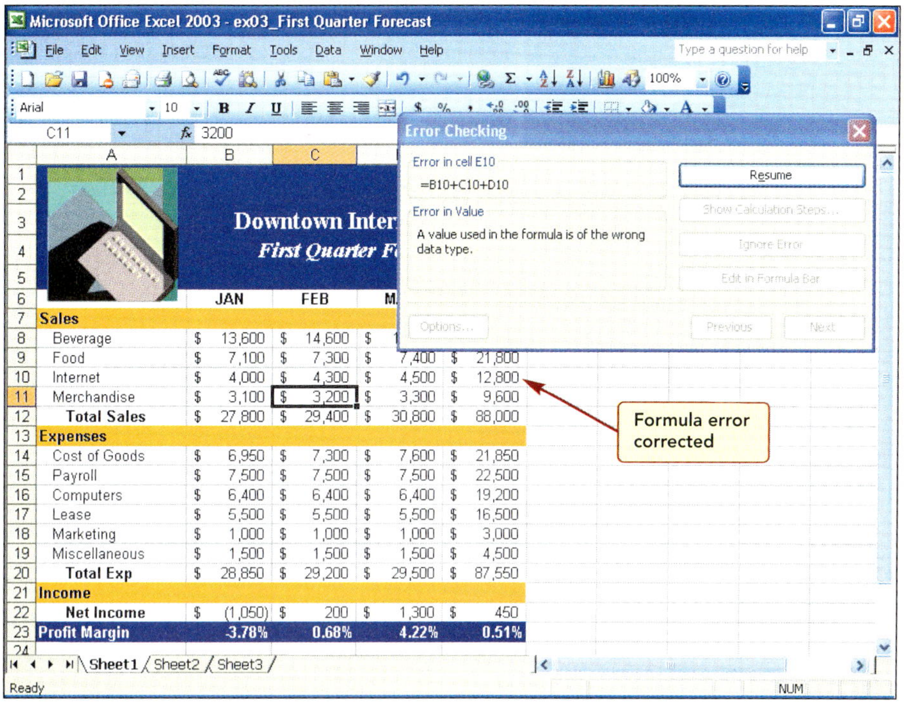

Figure 3.3

Cell E10 now displays the correctly calculated result. You will continue checking the worksheet for formula errors.

3 **Click Resume.**

Click OK.

No other errors were located. You are now ready to make several of the changes requested by Evan.

Calculating an Average

First you will add a column showing the average values for the first quarter.

1 **Enter the heading AVG in cell F6.**

Move to F8.

Your screen should be similar to Figure 3.4

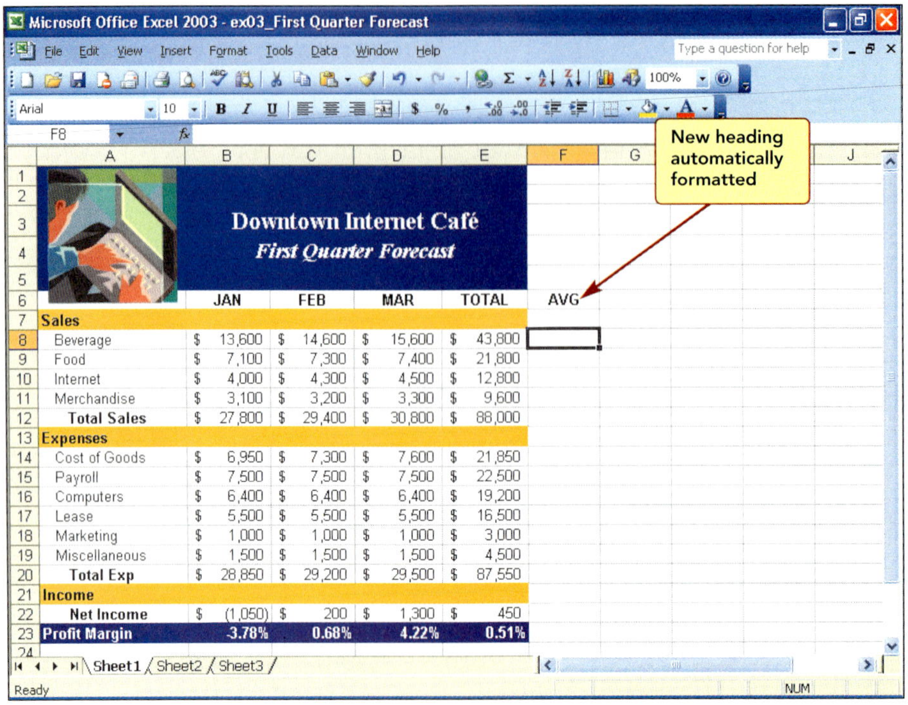

Figure 3.4

Notice that the new heading is already appropriately formatted to bold and centered. This is because Excel automatically extends formats to new cells if the format of at least three of the last five preceding cells in the row appears that way.

In addition to the SUM function, you can also use Σ AutoSum to enter several other commonly used functions. These include functions to calculate an Average, Minimum, Maximum, and Count.

2 **Open the Σ AutoSum drop-down menu.**

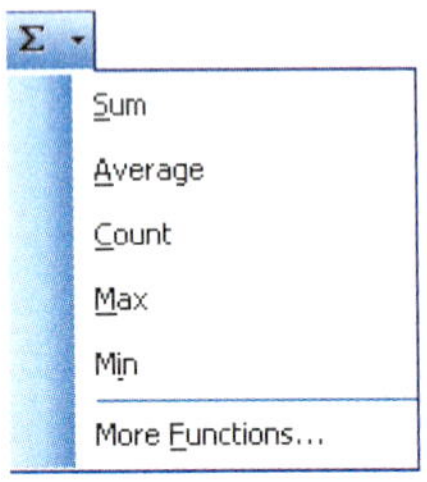

Choose Average.

Your screen should be similar to Figure 3.5

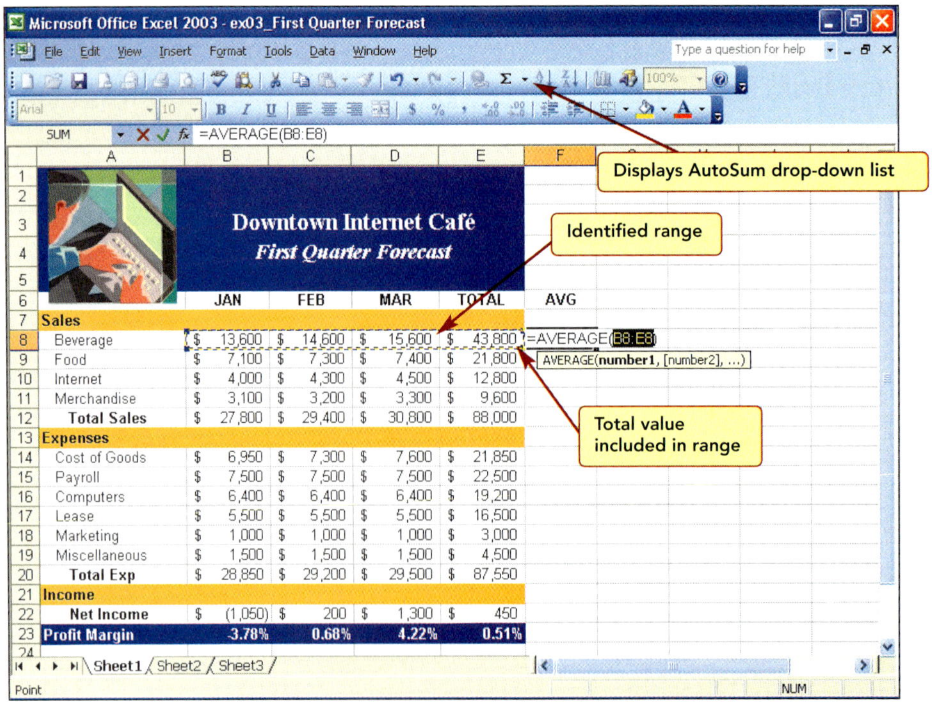

Figure 3.5

Excel identifies the range of cells B8 through E8 for the function argument. Because it incorrectly includes the total value in cell E8, you need to specify the correct range.

3 **Drag to select cells B8 through D8.**

Click ✓ Enter.

Your screen should be similar to Figure 3.6

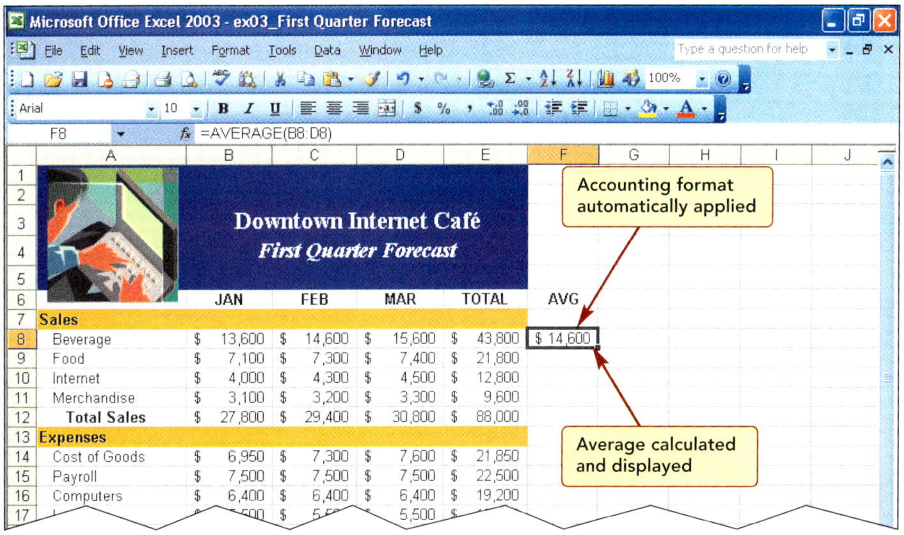

Figure 3.6

The average of the beverage sales for the quarter, $14,600, is calculated and displayed in cell F8. Notice that Excel again extended the format to the new cell, saving you the step of applying the Accounting format.

Next you need to copy the function down column F.

4 **Copy the function from cell F8 into cells F9 through F22.**

Your screen should be similar to Figure 3.7

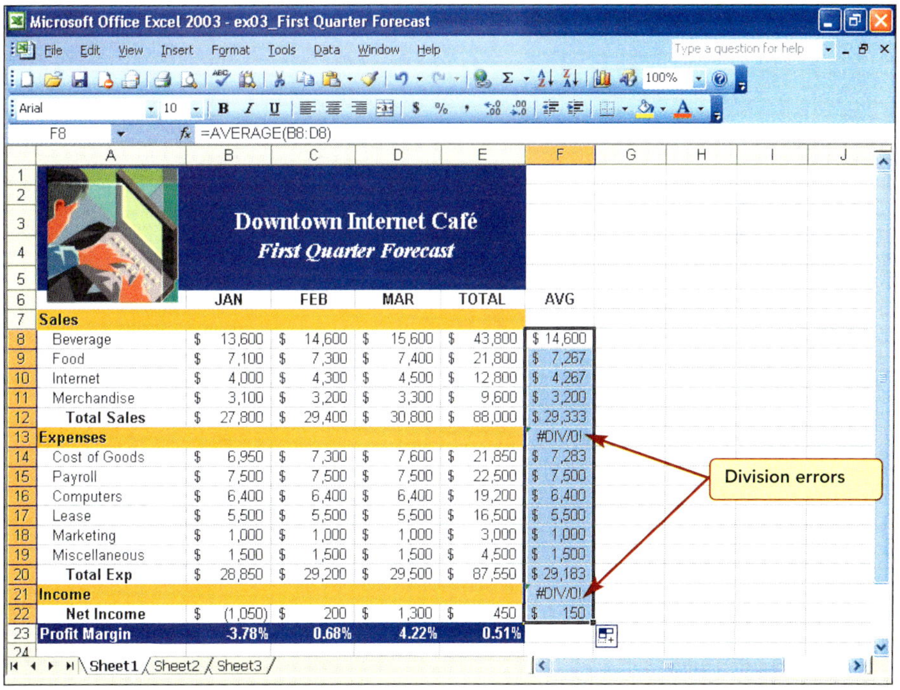

Figure 3.7

The average value has been correctly calculated for each row. Notice, however, that two cells display the error value #DIV/0!, indicating the cells contain a formula error.

Correcting Formula Errors Individually

To correct this problem, you need to find out the cause of the error.

1 **Move to cell F13.**

Point to Error Options.

Your screen should be similar to Figure 3.8

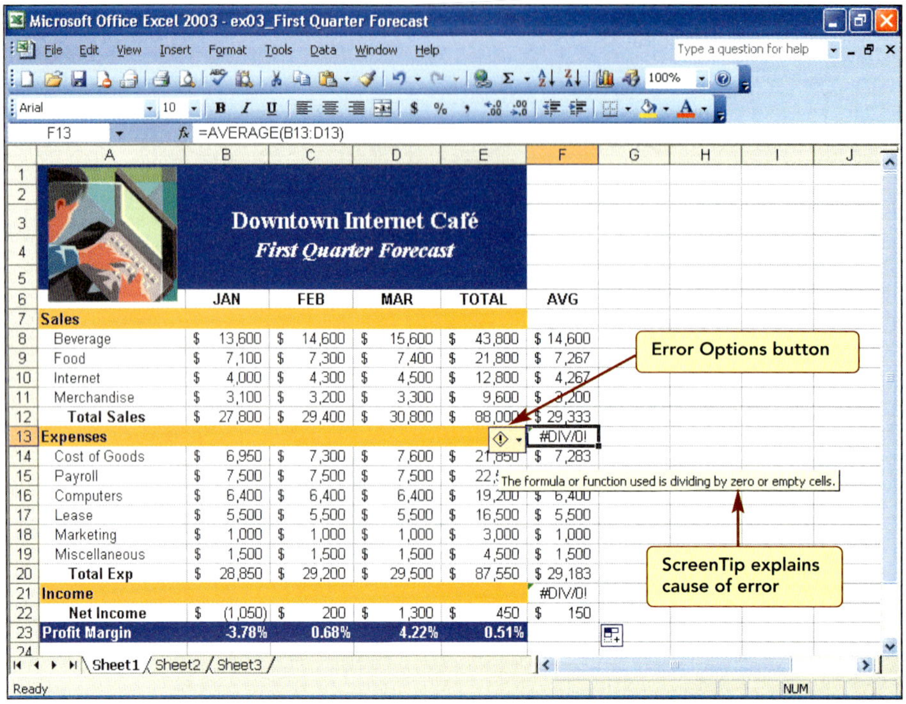

Figure 3.8

The Error Options button displays a ScreenTip identifying the cause of the error; in this case, the formula is attempting to divide by zero or empty cells. This time you will individually correct the error.

2 **Click Error Options.**

Choose Edit in Formula Bar.

> **Another Method**
>
> Using voice command, you can say "Options" to display the options menu when any options button is visible.

Your screen should be similar to Figure 3.9

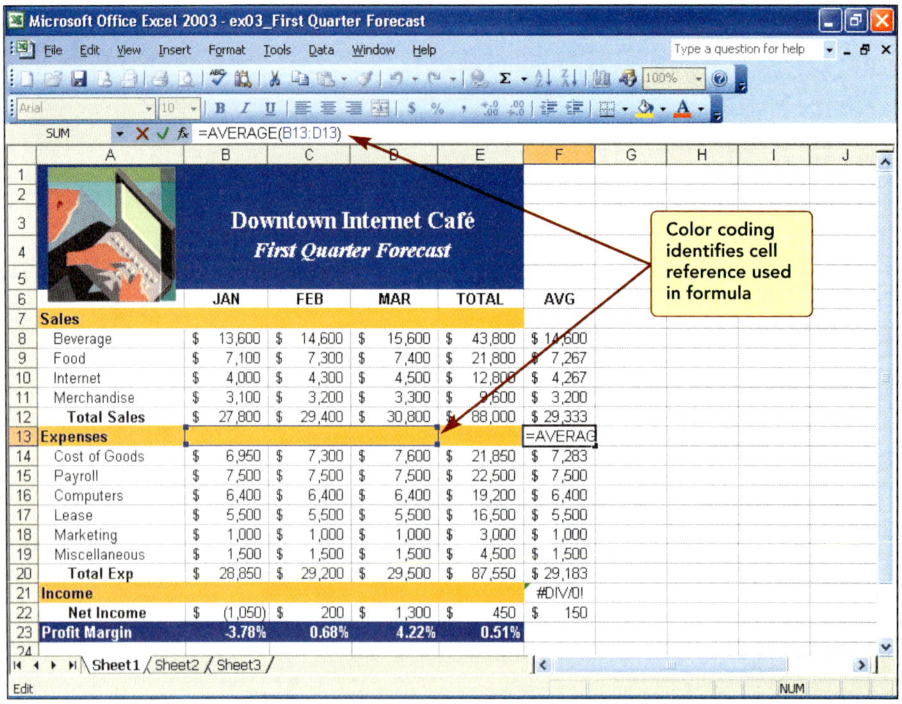

Figure 3.9

Notice that the cell references in the formula are color coded to match the borders Excel displays around the referenced worksheet cells. It is designed to provide visual cues to the relationships between the cells that provide values to the formulas or the cells that depend on the formulas. You can now easily see the error is caused by references to blank cells when the function was copied. Since you do not need this formula, you will delete it.

3

- **Press Esc.**
- **Press Delete.**

Your screen should be similar to Figure 3.10

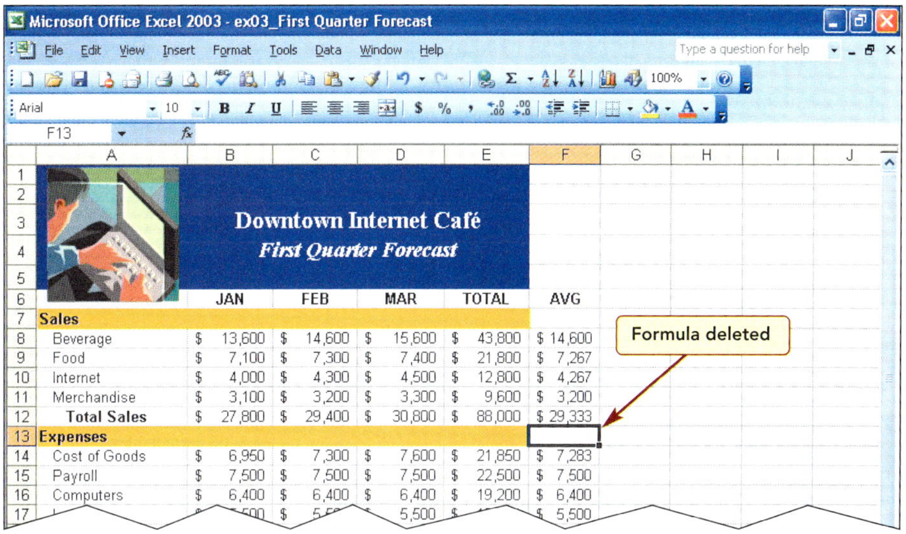

Figure 3.10

Likewise, you need to delete the function that was copied into cell F21. You will clear the entry in this cell using the fill handle.

4

- **Move to cell F21.**
- **Point to the fill handle and when the mouse pointer changes to +, drag upward until the cell is gray.**

- **Release the mouse button.**

Your screen should be similar to Figure 3.11

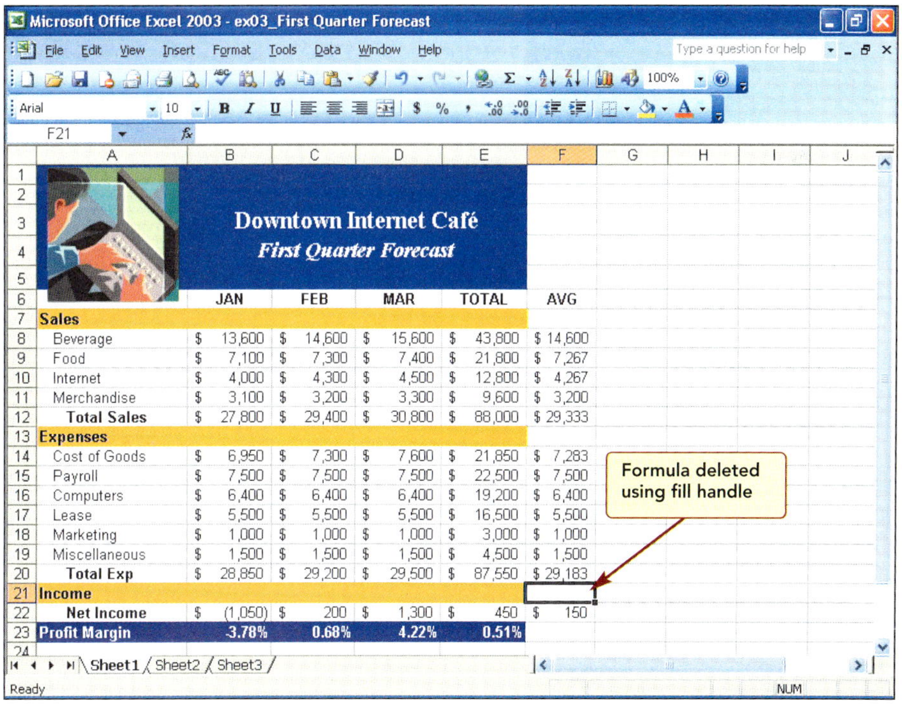

Figure 3.11

Using Absolute References

While looking at the sales data in the worksheet, you decide it may be interesting to find out what contribution each sales item makes to total sales. To find out, you will enter a formula to calculate the proportion of sales by each in column G. The formula to calculate the proportion for beverage sales is Total Beverage Sales/Total Sales.

1

- **Enter the heading Proportion in cell G6.**
- **Type the formula =E8/E12 in cell G8.**
- **Press ←Enter or click ✓ Enter.**
- **If necessary, move to G8.**

Your screen should be similar to Figure 3.12

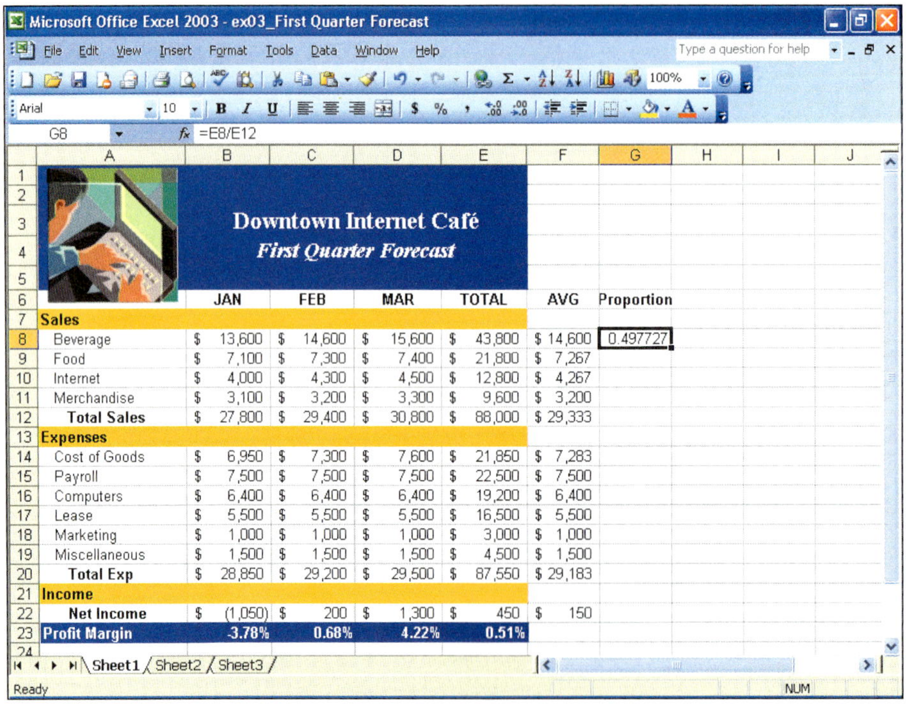

Figure 3.12

The value 0.497727 is displayed in cell G8. This shows that the beverage sales are approximately 50 percent of total sales.

Next, to calculate the proportion for Food Sales, you will copy the formula from G8 to G9. Another quick way to copy cell contents is to drag the cell border while holding down Ctrl. This method is most useful when the distance between cells is short and they are both visible in the window. It cannot be used if you are copying to a larger range than the source range.

2 **Point to the border of cell G8 and when the mouse pointer shape is** ✥, **hold down** `Ctrl` **and drag the mouse pointer to cell G9.**

Your screen should be similar to Figure 3.13

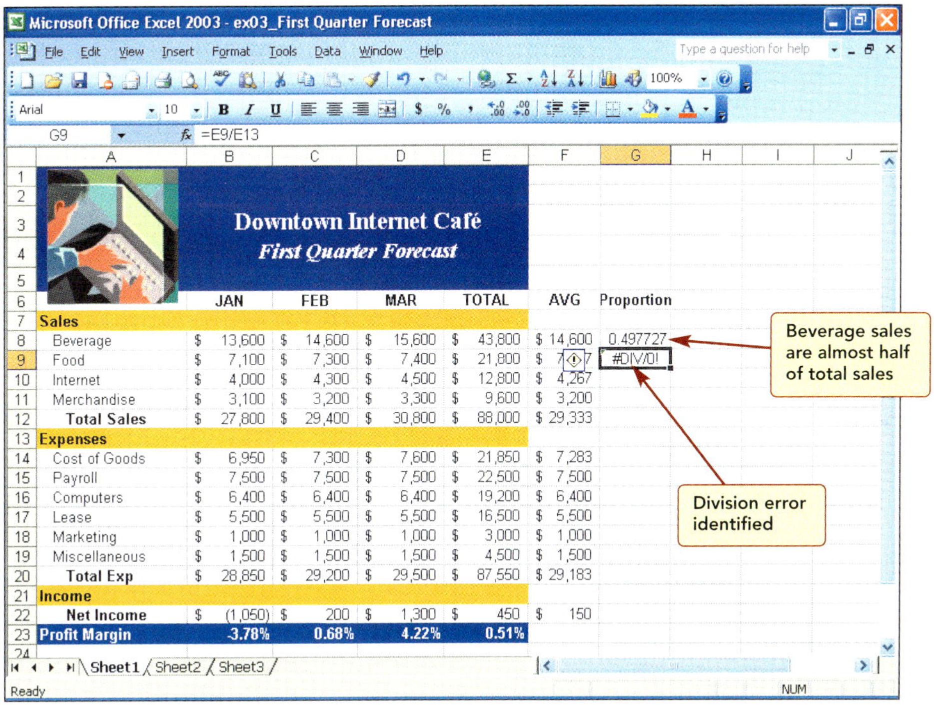

Figure 3.13

You see a #DIV/0! error value displayed in cell G9 and want to check the formula in that cell. Another way to quickly display the formula relationships is to change to Edit mode.

3 **Double-click on cell G9.**

Your screen should be similar to Figure 3.14

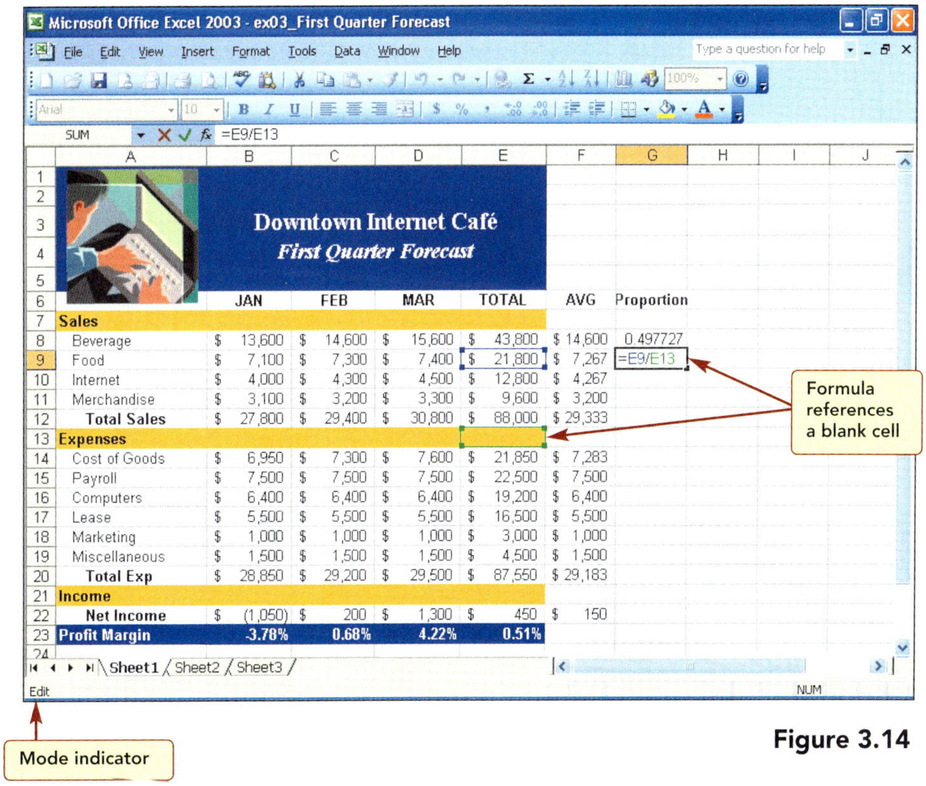

Figure 3.14

In Edit mode, the formula references are again color coded to the worksheet cells. You can now see the error occurred because the relative reference to cell E12 adjusted correctly to the new location when the formula was copied and now references cell E13, a blank cell. The formula in G8 needs to be entered so that the reference to the Total Sales value in cell E12 does not change when the formula is copied. To do this, you need to make the cell reference absolute.

Concept 1

Absolute Reference

1 An **absolute reference** is a cell or range reference in a formula whose location does not change when the formula is copied.

To stop the relative adjustment of cell references, enter a $ (dollar sign) character before the column letter and row number. This changes the cell reference to absolute. When a formula containing an absolute cell reference is copied to another row and column location in the worksheet, the cell reference does not change. It is an exact duplicate of the cell reference in the original formula.

A cell reference can also be a **mixed reference.** In this type of reference, either the column letter or the row number is preceded with the $. This makes only the row or column absolute. When a formula containing a mixed cell reference is copied to another location in the worksheet, only the part of the cell reference that is not absolute changes relative to its new location in the worksheet.

The table below shows examples of relative and absolute references and the results when a reference in cell G8 to cell E8 is copied to cell H9.

Cell Contents of G8	Copied to Cell H9	Type of Reference
$E$8	$E$8	Absolute reference
E$8	F$8	Mixed reference
$E8	$E9	Mixed reference
E8	F9	Relative reference

You will change the formula in cell G8 to include an absolute reference for cell E12. Then you will copy the formula to cells G9 through G11.

You can change a cell reference to absolute or mixed by typing in the dollar sign directly or by using the ABS (Absolute) key, F4. To use the ABS key, the program must be in Edit mode and the cell reference that you want to change must be selected.

4 **Press Esc to exit Edit mode.**

Move to G8.

Click on the reference to E12 in the formula bar to enter Edit mode and select the reference.

Press F4.

Your screen should be similar to Figure 3.15

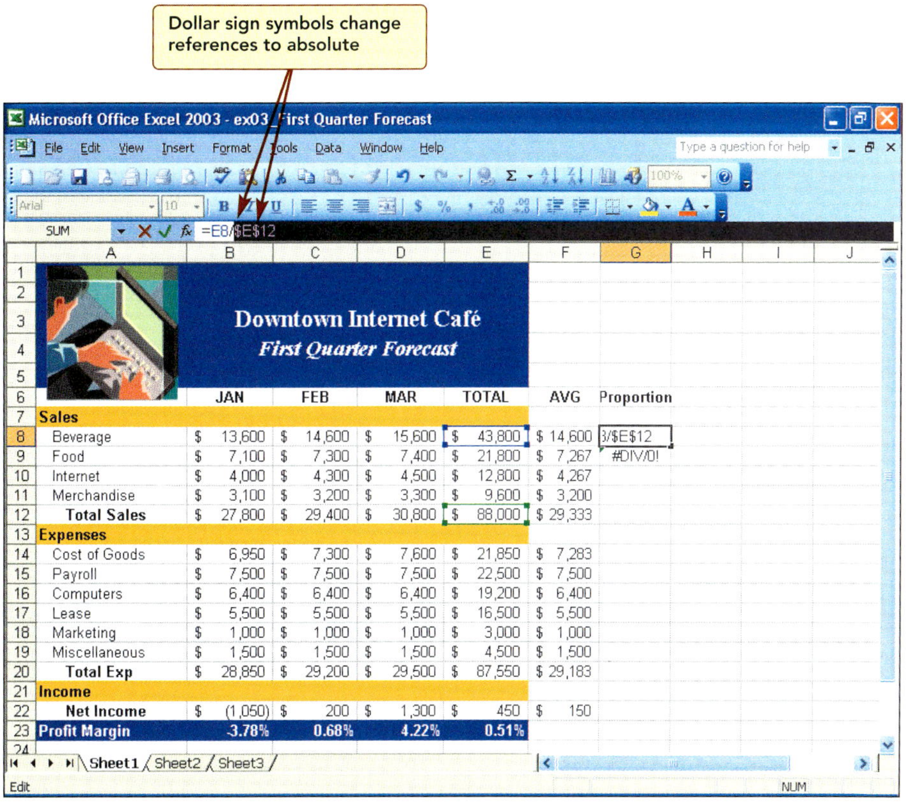

Figure 3.15

The cell reference now displays $ characters before the column letter and row number, making this cell reference absolute. If you continue to press F4, the cell reference will cycle through all possible combinations of cell reference types. Leaving the cell reference absolute, as it is now, will stop the relative adjustment of the cell reference when you copy it again.

5 Click ✓ Enter.

- Copy the revised formula to cells G9 through G11.
- Double-click on cell G9.

Your screen should be similar to Figure 3.16

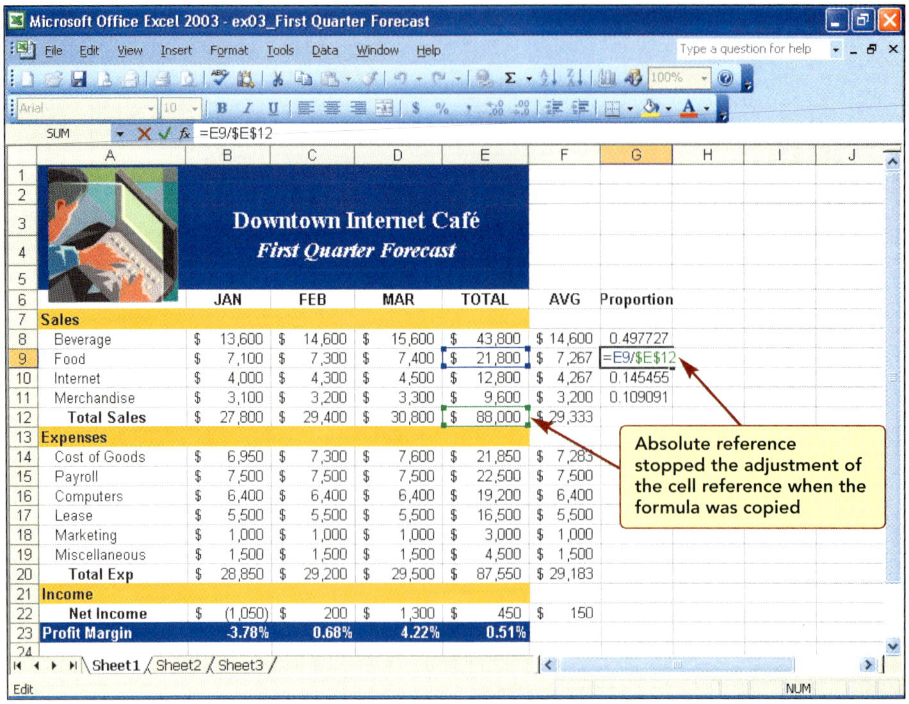

Figure 3.16

The formula when copied correctly adjusted the relative cell reference to Food sales in cell E9 and did not adjust the reference to E12 because it is an absolute reference.

The last change you need to make to the proportion data is to format it to the Percent style.

6 Press Esc.

- Select G8 through G11.
- Click % Percent Style.
- Click Increase Decimal (twice).
- Size column G to fit the contents.
- Move to cell A7 and save the workbook as **Forecast3** to your data file location.

Your screen should be similar to Figure 3.17

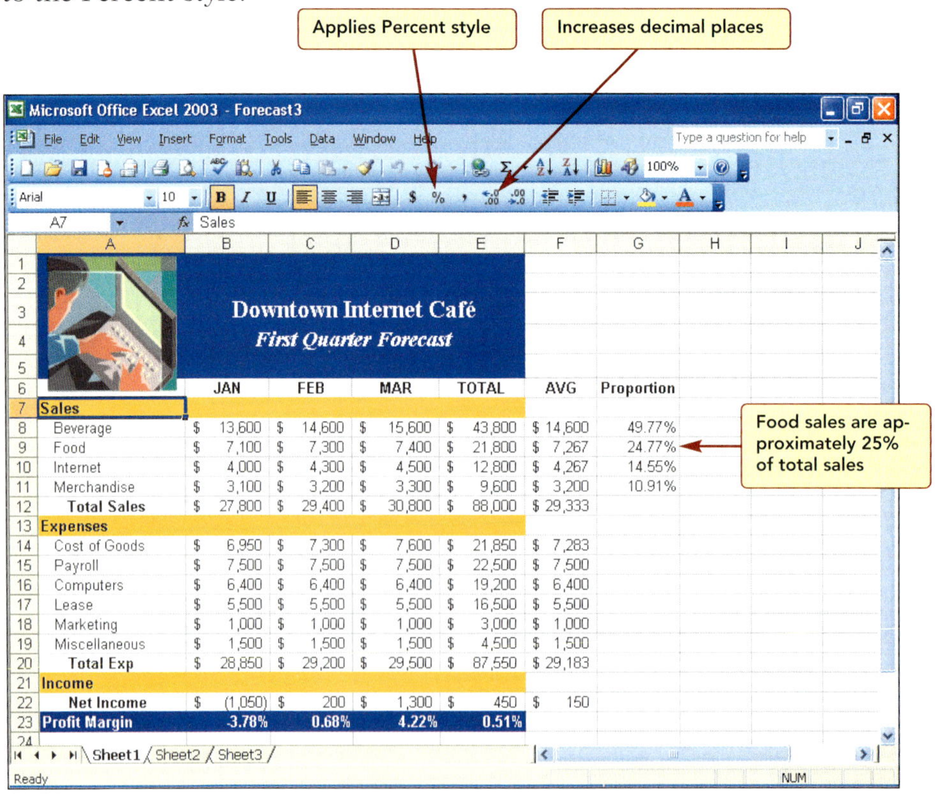

Figure 3.17

The calculated proportion shows the same values that a pie chart of this data would show.

Working with Sheets

Next, you want to add the second quarter forecast to the workbook. You want this data in a separate sheet in the same workbook file. To make it easier to enter the forecast for the next quarter, you will copy the contents of the first quarter forecast in Sheet1 into another sheet in the workbook. Then you will change the month headings, the title, and the number data for the second quarter. Finally, you want to include a formula to calculate a year-to-date total for the six months.

Copying Between Sheets

You want to copy the worksheet data from Sheet1 to Sheet2. Copying between sheets is the same as copying within a sheet, except that you switch to the new sheet to specify the destination.

1 **Select the worksheet range A1 through G23.**

Having Trouble?

A quick way to select this range is to move to cell A1, hold down ⇧Shift and click on cell G23.

Click Copy.

Click on the Sheet2 tab.

Click Paste.

Another Method

You can also use Edit/Move or Copy Sheet to move or copy a sheet into a new sheet in the workbook.

Your screen should be similar to Figure 3.18

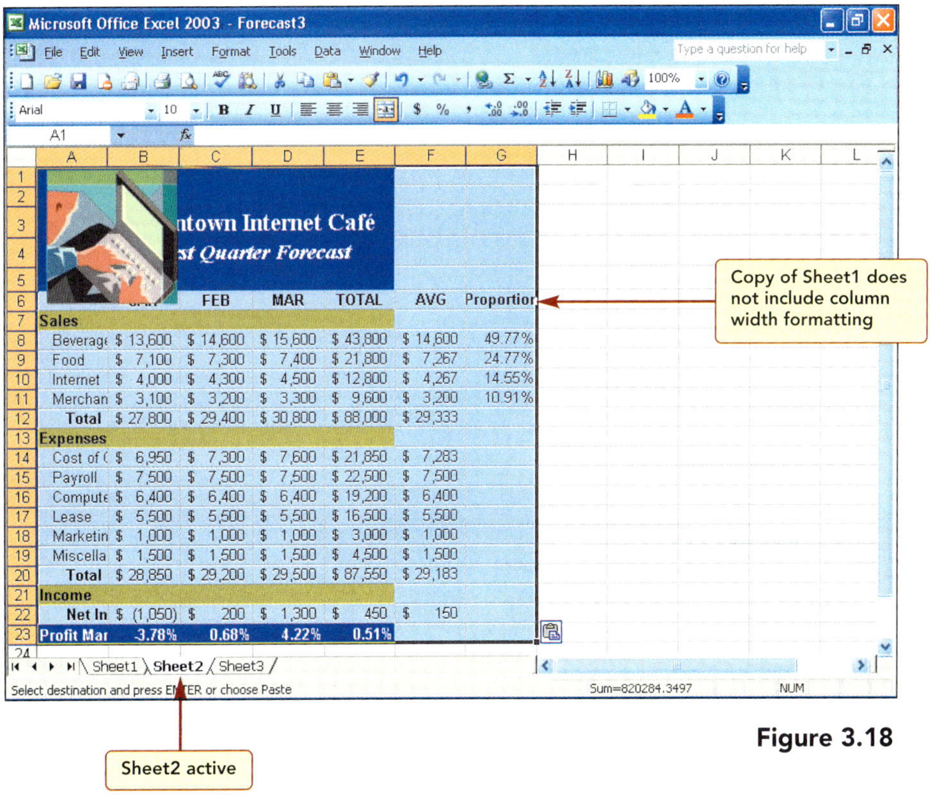

Figure 3.18

All the worksheet data and formatting, except for the column width settings, are copied into the existing Sheet2. You want to include the column width settings from the source.

2 Click Paste Options.

- Choose Keep Source Column Widths.

Your screen should be similar to Figure 3.19

Additional Information

If you select and copy the entire source sheet, all formatting including column widths is copied into the destination sheet.

Another Method

You can also create a copy of the active sheet in a new sheet by holding down Ctrl while dragging the active sheet tab to where you want the new sheet inserted.

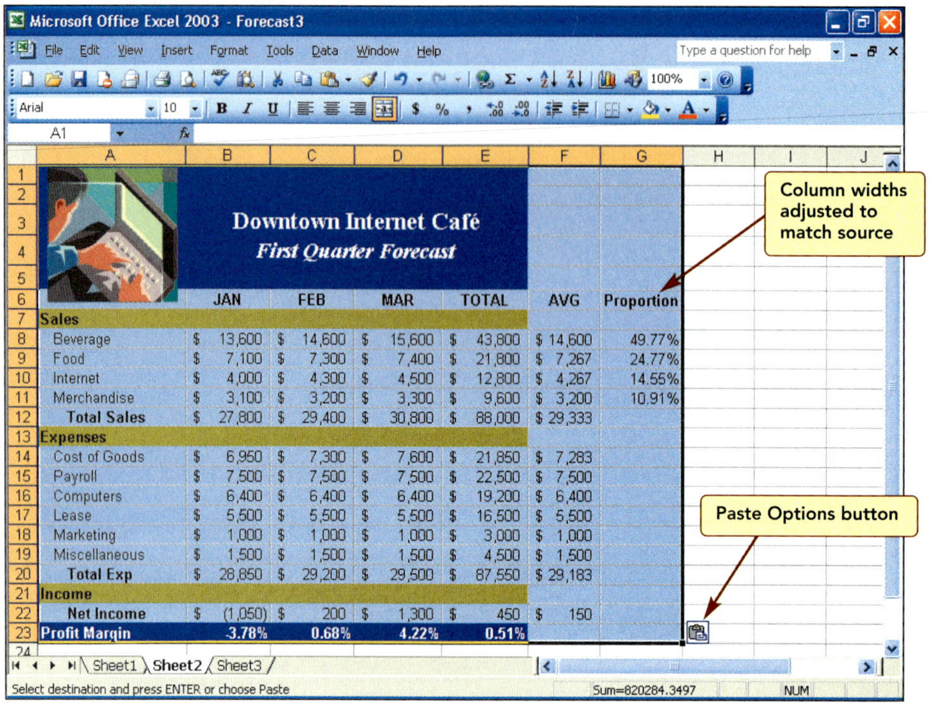

Figure 3.19

Sheet2 now contains a duplicate of the first quarter forecast in Sheet1.

Renaming Sheets and Coloring Sheet Tabs

As more sheets are added to a workbook, remembering what information is in each sheet becomes more difficult. To help clarify the contents of the sheets, you can rename the sheets.

Concept 2

Sheet Name

2 Each sheet in a workbook can be assigned a descriptive **sheet name** to help identify the contents of the sheet. The following guidelines should be followed when naming a sheet. A sheet name:

- Can be up to 31 characters
- Can be entered in uppercase or lowercase letters or a combination (it will appear as entered)
- Can contain any combination of letters, numbers, and spaces
- Cannot contain the characters : ? * / \
- Cannot be enclosed in square brackets [ ]

Double-clicking the sheet tab makes the sheet active and highlights the existing sheet name in the tab. The existing name is cleared as soon as you begin to type the new name. You will change the name of Sheet1 to First Quarter and Sheet2 to Second Quarter.

1
- **Double-click the Sheet1 tab.**
- **Type First Quarter.**
- **Press ←Enter.**
- **Change the name of the Sheet2 tab to Second Quarter.**

Another Method

The menu equivalent is Format/Sheet/Rename.

Your screen should be similar to Figure 3.20

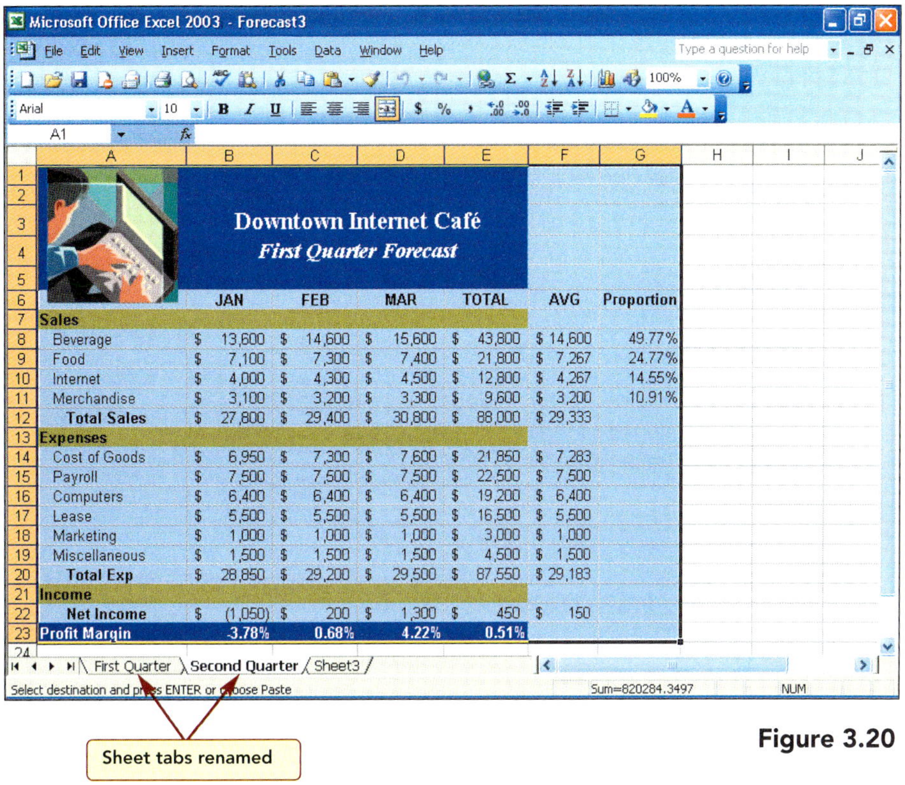

Figure 3.20

To further differentiate the sheets, you can add color to the sheet tabs.

2 Right-click on the First Quarter tab.

- Choose **Tab Color** from the shortcut menu.
- Select yellow from the color palette.
- Click OK.
- In the same manner, change the color of the Second Quarter sheet tab to blue.

Another Method

The menu equivalent is Format/Sheet/Tab Color.

Your screen should be similar to Figure 3.21

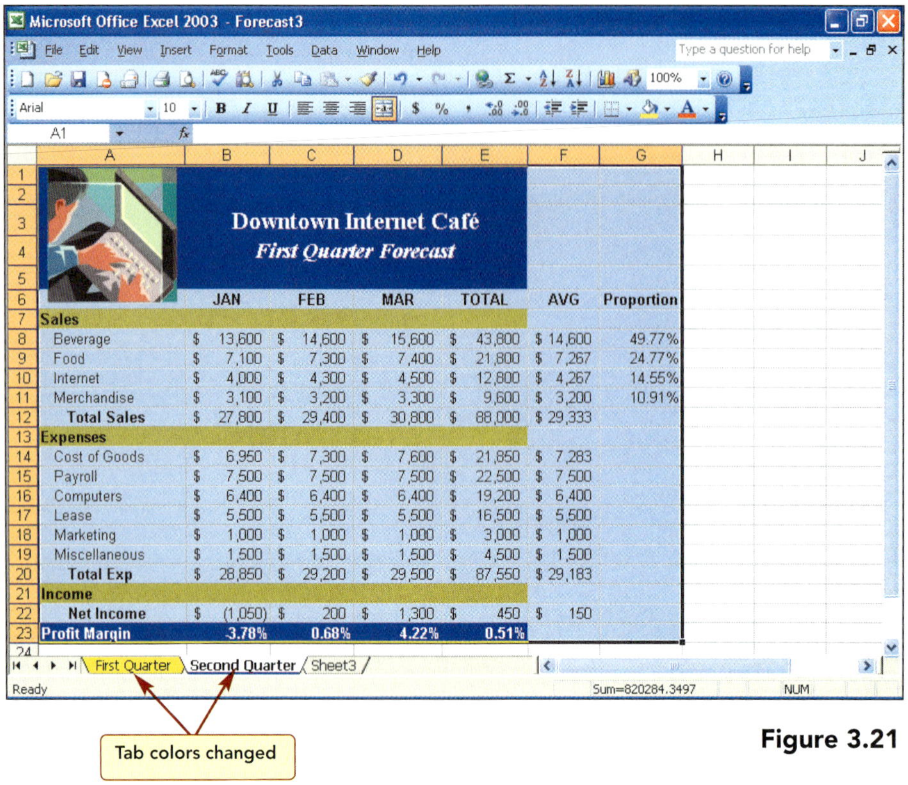

Figure 3.21

The sheet tab name of the selected sheet is underlined in the tab color of blue and the First Quarter sheet tab is yellow. When a sheet is not selected, the sheet tab is displayed with the background color.

Filling a Series

Now you can change the worksheet title and data in the Second Quarter sheet. First you will change the worksheet title to identify the worksheet contents as the second quarter forecast. Then you will change the month headings to the three months that make up the second quarter; April, May, and June.

1. Change the title in cell B4 to **Second Quarter Forecast**.
   - Change the month heading in cell B6 to **APR**.

Your screen should be similar to Figure 3.22

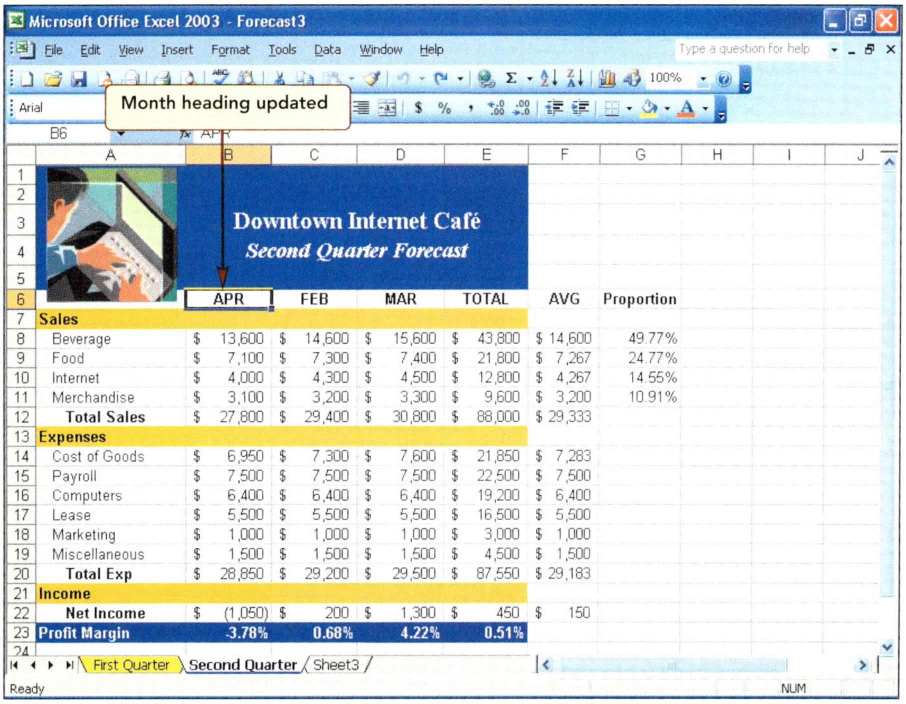

Figure 3.22

Now you need to change the remaining month headings to MAY and JUN. You will use the AutoFill feature to enter the month headings.

Concept 3

AutoFill

3 The **AutoFill** feature makes entering a series of headings easier by logically repeating and extending the series. AutoFill recognizes trends and automatically extends data and alphanumeric headings as far as you specify.

Dragging the fill handle activates the AutoFill feature if Excel recognizes the entry in the cell as an entry that can be incremented. When AutoFill extends the entries, it uses the same style as the original entry. For example, if you enter the heading for July as JUL (abbreviated with all letters uppercase), all the extended entries in the series will be abbreviated and uppercase. Dragging down or right increments in increasing order, and up or left increments in decreasing order. A linear series increases or decreases values by a constant value, and a growth series multiplies values by a constant factor. Examples of how AutoFill extends a series are shown in the table below.

Initial Selection	Extended Series
Qtr1	Qtr2, Qtr3, Qtr4
Mon	Tue Wed Thu
Jan, Apr	Jul, Oct, Jan

A starting value of a series may contain more than one item that can be incremented, such as JAN-02, in which both the month and year can increment. You can specify which value to increment by selecting the appropriate option from the AutoFill Options menu.

The entry in cell B6, APR, is the starting value of a series of months. You will drag the fill handle to the right to increment the months. The mouse pointer displays the entry that will appear in each cell as you drag.

2 **Drag the fill handle of cell B6 to extend the range from cell B6 through cell D6.**

> **Additional Information**
> If you do not want a series created when you drag the fill handle, hold down Ctrl as you drag and the entries will be copied, not incremented.

- **Save the workbook.**

Your screen should be similar to Figure 3.23

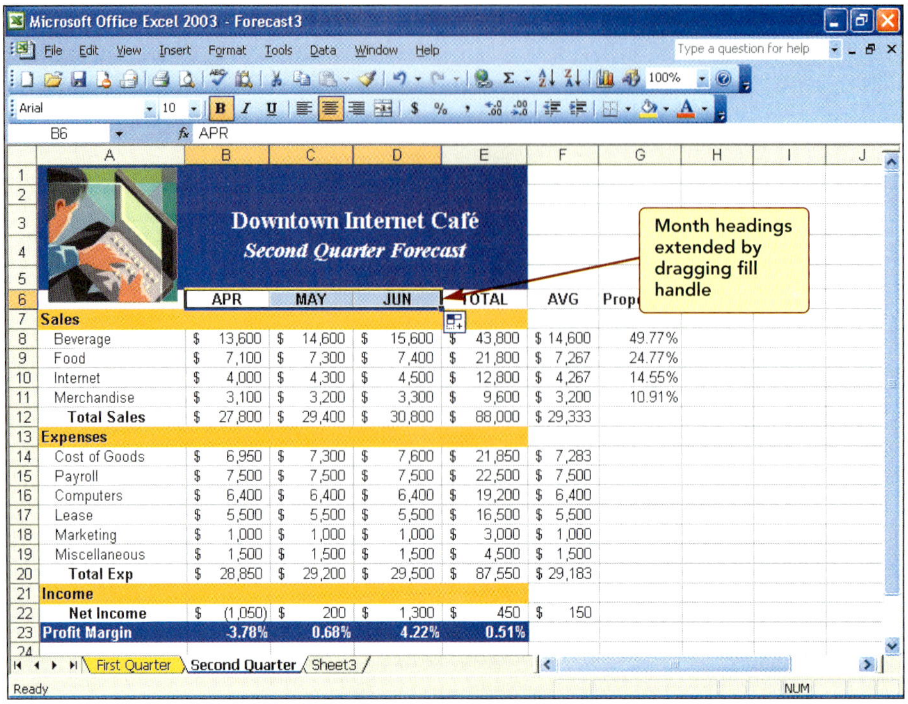

Figure 3.23

The month headings now correctly reflect the three months for the second quarter.

Referencing Multiple Sheets

Finally, you need to update the forecast for April through June beverage, food, Internet, and merchandise sales. Then you will enter a formula to calculate the year-to-date income total using data from both sheets.

1 **Enter the following values in the specified cells.**

Sales	Cell	Number
Beverage	B8	15700
	C8	15800
	D8	15900
Food	B9	7500
	C9	7600
	D9	7600
Internet	B10	4500
	C10	4500
	D10	4500
Merchandise	B11	3200
	C11	3200
	D11	3200

Your screen should be similar to Figure 3.24

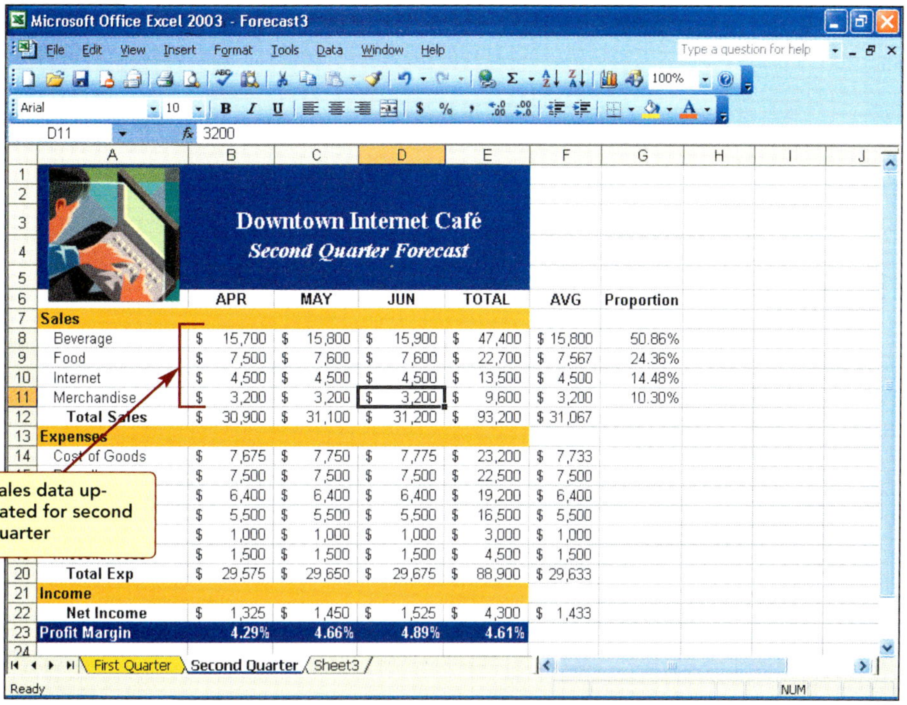

Figure 3.24

The worksheet now contains the data for the second quarter and all dependent formulas have been recalculated.

Now you can enter the formula to calculate a year-to-date income total. The formula to make this calculation will sum the total income numbers from cell E22 in the First Quarter sheet and cell E22 in the Second Quarter sheet. To reference data in another sheet in the same workbook, you enter a formula that references cells in other worksheets.

Concept 4

Sheet and 3-D References

4 A formula that contains references to cells in other sheets of a workbook allows you to use data from multiple sheets and to calculate new values based on this data. The formula contains a **sheet reference** consisting of the name of the sheet, followed by an exclamation point and the cell or range reference. If the sheet name contains nonalphabetic characters, such as a space, the sheet name (or path) must be enclosed in single quotation marks.

If you want to use the same cell or range of cells on multiple sheets, you can use a 3-D reference. A **3-D reference** consists of the names of the beginning and ending sheets enclosed in quotes and separated by a colon. This is followed by an exclamation point and the cell or range reference. The cell or range reference is the same on each sheet in the specified sheet range. If a sheet is inserted or deleted, the range is automatically updated. 3-D references make it easy to analyze data in the same cell or range of cells on multiple worksheets.

Reference	Description
=Sheet2!B17	Displays the entry in cell B17 of Sheet2 in the active cell of the current sheet
=Sheet1!A1+Sheet2!B2.	Sums the values in cell A1 of Sheet1 and B2 of Sheet2
=SUM(Sheet1:Sheet4!H6:K6)	Sums the values in cells H6 through K6 in Sheets 1, 2, 3, and 4
=SUM(Sheet1!H6:K6)	Sums the values in cells H6 through K6 in Sheet1
=SUM(Sheet1:Sheet4!H6)	Sums the values in cell H6 of Sheets 1, 2, 3, and 4

Just like a formula that references cells within a sheet, a formula that references cells in multiple sheets is automatically recalculated when data in a referenced cell changes.

You will enter a descriptive text entry in cell D24 and then use a 3-D reference in a SUM function to calculate the year-to-date total in cell E24.

The SUM function argument will consist of a 3-D reference to cell E22 in the First and Second Quarter sheets. Although a 3-D reference can be entered by typing it using the proper syntax, it is much easier to enter it by pointing to the cells on the sheets. To enter a 3-D reference, select the cell or range in the beginning sheet and then hold down ⇧Shift and click on the sheet tab of the last sheet in the range. This will include the indicated cell range on all sheets between and including the first and last sheet specified.

2

- In cell D24 enter and right-align the entry **Income Year-To-Date**.
- Move to E24.
- Click [Σ] AutoSum.
- Click cell E22.
- Hold down [⇧Shift] and click the First Quarter tab.
- Release [⇧Shift].
- Press [←Enter].
- Move to E24.

Your screen should be similar to Figure 3.25

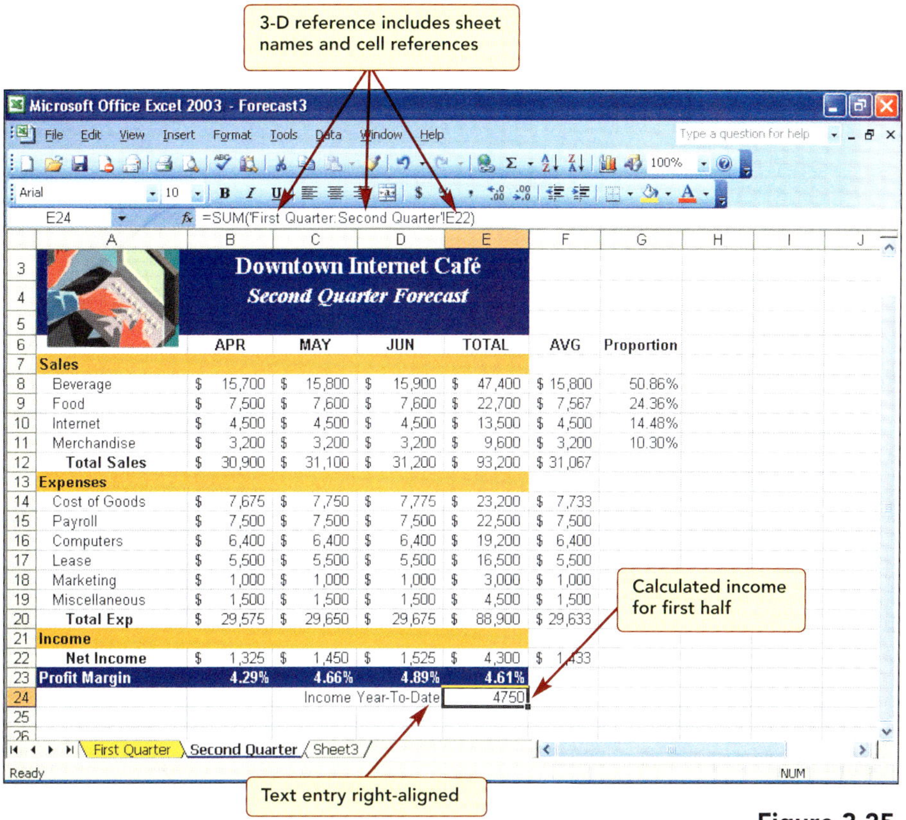

Figure 3.25

The calculated number 4750 appears in cell E24, and the function containing a 3-D reference appears in the formula bar.

You have now completed the forecast for the first half of the year.

3

- Change the format of cell E24 to Accounting with zero decimal places.
- Enter the following information in the Summary tab of the File Properties.

  Title **Downtown Internet Cafe**

  Subject **Quarterly Forecasts**

  Author **your name**

- Add a predefined header containing your name, page number, and the date to both sheets.
- Preview the entire workbook. Print both worksheets.
- Move to cell A7 in both sheets and save the workbook.
- Close the workbook.

Your printed output of the second quarter sheet should be similar to that shown here.

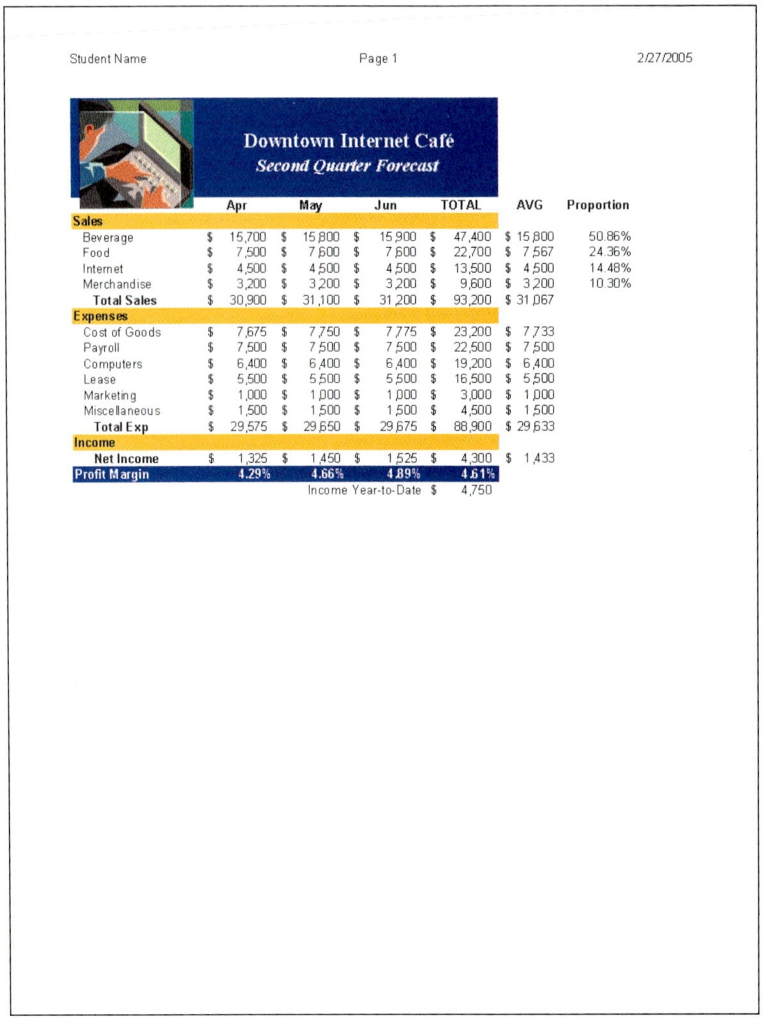

Student Name — Page 1 — 2/27/2005

Downtown Internet Café
Second Quarter Forecast

	Apr	May	Jun	TOTAL	AVG	Proportion
Sales						
Beverage	$ 15,700	$ 15,800	$ 15,900	$ 47,400	$ 15,800	50.86%
Food	$ 7,500	$ 7,600	$ 7,600	$ 22,700	$ 7,567	24.36%
Internet	$ 4,500	$ 4,500	$ 4,500	$ 13,500	$ 4,500	14.48%
Merchandise	$ 3,200	$ 3,200	$ 3,200	$ 9,600	$ 3,200	10.30%
Total Sales	$ 30,900	$ 31,100	$ 31,200	$ 93,200	$ 31,067	
Expenses						
Cost of Goods	$ 7,675	$ 7,750	$ 7,775	$ 23,200	$ 7,733	
Payroll	$ 7,500	$ 7,500	$ 7,500	$ 22,500	$ 7,500	
Computers	$ 6,400	$ 6,400	$ 6,400	$ 19,200	$ 6,400	
Lease	$ 5,500	$ 5,500	$ 5,500	$ 16,500	$ 5,500	
Marketing	$ 1,000	$ 1,000	$ 1,000	$ 3,000	$ 1,000	
Miscellaneous	$ 1,500	$ 1,500	$ 1,500	$ 4,500	$ 1,500	
Total Exp	$ 29,575	$ 29,650	$ 29,675	$ 88,900	$ 29,633	
Income						
Net Income	$ 1,325	$ 1,450	$ 1,525	$ 4,300	$ 1,433	
Profit Margin	4.29%	4.66%	4.89%	4.61%		
			Income Year-to-Date	$ 4,750		

Note: If you are running short on lab time, this is an appropriate place to end this session and begin again at a later time.

Deleting and Moving Sheets

You presented the completed first and second quarterly forecasts to Evan. He is very pleased with the results and now wants you to create worksheets for the third and fourth quarters and a combined annual forecast. Additionally, Evan has asked you to include a column chart of the data for each quarter. Finally, after looking at the forecast, Evan wants the forecast to show a profit margin of 5 percent for each month in the second quarter.

You have already made several of the changes requested and saved them as a workbook file. You will open this file to see the revised and expanded forecast.

1 Open the workbook file ex03_Annual Forecast**.**

Your screen should be similar to Figure 3.26

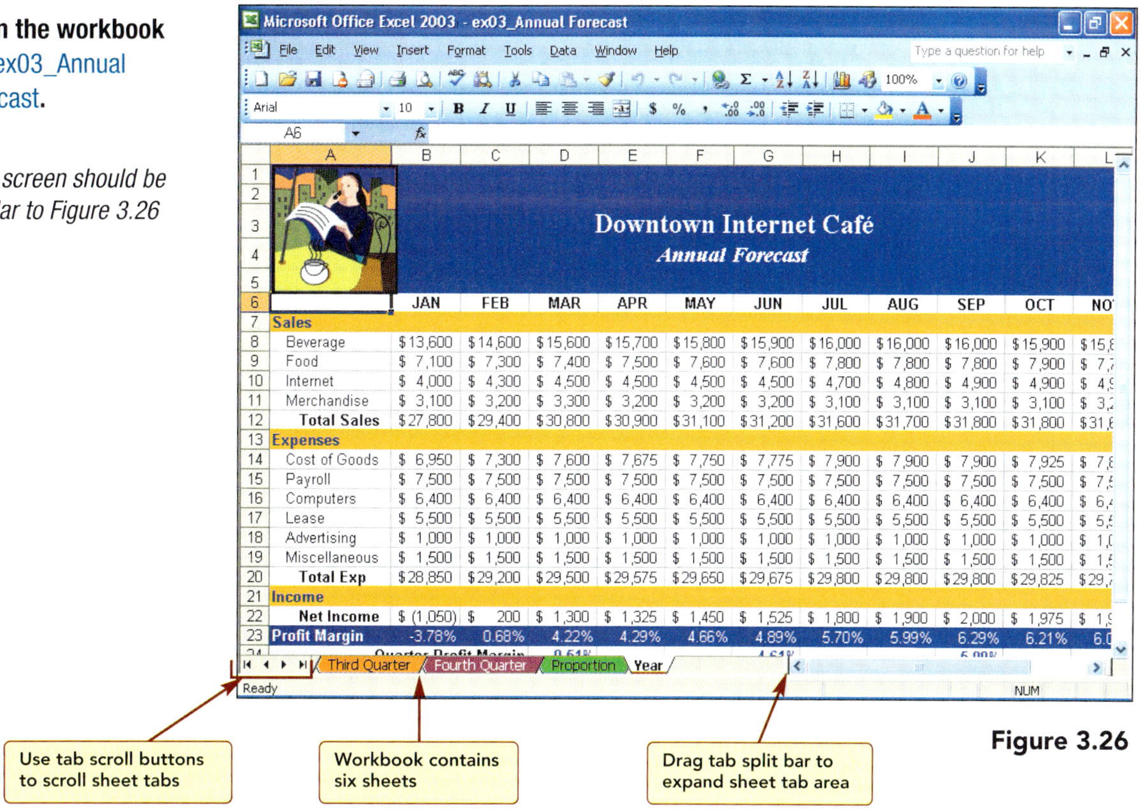

Figure 3.26

The workbook file now contains six sheets: First Quarter, Second Quarter, Third Quarter, Fourth Quarter, Proportion, and Year. The Proportion sheet contains the proportion of sales values from the first and second quarters. The Year sheet contains the forecast data for the entire 12 months. Each quarter sheet also includes a chart of the profit margin for that quarter. As you can now easily see, the profit margin by the end of the first quarter is showing a profit.

Notice also that the First Quarter and Second Quarter sheet tabs are not visible. This is because there is not enough space in the sheet tab area to display all the tabs. To see the tabs you can drag the tab split bar located at the right edge of the sheet tab area to expand the area or use the sheet tab scroll buttons to scroll the tabs into view.

2 • Click on each of the Quarter sheet tabs to view the quarterly data and profit margin chart.

• Display the Proportion sheet.

Your screen should be similar to Figure 3.27

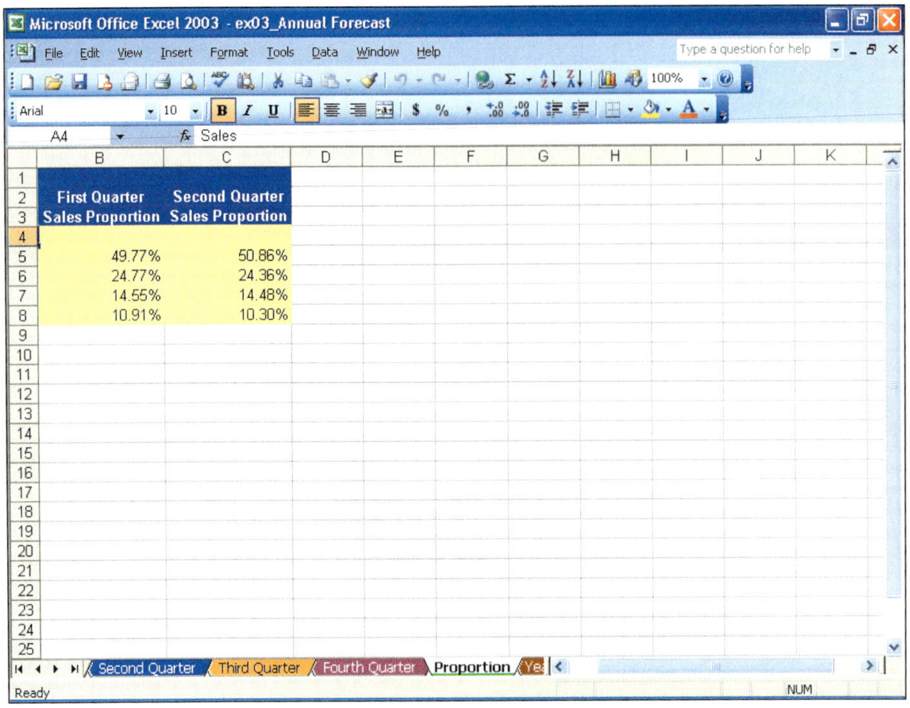

Figure 3.27

You decide this data, although interesting, is not needed in the forecast workbook and want to delete the entire sheet.

3 • Choose **Edit/Delete Sheet.**

• Click Delete to confirm that you want to permanently remove the sheet.

Another Method

You can also choose Delete from the sheet tab's shortcut menu to delete a sheet.

Your screen should be similar to Figure 3.28

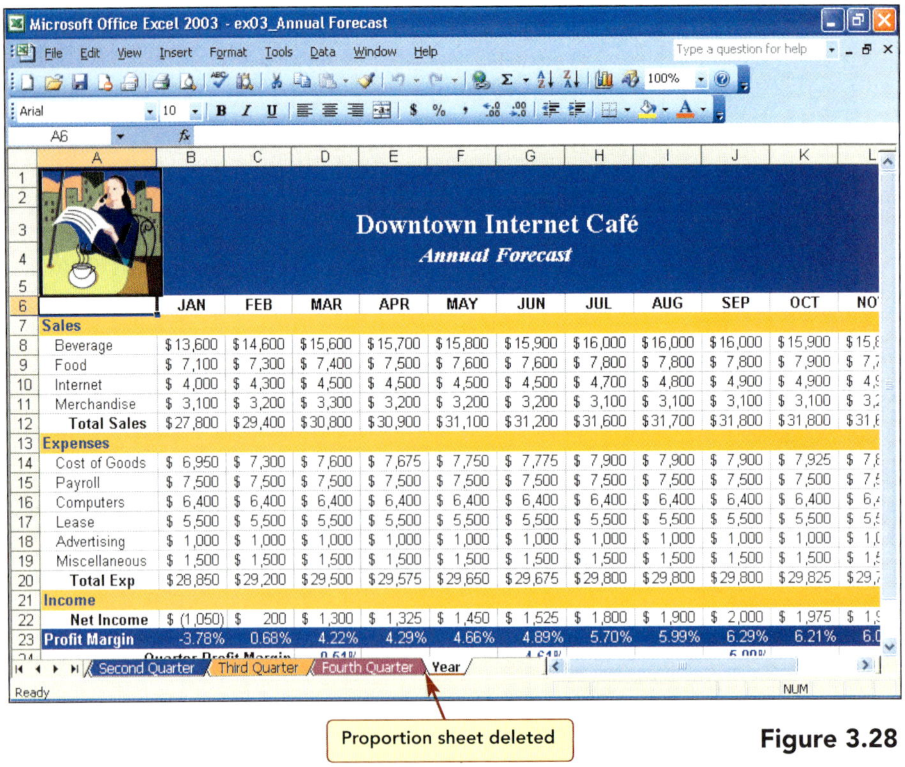

Figure 3.28

The entire sheet is deleted, and the Year sheet is now the active sheet. Next you want to move the Year sheet from the last position in the workbook to the first. You can quickly rearrange the order of sheets in a workbook by dragging the selected sheet tab along the row of sheet tabs to the new location. The symbol ▼ indicates the location where the sheet will be displayed.

Additional Information

You can insert a blank new sheet using **I**nsert/**W**orksheet. It is inserted to the left of the active sheet.

4 **Drag the Year tab to the left of the First Quarter tab.**

Another Method

You can also use **E**dit/**M**ove or Copy Sheet to move a sheet to another location in the workbook.

Your screen should be similar to Figure 3.29

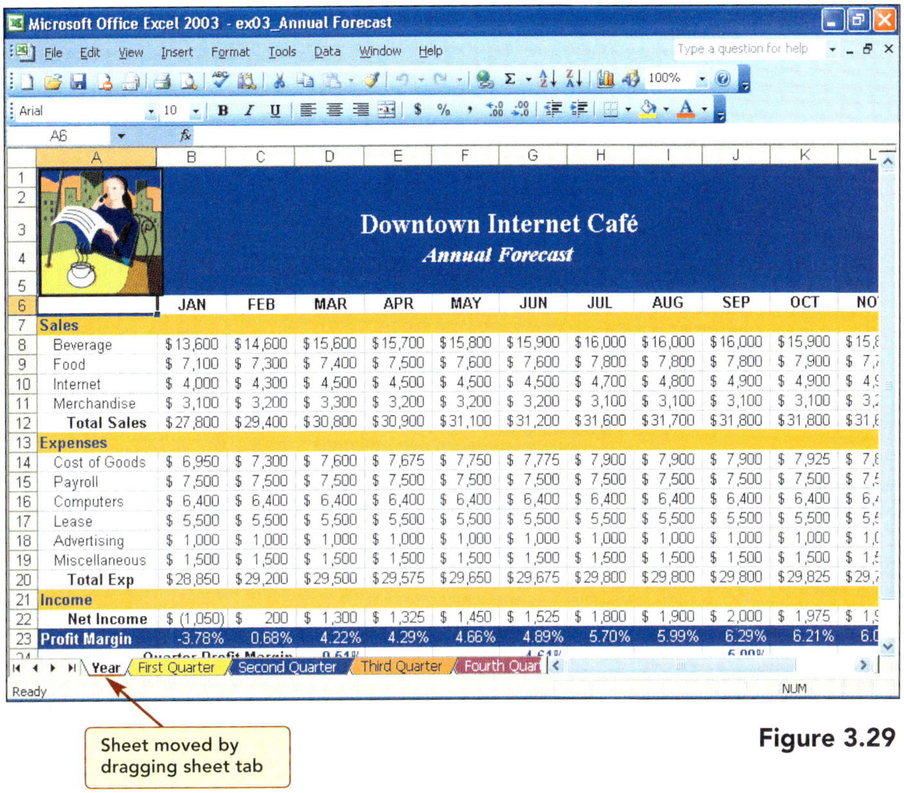

Figure 3.29

The Year sheet is now the first sheet in the workbook.

Finding and Replacing Information

As you look over the worksheets, you notice that the only abbreviation used in the entire workbook is for expenses in the Total Exp row heading. You want to change it to "Expenses" in all worksheets in the workbook.

You could change the word in each sheet by changing the text directly on the worksheet cells. However, the larger your workbook becomes, the more difficult it will be to find the data you want to modify. Therefore, you will use the Find and Replace feature to quickly locate the word and make the change.

Concept 5

Find and Replace

5 The **Find and Replace** feature helps you quickly find specific information and automatically replace it with new information. The Find command locates all occurrences of the text or numbers you specify. The Replace command is used with the Find command to locate the specified entries and replace the located occurrences with the replacement text you specify. You can also find cells that match a format you specify and replace the format with another. Finding and replacing data and formats is both fast and accurate, but you need to be careful when replacing that you do not replace unintended matches.

Finding Information

First, you will locate and correct the abbreviation using the Find command. This command can be used to locate data in any type of worksheet.

1 **Choose Edit/Find.**

> **Another Method**
>
> The keyboard shortcut is Ctrl + F.

If necessary, click Options >> to display the additional search options.

Your screen should be similar to Figure 3.30

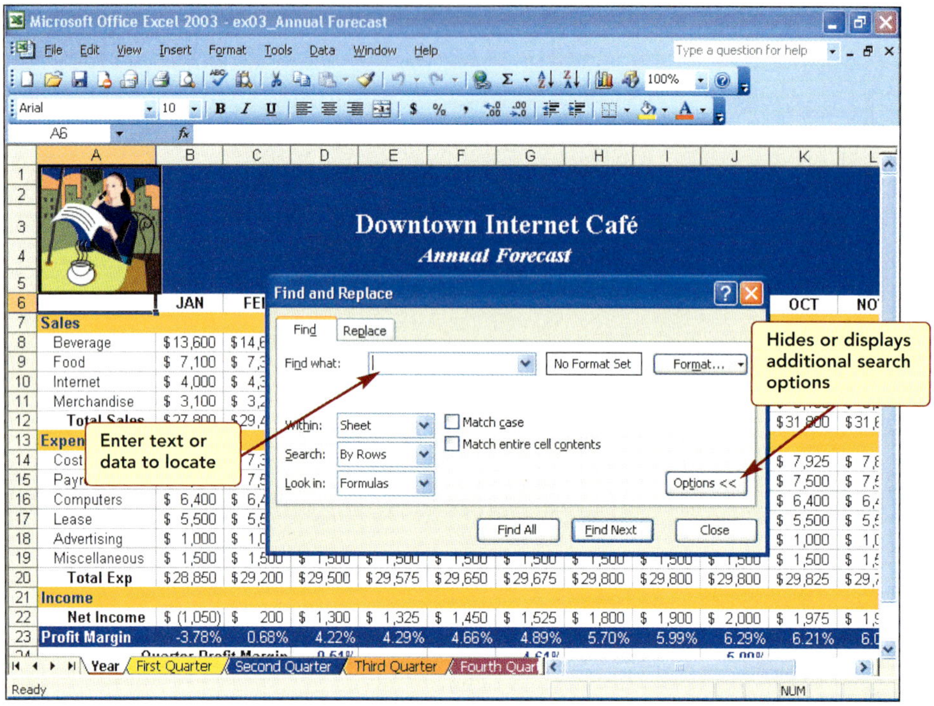

Figure 3.30

In the Find and Replace dialog box, you enter the information you want to locate in the Find What text box. It must be entered exactly as it appears in the worksheet. The additional options in the dialog box can be combined in many ways to help locate information. They are described in the table below.

Option	Effect
Within	Searches the active worksheet or workbook.
Search	Specifies the direction to search in the worksheet: By Columns searches down through columns and By Rows searches to the right across rows.
Look in	Looks for a match in the specified worksheet element: formulas, values, comments.
Match case	Finds words that have the same pattern of uppercase letters as entered in the Find What text box. Using this option makes the search case sensitive.
Match entire cell contents	Looks for an exact and complete match of the characters specified in the Find What text box.
Format	Used to specify a cell format to locate and replace. A sample of the selected format is displayed in the Preview box.

You will enter the text to find and will search using the default options.

2 **Type exp in the Find What box.**

Additional Information

Because the Match Case option is not selected, Find will look for an exact match regardless of whether the characters are uppercase or lowercase.

- **Click Options << to hide the additional search options.**
- **Click Find Next.**

Your screen should be similar to Figure 3.31

Additional Information

Clicking Find All displays all text or format matches in a list. Selecting an item from the list moves the cell selector to the cell containing the entry.

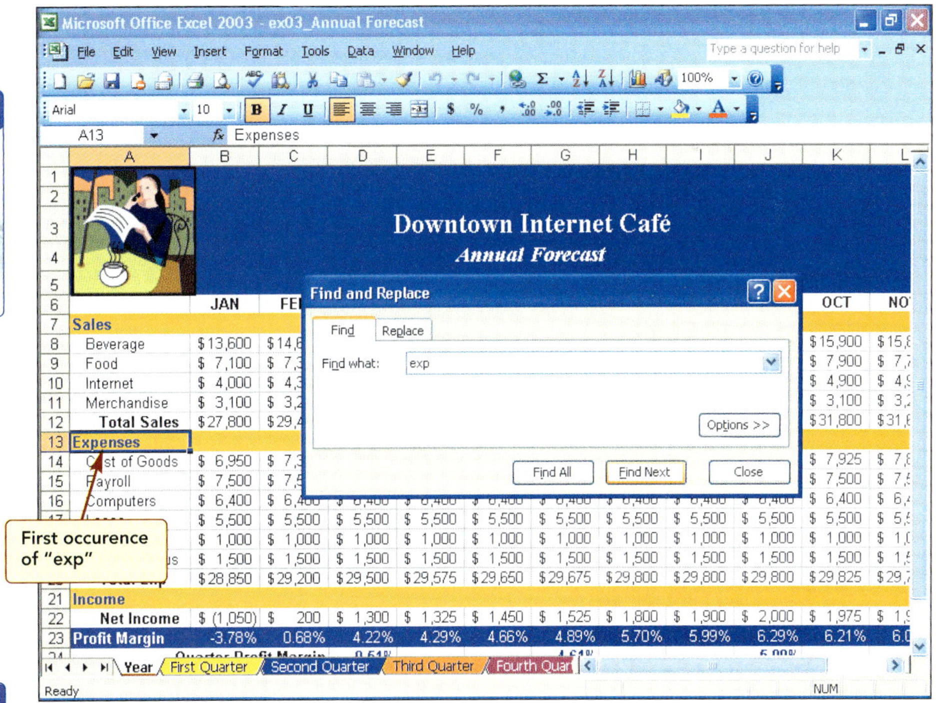

Figure 3.31

The cell selector jumps to the first occurrence of "exp," in cell A13, which contains the word "Expenses." It located this word because the first three letters match. However, this is not the entry you are trying to locate. You will continue the search to locate the next occurrence.

3 **Click Find Next.**

The Total Exp cell is located and selected. You can now edit the cell to display the word "Expenses."

4 **Double-click on the cell.**

Change Exp to **Expenses.**

Click .

Your screen should be similar to Figure 3.32

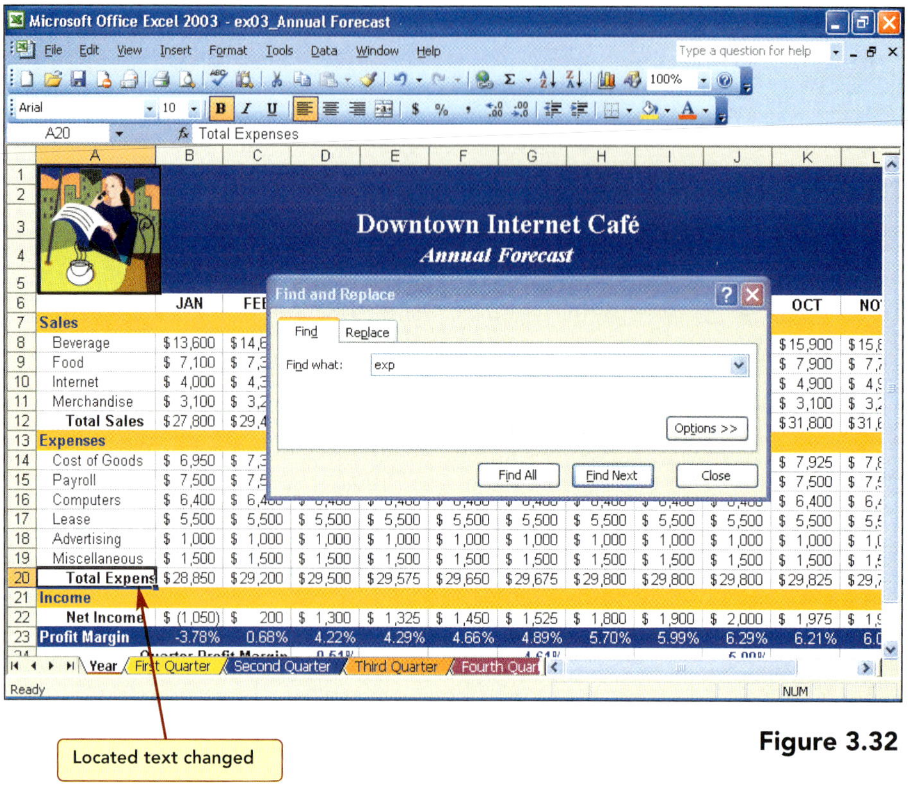

Figure 3.32

You manually made the correction to the label in cell A20. Next, you want to locate the word in all the other sheets and correct the entries.

Replacing Information

You realize that "exp" will be located twice in every worksheet. Since you want to change only the Total Exp headings you will refine your search term to locate only this heading and use the Replace command to make the correction automatically on the other sheets. The replacement text must be entered exactly as you want it to appear.

First, you will select all four quarter sheets as a group so that any changes you make are made to all selected sheets. To select two or more adjacent sheets click on the tab for the first sheet, and click on the last sheet tab while holding down ⇧Shift. You can select nonadjacent sheets by holding down Ctrl while clicking on each sheet. The title bar displays "[Group]" whenever multiple sheets are selected.

1 **Click on the First Quarter sheet tab, hold down ⇧Shift, and click on the Fourth Quarter tab.**

Additional Information

You can select all sheets using Select All Sheets from the tab shortcut menu.

Additional Information

The tabs of all sheets appear white, indicating they are selected; the active sheet tab name is bold.

- **Type total exp in the Find What box.**
- **Open the Replace tab.**

Another Method

The menu equivalent is Edit/Replace and the keyboard shortcut is Ctrl + H.

- **Type Total Expenses in the Replace With box.**
- **Click Find Next.**
- **Click Replace All.**

Your screen should be similar to Figure 3.33

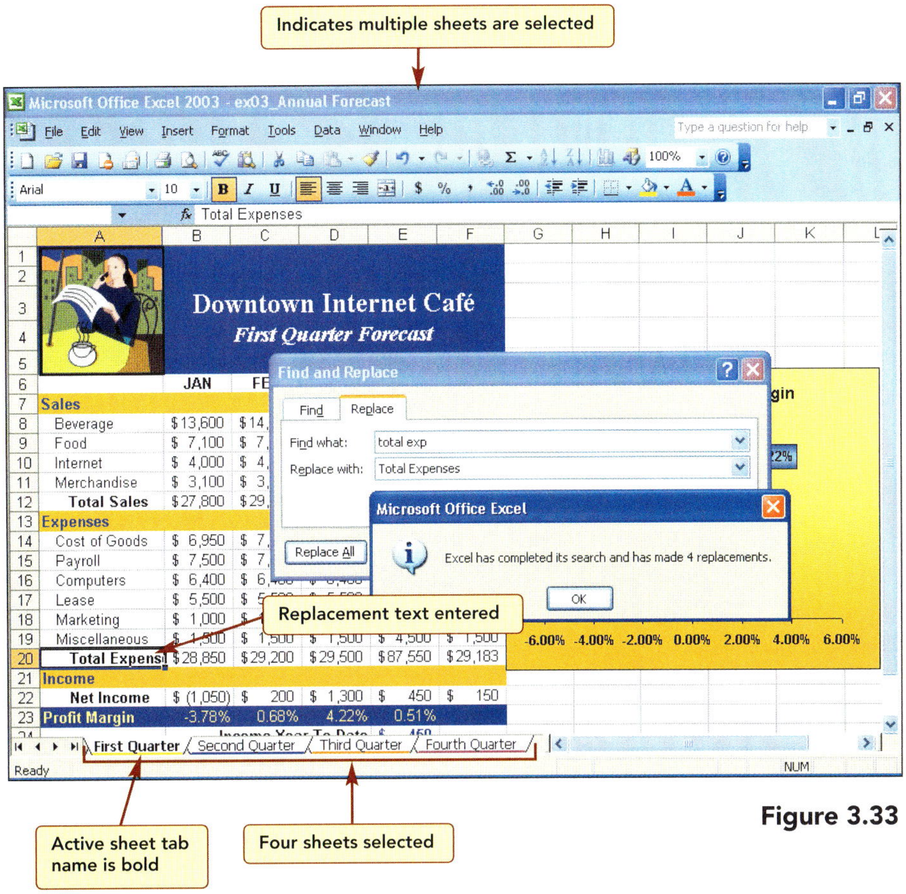

Figure 3.33

Four replacements were made, indicating that the heading was corrected on all four sheets. It is much faster to use Replace All than to confirm each match separately. However, exercise care when using Replace All because the search text you specify might be part of another word and you may accidentally replace text you want to keep.

2 Click OK.

Click Close.

Your screen should be similar to Figure 3.34

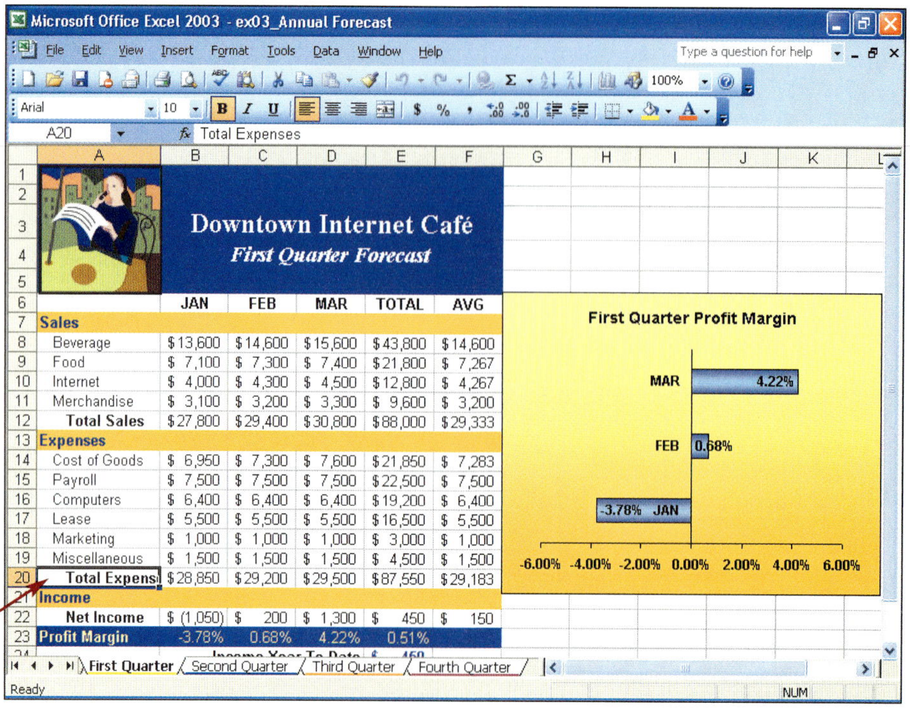

New heading too long for cell space

Figure 3.34

Because the new heading is longer than any other labels in column A, you will need to adjust the column width. You will expand the group selection to include the Year sheet and adjust the width of column A on all the worksheets at the same time.

3 Hold down Ctrl and click on the Year tab to add it to the group.

Having Trouble?

If you do not see the year tab, click the ◄ tab scroll button to display the tab.

AutoFit column A.

Having Trouble?

Double-click on the column border of column A when the mouse pointer is a ✛.

Right-click on the Year tab and choose Ungroup Sheets to cancel the group selection and make it active.

Additional Information

You can also click any unselected sheet to cancel a group selection.

Your screen should be similar to Figure 3.35

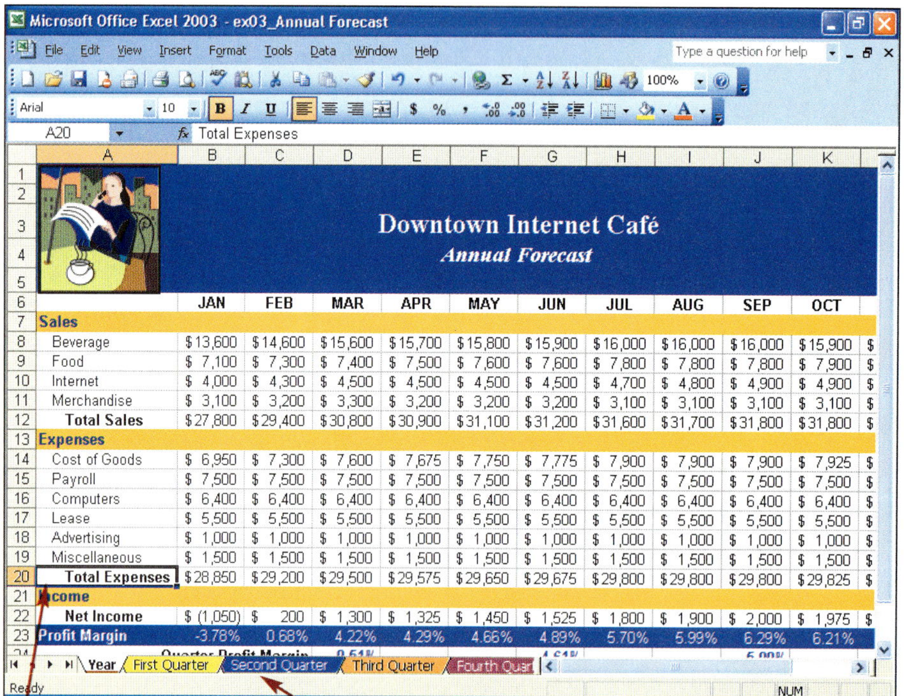

Column A sized to fit text

Group selection cancelled

Figure 3.35

You can now see that the A column width has been adjusted in the Year sheet, as it has in all other sheets. When multiple sheets are selected, be careful when making changes, as all selected sheets are affected.

Saving to a New Folder

You have made several changes to the workbook, and before continuing, you want to save it. Since the workbook is for projected forecasts, you decide to save it in a separate folder from the rest of the café's financial workbooks. You will save the file to a new folder named Forecasts.

1
- **Choose File/Save As.**
- **Enter as the file name Annual Forecast.**
- **If necessary, change the location to where you save your files.**
- **Click Create New Folder in the Save As dialog box.**

Your screen should be similar to Figure 3.36

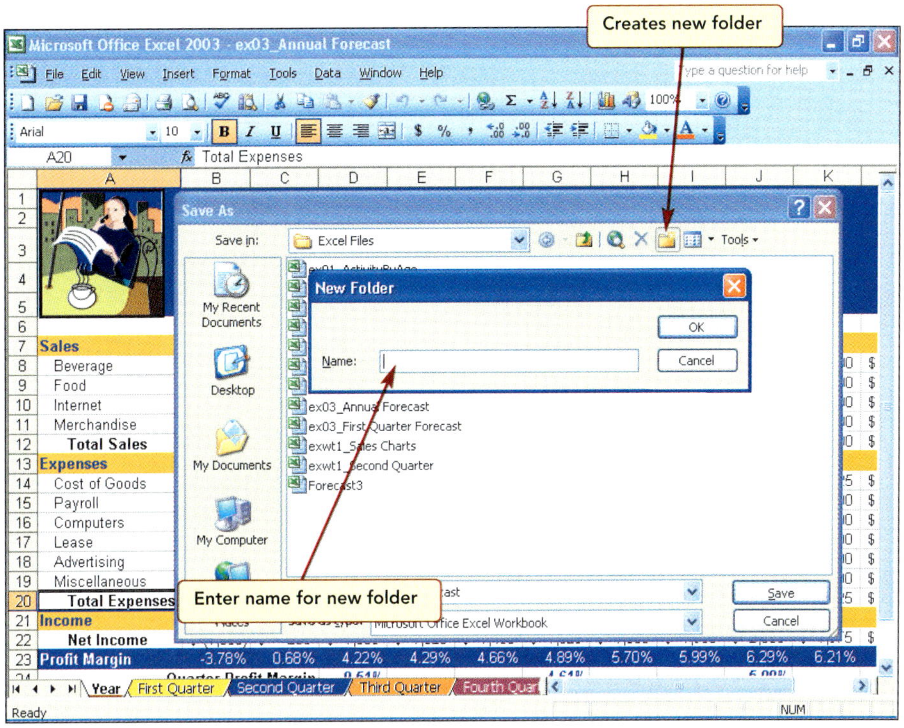

Figure 3.36

The New Folder dialog box enables you to create and name a new folder.

2
- **Type Forecasts in the Name text box.**
- **Click OK.**
- **Click Save.**

The Annual Forecast workbook is saved in the new Forecasts folder.

Additional Information

You can also rename an existing folder from the Save As dialog box by choosing Rename from the folder's shortcut menu and entering the new name.

Managing Large Worksheets

Now that the workbook is much larger, you are finding that it takes a lot of time to scroll to different areas within and between worksheets. To make managing large worksheets easier, you can zoom a worksheet, split the workbook window, and freeze panes.

Zooming the Worksheet

The Year worksheet displays all of the quarterly data. The entire worksheet, however, is not visible in the window. You can change how much information is displayed in the window to make it easier to navigate, view, and select worksheet data by adjusting the zoom percentage. The default zoom setting is 100 percent. This setting displays data onscreen the same size that it will appear on the printed page. You can reduce or enlarge the amount of information displayed onscreen by changing the magnification from between 10 to 400 percent. You want to decrease the zoom percent to display more information in the window.

Additional Information

The Zoom feature is common in all Office 2003 applications.

1 Open the 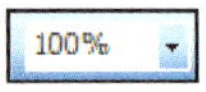 Zoom drop-down menu.

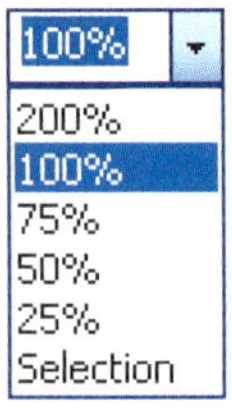

Additional Information

The Selection option adjusts the percentage to fit the selected range in the current window size.

- Choose 75%.

Another Method

The menu equivalent is View/Zoom and the voice command is "Zoom" followed by the percent value or zoom option.

Your screen should be similar to Figure 3.37

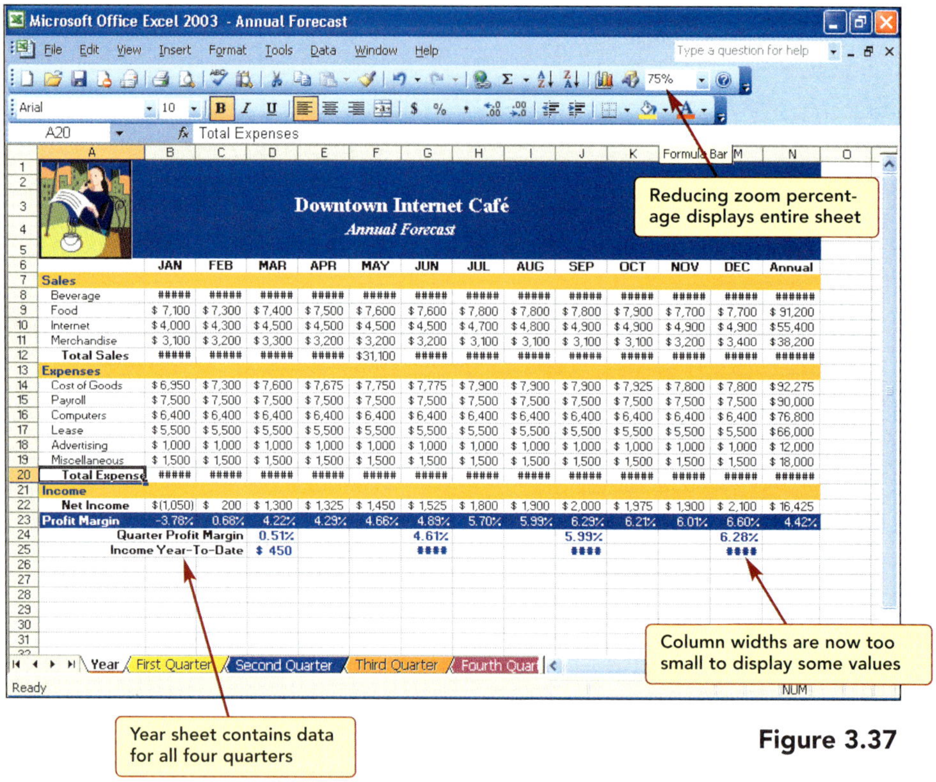

Figure 3.37

Additional Information

Pointing to the #### error value will display the cell value in a ScreenTip.

You can now see the entire worksheet. As you reduce the percentage, more worksheet area is visible in the window. However, it gets more difficult to read, and many cells display the error value ##### because the column width is not wide enough to fully display the entry.

Going to a Specific Cell

Most of the monthly values in the Year sheet, such as cell B8, contain linking formulas that reference the appropriate cells in the appropriate quarter sheets. Others, such as the total formulas and the formula to calculate the income, do not reference cells outside the Year worksheet. You will look at several of the formulas in cells that reference the quarter sheets.

1 **Return the zoom to 100%.**

Move to B8.

Move to E12.

Move to H16.

Your screen should be similar to Figure 3.38

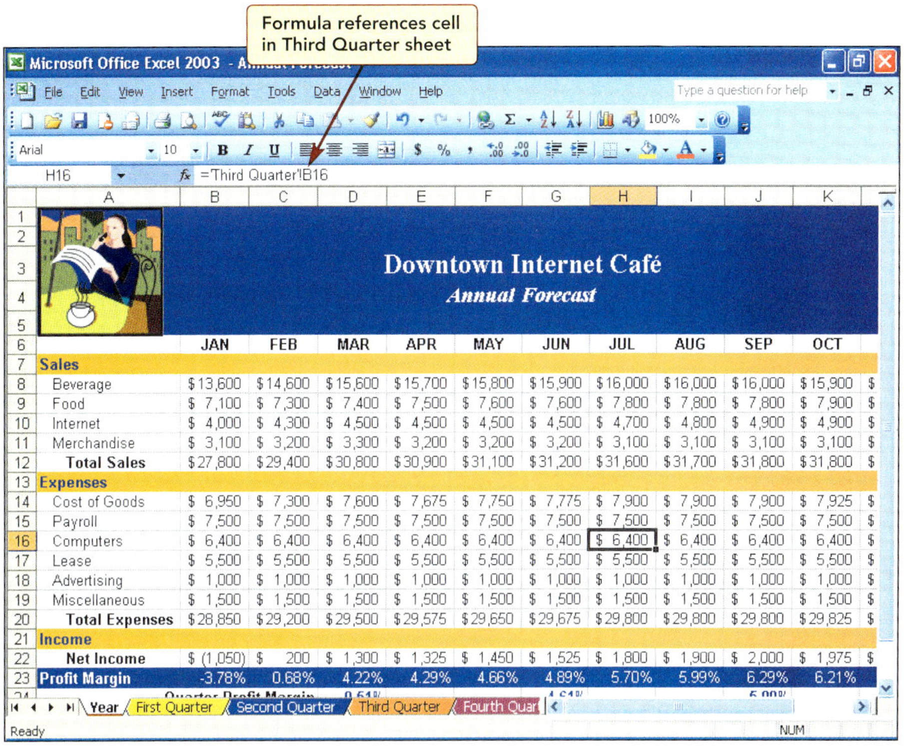

Figure 3.38

Each of these cells contains a formula that references a cell in the appropriate quarter sheet. To see the total formulas for the year in column N, you will move to cell N16 using the GoTo feature.

2 Type **N16** in the Name box.

Having Trouble?

The Name box is located at the left end of the formula bar.

Press ←Enter.

Another Method

The menu equivalent is **E**dit/**G**oTo and the keyboard shortcut is Ctrl + G or F5.

Your screen should be similar to Figure 3.39

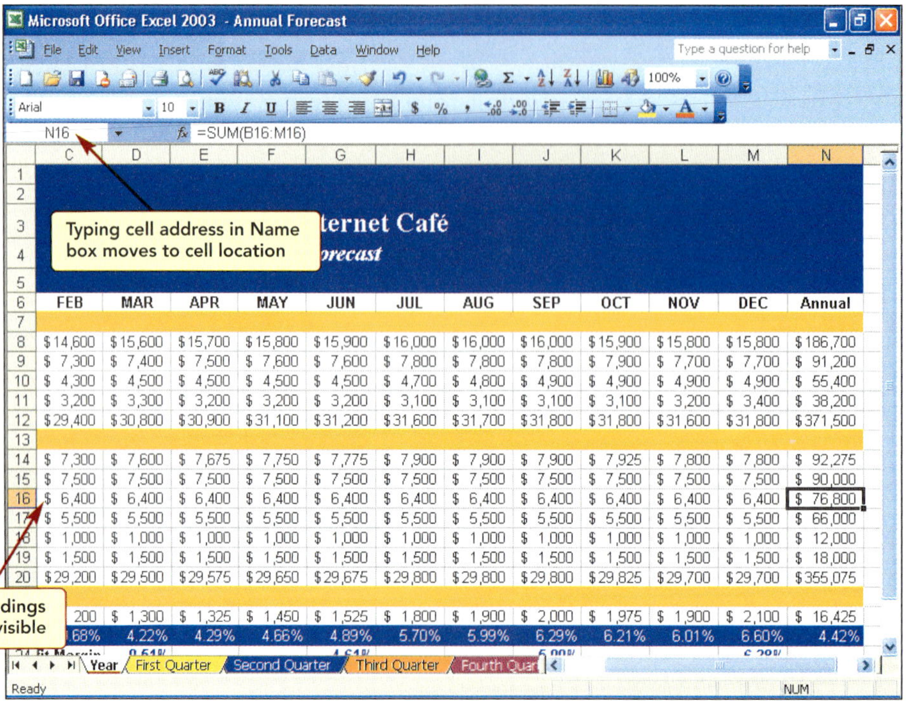

Figure 3.39

The cell selector jumps directly to cell N16 in the Annual column. The formula in this cell calculates the total of the values in row 16 and does not reference another sheet. However, it is difficult to know what the numbers represent in this row because the row headings are not visible. For example, is this number the total for the lease expenses, advertising expenses, or miscellaneous expenses? Without scrolling back to see the row headings, it is difficult to know.

Splitting Windows

Whenever you scroll a large worksheet, you will find that information you may need to view in one area scrolls out of view as you move to another area. Although you could reduce the zoom percent to view more of a worksheet in the window, you still may not be able to see the entire worksheet if it is very large. And as you saw, continuing to reduce the zoom makes the worksheet difficult to read and prevents some values from fully displaying. To view different areas of the same worksheet at the same time, you can split the window.

Concept 6

Split Window

6

The **split window** feature allows you to divide a worksheet window into sections, making it easier to view different parts of the worksheet at the same time. The sections of the window, called **panes**, can consist of any number of columns or rows along the top or left edge of the window. You can divide the worksheet into two panes either horizontally or vertically, or into four panes if you split the window both vertically and horizontally.

Each pane can be scrolled independently to display different areas of the worksheet. When split vertically, the panes scroll together when you scroll vertically, but scroll independently when you scroll horizontally. Horizontal panes scroll together when you scroll horizontally, but independently when you scroll vertically.

Panes are most useful for viewing a worksheet that consists of different areas or sections. Creating panes allows you to display the different sections of the worksheet in separate panes and then to quickly switch between panes to access the data in the different sections without having to repeatedly scroll to the areas.

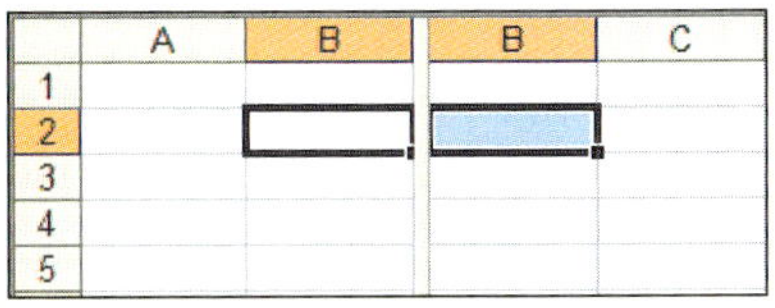

Two vertical panes

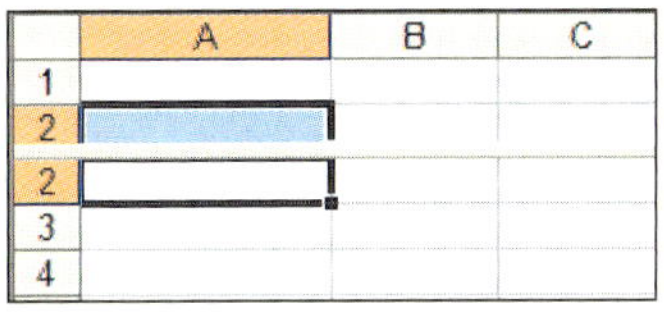

Two horizontal panes

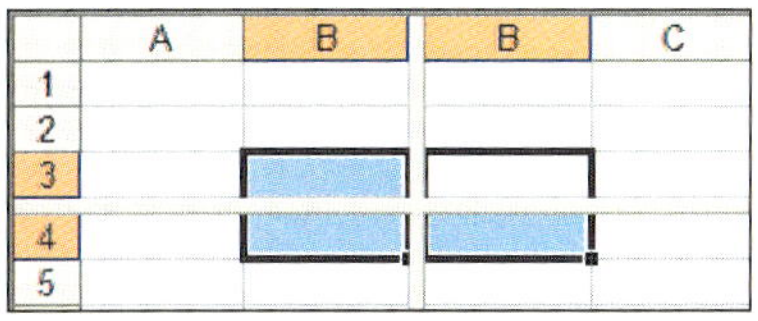

Four panes

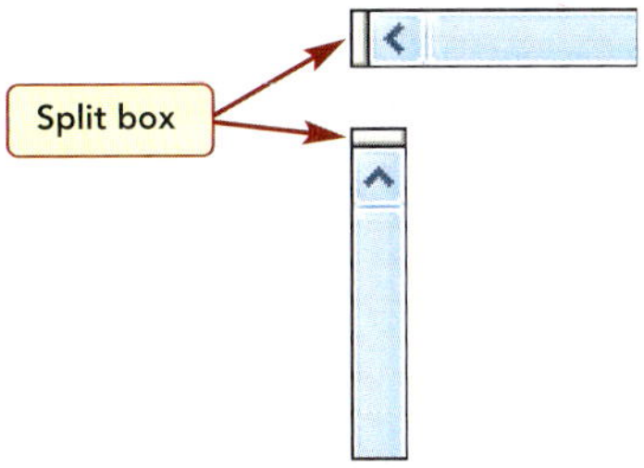

Dragging the split box at the top of the vertical scroll bar downward creates a horizontal split, and dragging the split box at the right end of the horizontal scroll bar leftward creates a vertical split.

You will split the window into two vertical panes. This will allow you to view the headings in column A at the same time as you are viewing data in column N.

1 Point to the vertical split box in the horizontal scroll bar.

Additional Information

The mouse pointer changes to a ◂||▸ to show you can drag to create a split.

Drag to the left and position the bar between columns D and E.

Your screen should be similar to Figure 3.40

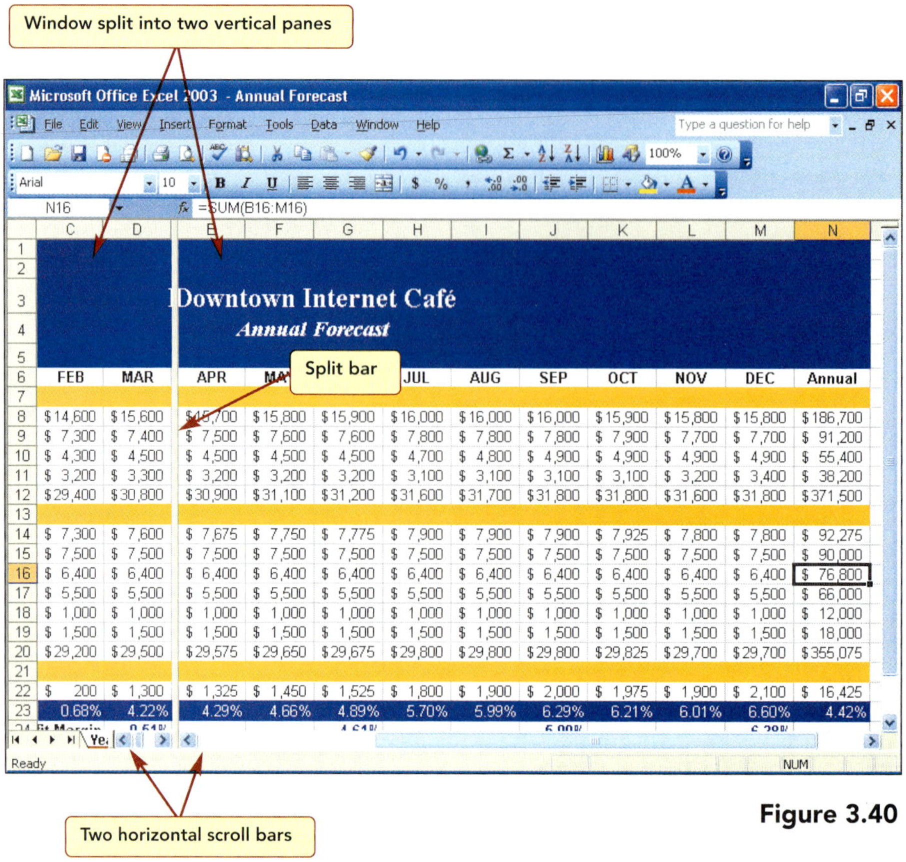

Figure 3.40

Additional Information

The Window/Split command can be used to quickly create a four-way split at the active cell.

There are now two vertical panes with two separate horizontal scroll bars. The highlighted cell selector is visible in the right pane. The left pane also has a cell selector in cell N16, but it is not visible because that area of the worksheet is not displayed in the pane. When the same area of a worksheet is visible in multiple panes, the cell selector in the panes that are not active is highlighted whereas the cell selector in the active pane is clear. The active pane will be affected by your movement horizontally. The cell selector moves in both panes, but only the active pane scrolls.

You will scroll the left pane horizontally to display the month headings in column A.

2 **Click C16 in the left pane to display the active cell selector in the pane.**

Press ← twice.

Your screen should be similar to Figure 3.41

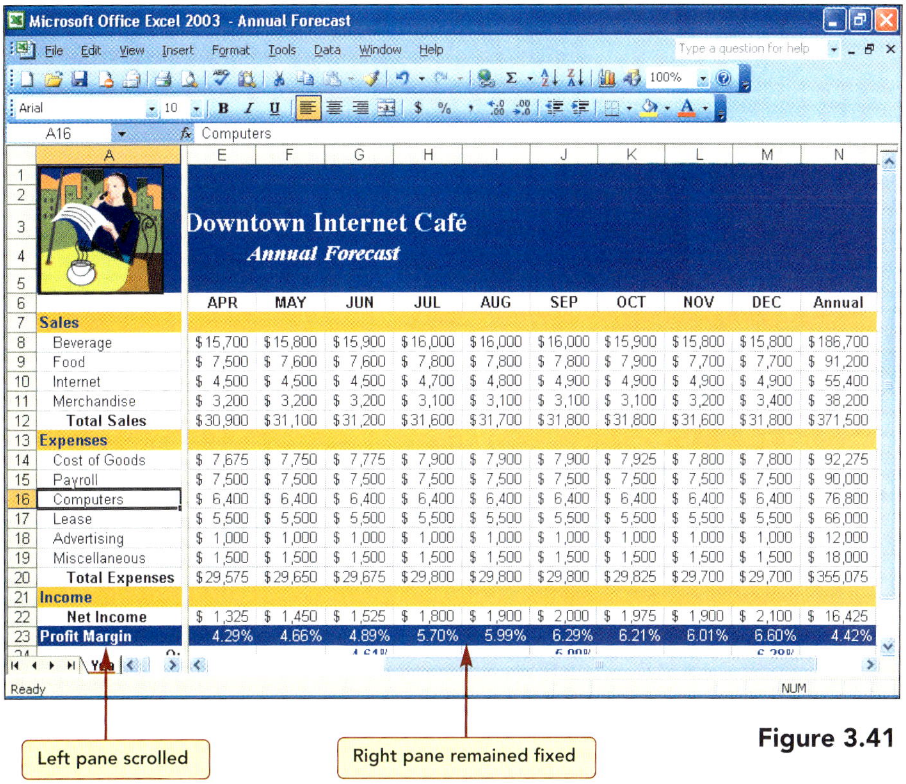

Figure 3.41

The right pane did not scroll when you moved horizontally through the left pane to display the row headings. The cell selector in the right pane is in the same cell location as in the left pane (A16), although it is not visible. You want to change the location of the split so that you can view an entire quarter in the left pane in order to more easily compare quarters.

3 **Drag the split bar to the right three columns.**

Click cell E16 in the right pane.

Press End →.

Press → (three times).

Your screen should be similar to Figure 3.42

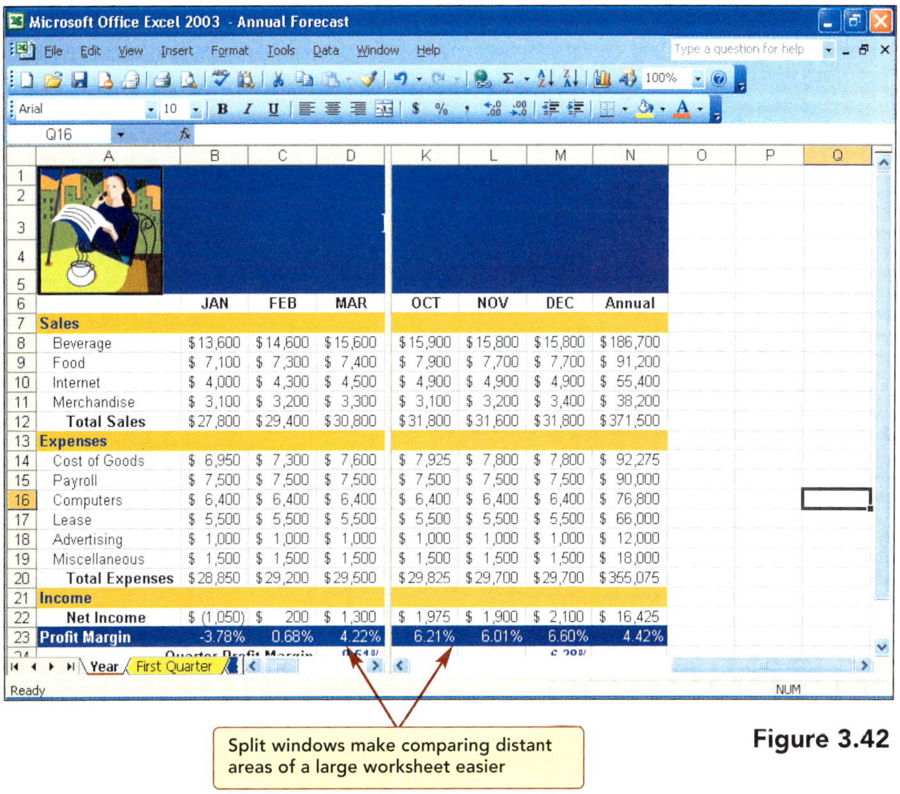

Figure 3.42

Now you can easily compare the first quarter data to the last quarter data. As you can see, creating panes is helpful when you want to display and access distant areas of a worksheet quickly. After scrolling the data in the panes to display the appropriate worksheet area, you can then quickly switch between panes to make changes to the data that is visible in the pane. This saves you the time of scrolling to the area each time you want to view it or make changes to it. You will clear the vertical split from the window.

4 **Double-click anywhere on the split bar.**

Another Method

The menu equivalent is Window/Remove Split.

Your screen should be similar to Figure 3.43

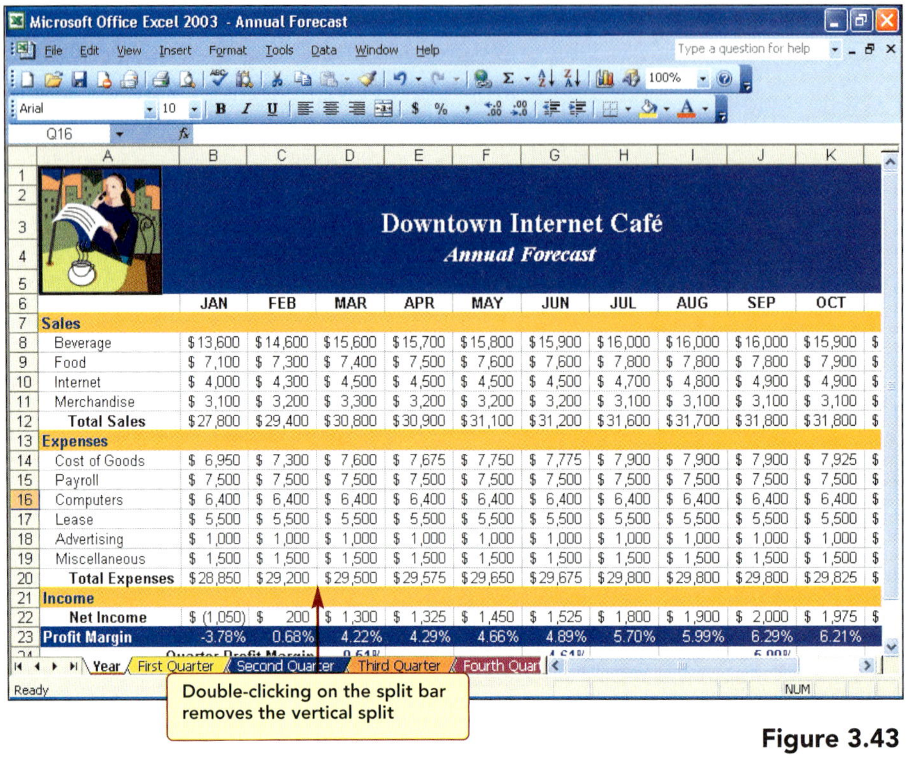

		JAN	FEB	MAR	APR	MAY	JUN	JUL	AUG	SEP	OCT	
7	Sales											
8	Beverage	$13,600	$14,600	$15,600	$15,700	$15,800	$15,900	$16,000	$16,000	$16,000	$15,900	$
9	Food	$ 7,100	$ 7,300	$ 7,400	$ 7,500	$ 7,600	$ 7,600	$ 7,800	$ 7,800	$ 7,800	$ 7,900	$
10	Internet	$ 4,000	$ 4,300	$ 4,500	$ 4,500	$ 4,500	$ 4,500	$ 4,700	$ 4,800	$ 4,900	$ 4,900	$
11	Merchandise	$ 3,100	$ 3,200	$ 3,300	$ 3,200	$ 3,200	$ 3,200	$ 3,100	$ 3,100	$ 3,100	$ 3,100	$
12	Total Sales	$27,800	$29,400	$30,800	$30,900	$31,100	$31,200	$31,600	$31,700	$31,800	$31,800	$
13	Expenses											
14	Cost of Goods	$ 6,950	$ 7,300	$ 7,600	$ 7,675	$ 7,750	$ 7,775	$ 7,900	$ 7,900	$ 7,900	$ 7,925	$
15	Payroll	$ 7,500	$ 7,500	$ 7,500	$ 7,500	$ 7,500	$ 7,500	$ 7,500	$ 7,500	$ 7,500	$ 7,500	$
16	Computers	$ 6,400	$ 6,400	$ 6,400	$ 6,400	$ 6,400	$ 6,400	$ 6,400	$ 6,400	$ 6,400	$ 6,400	$
17	Lease	$ 5,500	$ 5,500	$ 5,500	$ 5,500	$ 5,500	$ 5,500	$ 5,500	$ 5,500	$ 5,500	$ 5,500	$
18	Advertising	$ 1,000	$ 1,000	$ 1,000	$ 1,000	$ 1,000	$ 1,000	$ 1,000	$ 1,000	$ 1,000	$ 1,000	$
19	Miscellaneous	$ 1,500	$ 1,500	$ 1,500	$ 1,500	$ 1,500	$ 1,500	$ 1,500	$ 1,500	$ 1,500	$ 1,500	$
20	Total Expenses	$28,850	$29,200	$29,500	$29,575	$29,650	$29,675	$29,800	$29,800	$29,800	$29,825	$
21	Income											
22	Net Income	$ (1,050)	$ 200	$ 1,300	$ 1,325	$ 1,450	$ 1,525	$ 1,800	$ 1,900	$ 2,000	$ 1,975	$
23	Profit Margin	-3.78%	0.68%	4.22%	4.29%	4.66%	4.89%	5.70%	5.99%	6.29%	6.21%	

Figure 3.43

Freezing Panes

Another way to manage a large worksheet is to freeze panes.

Concept 7

Freeze Panes

7 **Freezing panes** prevents the data in the pane from scrolling as you move to different areas in a worksheet. You can freeze the information in the top and left panes of a window only. This feature is most useful when your worksheet is organized using row and column headings. It allows you to keep the titles on the top and left edge of your worksheet in view as you scroll horizontally and vertically through the worksheet data.

You want to keep the month headings in row 6 and the row headings in column A visible in the window at all times while looking at the Income and Profit Margin data beginning in row 21. To do this, you will create four panes with the upper and left panes frozen.

When creating frozen panes, first position the worksheet in the window to display the information you want to appear in the top and left panes. This is because data in the frozen panes cannot be scrolled like data in regular panes. Then move to the location specified in the following table before using the **W**indow/**F**reeze Panes command to create and freeze panes.

<table>
<tr><th>To Create</th><th>Cell Selector Location</th><th>Example</th></tr>
<tr><td>Two horizontal panes with the top pane frozen</td><td>Move to the leftmost column in the window and to the row below where you want the split to appear.</td><td>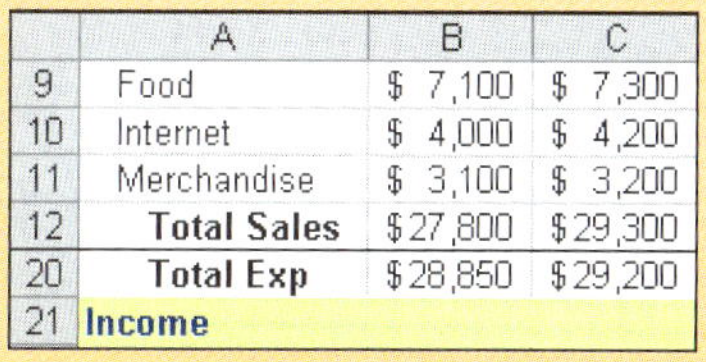
<table>
<tr><th></th><th>A</th><th>B</th><th>C</th></tr>
<tr><td>9</td><td>Food</td><td>$ 7,100</td><td>$ 7,300</td></tr>
<tr><td>10</td><td>Internet</td><td>$ 4,000</td><td>$ 4,200</td></tr>
<tr><td>11</td><td>Merchandise</td><td>$ 3,100</td><td>$ 3,200</td></tr>
<tr><td>12</td><td>Total Sales</td><td>$27,800</td><td>$29,300</td></tr>
<tr><td>20</td><td>Total Exp</td><td>$28,850</td><td>$29,200</td></tr>
<tr><td>21</td><td>Income</td><td></td><td></td></tr>
</table>
Top Pane Frozen</td></tr>
<tr><td>Two vertical panes with the left pane frozen</td><td>Move to the top row of the window and to the column to the right of where you want the split to appear.</td><td>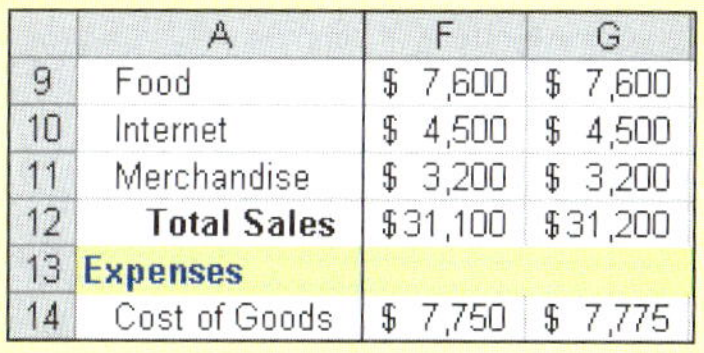
<table>
<tr><th></th><th>A</th><th>F</th><th>G</th></tr>
<tr><td>9</td><td>Food</td><td>$ 7,600</td><td>$ 7,600</td></tr>
<tr><td>10</td><td>Internet</td><td>$ 4,500</td><td>$ 4,500</td></tr>
<tr><td>11</td><td>Merchandise</td><td>$ 3,200</td><td>$ 3,200</td></tr>
<tr><td>12</td><td>Total Sales</td><td>$31,100</td><td>$31,200</td></tr>
<tr><td>13</td><td>Expenses</td><td></td><td></td></tr>
<tr><td>14</td><td>Cost of Goods</td><td>$ 7,750</td><td>$ 7,775</td></tr>
</table>
Left Pane Frozen</td></tr>
<tr><td>Four panes with the top and left panes frozen</td><td>Move to the cell below and to the right of where you want the split to appear.</td><td>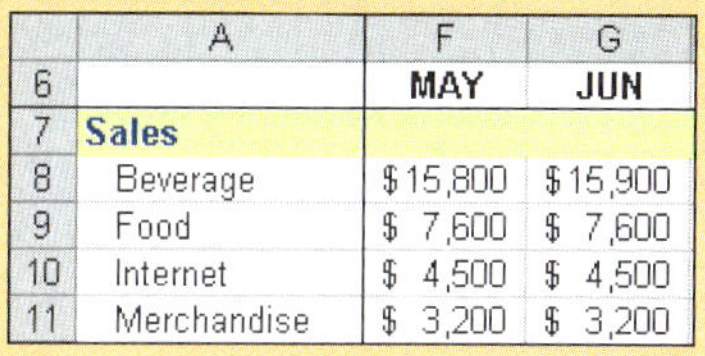
<table>
<tr><th></th><th>A</th><th>F</th><th>G</th></tr>
<tr><td>6</td><td></td><td>MAY</td><td>JUN</td></tr>
<tr><td>7</td><td>Sales</td><td></td><td></td></tr>
<tr><td>8</td><td>Beverage</td><td>$15,800</td><td>$15,900</td></tr>
<tr><td>9</td><td>Food</td><td>$ 7,600</td><td>$ 7,600</td></tr>
<tr><td>10</td><td>Internet</td><td>$ 4,500</td><td>$ 4,500</td></tr>
<tr><td>11</td><td>Merchandise</td><td>$ 3,200</td><td>$ 3,200</td></tr>
</table>
Top and Left Panes Frozen</td></tr>
</table>

You want to split the window into four panes with the month column headings at the top of the window and the row headings in column A at the left side of the window.

1 Scroll the window until row 6 is the top row in the window.

- Move to B7.
- Choose Window/Freeze Panes.

Your screen should be similar to Figure 3.44

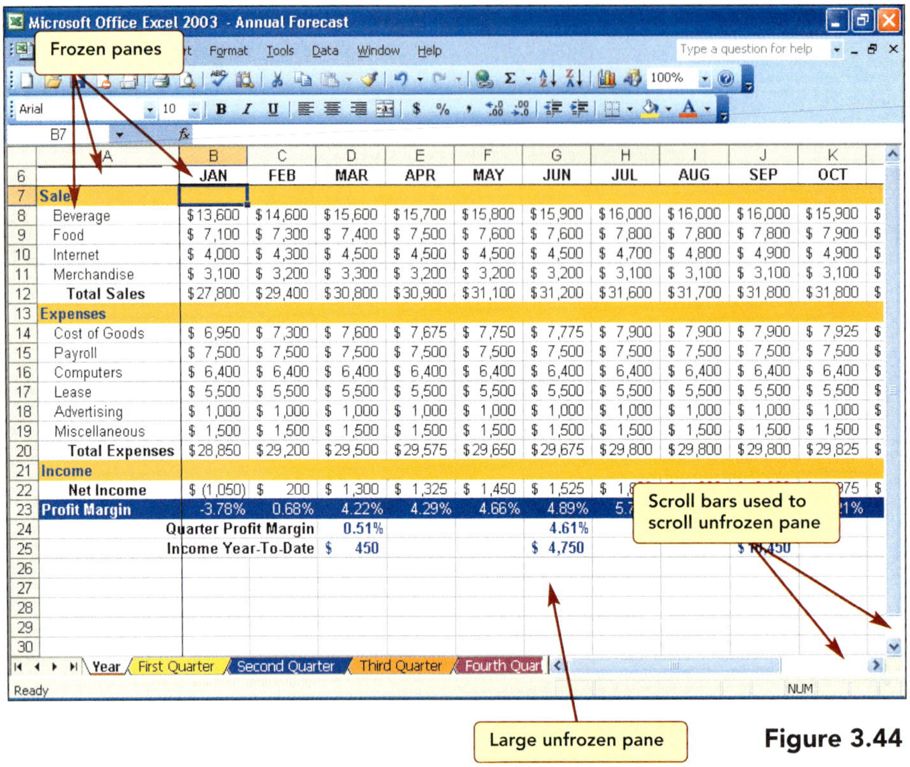

Figure 3.44

The window is divided into four panes at the cell selector location. Only one set of scroll bars is displayed because the only pane that can be scrolled is the larger lower-right pane. You can move the cell selector into a frozen pane, but the data in the frozen panes will not scroll. Also, there is only one cell selector that moves from one pane to another over the pane divider, making it unnecessary to click on the pane to make it active before moving the cell selector in it.

Because Evan has asked you to adjust the Profit Margin values, you want to view this area of the worksheet only.

2 Use the vertical scroll bar to scroll the window until row 21 is below row 6.

- Move to cell G24.

Your screen should be similar to Figure 3.45

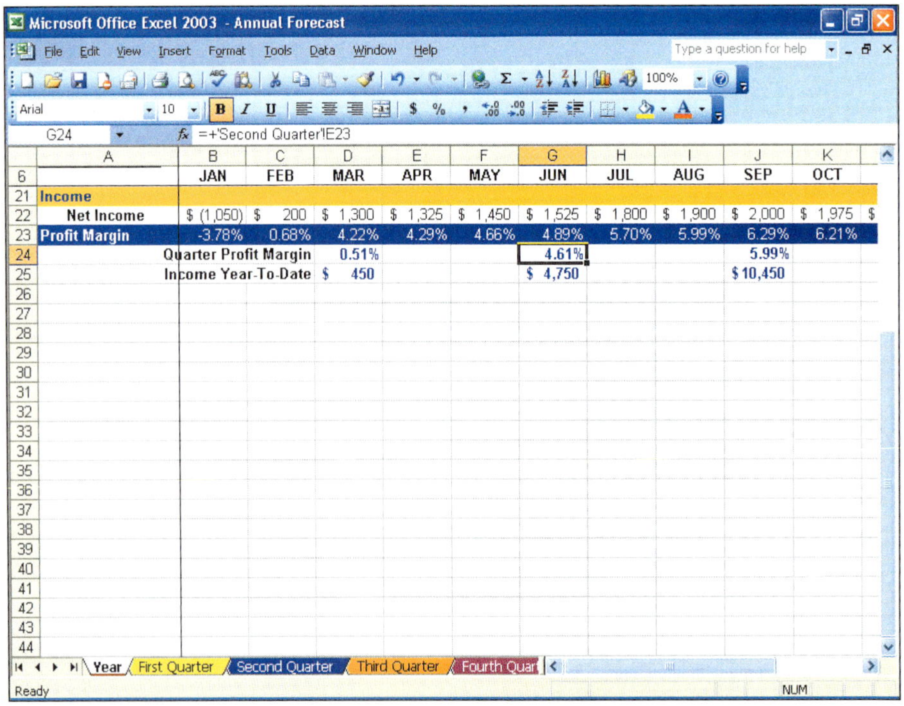

Figure 3.45

Now the Income and Profit Margin data is displayed immediately below the month headings in row 6. The data in rows 7 through 20 is no longer visible, allowing you to concentrate on this area of the worksheet.

Watching Cells

While using a workbook with large worksheets and/or multiple sheets, you may want to keep an eye on how changes you make to values in one area affect cells in another. For example, if you change a value in one sheet that is referenced in a formula in another, you can view the effect on the calculated value using the Watch Window toolbar.

You will be changing values in the Second Quarter sheet next and want to be able to see the effect on the linked formulas in the Year sheet at the same time.

1

- **Select cells G24 and N23.**
- **Choose Tools/Formula Auditing/Show Watch Window.**
- **If the Watch Window toolbar is docked along an edge of the window, drag it into the workbook window area.**

Another Method

You can also open the Watch Window toolbar from the toolbar shortcut menu.

- **Click** Add Watch... **from the Watch Window toolbar.**

Your screen should be similar to Figure 3.46

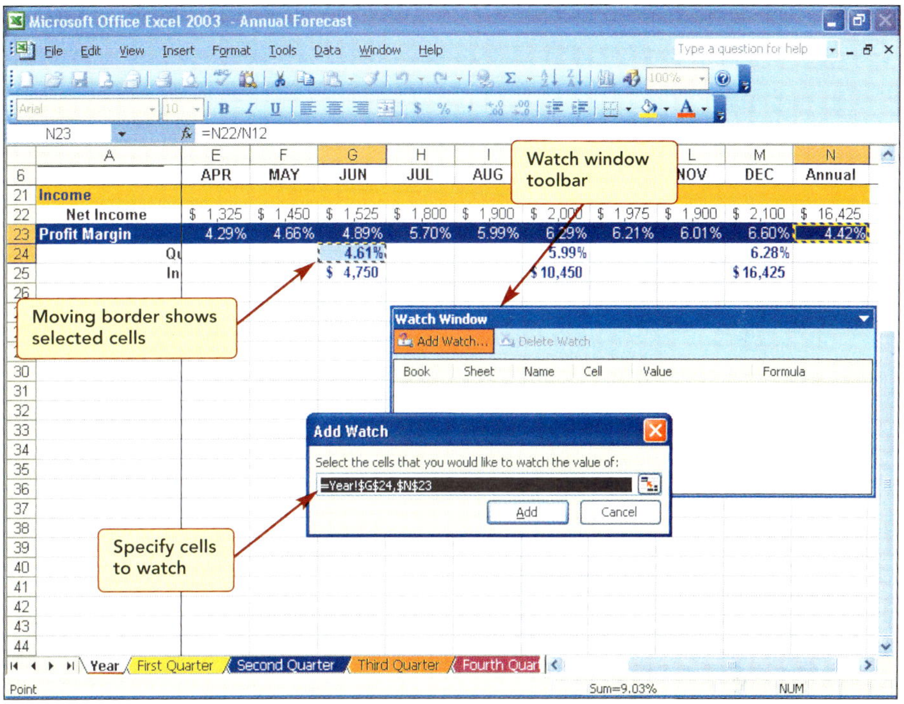

Figure 3.46

An empty Watch Window toolbar is displayed. The Add Watch dialog box is used to specify the cells you want to see in the Watch Window toolbar. The currently selected cells are identified with a moving border. You will add these cells to the Watch Window.

2 Click Add.

- Size the Watch Window toolbar to just large enough to display the two cell values rows.
- Move the Watch Window toolbar to the right corner of the workbook window below the formula bar.

Your screen should be similar to Figure 3.47

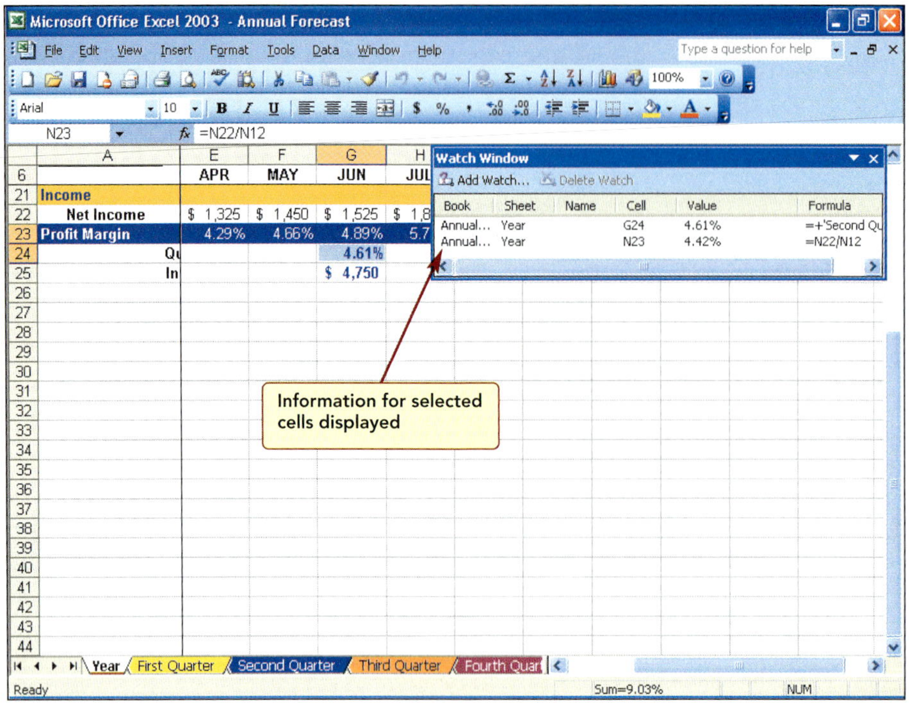

Figure 3.47

Additional Information

You can also watch linked cells in other open workbooks.

The values in the selected cells as well as the formula and location information are displayed in the Watch Window. The toolbar will remain open on top of the workbook as you move from one sheet to another.

Forecasting Values

Evan has asked you to adjust the forecast for the second quarter to show a profit margin of at least 5 percent for each month. After some consideration, you decide you can most easily reduce monthly payroll expenses by carefully scheduling employee work during these three months. Reducing the monthly expense will increase the profit margin for the quarter. You want to find out what the maximum payroll value you can spend during that period is for each month to accomplish this goal. The process of evaluating what effect changing the payroll expenses will have on the profit margin is called what-if analysis.

Concept 8

What-If Analysis

8 **What-if analysis** is a technique used to evaluate the effects of changing selected factors in a worksheet. This technique is a common accounting function that has been made much easier with the introduction of spreadsheet programs. By substituting different values in cells that are referenced by formulas, you can quickly see the effect of the changes when the formulas are recalculated.

You can perform what-if analysis by manually substituting values or by using one of the what-if analysis tools included with Excel.

Performing What-If Analysis Manually

To do this, you will enter different payroll expense values for each month and see what the effect is on that month's profit margin. You will adjust the May payroll value first.

1

- **Select the Second Quarter sheet.**
- **Type 7300 in cell C15.**
- **Click ✓.**

Your screen should be similar to Figure 3.48

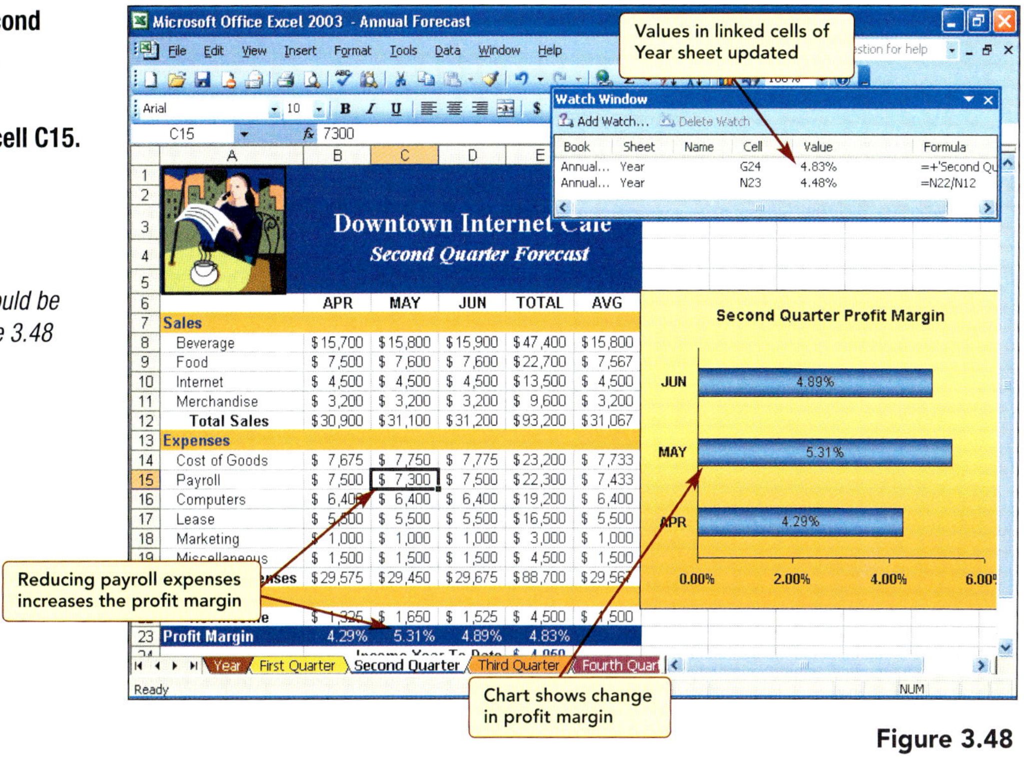

Figure 3.48

Now by looking in cell C23, you can see that decreasing the payroll expenses has increased the profit margin for the month to 5.31 percent. This is more than you need. Also notice the chart has changed to reflect the change in May's profit margin. The Watch Window shows that the values in the two linked cells in the Year sheet were updated accordingly.

You will continue to enter payroll values until the profit margin reaches the goal.

2 Type 7400 in cell C15.

Click ✓.

Type 7390 in cell C15.

Click ✓.

Type 7395 in cell C15.

Click ✓.

Save the workbook.

Your screen should be similar to Figure 3.49

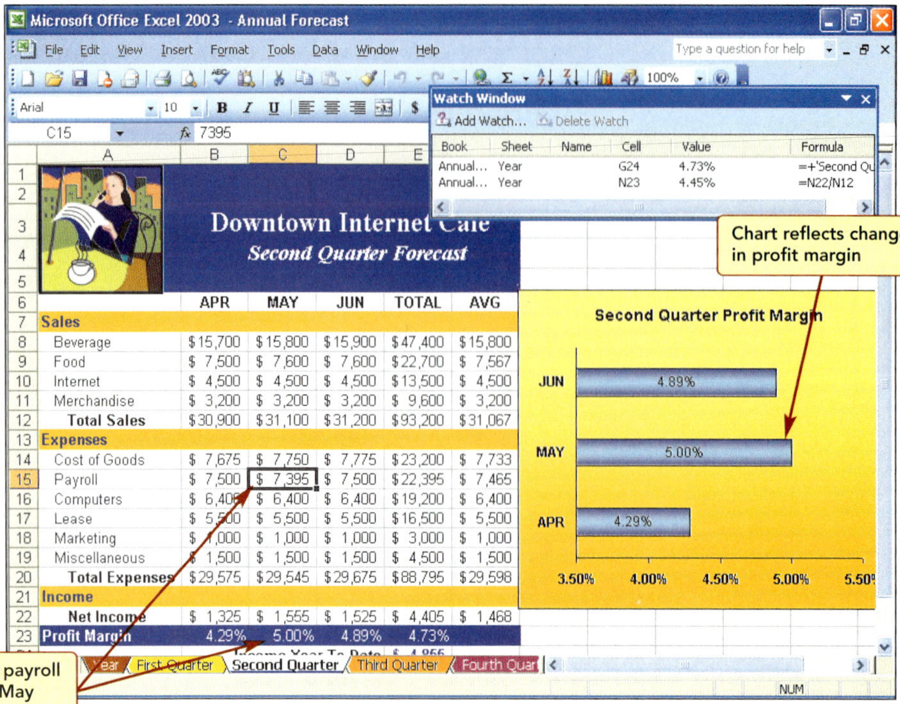

Figure 3.49

That's it! Reducing the payroll value from 7500 to 7395 will achieve the 5 percent profit margin goal for the month.

Using Goal Seek

It usually takes several tries to find the appropriate value when manually performing what-if analysis. A quicker way is to use the what-if analysis Goal Seek tool provided with Excel.

Concept 9

Goal Seek

9 The **Goal Seek** tool is used to find the value needed in one cell to attain a result you want in another cell. Goal Seek varies the value in the cell you specify until a formula that is dependent on that cell returns the desired result. The value of only one cell can be changed.

You will use this method to find the payroll value for April that will produce a 5 percent profit margin for that month. The current profit margin value is 4.29 percent in cell B23.

1 Move to B23.

Choose **T**ools/**G**oal Seek.

Your screen should be similar to Figure 3.50

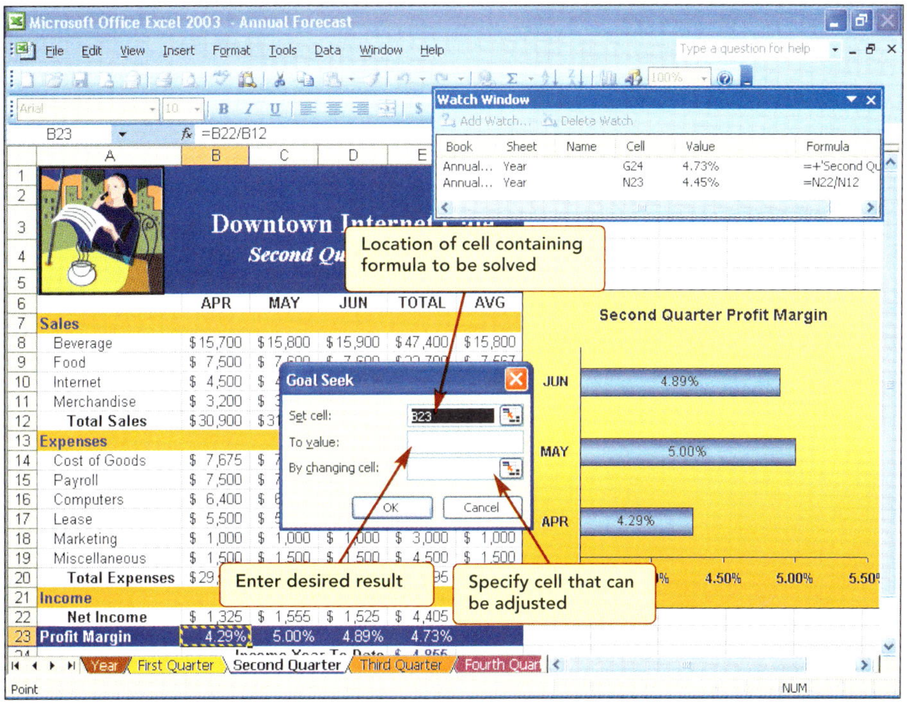

Figure 3.50

In the Goal Seek dialog box, you need to specify the location of the cell containing the formula to be solved, the desired calculated value, and the cell containing the number that can be adjusted to achieve the result. You want the formula in cell B23 to calculate a result of 5 percent by changing the payroll number in cell B15. The Set Cell text box correctly displays the current cell as the location of the formula to be solved. You will enter the information needed in the Goal Seek dialog box.

2 Click in the To Value text box and enter the value 5.00%.

Click in the By Changing Cell text box and then click on cell B15 in the worksheet to enter the cell reference.

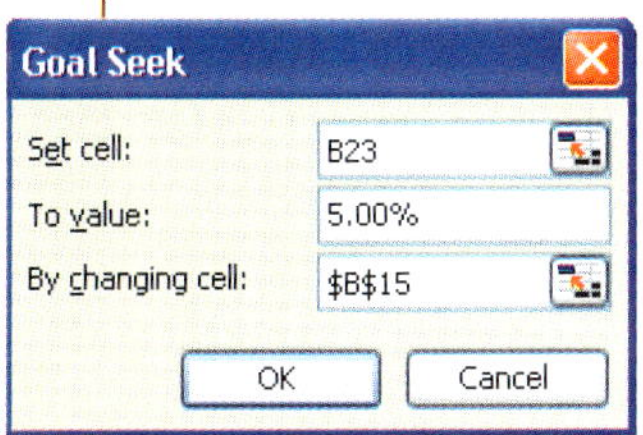

Click OK.

Your screen should be similar to Figure 3.51

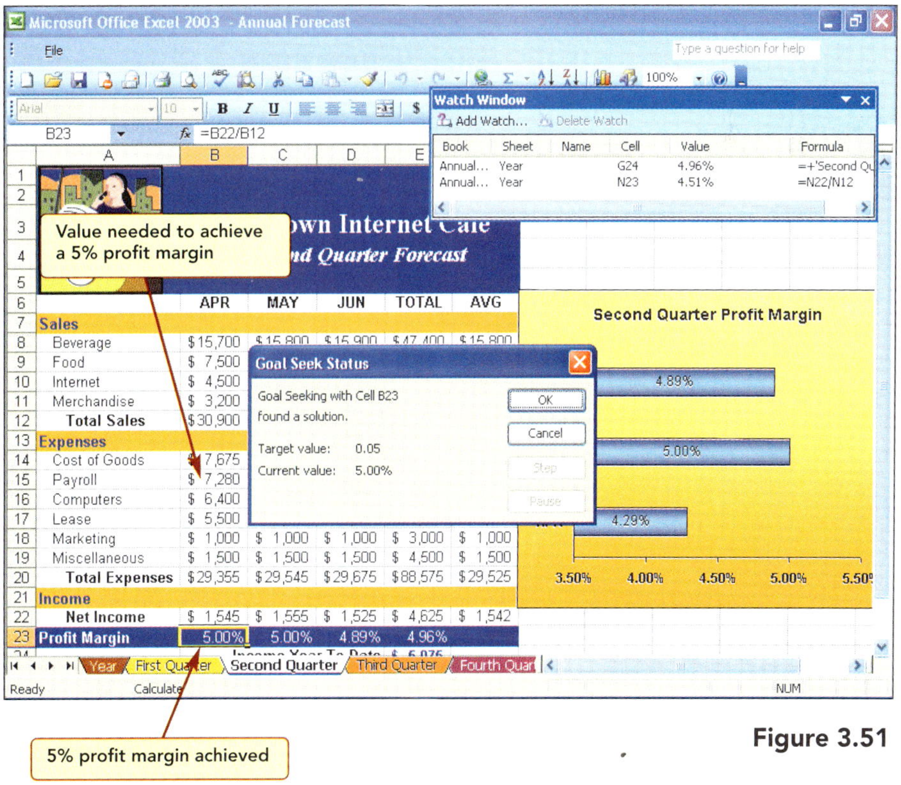

Figure 3.51

The Goal Seek dialog box tells you it found a solution that will achieve the 5 percent profit margin. The payroll value of 7280 that will achieve the desired result has been temporarily entered in the worksheet. You can reject the solution and restore the original value by choosing Cancel. In this case, however, you want to accept the solution.

3 Click OK.

Your screen should be similar to Figure 3.52

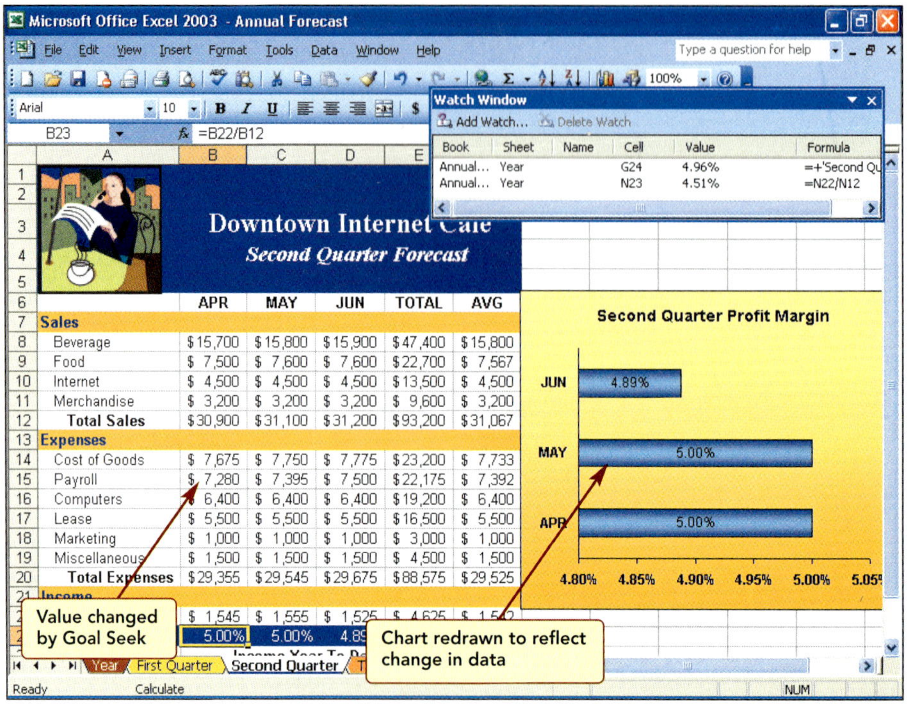

Figure 3.52

The payroll value is permanently updated and the chart redrawn to reflect the change in profit margin for April.

Changing Values Using a Chart

Finally, you need to adjust the June payroll value. This time you will find the value by dragging the June chart data marker to the 5.00% position on the chart. As you drag the data marker, a dotted bar line will show the new bar length and a ChartTip will display the new profit margin value. An indicator on the X axis also marks your location. Releasing the mouse button with the bar at the new position specifies the new value and opens the Goal Seek dialog box.

1 Click on the June data series bar twice (slowly) to select the individual bar.

Additional Information

The bar is surrounded by eight selection handles.

- Drag the middle selection handle on the right end of the bar to increase the length of the bar. When the bar ChartTip value is 0.05 or as close as you can get, release the mouse button.

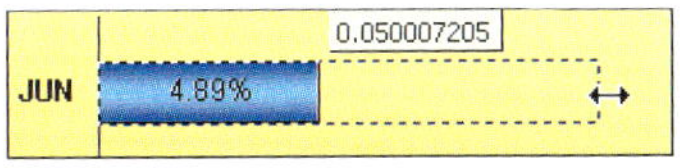

Your screen should be similar to Figure 3.53

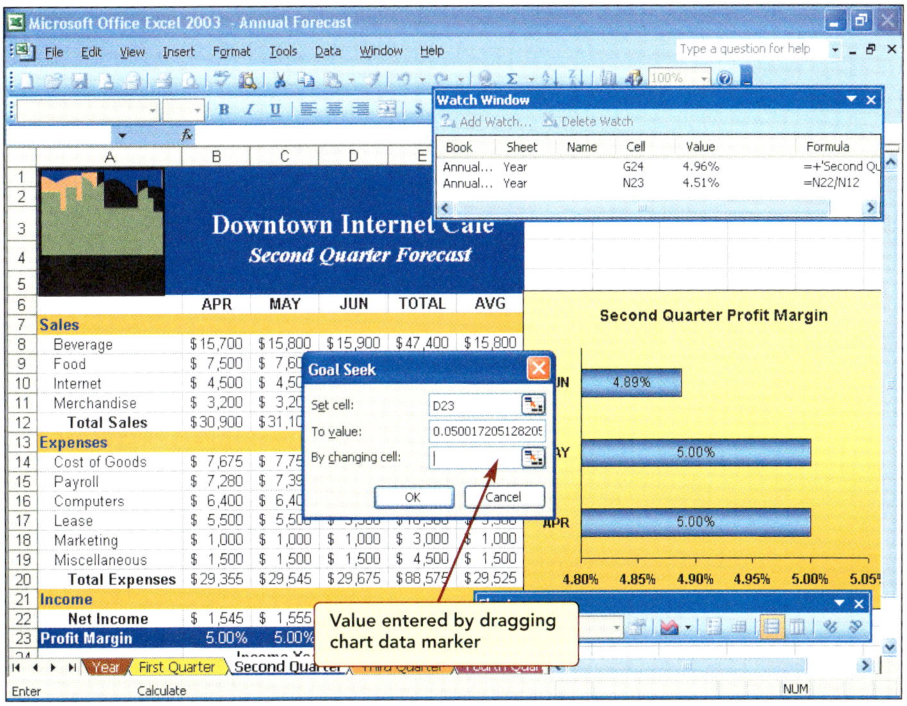

Figure 3.53

Dragging the data marker specifies the value you want to change to and the location of the cell containing the formula. The Goal Seek dialog box is displayed. The Set Cell location and value to attain are entered. Depending on the value you were able to attain by dragging the data marker, you may still need to adjust the value to the exact value of 0.05. You also need to specify the cell location of the value to change.

2 If necessary, edit the To Value contents to 0.05.

- Enter cell D15 in the By Changing Cell text box.
- Click OK.
- Click OK to accept the solution.

Your screen should be similar to Figure 3.54

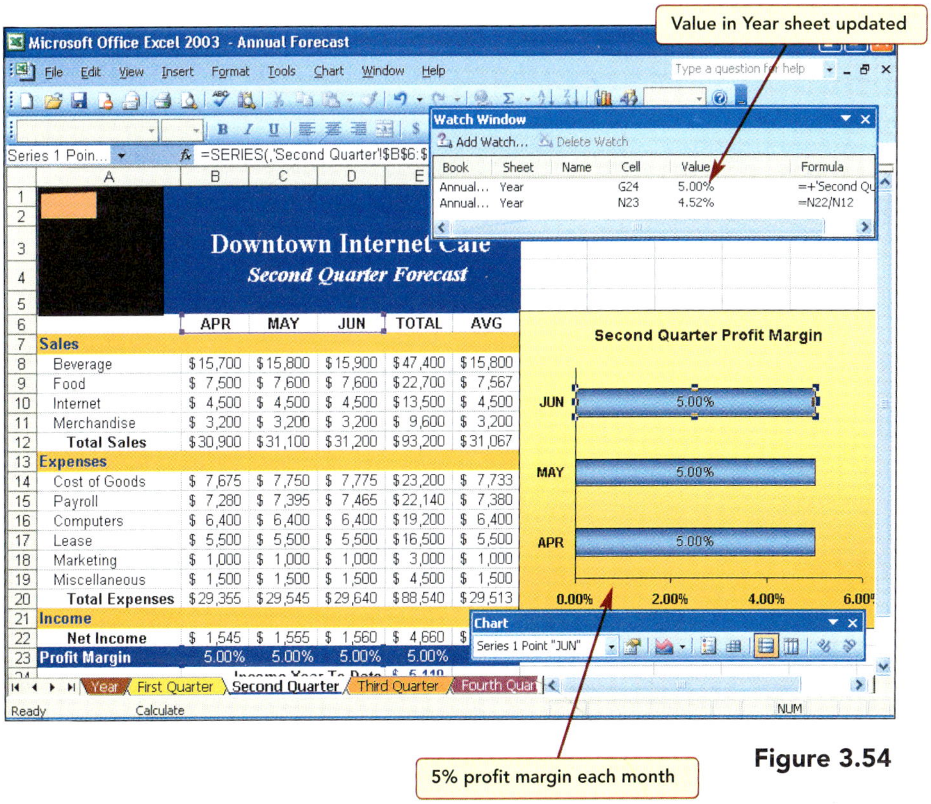

Figure 3.54

The second quarter values are now at the 5 percent profit margin objective. The Watch Window also reflects the change in cell G24.

3
- **Click ☒ Close to close the Watch Window toolbar.**
- **Make the Year sheet active to further verify that the profit margin values for the second quarter were updated.**
- **Choose Window/Unfreeze Panes.**
- **Update the workbook properties by entering a title and your name as author.**
- **Save the workbook again.**

Customizing Print Settings

Now you are ready to print the workbook. Because your worksheet looks great on your screen, this does not mean it will look good when printed. Many times you will want to change the default print and layout settings to improve the appearance of the output. Customizing the print settings by controlling page breaks, changing the orientation of the page, centering the worksheet on the page, hiding gridlines, and adding custom header and footer information are just a few of the ways you can make your printed output look more professional.

Controlling Page Breaks

First you want to preview the Year sheet.

1
- **If necessary, select the Year sheet.**
- **Click Print Preview.**
- **Click Next.**

Your screen should be similar to Figure 3.55

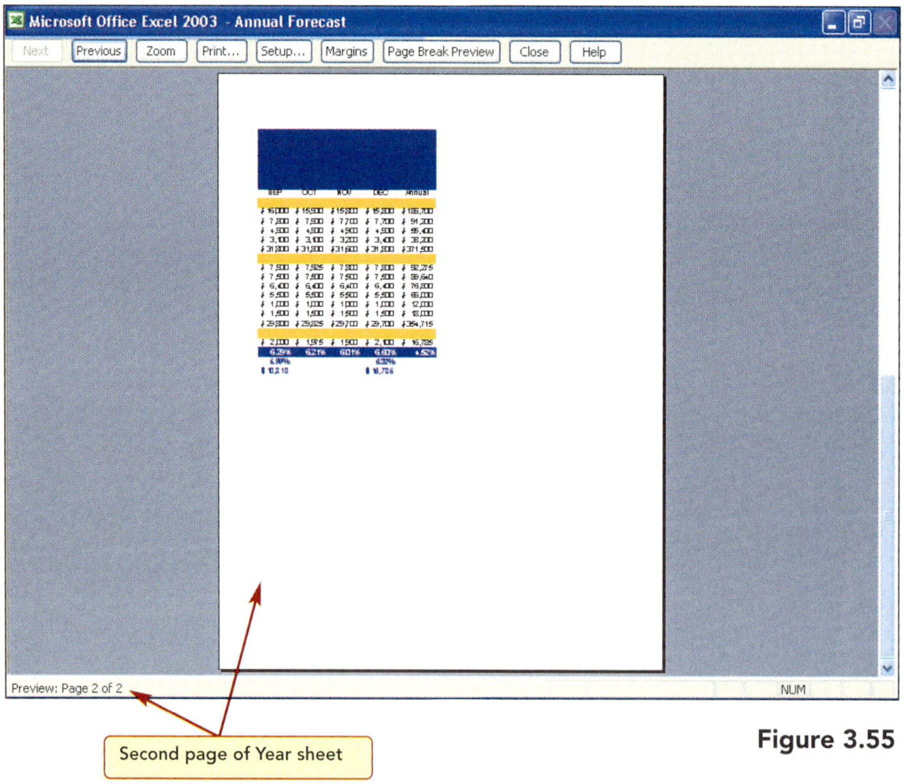

Figure 3.55

The first page of the Year worksheet displays the first eight months, and the second page the last four months and the Annual total. Although you could use the Fit To feature to compress the worksheet to a single page, this would make the data small and difficult to read. Instead, you decide to leave the printout as two pages, but, you want the second six months to appear on the second page. To do this, you will change the location of the **page break**, the place where one printed page ends and another starts. Excel inserts automatic page breaks based on the paper size, margin settings and orientation when the worksheet exceeds the width of a page. Excel includes a third view, Page Break Preview that shows you what data will go on each page when you print the worksheet. Using this view, you can adjust the location of page breaks.

2 Click Page Break Preview.

Your screen should be similar to Figure 3.56

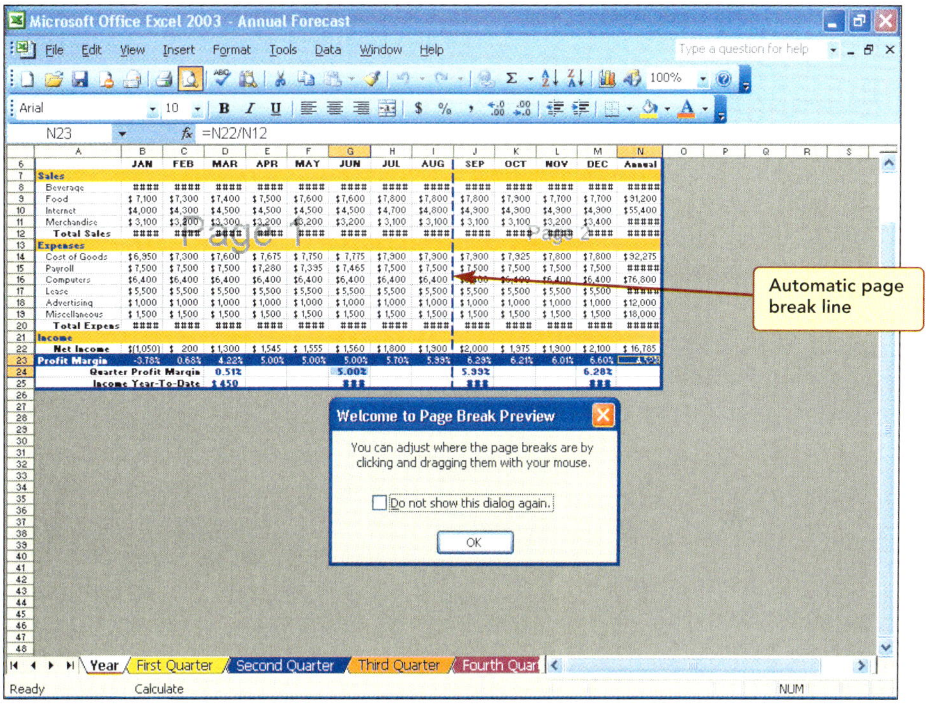

Figure 3.56

Additional Information

You can work in Page Break view just like in Normal view.

Now you can see the page break location. The dashed line indicates the location of the automatic page break. You can change the location by dragging the page break line. When you move an automatic page break location to another location, the page break line changes to a solid line, indicating it is a manual page break.

3 If necessary, click OK to close the Welcome to Page Break Preview dialog box.

- Point to the page break line and when the mouse pointer is ↔, drag the line to the left between columns G and H.

Your screen should be similar to Figure 3.57

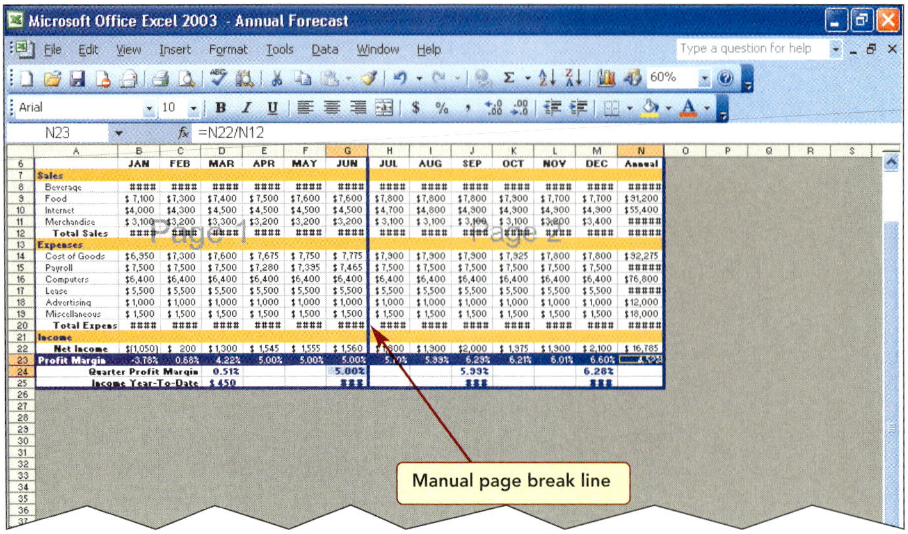

Figure 3.57

You can now either return to Normal view or to Print Preview. You again want to see how the page will look when printed.

4 Click Print Preview.

Your screen should be similar to Figure 3.58

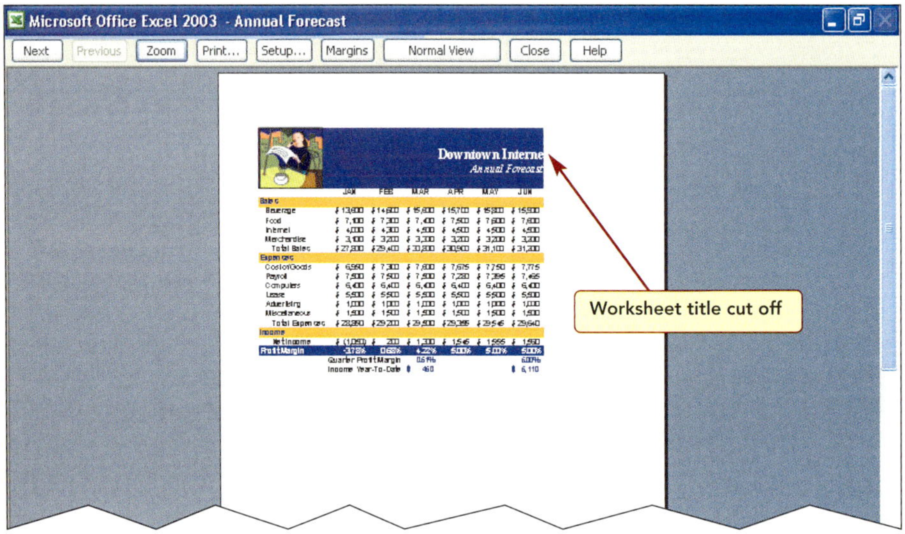

Figure 3.58

Unfortunately, moving the page break to this position cuts the worksheet title between the two pages.

Changing Page Orientation

Instead, you decide to change the orientation or the direction the output is printed on a page. The default orientation is **portrait**. This setting prints across the width of the paper. You will change the orientation to **landscape**, which prints across the length of the paper. Then you will use the Fit To feature to make sure the worksheet fits on one page with the new orientation.

1. Click Setup....
   - If necessary, open the Page tab.
   - Select **L**andscape.
   - Select Fit to.
   - Click OK.

Your screen should be similar to Figure 3.59

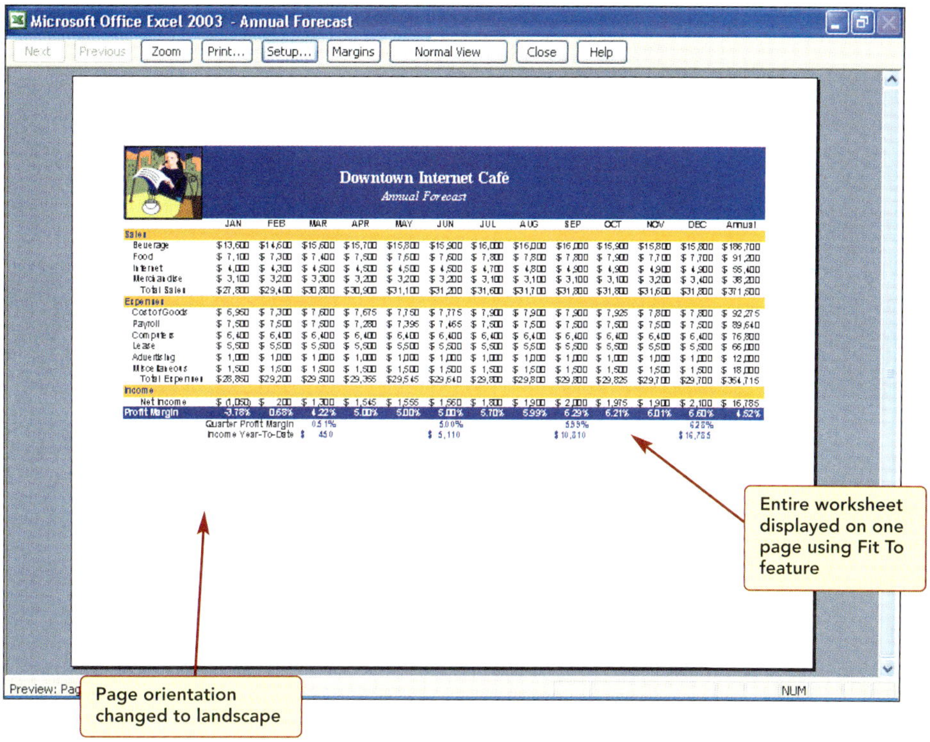

Figure 3.59

Additional Information

You can remove a manual page break using **I**nsert/Remove Page **B**reak or by dragging the page break outside of the print area in Page Break Preview.

Using Fit To ignores the manual page break and reduces the worksheet to a single page.

Displaying Gridlines and Centering on a Page

The entire worksheet now easily fits across the length of the page. Because the worksheet is large, you also feel the worksheet may be easier to read if the row and column gridlines were printed. In addition, you want the worksheet to be centered vertically on the page.

1. Click Setup....
   - From the Sheet tab, select **G**ridlines.
   - From the Margins tab, select **V**ertically.
   - Click OK.

Your screen should be similar to Figure 3.60

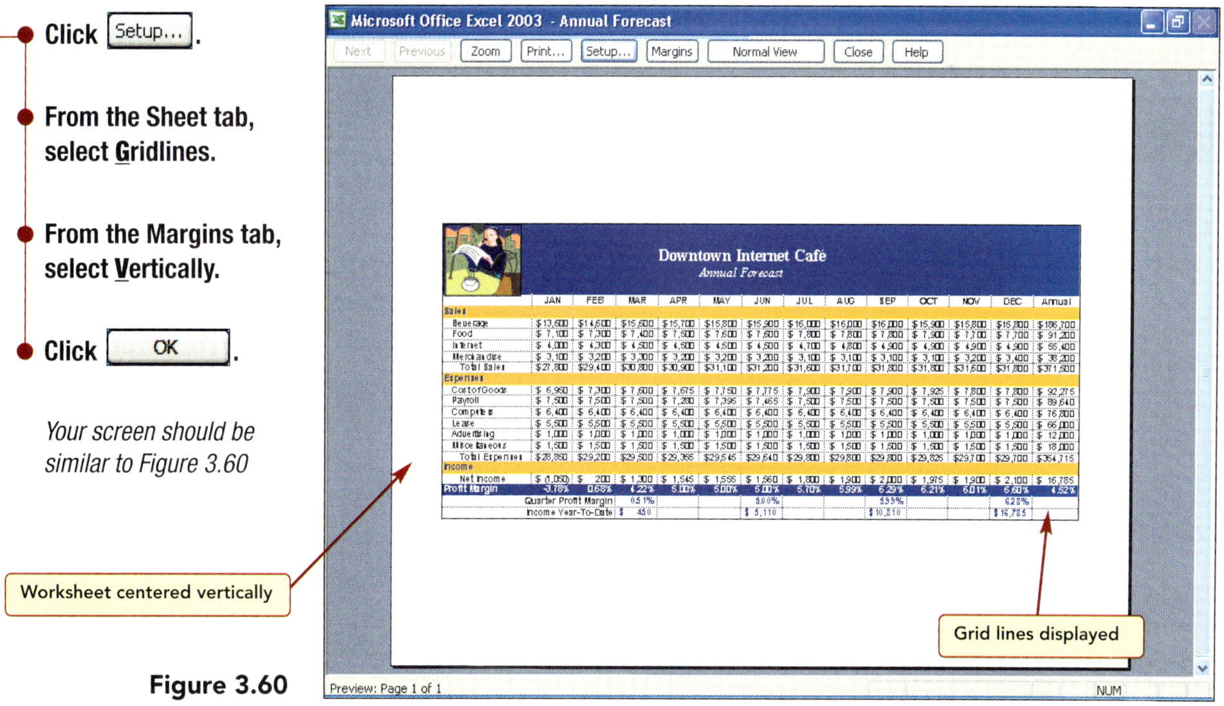

Figure 3.60

The preview screen is recreated showing how the sheet will appear centered vertically and with gridlines. You will return the view to Normal view and then preview the rest of the worksheet.

2 **Click** Normal View.

Additional Information

When in Page Break Preview, you can use **V**iew/**N**ormal to return to Normal view.

- **Select the four quarter sheets.**
- **Click** Print **Preview.**

Your screen should be similar to Figure 3.61

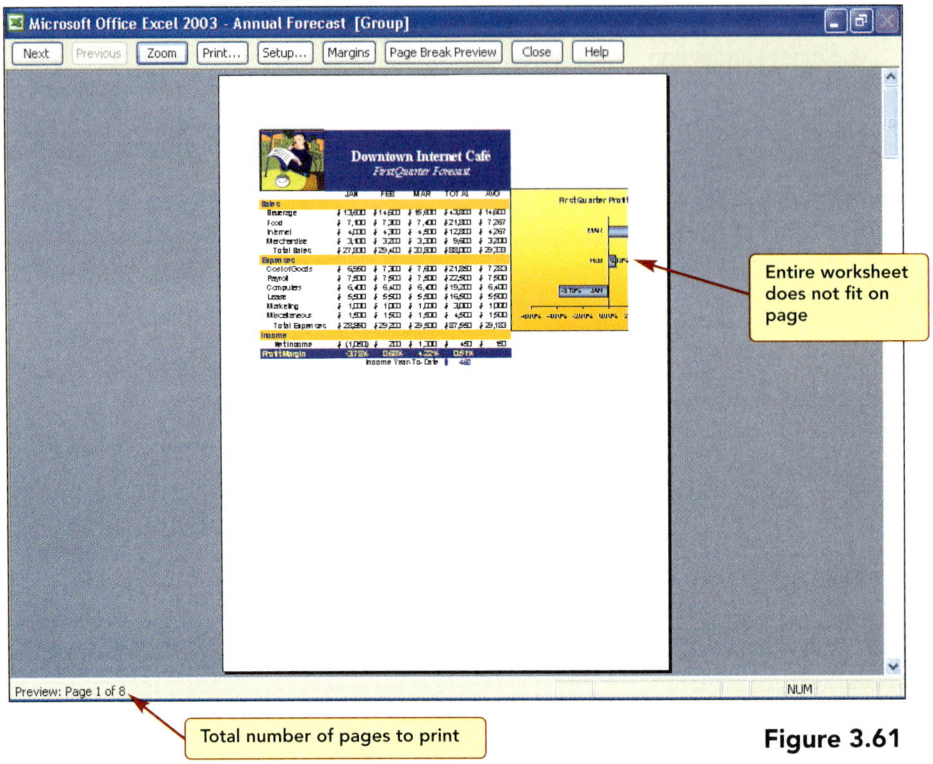

Figure 3.61

Again, notice the worksheet does not fit on the page. In addition, notice that the total number of pages to be printed is eight. This is because each quarter sheet requires two pages to print in portrait orientation. You will also change the orientation of these sheets to landscape and center them both horizontally and vertically on the page. Rather than change each sheet individually in the preview window, you can make this change to the four sheets at the same time in the worksheet window.

3

- Click **Close**.
- Choose **File/Page Setup**.
- From the Page tab select **Landscape**.
- From the Margins tab select **Horizontally** and **Vertically**.
- Click **Print Preview**.

Your screen should be similar to Figure 3.62

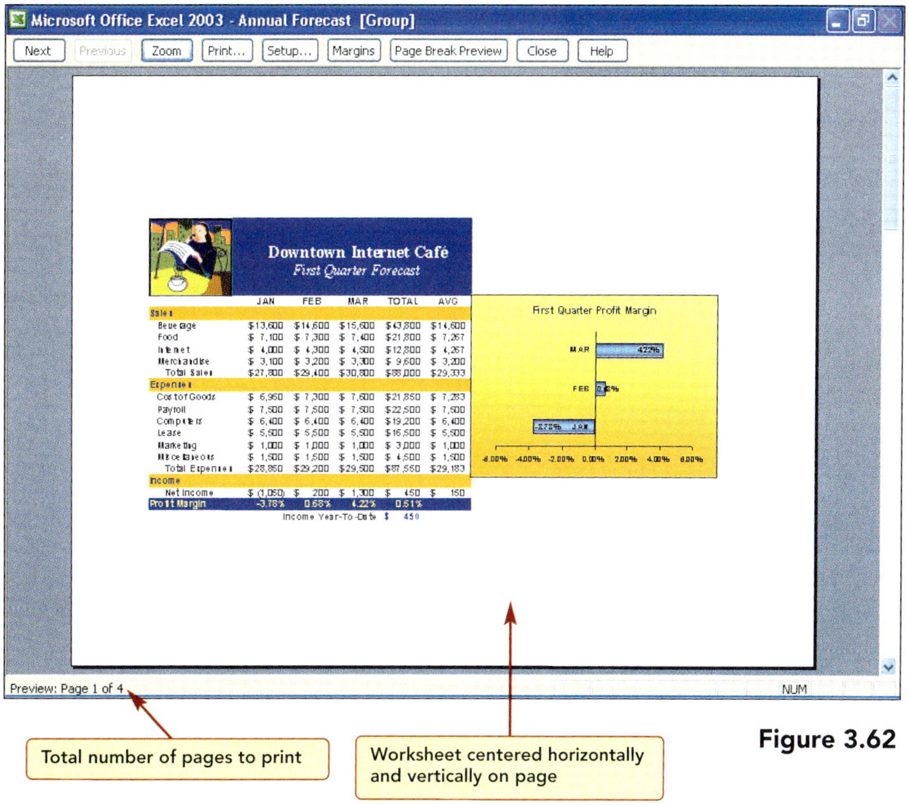

Figure 3.62

The worksheet is displayed in landscape orientation and centered both horizontally and vertically on the page. You can also see from the total number of pages to print (four) that the same changes have been made to the four selected sheets.

Adding Custom Headers and Footers

You would also like to add a custom footer to all the sheets. It is faster to add the footer to all sheets at the same time. If you make changes to the active sheet when multiple sheets are selected, the changes are made to all other selected sheets.

Additional Information

Be careful when making changes to multiple sheets as these changes may replace data on other sheets.

1 Click [Close].

- Hold down [Ctrl] and click the Year sheet tab to add it to the selection.
- Choose File/Page Setup.
- Open the Header/Footer tab.
- Click [Custom Footer...].

Your screen should be similar to Figure 3.63

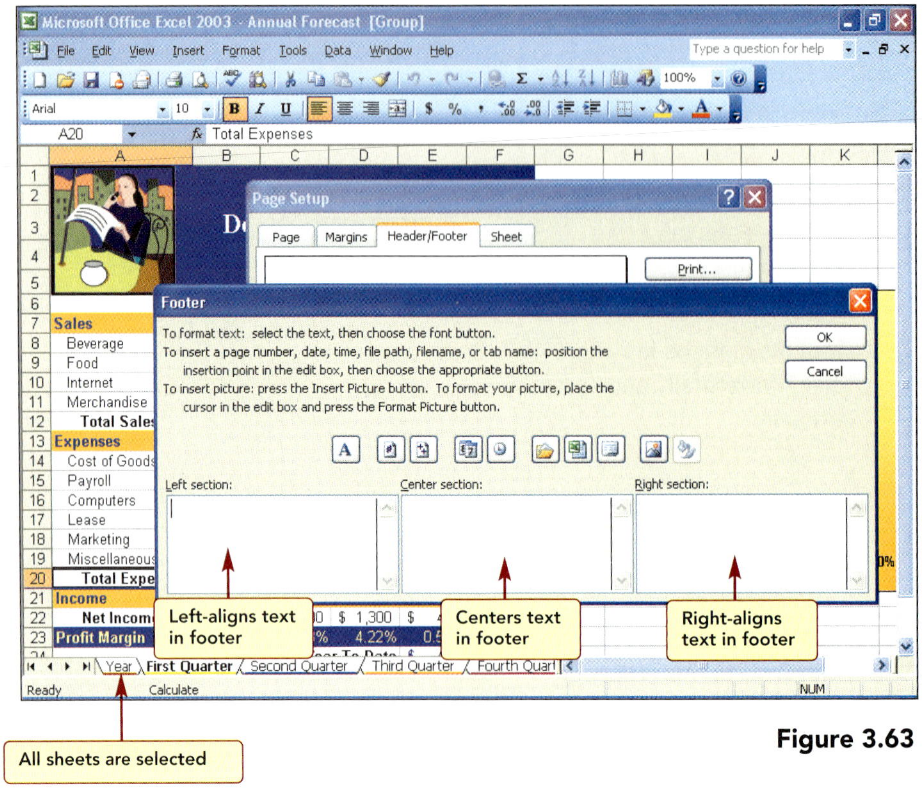

Figure 3.63

The Left Section text box will display the footer text you enter aligned with the left margin; the Center Section will center the text; and the Right Section will right-align the text. The insertion point is currently positioned in the Left Section text box. You want to enter your name, class, and the date in this box. You will enter your name and class by typing it directly in the box. Instead of typing the date, however, you will enter a code that will automatically insert the current date whenever the worksheet is printed.

The buttons above the section boxes (identified below) are used to enter the codes for common header and footer information.

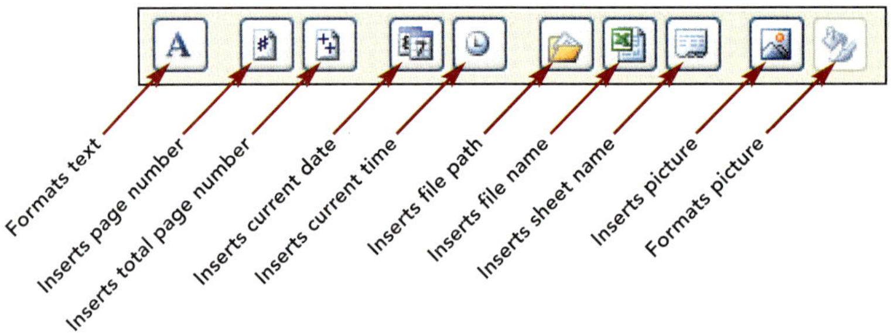

2

- Type **Created by your name.**
- Press Tab.
- Enter the **name of your class** and the **section or time.**
- Press Tab.
- Click **Date.**

Your screen should be similar to Figure 3.64

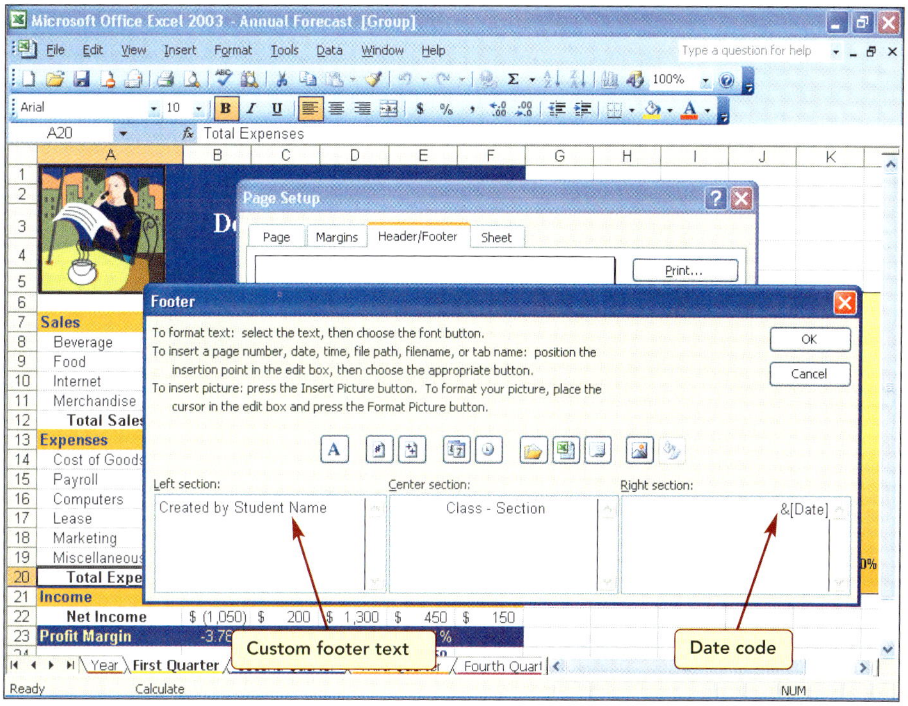

Figure 3.64

You want to make one final check to see how the footer will look before printing the workbook. When you do, you will see that the Year sheet setup changes have changed to the same settings used in the other sheets. You will need to respecify that sheet's settings.

3

- Click OK.
- Click Print Preview.
- Fit the Year sheet to one page and display gridlines again.
- Look at the other sheets to confirm that the footer was added to them as well.
- Display the Year sheet again.

Your screen should be similar to Figure 3.65

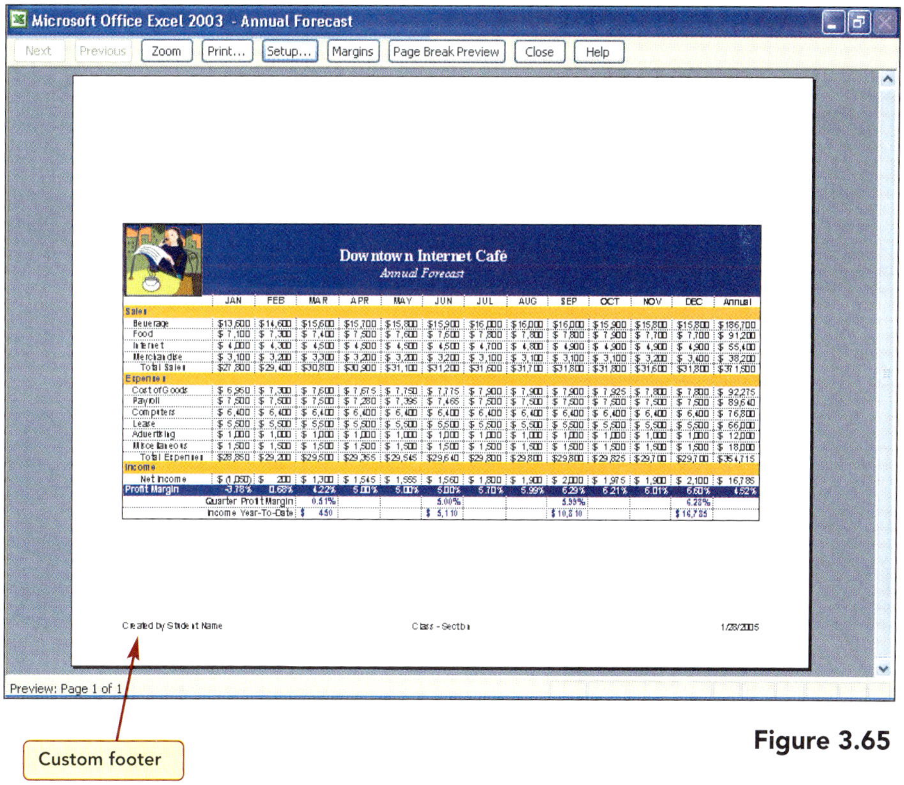

Figure 3.65

The footer as you entered it appears on all selected worksheets.

Printing Selected Sheets

You want to print the Year and Second Quarter worksheets only.

1

- **Close the preview window.**
- **Right-click on a sheet tab and choose Ungroup Sheets.**
- **If necessary, make the Year sheet active.**
- **Save the file again.**
- **Hold down Ctrl and click the Second Quarter sheet tab to add it to the selection of sheets to print.**
- **Click Print.**

Having Trouble?

If you need to specify print settings that are different from the default settings on your system, use File/Print to print the worksheet.

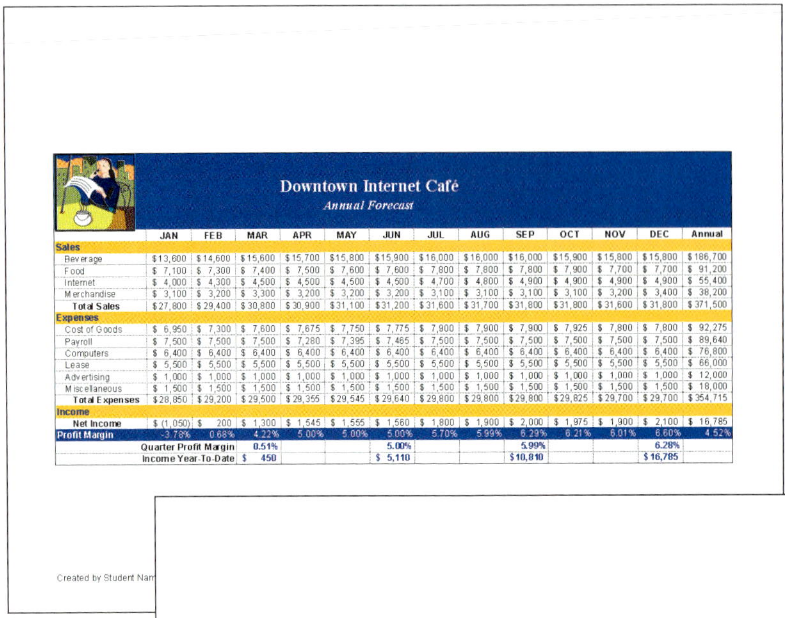

Downtown Internet Café

Annual Forecast

	JAN	FEB	MAR	APR	MAY	JUN	JUL	AUG	SEP	OCT	NOV	DEC	Annual
Sales													
Beverage	$13,600	$14,600	$15,600	$15,700	$15,800	$15,900	$16,000	$16,000	$16,000	$15,900	$15,800	$15,800	$186,700
Food	$ 7,100	$ 7,300	$ 7,400	$ 7,500	$ 7,600	$ 7,600	$ 7,800	$ 7,800	$ 7,800	$ 7,900	$ 7,700	$ 7,700	$ 91,200
Internet	$ 4,000	$ 4,300	$ 4,500	$ 4,500	$ 4,500	$ 4,500	$ 4,700	$ 4,800	$ 4,900	$ 4,900	$ 4,900	$ 4,900	$ 55,400
Merchandise	$ 3,100	$ 3,200	$ 3,300	$ 3,200	$ 3,200	$ 3,200	$ 3,100	$ 3,100	$ 3,100	$ 3,100	$ 3,200	$ 3,400	$ 38,200
Total Sales	$27,800	$29,400	$30,800	$30,900	$31,100	$31,200	$31,600	$31,700	$31,800	$31,800	$31,600	$31,800	$371,500
Expenses													
Cost of Goods	$ 6,950	$ 7,300	$ 7,600	$ 7,675	$ 7,750	$ 7,775	$ 7,900	$ 7,900	$ 7,900	$ 7,925	$ 7,800	$ 7,800	$ 92,275
Payroll	$ 7,500	$ 7,500	$ 7,500	$ 7,280	$ 7,395	$ 7,465	$ 7,500	$ 7,500	$ 7,500	$ 7,500	$ 7,500	$ 7,500	$ 89,640
Computers	$ 6,400	$ 6,400	$ 6,400	$ 6,400	$ 6,400	$ 6,400	$ 6,400	$ 6,400	$ 6,400	$ 6,400	$ 6,400	$ 6,400	$ 76,800
Lease	$ 5,500	$ 5,500	$ 5,500	$ 5,500	$ 5,500	$ 5,500	$ 5,500	$ 5,500	$ 5,500	$ 5,500	$ 5,500	$ 5,500	$ 66,000
Advertising	$ 1,000	$ 1,000	$ 1,000	$ 1,000	$ 1,000	$ 1,000	$ 1,000	$ 1,000	$ 1,000	$ 1,000	$ 1,000	$ 1,000	$ 12,000
Miscellaneous	$ 1,500	$ 1,500	$ 1,500	$ 1,500	$ 1,500	$ 1,500	$ 1,500	$ 1,500	$ 1,500	$ 1,500	$ 1,500	$ 1,500	$ 18,000
Total Expenses	$28,850	$29,200	$29,500	$29,355	$29,545	$29,640	$29,800	$29,800	$29,800	$29,825	$29,700	$29,700	$354,715
Income													
Net Income	$ (1,050)	$ 200	$ 1,300	$ 1,545	$ 1,555	$ 1,560	$ 1,800	$ 1,900	$ 2,000	$ 1,975	$ 1,900	$ 2,100	$ 16,785
Profit Margin	-3.78%	0.68%	4.22%	5.00%	5.00%	5.00%	5.70%	5.99%	6.29%	6.21%	6.01%	6.60%	4.52%
Quarter Profit Margin			0.51%			5.00%			5.99%			6.28%	
Income Year-To-Date			$ 450			$ 5,110			$10,810			$16,785	

Created by Student Name

Downtown Internet Café

Second Quarter Forecast

	APR	MAY	JUN	TOTAL	AVG
Sales					
Beverage	$15,700	$15,800	$15,900	$47,400	$15,800
Food	$ 7,500	$ 7,600	$ 7,600	$22,700	$ 7,567
Internet	$ 4,500	$ 4,500	$ 4,500	$13,500	$ 4,500
Merchandise	$ 3,200	$ 3,200	$ 3,200	$ 9,600	$ 3,200
Total Sales	$30,900	$31,100	$31,200	$93,200	$31,067
Expenses					
Cost of Goods	$ 7,675	$ 7,750	$ 7,775	$23,200	$ 7,733
Payroll	$ 7,280	$ 7,395	$ 7,465	$22,140	$ 7,380
Computers	$ 6,400	$ 6,400	$ 6,400	$19,200	$ 6,400
Lease	$ 5,500	$ 5,500	$ 5,500	$16,500	$ 5,500
Marketing	$ 1,000	$ 1,000	$ 1,000	$ 3,000	$ 1,000
Miscellaneous	$ 1,500	$ 1,500	$ 1,500	$ 4,500	$ 1,500
Total Expenses	$29,355	$29,545	$29,640	$88,540	$29,513
Income					
Net Income	$ 1,545	$ 1,555	$ 1,560	$ 4,660	$ 1,553
Profit Margin	5.00%	5.00%	5.00%	5.00%	
			Income Year-To-Date	$ 5,110	

Your printed output should look like that shown here.

Printing Selected Areas

You are finished printing the Annual and Second Quarter sheets and you have the information Evan requested. However, you think Evan would also like a printout of the First Quarter worksheet without the chart displayed. To print a selected area, you first select the cell range that you want to print.

1 **Select the First Quarter sheet**

Select cells A1 through F24.

Having Trouble?

Because the graphic covers cell A1, move to cell A1 then hold down ⇧Shift and click cell F24 to select the range.

Choose File/Print Area/Set Print Area.

Your screen should be similar to Figure 3.66

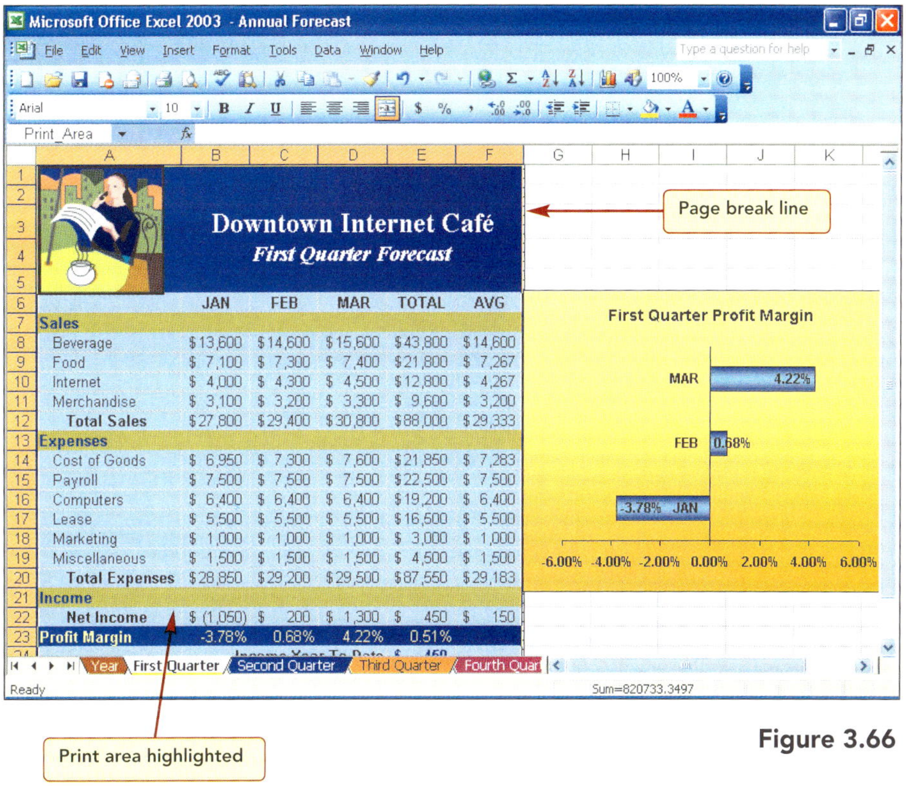

Figure 3.66

The area you selected, called the **print area**, is highlighted, and a page break line shows where the selected range will print on a page.

2 **Click [Print Preview icon] Print Preview.**

Your screen should be similar to Figure 3.67

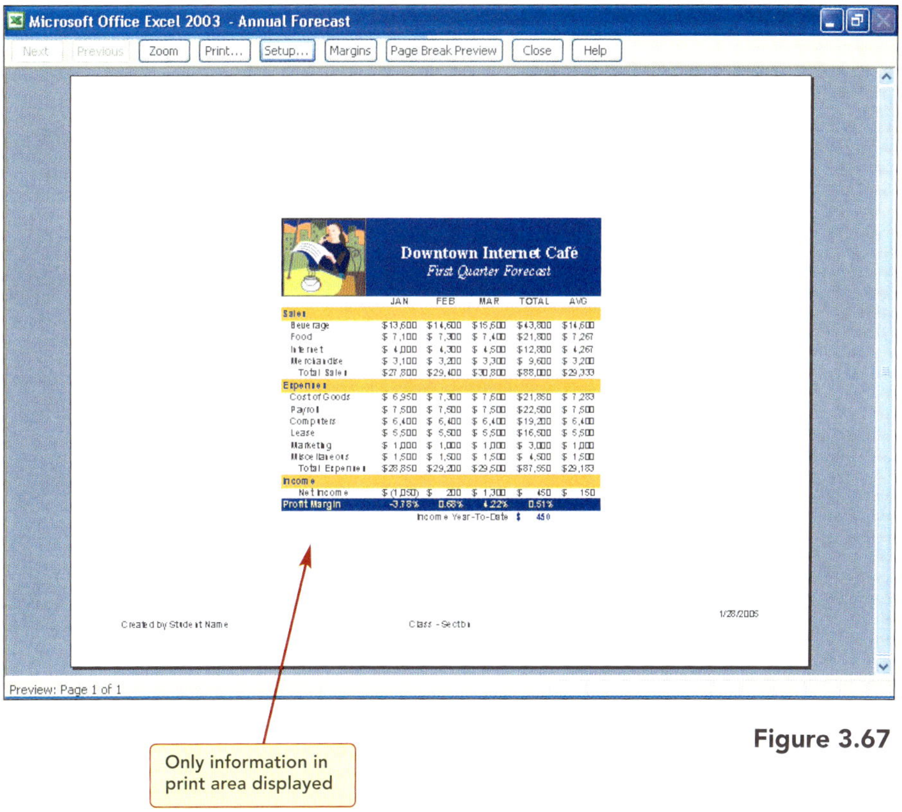

Figure 3.67

The preview window displays only the information contained in the defined print area. The print area is saved with the worksheet and will be used automatically whenever you print the worksheet.

3. Click Print... .
   - Specify any print settings and click OK .
   - Close and save the workbook and exit Excel.

Focus on Careers

EXPLORE YOUR CAREER OPTIONS

Medical Sales Accountant

A medical sales accountant visits doctors and clinics to promote the pharmaceuticals and supplies their company makes. The accountants usually specialize in a few pharmaceuticals or products so that they can help the doctor understand the benefits and risks associated with their products. Medical sales accountants must keep careful and complete records of the samples they have in inventory and what they have delivered to doctors. An Excel workbook is a useful tool to keep track of the many doctors and deliveries made. A career as a medical sales accountant can start with a salary of $35,000 and go up to over $90,000 plus car and travel benefits.

LAB 3
Managing and Analyzing a Workbook

Absolute Reference (EX3.14)

An absolute reference is a cell or range reference in a formula whose location does not change when the formula is copied.

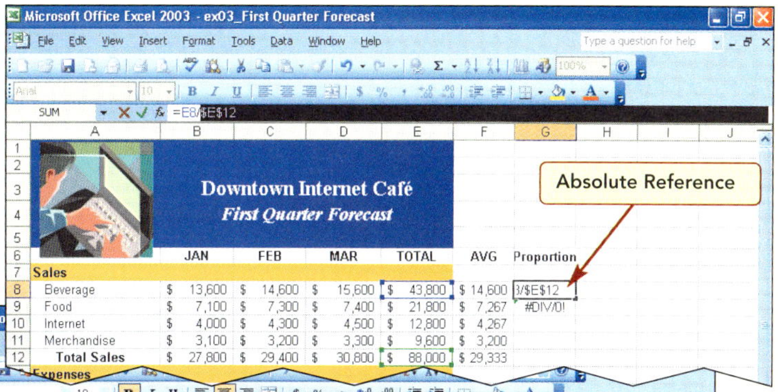

Sheet Name (EX3.18)

Each sheet in a workbook can be assigned a descriptive sheet name to identify the contents of the sheet.

AutoFill (EX3.21)

The AutoFill feature makes entering long or complicated headings easier by logically repeating and extending the series.

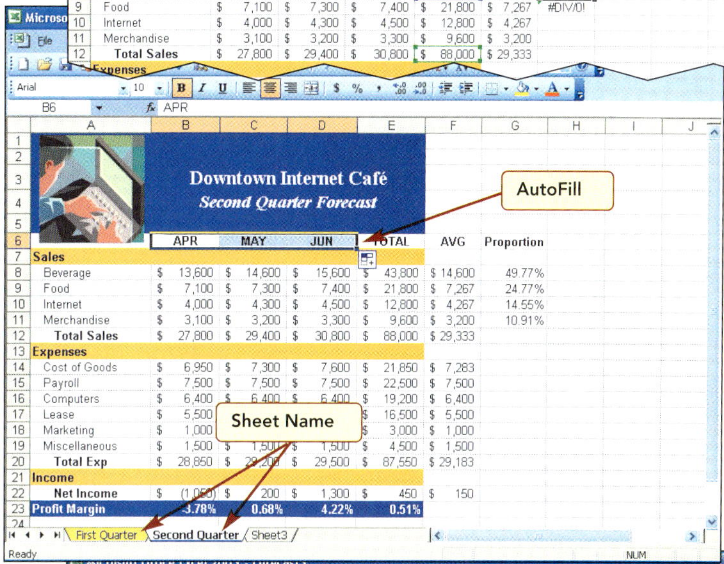

Sheet and 3-D References (EX3.24)

A formula containing sheet and 3-D references to cells in different worksheets in a workbook allows you to use data from other worksheets and to calculate new values based on this data.

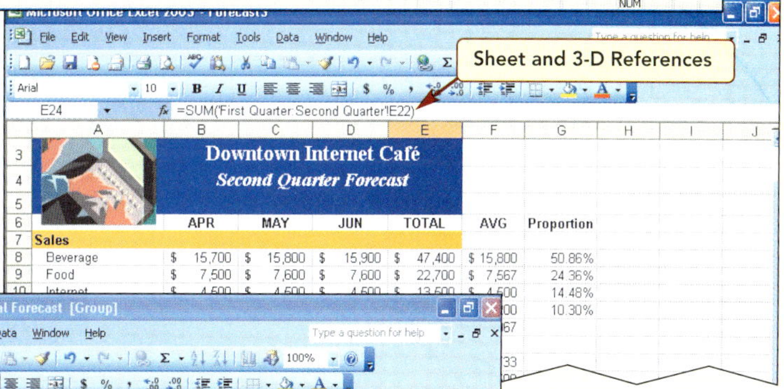

Find and Replace (EX3.30)

The Find and Replace feature helps you quickly find specific information and automatically replace it with new information.

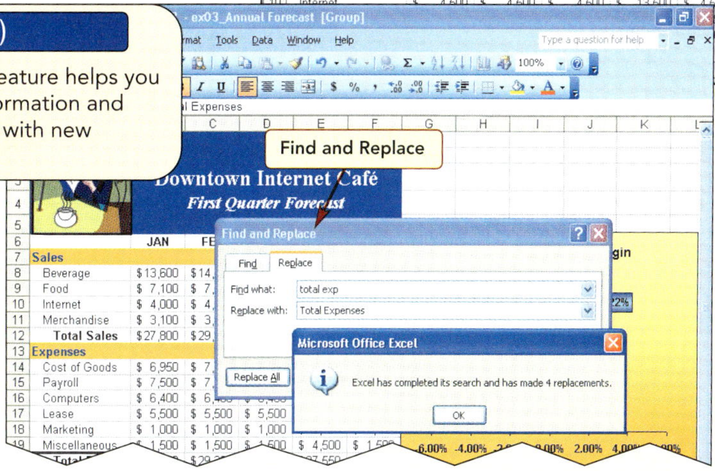

concept summary

Split Window (EX3.39)

The split window feature allows you to divide a worksheet window into sections, making it easier to view different parts of the worksheet at the same time.

Freeze Panes (EX3.42)

Freezing panes prevents the data in the panes from scrolling as you move to different areas in the worksheet.

What-If Analysis (EX3.46)

What-if analysis is a technique used to evaluate the effects of changing selected factors in a worksheet.

Goal Seek (EX3.48)

The Goal Seek tool is used to find the value needed in one cell to attain a result you want in another cell.

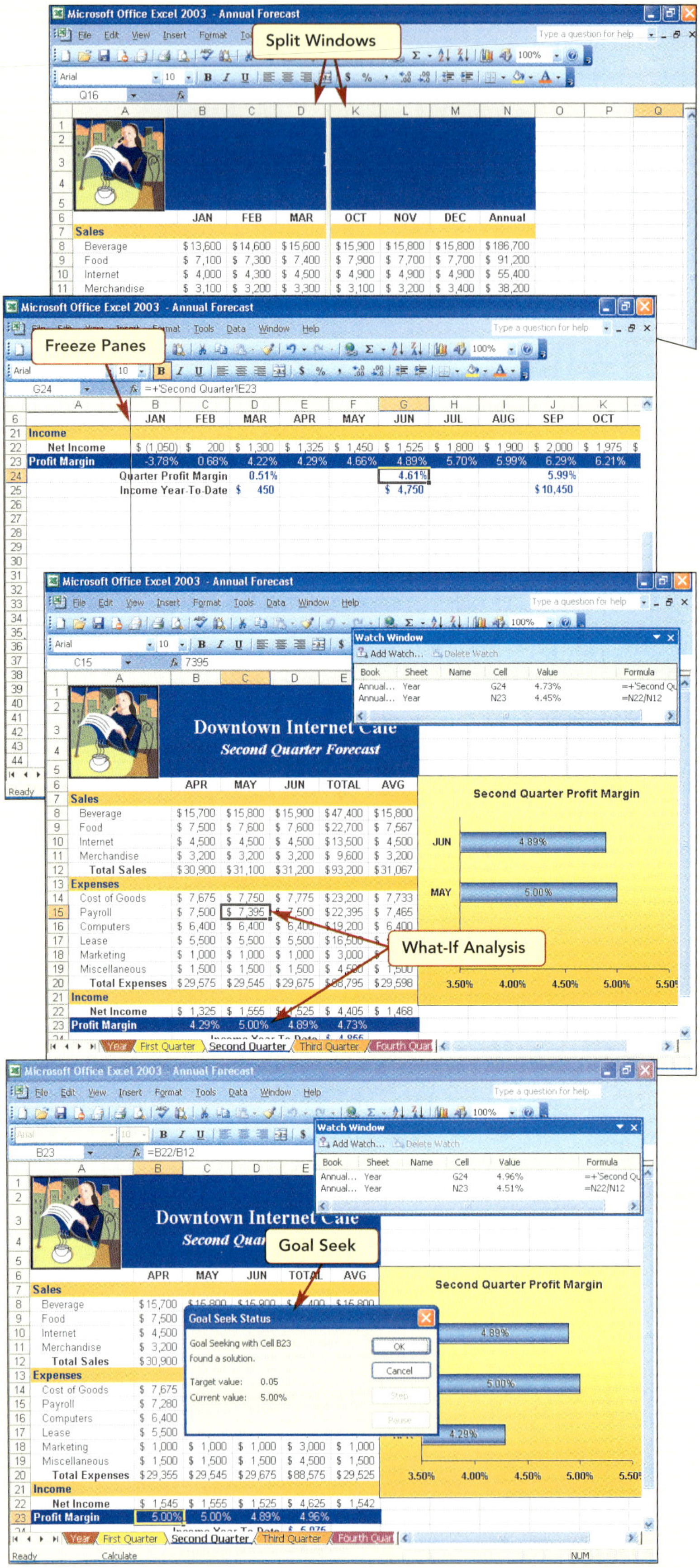

LAB 3

Managing and Analyzing a Workbook

key terms

3-D reference EX3.24
absolute reference EX3.14
AutoFill EX3.21
Find and Replace EX3.30
freeze panes EX3.42
Goal Seek EX3.48
landscape EX3.54
mixed reference EX3.14
page break EX3.53
pane EX3.39
portrait EX3.54
print area EX3.61
sheet name EX3.18
sheet reference EX3.24
split window EX3.39
what-if analysis EX3.46

microsoft office specialist skills

The Microsoft Office Specialist certification program is designed to measure your proficiency in performing basic tasks using the Office 2003 applications. Certification demonstrates that you have the skills and provides a valuable industry credential for employment. After completing this lab, you have learned the following Microsoft Office Excel 2003 Specialist skills:

Skill Sets	Skill Standards	Page
Creating Data and Content	Enter and edit cell content	EX3.11,3.20
	Navigate to specific cell content	EX3.29,3.27
Analyzing Data	Insert and modify formulas	EX3.6,3.10,3.12
	Use statistical, date and time, financial and logical functions in formulas	EX3.7
Formatting Data and Content	Apply and modify cell formats	EX3.16
	Format worksheets	EX3.18
Managing Workbooks	Organize worksheets	EX3.26
	Preview data in other views	EX3.52
	Customize Window layout	EX3.38
	Set up pages for printing	EX3.52
	Print data	EX3.60
	Organize workbooks using file folders	EX3.35

command summary

Command	Shortcut Key	Button	Voice	Action
File/Page Setup/Page/ Landscape				Changes page orientation to landscape
File/Page Setup/Sheet/ Gridlines				Displays/hides gridlines
File/Page Setup/Margins/ Horizontally				Centers worksheet horizontally on page
File/Page Setup/Margins/ Vertically				Centers worksheet vertically on page
Edit/Delete Sheet				Deletes entire sheet
Edit/Move or Copy Sheet				Moves or copies selected sheet
Edit/Find	Ctrl + F			Locates specified text, numbers, and/or formats
Edit/Replace	Ctrl + H			Locates specified characters or formats and replaces them with specified replacement characters or format
Edit/Go To	Ctrl + G			Goes to a specified cell location in worksheet
View/Page Break Preview				Displays worksheet in Page Break view
View/Normal		Apply		Changes view of window to Normal view
View/Zoom		100%	Zoom	Changes magnification of window
Insert/Remove Page Break				Removes page break
Format/Sheet/Rename				Renames sheet
Format/Sheet/Tab Color				Changes color of sheet tabs
Tools/Error Checking				Checks worksheet for formula errors

command summary

Command	Shortcut Key	Button	Voice	Action
Tools/Goal Seek				Adjusts value in specified cell until a formula dependent on that cell reaches specified result
Tools/Formula Auditing/Show Watch Window				Opens Watch Window toolbar
Window/Freeze Panes				Freezes top and/or leftmost panes
Window/Unfreeze Panes				Unfreezes window panes
Window/Split				Divides window into four panes at active cell
Window/Remove Split				Removes split from active worksheet

lab exercises

matching

Match the lettered item on the right with the numbered item on the left.

1. 'Second Quarter!'A13	______	**a.** default page orientation
2. panes	______	**b.** prevents data in pane from scrolling
3. portrait	______	**c.** pane that contains the cell selector
4. freezing panes	______	**d.** the sections of a divided window
5. Sheet1:Sheet3!H3:K5	______	**e.** sheet reference
6. Watch window	______	**f.** mixed cell reference
7. landscape	______	**g.** 3-D reference
8. $M$34	______	**h.** indicates division by zero error
9. active pane	______	**i.** prints across the length of the paper
10. $B12	______	**j.** absolute cell reference
11. #DIV/0!		

true/false

Circle the correct answer to the following questions.

1. =SUM(Sheet15:Sheet50!H6) averages the values in cell H6 of sheets 15 and 50. True False
2. A relative reference is a cell or range reference in a formula whose location does not change when the formula is copied. True False
3. $G8 is an absolute reference. True False
4. If you hold down Ctrl while you drag the fill handle, the entries will not be incremented. True False
5. You can freeze the information in the top and right panes of a window only. True False
6. The sheet reference consists of the name of the sheet separated from the cell reference by a question mark. True False
7. The Window/Split command can be used to quickly create a four-way split at the top left of the worksheet. True False
8. To create two horizontal panes with the left pane frozen, move the cell selector in the top row of the window and select the column to the right of where you want the split to appear. True False
9. Dragging the sizing handle activates the AutoFill feature and recognizes the cell entry as one that can be incremented. True False
10. What-if analysis varies the value in the cell you specify until a formula that is dependent on that cell returns the desired result. True False

fill-in

Complete the following statements by filling in the blanks with the correct key terms.

1. A(n) ___________ reference is created when the reference is to the same cell or range on multiple sheets in the same workbook.
2. A $ character in front of both the column and row reference in a formula creates a(n) ____________ reference.
3. The __________ tool is used to find the value needed in one cell to attain a result you want in another cell.
4. _______________ orientation prints a document sideways across the length of the page.
5. A(n) __________ reference is made when part of the cell address is absolute and the other part is relative.
6. A worksheet window can be divided into _________, either horizontal or vertical, through which different areas of the worksheet can be viewed at the same time.
7. ________________ consist of the name of the sheet enclosed in quotes, and are separated from the cell reference by an exclamation point.
8. A technique used to evaluate what effect changing one or more values in formulas has on other values in the worksheet is called ___________________.
9. When specified rows and columns are _________, they are fixed when you scroll.
10. The ____________ feature logically repeats and extends a series.

multiple choice

Circle the correct response to the questions below.

1. The ______________ error value indicates that the wrong type of argument or operand was used.
   a. #####
   b. #DIV/0
   c. #N/A
   d. #VALUE!
2. The ______________ function key will change a selected cell reference to absolute.
   a. F3
   b. F4
   c. F7
   d. F10
3. The number 32534 displayed with the Currency[0] style would appear as ______________ in a cell.
   a. 32,534
   b. $32534
   c. $32,534
   d. $32,534.00
4. The cell reference to adjust row 8 without adjusting column E is:
   a. $E$8
   b. E8
   c. $E8
   d. E$8
5. Which of the following is NOT a valid sheet name?
   a. Second Quarter
   b. Qtr 1
   c. 3/12/04
   d. Week 8 - 10
6. The ______________ feature enters a series of headings by logically repeating and extending the series.
   a. AutoFill
   b. AutoRepeat
   c. ExtendSelect
   d. ExtendFill
7. A division of the worksheet window that allows different areas of the worksheet to be viewed at the same time is called a:
   a. window
   b. part
   c. pane
   d. section
8. The information in the worksheet can be ____________ in the top and left panes of a window only.
   a. frozen
   b. fixed
   c. aligned
   d. adjusted

9. ______________ is used to evaluate the effects of changing selected factors in a worksheet.
   a. AutoCalculate
   b. What-if analysis
   c. AutoFill
   d. Value analysis

10. A cell address that is part absolute and part relative is a(n): ______________________
    a. absolute reference
    b. frozen cell
    c. mixed reference
    d. relative reference

rating system
★ Easy
★★ Moderate
★★★ Difficult

step-by-step

Sandwich Shop Sales Forecast ★

1. Jin Lee owns seven Ice Cream franchises. She has created a worksheet to record each store's first quarter sales. Jin would like you to extend this first quarter sales worksheet to another worksheet that provides a sales forecast for the second quarter. The completed worksheets are shown here.
   a. Open the workbook ex03_Ice Cream Shop.
   b. Total the row and columns using the SUM function. Copy the worksheet data from Sheet1 to Sheet2. Rename the Sheet1 tab to **1st Quarter Sales** and rename Sheet1(2) tab to **2nd Quarter Sales**. Add color to the tabs. Delete Sheet3.
   c. In the 2nd Quarter Sales sheet, change the monthly labels to Apr, May, and June using AutoFill.

Student Name
5/2/2005

The Ice Cream Shop

Location	Jan	Feb	Mar	Total
Three Palms Place	$7,500.00	$7,750.00	$8,000.00	$23,250.00
Mahoney Square	$14,300.00	$14,250.00	$13,900.00	$42,450.00
Mountain Park Court	$10,000.00	$10,200.00	$10,000.00	$30,200.00
Valley Mall	$12,200.00	$12,500.00	$12,950.00	$37,650.00
Fashion Court	$4,500.00	$3,750.00	$4,150.00	$12,400.00
Sunland Place	$5,300.00	$5,350.00	$5,000.00	$15,650.00
Tri-City Mall	$10,000.00	$10,500.00	$9,750.00	$30,250.00
Total	$63,800.00	$64,300.00	$63,750.00	$191,850.00

Student Name
5/2/2005

The Ice Cream Shop

Projected Sales

Location	Apr	May	Jun	Total
Three Palms Place	$9,500.00	$10,450.00	$12,017.50	$31,967.50
Mahoney Square	$14,250.00	$15,675.00	$18,026.25	$47,951.25
Mountain Park Court	$13,000.00	$14,300.00	$16,445.00	$43,745.00
Valley Mall	$14,000.00	$15,400.00	$17,710.00	$47,110.00
Fashion Court	$5,250.00	$5,775.00	$6,641.25	$17,666.25
Sunland Place	$3,500.00	$3,850.00	$4,427.50	$11,777.50
Tri-City Mall	$7,800.00	$8,580.00	$9,867.00	$26,247.00
Total	$67,300.00	$74,030.00	$85,134.50	$226,464.50

Sales Year-To-Date $418,314.50

d. Enter the following projected April sales figures:

Location	Number
Three Palms Plaza	9500
Mahoney Square	14250
Mountain Park Court	13000
Valley Mall	14000
Fashion Court	5250
Sunland Plaza	3500
Tri-City Mall	7800

e. A new advertising campaign for May and June is expected to increase monthly sales. May sales for each location are expected to be 10 percent more than April sales, and June sales are expected to be 15 percent more than May. Enter formulas to calculate May and June sales for the Three Palms Plaza location and then copy these formulas into the other appropriate cells.

f. Enter and bold the heading **Projected Sales** in cell C2. Center the heading over columns C and D.

g. Enter, bold, italicize, and right-align the heading **Sales Year-To-Date:** in cell D13. In cell E13, enter a formula to calculate the total sales for the first six months by summing cells E11 on both sheets. Format the value to Currency with two decimal places.

h. Make the following changes in both sheets:

- Format the numbers to currency with two decimal places.
- Format the column headings to centered, bold, and underlined.
- Center the worksheet title across columns A through E, and add a color and font of your choice.
- Add a fill color of your choice behind the worksheet data.
- Bold and italicize the Total row heading and Total row values.
- Document the workbook to include your name as the author.
- Add a custom header with your name and the date right-aligned to both worksheets.
- Add fill color, graphics, and additional formatting of your choice to the sheet.

i. Use the Find and Replace command to change "Plaza" to **Place**.

j. Preview the workbook. Save the workbook as Ice Cream Shop2. Print the 2nd-Quarter Sales worksheet.

Forecasting Sales ★ ★

2. The Animal Angels rescue group has started a new pet supply retail store to meet the needs of adopting families. Their accountant, Jeremy, has just completed the sales analysis of the first six months of sales. The completed worksheet is shown here.

Student Name
3/24/2005

Animal Angel Pet Supplies

Sales Analysis

	JAN	FEB	MAR	APR	MAY	JUN	TOTAL	AVG.
Income								
Dog Food	$ 728.03	$ 678.43	$ 712.49	$ 653.51	$ 562.12	$ 622.31	$ 3,956.89	$ 659.48
Dog Dishes	$ 325.22	$ 330.13	$ 308.40	$ 440.14	$ 370.59	$ 519.08	$ 2,293.56	$ 382.26
Dog Leash/Collar	$ 617.07	$ 697.64	$ 653.71	$ 692.27	$ 538.59	$ 692.26	$ 3,891.54	$ 648.59
Dog Bed	$ 391.34	$ 389.67	$ 377.76	$ 324.88	$ 279.75	$ 330.00	$ 2,093.40	$ 348.90
Dog Toys	$ 949.41	$ 993.30	$ 866.49	$ 893.01	$ 831.29	$ 844.02	$ 5,377.52	$ 896.25
Cat Food	$ 606.33	$ 624.96	$ 619.70	$ 613.18	$ 503.40	$ 589.91	$ 3,557.48	$ 592.91
Cat Dishes	$ 331.63	$ 299.84	$ 311.29	$ 408.95	$ 352.23	$ 445.76	$ 2,149.70	$ 358.28
Cat Leash/Collar	$ 576.82	$ 555.03	$ 560.16	$ 535.35	$ 474.15	$ 557.47	$ 3,258.98	$ 543.16
Cat Toys	$ 741.13	$ 719.34	$ 739.47	$ 762.66	$ 618.58	$ 759.78	$ 4,340.96	$ 723.49
Scratching Post	$ 317.12	$ 325.33	$ 280.46	$ 250.65	$ 222.45	$ 335.77	$ 1,731.78	$ 288.63
Litter box	$ 451.96	$ 420.17	$ 565.30	$ 385.50	$ 767.30	$ 390.62	$ 2,980.85	$ 496.81
10 Gallon Aquarium	$ 321.14	$ 289.35	$ 234.48	$ 254.67	$ 236.47	$ 259.79	$ 1,595.90	$ 265.98
ID Tags	$ 746.64	$ 790.10	$ 1,009.78	$ 954.92	$ 836.72	$ 935.54	$ 5,273.70	$ 878.95
Donations	$ 316.14	$ 364.35	$ 309.48	$ 1,276.13	$ 2,413.98	$ 1,777.02	$ 6,457.10	$ 1,076.18
Total Income	$ 7,419.98	$ 7,477.64	$ 7,548.97	$ 8,445.82	$ 9,007.62	$ 9,059.33	$ 48,959.36	$ 8,159.89
EXPENSES								
Payroll	$ 3,589.94	$ 3,572.01	$ 3,580.63	$ 3,589.00	$ 3,558.29	$ 3,560.91	$ 21,450.78	$ 3,575.13
Loss	$ 65.94	$ 34.21	$ 76.95	$ 20.99	$ 14.50	$ 3.59	$ 216.18	$ 36.03
Acquisitions	$ 3,532.83	$ 3,723.83	$ 3,826.83	$ 3,835.83	$ 3,934.83	$ 3,494.83	$ 22,348.98	$ 3,724.83
Total Expenses	$ 7,188.71	$ 7,330.05	$ 7,484.41	$ 7,445.82	$ 7,507.62	$ 7,059.33	$ 44,015.94	$ 7,335.99
INCOME	$ 231.27	$ 147.59	$ 64.56	$ 1,000.00	$ 1,500.00	$ 2,000.00	$ 4,943.42	$ 823.90

a. Open the workbook ex03_ Animal Angels. Adjust the zoom to display the entire worksheet. Correct the formula errors in row 28. Change the font color of the title to light orange.

b. Use AutoFill to complete the month headings. Save the workbook as Animal Angels2.

c. Enter the formulas to calculate the figures for the Total column, and Total Income and Total Expenses rows.

d. Enter the function to calculate the Average in cell I6. Copy the function down the column. Clear any cells that contain division by zero errors.

e. Freeze the window to keep the Total and Average columns on the screen with the titles in column A and row 4.

f. Jeremy would like to know the amount of donations that would be necessary to generate an April Net Income of $1000, May of $1500, and $2000 for June. Use Goal Seek to answer these questions and update the donations figures. (Hint: Net income is displayed in row 28.)

g. Jeremy will soon be working on sales figures for the second six months. He does not have the new figures for the July through December sheet, but he will enter the formulas that will calculate the year-to-date totals now. Select cells A1:I28 and copy them to Sheet2. Use Paste Options to retain the original column widths.

h. Delete the figures in cells B6:G19 and B23:G25. In cell H6, enter a formula that adds the total from January through June with the monthly figures from July through December. Copy the formula down the column. Change the month headings using AutoFill for the second six months. Change the average formula to average the 12 months. Change the label in H4 to **Annual TOTAL** and I4 to **Annual AVG**.

i. Delete the extra sheet in the workbook. Rename Sheet1 **January-June Sales**. Rename Sheet2 **July-December Sales**. Add tab colors of your choice. Adjust the sheet formatting as needed.

j. Add a custom header with your name and the date left-aligned. Change the print orientation to landscape. Save the workbook. Print the January-June Sales worksheet.

Thailand Tour Cost Analysis ★★

3. Alice, a travel analyst for Adventure Travel Tours, is evaluating the profitability of a planned Thailand Tour package. She has researched competing tours and has determined that a price of $5,900 is appropriate. Alice has determined the following costs for the package.

Item	Cost
Air transport	$1,800 per person
Ground transportation	$460 per person
Lodging	$1,475 per person
Food	$900 per person
Tour Guides	$3,000
Administrative	$1,200
Miscellaneous	$2,000

Alice has started a worksheet to evaluate the revenues and costs for the Thailand Tour. She wants to know how many travelers are needed to break even (revenues equal costs), how many are needed to make $5,000, and how many are needed to make $10,000. The three worksheets of the completed analysis are shown here.

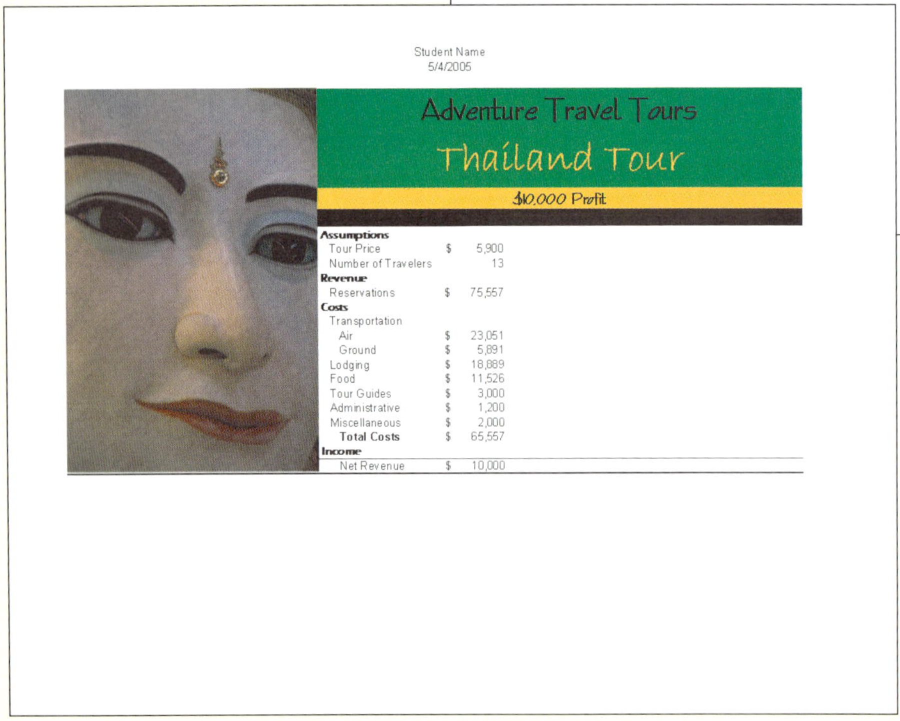

a. Open the workbook ex03_Thai Tour. Notice that Alice has already entered the tour price and an estimated number of travelers. Zoom the worksheet to display the entire sheet.

b. Revenue from reservations is calculated by multiplying the tour price times the number of travelers. Enter this formula into C9. Save the workbook as Thai Tour2 in a folder named Tour Analysis.

c. Based on Alice's cost information, air transportation is $1,800 times the number of travelers. Enter this formula into C12. Enter formulas into C13, C14, and C15 for the other expenses (see table above) related to the number of travelers.

d. Enter the remaining expenses into cells C16, C17, and C18.

e. Calculate total costs in cell C19. Net revenue is the difference between revenue from reservations and total costs. Enter this formula into cell C21.

f. Format the currency values in the worksheet to Accounting with no decimal places.

g. Use Goal Seek to determine the number of travelers required to just break even (net revenue equals zero).

h. Rename the sheet tab to **Break Even**. Copy the Break Even sheet data to Sheet2 and rename the tab of the copy **$5000**. Add color to the tabs.

i. In the $5000 sheet, change the title in B3 to **$5,000 Profit**. Use Goal Seek to determine the number of travelers needed to produce a net revenue of $5,000.

j. Copy the **$5000** sheet data to Sheet3 and rename the tab of the copy to **$10,000**. Change the tab color. Change the title in B3 to **$10,000 Profit**. Use Goal Seek to determine the number of travelers needed to produce a net revenue of $10,000.

k. Use the Find and Replace command to change Trip Guides to **Tour Guides**.

l. Preview the workbook. Add a custom header with your name and the date center-aligned to the three sheets. Change the page layout to landscape. Adjust the column widths so each sheet prints on one page. Center the worksheet horizontally. Save the workbook. Print the Break Even sheet and the $10,000 sheet.

Calculating Total Points and GPA ★★★

4. Ray Schultz is a college student who has just completed the first two years of his undergraduate program as a business major. In this exercise, you will calculate semester and cumulative totals and GPA for each semester. The completed worksheet for Spring 2004 is shown here.

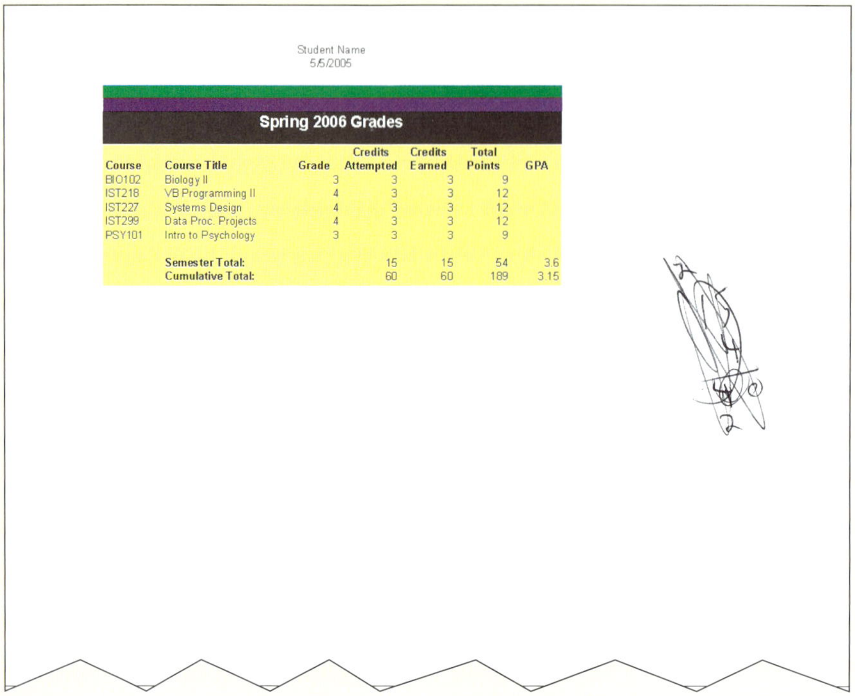

Student Name
5/5/2005

Course	Course Title	Grade	Credits Attempted	Credits Earned	Total Points	GPA
	Spring 2006 Grades					
BIO102	Biology II	3	3	3	9	
IST218	VB Programming II	4	3	3	12	
IST227	Systems Design	4	3	3	12	
IST299	Data Proc. Projects	4	3	3	12	
PSY101	Intro to Psychology	3	3	3	9	
	Semester Total:		15	15	54	3.6
	Cumulative Total:		60	60	189	3.15

a. Open the workbook ex03_Grade Report. Look at the four sheets. Rename the sheet tabs **Fall 2004**, **Spring 2005**, **Fall 2005**, and **Spring 2006**. Add color to the tabs.

b. Use Find and Replace to change Survey of Math to **Math 101**. Save the workbook as Grade Report2 in a folder named Grade Analysis.

c. You need to enter the formulas to calculate the Total Points and GPA for the four semesters. You will do this for all four sheets at the same time. Select the four sheets. In the Fall 2004 sheet, multiply the Grade by the Credits Earned to calculate Total Points for Intro to Business. Copy that formula down the column. Sum the Credits Attempted, Credits Earned, and Total Points columns and display the results in the Semester Total row.

d. In cell G13, divide the Semester Total's Total Points by the Semester Total's Credits Earned to calculate the GPA for the semester. Ungroup the sheets.

e. Use what-if analysis to see what Amy's GPA would be if she had earned a 3 instead of a 2 in Western Civilization. Change the grade back to a 2.

f. Look at each sheet to see that the formulas were entered and the calculations performed.

g. Go to cell D14 in the Fall 2004 sheet. Enter the reference formula =D13 to copy the Semester Total Credits Attempted number to the Cumulative Total row. Copy the formula to cells E14 and F14 to calculate Credits Earned and Total Points.

h. Go to the Spring 2005 sheet and calculate a Cumulative Total for Credits Attempted by summing the Spring 2005 Semester Total and the Fall 2004 Cumulative Total. (Hint: You can use pointing to enter the Cumulative Totals formula.)

i. Copy that formula to the adjacent cells to calculate Cumulative Totals for Credits Earned and Total Points. Repeat this procedure on the Fall 2005 and Spring 2006 sheets.

j. Go to the Fall 2004 sheet. Select all four sheets. In cell G14, calculate the GPA for the Cumulative Total. Format the Semester Total GPA and the Cumulative Total GPA to display two decimals. Look at each sheet to see the cumulative GPA for each semester. (Hint: Amy's cumulative GPA at the end of the Spring 2006 semester is 3.15.)

k. Display the sheet tab shortcut menu and ungroup the sheets. Go to the Fall 2004 sheet and preview the workbook. Add a custom header with your name and the date center-aligned to the sheets.

l. Add any additional formatting of your choice to the sheets.

m. Save the workbook. Print the Spring 2006 sheet centered horizontally on the page.

Year-to-Date Sales Analysis ★ ★ ★

5. Madeline Singh works in the Accounting department at DVD Direct, a DVD-by-mail rental company. She has been asked to prepare a report on the year-to-date accounting totals. She has already entered the figures for January through June. Next, she will create a worksheet for July through December and compile the year's totals. Your completed worksheet is shown here.

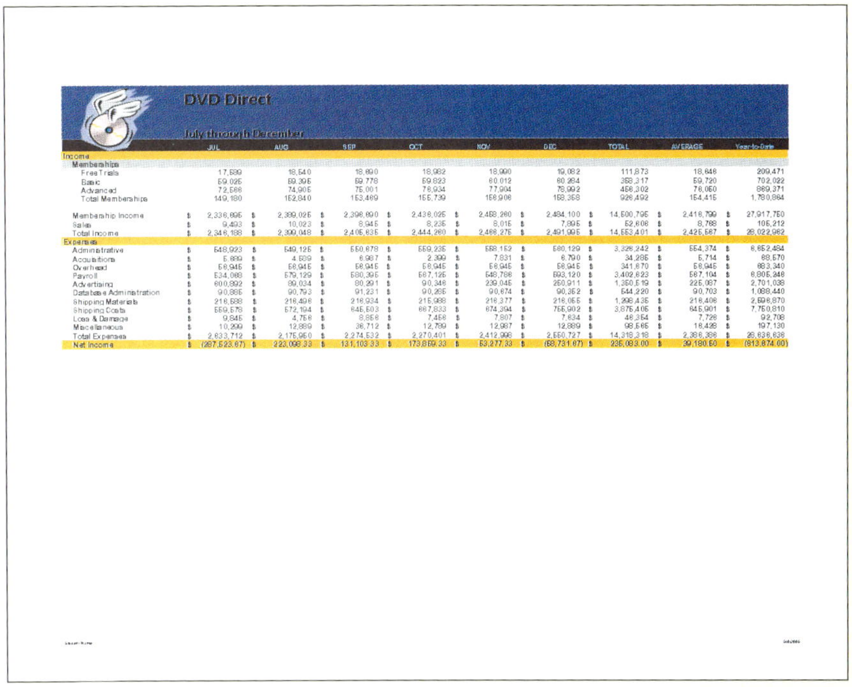

a. Open the file ex03_DVD Direct. Adjust the zoom to display all the data. Correct the formula errors. Save the workbook as DVD Direct2.

b. Enter formulas in cells H6:H9 to calculate the membership totals. Now enter formulas in cells H11:H13 for these totals.

c. Enter the following formula in cell B11 to calculate the income from memberships for January: **=(B7*$B$28)+(B8*$B$29)**. Copy the formula down the row to calculate the Membership income. Enter the appropriate formulas in the Total column to calculate the total income figures.

d. Enter formulas in cells H15:H24 to calculate the total expenses. In cell H25, total the expenses.

e. Move to cell B26 and enter a formula that subtracts the Total Expenses from the Total Income. Copy the formula across the row.

f. Enter the heading **AVERAGE** in cell I3. Adjust the formatting of the new column to match the other columns in the sheet. Enter a formula to calculate the average number of free trials in cell I6. Copy the formula down the column. Delete the division by zero errors. Adjust the formatting of the sheet as needed.

g. Select the range A1:I26 and copy the sheet to Sheet2. Use Paste Options to keep the source column widths. Adjust the row height to accomodate the graphic. Rename the new sheet **Jul-Dec**. Add tab colors to both sheets.

h. Change the title in the Jul-Dec sheet to **July through December**. Change the month heading in cell B3 to **JUL**. Use AutoFill to change the remaining month headings.

i. Adjust the references in the formulas of row 11.

j. Select cells I13 and I26 and use Watch Window to view the changes made when you enter the following values in the specified cells:

	Jul	Aug	Sep	Oct	Nov	Dec
Free Trial	17,589	18,540	18,690	18,982	18,990	19,082
Basic	59,025	59,395	59,778	59,823	60,012	60,284
Advanced	72,566	74,905	75,001	76,934	77,904	78,992

k. Close the Watch Window. Move to cell J3 and enter the heading **Year-to-Date**. In cell J6, enter a formula to compute the total free trial memberships in the first and second six-month periods. Copy the formula down the column to find the year-to-date totals for all of the rows. Adjust the formatting in column J to match the others in the sheet.

l. Delete Sheet3. Use Find and Replace to change the New Products labels to **Acquisitions**.

m. Use Goal Seek to calculate the number of Advanced Memberships needed to break even in the Net Income cell for December.

n. Change the page orientation to landscape. Adjust the formatting so all of the Jul-Dec sheet prints on one page.

o. Add a custom footer with your name and the date to both sheets. Save the workbook. Print the Jul-Dec sheet.

on your own

Expanding Budget Projections ★

CONTINUING EXERCISES

1. In On Your Own exercise 2 of Lab 1, you created a Personal Budget workbook for a three-month budget. Extend this workbook by adding two additional sheets. One sheet will contain a budget for the next six months. The final sheet will present a full year's summary using 3-D references to the values in the appropriate sheets.

   Consider making a special purchase, such as a car, a new computer, or perhaps taking a trip. On a separate line below the total balance in the summary sheet, enter the amount you would need. Subtract this value from the total balance. If this value is negative, reevaluate your expenses and adjust them appropriately. Format the sheets using the features you have learned in the first three labs. Add your name in a custom header on all sheets. Preview, print, and save the workbook as Personal Budget2.

Program Expense Comparisons ★

2. Obtain yearly income and expense data for three major art programs at your college or university. In a workbook, record each program's data in a separate sheet. In a fourth sheet, calculate the total income, total expenses, and net income for each program. Also in this sheet, calculate the overall totals for income, expense, and net income. Format the sheets using the features you have learned in the first three labs. Add your name in a custom header on all sheets. Preview, print, and save the workbook as Art Expenses in a folder named College Programs.

Stock Data Analysis ★ ★

3. Select three stocks listed on the New York Stock Exchange. Using the Internet or the library, determine each stock's month-ending price for the past year. In a workbook containing four sheets, record each stock's prices in separate worksheets. In a fourth sheet, calculate the average, standard deviation, and maximum and minimum for each of the three stocks. Also, in the final sheet, chart the average data for the three stocks. Format the sheets using the features you have learned in the first three labs. Add your name in a custom header on all sheets that includes your name. Preview, print, and save the workbook as Stock Analysis in a folder named Stocks.

Inventory Tracking ★ ★ ★

4. Many companies have a central location for employees to pick up office supplies. Design a worksheet that will keep track of the items in inventory divided by category; for example: pens, paper, staples, etc. Each category may have as many detail lines as needed to represent the items. For example: blue pens, red pens, markers, etc.

The worksheet should keep track of the number of items in inventory, the price paid for each unit, and the extended price (items * price). Sum the number of items in inventory and the total inventory on hand. Sum each category and calculate the percent each category is of total sales. Format the sheet using the features you have learned in the first three labs. Add your name in a custom header on all sheets. Change the worksheet orientation if necessary, preview, print, and save the workbook as Inventory Tracking.

Start Your Own Business ★ ★ ★

5. Owning and managing a small business is a dream of many college students. Do some research on the Web or in the library and choose a business that interests you. Create a projected worksheet for four quarters in separate worksheets. In a fifth sheet, show the total for the year. Include a year-to-date value in each quarterly sheet. In the last quarter sheet, select one expense and determine what value the expense would have to have been so that the net income for that quarter would have been 10 percent higher than the current level. Format the sheets using the features you have learned in the first three labs. Add your name in a custom header on all sheets. Preview, print, and save the workbook as My Business.

Working Together 1: Linking, Embedding, and E-Mailing

Case Study

Downtown Internet Café

Evan, the Cafe owner, is particularly concerned about the first quarter forecast. Your analysis of the sales data for the first quarter shows a steady increase in total sales. However, as you suggested, if a strong sales promotion is mounted, Internet sales will increase sharply. Evan has asked you to send him a memo containing the worksheet data showing the expected sales without a strong sales promotion and the chart showing the projected sales with a sales promotion.

Additionally, Evan wants a copy of the second quarter forecast showing the five percent profit margins for each month. He also wants a copy of the workbook file so that he can play with the sales values to their effects on the profit margin.

You will learn how to share information between applications while you create these memos. Additionally, you will learn how to convert the workbook to an .XML file format and to send the workbook via e-mail. Your completed documents will look like those shown below.

Note: This lab assumes that you already know how to use Word and that you have completed Labs 2 and 3 of Excel.

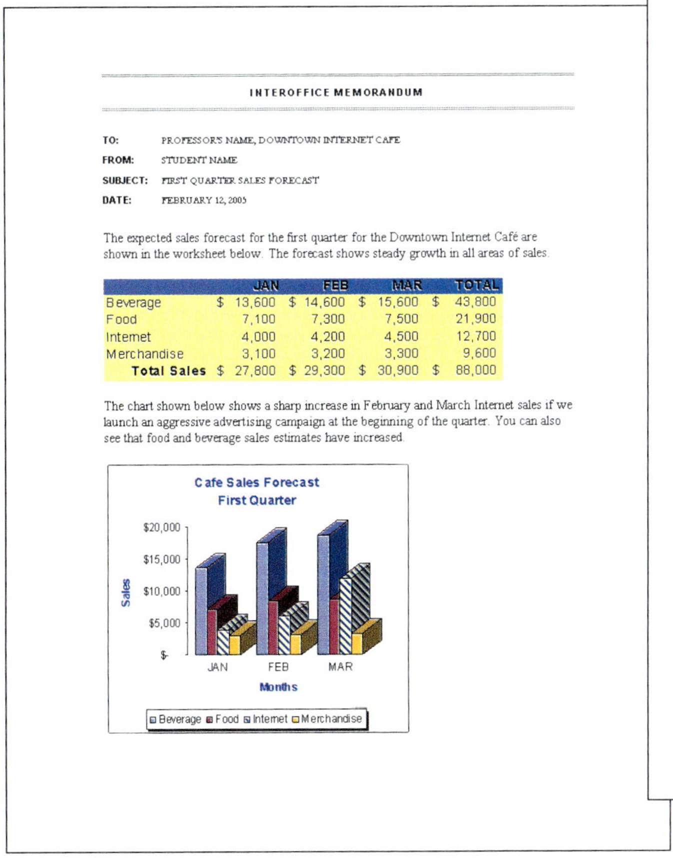

INTEROFFICE MEMORANDUM

TO: PROFESSOR'S NAME, DOWNTOWN INTERNET CAFE
FROM: STUDENT NAME
SUBJECT: FIRST QUARTER SALES FORECAST
DATE: FEBRUARY 12, 2005

The expected sales forecast for the first quarter for the Downtown Internet Café are shown in the worksheet below. The forecast shows steady growth in all areas of sales.

	JAN	FEB	MAR	TOTAL
Beverage	$ 13,600	$ 14,600	$ 15,600	$ 43,800
Food	7,100	7,300	7,500	21,900
Internet	4,000	4,200	4,500	12,700
Merchandise	3,100	3,200	3,300	9,600
Total Sales	$ 27,800	$ 29,300	$ 30,900	$ 88,000

The chart shown below shows a sharp increase in February and March Internet sales if we launch an aggressive advertising campaign at the beginning of the quarter. You can also see that food and beverage sales estimates have increased.

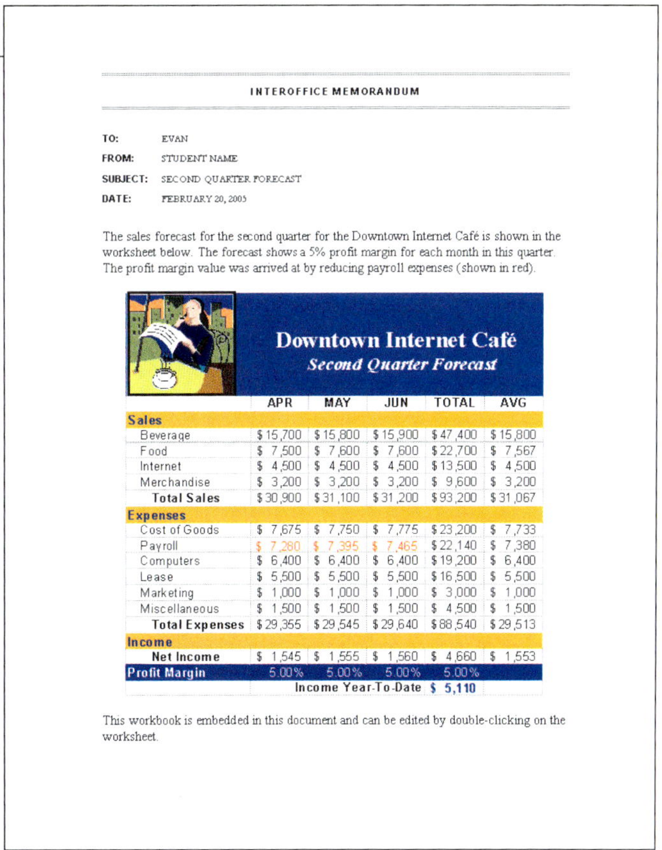

INTEROFFICE MEMORANDUM

TO: EVAN
FROM: STUDENT NAME
SUBJECT: SECOND QUARTER FORECAST
DATE: FEBRUARY 20, 2005

The sales forecast for the second quarter for the Downtown Internet Café is shown in the worksheet below. The forecast shows a 5% profit margin for each month in this quarter. The profit margin value was arrived at by reducing payroll expenses (shown in red).

Downtown Internet Café
Second Quarter Forecast

	APR	MAY	JUN	TOTAL	AVG
Sales					
Beverage	$ 15,700	$ 15,800	$ 15,900	$ 47,400	$ 15,800
Food	$ 7,500	$ 7,600	$ 7,600	$ 22,700	$ 7,567
Internet	$ 4,500	$ 4,500	$ 4,500	$ 13,500	$ 4,500
Merchandise	$ 3,200	$ 3,200	$ 3,200	$ 9,600	$ 3,200
Total Sales	$ 30,900	$ 31,100	$ 31,200	$ 93,200	$ 31,067
Expenses					
Cost of Goods	$ 7,675	$ 7,750	$ 7,775	$ 23,200	$ 7,733
Payroll	$ 7,280	$ 7,395	$ 7,465	$ 22,140	$ 7,380
Computers	$ 6,400	$ 6,400	$ 6,400	$ 19,200	$ 6,400
Lease	$ 5,500	$ 5,500	$ 5,500	$ 16,500	$ 5,500
Marketing	$ 1,000	$ 1,000	$ 1,000	$ 3,000	$ 1,000
Miscellaneous	$ 1,500	$ 1,500	$ 1,500	$ 4,500	$ 1,500
Total Expenses	$ 29,355	$ 29,545	$ 29,640	$ 88,540	$ 29,513
Income					
Net Income	$ 1,545	$ 1,555	$ 1,560	$ 4,660	$ 1,553
Profit Margin	5.00%	5.00%	5.00%	5.00%	
			Income Year-To-Date	$ 5,110	

This workbook is embedded in this document and can be edited by double-clicking on the worksheet.

Sharing Information Between Applications

All Microsoft Office 2003 applications have a common user interface such as similar commands and menu structures. In addition to these obvious features, they have been designed to work together, making it easy to share and exchange information between applications. For example, the same commands and procedures to copy information within an Office Excel 2003 worksheet are used to copy information to other Office 2003 applications such as Word. The information is pasted in a format the application can edit, if possible. Information can also be copied as a linked object or an embedded object. You will use each of these three methods to copy information between Word 2003 and Excel 2003.

Copying a Worksheet to a Word Document

The memo to Evan about the analysis of the sales data has already been created using Word 2003 and saved as a document file.

1

- **Start Office Word 2003 and open the document exwt1_Sales Forecast Memo.**
- **In the memo header, replace [Professor's Name] with your instructor's name and Student Name with your name.**
- **Save the file as Sales Forecast Memo.**
- **Reduce the zoom to 75%.**

Your screen should be similar to Figure 1

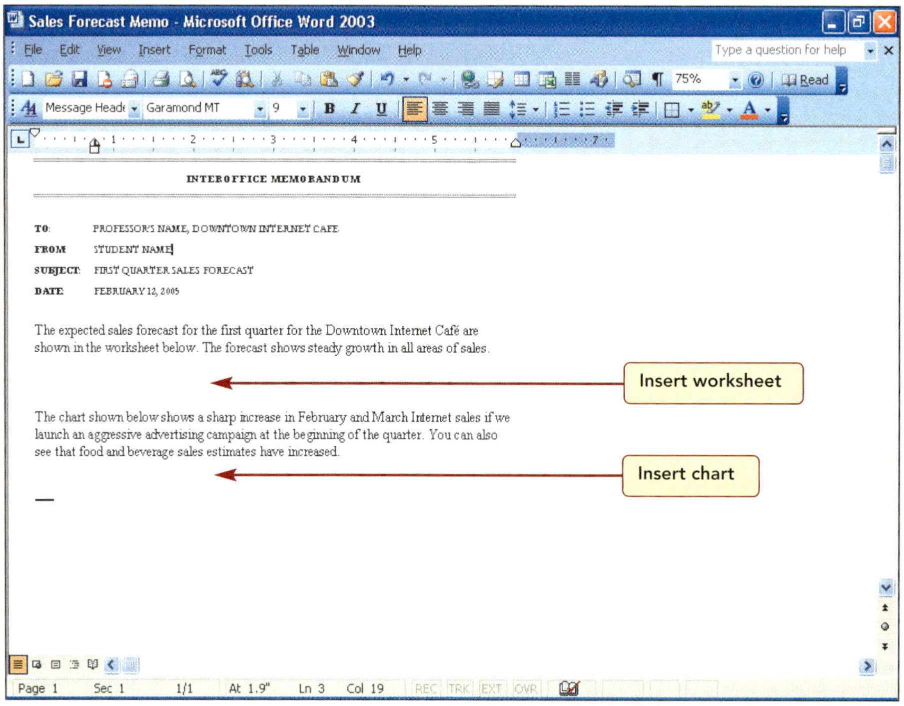

Figure 1

As you can see, you still need to add the Excel worksheet data and chart to the memo. To insert the information from the Excel workbook file into the Word memo, you need to open the workbook. You will then tile the two open application windows to make it easier to see and work with both files.

2

- **Start Excel and open the workbook exwt1_Sales Charts.**
- **Reduce the zoom to 75%.**
- **Tile the two open windows vertically.**

Having Trouble?
Select Tile Windows Vertically from the taskbar shortcut menu.

Your screen should be similar to Figure 2

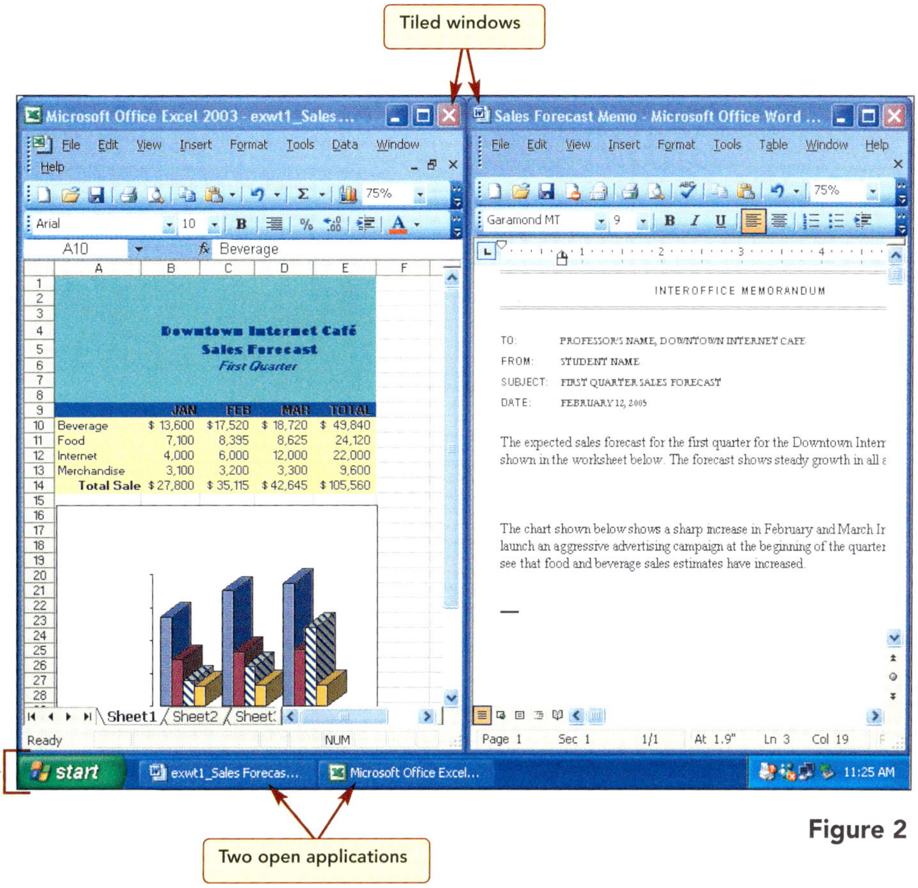

Figure 2

There are now two open applications, Word and Excel. Because both applications are visible at the same time, simply clicking on the application window makes that application active. Then you can work in the active application using the application's tools and commands. You will insert the worksheet data of the first quarter sales forecast below the first paragraph. Below the second paragraph, you will display the chart.

You will begin by copying the chart from Excel into the Word document. While using Excel, you have learned how to use cut, copy, and paste to move or copy information within and between worksheets. You can also perform these operations between files in the same application and between files in different Office applications.

3 Click in the Excel application window to make it active.

Additional Information

The window title bar is bold when the application is active.

- **Select the column chart.**
- **Click Copy to copy the selected chart object to the Clipboard.**
- **Switch to the Word application and move the insertion point to the second blank line below the second paragraph of the memo.**
- **Click Paste to copy the contents from Clipboard into the memo.**

Your screen should be similar to Figure 3

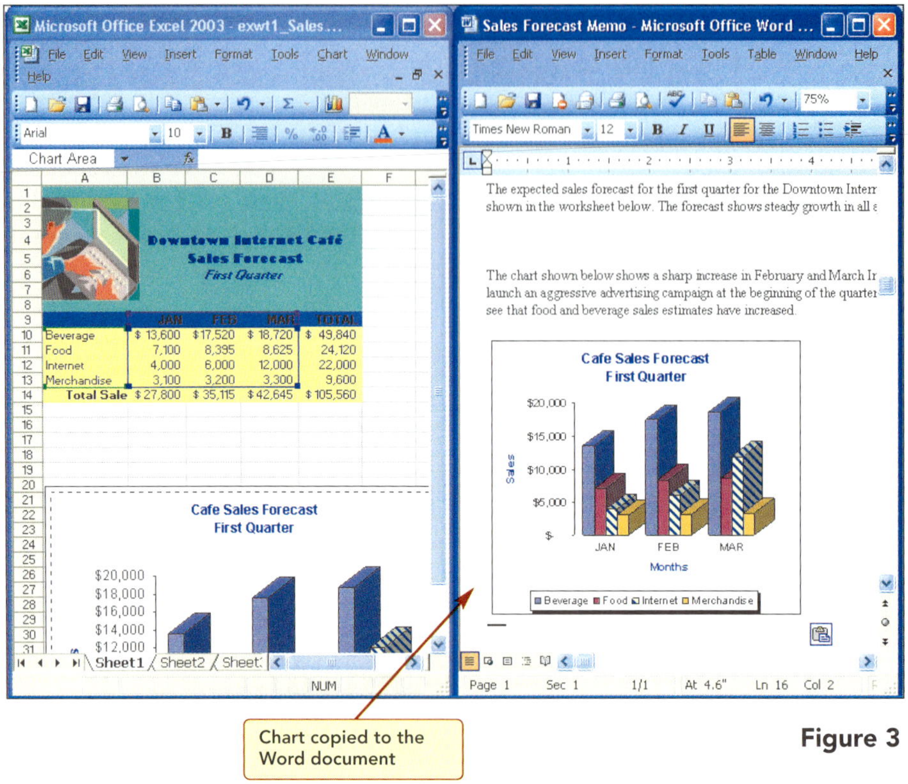

Figure 3

A copy of the chart has been inserted as an object into the Word document. It can be sized and moved like any other graphic object.

Linking Between Applications

Next, you want to copy the worksheet showing the sales trends below the first paragraph in the memo. You will insert the worksheet into the memo as a **linked object**. Information created in one application can also be inserted as a linked object into a document created by another application. When an object is linked, the data is stored in the **source file** (the document in which it was created). A graphic representation or picture of the data is displayed in the **destination file** (the document in which the object is inserted). A connection between the information in the destination file to the source file is established by the creation of a link. The link contains references to the location of the source file and the selection within the document that is linked to the destination file.

When changes are made in the source file that affect the linked object, the changes are reflected automatically in the destination file when it is opened. This is called a **live link**. When you create linked objects, the date and time on your machine should be accurate. This is because the program refers to the date of the source file to determine whether updates are needed when you open the destination file.

You will copy the worksheet as a linked object so that it will be updated automatically if the source file is edited.

1 Click in the Excel application window to make it active.

- Select cells A9 through E14.
- Click Copy.

Having Trouble?

If the Clipboard task pane opens, close it.

- Switch to the Word document and move the insertion point to the second blank line below the first paragraph of the memo.
- Choose Edit/Paste Special.
- Select Paste link.

Your screen should be similar to Figure 4

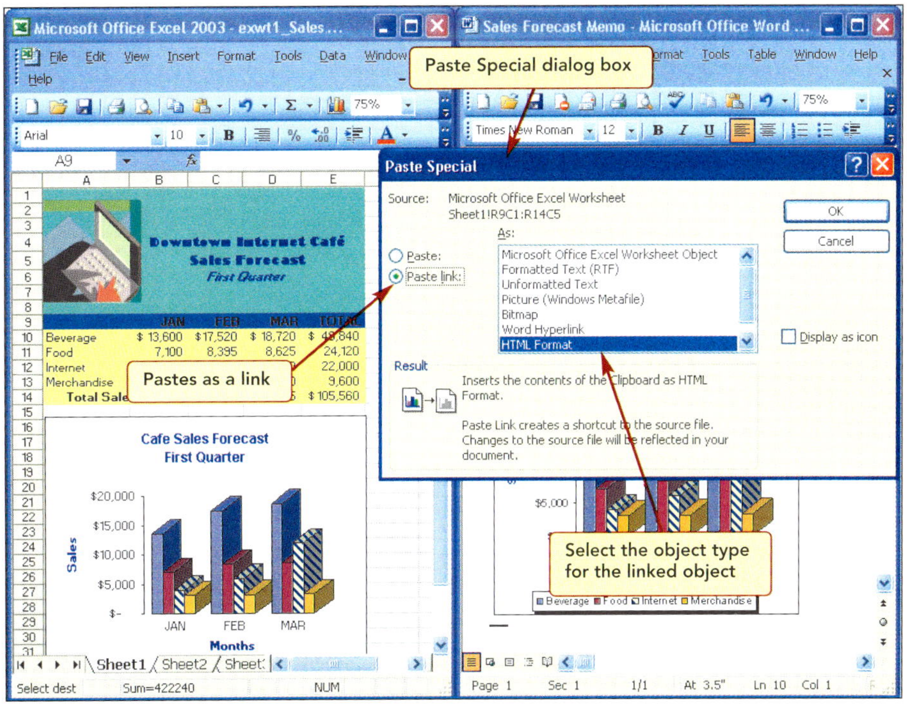

Figure 4

The Paste Special dialog box displays the type of object contained in the Clipboard and its location in the Source area. From the As list box, you select the type of format in which you want the object inserted into the destination file. There are many different object types from which you can select. It is important to select the appropriate object format so that the link works correctly when inserted in the destination. In this case, you want to use the Microsoft Office Excel Worksheet Object format.

The Result area describes the effect of your selections. In this case, the object will be inserted as a picture, and a link will be created to the chart in the source file. Selecting the Display as Icon option changes the display of the object in the destination file from a picture to an icon. When inserted in this manner, double-clicking the icon displays the object picture.

2 Select Microsoft Office Excel Worksheet Object.

Click OK.

Your screen should be similar to Figure 5

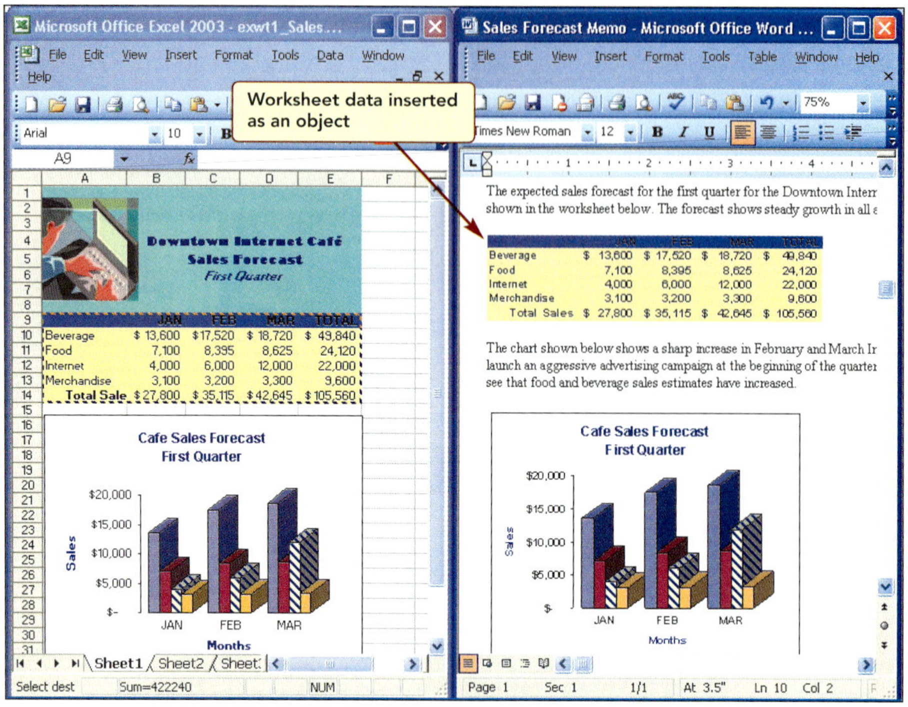

Figure 5

The worksheet data has been copied into the Word document as an object that can be sized and moved like any other object. You want to make the worksheet larger.

3 Select the worksheet object and increase its size as in Figure 6.

Deselect the worksheet object.

Your screen should be similar to Figure 6

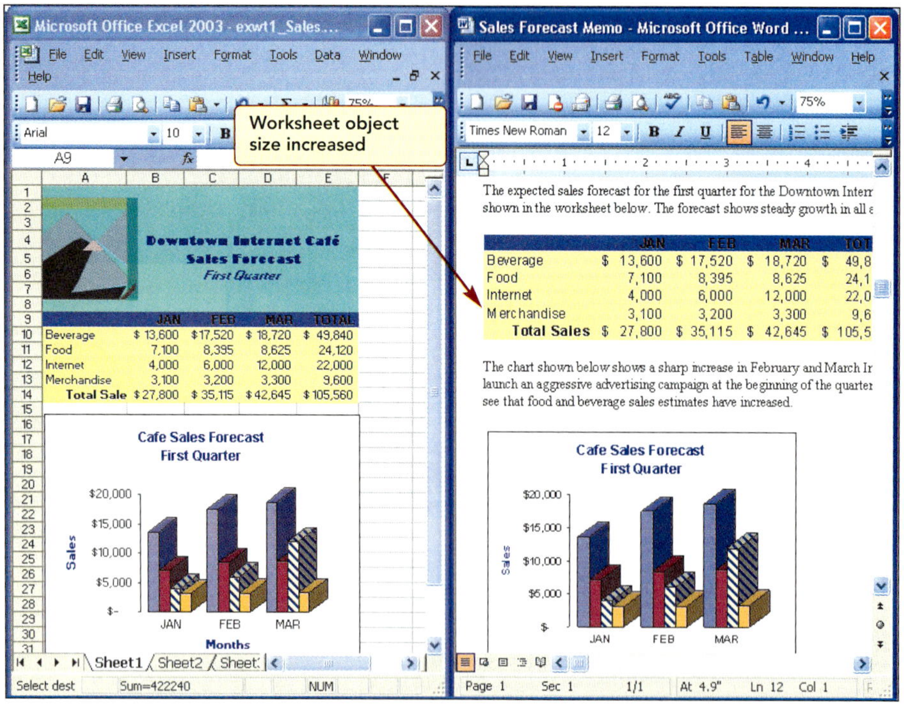

Figure 6

Updating a Linked Object

Next, you want to return the sales data in the Excel worksheet to the original forecasted values assuming an aggressive marketing campaign is not mounted.

1

- **Switch to the Excel window.**
- **Press Esc to clear the moving border.**
- **Change the sales values in the cells indicated below.**

	Cell	Value
Beverage	C10	14600
	D10	15600
Food	C11	7300
	D11	7500
Internet	C12	4200
	D12	4500

- **Switch to the Word window.**
- **Press F9 to update the linked object.**

Another Method

The menu equivalent is Edit/Update Link.

Your screen should be similar to Figure 7

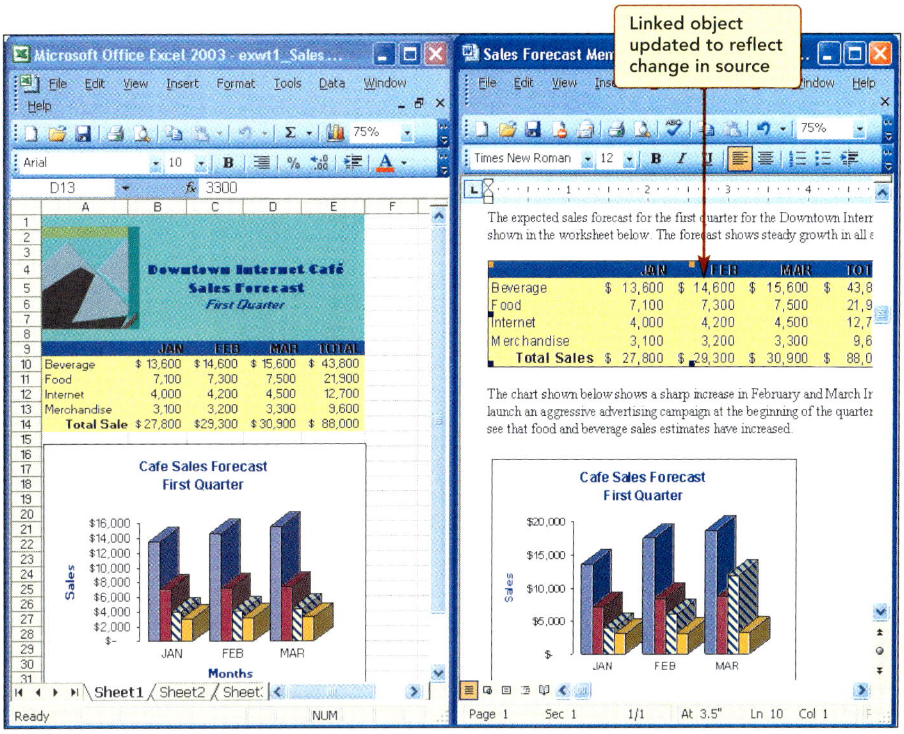

Figure 7

Notice that the chart in Excel has been updated to reflect the change in the worksheet data. Likewise, the worksheet in the memo reflects the changes you made in Excel for the sales data. This is because any changes you make in Excel will be reflected in the linked object in the Word document. However, because the chart in the Word document is not a linked object, it does not reflect the changes in data made in Excel.

Editing Links

When a document is opened that contains links, the application looks for the source file and automatically updates the linked objects. If the document contains many links, updating can take a lot of time. Additionally, if you move the source file to another location or perform other operations that may interfere with the link, your link will not work. To help with situations like these, you can edit the settings associated with links. You will look at the links to the worksheet data created in the Word document.

1 Choose Edit/Links.

Your screen should be similar to Figure 8

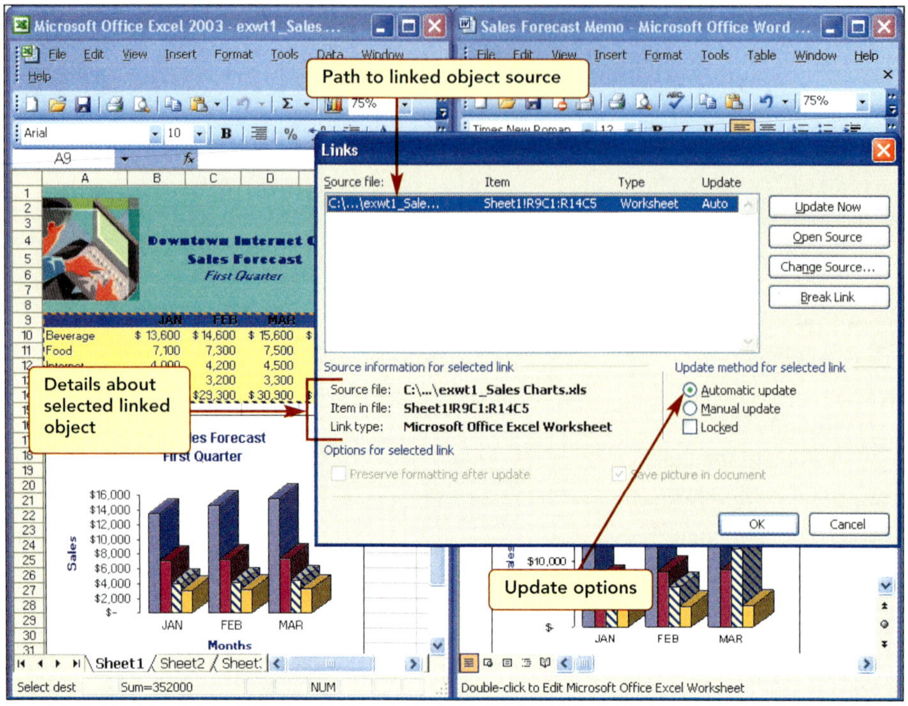

Figure 8

The Links dialog box displays the object path for all links in the document in the list box. The field code specifies the path and name of the source file, the range of linked cells or object name, the type of file, and the update status. Below the list box, the details for the selected link are displayed.

The other options in this dialog box are described in the table below.

Option	Effect
Automatic update	Updates the linked object whenever the destination document is opened or the source file changes. This is the default.
Manual update	The destination document is not automatically updated and you must use the Update Now command button to update the link.
Locked	Prevents a linked object from being updated.
Open Source	Opens the source document for the selected link.
Change Source	Used to modify the path to the source document.
Break Link	Breaks the connection between the source document and the active document.

The links in the Word document are to the exwt1_Sales Charts workbook file. Now that the memo is complete, you will untile the windows and save the documents.

2 Click [Cancel].

- **Switch to the Excel window.**
- **Undo the tiled windows.**

Having Trouble?

Choose Undo Tile from the taskbar shortcut menu.

- **Save the Excel workbook as Sales Forecast Linked.**
- **Close the file.**
- **Switch to the Word window.**

Having Trouble?

Click the taskbar button to switch to the Word document.

- **Choose Edit/Links.**

Your screen should be similar to Figure 9

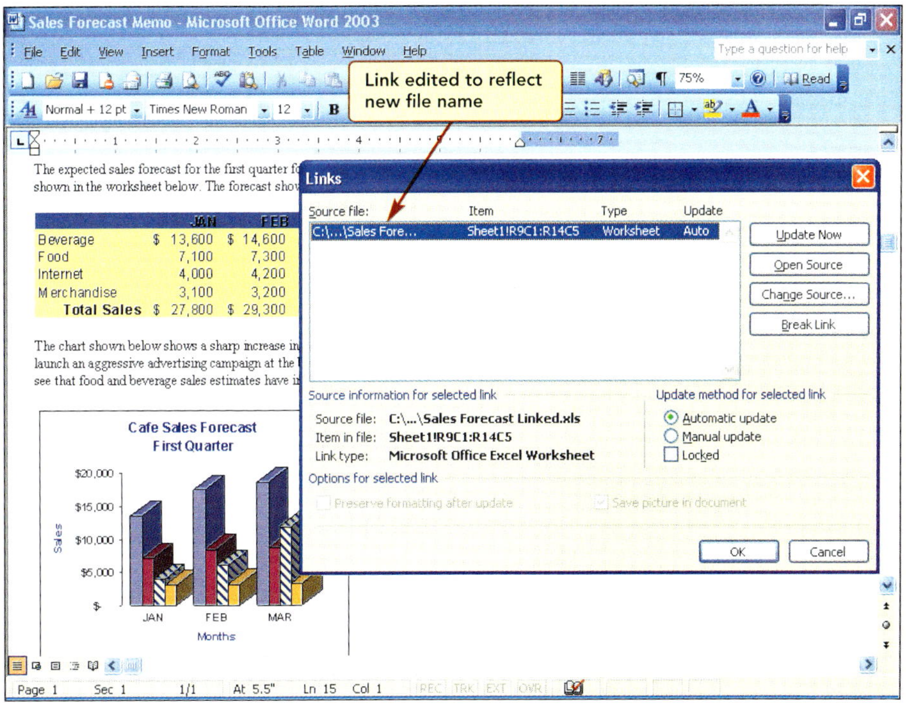

Figure 9

You can now see that the link has been edited to reflect the new workbook file name.

3 Click [OK].

- **Save, preview, print, and then close the Word document.**

Embedding an Object in Another Application

Having Trouble?

Refer to Concept 2: Graphics in Lab 2 to review embedded objects.

The last thing you need to send Evan is a memo that describes and shows the second quarter forecast. To do this, you will open the memo already created for you in Word and **embed** the sections from the Annual Forecast Revised workbook that Evan wants in the appropriate locations. An object that is embedded is stored in the destination file and becomes part of that document. The entire file, not just the selection that is displayed in the destination file, becomes part of the document. This means that you can modify it without affecting the source document where the original object resides.

1. Open the Word document exwt1_Second Quarter Memo.
   - In the memo header, replace Student Name with your name.
   - Save the document as Second Quarter Memo.
   - Switch to Excel and open the workbook file exwt1_Second Quarter.

Your screen should be similar to Figure 10

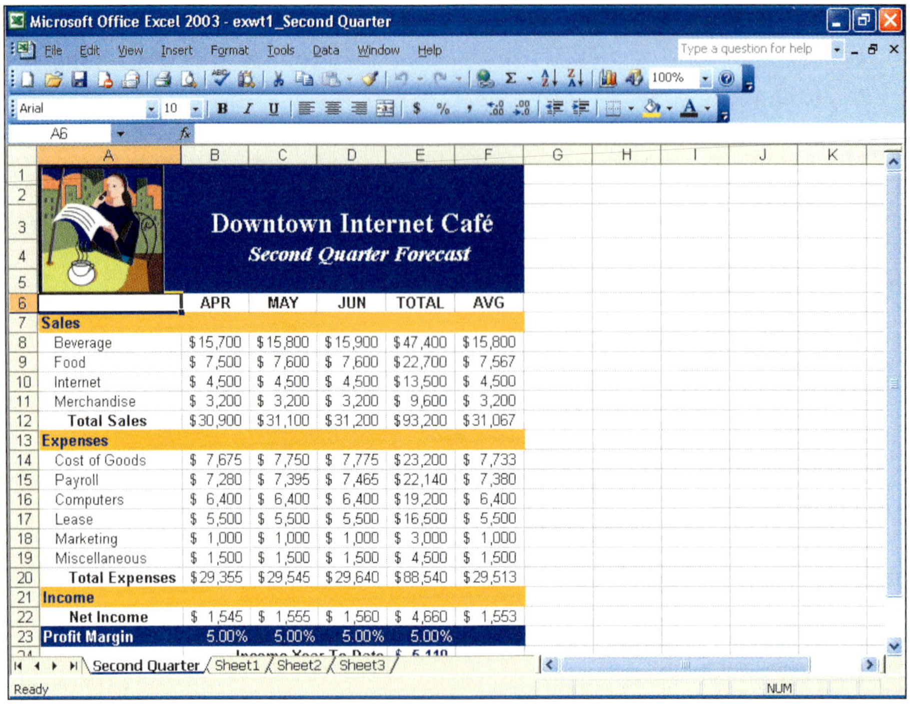

Figure 10

You will embed the second quarter forecast worksheet in the Word document.

2. Copy the range A1 through F24.
   - Switch to the Word window.
   - Move to the second blank line below the first paragraph of the memo.
   - Choose Edit/Paste Special.

Additional Information

To embed an entire file, use Insert/Object.

Your screen should be similar to Figure 11

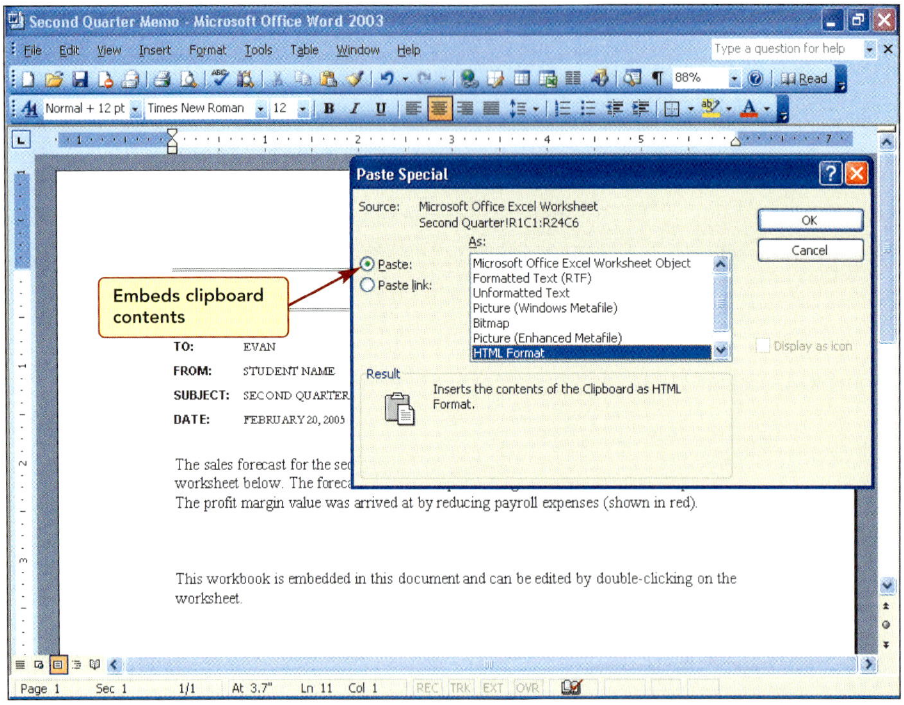

Figure 11

The Paste option inserts or embeds the Clipboard contents in the format you specify from the As list box. To embed the contents of the Clipboard into a document so it can be edited using the source program, select the option that displays the server name, in this case Excel.

3
- **Select Microsoft Office Excel Worksheet Object.**
- **Click OK.**
- **Click on the worksheet to select the object and increase its size to almost the full text width.**

Your screen should be similar to Figure 12

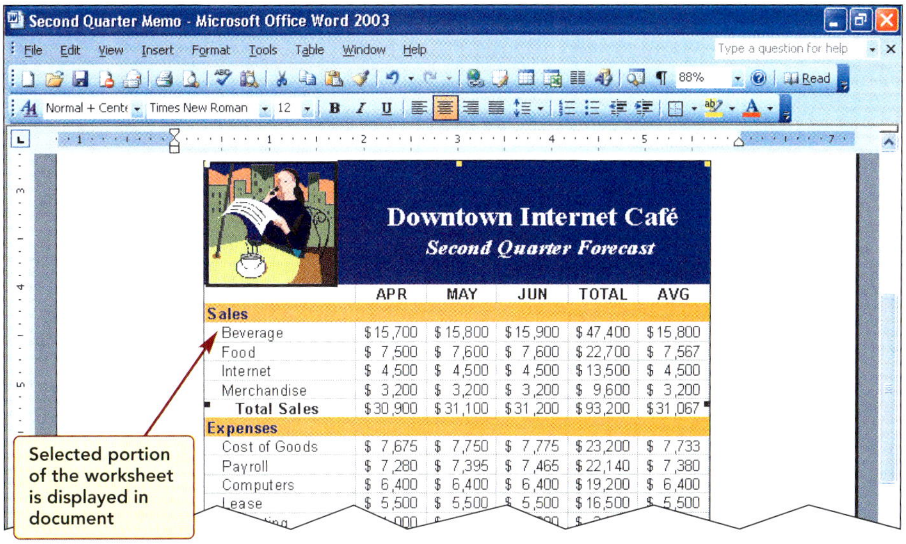

Figure 12

The selected portion of the worksheet is displayed in the memo at the location of the insertion point.

Updating an Embedded Object

You want to add color to the payroll range of cells you adjusted to arrive at the five percent profit margin. Because the worksheet is embedded, you can do this from within the Word document. The source program is used to edit data in an embedded object. To open the source program and edit the worksheet, you double-click the embedded object.

1
- **Double-click the worksheet object in Word.**

Having Trouble?

If the worksheet does not fully display the numbers, click outside the worksheet to return to the document, make the worksheet object larger, and then open the source program again.

Your screen should be similar to Figure 13

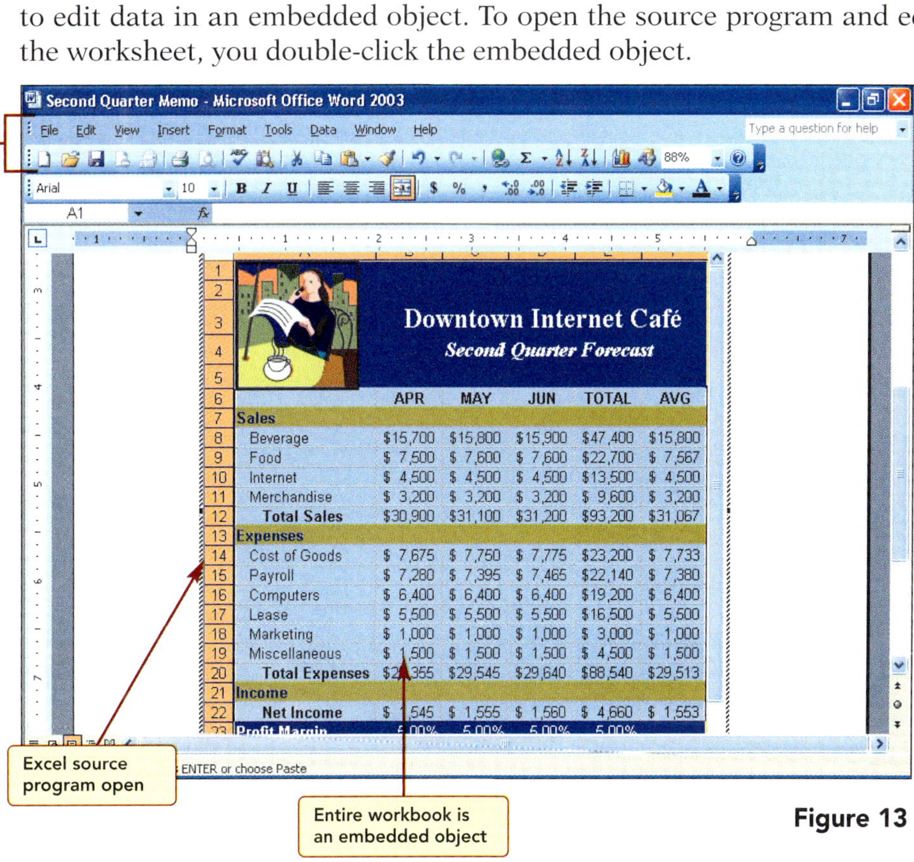

Figure 13

> **Additional Information**
> The user must have the source program on his or her system to be able to open and edit the embedded object.

The source program, in this case Excel, is opened. The Excel menus and toolbars replace the menus and toolbars in the Word application window. The selected portion of the embedded object is displayed in an editing worksheet window. Now, you can use the source program commands to edit the object.

2
- **Change the font color of cells B15 through D15 to red.**
- **Close the source program by clicking anywhere outside the object.**
- **Save the document.**

Your screen should be similar to Figure 14

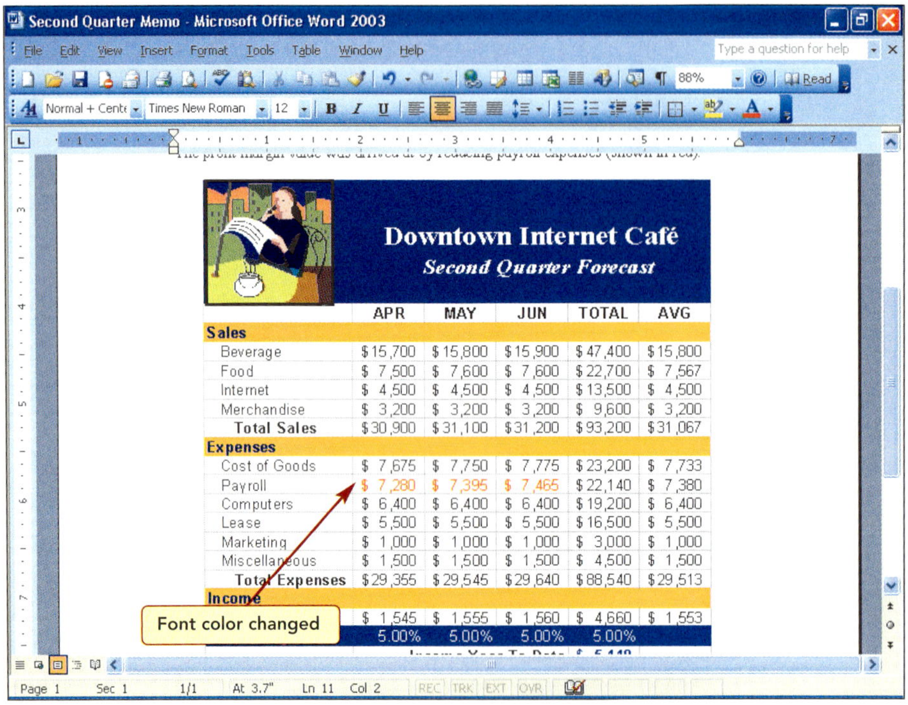

Figure 14

The embedded object in the memo is updated to reflect the changes you made.

Saving a Worksheet as XML

Evan has also asked that you send him a copy of the workbook file that he can give to his financial advisor to examine. Because he does not know what software the advisor uses, you will save the file using XML (Extensible Markup Language) format. **XML** converts a structured file, such as a worksheet, into a text file that follows standard guidelines and can be read by a variety of applications.

1
- **Switch to the Excel window.**
- **Choose File/Save As and enter the file name of** Second Quarter.
- **Change the file type to XML Spreadsheet.**
- **Click** Save.
- **Click** Yes **to confirm that you want to continue.**
- **Close the workbook file and exit Excel.**

The worksheet data has been saved in a file using the XML format without the picture or chart. Now, this file can be read by a variety of different applications.

E-Mailing a Memo

Finally, you want to send the memo and the XML file via e-mail to Evan. All the Office System applications have the capability to access and send e-mail using an e-mail program on your system.

Having Trouble?

If you do not have an e-mail program installed, the button is not displayed and you will need to skip this section.

1 **Switch to the Word memo.**

Click E-mail.

Another Method

The menu equivalent is File/Send to/Mail Recipient.

Your screen should look similar to Figure 15

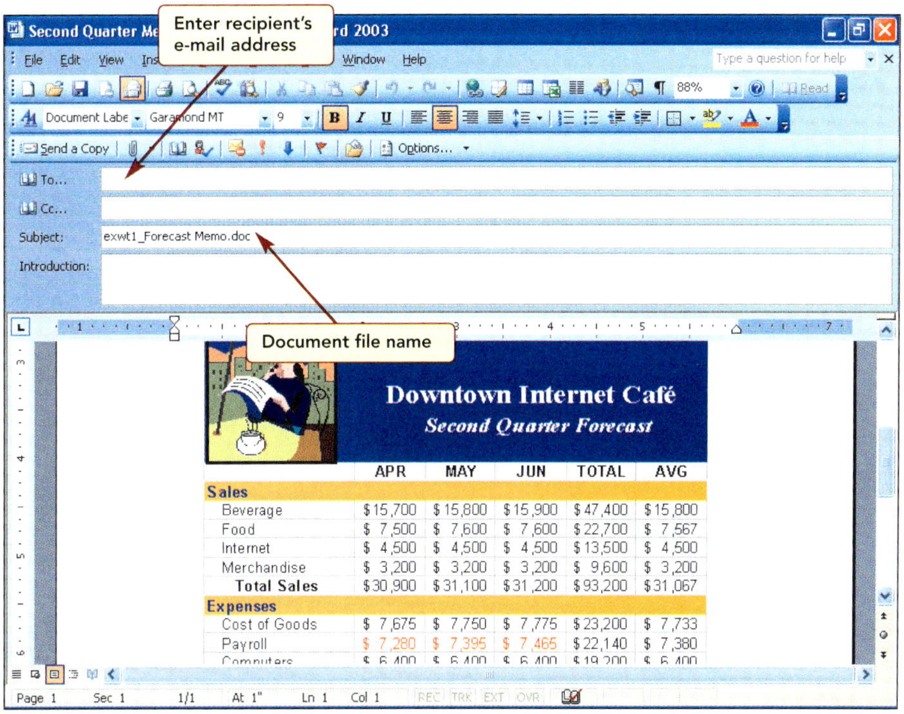

Figure 15

Additional Information

The original document filename is displayed because the new filename will not be recognized until you close the file.

An e-mail message box is displayed at the top of the document. You use the message box to specify the recipient's e-mail address, the e-mail address of anyone to whom you want to send a copy of this message (cc:), and the subject of the message. You can also use the toolbar buttons to select recipient names from your e-mail address book, attach a file to the message, set the message priority (high, normal, or low priority), include a follow-up message flag, and set other e-mail options. The name of the document appears in the Subject box by default. Finally, you can use the Introduction box to include a brief note along with the copy of the memo.

You will enter the e-mail address, a subject, and brief note.

Additional Information

To send an e-mail message to multiple recipients, separate the e-mail addresses with semicolons.

2 Enter the e-mail address of the person to whom you want to send the message in the To box.

Having Trouble?

Ask your instructor what e-mail address to use. For example, if you have a personal e-mail address, your instructor may want you to use it for this exercise.

- In place of the information displayed in the Subject box, enter **Second Quarter Forecast**.
- In the Introduction box, type **Attached is the Second Quarter worksheet saved in XML file format**.

Your screen should look similar to Figure 16

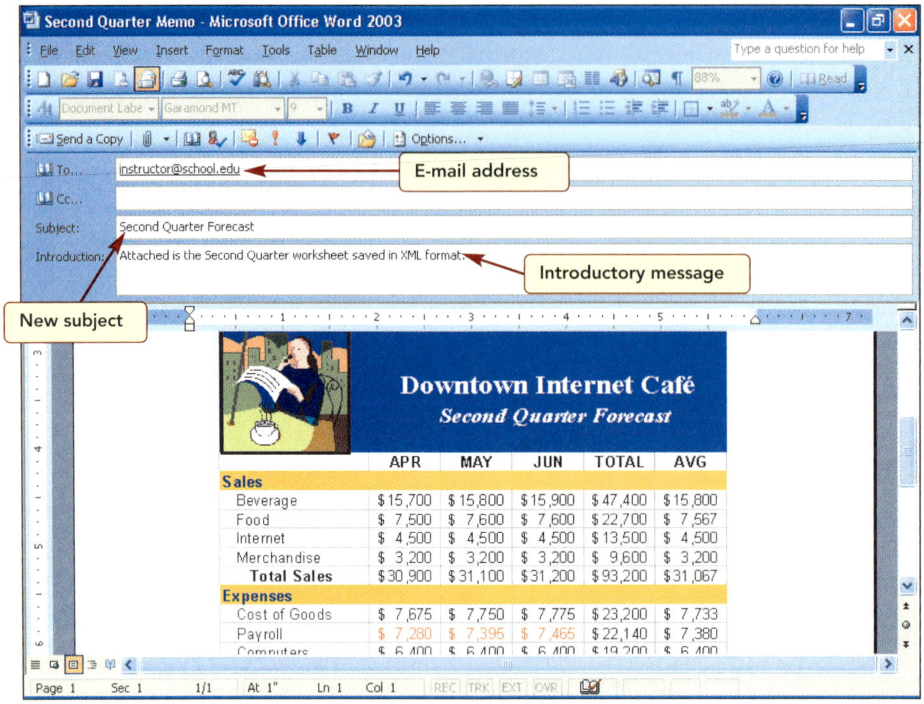

Figure 16

Next, you need to send the XML file as an attachment along with the e-mail message. An **attachment** is a copy of a file that is included with an e-mail message. The attached file can then be opened by the recipient using the appropriate application software.

3 Click [Insert File button] Insert File.

- From the Insert File dialog box, change the file types to XML Files and select Second Quarter.
- Click Insert.

Your screen should look similar to Figure 17

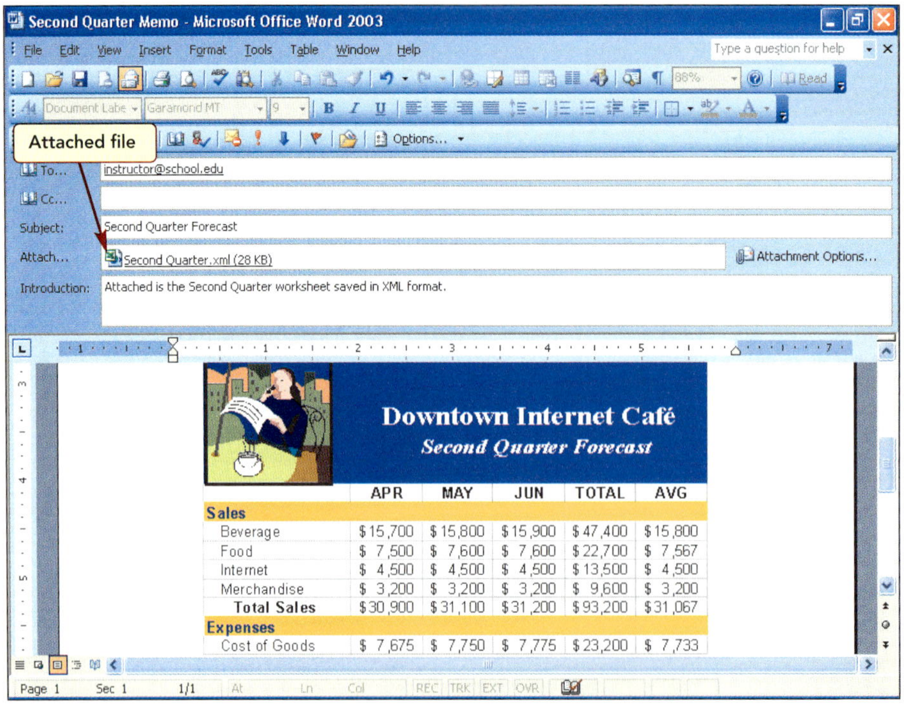

Figure 17

The name of the file that will be sent along with the e-mail message is displayed in the Attachment line. You are now ready to send the e-mail message.

4 Click Send a Copy.

Having Trouble?

If you do not have an Internet connection established, you will not be able to send this message. Click Cancel to cancel the connection message.

Your message is sent and the e-mail message box is removed from the screen. When the e-mail message is received, the memo will appear in the body of the message. The procedure for opening a file attachment depends upon the e-mail program being used. Typically, clicking on the attachment symbol or name provides a menu of options that allows you to open or save the file to your disk.

5 Preview and print the memo.

Exit Word.

Deciding When to Link or Embed Objects

Linking documents is a very handy feature, particularly in documents whose information is updated frequently. If you include a linked object in a document that you are giving to another person, make sure the user has access to the source file and application. Otherwise the links will not operate correctly.

Keep the following in mind when deciding whether to link or embed objects.

Use linking when:	Use embedding when:
File size is important.	File size is not important.
Users have access to the source file and application.	Users have access to the application but not to the source file.
The information is updated frequently.	The data changes infrequently.

WORKING TOGETHER 1
Linking, Embedding, and E-Mailing

key terms

attachment EXWT1.14
destination file EXWT1.4
embed EXWT1.9
linked object EXWT1.4
live link EXWT1.4
source file EXWT1.4
XML EXWT1.12

microsoft office specialist skills

The Microsoft Office Specialist certification program is designed to measure your proficiency in performing basic tasks using the Office 2003 applications. Getting certified demonstrates that you have the skills and provides a valuable industry credential for employment. After completing this lab, you have learned the following Microsoft Office Excel 2003 Specialist skills:

Skill Sets	Skill Standards	Page
Managing Workbooks	Insert, delete, and move cells	EXWT1.5,1.10
	Save data in appropriate formats for different uses	EXWT1.12

command summary

Command	Button	Action
File/Send to/Mail Recipient		Sends active document to e-mail recipient
Edit/Paste Special		Inserts object as an embedded object
Edit/Links		Modifies selected link
Insert/Object		Inserts objects of different types

rating system

★ Easy

★★ Moderate

★★★ Difficult

step-by-step

Rescue Foundation Income Memo ★★

1. The Animal Rescue Foundation's agency director has asked you to provide her with information about income for 2004. You want to create a memo to her and include a copy of the worksheet analysis of this data in the memo. The completed memo is shown below.

   a. Start Word and open the document exwt1_Rescue Memo.

   b. In the header, replace the From placeholder with your name. Add your instructor's name to the To line.

   c. Start Excel and open the workbook exwt1_Contributions.

   d. Insert both worksheets as Microsoft Excel Worksheet Object links below the first paragraph in the Word memo. Size and center the worksheets below the paragraph.

   e. In Excel enter the income of **$2,650** for May raffle ticket sales. In the memo update the linked worksheet.

   f. Save the Excel workbook in XML file format as Contributions2. Exit Excel.

   g. If necessary, adjust the size and placement of the worksheets in the memo. Save the Word document as Rescue Memo Linked. Preview and print the document.

   h. Print or e-mail the memo to your instructor and carbon copy yourself. Include appropriate information in the subject. Include the worksheet as an attachment.

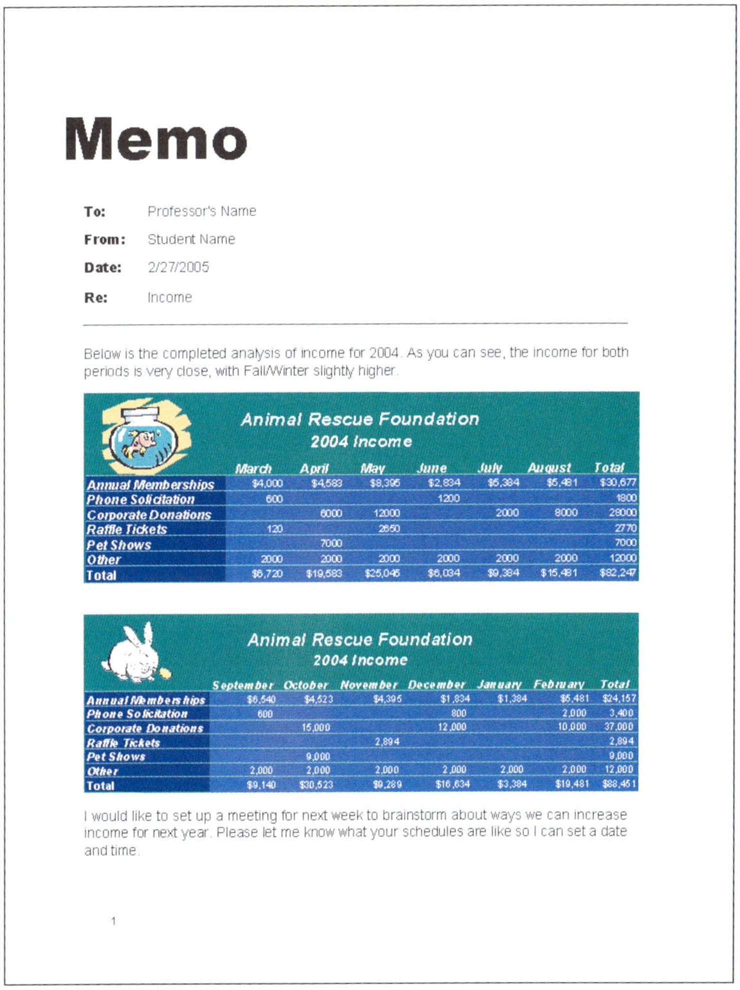

Memo

To: Professor's Name

From: Student Name

Date: 2/27/2005

Re: Income

Below is the completed analysis of income for 2004. As you can see, the income for both periods is very close, with Fall/Winter slightly higher.

Animal Rescue Foundation
2004 Income

	March	April	May	June	July	August	Total
Annual Memberships	$4,000	$4,583	$8,395	$2,834	$5,384	$5,481	$30,677
Phone Solicitation	600			1200			1800
Corporate Donations		6000	12000		2000	8000	28000
Raffle Tickets	120		2650				2770
Pet Shows		7000					7000
Other	2000	2000	2000	2000	2000	2000	12000
Total	$6,720	$19,583	$25,046	$6,034	$9,384	$15,481	$82,247

Animal Rescue Foundation
2004 Income

	September	October	November	December	January	February	Total
Annual Memberships	$6,540	$4,523	$4,395	$1,834	$1,384	$5,481	$24,157
Phone Solicitation	600			800		2,000	3,400
Corporate Donations		15,000		12,000		10,000	37,000
Raffle Tickets			2,894				2,894
Pet Shows		9,000					9,000
Other	2,000	2,000	2,000	2,000	2,000	2,000	12,000
Total	$9,140	$30,523	$9,289	$16,634	$3,384	$19,481	$88,461

I would like to set up a meeting for next week to brainstorm about ways we can increase income for next year. Please let me know what your schedules are like so I can set a date and time.

1

Tour Status Memo ★ ★

2. Adventure Travel Tours travel agency sends a monthly status report to all subsidiary offices showing the bookings for the specialty tours offered by the company. Previously the worksheet data was printed separately from the memo. Now you want to include the worksheet in the same document as the memo. Your completed memo is shown here.

   a. Start Word and open the exwt1_Tour Status Report document. Replace Student Name with your name on the From line in the heading.

   b. Start Excel and open the exwt1_Adventure Travel Status workbook.

   c. Copy the worksheet as a linked object into the memo below the paragraph.

   d. In Excel enter the data shown below for the March bookings worksheet.

Tour	March Data
The Land of the Midnight Sun	2
Costa Rica Rainforest	4
Vail Ski Mountain	4
Machu Picchu	3
Imperial China	6
Tanzania Safari	6

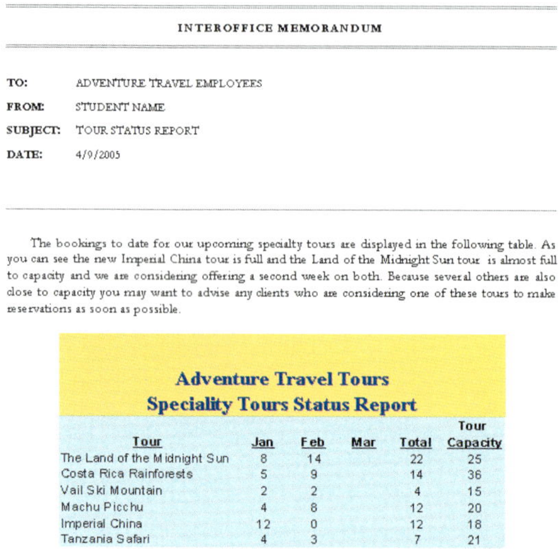

INTEROFFICE MEMORANDUM

TO: ADVENTURE TRAVEL EMPLOYEES
FROM: STUDENT NAME
SUBJECT: TOUR STATUS REPORT
DATE: 4/9/2005

The bookings to date for our upcoming specialty tours are displayed in the following table. As you can see the new Imperial China tour is full and the Land of the Midnight Sun tour is almost full to capacity and we are considering offering a second week on both. Because several others are also close to capacity you may want to advise any clients who are considering one of these tours to make reservations as soon as possible.

Adventure Travel Tours
Speciality Tours Status Report

Tour	Jan	Feb	Mar	Total	Tour Capacity
The Land of the Midnight Sun	8	14		22	25
Costa Rica Rainforests	5	9		14	36
Vail Ski Mountain	2	2		4	15
Machu Picchu	4	8		12	20
Imperial China	12	0		12	18
Tanzania Safari	4	3		7	21

   e. Save the workbook in XML file format as Adventure Travel Status2. Exit Excel.

   f. Center the worksheet object in the word document.

   g. Save the Word document as March Status Report. Print the memo.

   h. Print or e-mail the memo to your instructor and carbon copy yourself. Include appropriate information in the subject. Include the worksheet as an attachment.

Home Sale Price Memo ★ ★

3. Jennifer works for a large real estate company in the marketing department. She has recently researched the average home prices for existing homes in four regions and has created a worksheet and column chart of the data. Now Jennifer wants to send a memo containing the chart to her supervisor. The completed memo is shown below.

   a. Start Word and open the document exwt1_Home Price Memo.

   b. In the header, replace the placeholder information in brackets with the following:

TO:	**Mel Stocker**
FROM:	**Jennifer Pizzaro**
CC:	**[your name]**
RE:	**Average Existing Home Prices**

   c. Start Excel and open the workbook exwt1_Real Estate Prices. Embed the column chart below the paragraph in the Word memo. Center the chart in the memo. Exit Excel.

   d. You decide you need to clarify that the data for 2005 and 2006 is projected. Add a second title line **(2005–2006 Projected)** to the embedded chart in 12 point, italic, no bold.

   e. Save the Word document as Home Price Memo2. Preview and print the document.

   f. Print or e-mail the memo to your instructor and carbon copy yourself. Include appropriate information in the subject.

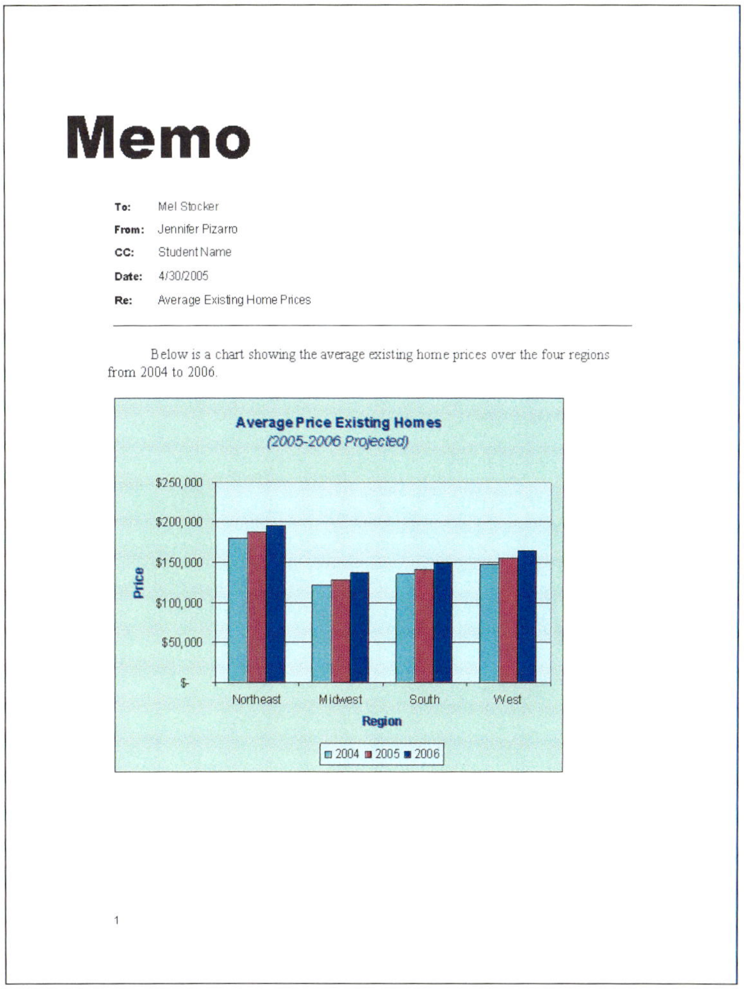
Memo

To: Mel Stocker
From: Jennifer Pizarro
CC: Student Name
Date: 4/30/2005
Re: Average Existing Home Prices

Below is a chart showing the average existing home prices over the four regions from 2004 to 2006.

1

Using Solver, Creating Templates, and Evaluating Scenarios

LAB 4

Objectives

After you have read this chapter, you should be able to:

1. Use Solver.
2. Create an Answer report.
3. Create and use workbook templates.
4. Protect a worksheet.
5. Open and use multiple workbooks.
6. Link workbooks.
7. Hide worksheets.
8. Create diagrams
9. Create, edit, and use scenarios.
10. Create a Scenario Summary report.
11. Display the current date and time.

Case Study

Downtown Internet Café

After further discussion with Evan, the owner of the Downtown Internet Café, you continued to refine the forecast analysis for the year. Based on Evan's input, you used Goal Seek to revise the third quarter sales to show a 6 percent monthly profit margin. In the fourth quarter, because Evan expects sales to increase approximately 10 percent over third quarter sales, you adjusted the sales to reflect the expected increase. You also increased the payroll expenses to manage the larger sales volume.

Evan thinks these changes are more realistic but wants you to further refine the fourth quarter analysis to show a quarterly profit margin of 8.5 percent. You will use the Solver tool to determine the values.

Once the annual forecast for the current year (2005) is complete, Evan wants you to use the same procedure to create the forecast for the following year (2006). You will use the current year annual forecast worksheet to create a template for the next year's forecast. Then you will use the template to create the first quarter forecast for that year.

Additionally, Evan wants to see a visualization of the sales in the form of a diagram. You will use Office Excel 2003 to create a drawing of a pyramid to show how the four sales are related.

Finally, you have been asked to create three different scenarios that will show the best, worst, and most likely scenarios for the first-quarter forecast for the following year. The completed scenario summary report is shown here.

Brand X pictures/Getty Images

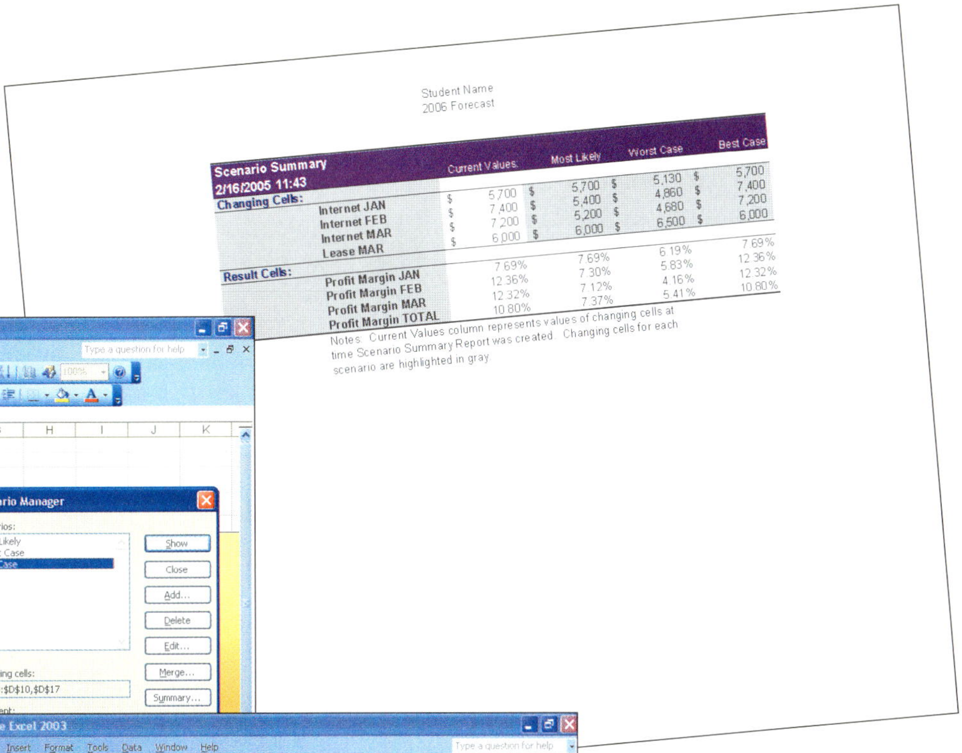

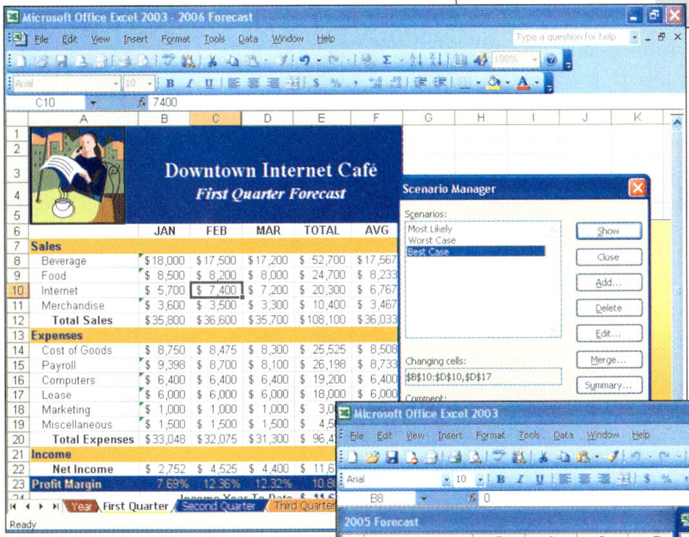

Using Scenario Manager, you can analyze various possible outcomes to help plan for the future.

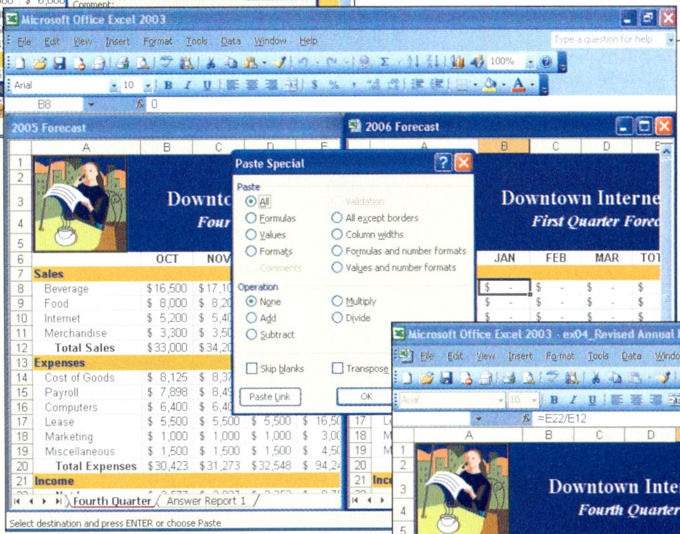

Creating links between workbooks allows changes you make in one workbook file to be automatically reflected in another workbook file.

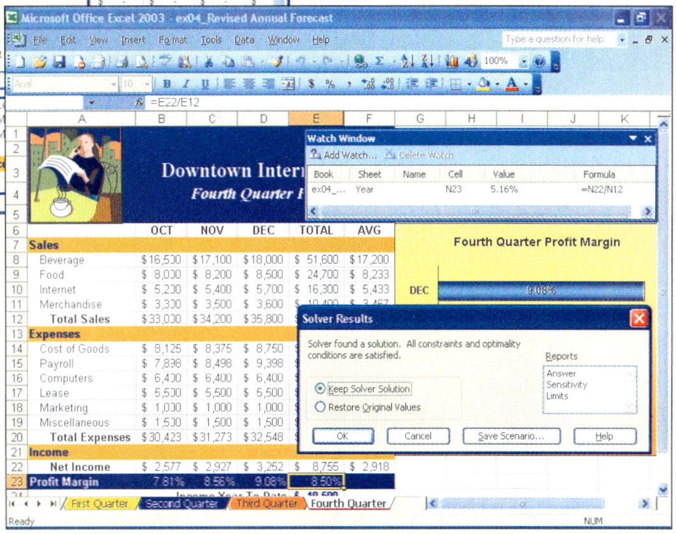

Using Solver, you can quickly determine the effect of changing values in two or more cells on another cell.

Concept Preview

The following concepts will be introduced in this lab:

1. **Solver** Solver is a tool used to perform what-if analysis to determine the effect of changing values in two or more cells on another cell.
2. **Workbook Template** A workbook template is a workbook file that contains predesigned worksheets that can be used as a pattern for creating similar worksheets in new workbooks.
3. **Protection** The protection feature controls what information can be changed in a workbook.
4. **Window Arrangement** The window arrangement feature displays all open workbook files in separate windows on the screen, making it easy to view and work with information in different workbooks.
5. **Link** A link creates a connection between files that automatically updates the data in one file whenever the data in the other file changes.
6. **Diagram** A diagram is a graphic object that can be used to illustrate concepts and to enhance the workbook.
7. **Scenario** A scenario is a named set of input values that you can substitute in a worksheet to see the effects of a possible alternative course of action.

Analyzing the Worksheet

After seeing how the payroll values changed each month to achieve higher second and third quarter profit margins, Evan would like you to do a similar analysis on the fourth quarter. First you want to look at the current profit margin value for the fourth quarter.

1

- **Start Office Excel 2003.**
- **Open the workbook file ex04_Revised Annual Forecast.**
- **Make the Fourth Quarter sheet active.**
- **Select cell E23.**

Your screen should be similar to Figure 4.1

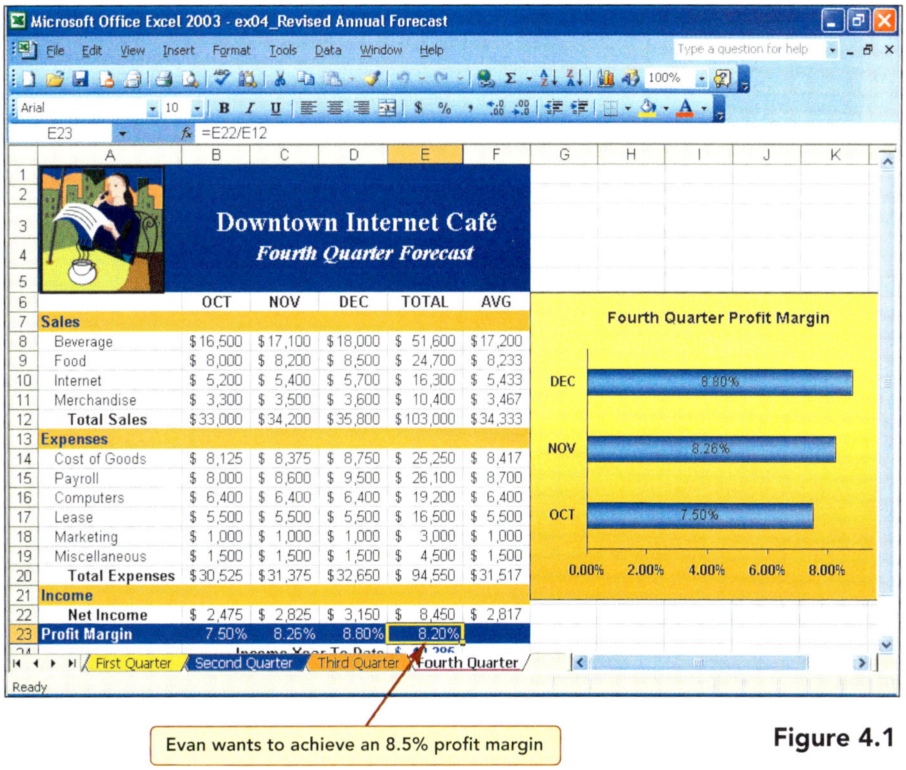

Figure 4.1

The current total profit margin for the fourth quarter is 8.20 percent. Evan would like to achieve an 8.5 percent quarterly profit margin. Again, to do this, you will need to reduce the monthly payroll expenses. While you are making changes to the quarterly worksheet, you will display the Watch Window to see how the changes affect the annual profit margin.

2

- **Move to the Year sheet.**
- **Select cell N23.**
- **Open the Watch Window toolbar.**

Having Trouble?

Open the Watch Window toolbar from the toolbar shortcut menu. Click Add Watch... to set the watch cell.

- **If necessary, select any existing watch cells in the toolbar and click Delete Watch to delete them.**
- **Add cell N23 to the Watch Window toolbar.**
- **Size and position the Watch Window as in Figure 4.2.**

Your screen should be similar to Figure 4.2

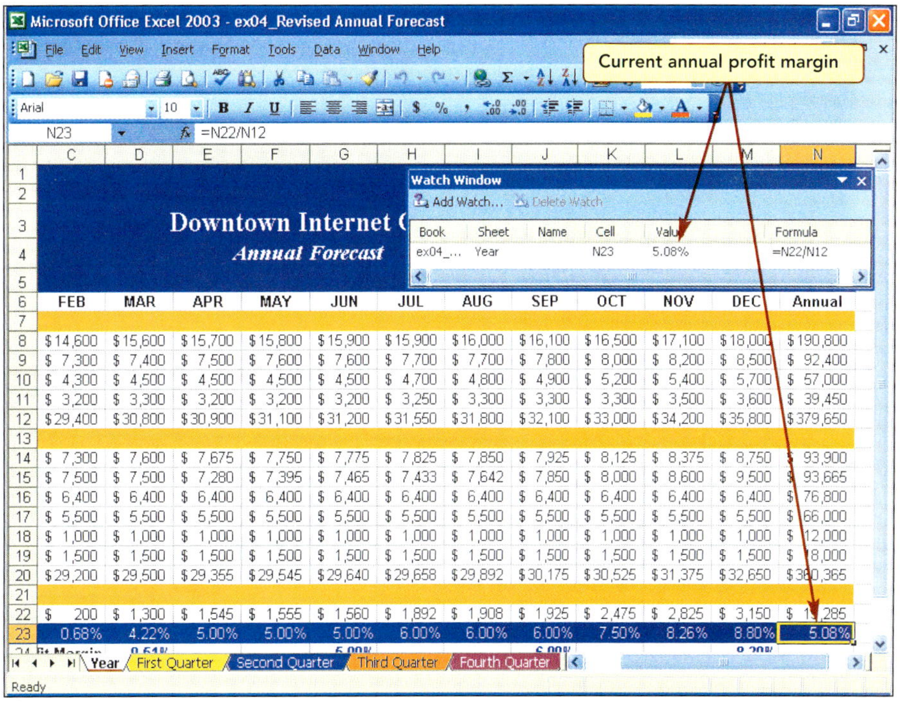

Figure 4.2

Using Solver

Although you could manually perform what-if analysis or use the Goal Seek feature to determine the desired profit margin value, it would be much quicker to use the Solver tool.

Concept 1

Solver

1 **Solver** is a tool used to perform what-if analysis to determine the effect of changing values in two or more cells, called the **adjustable cells,** on another cell, called the **target cell.** Solver calculates a formula to achieve a given value by changing one of the variables that affect the formula. To do this, Solver works backward from the result of a formula to find the numbers. The cells you select must be related through formulas on the worksheet. If they are not related, changing one will not change the other. You can also include constraints to restrict the values Solver can use. The constraints can refer to other cells that affect the target cell formula.

Solver can also produce three types of reports about the solution: Answer, Sensitivity, and Limits. In an Answer report, the original and final values of the target cell and adjustable cells are listed along with any constraints and information about the constraints. Information about how sensitive the solution is to small changes in the target cell formula or in the constraints is provided in a Sensitivity report. A Limits report includes the original and target values of the target cell and adjustable cells. It also lists the lower limit, or the smallest value that the adjustable cell can take while holding all other adjustable cells fixed and still satisfying the constraints and upper or greatest value.

1 **Display the Fourth Quarter sheet.**

Choose Tools/Solver.

Having Trouble?

The first time you try to use Solver it may not appear on the menu. To add the Solver option to the menu, choose Tools/Add-Ins/Solver Add-in. Note: You may need the original install CD if you are using your own computer to load this add-in.

Move the Solver Parameters dialog box to the right side of the screen.

Your screen should be similar to Figure 4.3

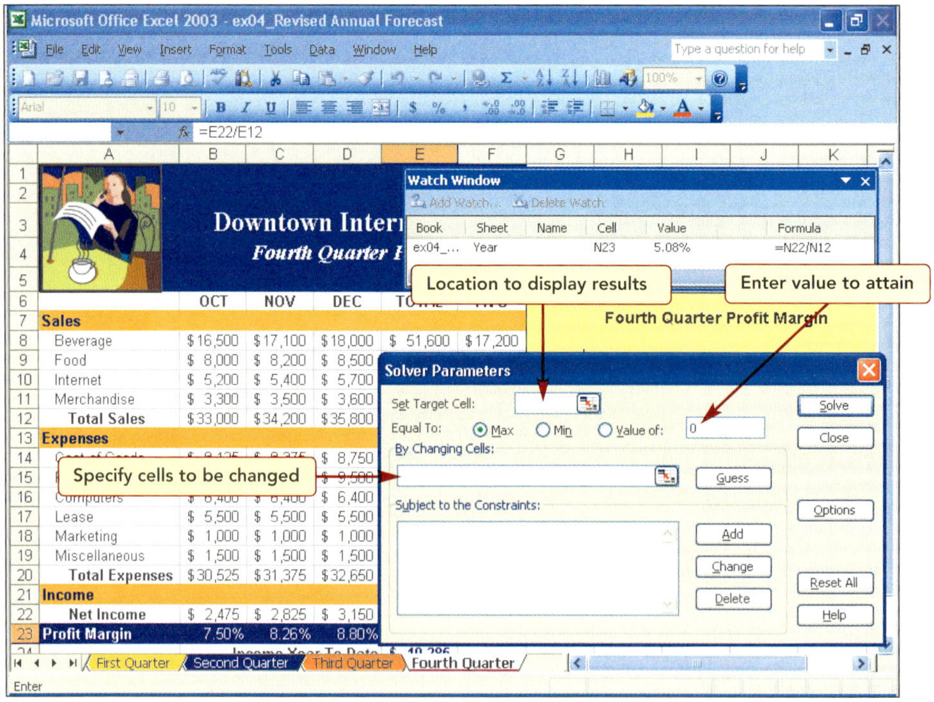

Figure 4.3

In the Solver Parameters dialog box, you need to supply three items of information: the target cell where the result will appear, the desired result value, and the cell or cells that will be changed to achieve the result.

The cell reference of the cell containing the formula you want to solve is entered in the Set Target Cell text box. The number you want as the result of the formula is entered in the Equal To text box. You can set the number to be a maximum, minimum, or an exact number. The maximum option sets the target cell to the highest possible number, while the minimum option sets the target cell to the lowest possible number.

The final information needed is the cell or cell range whose contents can be changed when the formula is computed. This range is entered in the By Changing Cells text box. In the fourth quarter, you are looking for a value of 8.5 percent by changing the values in the range of cells B15 through D15.

2

- **Specify cell E23 as the Set target cell.**
- **Select Value of.**
- **Type .085 in the Value Of text box.**
- **Specify the range B15 through D15 in the By Changing Cells text box.**

Having Trouble?

You can minimize the dialog box using the [button] button and select the range by highlighting it in the worksheet.

Your screen should be similar to Figure 4.4

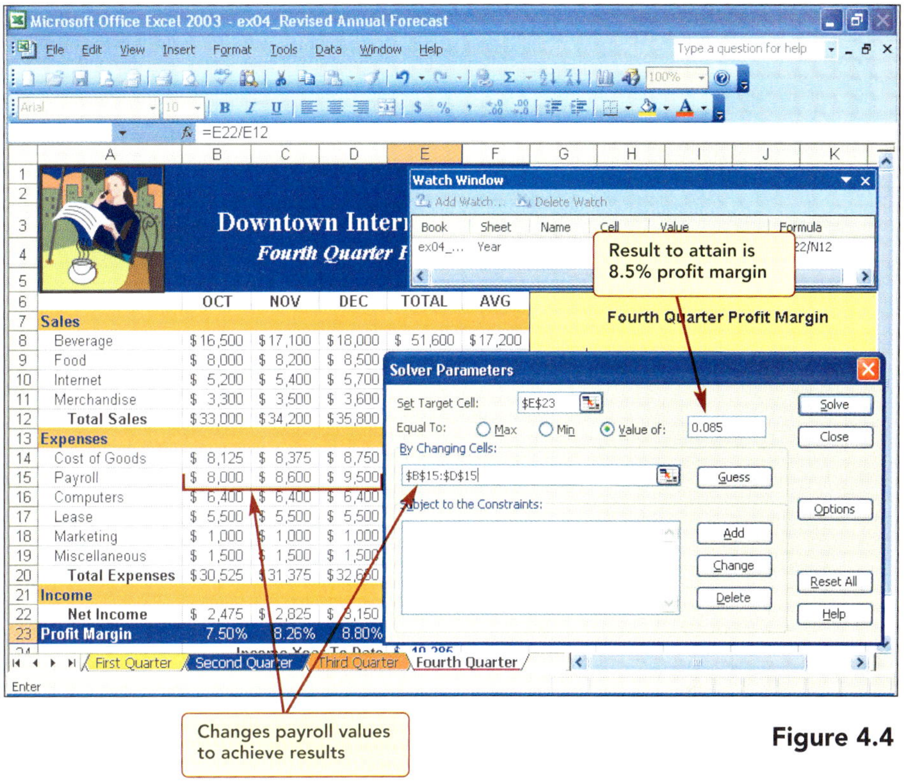

Figure 4.4

Now you are ready to have Solver find the values to meet the parameters you specified.

3 Click Solve.

Your screen should be similar to Figure 4.5

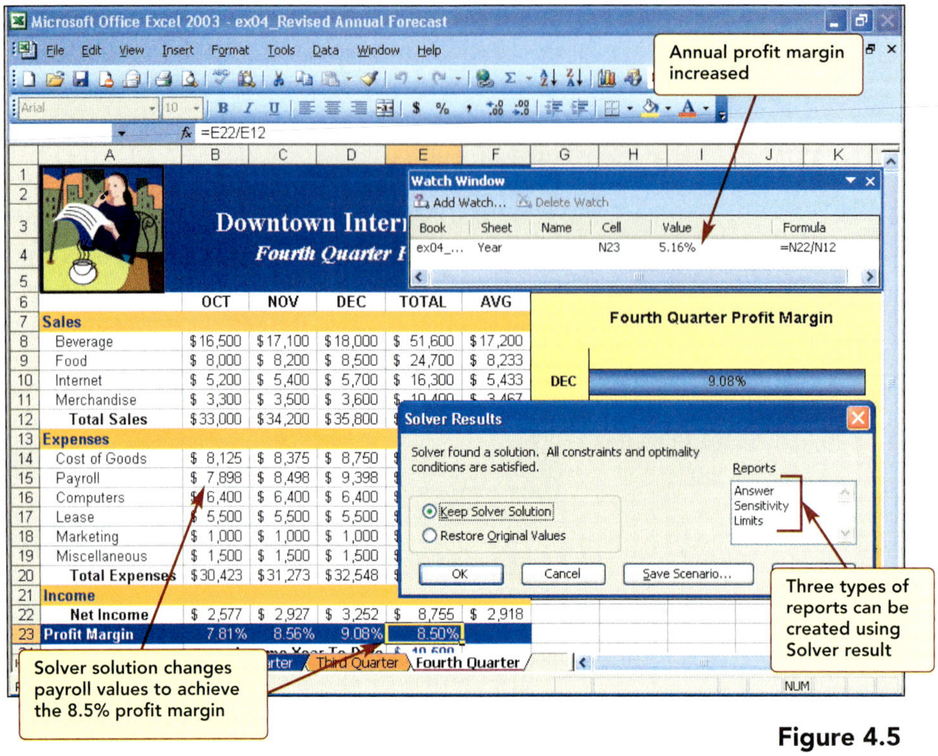

Figure 4.5

The Solver Results dialog box tells you that Solver found a solution. The new payroll numbers are entered in the worksheet range and the worksheet is automatically recalculated. By reducing the payroll expenses slightly each month, the total profit margin for the quarter is 8.5 percent. As you can see in the Watch Window, the profit margin for the year increased from 5.08 to 5.16 percent as a result of reducing payroll expenses in the fourth quarter.

Creating an Answer Report

From the Solver Results dialog box, you can choose whether to keep the solution or restore the original values. In addition, you can have Solver create Answer, Sensitivity, and Limits Reports. You decide to keep the solution and create an Answer report.

1

- **Select Answer from the Reports list box.**
- **Click OK.**
- **Make the Answer Report 1 sheet active.**

Your screen should be similar to Figure 4.6

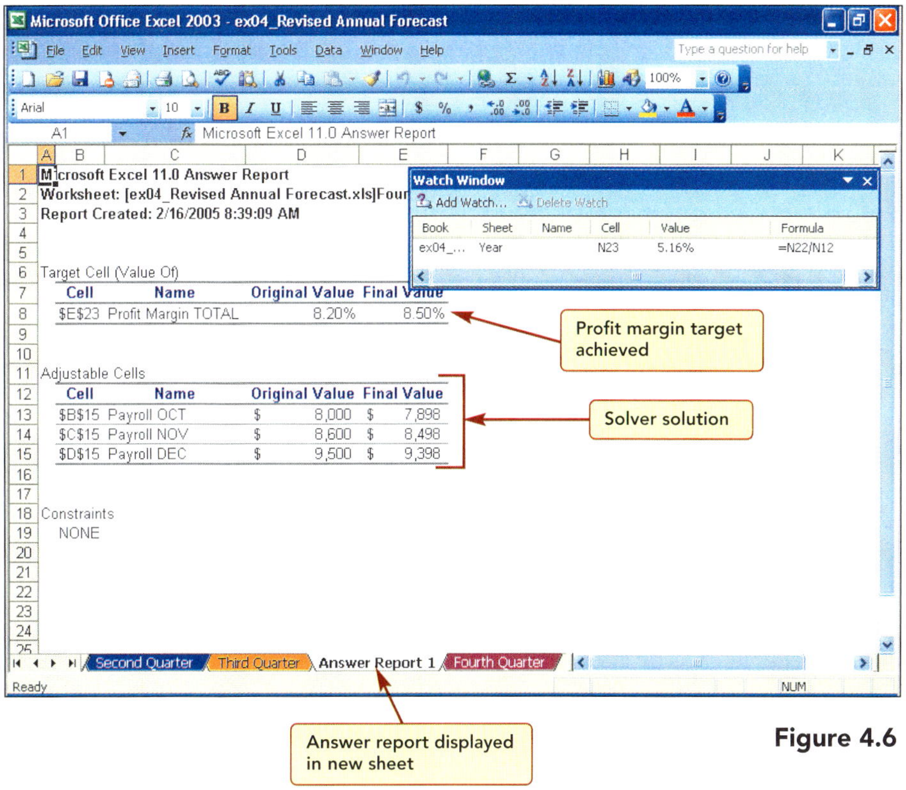

Figure 4.6

The Answer Report 1 sheet displays the Answer report that was generated. The target cell section of the report shows the original profit margin value of 8.20 percent and the final value of 8.50 percent. The Adjustable Cells area shows the original and final values for each cell that was changed to achieve the profit margin of 8.50 percent. The forecast for 2005 is now complete.

2

- **Move the Answer Report 1 sheet after the Fourth Quarter sheet.**
- **Close the Watch Window toolbar.**
- **Make the Year sheet active.**
- **Move to cell A6 and save the workbook file as 2005 Forecast.**

Creating a Custom Template

After seeing the effects of your analyses on the Year sheet, Evan has found Solver to be a valuable tool for planning and managing operations. He has asked you to create a new workbook containing a forecast for the following year. You could create this new forecast workbook by starting all over again, specifying the formats and formulas. However, as the current workbook already contains this information, you decide to use it as a model or template for future forecasts.

Concept 2

Workbook Template

2 A workbook **template** is a workbook file that contains predesigned worksheets that can be used as a pattern for creating similar worksheets in new workbooks. Every Excel workbook is based on a template. The default settings for a basic blank workbook are stored in the Book.xlt template file. Whenever you create a new workbook using this template, the same default settings are used. Templates can contain text, graphics, formats, page layouts, headers and footers, functions and formulas, and macros.

Templates are useful in any application where input and output are required using the same format. By not having to redesign the worksheet form each time the report is needed, you save time and increase accuracy. You can go back to the original design repeatedly by saving the workbook containing the data under a different file name than the one you used to save the workbook template.

Many other templates are available within Excel and on the Microsoft Internet site that are designed to help you create professional-looking workbooks. They include templates that create different styles of balance sheets, expense statements, loan amortizations, sales invoices, and timecards. You can also design and save your own workbook templates.

Excel saves a workbook template using a special file format with the file extension .xlt. Workbook templates are also stored in a special Templates folder. To use a workbook template, you select the template file name from the General tab of the New File dialog box. When you save the workbook after entering data in the template, Excel automatically displays the Save As dialog box so that you can specify the new file name. It also changes the file type to an Excel workbook (.xls). This ensures that you do not unintentionally save over the template file.

Designing the Template

A well-designed template allows you to enter information into the appropriate locations while protecting formulas and basic formats. Since the basic workbook design you want to use for your template is already in place, you will modify the worksheets in the workbook to create the template. The first steps are to eliminate the Answer Report 1 sheet and to change the values in the quarter sheets to zeros.

1 Delete the Answer Report 1 sheet.

Select the First Quarter through Fourth Quarter sheets.

Having Trouble?

Hold down ⇧Shift to extend the sheet selection.

Enter **0** in cells B8 through D11 and cells B15 through D19 in the First Quarter sheet.

Move to cell B20.

Your screen should be similar to Figure 4.7

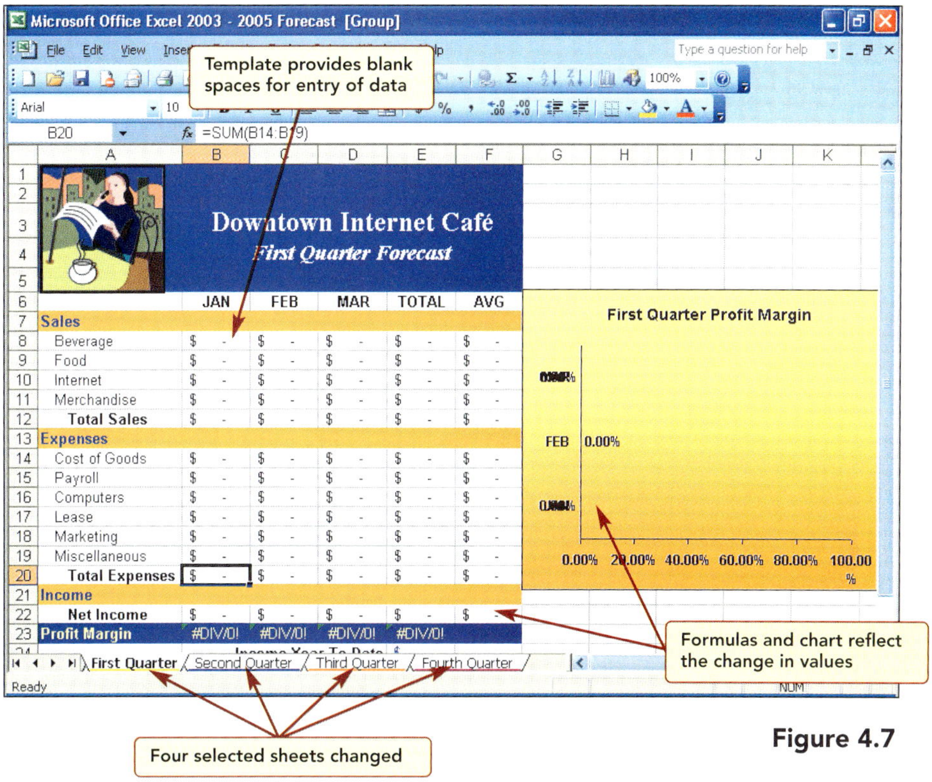

Figure 4.7

The selected cell format displays cells containing zero values with a dash symbol. All other worksheet cells containing formulas as well as the chart reflect the change in the values.

2 Look at each of the three other quarter sheets to verify that the values have been replaced.

Make the Year sheet active and move to cell B8.

Your screen should be similar to Figure 4.8

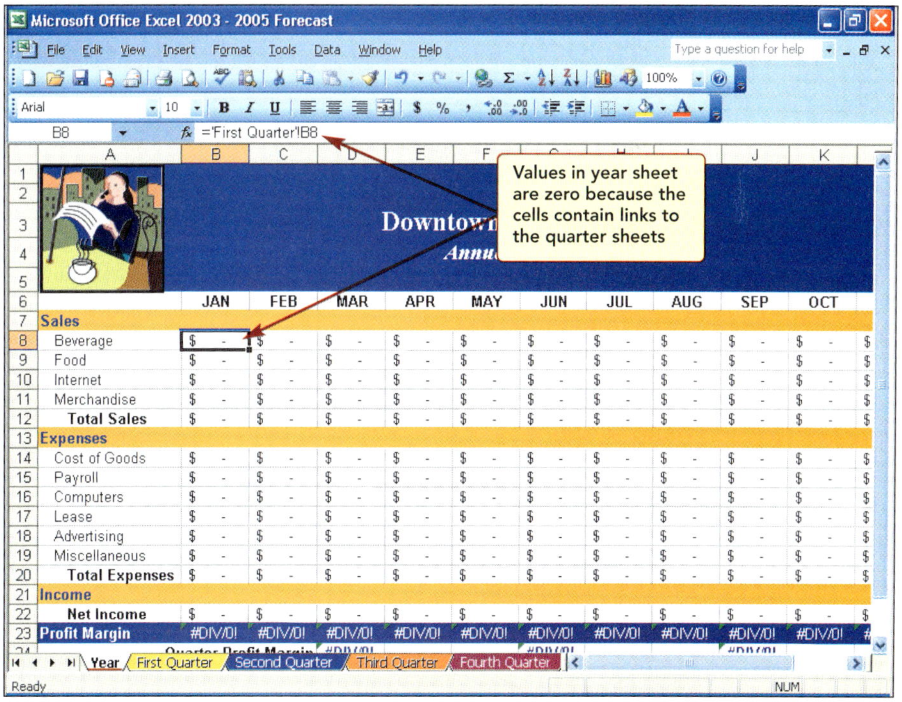

Figure 4.8

Because the Year sheet contains formulas that link to the values in the quarter sheets, this sheet also displays zero values. Now, whenever you are creating another annual forecast, you will simply enter the new values in place of the blanks in the quarter sheets and the annual sheet will automatically be completed.

Protecting the Worksheet

Now that all the values have been removed and the template is ready to use, you want to prevent unwanted changes to the worksheets that would cause headings and formulas to be altered or cleared. To do this, you can protect the worksheet.

Concept 3

Protection

3 The **protection** feature controls what information can be changed in a workbook. Excel includes two levels of protection: worksheet protection and workbook protection.

Worksheet protection prevents users from changing a worksheet's contents by protecting the entire worksheet or specified areas of it. When a worksheet is protected, all cells and graphic objects on it are locked. The contents of a locked cell cannot be changed. If you want to leave some cells unlocked for editing, such as in a worksheet that you use as an entry form, you can lock cells containing labels and formulas but unlock the entry fields so that other users can fill them in. This type of protection prevents you from entering or changing an entry in any locked cells.

Workbook-level protection prevents changes to an entire workbook in two ways. First, you can protect the structure of a workbook so that sheets cannot be moved or deleted or new sheets inserted. Second, you can protect a workbook's windows. This prevents changes to the size and position of windows and ensures that they appear the same way each time the workbook is opened.

In addition, you can include a **password** that prevents any unauthorized person from either viewing or saving changes to the workbook. Two separate passwords can be used: one to open and view the file and another to edit and save the file. If you use a password, you must remember the password in order to turn protection off in the future.

Initially all cells in a worksheet are locked. However, you can enter data in the cells because the worksheet protection feature is not on. When protection is turned on, all locked cells are protected. Therefore, before protecting this sheet, you need to unlock the areas in the worksheet where you want to allow users to make changes to information.

The only area of the Year sheet that needs to be unprotected is the subtitle where the year will be entered when the template is used. You will unlock the cell containing the subtitle and add protection to the rest of the worksheet.

1. Move to cell D4.
   - Choose F**o**rmat/C**e**lls.
   - Open the Protection tab.
   - Clear the **L**ocked option.

Your screen should be similar to Figure 4.9

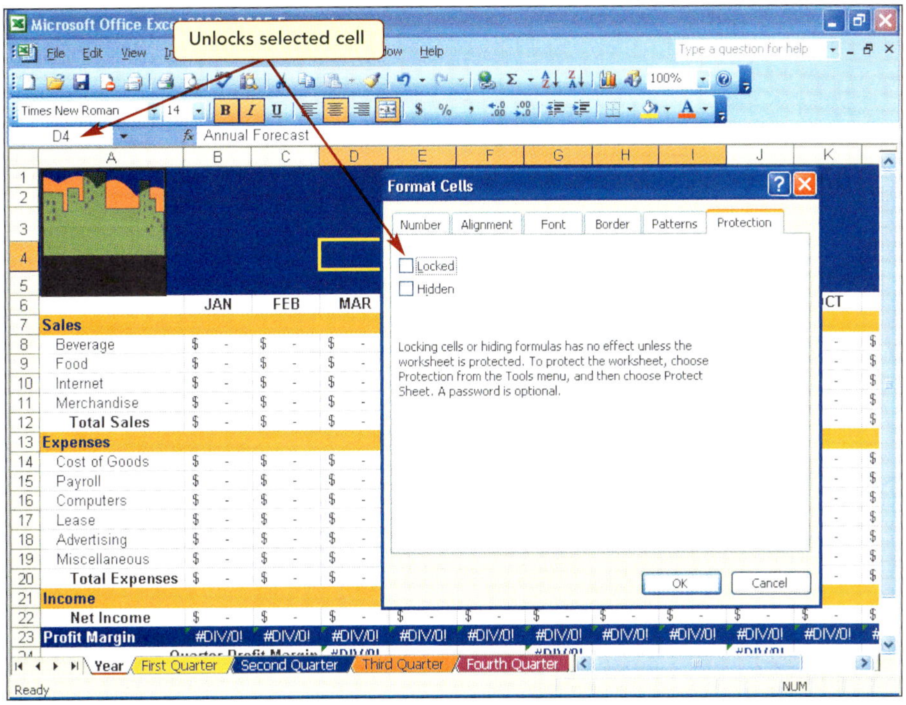

Figure 4.9

Once the cells you want to allow changes to in a worksheet are unlocked, you can add protection.

2. Click OK.
   - Display the Protection toolbar.
   - Click Protect Sheet.

Another Method

The menu equivalent is **T**ools/**P**rotection/**P**rotect Sheet.

Your screen should be similar to Figure 4.10

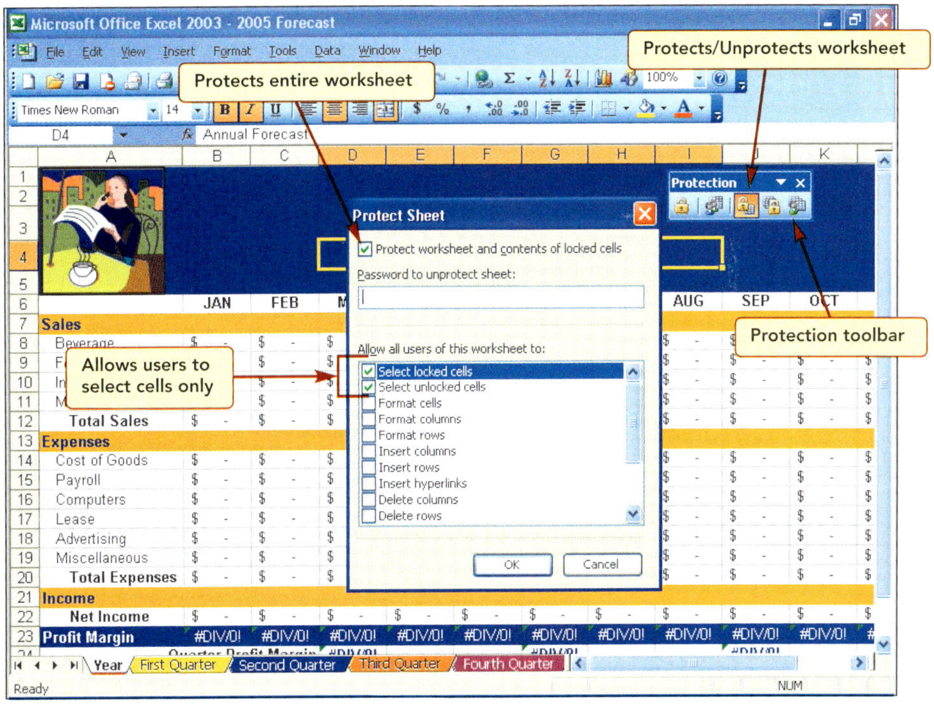

Figure 4.10

In the Protect Sheet dialog box, you can enter a password to prevent unauthorized people from removing protection from the sheet and specify the options that you want to enable for all users of the template. The

Select Locked Cells and Select Unlocked Cells options are enabled by default. Leaving these selected and the others unselected provides complete protection for the worksheet. You will complete the command to protect this sheet and then you will unlock the data entry areas of the four quarter sheets.

3 Click OK.

- **Select the First Quarter through Fourth Quarter sheets.**
- **Select cells B8 through D11 and B15 through D19.**

Having Trouble?

Hold down Ctrl to select nonadjacent ranges.

- **Choose Format/Cells.**
- **Clear the Locked option in the Protection tab.**
- **Click OK.**

Your screen should be similar to Figure 4.11

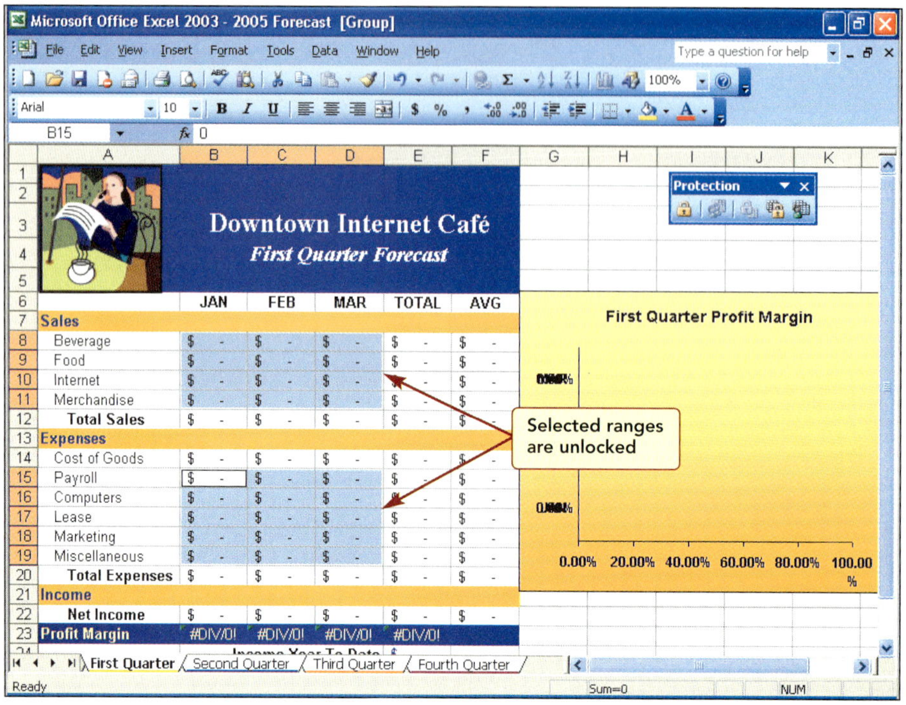

Figure 4.11

When protecting worksheets, you must protect each sheet individually. You will ungroup the sheets and protect each sheet.

4 Select **Ungroup Sheets** from the sheet tab shortcut menu.

Another Method

You can also hold down ⇧Shift while clicking a sheet tab to ungroup sheets.

- If necessary, make the First Quarter sheet active.
- Click Protect Sheet.
- Click OK.
- In a similar manner protect the other three quarter sheets.

Your screen should be similar to Figure 4.12

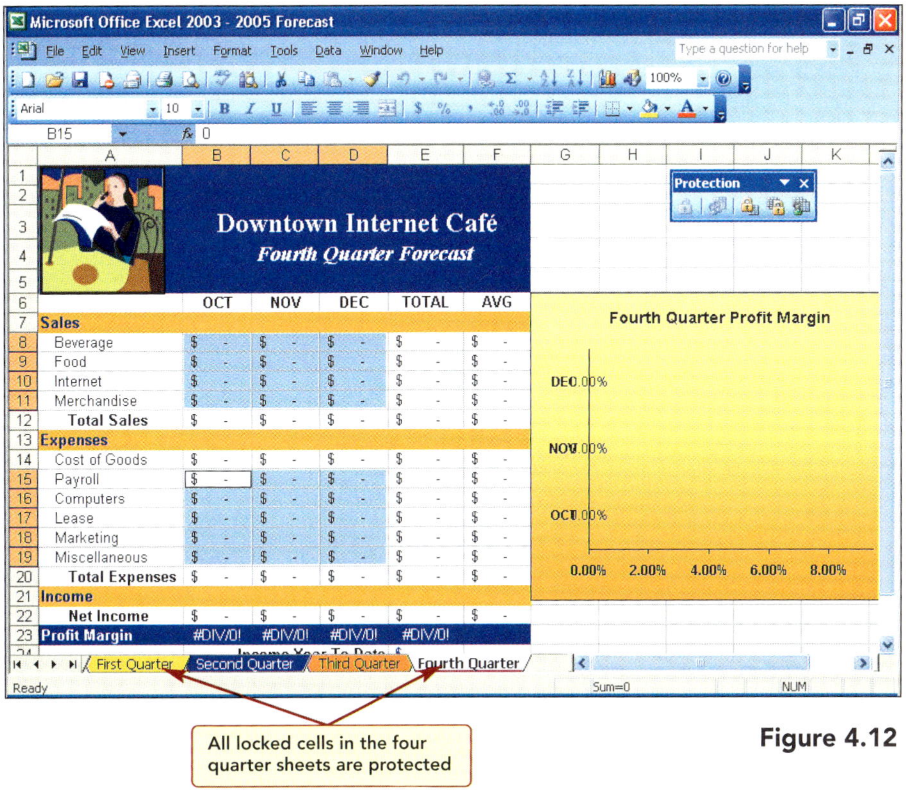

Figure 4.12

Now all locked cells in the four quarter sheets are protected. Only those cells you unlocked prior to turning on protection can be changed. To test this out, you will try to make an entry in a protected cell.

5 Type any character in cell B6 of the Fourth Quarter sheet.

Your screen should be similar to Figure 4.13

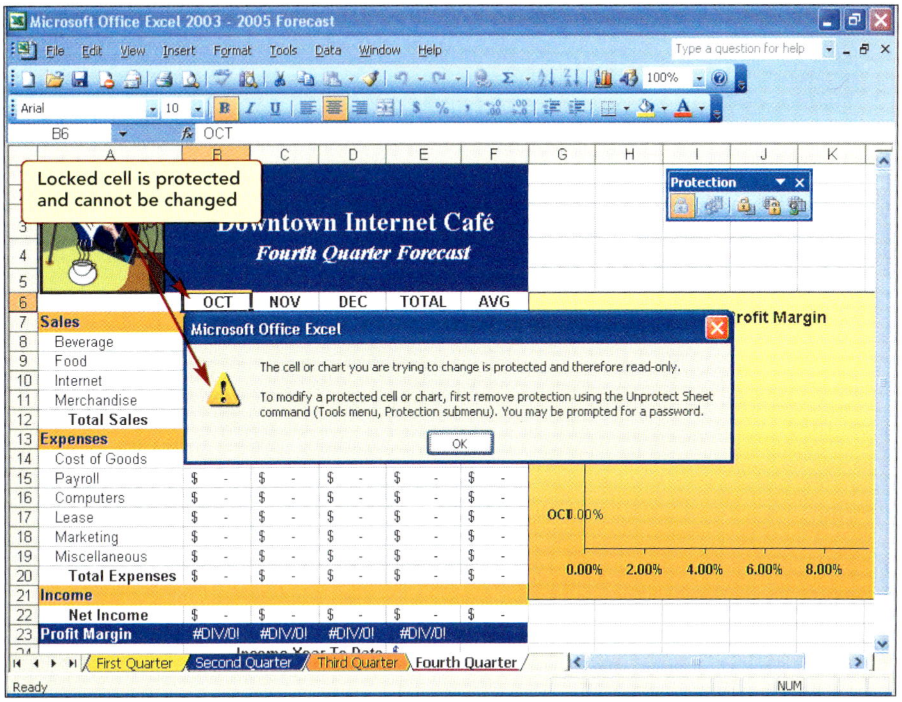

Figure 4.13

The warning dialog box informs you that you cannot change entries in locked cells. Next, you will enter a value in an unlocked cell.

6 Click OK to clear the message.

- Type 1250 in cell B8 and press ←Enter.

Your screen should be similar to Figure 4.14

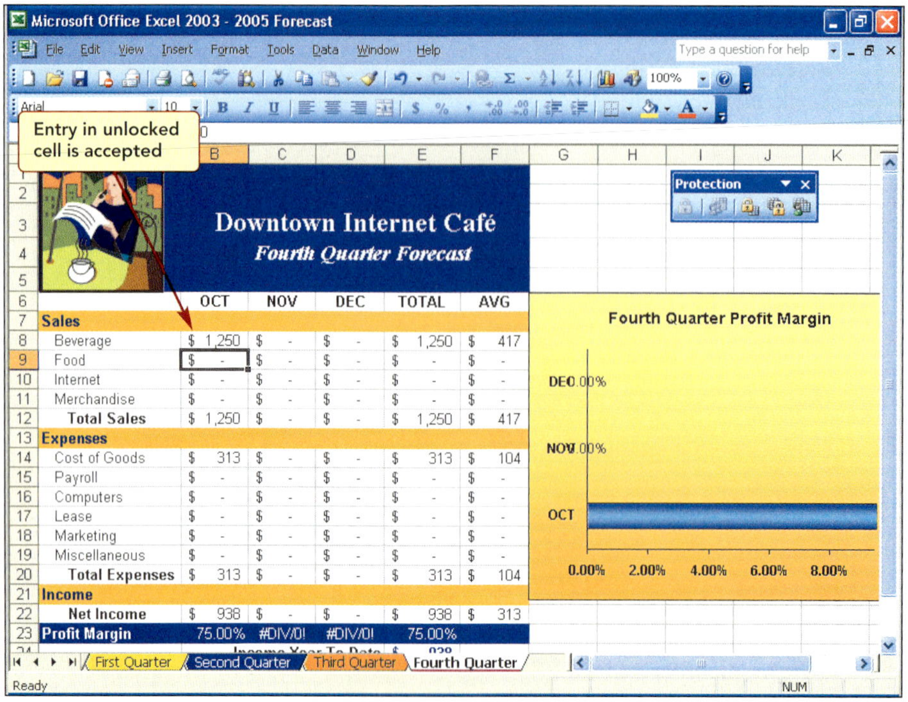

Figure 4.14

The entry is accepted because the cell was unlocked before protection was applied to the sheet.

Saving the Template

Now that the sheets are protected, you will save this workbook as a template file. First, you will clear the test entry and move the cell pointer to the location in the worksheet where you want it to appear when opened.

1 Click [Undo button] Undo to remove the test entry.

- Move to cell B8 in each of the other quarter sheets.
- Move to cell D4 in the Year sheet.
- Close the Protection toolbar.
- Choose **File/Save As**.
- Enter the new name, Forecast Template, in the File Name text box.
- From the Save As Type list box, select Template.

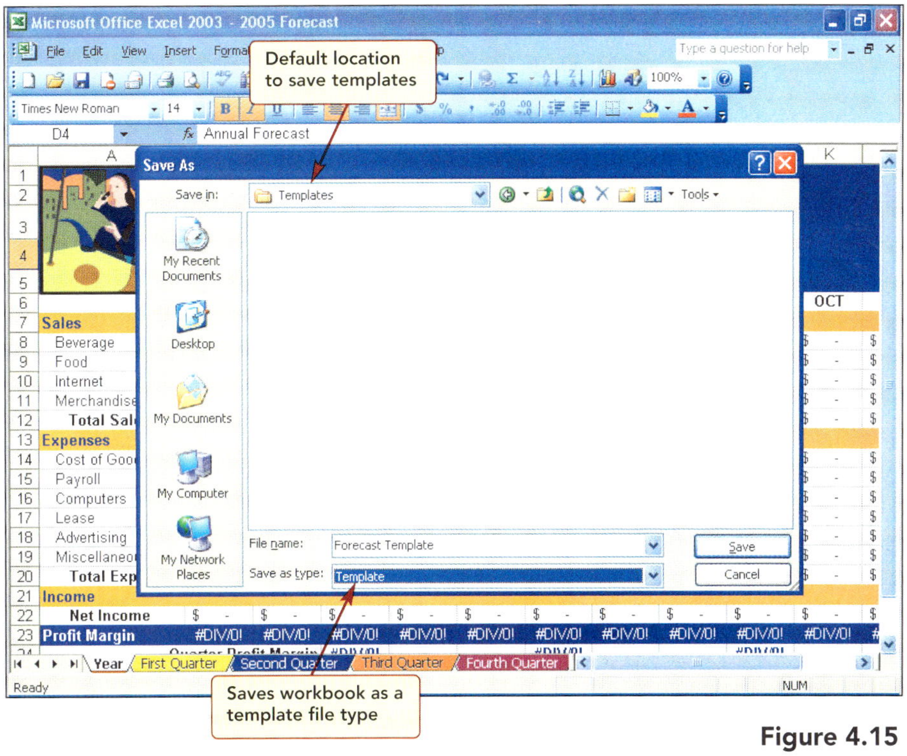

Figure 4.15

Additional Information

You cannot save a workbook as a template by typing the file extension .xlt in a file name. You must select the Template file type from the Save As Type list box.

Your screen should be similar to Figure 4.15

Templates are saved by default to the Templates folder on your system. You can also save templates to other locations just like any other workbook file.

2 Click [Save].

Having Trouble?

If a file already exists with this name, click [Yes] to replace it.

- Close the Forecast Template file.

The Forecast Template workbook is now ready to use.

Using the Template

Now you will use the Forecast Template file to create a new forecast workbook for the following year, 2006.

1 **Choose File/New.**

Click On my computer from the Templates section of the New Workbook task pane.

Your screen should be similar to Figure 4.16

Additional Information

Only templates saved to the Template folder will be listed.

Additional Information

Your General tab may display additional icons depending on how many and what kind of templates have been created and saved in Excel.

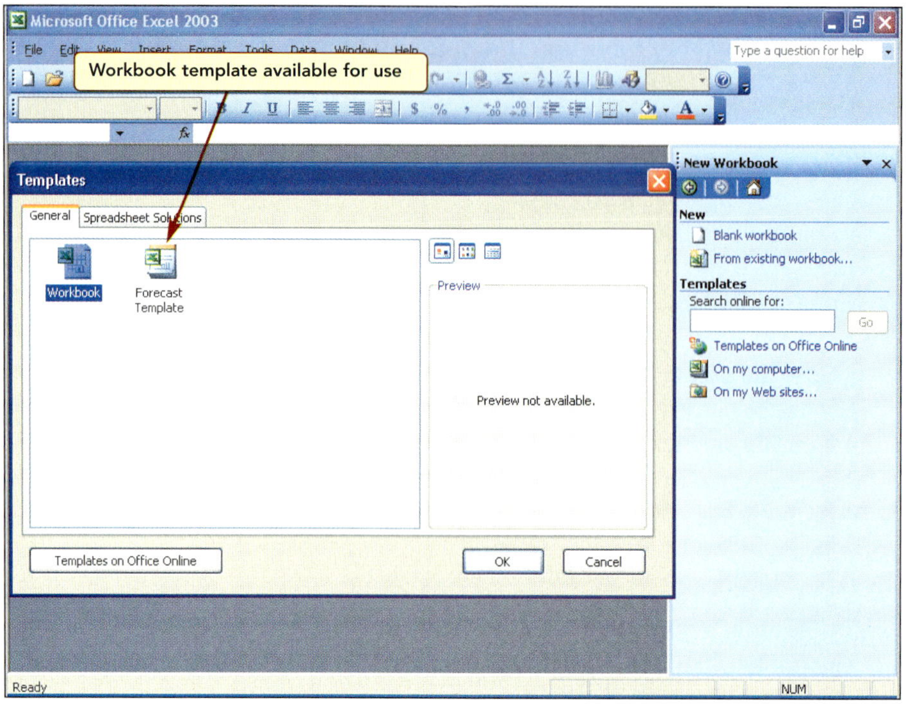

Figure 4.16

The Forecast Template file name appears in the General tab of the Templates dialog box. You will open the template and change the subtitle in the Year sheet to display the year 2006.

2 **Select Forecast Template.**

Click OK.

Change the subtitle in cell D4 of the Year sheet to 2006 Annual Forecast.

Your screen should be similar to Figure 4.17

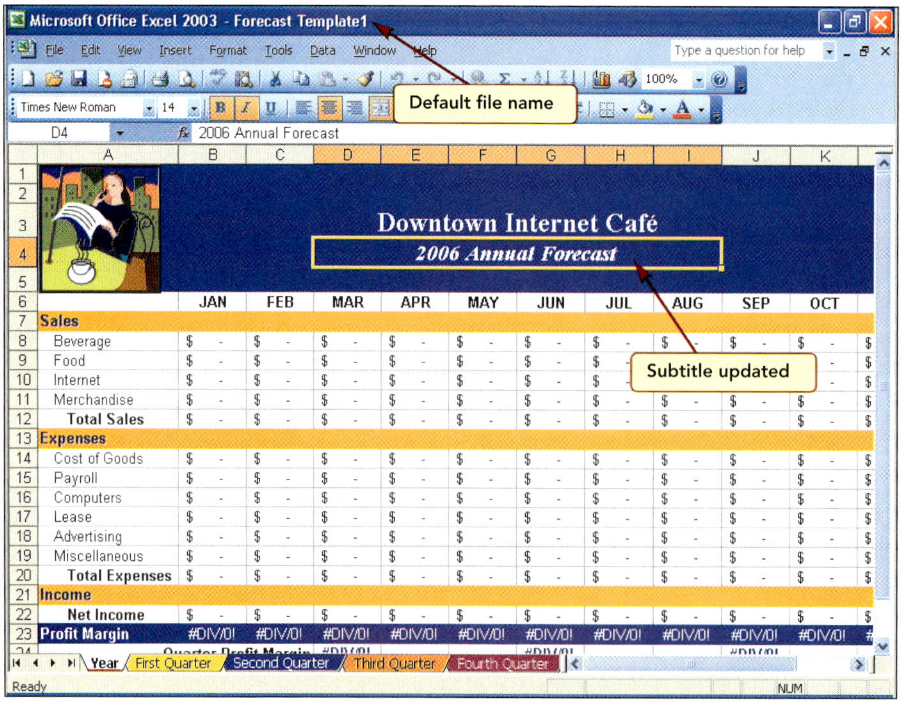

Figure 4.17

Before continuing, you want to save the revised template file as a new workbook file for use in entering the 2006 forecast data. Notice the file name in the title bar is Forecast Template1. Excel automatically adds a number to the file name when the template is opened to prevent you from accidentally overwriting the original template file when saving. Additionally, when using a template to create a new workbook file, even if you use the Save command, Excel automatically displays the Save As dialog box so that you can specify a new file name.

3 **Click Save.**

- **Enter the new name, 2006 Forecast, in the File Name text box.**

Additional Information

To ensure that you do not unintentionally save over the template file, Excel automatically assigns the .xls workbook extension as the file type.

- **Change the Save In location to the appropriate location to save your files.**
- **Click Save.**

Your screen should be similar to Figure 4.18

Figure 4.18

Working with Multiple Workbooks

Evan wants you to focus on the 2006 first quarter forecast. Because he expects all sales and expenses to remain the same as the December 2005 values, you can obtain this data from the 2005 Forecast workbook. To do this, you want to copy the data from one workbook to the other. In Excel, you can open multiple workbook files at the same time. Each workbook is opened in its own window. You can also open additional separate windows to display different parts of the active workbook. The open windows can be arranged so that you can see them simultaneously to make it easy to work with data in multiple workbooks at the same time.

Opening a Second Workbook File

You will open the workbook file containing the 2005 forecast data you saved earlier.

1 **Open the** 2005 Forecast **workbook file.**

Your screen should be similar to Figure 4.19

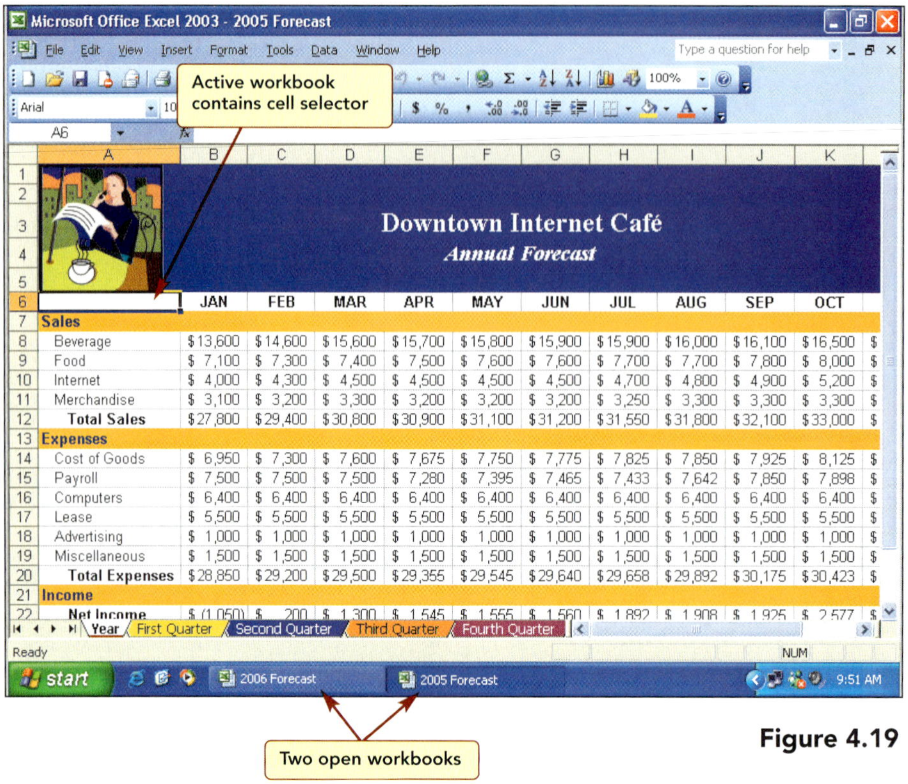

Figure 4.19

Now there are two active workbook files, and the taskbar displays a button for each open window. The 2005 Forecast workbook file window is open on top of the 2006 Forecast workbook file window. The newly opened file is the **active workbook** file. It is the file that will be affected by changes and the file that contains the cell selector.

Arranging Workbook Windows

The way the workbooks are currently displayed makes it difficult to work with both files simultaneously. To make it easier to work with both files at the same time, you can change the arrangement of the windows.

Concept 4

Window Arrangement

4 The **window arrangement** feature displays all open workbook files in separate windows on the screen, making it easy to view and work with information in different workbooks. When new workbook windows are opened, they appear in the same size and on top of any other open windows. Open windows can be arranged in the following ways:

Tiled: The windows are displayed one after the other in succession, across and down the screen

Vertical: The windows are displayed side by side.

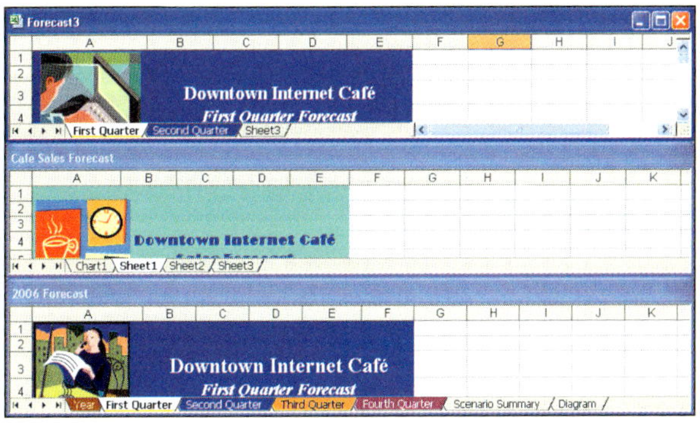

Horizontal: The windows are displayed one above the other.

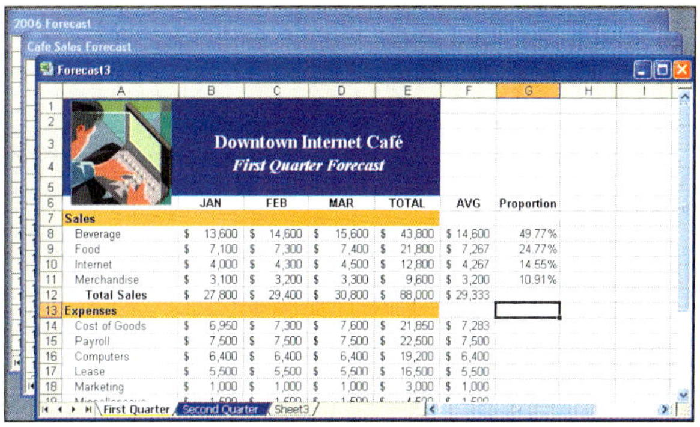

Cascade: The windows are displayed one on top of the other, cascading down from the top of the screen.

You decide that the easiest way to work with the two files is to tile them.

1 Choose **Window/Arrange**.

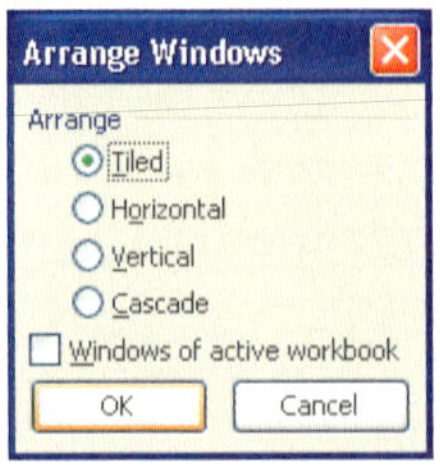

If necessary, select **Tiled**.

Additional Information

The Windows of Active Workbook option arranges the windows of only the active workbook.

Click OK.

Your screen should be similar to Figure 4.20

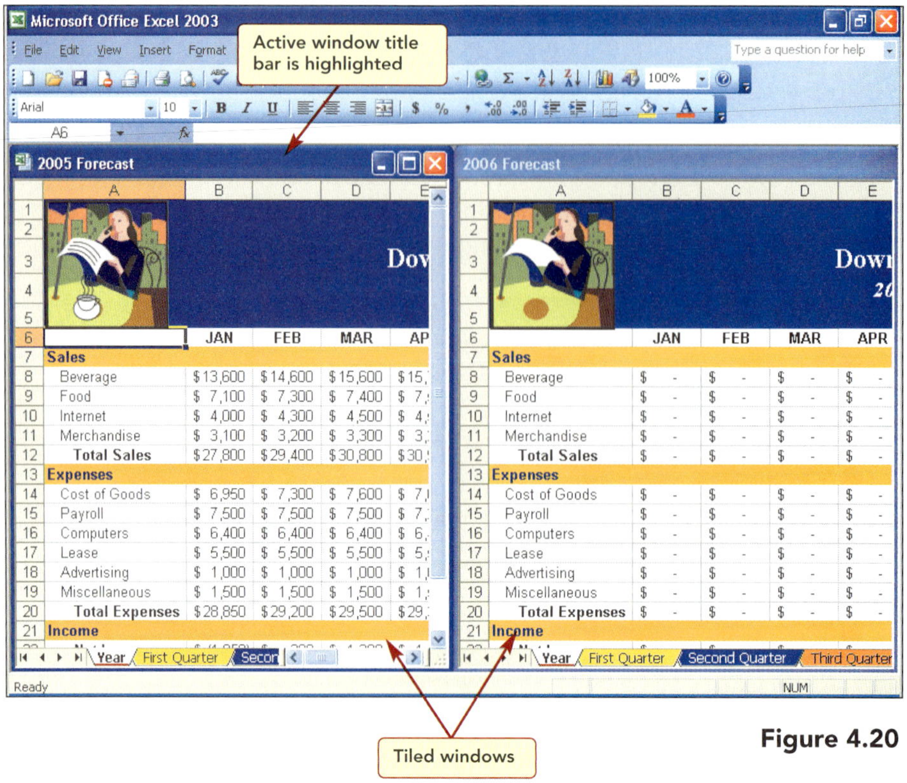

Figure 4.20

The two workbook windows appear next to each other. The title bar of the active workbook file is highlighted. You want to see the December values in the Fourth Quarter sheet of the 2005 Forecast and the First Quarter sheet from the 2006 Forecast.

2 Display the Fourth Quarter sheet in the 2005 Forecast workbook.

Click in the 2006 Forecast workbook window to make it active.

Display the First Quarter sheet.

Your screen should be similar to Figure 4.21

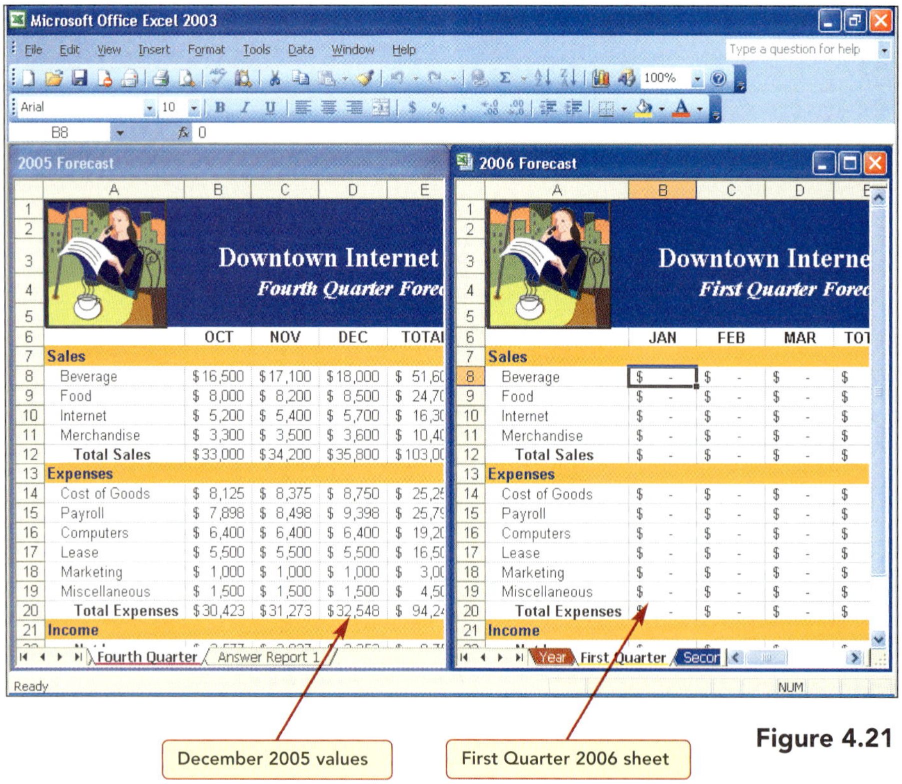

Figure 4.21

Linking Workbooks

You decide to use the December data from the 2005 Forecast workbook as the data for the first quarter of the 2006 Forecast workbook. Additionally, you want the data in the 2006 forecast to update automatically if the data in the 2005 forecast changes. To do this, you will create a link between the two workbook files.

Concept 5

Link

5 A **link** creates a connection between files that automatically updates the linked data in one file whenever the data in the other file changes. When data in a linked cell changes, the workbook that is affected by this change is automatically updated when it is opened.

The link between the workbook files is formed by entering an **external reference formula** in one workbook that refers to a cell in another workbook. The formula is entered in the workbook that receives the data. This workbook file is called the **destination workbook.** The workbook that supplies the data is called the **source** workbook. The cell containing the external reference formula (the **destination cell**) refers to the cell (the **source cell**) in the source file that contains the data to be copied.

An external reference formula uses the following format:

= [2005 Forecast]Fourth Quarter!$D$8

[workbook file reference]sheet reference!cell reference

The file reference consists of the file name of the source workbook followed by the name of the worksheet. The cell reference of the cell or range of cells containing the number to be copied into the destination workbook follows the file reference. The two parts of the formula are separated by an exclamation point.

You will create a link between the two workbook files by entering external reference formulas in the 2006 First Quarter worksheet that reference the cells containing the values in the Fourth Quarter sheet of the 2005 Forecast workbook. The 2005 Forecast workbook is the source workbook, and the 2006 Forecast workbook is the destination workbook.

The first external reference formula you will enter will link the beverage sales numbers. To create an external reference formula, you copy the contents of the source cell to the Clipboard, switch to the dependent workbook, and then use the Edit/Paste Special command to create the external reference formula link in the specified cell of the dependent workbook.

The source cell is cell D8 of the Fourth Quarter sheet in the 2005 Forecast workbook. You will copy the contents of the source cell and paste it into the destination cell.

1 Select cell D8 of the Fourth Quarter sheet in the 2005 Forecast workbook.

- Click Copy.
- Select cell B8 in the First Quarter sheet of the 2006 Forecast workbook.
- Choose **E**dit/Paste **S**pecial.

Your screen should be similar to Figure 4.22

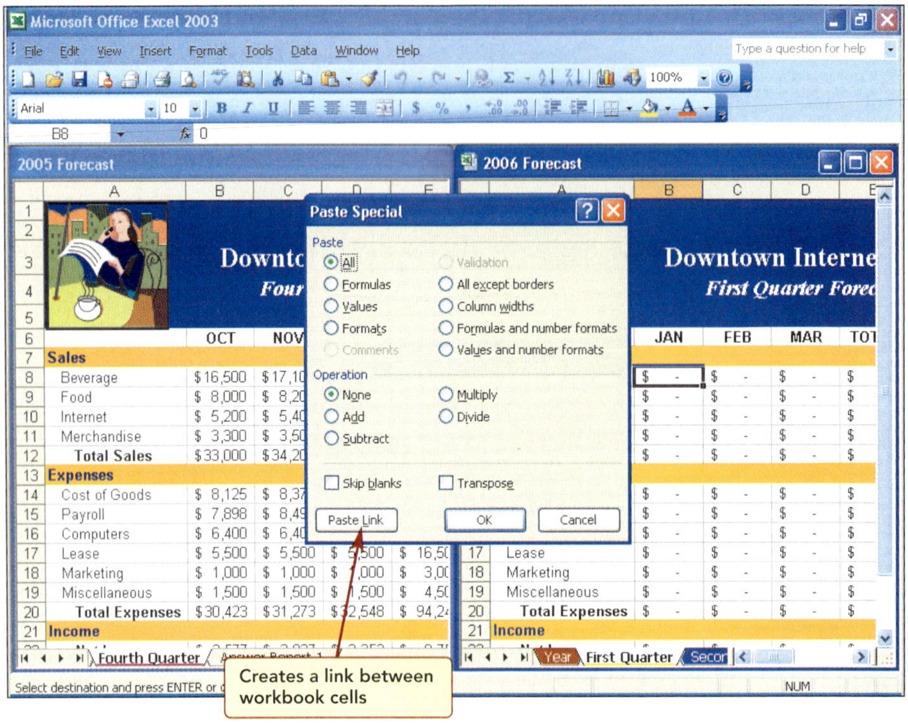

Figure 4.22

From the Paste Special dialog box, you specify how much of the cell contents you want pasted. You can paste either the entire cell contents (including formatting), or selected attributes associated with the cell, such as only the formula, value, format, comments, validation, or column width of the cell. You can also perform an addition, subtraction, multiplication, or division operation on the pasted cell. Finally, you can create a link to the source cell contents so that when the source cell is changed, the destination cell is automatically changed as well.

2 Click Paste Link.

Additional Information

The Paste Options button also includes the Link Cells option.

Your screen should be similar to Figure 4.23

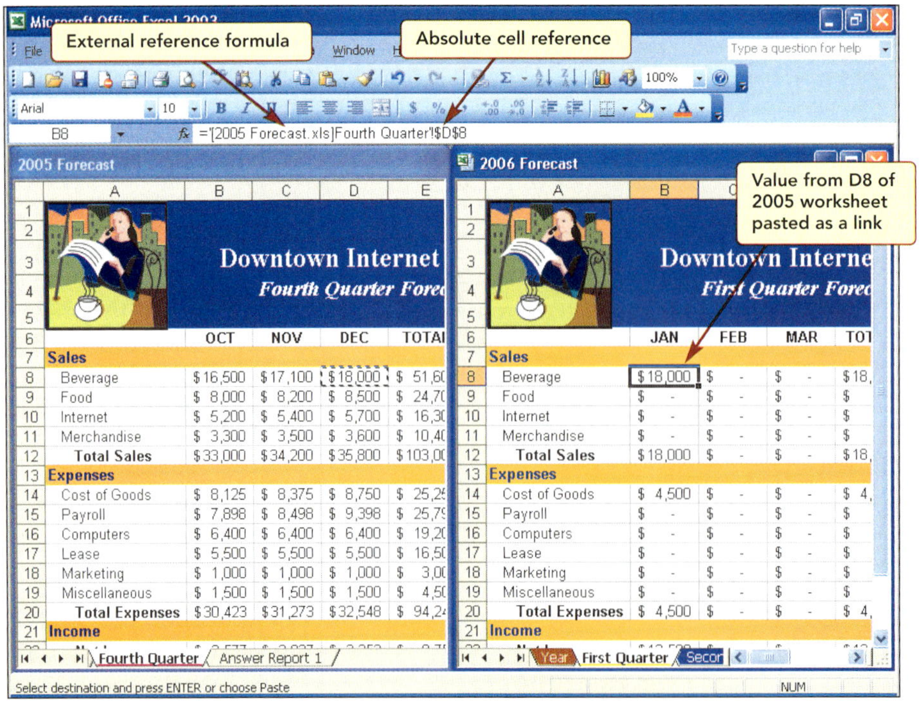

Figure 4.23

The link has been established and an external reference formula has been entered into the selected cell of the destination workbook. The formula is displayed in the formula bar, and the number in cell D8 of the source workbook is entered into the destination workbook and displayed in cell B8. Notice that Excel uses absolute references in the external reference formula.

Next, you want to create a link between the other December values in the source workbook. To do this quickly, you can copy the external reference formula down the column. However, you must first change the cell reference $D$8 in the external reference formula to a mixed reference of ($D8) so that it will adjust appropriately as the formula is copied.

3

- **In cell B8 of the 2006 Forecast workbook, edit the absolute reference ($D$8) in the formula to $D8.**
- **Copy the external reference formula in cell B8 to cells B9 through B11 and B15 through B19.**
- **Click cell B19 to deselect the range.**

Your screen should be similar to Figure 4.24

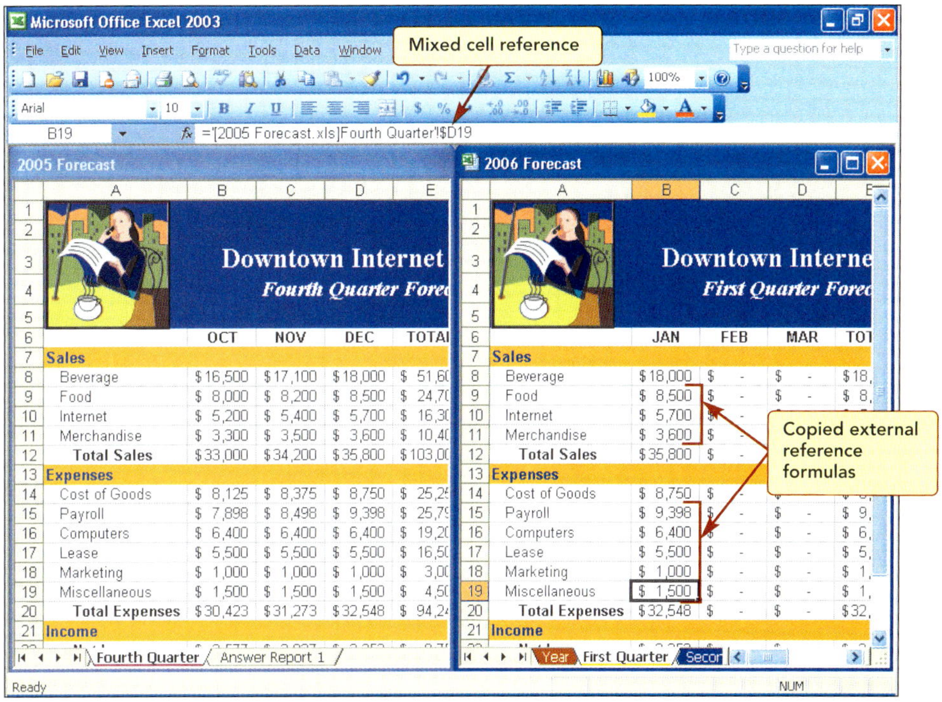

Figure 4.24

The data for January 2006 is now complete. It is the same as the December 2005 data. Because the data in the worksheets is linked, a change in the December 2005 worksheet values will automatically be reflected in the First Quarter 2006 worksheet.

Updating Linked Data

Evan advises you that the lease for the café will increase to $6,000 a month beginning in October of 2005. You want to enter this new amount and see the effect of this change.

1 Switch to the 2005 Forecast workbook window.

- Enter **6,000** into cells B17, C17, and D17 in the Fourth Quarter sheet.

Your screen should be similar to Figure 4.25

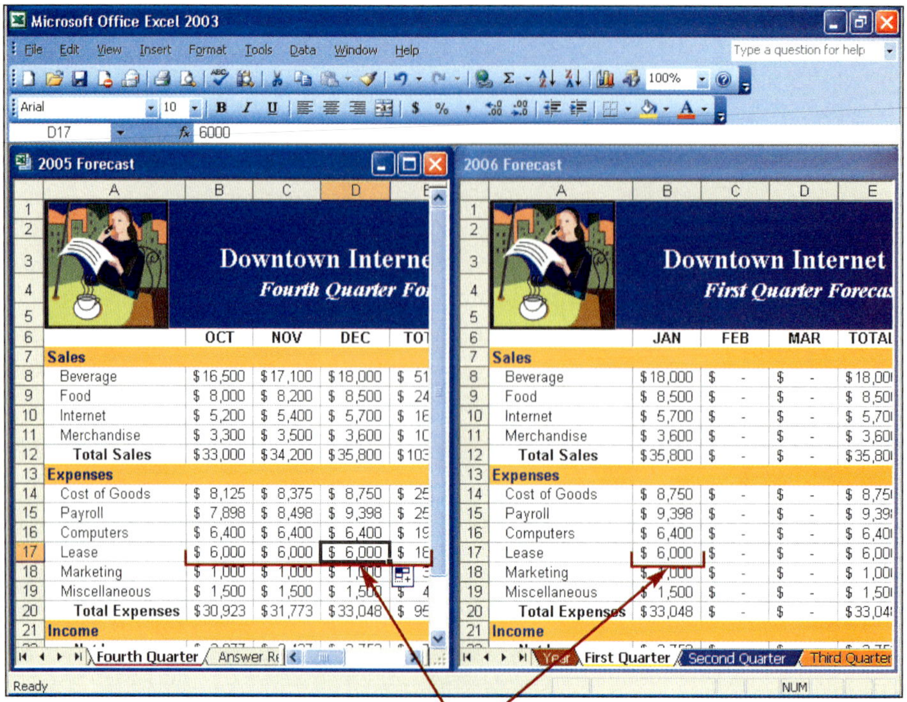

Figure 4.25

All affected formulas are recalculated. Because the workbooks are linked, the change in the 2005 Forecast is automatically reflected in the 2006 Forecast. Once an external reference formula is entered in a worksheet, whenever the data in the cell referenced in the source file changes, the dependent file is automatically updated if it is open.

If the dependent file is not open, it is not updated. To ensure that a dependent file gets updated when you open the source file, Excel displays an alert message asking if you want to update references to unopened documents. If you respond Yes, Excel checks the source documents and updates all references to them so that you will have the latest values from the source worksheet.

You do not need to obtain any further data from the 2005 Forecast workbook at this time. You will save it and enlarge the 2006 Forecast window to make it easier to work with.

2 • **Save the** 2005 Forecast **file.**

• **Maximize the 2006 Forecast window.**

• **Save the** 2006 Forecast **file.**

Your screen should be similar to Figure 4.26

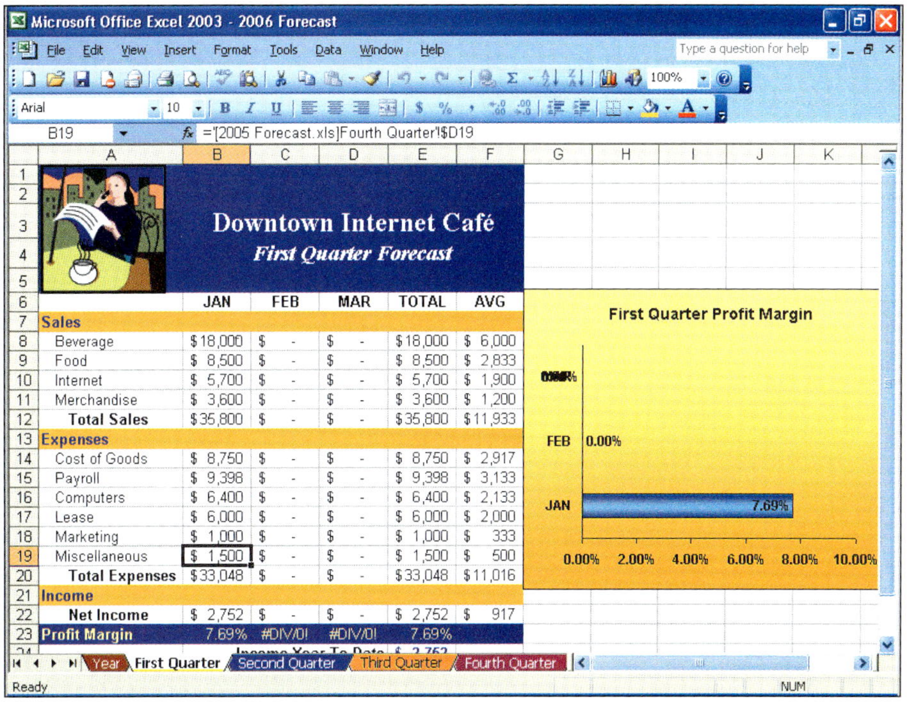

Figure 4.26

Hiding Workbooks and Worksheets

Evan has suggested that you create a drawing to illustrate the relationship between the four sales categories. You decide to do this in the 2006 Forecast workbook. When you are working with two workbooks that have similar data in them you might easily confuse them. to help in situations like this, Excel allows you to hide a workbook. By hiding a workbook it stays in memory but is not visible to the user. To further simplify the display you can also hide worksheets in a workbook file.

You will hide the 2005 Forecast file while you work with the 2006 Forecast. In addition, you will hide all sheets except the First Quarter sheet in the 2006 Forecast workbook.

1. **Make the 2005 Forecast window active.**

- **Choose Window/Hide.**

- **Select the Year, Second Quarter, Third Quarter, and Fourth Quarter sheets.**

> **Having Trouble?**
> Hold down (Ctrl) while clicking the worksheet tabs to select them.

- **Choose Format/Sheet/Hide.**

Your screen should be similar to Figure 4.27

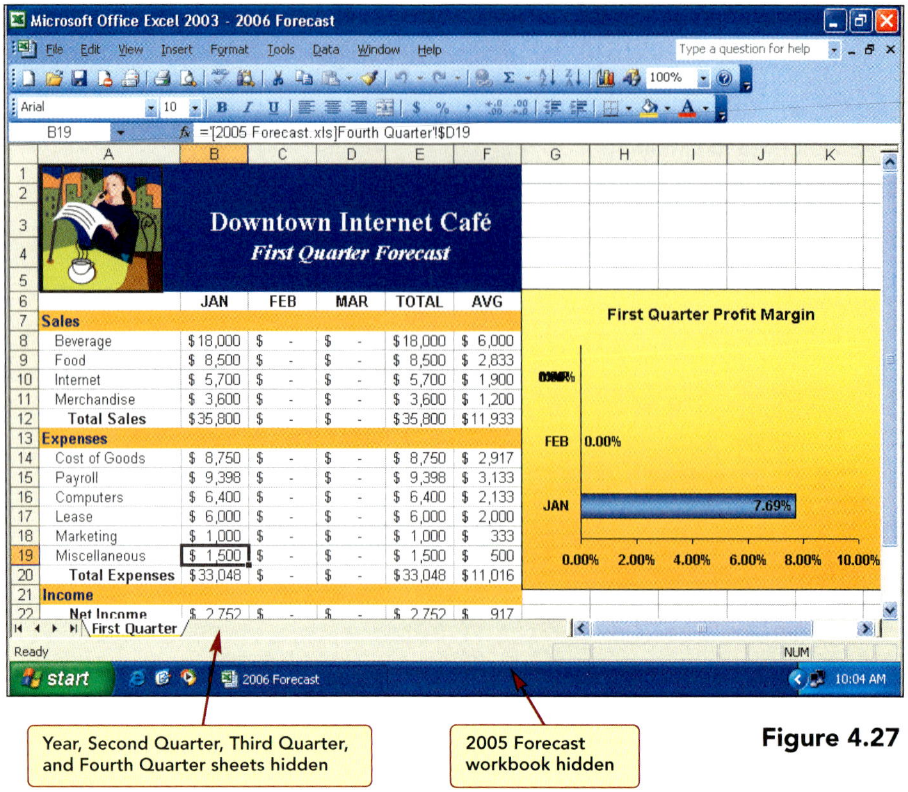

Figure 4.27

The 2005 Forecast workbook file is no longer displayed and the taskbar button for the workbook file is removed. The only worksheet that is displayed is the First Quarter sheet in the 2006 Forecast workbook.

Inserting a Worksheet

You will create the drawing on a separate worksheet in the 2006 Forecast workbook. To do this, you will insert a new worksheet in the workbook and name it. New Sheets are automatically inserted to the left of the active sheet.

1 **Choose Insert/Worksheet.**

Name the sheet Diagram.

Your screen should be similar to Figure 4.28

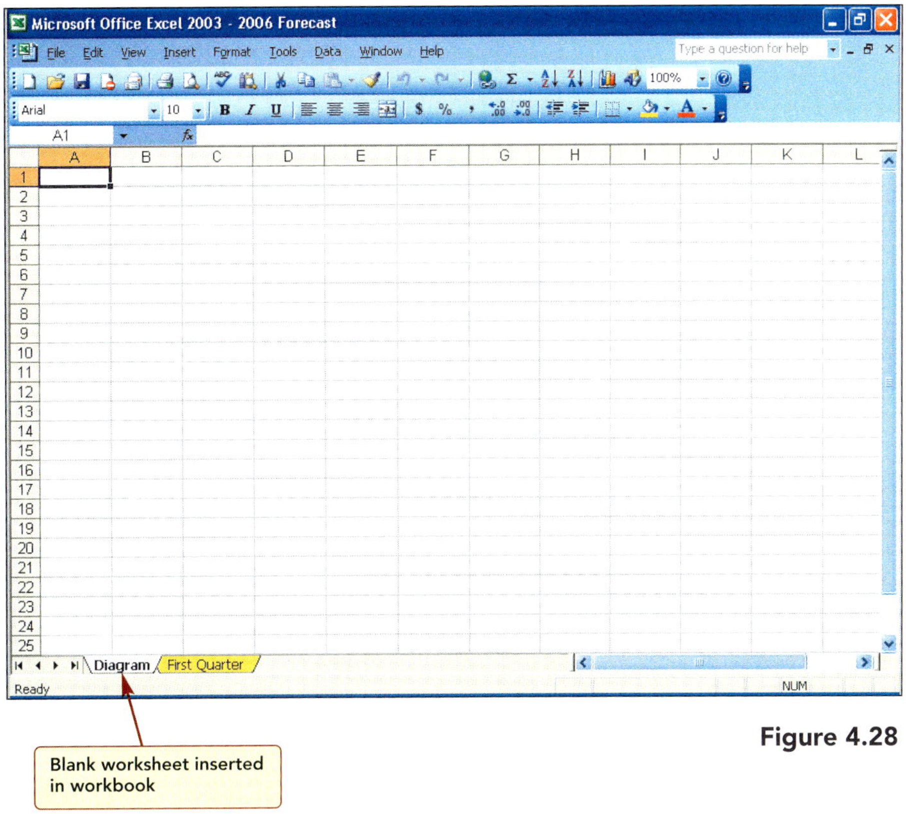

Figure 4.28

A blank worksheet has been inserted into the workbook.

Arranging Worksheet Windows

You want to be able to see the data in the First Quarter worksheet while you create the diagram. Just like workbook windows, you can arrange displayed worksheets in the workspace. To do this, each worksheet you want to arrange must be open in a separate window. Then, you can specify the window arrangement.

1 Choose **W**indow/**N**ew Window.

- Choose **W**indow/**A**rrange.
- Select **W**indows of active workbook.
- Click OK.

Your screen should be similar to Figure 4.29

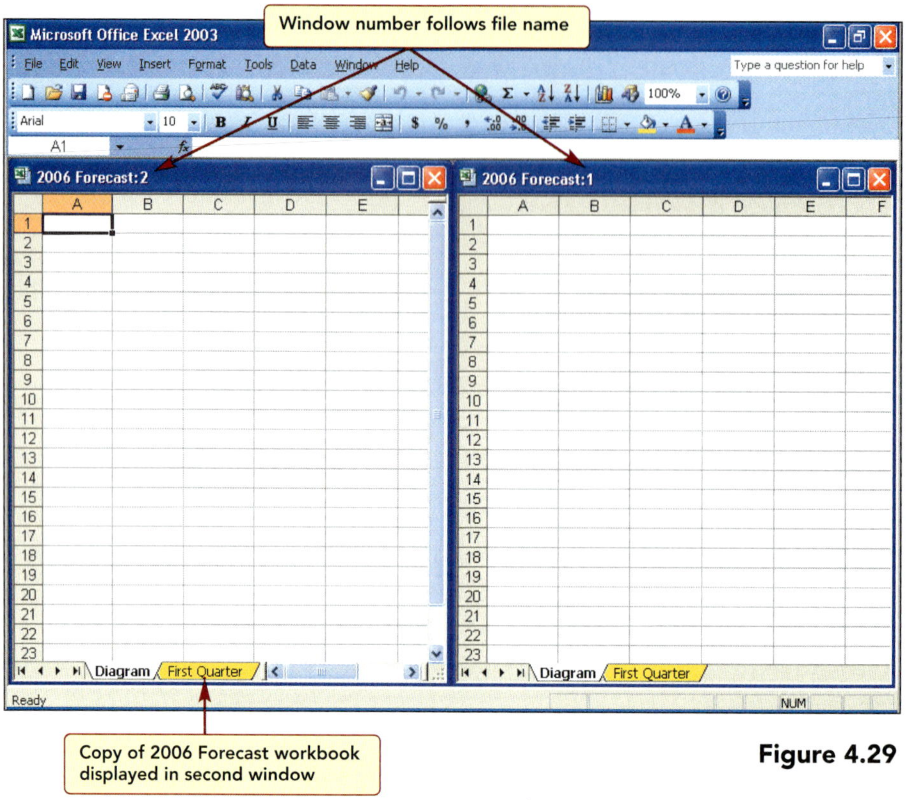

Figure 4.29

A copy of the 2006 Forecast workbook is displayed in the second window. The window title bar displays the file name followed by the window number to help you identify the windows.

Now you will display the First Quarter sheet in the right window (window 1).

2 Click on the 2006 Forecast:1 window to make it active.

- Display the First Quarter sheet.

Your screen should be similar to Figure 4.30

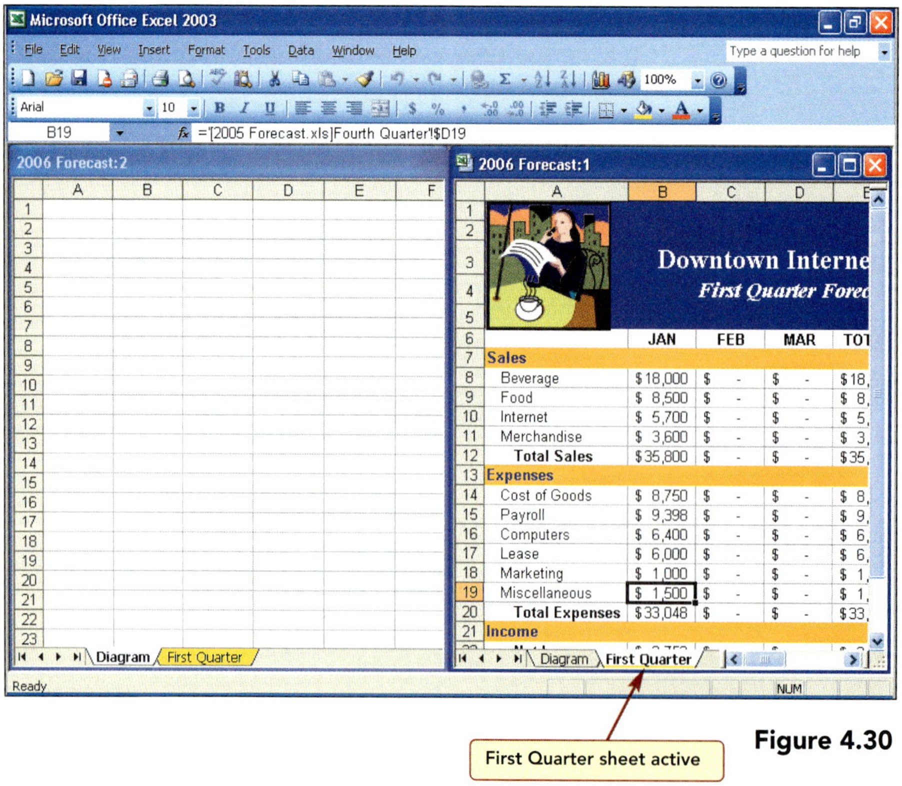

Figure 4.30

Creating Diagrams

You want to create a drawing that will display the importance of the four sales categories relative to each other. Excel includes several ready-made diagrams that help you quickly create a drawing to show this type of information.

Concept 6

Diagram

6 A **diagram** is a graphic object that can be used to illustrate concepts and to enhance your workbook. Diagrams are based on text rather than numeric information. There are six predesigned diagrams you can use. The type of diagram you choose depends on the purpose of the diagram and the type of concept you want to illustrate. The table below describes the diagram types and uses.

	Type	Use
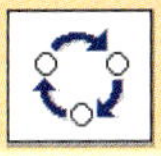	Cycle	Shows a process that has a continuous cycle
	Target	Shows steps toward a goal
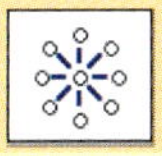	Radial	Shows relationships of elements to a core element
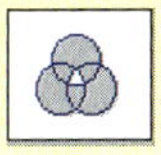	Venn	Shows areas of overlap between and among elements
	Pyramid	Shows foundation-based relationships
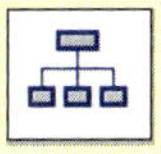	Organization	Shows hierarchical-based relationships

Additionally, you can create flowcharts (or flow diagrams) using a combination of shapes on the Drawing toolbar, including flowchart shapes and connectors. Flowcharts show a process that has a beginning and an end.

You will use the Pyramid diagram type to illustrate how the four sales categories relate.

1 Click on the Diagram sheet in the 2006 Forecast:2 window to make it active.

- Choose **Insert/Diagram**.
- From the Diagram Gallery, click Pyramid Diagram.
- Click OK.
- If necessary move the Diagram toolbar so it does not cover the pyramid.

Your screen should be similar to Figure 4.31

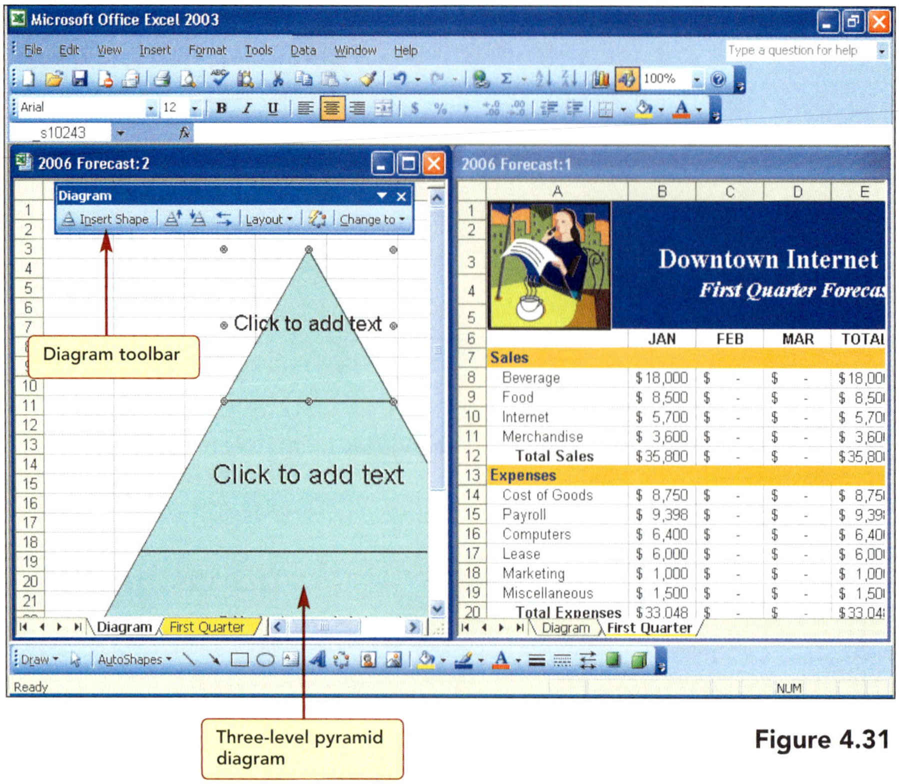

Figure 4.31

A pyramid diagram consisting of three levels is created by default. Each level is a separate element of the diagram that can be modified independently. The Diagram toolbar is also displayed and contains buttons to add shapes, modify the layout, and enhance the diagram.

2 Scroll the window to see the bottom of the pyramid.

Your screen should be similar to Figure 4.32

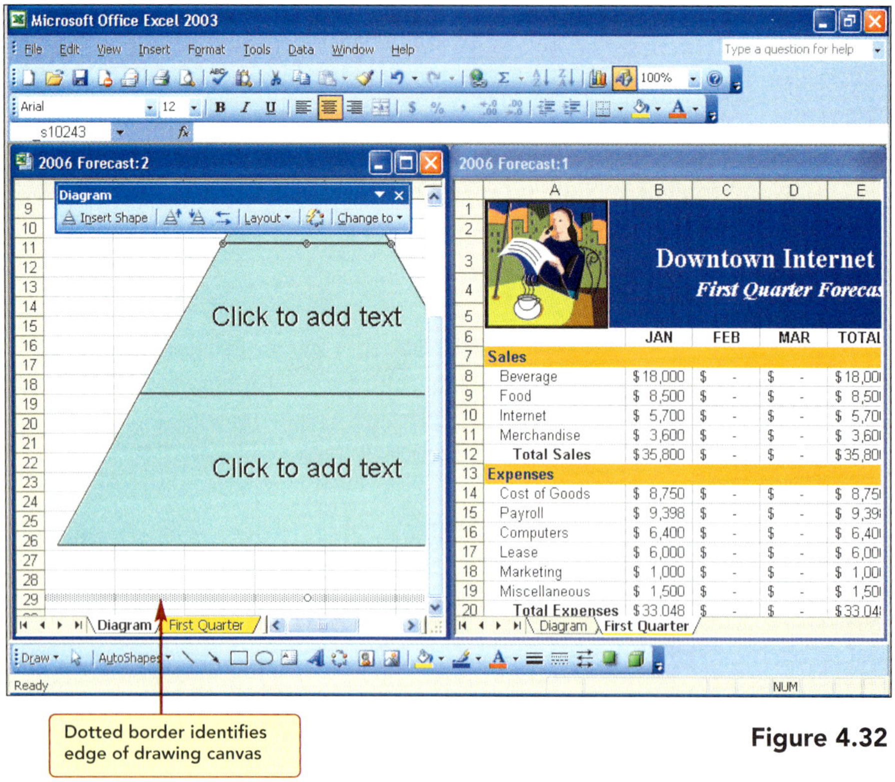

Figure 4.32

Notice the dotted border below the diagram. This identifies the outside edge of the **drawing canvas**, an area that surrounds the entire diagram and keeps all pieces of the diagram together as a unit. All items drawn in the drawing canvas stay as a complete picture within the worksheet and can be moved and resized as a unit.

Adding Shapes to a Diagram

Because you want the pyramid to represent the four sales categories, you first need to add another level to the pyramid for the fourth sales category. As you add elements to a diagram, the diagram will automatically resize to fit the drawing canvas. If you do not want the diagram to resize, you can expand the drawing canvas before adding more elements by dragging the drawing canvas handles, or by using the options in the Layout drop-down menu described below.

Option	Effect
Fit Diagram to Contents	Reduces the size of the drawing canvas to fit the size of the diagram.
Expand Diagram	Increases the size of the drawing canvas to add space around the diagram
Resize Diagram	Increases the size of both the diagram and the drawing canvas.

You will let the pyramid resize to the current drawing canvas size, as there is still plenty of space. You will also increase the size of the Diagram window so you can see more of the diagram.

1
- **Drag the left edge of the Forecast:1 window to the right to reduce the window size to about a third of the workspace.**
- **Drag the right edge of the Forecast:2 window to the right to fill in the blank workspace area as in Figure 4.33.**
- **Click Insert Shape on the diagram toolbar.**

Your screen should be similar to Figure 4.33

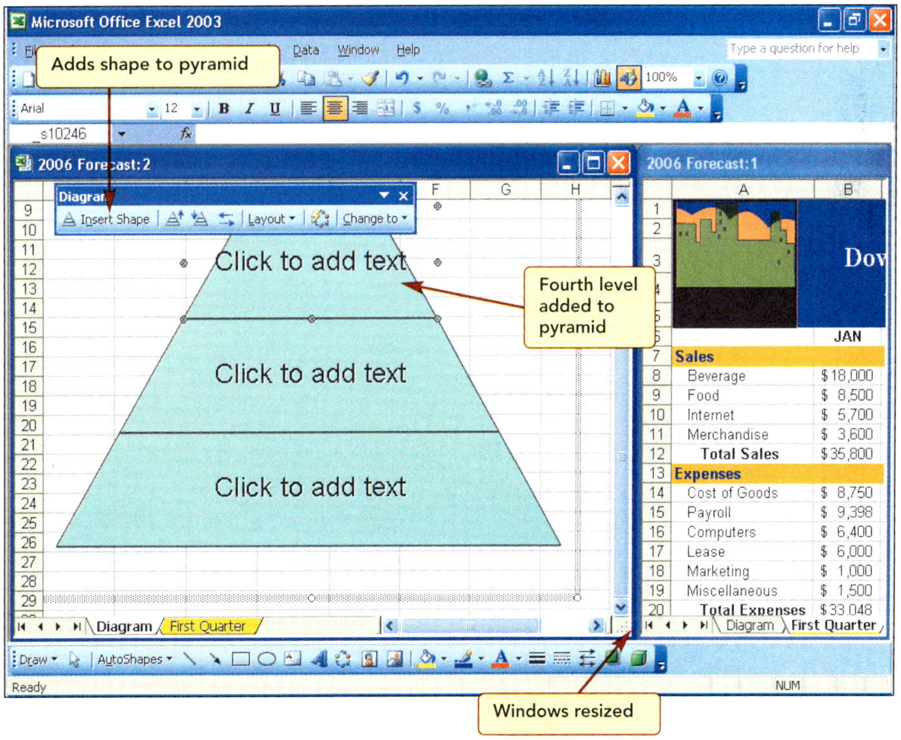

Figure 4.33

The pyramid shape now consists of four levels.

Adding Text to a Diagram

Each segment of the pyramid contains placeholder text consisting of instructions on how to add text to the diagram. To add text, you click on the diagram element to select it and type the text you want to insert. When an element is selected, it is surrounded by sizing handles that are used to decrease or enlarge the shape, and a hatched border or a dotted border. A hatched border indicates the object is a text box in which you can enter, delete, select, and format text. A dotted border indicates you can format the entire element. Clicking on the hatched border changes it to a dotted border.

You will replace the placeholder text with text that will identify the four sales categories. As you can see from the First Quarter worksheet, the largest sales category is Beverages. This category will be represented in the largest (bottom) section of the pyramid. The next largest sales category will be represented in the next level, and so forth.

1 **Click on "Click to add text" in the bottom level.**

Type Beverage Sales.

Your screen should be similar to Figure 4.34

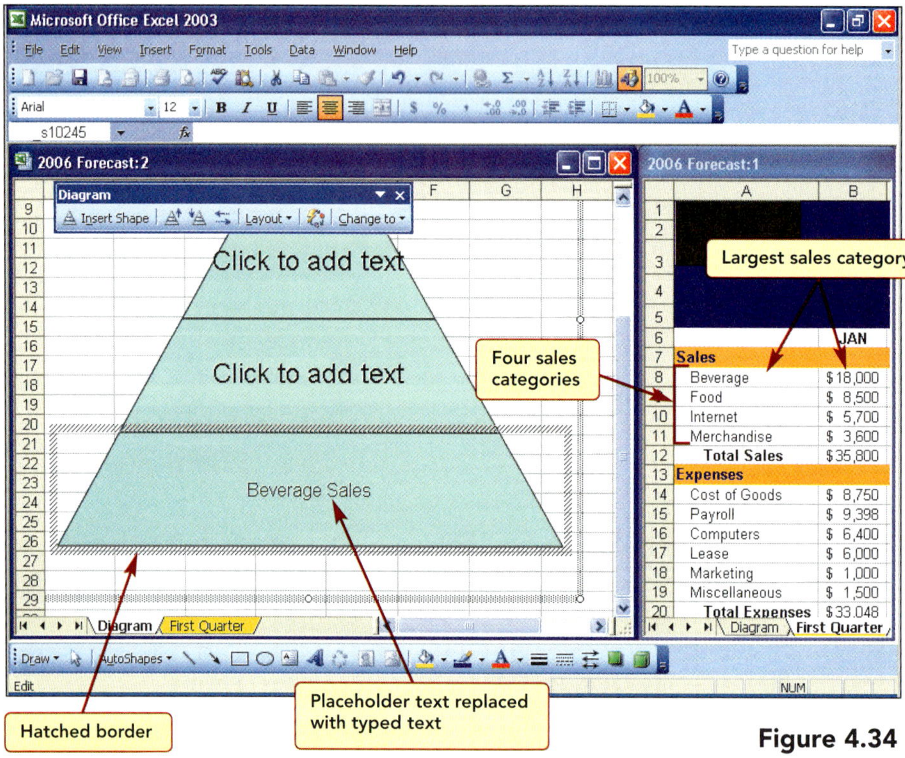

Figure 4.34

The placeholder text has been replaced with the text you entered. It is centered both horizontally and vertically in the text box. Using the First Quarter sheet as a reference, you will enter the remaining sales category names into the pyramid.

2 In a similar manner add the text **Food Sales**, **Internet Sales** and **Merchandise** to the other levels.

Your screen should be similar to Figure 4.35

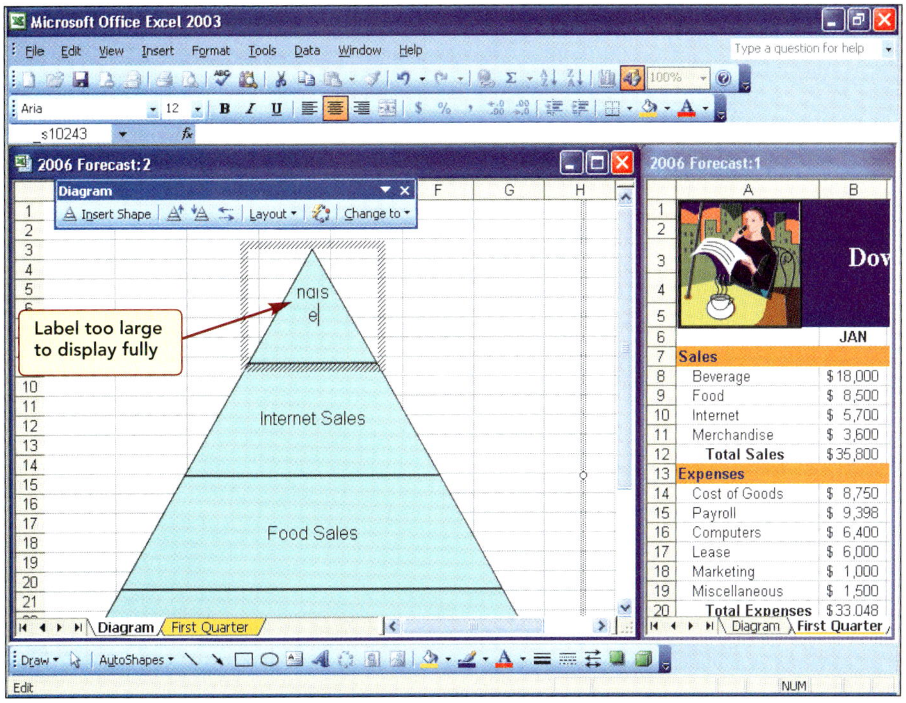

Figure 4.35

Formatting the Diagram

Notice that the Merchandise label is not fully displayed because it is too large for the available space. To fix this you will reduce the font size of the text in the top shape to 8 points.

You also think the pyramid would look better if the four levels were different colors. You could apply colors individually to each element or use one of the preset design schemes, called **AutoFormats**, to improve the appearance of the diagram. There are nine diagram AutoFormat styles consisting of different line and color combinations that can be applied to the pyramid diagram.

Additional Information

AutoFormats can also be applied to a range. You will learn about this feature in Lab 5.

1

- Drag to select the text in the top shape.
- Open the 12 Font Size menu and change the font size to 8.
- Click outside the pyramid to deselect the element.
- Click AutoFormat on the Diagram toolbar.
- Select the Fire style.
- Click OK.

Your screen should be similar to Figure 4.36

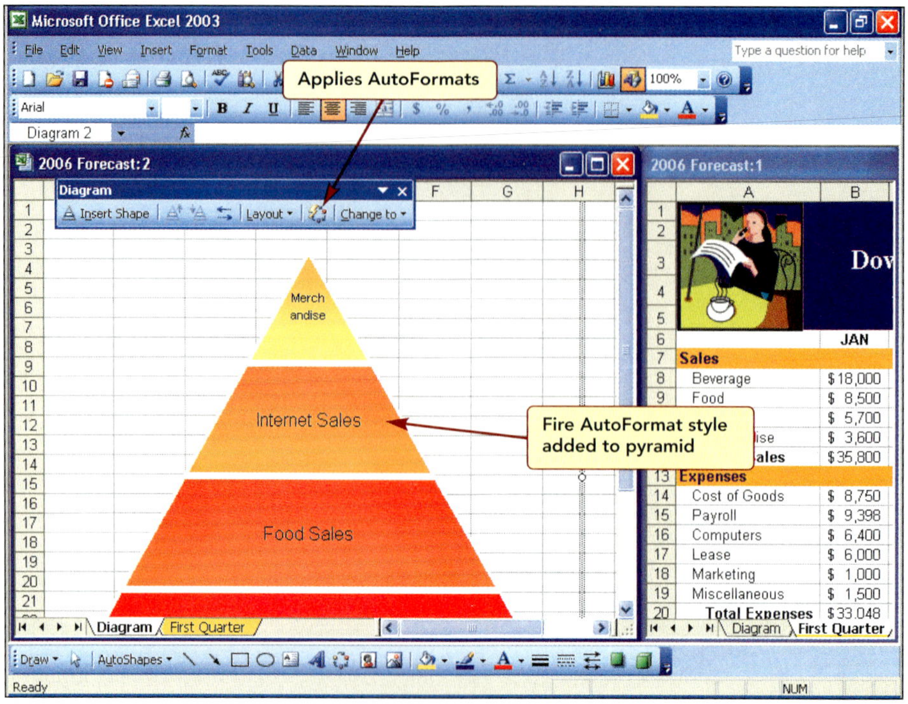

Figure 4.36

The addition of the AutoFormat style to the pyramid has made it much more interesting.

Unhiding Sheets and Workbooks

Now that you are finished working on the diagram, you will close the Forecast:2 window and maximize the remaining window. Then you will redisplay the other sheets in the workbook.

1

- Click ✕ to close the Forecast:2 window.
- Maximize the 2006 Forecast window.
- Choose Format/Sheet/Unhide.
- Select the Year sheet from the Unhide dialog box and click OK.
- In a similar manner, unhide the three other sheets.
- Move the Diagram sheet to after the Fourth Quarter sheet.

Your screen should be similar to Figure 4.37

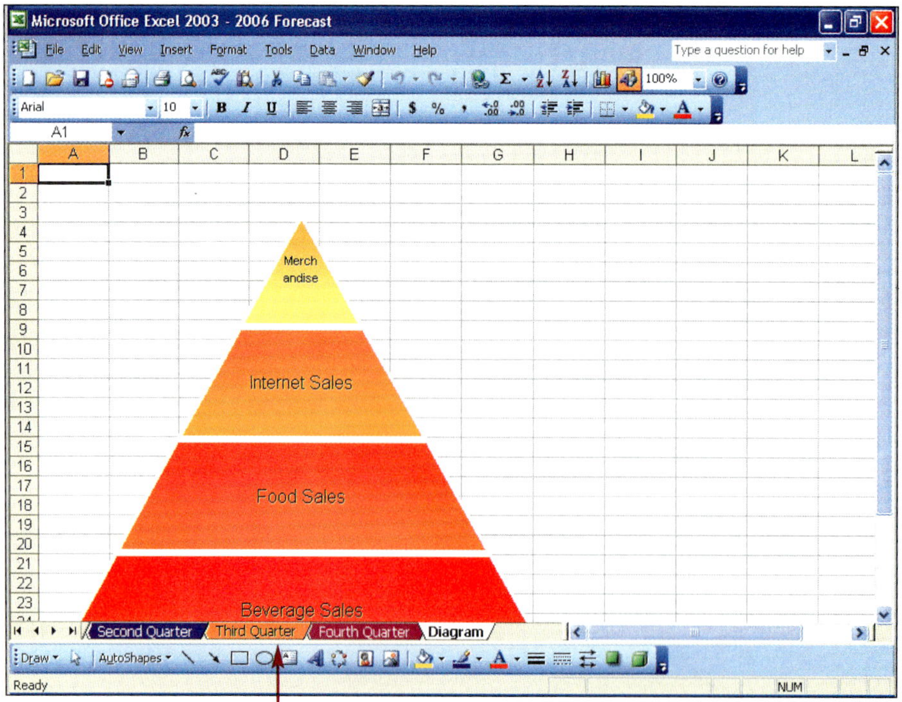

Figure 4.37

Finally, you want to include a copy of the Diagram sheet in the 2005 workbook file. You will redisplay this file, tile the workbook windows and copy the Diagram sheet.

2

- **Choose Window/ Unhide/2005 Forecast/ OK .**
- **Choose Window/Arrange.**
- **Clear the Windows of Active Workbook option.**
- **Click OK .**
- **From the Diagram tab shortcut menu, choose Move or Copy.**
- **From the To Book list, select 2005 Forecast.**
- **From the Before Sheet list, select (move to end).**
- **Select Create a copy.**
- **Click OK .**

Your screen should be similar to Figure 4.38

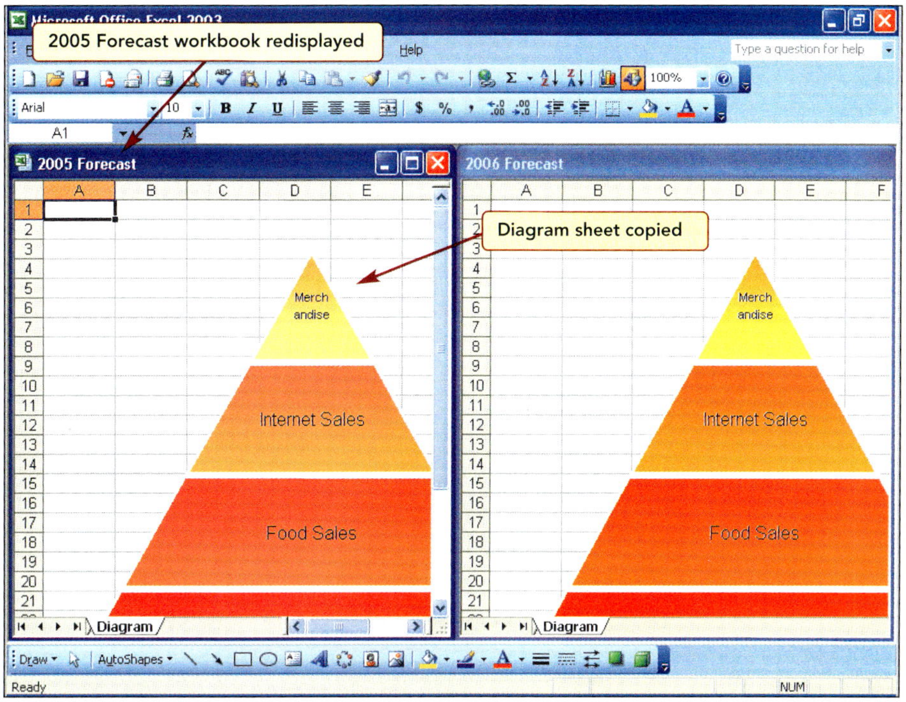

Figure 4.38

Now both workbooks include the pyramid diagram sheet.

3

- **Save and close the** 2005 Forecast **workbook file.**
- **Maximize the** 2006 Forecast **workbook window.**
- **Turn off the display of the Drawing toolbar.**
- **Preview the Diagram sheet.**
- **Add your name, left aligned, and the current date, right aligned, in the header.**
- **Center the pyramid horizontally on the page.**
- **Print the pyramid.**

Your printed output should be similar to that shown here.

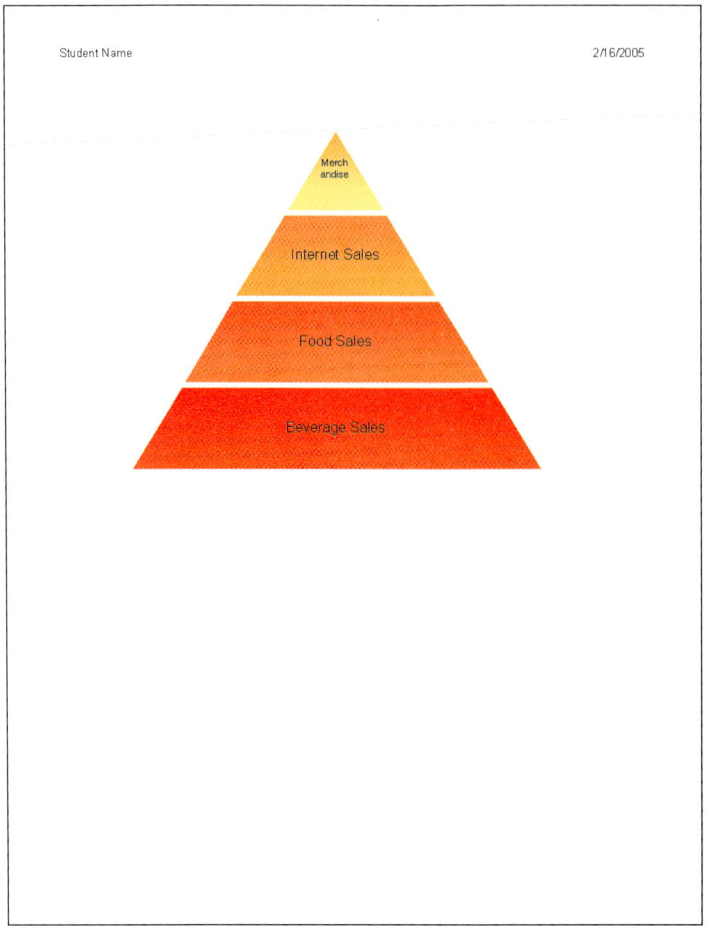

Using Scenarios

Evan has reviewed the January 2006 values and is comfortable with them. He predicts, however, that post-holiday sales in February and March will decline. He has asked you to complete the First Quarter forecast with the following data:

	February	March
Beverage	17,500	17,200
Food	8,200	8,000
Internet	5,400	5,200
Merchandise	3,500	3,300
Payroll	8,700	8,100
Computers	6,400	6,400
Lease	6,000	6,000
Marketing	1,000	1,000
Miscellaneous	1,500	1,500

1. **Display the First Quarter sheet.**

   Enter the values shown in the table on the previous page to update the First Quarter forecast.

   Choose Tools/Protection/Unprotect Sheet and AutoFit column E.

Your screen should be similar to Figure 4.39

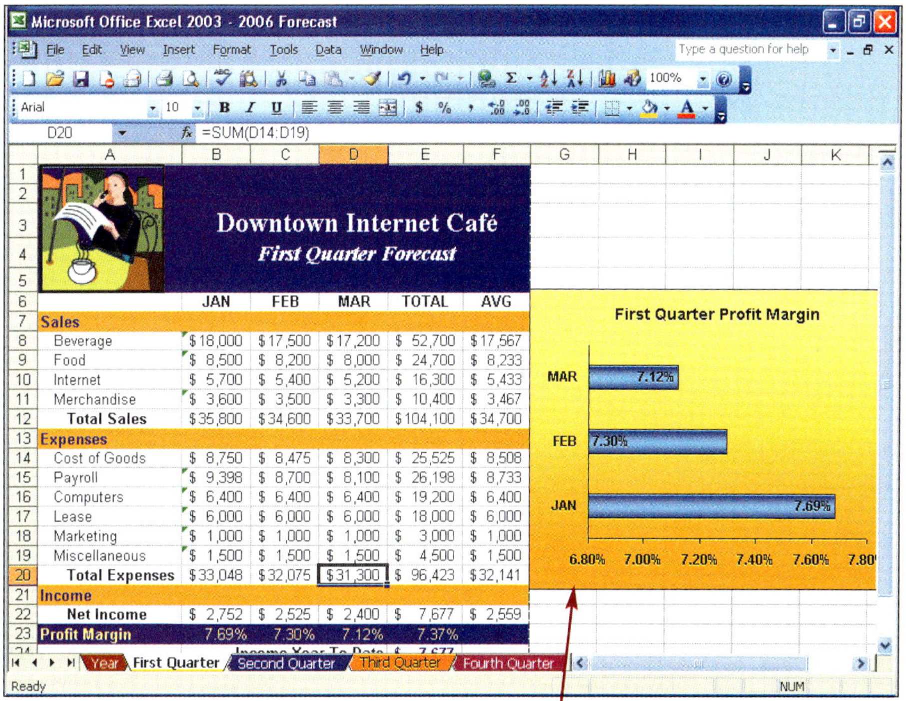

First quarter 2006 complete

Figure 4.39

While he realizes that sales and costs may be higher or lower than those presented, Evan believes the most likely scenario, or set of values, is reflected in the First Quarter worksheet. He has asked you to evaluate a best-case scenario and a worst-case scenario.

Concept 7

Scenario

7 A **scenario** is a named set of input values that you can substitute in a worksheet to see the effects of a possible alternative course of action. Scenarios are designed to help forecast the outcome of various possible actions. You can create and save different groups of scenario values on a worksheet and then switch to any of these scenarios to view the results.

For example, if you want to create a budget forecast based on various revenue values, you could define the potential values and then switch between the scenarios to perform what-if analyses. You can also create reports in separate sheets that summarize the scenarios you create.

The current data in the First Quarter worksheet reflects the most likely scenario. Evan has identified the best-case scenario as one where Internet sales increase 25 percent above the current estimate in February and March and all other values remain unchanged. His worst-case scenario is if Internet sales decrease 10 percent below the current estimate for the entire quarter and the lease in March increases from $6,000 to $6,500.

Creating Scenarios

You will use the Scenario Manager tool to evaluate the alternative scenarios by changing the values for Internet sales for January (cell B10), February (cell C10), and March (cell D10), and for March Lease Expense (cell D17). You could create separate worksheets to evaluate each scenario. However, using the Scenario Manager tool, you can create different scenarios and insert these scenarios directly into the workbook to see how each affects the worksheet.

1. **Move to cell B10.**
   - **Choose Tools/ Scenarios.**
   - **Move the Scenario Manager dialog box to the right of column F.**

Your screen should be similar to Figure 4.40

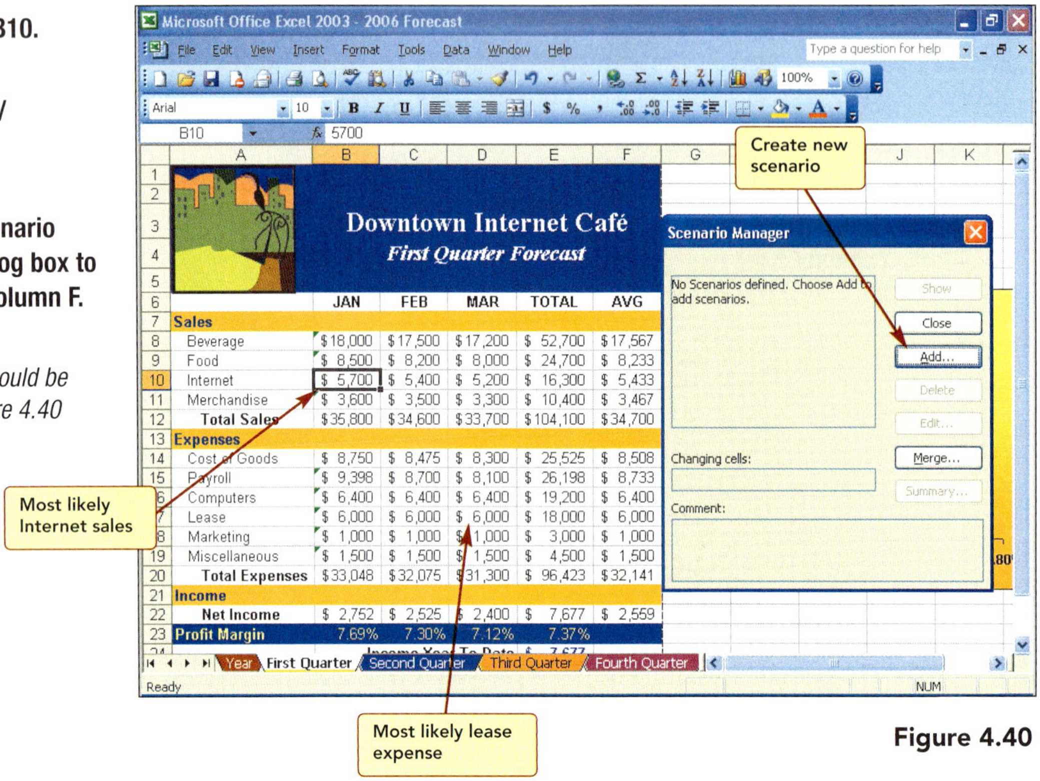

Figure 4.40

The Scenario Manager dialog box is used to add, delete, and edit scenarios. There are no scenarios named yet. First, you will define the most likely scenario.

2 **Click** Add... .

Your screen should be similar to Figure 4.41

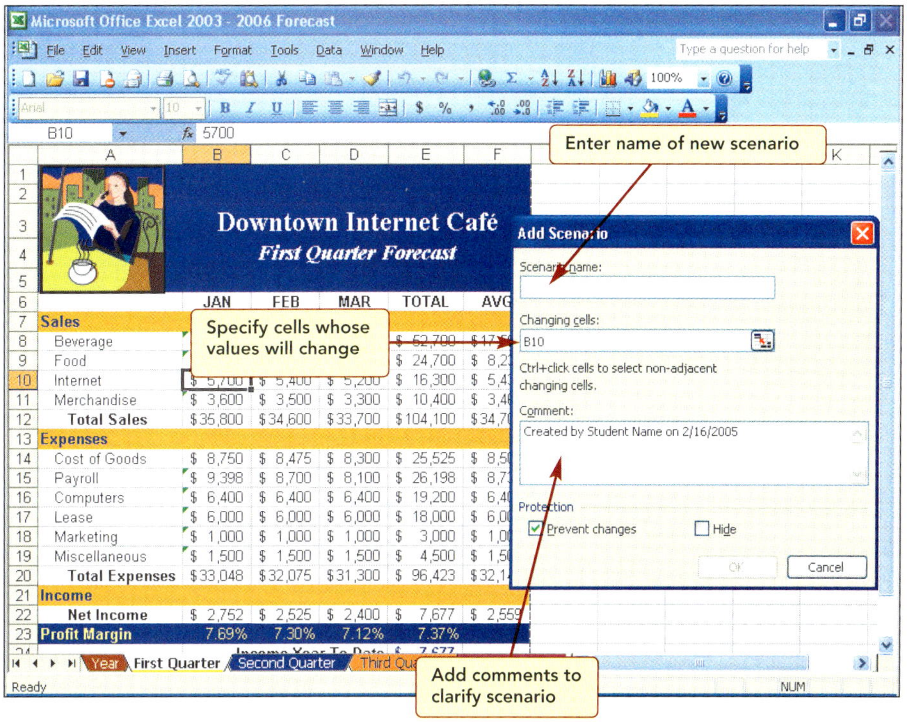

Figure 4.41

In the Add Scenario dialog box, you enter a name for the first scenario and the range of cells that will contain the changing values.

3 **Type Most Likely in the Scenario Name text box.**

Specify the range B10 through D10 and cell D17 as the changing cells in the Changing Cell text box.

Additional Information

Click [button] to reduce the dialog box and select the range from the worksheet. Hold down Ctrl while selecting nonadjacent cells.

Your screen should be similar to Figure 4.42

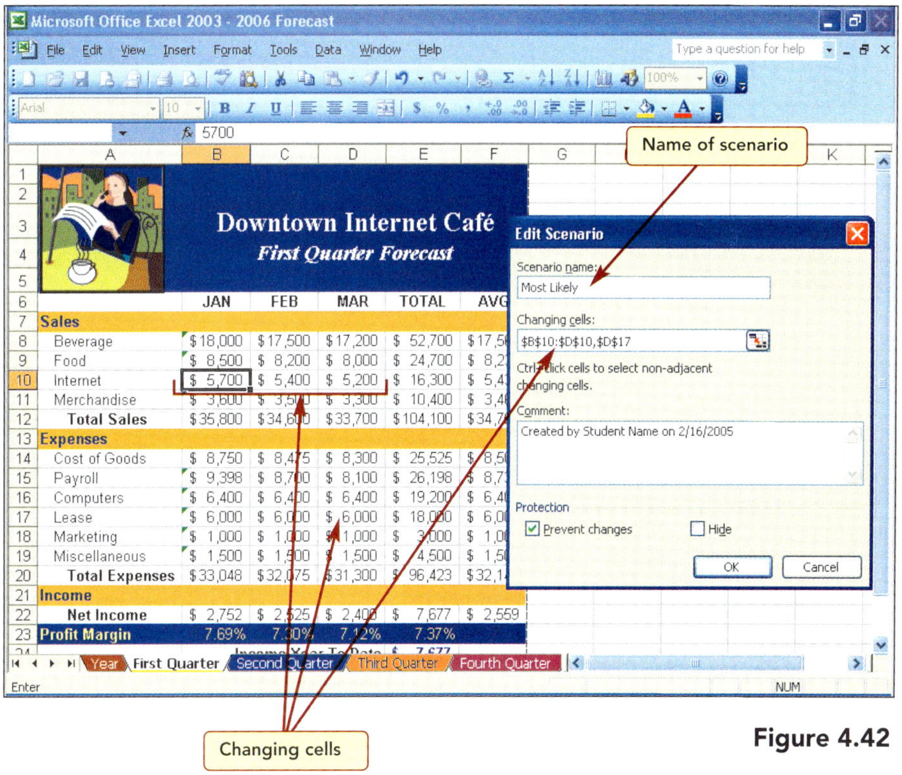

Figure 4.42

It is often helpful to add a comment to clarify the data included in the scenario. The default comment in the Comment text box is "Created by [name] on [date]." You will include additional information to clarify the meaning of the scenario.

4 • Click in the Comment text box.

• If necessary, replace the name with your name.

• Press ←Enter at the end of the date.

• Type **Expected first quarter sales and expenses.**

• Click OK.

• Click OK to accept that formulas will be replaced by values.

Your screen should be similar to Figure 4.43

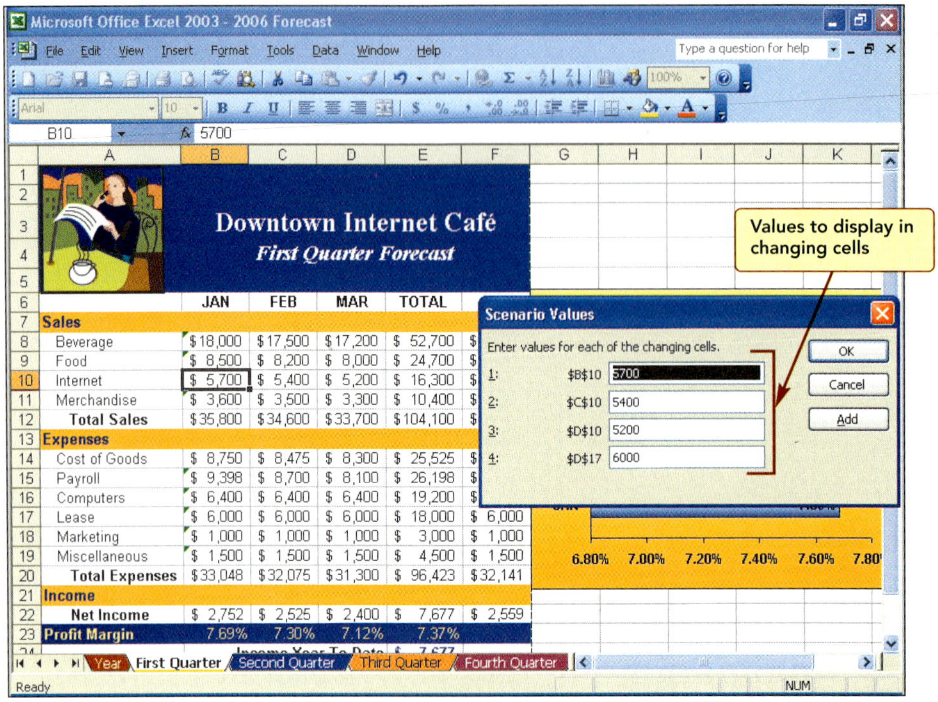

Figure 4.43

Additional Information

It is always a good idea to create a scenario of your original data as this will allow you to redisplay this information at any time.

The Scenario Values dialog box is used to enter the values to be varied for the different scenarios. The current worksheet values are displayed. These are the values you want to use for the Most Likely scenario.

5 • Click OK.

Your screen should be similar to Figure 4.44

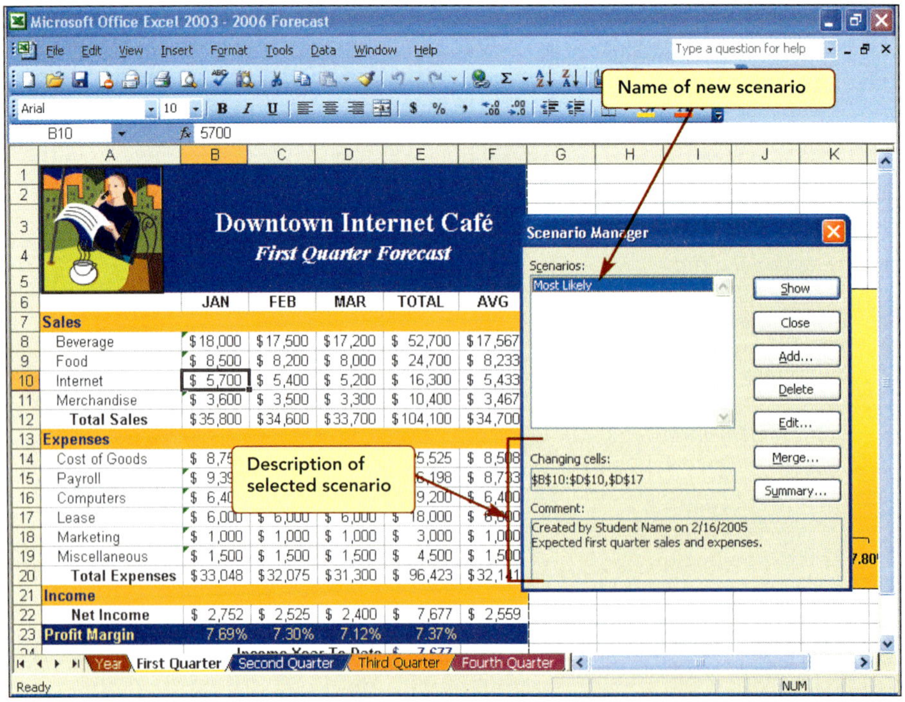

Figure 4.44

You are returned to the Scenario Manager dialog box and the name of the new scenario is displayed in the Scenarios list box.

Next, you will create the worst-case scenario. In this scenario there would be a 10 percent decrease in Internet sales and an increase in the lease expense.

6 Click Add... .

- In the Scenario Name text box, type **Worst Case**.
- In the Comment text box, change the name if necessary and enter the following: **Internet sales are 10% less than the most likely values and March lease expense increases to $6,500.**.
- Click OK twice.
- Enter the following values in the corresponding changing cells text boxes.

$B$10 5130

$C$10 4860

SDS10 4680

SD$17 6500

Your screen should be similar to Figure 4.45

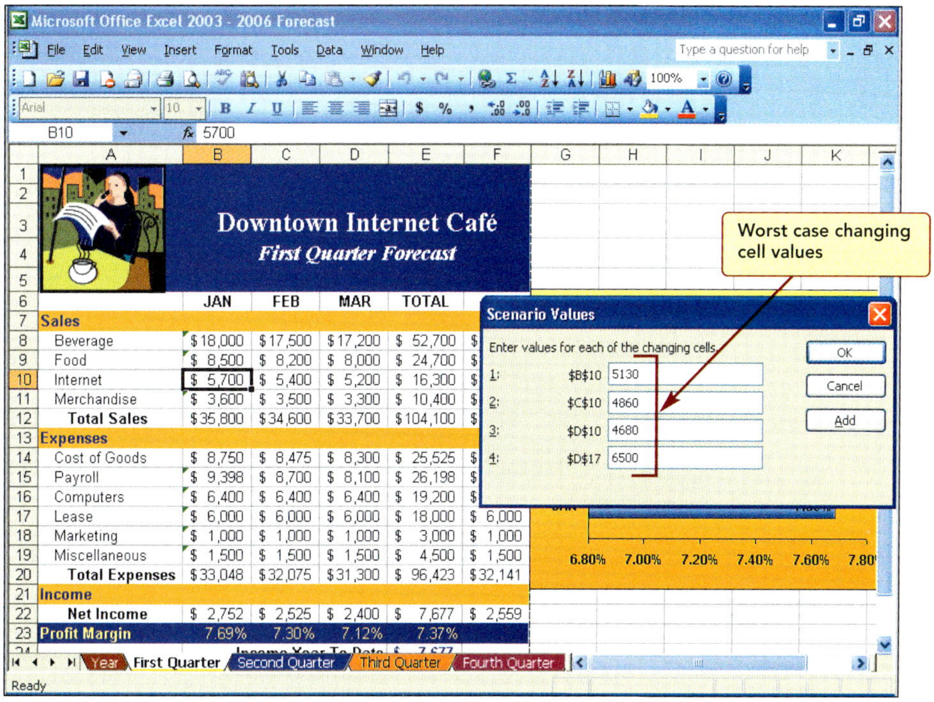

Figure 4.45

Next, you will create the best-case scenario. In this scenario, Evan anticipates that Internet sales will increase 25 percent for February and March above the most likely values and the March lease expense will remain the same. You could create the scenario in the same way by entering the new values in the changing cells. Another way is to use Solver to calculate the expected values for you and then create the scenario from the Solver result.

1 Click OK.

Click Close.

Save the workbook file.

Choose **T**ools/So**l**ver.

Set the target cell as E10, the value equal to **20300**, and the changing cells as C10:D10.

Additional Information

The value is an estimate of a 25 percent increase.

Click **S**olve.

Your screen should be similar to Figure 4.46

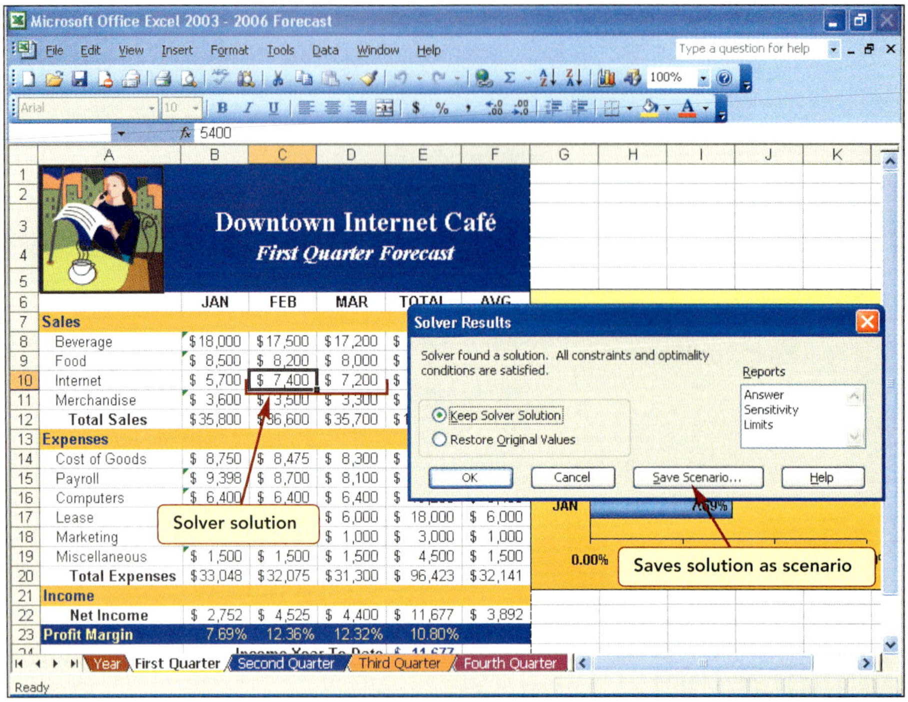

Figure 4.46

The Solver solution increases the February Internet sales to $7,400 and March to $7,200. You will create the scenario from these results. You will not keep the Solver solution, as you want the original values maintained in the worksheet.

2 Click Save Scenario....

Enter the scenario name of **Best Case**.

Click OK.

Select Restore **O**riginal Values.

Click OK.

Your screen should be similar to Figure 4.47

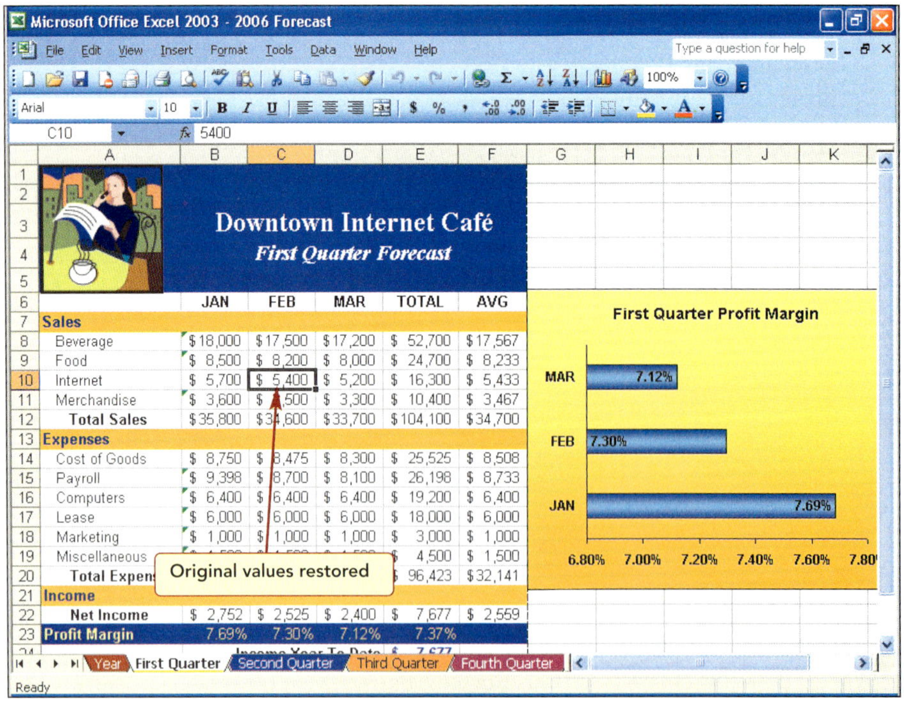

Figure 4.47

The original values are displayed in the worksheet again and the Solver results have been stored as a scenario.

Showing and Editing Scenarios

There are now three different scenarios in the worksheet. You want to see the effects of the worst-case and best-case scenarios.

1 Choose **Tools/Scenarios.**

From the Scenario Manager dialog box, select Worst Case.

Click **Show**.

Move the Scenario Manager dialog box down so that you can see the chart.

Your screen should be similar to Figure 4.48

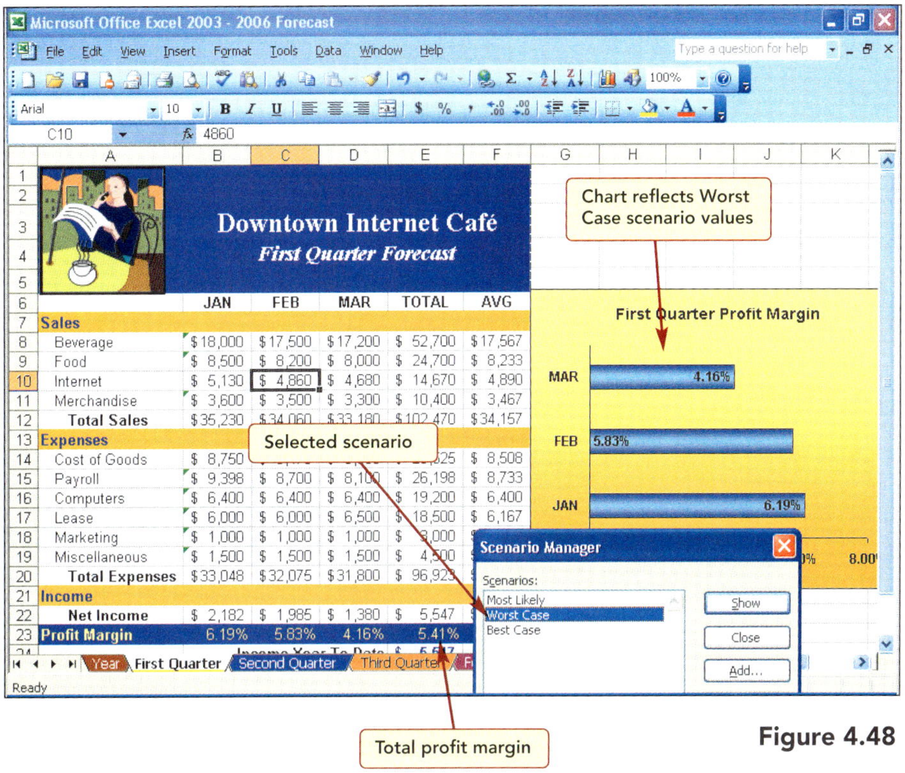

Figure 4.48

The worksheet displays the worst-case values. These values result in a total profit margin of 5.41 percent. The chart reflects the change in monthly profit margins.

2 In a similar manner, display the Best Case scenario.

Having Trouble?

If Excel did not update the chart, move the Scenario Manager box slightly to refresh the window.

Your screen should be similar to Figure 4.49

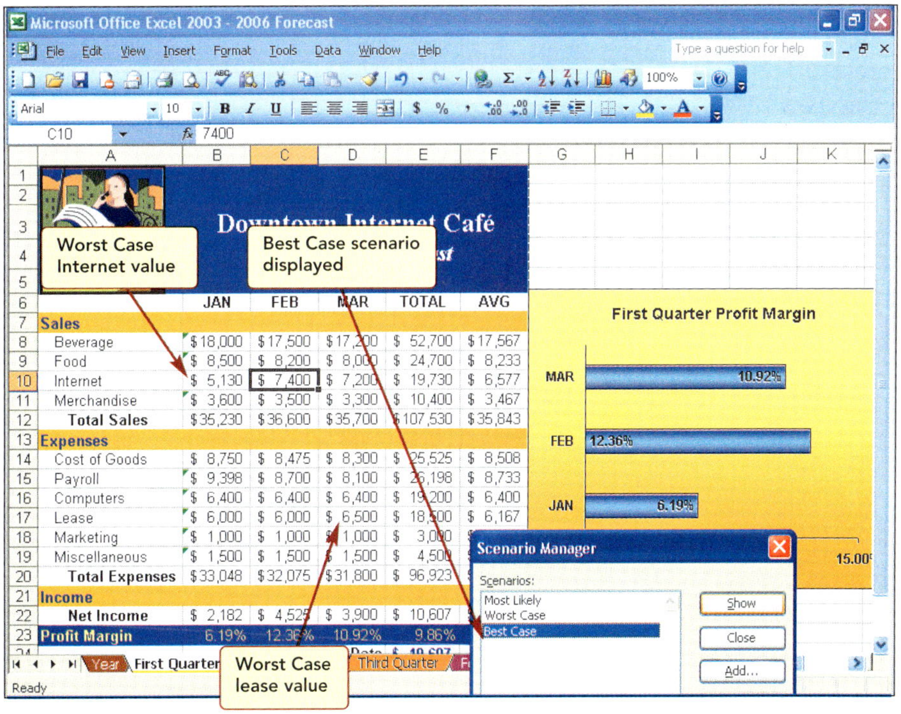

Figure 4.49

The best-case values are displayed in the worksheet. You notice, however, that the January Internet sales and the March lease expense values are the values that were last used in the Worst Case scenario. You need to edit the Best Case scenario to reset the January Internet sales to $5,700 and the March Lease to $6,000. You will also add a comment to the scenario.

3

- **Move the Scenario Manager dialog box to the right of column F again.**
- **Click Edit... .**
- **Specify the Changing Cells range as B10:D10 and cell D17.**
- **In the Comment text box, if necessary, change the name and enter the following: Internet sales increase 25% in February and March over the most likely values and March lease expense remains the same.**
- **Click OK .**
- **Enter 5700 as the value for cell B10 and 6000 as the value for D17.**
- **Click OK .**
- **Click Show .**

Your screen should be similar to Figure 4.50

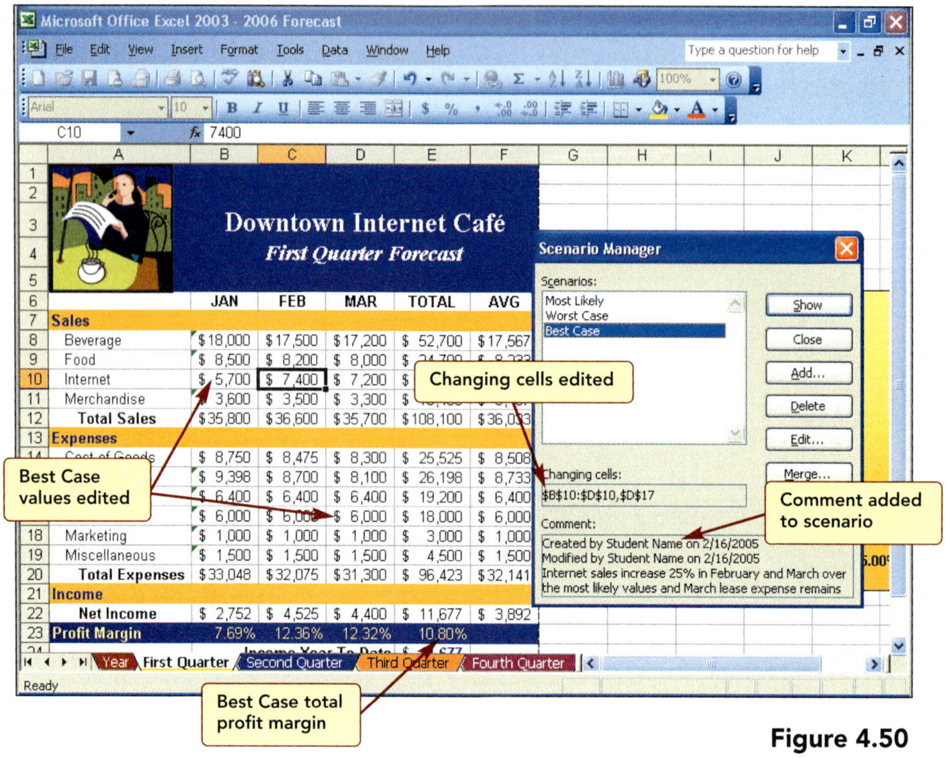

Figure 4.50

The Best Case scenario now shows a total profit margin of 10.80 percent.

Creating a Scenario Report

Another way to evaluate the scenarios is to create a summary report that will display the effect on the profit margins for each scenario.

1 Click Summary... .

- **Specify the Result Cells range as B23 through E23 (containing the profit margin values) as the range of cells whose results you want summarized.**
- **Click OK .**
- **Save the workbook file.**

Your screen should be similar to Figure 4.51

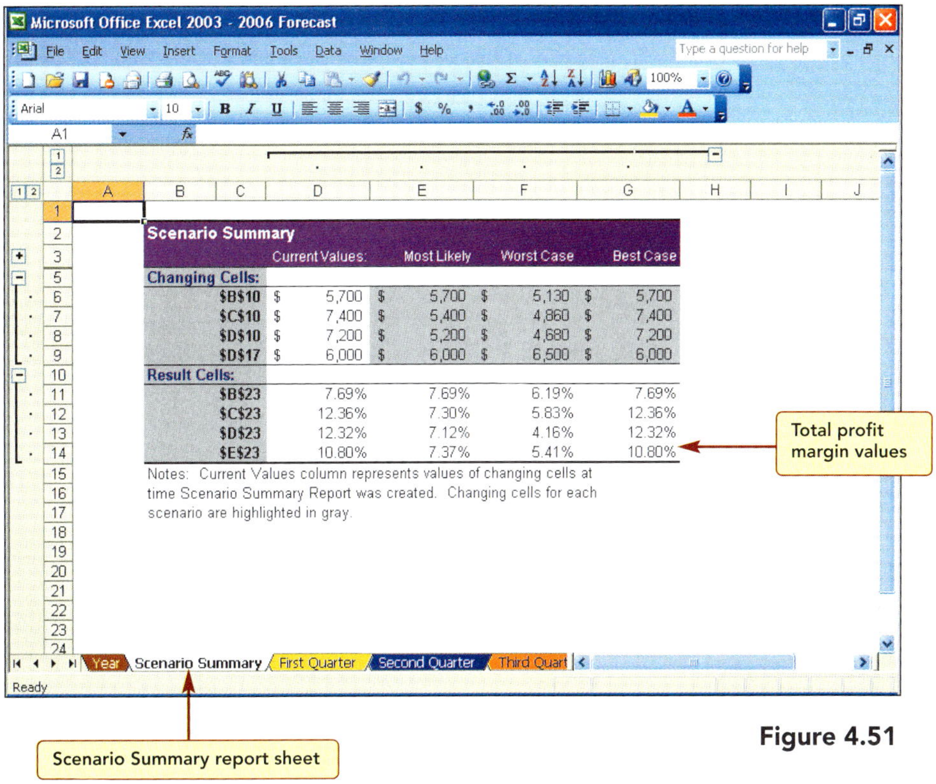

Figure 4.51

The Scenario Summary report is created and displayed in a separate sheet. It displays the values for the three scenarios and the profit margin results for each scenario. As you can see from the summary, the Most Likely scenario shows a total profit margin of 7.37 percent. The Best Case scenario yields higher profit margins, with a total profit margin of 10.80 percent for the quarter. The Worst Case scenario yields lower profit margins, with a total profit margin of 5.41 percent.

The report however, is hard to understand because it uses cell references as the labels. To clarify the meaning of the report, you will edit the row labels.

2 Enter the labels in the following cells:

C6	Internet JAN	C11	Profit Margin JAN
C7	Internet FEB	C12	Profit Margin FEB
C8	Internet MAR	C13	Profit Margin MAR
C9	Lease MAR	C14	Profit Margin TOTAL

- AutoFit column C.

Your screen should be similar to Figure 4.52

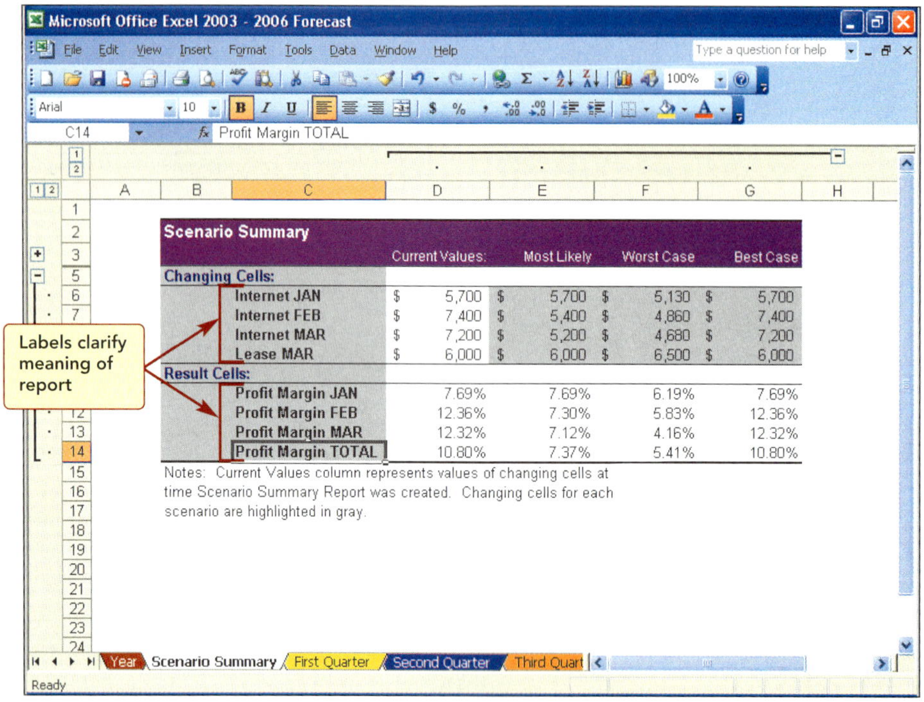

Figure 4.52

You have now completed best- and worst-case scenarios for the first quarter for 2006, as Evan requested.

Displaying the Current Date and Time

You would like to include a date and time stamp on the Scenario Summary worksheet to identify when the values were entered and the scenarios applied. You could just enter the current date and time on the worksheet, but you want to ensure that it reflects exactly when the most recent changes and analyses are done. To have the date and time automatically update whenever a worksheet is recalculated, the **NOW function** is used.

Using the Insert Function Feature

You will enter the function in cell B3. You could enter the function directly by typing it. However, another way is to use the Insert Function feature. This feature simplifies entering functions by prompting you to select a function from a list and then helps you enter the arguments correctly.

1 Move to cell B3 on the Scenario worksheet.

Click Insert Function.

Another Method

The menu equivalent is Insert/Function and the keyboard shortcut is ⇧Shift + F3.

Your screen should be similar to Figure 4.53

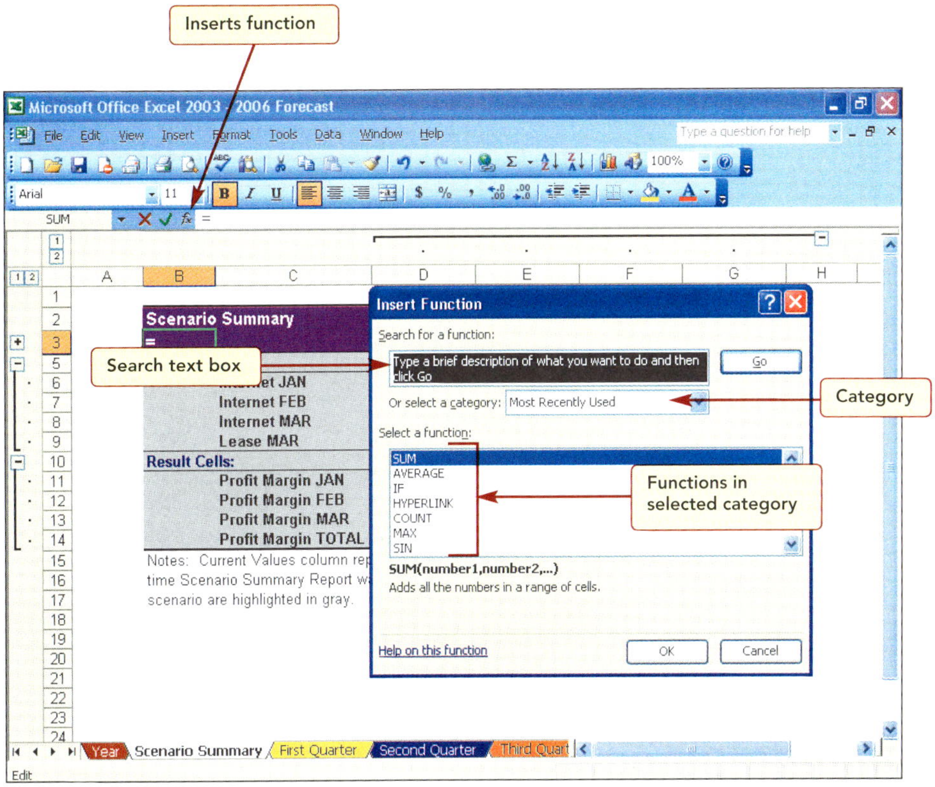

Figure 4.53

The NOW function may not be displayed in the most recently used category. Any function you want to use can be found by typing a description of what you want to do in the Search text box or by selecting a category.

2 From the Or select a Category drop-down list, select Date & Time.

Scroll the Select a function list and select NOW.

Click OK.

Your screen should be similar to Figure 4.54

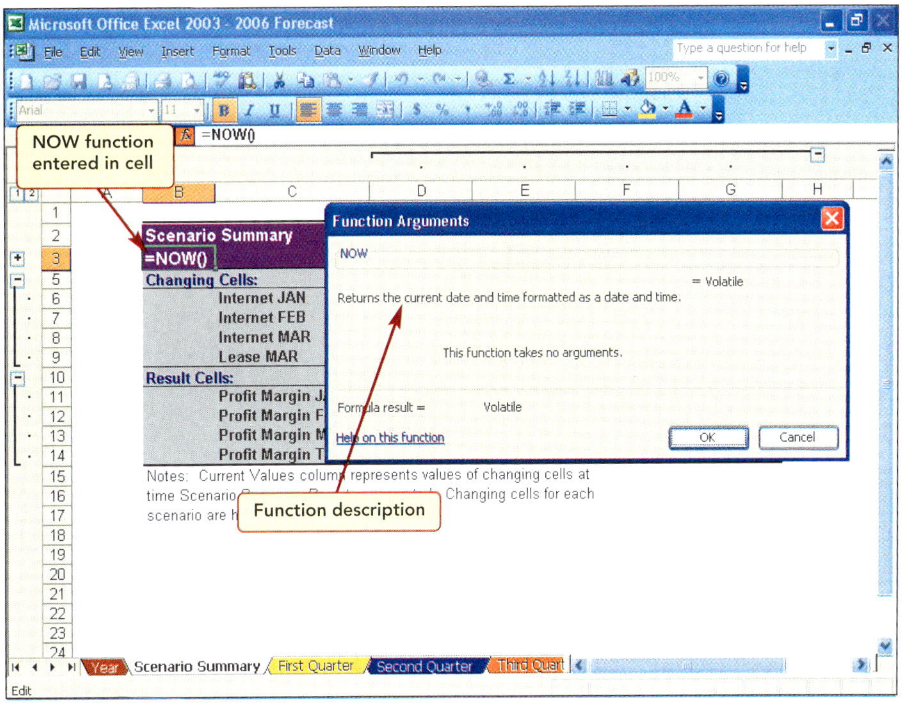

Figure 4.54

The Function Arguments dialog box displays a message telling you that this function displays the current date and time, and requires no arguments. To complete the function,

3 Click OK.

Your screen should be similar to Figure 4.55

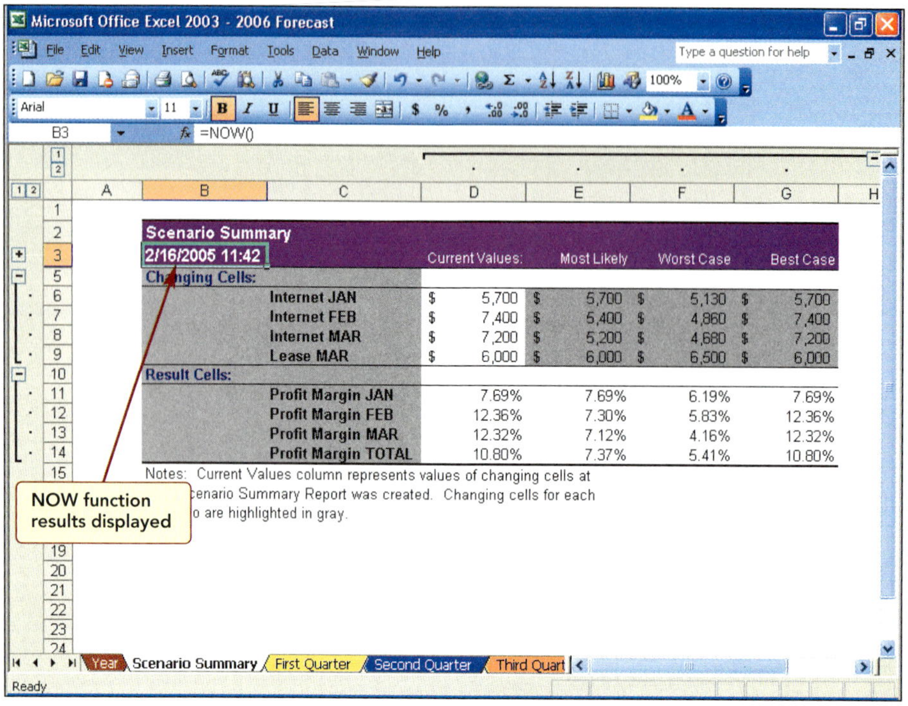

Figure 4.55

The current date and time are displayed in cell B3.

Shifting Cells

Additional Information

You can also shift cells down the worksheet when inserting new cells.

A final change you want to make is to move the Note at the bottom of the Scenario Summary to the right. Rather than cutting and pasting the cell contents, you will insert blank cells before the cells and shift the existing cells to the right.

1. **Select cells B15:B17.**
   - **Choose Insert/Cells/Shift Cells Right.**
   - **Click OK.**

Your screen should be similar to Figure 4.56

Additional Information

You can also delete cells using Edit/Delete and shift them to the left or up in the worksheet.

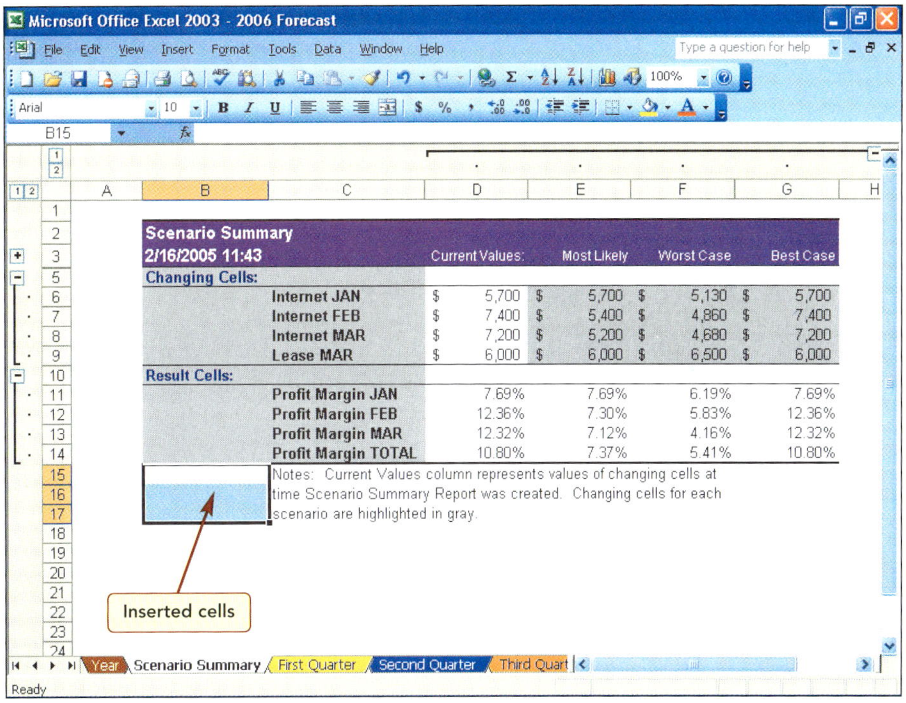

Figure 4.56

Three new cells have been inserted and the existing cells have shifted to the right. Now you are ready to print the worksheet.

2. **Move the Scenario Summary sheet to after the Fourth Quarter sheet.**
   - **Preview the Scenario Summary sheet.**
   - **Include your name and the workbook name on separate lines centered in a custom header.**
   - **Print the worksheet centered horizontally in landscape orientation.**
   - **Move to cell A6 in the First Quarter sheet.**
   - **Protect the sheet, save the workbook, and exit Excel.**

Focus on Careers

EXPLORE YOUR CAREER OPTIONS

Cage Cashier

Do you like to count money? Have you ever wondered who handles the money in a casino behind the scenes? Cage cashiers manage the cash, chips, and all the paperwork needed to track the large amounts of money that change hands every day. Some cage cashiers work to verify guests' financial records so they can open house credit lines. Other cashiers are primarily responsible for using computer spreadsheet programs to access and reconcile the books. Cage cashiers must have good math skills and have experience with accounting or bookkeeping. Salary is dependent on experience, and cage cashiers typically make tips in addition to an hourly wage. The demand for cage cashiers is expected to increase as gaming expands beyond the traditional centers in Nevada and New Jersey.

concept summary

LAB 4

Using Solver, Creating Templates, and Evaluating Scenarios

Solver (EX4.6)

Solver is a tool used to perform what-if analysis to determine the effect of changing values in two or more cells on another cell.

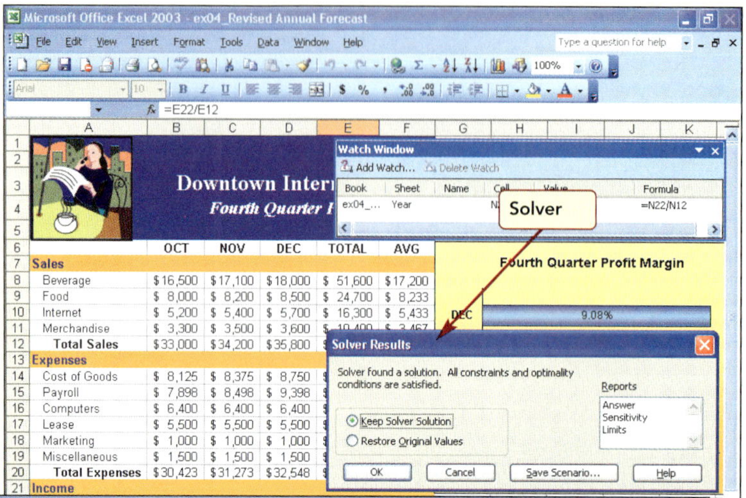

Workbook Template (EX4.10)

A workbook template is a workbook file that contains predesigned worksheets that can be used as a pattern for creating similar worksheets in a new workbooks.

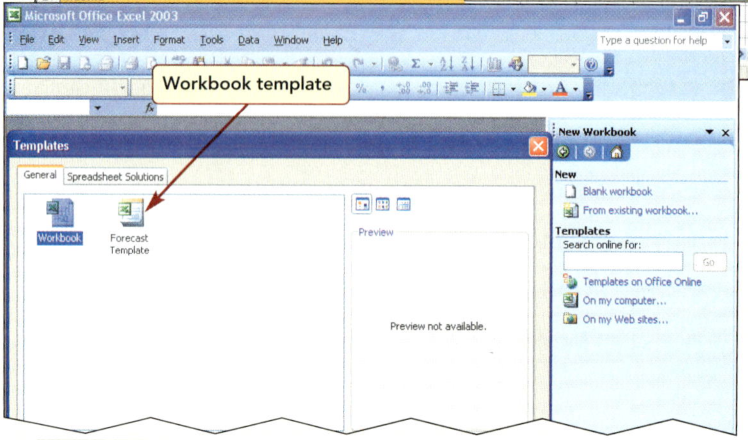

Protection (EX4.12)

The protection feature controls what information can be changed in a workbook.

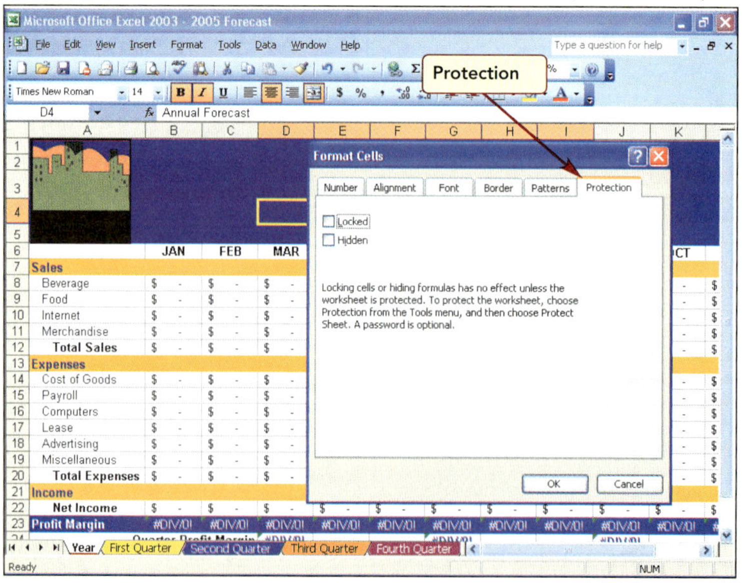

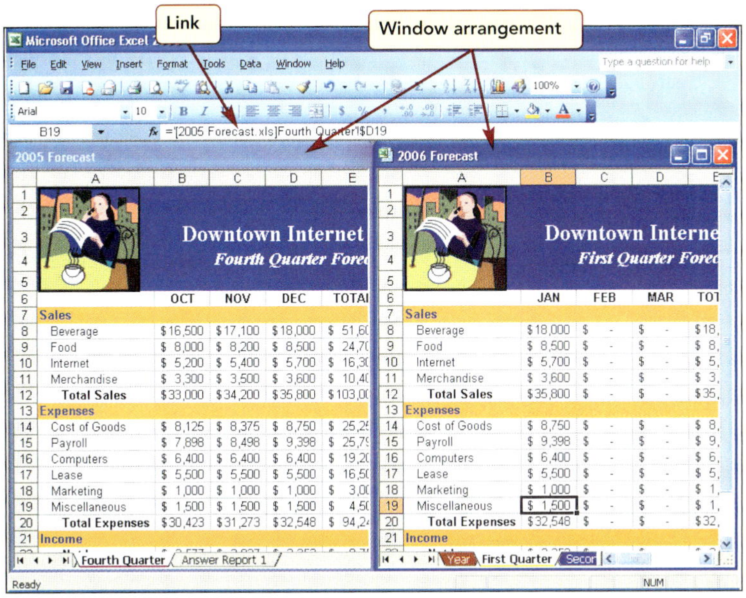

Window Arrangement (EX4.21)

The window arrangement feature displays all open workbook files in separate windows on the screen, making it easy to view and work with information in different workbooks.

Link (EX4.23)

A link creates a connection between files that automatically updates the data in one file whenever the data in the other file changes.

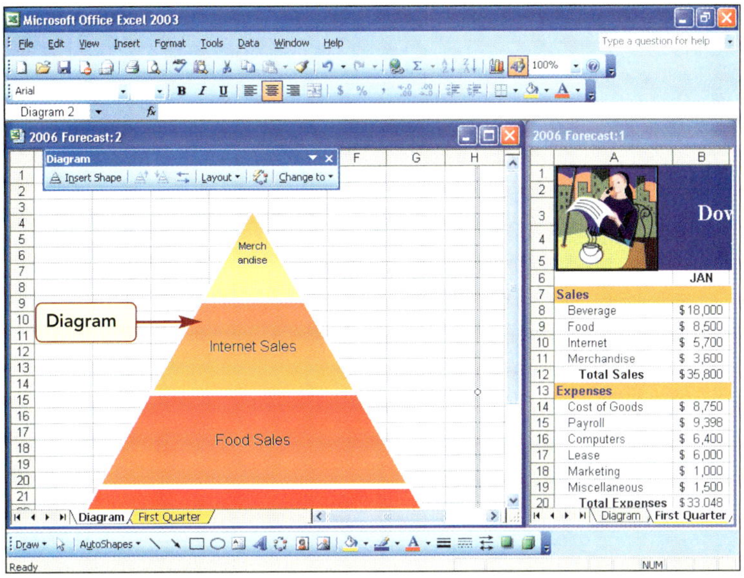

Diagram (EX4.31)

A diagram is a graphic object that can be used to illustrate concepts and to enhance your workbook.

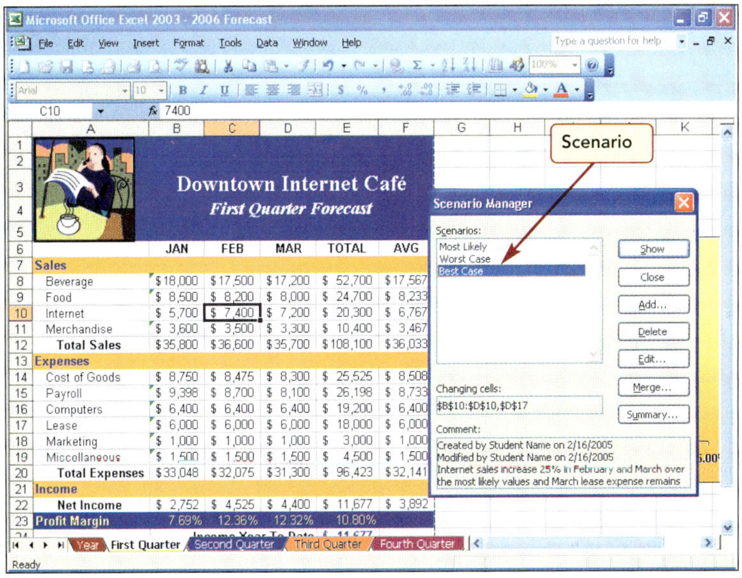

Scenario (EX4.39)

A scenario is a named set of input values that you can substitute in a worksheet to see the effects of a possible alternative course of action.

lab review

LAB 4

Using Solver, Creating Templates, and Evaluating Scenarios

key terms

active workbook EX4.20
adjustable cell EX4.6
AutoFormat EX4.35
cascade EX4.21
destination cell EX4.23
destination workbook EX4.23
diagram EX4.31
drawing canvas EX4.33
external reference formula EX4.23
horizontal EX4.21
link EX4.23
NOW function EX4.48
password EX4.12
protection EX4.12
scenario EX4.39
Solver EX4.6
source cell EX4.23
source workbook EX4.23
target cell EX4.6
template EX4.10
tiled EX4.21
vertical EX4.21
window arrangement EX4.21

microsoft office specialist skills

The Microsoft Office Specialist certification program is designed to measure your proficiency in performing basic tasks using the Office 2003 applications. Getting certified demonstrates that you have the skills and provides a valuable industry credential for employment. After completing this lab, you have learned the following Microsoft Office Excel 2003 Specialist skills:

Skill Sets	Skill Standards	Page
Analyzing Data	Use statistical, date and time, financial, and logical functions	EX4.48
	Create, modify, and position diagrams and charts based on worksheet data	EX4.31
Formatting Data and Content	Format worksheets	EX4.27,4.36
Managing Workbooks	Create new workbooks from templates	EX4.18
	Organize worksheets	EX4.28
	Customize window layout	EX4.29

command summary

Command	Shortcut Keys	Button	Action
Edit/Delete/Shift Cells Left			Deletes selected cells and shifts remaining cells to left
Edit/Delete/Shift Cells Up			Deletes selected cells and shifts remaining cells up
Insert/Cells/Shift Cells Right			Moves existing cells to right when new cells are inserted
Insert/Cells/Shift Cells Down			Moves existing cells down when new cells are inserted
Insert/Worksheet			Inserts a new worksheet into the workbook
Insert/Function			Inserts a function into a cell
Insert/Diagram			Inserts a diagram in worksheet
Format/Cells/Protection/Locked			Toggles between locking and unlocking a cell
Format/Sheet/Hide			Hides selected sheets
Format/Sheet/Unhide			Unhides selected sheet
Tools/Protection/Protect Sheet			Prevents unauthorized users from changing a worksheet's contents
Tools/Protection/ Unprotect Sheet			Unprotects worksheet and allows modification of contents
Tools/Scenarios			Starts Scenario Manager tool to create sets of data for what-if analysis
Tools/Solver			Starts Solver tool to perform what-if-analysis
Tools/Add-Ins/Solver Add-In			Adds Solver tool to menu
Window/New Window			Displays a new window
Window/Arrange			Arranges open windows vertically, horizontally, tiled, or cascaded
Window/Hide			Hides current workbook
Window/Unhide			Unhides selected workbook

lab exercises

matching

Match the lettered item on the right with the numbered list on the left.

1. Solver	______	**a.** prevents unauthorized users from viewing or changing a workbook
2. source workbook	______	**b.** used as a pattern for creating new workbooks
3. template	______	**c.** cell containing the external reference formula
4. cascade	______	**d.** forecasts the outcome of various possible actions
5. target cell	______	**e.** creates a link between workbook files
6. source cell	______	**f.** determines the effects of changed values in adjustable cells
7. external reference formula	______	**g.** creates a connection between files that automatically updates the data in one file when a change is made in another file
8. password	______	**h.** supplies the data in a linked workbook
9. destination cell	______	**i.** cell containing the value you want to solve for
10. link	______	**j.** windows displayed one on top of another
11. scenario		

multiple choice

Circle the correct response to the questions below.

1. __________ is a tool used for what-if analysis.
- **a.** Scenario
- **b.** Solver
- **c.** Adjustable cell
- **d.** Template

2. In the external reference formula [Forecast.xls]Year$N$8, Year is the ______________.
- **a.** source file
- **b.** destination file
- **c.** active reference
- **d.** sheet reference

3. The workbook that receives the data is called the ______________.
- **a.** source workbook
- **b.** destination workbook
- **c.** link
- **d.** dependent cell

4. A(n) ____________ is entered in one worksheet to create a link to another worksheet.
   a. dependent value
   b. linking formula
   c. internal reference formula
   d. external reference formula

5. ___________ calculate(s) a formula to achieve a given value.
   a. Target cells
   b. Scenario Manager
   c. Solver
   d. Source cells

6. The ______________ tool lets you view the effect of varying values applied to a worksheet.
   a. Scenario Manager
   b. Solver
   c. What-If Analysis
   d. Goal Seek

7. The ______________ command removes the selected worksheet from the user view.
   a. Format/Sheet/Hide
   b. Format/Sheet/Remove
   c. Window/Sheet/Hide
   d. Window/Hide

8. ______________ prevents users from changing the contents of a worksheet.
   a. Locking cells
   b. Protecting a worksheet
   c. Unlocking cells
   d. A password

9. A workbook _____________ is a workbook file that contains predesigned worksheets that can be used as a pattern for creating similar sheets in new workbooks.
   a. template
   b. arrangement
   c. design
   d. diagram

10. ________________ are used to illustrate various conceptual material and to enliven documents.
   a. Graphics
   b. Pictures
   c. Diagrams
   d. Icons

lab exercises

true/false

Circle the correct answer to the following questions.

1. A scenario report shows the results of all scenarios created for a worksheet.	True	False
2. Templates can contain graphics.	True	False
3. Cells you select as variables in Solver must be related through formulas on a worksheet.	True	False
4. A template is created by adding the .xlt extension to the file name.	True	False
5. Solver can produce a report about a solution.	True	False
6. When the worksheet is protected, the contents of unlocked cells cannot be changed.	True	False
7. A password prevents unauthorized users from viewing or saving changes to a workbook.	True	False
8. The vertical window arrangement displays windows side-by-side.	True	False
9. Whenever data in an external reference formula is changed in the source workbook, data in the linked cell in the destination workbook is automatically changed as well.	True	False
10. Diagrams are normally used to display numerical data.	True	False

fill-in

Complete the following statements by filling in the blanks with the correct key terms.

1. The ______________ is the workbook that the next action you take affects.
2. ___________________ is a tool used to perform what-if analyses to determine the effect of changing values in two or more cells.
3. The cells that contain the values to be changed when using Solver are called the ___________________.
4. To protect a worksheet from changes by an unauthorized person, you should include a ___________.
5. The cell containing a formula you want to solve is called the ______________.
6. You cannot save a workbook as a __________ by typing the file extension .xlt.
7. Once a(n) ___________ formula is entered in a worksheet the ___________ file is automatically updated if it is open.
8. A ____________ is a named set of input values used to help forecast the outcome of various possible actions.
9. Windows are ____________ when they are displayed one after the other in succession, across and down the screen.
10. The workbook that supplies data to another workbook is called the ______________.

rating system

★ Easy

★★ Moderate

★★★ Difficult

step-by-step

IronWorks Income Analysis ★

1. IronWorks creates unique wrought iron home accents. The accounting manager uses a six-month income worksheet that tracks the amount of income from different sources. The company would like to create a template that it can use each year to track the information. Your completed worksheets will be similar to the one shown here.

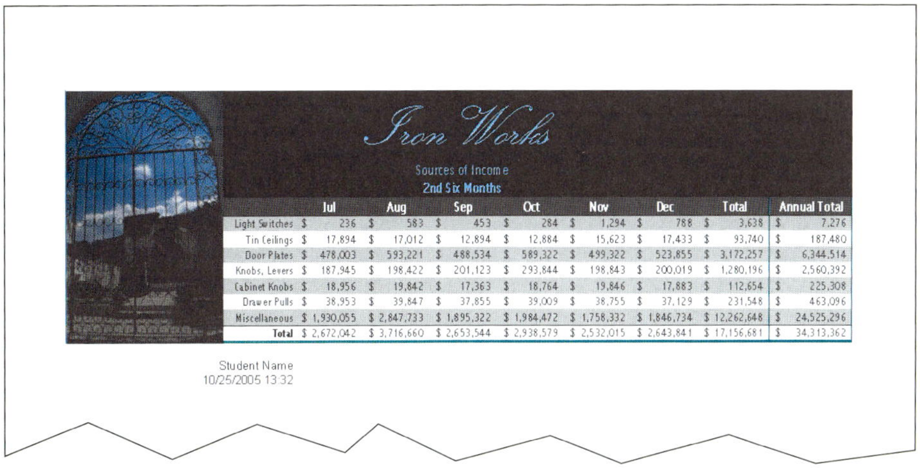
Iron Works

Sources of Income

2nd Six Months

	Jul	Aug	Sep	Oct	Nov	Dec	Total	Annual Total
Light Switches	$ 236	$ 583	$ 453	$ 284	$ 1,294	$ 788	$ 3,638	$ 7,276
Tin Ceilings	$ 17,894	$ 17,012	$ 12,894	$ 12,884	$ 15,623	$ 17,433	$ 93,740	$ 187,480
Door Plates	$ 478,003	$ 593,221	$ 488,534	$ 589,322	$ 499,322	$ 523,855	$ 3,172,257	$ 6,344,514
Knobs, Levers	$ 187,945	$ 198,422	$ 201,123	$ 293,844	$ 198,843	$ 200,019	$ 1,280,196	$ 2,560,392
Cabinet Knobs	$ 18,956	$ 19,842	$ 17,363	$ 18,764	$ 19,846	$ 17,883	$ 112,654	$ 225,308
Drawer Pulls	$ 38,953	$ 39,847	$ 37,855	$ 39,009	$ 38,755	$ 37,129	$ 231,548	$ 463,096
Miscellaneous	$ 1,930,055	$ 2,847,733	$ 1,895,322	$ 1,984,472	$ 1,758,332	$ 1,846,734	$ 12,262,648	$ 24,525,296
Total	$ 2,672,042	$ 3,716,660	$ 2,653,544	$ 2,938,579	$ 2,532,015	$ 2,643,841	$ 17,156,681	$ 34,313,362

Student Name
10/25/2005 13:32

a. Open the file ex04_IronWorks Income.

b. Make a copy of Sheet1. Rename Sheet1 **First Six Months** and Sheet 1(2) **Second Six Months**. Delete Sheet2 and Sheet3.

c. Modify the month column labels in the Second Six Months sheet to reflect the last six months of the year. Change the title of the sheet in cell A3 to **2nd Six Months**.

d. Add the column label **Annual Total** in cell I4. AutoFit the column. Enter formulas in the Annual total column to calculate the totals for the year.

e. Extend the worksheet formatting to the new column. Re-center the worksheet titles.

f. Enter your name and the current date using the NOW function in cells A15 and A16, respectively, of both sheets in the open book.

g. Select both sheets. Select cell A3 and cells B5 through G11 and unlock the cells. Deselect the selection. Ungroup the worksheets. Protect both worksheets.

h. Move to cell B5 of the First Six Months sheet.

i. Preview the workbook. Center the worksheets horizontally. Print the Second Six Months worksheet in landscape orientation, each on a single page.

j. Save the workbook as IronWorks Income1.

k. Delete the values in cells B5 through G11 on both worksheets. Save the workbook as a template with the name IronWorks Income. Close the workbook.

Art Department Expense Projections ★ ★

2. The College of Fine Arts would like to use the data it collected to do some analysis for the coming year. It would like to remodel one of the art galleries and purchase new equipment for another, but it is concerned about the rising costs of utilities. Your completed scenario summary should be similar to the example shown.

Student Name

Scenario Summary 10/25/2005 13:36		Current Values:	Worst Case	Most Likely	Best Case
Changing Cells:					
	Harry Wood Electricity	1,020.00	1,244.67	1,132.33	1,020.00
	Northlight electricity	1,550.00	1,774.67	1,662.33	1,550.00
	Step Electricity	800.00	1,024.67	912.33	800.00
Result Cells:					
	Total Costs--Harry Wood	$ 41,765.00	$ 41,989.67	$ 41,877.33	$ 41,765.00
	Total Costs--Northlight	$ 47,655.00	$ 47,879.67	$ 47,767.33	$ 47,655.00
	Total Costs--Step	$ 1,120.00	$ 1,344.67	$ 1,232.33	$ 1,120.00

a. Open the file ex04_Art Department.

b. The college expects an increase in total electricity costs for next year. They have determined that the Worst Case would be $4,044 (20 percent increase). Use Solver to calculate the electricity cost for each gallery. Save the results as a scenario and restore the original values.

c. The Most Likely Case will be $3,707 (10 percent increase). Use Solver to determine the costs for each gallery. Save the results as a scenario and restore the original values.

d. Add a scenario using the original values as the Best Case. Add comments to each of the scenarios.

e. Create a Scenario Summary for the electricity expenses. Delete the notes below the summary table. Delete the cell references and replace them with the names of the galleries. Size column C to fully display the gallery names.

f. Delete Sheet2 and Sheet3. Rename Sheet1 **Budget**. Include your name in a custom header on both sheets. Insert the current date in cell B3 using the NOW function of the Scenario Summary. Protect the worksheet.

g. Save the workbook as Art Department. Print the Scenario Summary in landscape orientation.

Adventure Travel Tours Revenue Analysis ★ ★

3. Adventure Travel Tours has begun a new marketing program that emphasizes the tour packages. It expects this campaign to increase the annual income earned in this division by as much as 15 percent over last year's earnings. You have been asked to create a Scenario Summary that analyzes quarterly profits in three scenarios. The company would also like to create a template to allow easy analysis of next year's performance. Your completed worksheets should be similar to the one shown here.

Student Name [Current Date]

Adventure Travel
Projected Annual Sources of Income

	1st Qtr	2nd Qtr	3rd Qtr	4th Qtr	Total
Car Rentals	$ 124,650	$ 124,875	$ 126,500	$ 129,145	$ 505,170
Airlines	$ 236,466	$ 238,368	$ 241,461	$ 246,856	$ 963,151
Tour Packages	$ 1,125,530	$ 1,350,655	$ 1,500,675	$ 1,755,850	$ 5,732,710
Hotels	$ 550,000	$ 550,545	$ 595,655	$ 605,115	$ 2,301,315
Total	$ 2,036,646	$ 2,264,443	$ 2,464,291	$ 2,736,966	$ 9,502,346

a. Open the file ex04_Travel Analysis.

b. Make a copy of Sheet1. Rename Sheet1 **Yearly Income** and Sheet1(2) **Projected Income**.

c. Delete the other blank sheets from the workbook.

d. Change the subtitle of the Projected Income Sheet to **Projected Annual Sources of Income**.

e. The company expects to see the total profit margin remain $917,287 in the Airlines category. They have determined that Worst Case Airlines revenue would be $871,423 (95 percent). The Best Case scenario puts the profits at $963,151 (5 percent increase). Use Solver to calculate the quarterly profits needed to achieve these goals in the Projected Income sheet. Create a scenario for each case using the values you found with Solver with the appropriate title and comments and restore the original values.

f. Create a Scenario Summary for the total airline revenue. Delete the notes below the summary table. Delete the cell references and replace them with the names of the quarters ($B$6=First Quarter).

g. Add the worksheet title **Airline Revenue Scenarios** in cell B2. Insert the current date in cell B3 using the NOW function.

h. Move the Summary worksheet to the third tab position. Include your name and the date in a custom header on all sheets. Save the workbook as Air Revenue Analysis.

i. Delete the values in the Projected Income and Yearly Income sheets. Unlock the appropriate cells and protect the worksheet. Save the workbook as a template named ATT Projected Income.

j. Print the workbook with the best-case values showing centered horizontally in landscape orientation.

Book Ends Financial Projections ★★★

4. Dennis Ma owns and operates Book Ends, an independent bookstore. He is reviewing his quarterly sales and is preparing his projections for the fourth quarter. He will need to review the previous year's totals to make his projections. Your completed sheets and scenario summary should be similar to those shown here.

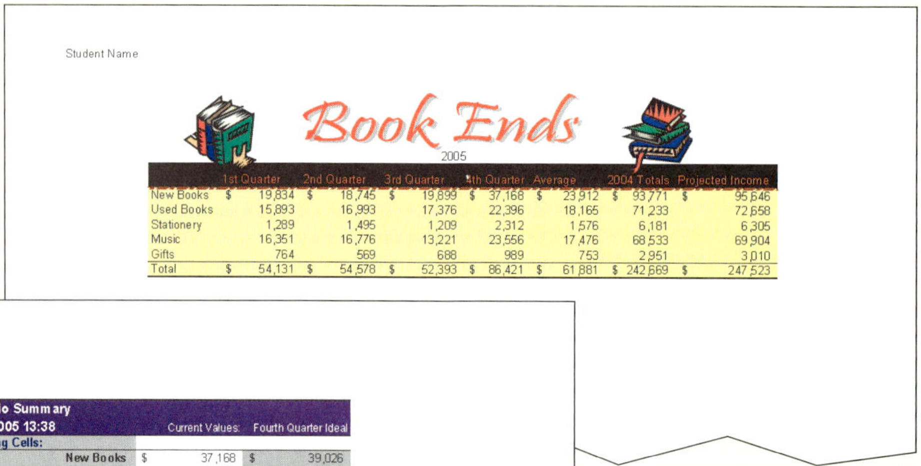
Student Name

Book Ends

2005

	1st Quarter	2nd Quarter	3rd Quarter	4th Quarter	Average	2004 Totals	Projected Income
New Books	$ 19,834	$ 18,745	$ 19,899	$ 37,168	$ 23,912	$ 93,771	$ 95,646
Used Books	15,893	16,993	17,376	22,396	18,165	71,233	72,658
Stationery	1,289	1,495	1,209	2,312	1,576	6,181	6,305
Music	16,351	16,776	13,221	23,556	17,476	68,533	69,904
Gifts	764	569	688	989	753	2,951	3,010
Total	$ 54,131	$ 54,578	$ 52,393	$ 86,421	$ 61,881	$ 242,669	$ 247,523

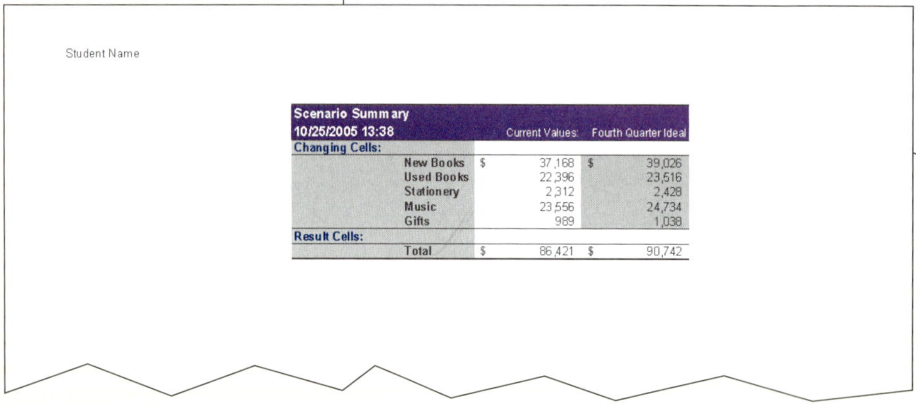
Student Name

Scenario Summary 10/25/2005 13:38		Current Values:	Fourth Quarter Ideal
Changing Cells:			
	New Books	$ 37,168	$ 39,026
	Used Books	22,396	23,516
	Stationery	2,312	2,428
	Music	23,556	24,734
	Gifts	989	1,038
Result Cells:			
	Total	$ 86,421	$ 90,742

a. Start Excel 2003 and open the file ex04_Book Ends. Change the name of Sheet1 to **2005**. Delete the blank sheets.

b. Insert formulas in columns F and H to calculate the average quarterly sales and yearly totals in column F and H, respectively.

c. Open the file ex04_Book Ends 2004. Paste links to the total values in column G to column G of the Book Ends 2005 Financial Analysis.

d. Dennis would like to project the income for the fourth quarter so he can see a 2 percent increase in yearly sales totals over the 2004 values. Use Solver to calculate the totals needed to see the following increases in the projected income values:

New Books	**$95,646**
Used Books	**$72,658**
Stationery	**$6,305**
Music	**$69,904**
Gifts	**$3,010**

e. Dennis is planning a new marketing campaign he hopes will increase sales by 5 percent. Using the new fourth quarter sales goals shown below, create a scenario called **Fourth Quarter Ideal**. Add the following comment: **Created by [Your Name] on [Date]—5% Sales Increase**.

New Books	**$39,026**
Used Books	**$23,516**

Stationery **$2,428**

Music **$24,734**

Gifts **$1,038**

f. Create a Scenario Summary displaying the results for cell E10. Delete the note below the summary report. Change the cell references to appropriate labels.

g. Enter your name in the header of both sheets. Enter a function to display the current date in cell B3 of the Scenario Summary.

h. Save the workbook as Book Ends 2005.

i. Print the Scenario Summary worksheet and the updated worksheet centered horizontally in landscape orientation.

j. Delete the Scenario Summary sheet. Delete the values in cells B5 through E9 and G5 to G9. Unlock the same cells. Protect the sheet. Save the workbook as a template named Book Ends Analysis Template.

Animal Rescue Foundation Contributions ★★★

5. The Animal Rescue Foundation, a nonprofit animal rescue agency, relies on donations to cover all its expenses. You would like to do some analysis on the data and project the amount that will be needed for next year based on scenarios that the committee feels are likely. Your completed income analysis will be similar to the one shown here.

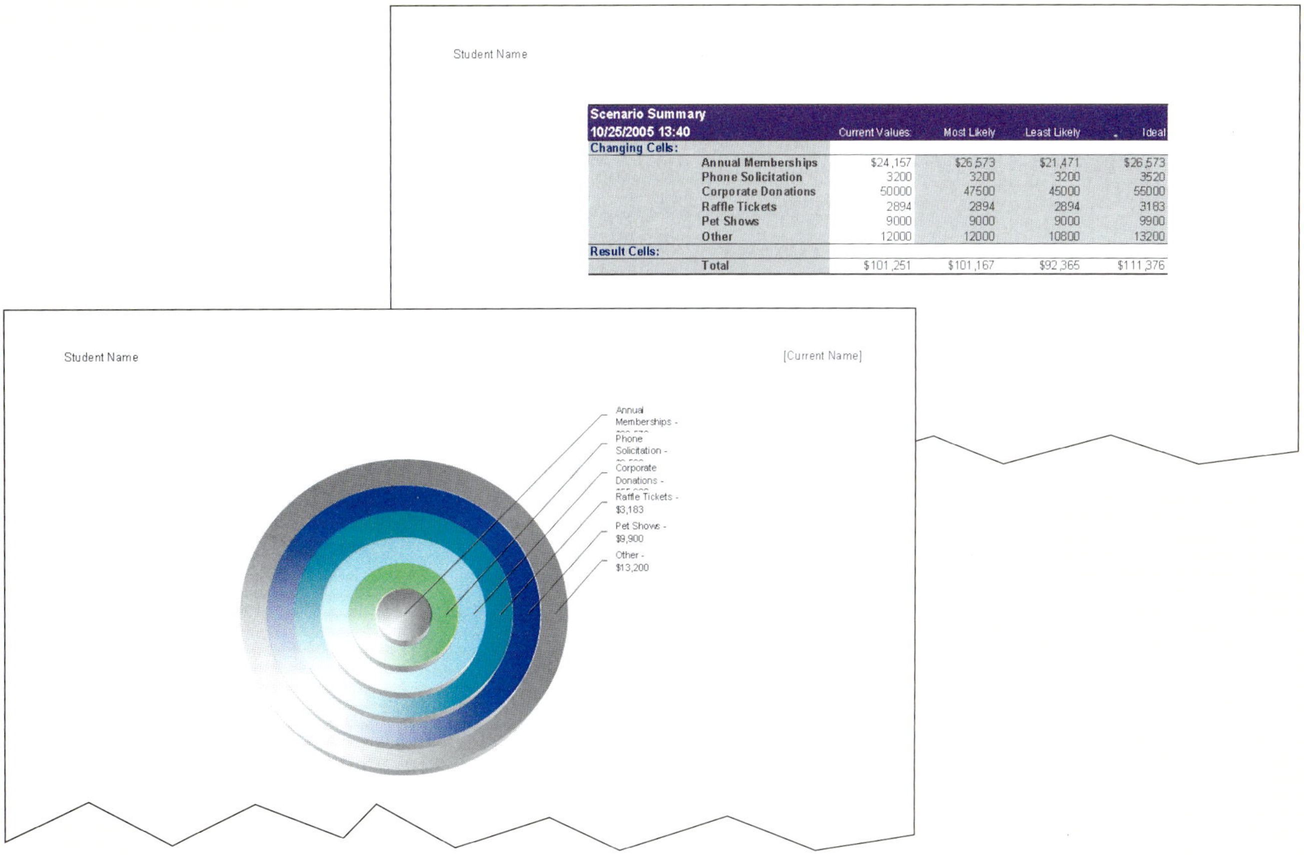
Student Name

Scenario Summary 10/25/2005 13:40		Current Values:	Most Likely	Least Likely	Ideal
Changing Cells:					
	Annual Memberships	$24,157	$26,573	$21,471	$26,573
	Phone Solicitation	3200	3200	3200	3520
	Corporate Donations	50000	47500	45000	55000
	Raffle Tickets	2894	2894	2894	3183
	Pet Shows	9000	9000	9000	9900
	Other	12000	12000	10800	13200
Result Cells:					
	Total	$101,251	$101,167	$92,365	$111,376

a. Open the file ex04_ARF Contributions to see last year's income. Save the file as ARF Contributions Reviewed.

b. Copy the Fall-Winter sheet to a new workbook. Rename the tab for the new sheet **Analysis**. Delete the extra sheets if necessary. Delete column H. Adjust the formatting as needed.

c. Insert a new row above row 5. Adjust the title as needed to add a subtitle. Merge cells A5 through G5 when you center the new title **Analysis and Projections**.

d. Enter the labels **2003 Income**, **5% Increase, 10% Increase**, **10% Decrease, 5% Decrease**, and **Current Scenario** in cells B6 through G6. Adjust the size of the columns to fully display the labels.

e. Select cells H6 through H11 of the Fall-Winter sheet in the ARF Contributions Reviewed file. Create a link to this data in cells B7 through B12 of the new worksheet. Close the ARF Contributions Reviewed workbook.

f. Delete the values in cells C7 through G12.

g. Use the number in cell B7 to calculate the values for cells C7 through F7. Copy the formulas down the columns to row 11. (Hint: Cell C7 should contain the formula =B7*1.05, cell F7 should contain the formula =B7*.95.)

h. Copy and paste just the values from column B to column G.

i. Create the following scenarios using cells G7 through G12 as the changing cells and the following calculated values in the worksheet:

Most Likely

Annual Memberships	10% increase
Phone Solicitation	Current
Corporate Donations	5% decrease
Raffle Tickets	Current
Pet Shows	Current
Other	Current

Least Likely

Annual Memberships	10% decrease
Phone Solicitation	Current
Corporate Donations	10% decrease
Raffle Tickets	Current
Pet Shows	Current
Other	10% decrease

Ideal

Annual Memberships	10% increase
Phone Solicitation	10% increase
Corporate Donations	10% increase
Raffle Tickets	10% increase
Pet Shows	10% increase
Other	10% increase

j. Create a Scenario Summary displaying the results for cell G13. Delete the note below the summary report. Change the cell references to appropriate labels.

k. Enter your name in the header of the sheet. Enter a function to display the current date in cell B3 of the Scenario Summary.

l. Insert a new sheet called **Target**. Insert a Target Diagram and add three shapes. Include the labels and values for the 10 percent overall increase in the text placeholders. Add an AutoFormat of your choice to the diagram. Adjust the font and placement of the diagram as needed.

m. Add your name to the worksheets in a custom header. Print the Scenario Summary and diagram worksheets centered horizontally in landscape orientation.

n. Delete the Scenario Summary and Target sheets. Delete the values in cells B7:B12 and G7:G12. Unlock the cells in columns B and G. Protect the sheet. Save the sheet as ARF Analysis Template.

on your own

Games Growth Projections ★

1. You have been hired as a consultant by a video game manufacturer to help the company project expected growth over the next five years based on its research. Assume that the company currently has 35 percent of the market. The current number of customers is 300,500, and available research estimates an increase of 2 percent in year 2; 4 percent in year 3; 7 percent in year 4; and 12 percent in year 5. Create a worksheet that shows the current customer figure and the projected increases for the next five years. Use these numbers to create revenue figures based on a yearly profit of $175 per customer. Create scenarios with the calculated values as the baseline, a 2 percent decrease in customers and revenue per year as the worst case, and an additional 4 percent increase per year as the best case. Create a Scenario Summary report. Enter your name and the current date in all the worksheets. Save the file as Video Game Projections. Print the worksheets.

Spring Break Scenarios ★★

2. Now that your personal budget is complete, you have decided to do some analysis to determine whether a trip during spring semester break is possible. Use the budget you created in Lab 3, On Your Own exercise 1, and evaluate your yearly budget to determine whether you will have enough money to pay for a spring break trip next year. Use Solver to determine the number of hours you need to work to earn enough money for the trip in addition to the rest of your expenses. Create three scenarios: one showing the current values, a second showing a 5 percent decrease in entertainment expenses, and a third showing a decrease in one of your other expenses. Create a Scenario Summary. Enter your name and the current date in a header for all the worksheets. Save the file as Spring Break Analysis. Print the worksheets.

Small Business Expansion Projections ★★

3. You believe the small business you created in Lab 3, On Your Own exercise 5 could see greater profits with an additional location. Use the information you gathered in the previous workbook and Solver to determine what variables would increase profits by 25 percent. Create three scenarios to determine the effects of a 5 percent, 10 percent, and 15 percent increase in profits in each quarter on the total yearly profits. Create a Scenario Summary. Save your file as Expansion Projections. Print the summary.

Stock Portfolio Analysis ★ ★ ★

4. You have been studying the stock market in your economics class and would like to evaluate a portfolio of four different stocks. Using the Web or other news source, choose four stocks listed on the New York Stock Exchange and enter the following information about each stock in separate sheets of a workbook: stock exchange number, cost per share, brokerage fee, total cost per share, price/earnings ratio, dividend return percentage, and week-ending price. Track your stocks (or use historical values) for a month. Create scenarios of good, bad, and expected market changes in the current month-ending price over the next month. Enter your name and the current date in headers in the worksheets. Save the file as Stock Analysis. Print the workbook.

Using Excel Templates ★ ★ ★

5. You would like to analyze the costs of a new car loan. Use the Excel Loan Amortization template and conduct research into new car prices and loan rates. Insert a new sheet and do a cost comparison of several cars you have analyzed. Create scenarios for different loan rates and create a Scenario Summary using the techniques you learned in the lab. Save the file as New Car Loan. Print the workbook. Save your sheet as a template named Loan Analysis Template, with the values removed.

Using Data Tables, Creating Macros, and Designing Onscreen Forms

LAB 5

Objectives

After you have read this chapter, you should be able to:

1. Use the PMT function.
2. Research information on the Web.
3. Create a data table.
4. Automatically format a worksheet.
5. Add text boxes and arrows.
6. Create a command button control.
7. Create a macro with the Macro Recorder.
8. Create a form.
9. Name cell references.
10. Use the IF function.
11. Create a combo box control.
12. Add cell comments.

Case Study

Downtown Internet Café

Evan, the owner of the Downtown Internet Café, has been impressed with your use of Office Excel 2003 to forecast the café's future for the next two years. Now, he has two new projects that he wants you to complete.

First, he is considering the purchase of a new espresso machine to replace the current machine, which is leased. Evan plans to finance the purchase and would like you to evaluate several different loan options. You will create a loan analysis spreadsheet that incorporates Office Excel's PMT function, macros, and Data Table feature.

Next, Evan would like you to develop a spreadsheet to calculate and record customer Bonus Dollars. Bonus Dollars are awarded to customers based on their monthly Internet connection-time usage and can be redeemed for more connection time or other merchandise at the café. They are an incentive for customers to extend their stay at the café and, of course, spend more money while they're there. You will create an onscreen form to calculate and record customer Bonus Dollars. The completed loan analysis and Bonus Dollars form are shown on the opposite page.

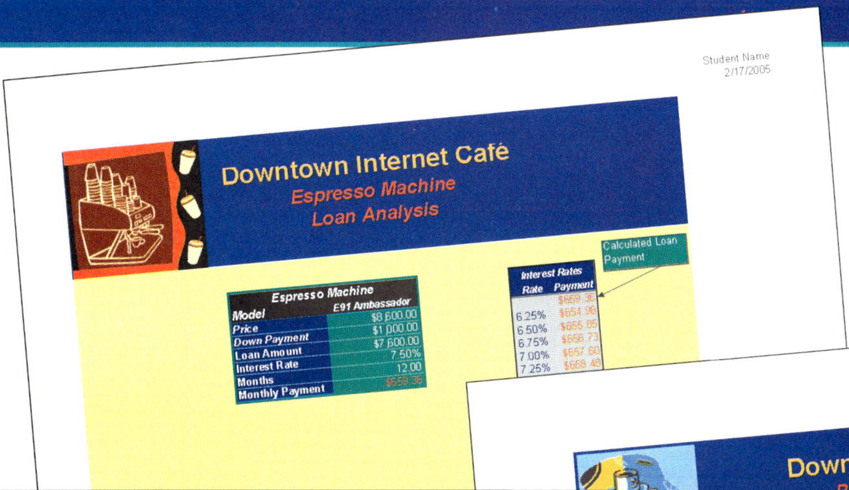

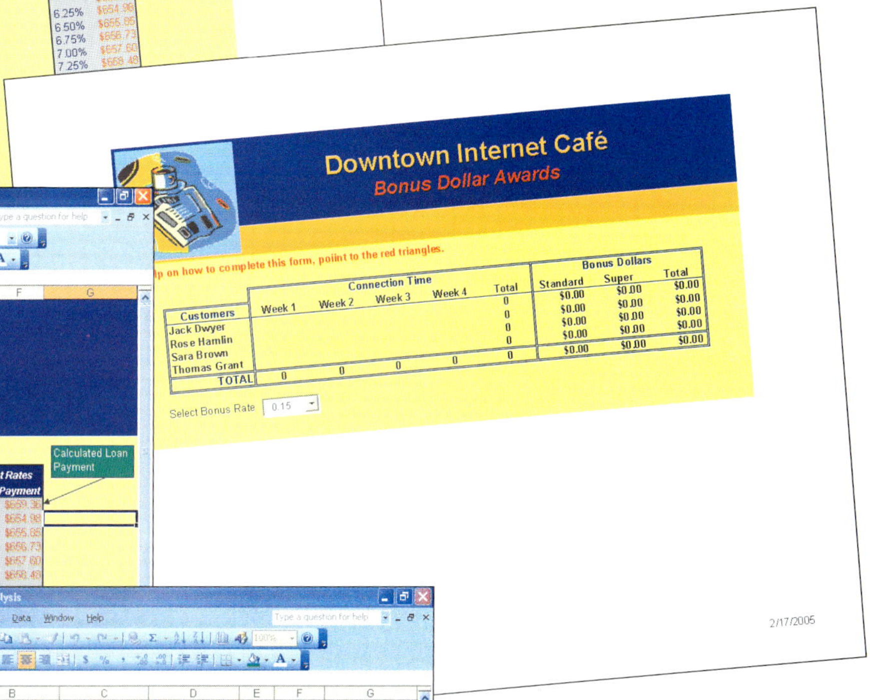

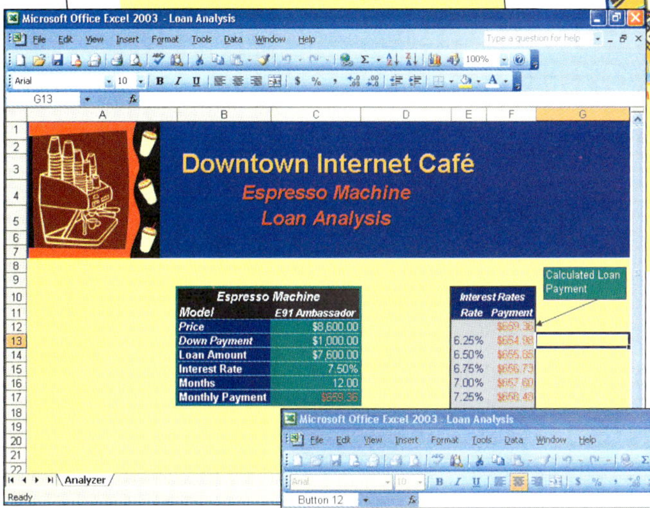

Using a data table is another method to perform what-if analysis.

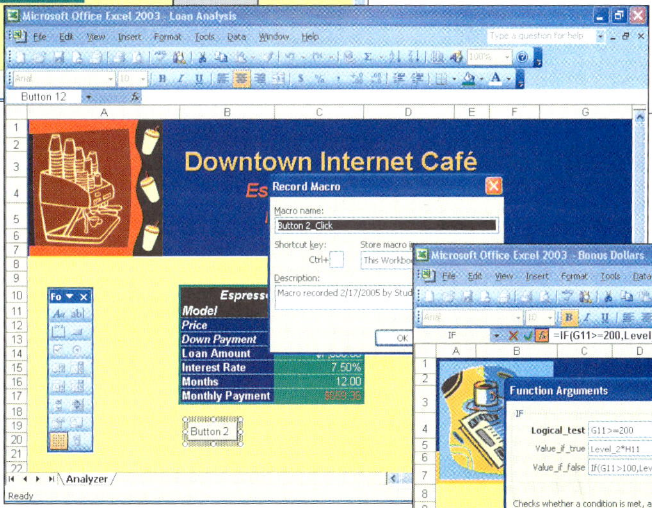

Macros automate repetitive tasks, saving both time and effort.

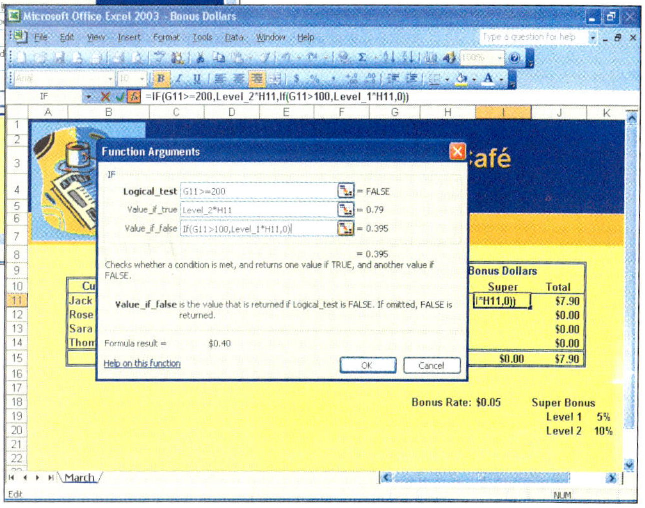

Using an IF function allows different calculations to be performed if certain conditions are met.

Concept Preview

The following concepts will be introduced in this lab:

1. **Data Table** A data table is a range of cells that is used to quickly calculate multiple what-if versions in one operation and to show the results of all together in the worksheet.
2. **Macro** A macro is a series of keystrokes and commands that are stored as instructions in a unit or module of Microsoft Visual Basic, a programming language.
3. **Control** Controls are graphic objects that are designed to help the user interact with the worksheet.
4. **Macro Recorder** The Macro Recorder automatically creates a macro by recording a series of actions as macro commands.
5. **Form** A form is a formatted worksheet with blank spaces that can be filled in online on an individual computer or on a network, or printed and completed on paper
6. **IF Function** The IF function checks to see if certain conditions are met and then takes action based on the results of the check.
7. **Comment** Comments are notes attached to cells that can be used to clarify the meaning of the cell contents, provide documentation, or ask a question.

Calculating a Loan Payment

Evan has read several reviews in the *Tea and Coffee Trade Journal* and looked at several different models of commercial espresso makers at restaurant supply stores. He is still undecided about the model to purchase and wants to see an analysis of what the monthly loan payments would be for different down payments, interest rates, and repayment periods for each kind.

Based on the information Evan has given you, you started a workbook for the loan analysis by entering some descriptive labels and formats in a worksheet. You will open the workbook file and continue to work on the loan analysis.

1 • **Start Office Excel 2003 and open the workbook file** ex05_Loan Analysis**.**

• **If necessary, maximize the application and worksheet windows.**

Your screen should be similar to Figure 5.1

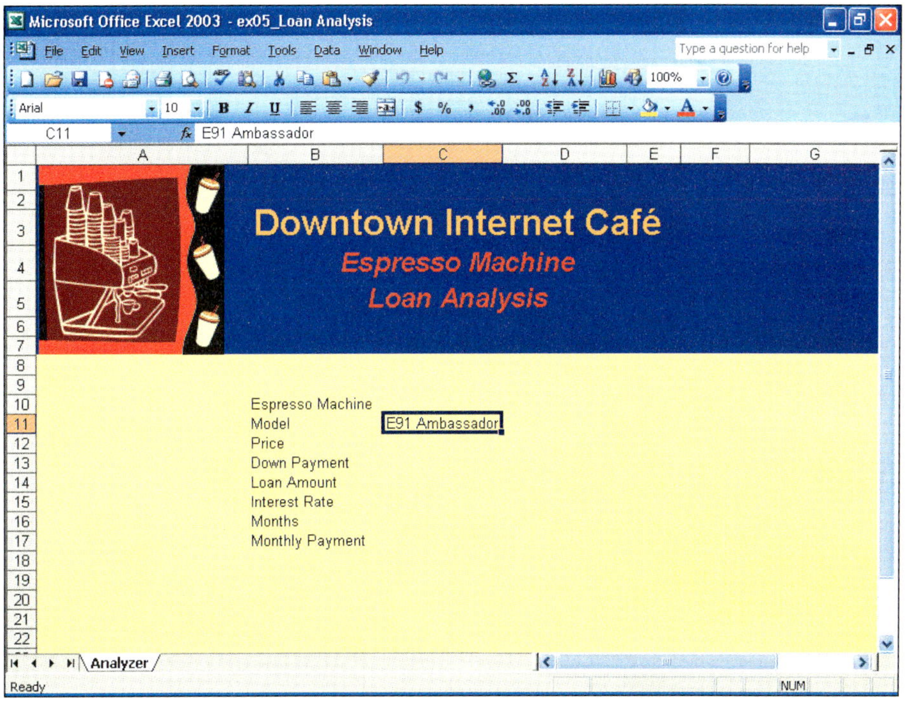

Figure 5.1

Much of the structure and formatting for the worksheet has already been completed. To continue to create the worksheet, you need to enter a formula to calculate the loan amount. The amount of the loan is the price of the item minus the down payment. Then you will enter the data for the first espresso machine Evan is considering, the E91 Ambassador, and he wants to repay the loan in monthly payments over a one-year period.

First you decide to calculate loan payments using a 7.25 percent loan rate.

2 • **In cell C14 enter the formula =C12-C13.**

• **In cell C12 enter 8600.**

• **In cell C13 enter 1000.**

• **In cell C15 enter .075.**

• **In cell C16 enter 12.**

Your screen should be similar to Figure 5.2

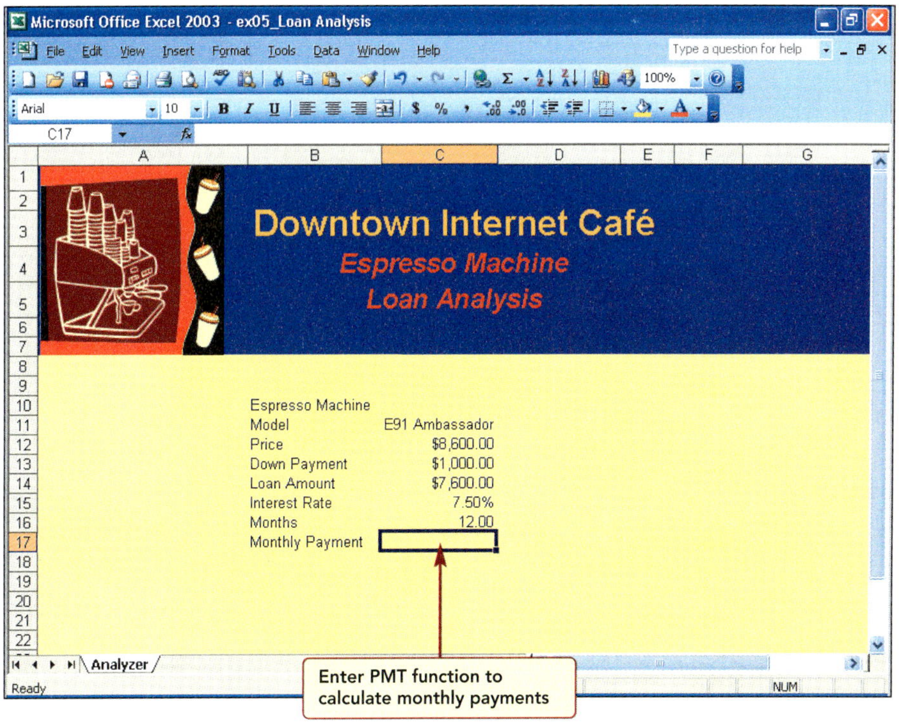

Figure 5.2

Using the PMT Function

The next thing that needs to be entered is the monthly payment. To calculate this value, you use the PMT function. The **PMT function** calculates a periodic payment on a loan. The value returned includes the loan amount and interest but no taxes, reserve payments, or fees sometimes associated with loans. The PMT function uses the following syntax:

Additional Information

When using the PMT function, it is important to use consistent units for specifying rate and nper.

PMT(rate, nper, pv)

This function contains three arguments: rate, nper, and pv. The rate argument is the interest rate of the loan. The nper argument is the total number of payments for the loan. The pv argument is the amount of the loan, also referred to as the principal or preset value.

The rate in the PMT function you will use to calculate the monthly loan payment for the espresso machine is the yearly interest rate (C15) divided by 12. This converts the yearly rate to a monthly rate. The nper argument is the length of the loan in months (C16). The pv argument is the loan amount in cell C14. As you enter the function, a ScreenTip will be displayed that shows you the arguments that are needed to complete the function.

Additional Information

If the loan payment was in years, you would need to multiply the value by 12 to calculate the number of monthly payments.

1. **In cell C17 enter the function =PMT(C15/12, C16,C14).**

Having Trouble?

You can use the Insert Function feature to help enter this function.

Your screen should be similar to Figure 5.3

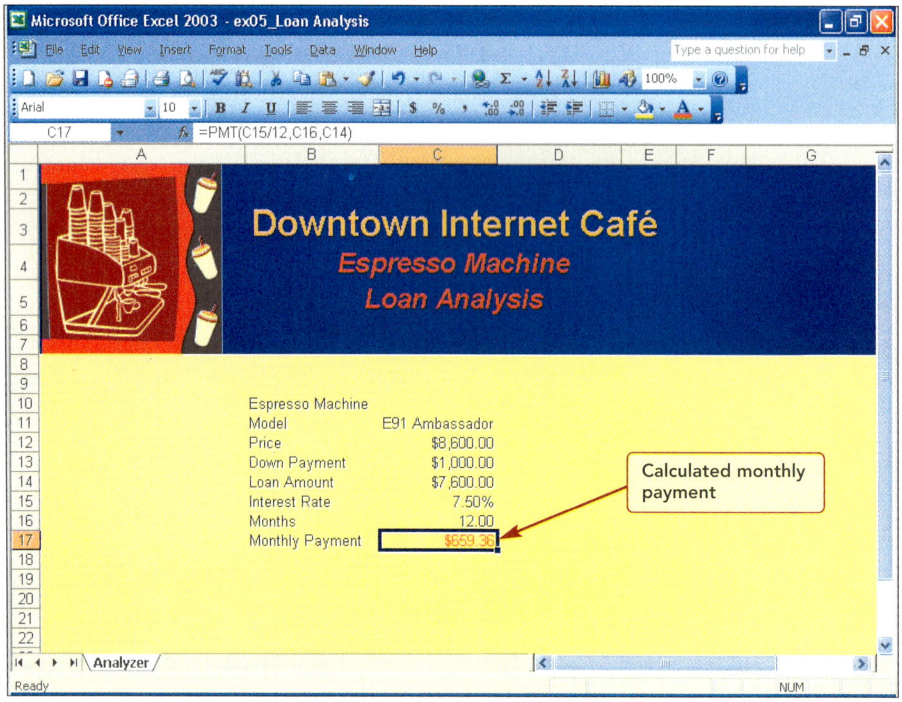

Figure 5.3

Excel calculates the monthly payment and displays it in cell C17 based on a 7.5 percent interest rate. Notice the payment value is displayed in red. This is because a payment is considered a negative value.

Researching Information on the Web

Evan has checked with a local bank for information on short-term, small-business loan rates. He found that for loans less than $25,000, the maximum interest rate must not exceed the prime rate plus 4.25 percent when maturity is less than 7 years. Prime rate is the lowest rate of interest on loans that is available from a bank set at a given time.

Before you can continue much further, you need to find out the current prime rate. You can do this quickly using the Research tool to research the prime rate on the Internet.

Note: You need an Internet connection, and the Online Services feature must be activated. Click Research Options in the Research task pane and select the services you want to access. If you do not have this feature available, continue to the next section.

1 Click Research.

Another Method

The menu equivalent is Tools/Research.

- **In the Search For text box, type prime rate.**
- **Select MSN Search from the Show Results From drop-down list box.**
- **If necessary, click Start Searching.**

Your screen should be similar to Figure 5.4

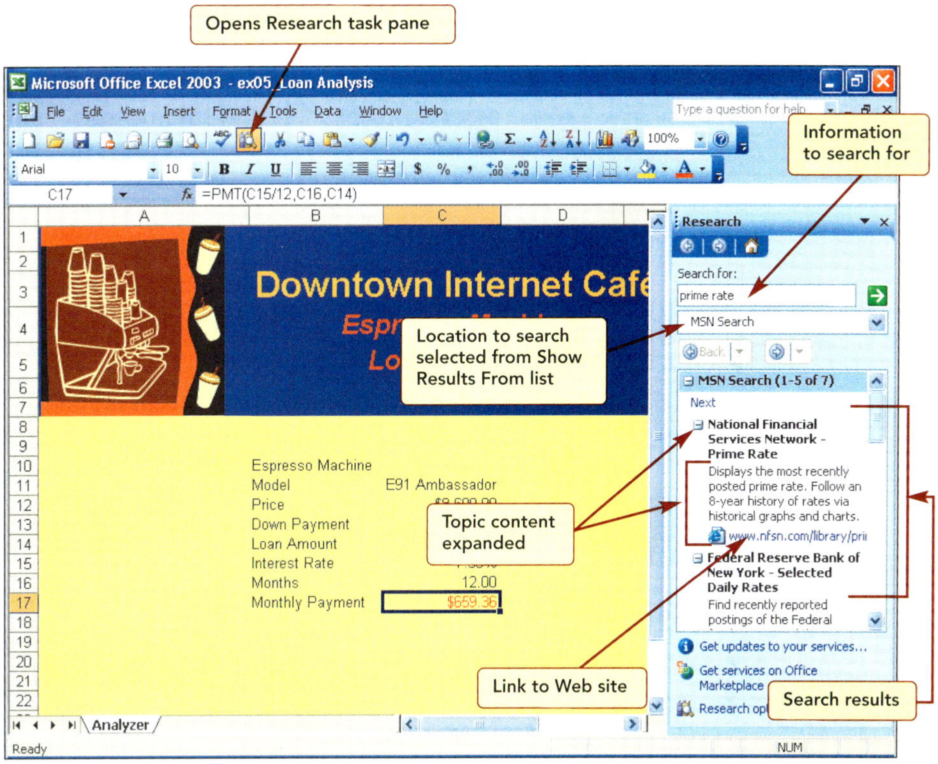

Figure 5.4

The Research task pane displays the first five Web sites that meet your search terms. You will locate the information about the National Financial Services Network Web site and then click on the link to that site.

2 If necessary, scroll the results list to locate the National Financial Services Network – Prime Rate topic and click on it to expand it.

Additional Information

If a topic is not expanded a ⊞ appears to the left of the topic heading. A ⊟ appears when the topic is expanded.

- Click the www.nfsn.com/library/prime.htm link.

Having Trouble?

If the National Financial Services topic is not available, select another of your choice. Then select the link at the bottom of the description. Your screen will display different information than in Figure 5.5, but it should include information about the current prime rate.

Your screen should be similar to Figure 5.5

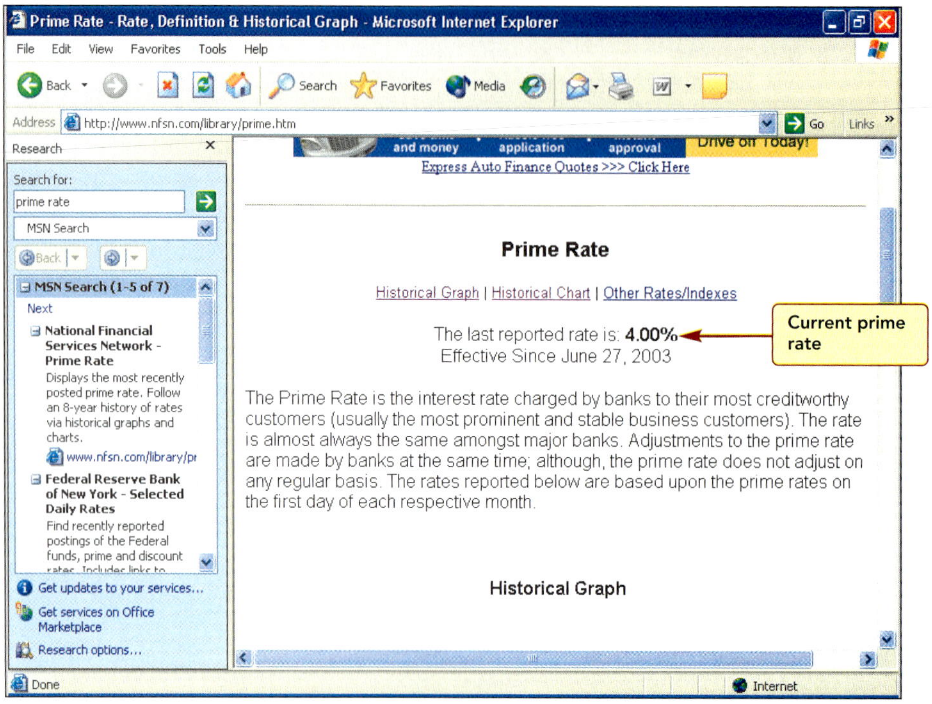

Figure 5.5

Having Trouble?

Because the prime rate changes over time, the rate shown on your screen is most likely different than the rate shown in Figure 5.5.

The browser program on your computer opens and displays the Web site for the selected page. The information you are looking for about the last reported prime rate is displayed. If your browser is Internet Explorer, the Research task pane is displayed along the left side of the screen to allow you to select and view other sites. Now that you know what the current prime rate is, you can continue to enter the information needed for the analysis.

3 Close the browser window.

- Close the Research task pane.

Additional Information

The text will base the following loan analysis using a maximum loan rate of 8.25 percent (4.00 Prime plus a maximum of 4.25%).

Now that you know what the prime rate is, you can expand the worksheet to evaluate the loan payments based on a range of possible loan rates.

Using a Data Table

Because interest rates will vary depending on which loan institution finances the purchase and when the loan is obtained, you want to set up a data table that shows the effect of different interest rates on the monthly loan payment amount.

Concept 1

Data Table

1 A **data table** is a range of cells that is used to quickly calculate multiple what-if versions in one operation and to show the results of all variations in the worksheet. Data tables perform a type of what-if analysis in which one or more variables are changed to see the effect on the formulas that include these variables.

Espresso Machine	
Model	*ES1500 Royal*
Price	$10,500.00
Down Payment	$1,000.00
Loan Amount	$9,500.00
Interest Rate	7.50%
Months	18.00
Monthly Payment	$559.67

One-variable Table *Varying Interest Rates Only* *Rate*	
	$559.67
6.25%	$554.28
6.50%	$555.35
6.75%	$556.43
7.00%	$557.51
7.25%	$558.59
7.50%	$559.67
7.75%	$560.75
8.00%	$561.83
8.25%	$562.92

Two-variable table *Varying Interest Rates and Length of Loan* *Rate*		*Months*	
$559.67	12	18	24
6.25%	$818.72	$554.28	$422.12
6.50%	$819.82	$555.35	$423.19
6.75%	$820.91	$556.43	$424.26
7.00%	$822.00	$557.51	$425.34
7.25%	$823.10	$558.59	$426.42
7.50%	$824.20	$559.67	$427.50
7.75%	$825.29	$560.75	$428.58
8.00%	$826.39	$561.83	$429.66
8.25%	$827.49	$562.92	$430.74

A **one-variable data table** can contain one or more formulas, and each formula refers to one input cell. An **input cell** is a cell in which a list of values is substituted to see the resulting effect on the related formulas. Input values can be listed down a column (**column-oriented**) or across a row (**row-oriented**).

A **two-variable data table** uses only one formula that refers to two different input cells, one column-oriented and one row-oriented. The purpose of this table is to show the resulting effect on the formula when the values in both of these cells are changed.

Since you are interested in seeing the effects of changing the interest rate only, you will create a one-variable data table. When designing a one-variable data table, the input values and formulas must be in adjacent rows or columns. First, you need to set up the data table in an unused portion of the worksheet by entering a title, column headings, and a series of interest rate percentages.

1. In cell E10 enter the title **Interest Rates**.
   - In cell E11 enter the column heading **Rate**, and in cell F11 enter **Payment**.
   - In cell E13 enter **6.25%** and in cell E14 enter **6.5%**.
   - Select the range E13 through E14 and drag the fill handle through cell E21.

Your screen should be similar to Figure 5.6

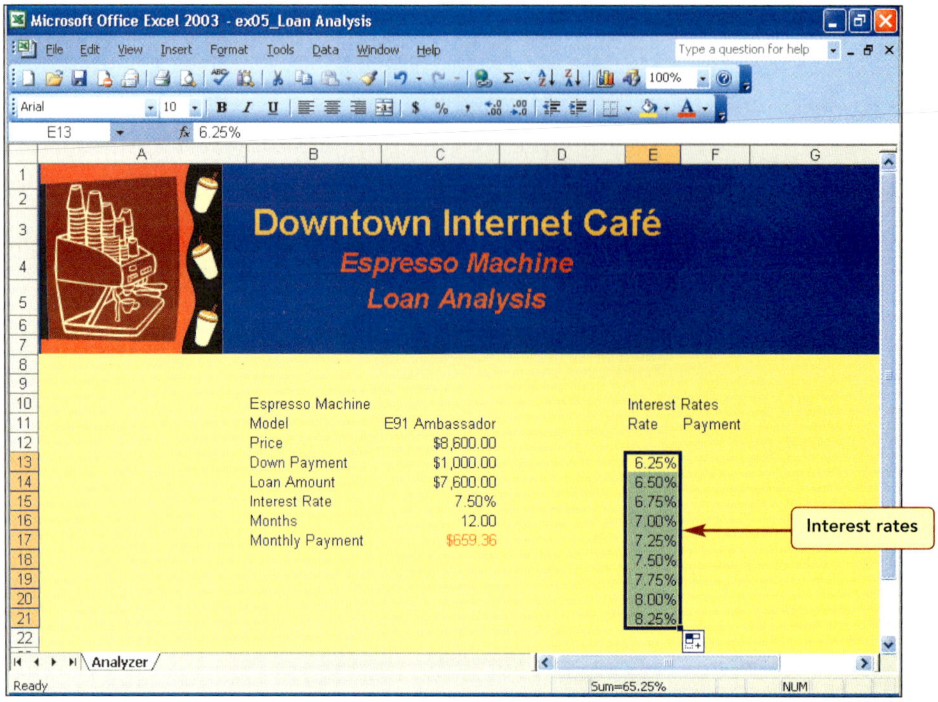

Figure 5.6

Dragging the fill handle filled column E with interest rates that range from 6.5 percent to 8.5 percent in 0.25 percent increments.

Next, you enter the monthly payment formula to be used in calculating the various payments. The formula is always entered in the row above the first input value and one cell to the right of the column of values. In this case, you will enter the formula in cell F12. You could copy this formula from the monthly payment cell in the loan analysis section of the worksheet. Instead, you will define the new formula as equal to that cell. This way, the data table formula will be automatically updated if the original formula (the one in the loan analysis section of the worksheet) is changed.

Additional Information

If the input values are listed across the row, the formula is entered in the column to the left of the first value and one cell below the row of values.

2 **In cell F12 enter =C17.**

Your screen should be similar to Figure 5.7

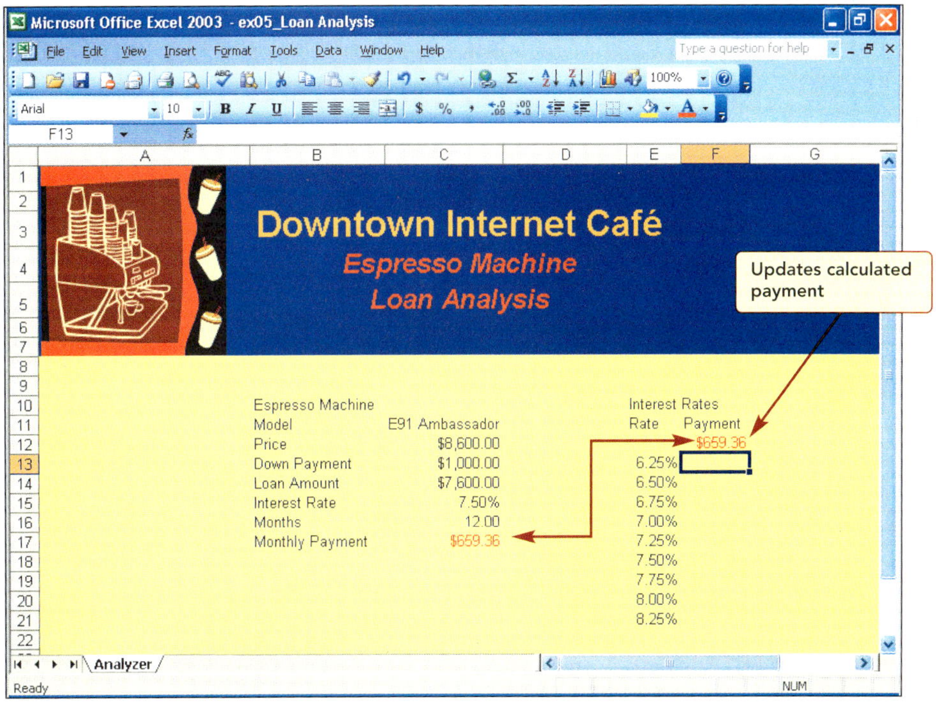

Figure 5.7

Finally, you need to define the range of cells that comprise the data table. The data table range consists of all cells except the ones containing the title and headings.

3 **Select the range E12 through F21.**

Choose Data/Table.

Your screen should be similar to Figure 5.8

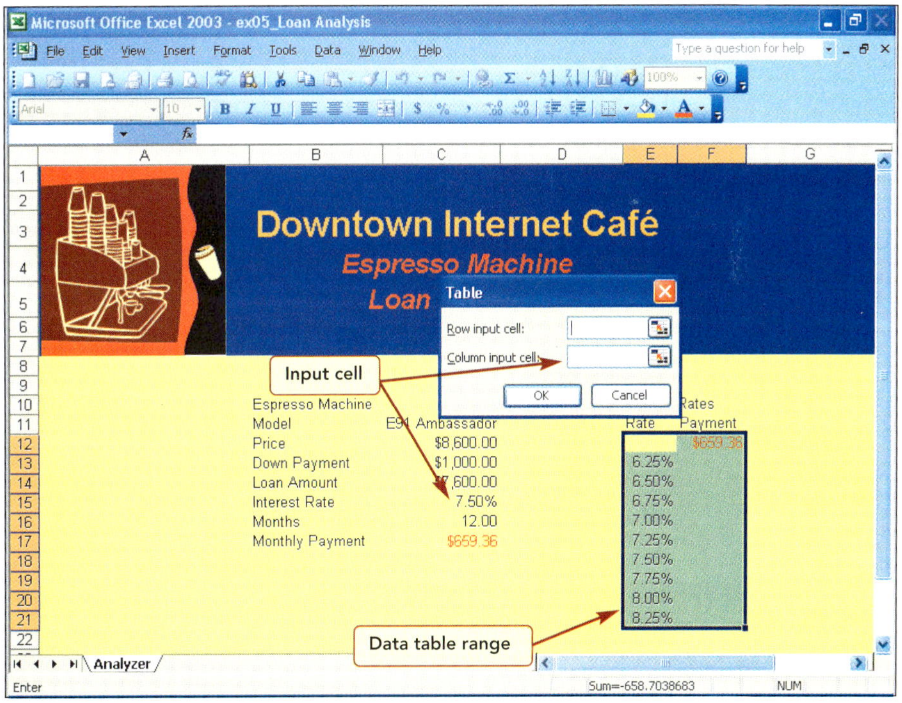

Figure 5.8

In the Table dialog box, you define the input cell in which values from the data table are substituted. Because the values in the data table are listed down a column, the input cell is entered as a Column Input Cell. In this case, the input cell is cell C15, the Interest Rate cell from the loan analysis section of the worksheet.

4 **Enter C15 in the Column Input Cell text box.**

Another Method

You can also define the input cell by reducing the dialog box and selecting the input cell in the worksheet.

- **Click** OK.
- **Deselect the table.**

Your screen should be similar to Figure 5.9

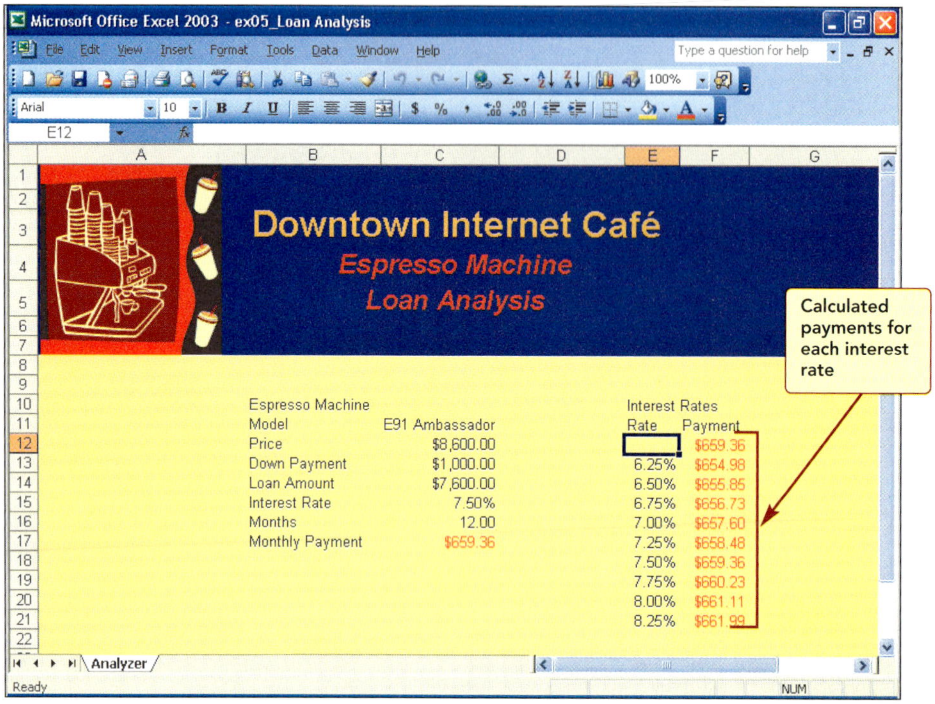

Figure 5.9

The data table shows the calculated monthly payments for each interest rate.

Automatically Formatting Worksheet Data

To quickly improve the appearance of the worksheet, you will apply an AutoFormat to the worksheet data and data table. An AutoFormat can be applied to a range of cells that has distinct elements, such as row and column labels, summary data and detail information. These AutoFormats consist of a combination of number formats, fonts and attributes, colors, patterns, borders, frames, and alignment settings.

Applying an AutoFormat

To apply an AutoFormat, you first specify the range you want affected by the formatting. In this case, you want to apply an AutoFormat to cells B10 through C17. You can select the range or you can let Excel select the range for you. To have Excel automatically select the range, the cell selector must be on any cell in the range. Excel determines that the range you want to AutoFormat is the range of cells that includes the active cell and is surrounded by blank cells.

1 Move to any cell in the worksheet range B10 through C17.

Choose Format/AutoFormat.

Your screen should be similar to Figure 5.10

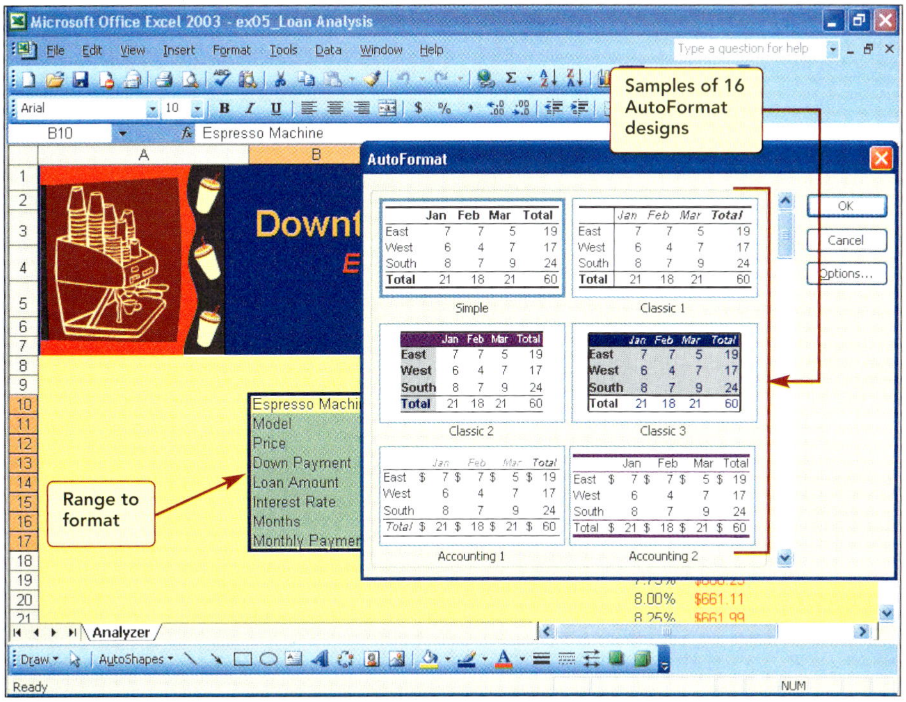

Figure 5.10

Additional Information

Use the None AutoFormat (located at the bottom of the list) to remove an existing AutoFormat.

The range B10 through C17 is correctly selected as the range to format. The AutoFormat dialog box displays samples of the 16 different format designs with the names assigned to the design below the sample.

2 Scroll the list to see all the formats.

Select the Colorful 1 AutoFormat.

Click OK.

Your screen should be similar to Figure 5.11

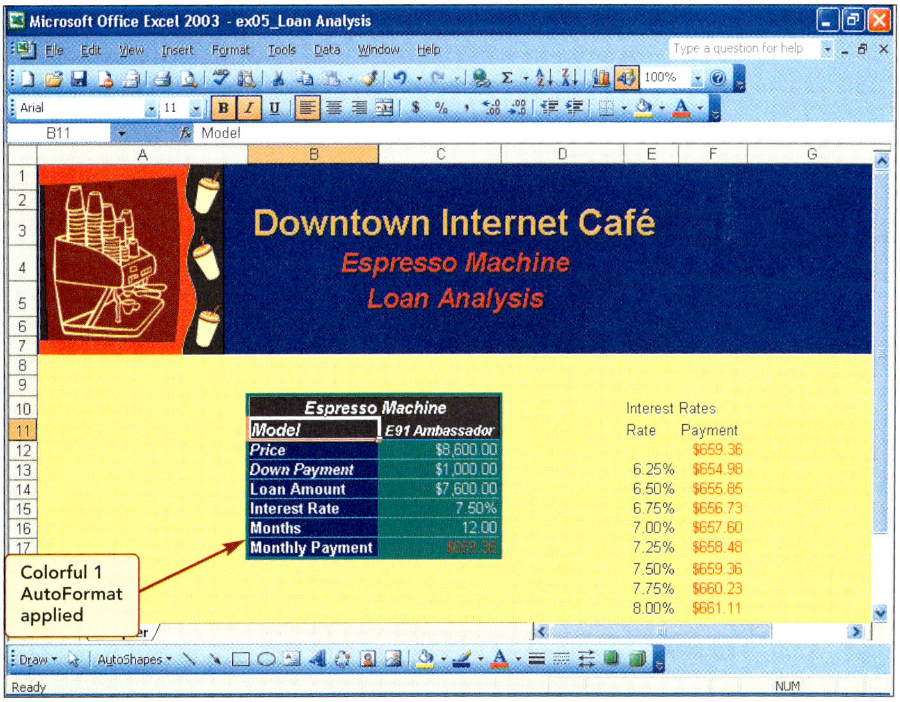

Figure 5.11

The Colorful 1 AutoFormat has been applied to the worksheet range. This format includes border lines, fill and font colors, and adjustment of column widths to fit the entries in the selected range.

3 Format the data table in cells E10 through F21 to the Classic 3 AutoFormat.

Your screen should be similar to Figure 5.12

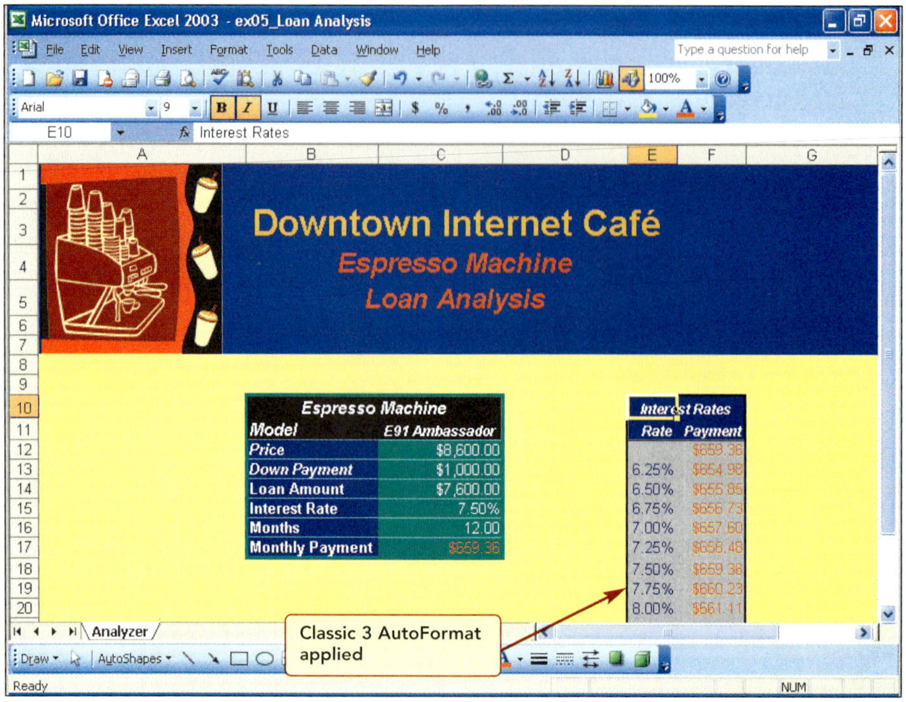

Figure 5.12

Adding a Text Box and Arrow

To emphasize the first value in the data table as the value calculated by the worksheet, you will add a text box that identifies the calculated monthly payment. A **text box** is a graphic object that displays text.

1

- If necessary, click Drawing to display the Drawing toolbar.
- Click Text Box.
- Click in column G to the right of the data table.
- Drag the right corner sizing handle down and to the right to create a box slightly less than the width of column G and two cells high.
- Click inside the text box to allow entry of text in the box.
- Type **Calculated Loan Payment**.

Having Trouble?

If the box is not large enough to fully display the text on two lines, use the sizing handles to adjust the size again.

Your screen should be similar to Figure 5.13

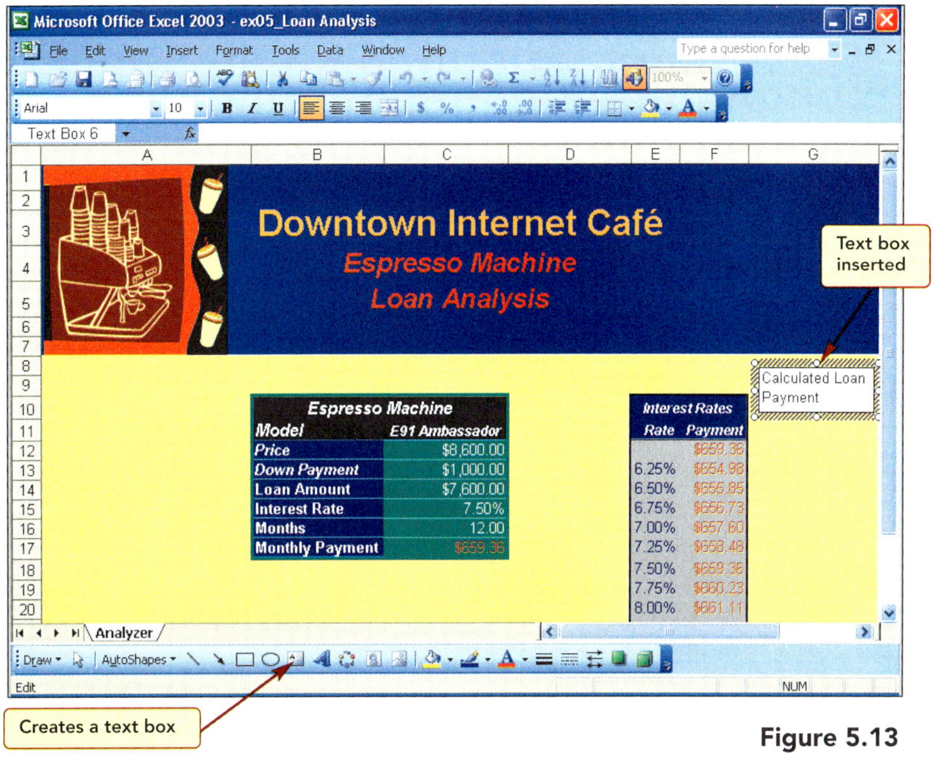

Figure 5.13

Additional Information

To start a new line inside the text box, press ←Enter.

As you type, the text in the box wraps within the box to the next line. The text box can be enhanced using many of the features on the Drawing toolbar. You will add a background fill color, border line color, and text color.

2 Click on the text box border to select the entire text box object.

- Click Fill Color and select the teal color.

Having Trouble?

The name of the colors appears in a ScreenTip as you point to the color.

- Click Line Color and select black.
- Click Font Color and select white.

Your screen should be similar to Figure 5.14

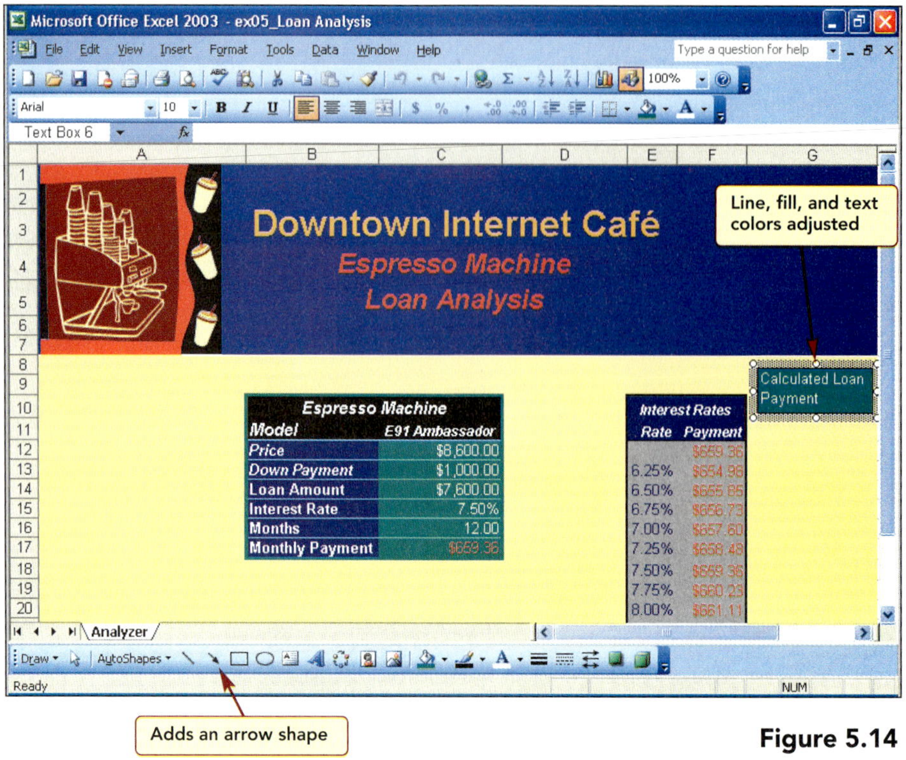

Figure 5.14

Finally, you will add an arrow from the text box to the value in cell F12.

3 If necessary, size and position the text box as in Figure 5.15.

Having Trouble?

Drag the text box border to move the object.

- Click Arrow.
- Draw an arrow by clicking on the bottom edge of the text box and dragging from the text box to the right edge of cell F12.
- Deselect the arrow.
- Close the Drawing toolbar.
- Save the workbook as Loan Analysis.

Your screen should be similar to Figure 5.15

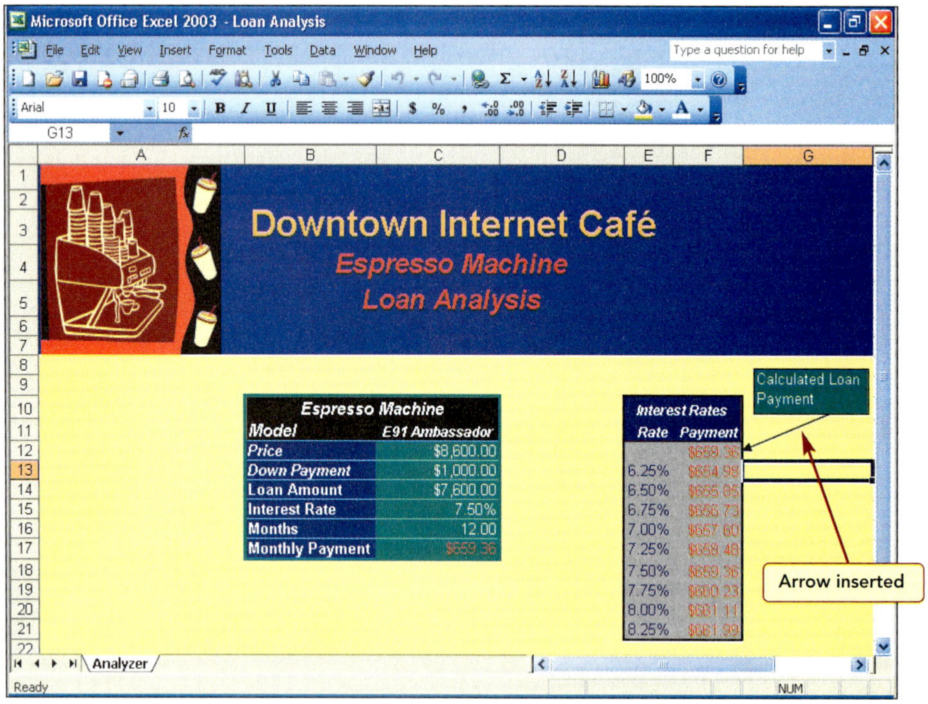

Figure 5.15

You have completed the loan analysis for the E91 Ambassador model espresso machine that Evan requested. Evan can now easily see what the monthly payment would be for a range of possible interest rates.

Automating Tasks with Macros

Evan is pleased with the worksheet you creeated, and would like to see the same loan analysis applied to other espresso machines he is considering. He also wants to use the worksheet to evaluate other potential purchases.

Each time you enter new product data, you plan to print the worksheet for Evan. Because you expect to use the worksheet frequently, you would like to create a macro to automate the printing process.

Concept 2

Macro

2 A **macro** is a series of keystrokes and commands that are stored as instructions in a unit or **module of** Microsoft Visual Basic, a programming language. When the macro is executed, or run, the stored actions are performed automatically. Macros are very useful for replacing a series of commands that are performed repeatedly. Instead of performing the same actions every time you need to perform a task, you use the macro, which performs the task automatically for you.

Some macros are very simple and merely duplicate a series of keystrokes. For example, a macro can be written that selects a range of cells. A more complex macro may perform a command, such as copying data from one cell to another or changing column widths. Even more complex macros can be written that let you create customized functions that combine math expressions, Excel functions, and programming code to perform special calculations. Other macros can be used to create your own customized menus and dialog boxes.

Changing the Macro Security Level

When a workbook contains macros, a macro virus warning may be displayed when the file is opened advising you that macros are detected and asking you to confirm that you want them enabled. This is because macros can contain viruses that may adversely affect your system. As a protection, Excel includes three security levels—high, medium, and low.

1 **Choose Tools/Macro/Security.**

Your screen should be similar to Figure 5.16

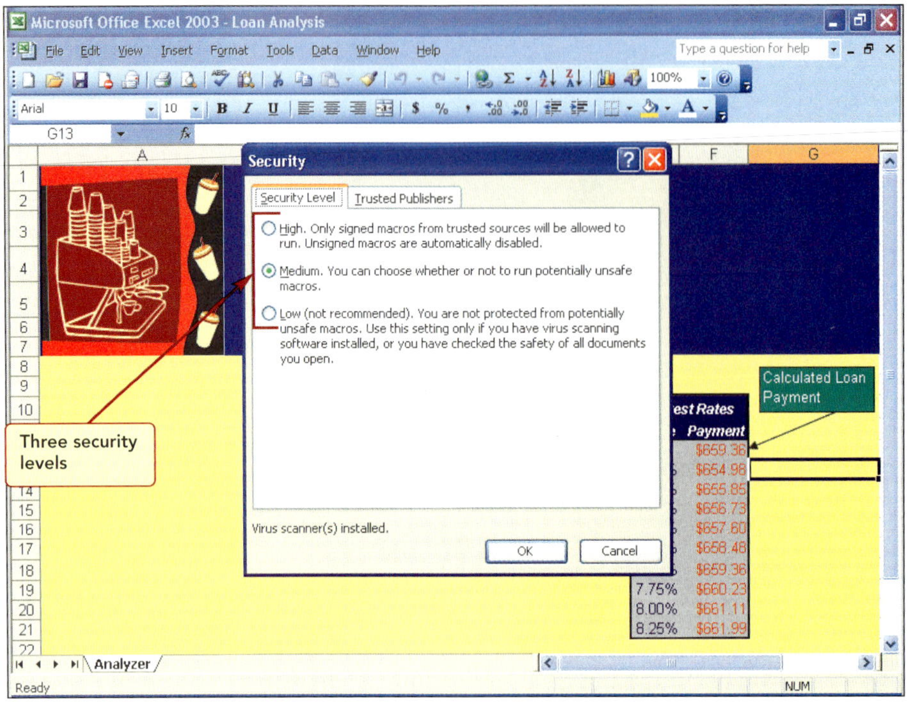

Figure 5.16

Additional Information

Under all levels, if anti-virus software is installed on your system, the workbook is scanned for viruses before it is opened.

Initially, the security level is set to Medium. Changing the setting to High provides the greatest amount of protection. This setting automatically disables macros if they are not digitally signed. A **digital signature** is an electronic encryption-based stamp of authentication that confirms the macro or document originated from the signer and has not been changed. The current security level, Medium, allows the user to decide to enable or disable unsigned macros. This is an appropriate level for this workbook.

2 **If necessary, change the security level to Medium.**

Click OK.

Creating a Command Button

Additional Information

Toolbar buttons are simply macro statements that are executed when the button to which they are assigned is selected.

One of the most common ways to run a macro is to create a command button in the worksheet that, when clicked, runs the macro instructions. You want to create a command button that will print the worksheet. You will create the command button before creating the macro so that the macro instructions can be assigned to the button.

A command button is one of many different controls that can be added to a worksheet.

Concept 3

Control

3 A **control** is a graphic object that is designed to help the user interact with the worksheet. They can be used to display or enter data, perform an action, or make the sheet easier to read. Examples of controls are check boxes, list boxes, option buttons, and command buttons. Controls include **property** settings that affect how they behave and work. The properties associated with many controls can be changed to customize the control for your own use.

Excel includes two ways to add controls to a worksheet: with the Forms toolbar or the Control Toolbox toolbar. The controls on the Forms toolbar are for use with Excel macros and work best on worksheets that will be used only in Excel. The Control Toolbox controls are ActiveX. These controls can be made "active" by defining the properties of the control. They do not need to be associated with a macro. The Control Toolbox controls are used when the worksheet will be used in interaction with other Office programs or on an Internet location.

You will create the command button using the Forms toolbar.

1 **Display the Forms toolbar and move it into column A.**

- **Click Button.**
- **Click on cell B19 to create the button.**

Your screen should be similar to Figure 5.17

Having Trouble?

Do not be concerned if your command button displays a different button number.

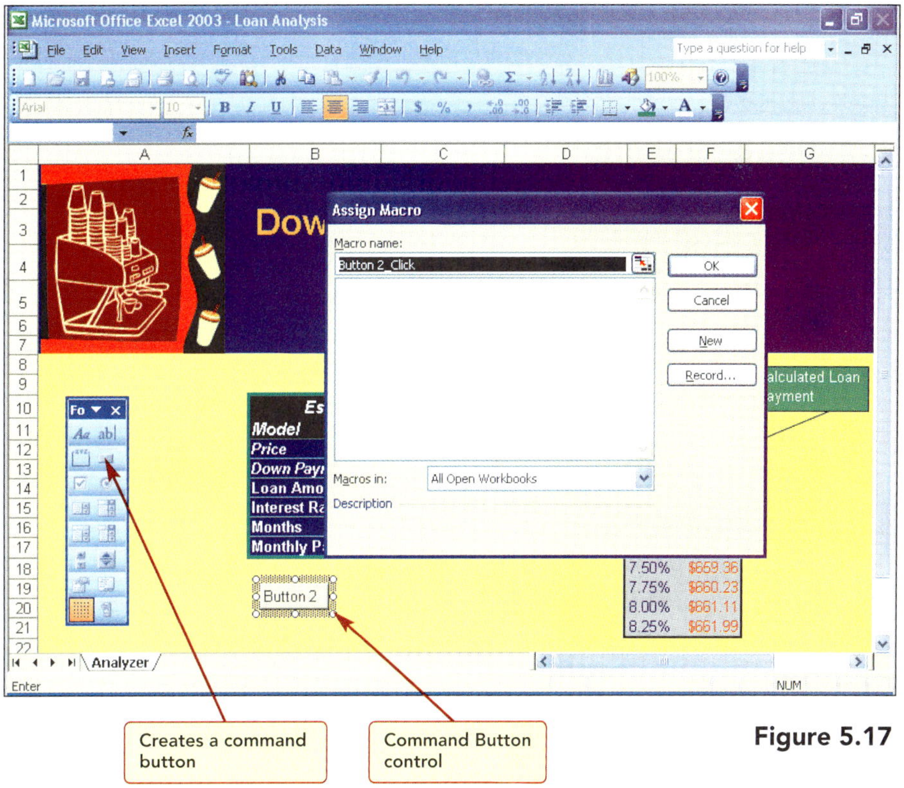

Figure 5.17

When you first create a control, Excel automatically displays the Assign Macro dialog box. This dialog box is used to modify the macro name and to create or assign the macro to associate with the button.

2 **In the Macro name text box, type PrintLandscape.**

Additional Information

A macro name must begin with a letter, cannot exceed 255 characters, and cannot include a space or period or the following characters: ! @ & $ #. Do not use a name that is a cell reference because it may result in an error message.

Your screen should be similar to Figure 5.18

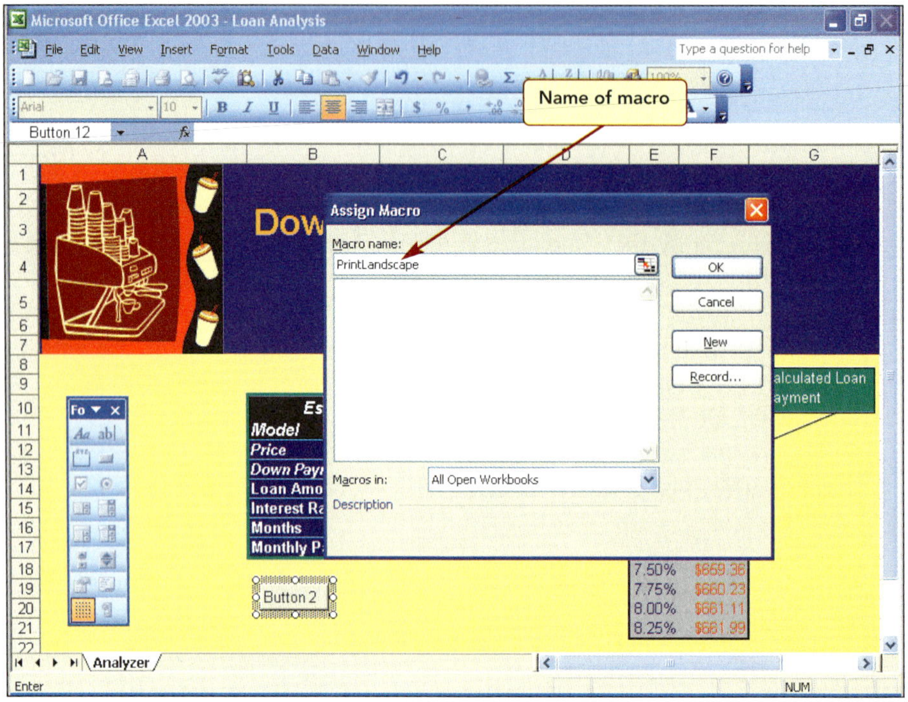

Figure 5.18

Additional Information

You will learn about entering macros using the Visual Basic Editor in Working Together 2.

Next, you need to create a new macro or select an existing macro to associate with the button. You can create a new macro by writing the instructions using Microsoft Visual Basic Editor or by using the Macro Recorder feature.

Using the Macro Recorder

You will create the macro instructions to print the worksheet using the Macro Recorder.

Concept 4

Macro Recorder

4 The **Macro Recorder** automatically creates a macro by recording a series of actions as macro commands. When the recorder is on, Excel automatically records every action you perform and stores it as a Microsoft Visual Basic instruction. You can then easily select the recorded macro by name and play it back, or execute it, as often as you like.

Once the macro is created, it can be viewed and changed using the Microsoft Visual Basic Editor program. However, it is recommended that the Macro Recorder method be used for short procedures, such as basic worksheet functions like formatting and printing, because it can be difficult to decipher and troubleshoot complex Visual Basic instructions after they have been recorded.

Additional Information

The worksheet will print when you are finished recording the macro, so make any needed printer setup preparations before you begin.

The macro you will create will print the worksheet in landscape orientation.

1 Click Record... .

Your screen should be similar to Figure 5.19

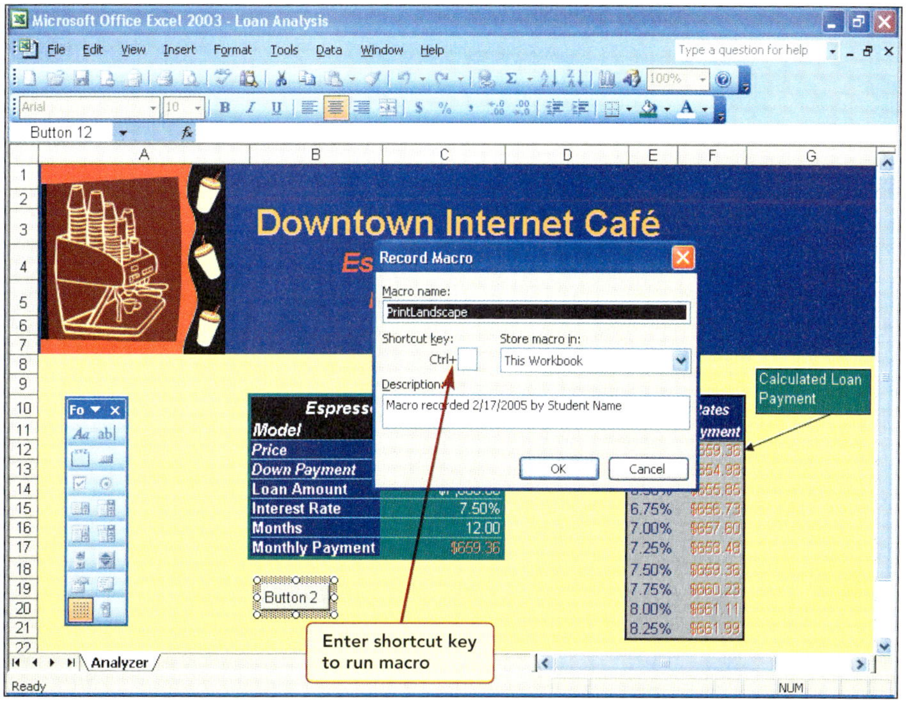

Figure 5.19

In the Record Macro dialog box, you assign a shortcut key that can be used to start the macro, select a location where it will be stored if other than in the active workbook, and enter a description of the macro. You will name this macro PrintLandscape. Since you have created a button to run this macro, you do not need to assign it a shortcut key and you will leave all the other selections as they are.

2 Click OK .

Your screen should be similar to Figure 5.20

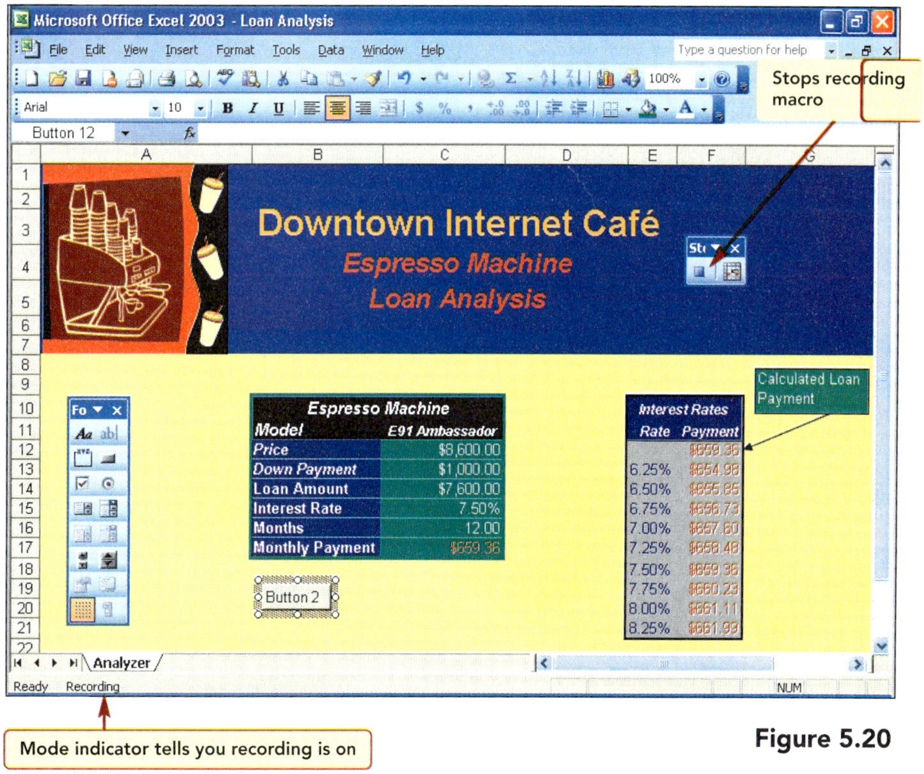

Figure 5.20

The message "Recording" is displayed in the status bar, and the Stop Recording toolbar appears. Now any action you perform will be recorded as a macro.

3
- Choose File/Page Setup.
- Open the Page tab.
- Select Landscape.
- Open the Header/Footer tab.
- Click Custom Header... .
- In the Right section enter your name.
- Press ←Enter.
- Type the current date.
- Click OK.
- Click Print... .
- If necessary, select the printer to use.
- Click OK.
- Click Stop Recording on the Recording toolbar.

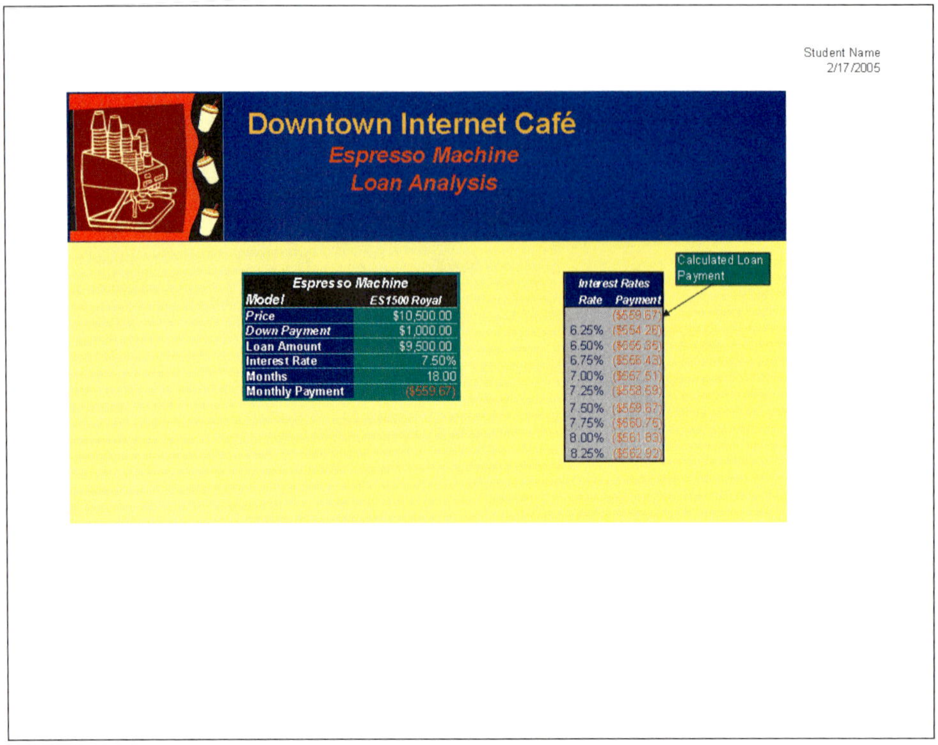

Another Method

The menu equivalent is Tools/Macro/Stop Recording.

Your printed worksheet should be similar to that shown here. Notice that the button control does not print, just like other worksheet features such as toolbars, that are designed to help you interact with the program.

Editing a Macro

Next, you will look at the macro statements for the macro that was just recorded.

1 **Click Edit Code on the Forms toolbar.**

If necessary, maximize the Code window.

> **Another Method**
>
> When a Form object is not selected, you can use Tools/Macro/Macros or the keyboard shortcut Alt + F8, select the macro name, and click Edit... to display macro code.

Your screen should be similar to Figure 5.21

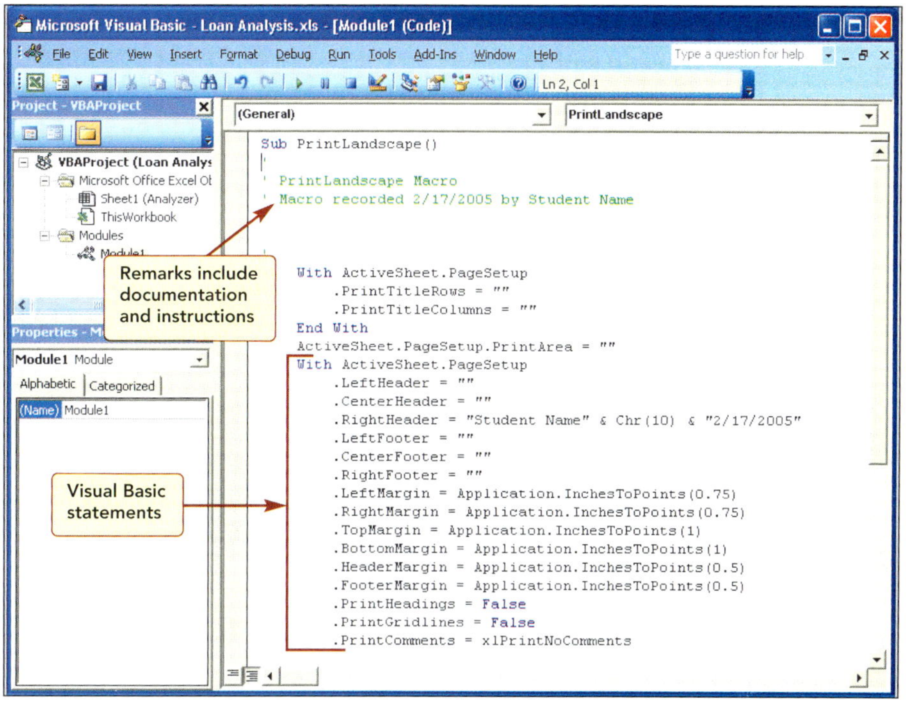

Figure 5.21

The Visual Basic Editor program is opened, and the Code window displays the Visual Basic statements that were recorded as you created the PrintLandscape macro. It contains the recorded macro statements for all settings that are on by default in the Page Setup dialog box as well as those you changed. The first statement line starts the macro and the last ends the macro. Notice that there are several lines below the first line that are green and begin with an apostrophe. The text on these lines are comments or remarks that describe the macro. They are not processed as part of the macro. You can edit the macro statements directly in the Visual Basic Editor Code window. In this case, you want to add a remark about the purpose of the macro to the documentation.

2 On the line below the "Macro recorded" line to the right of the apostrophe, type **Purpose: Prints the loan analysis.**

Your screen should be similar to Figure 5.22

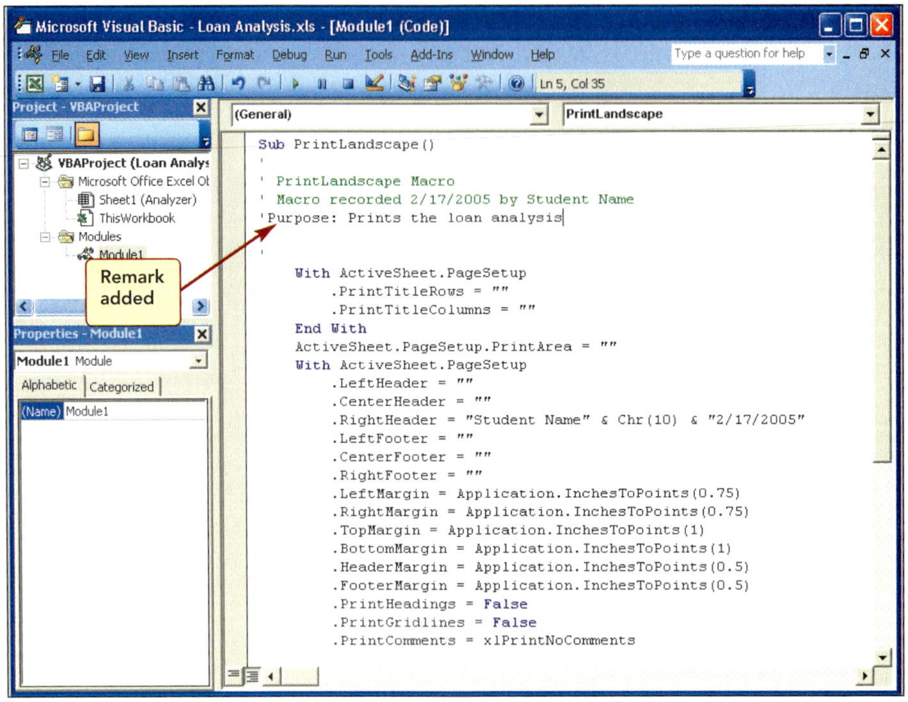

Figure 5.22

3 Close the Visual Basic Editor window.

Changing the Button Name

Although you named the macro associated with the button, the button still displays the default button name. Each graphic object as it is added to a worksheet is assigned an image number. You will change the default button name to a name that is descriptive of the action it will perform.

1 Click in the text in the button to change to text editing.

Another Method

You can also choose Edit Text from the object's shortcut menu.

- Select the text in the button.
- Type **Print**.
- Click outside the button to deselect it.

Your screen should be similar to Figure 5.23

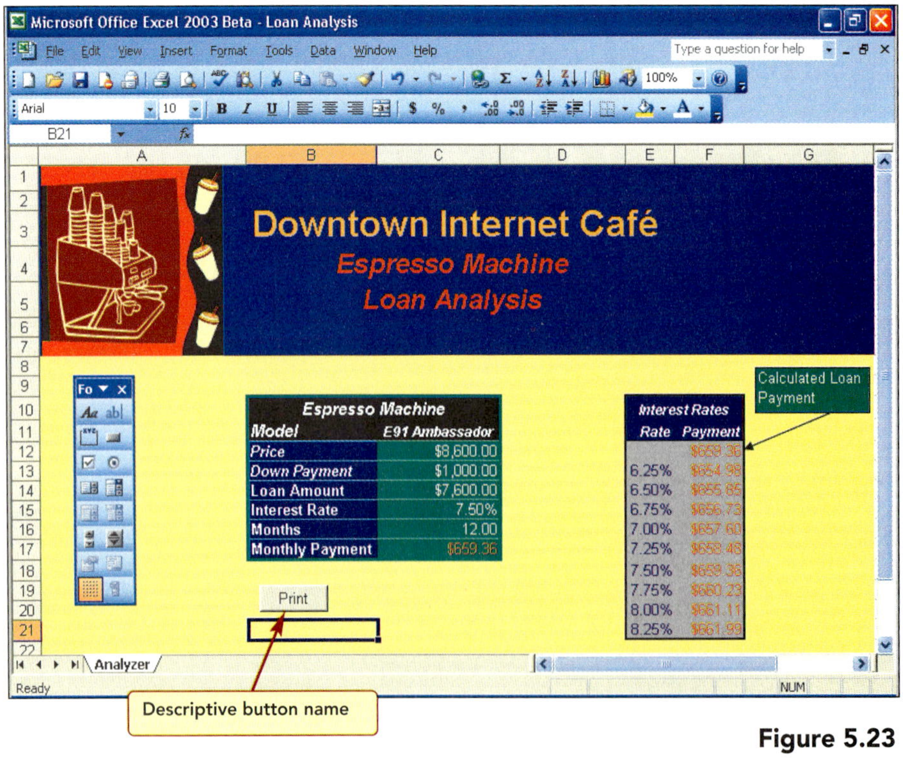

Figure 5.23

Using the Print Button

Evan is also considering another espresso machine and wants to see what the loan payments would be for this model. The machine model is ES1500 Royal that costs $10,500. Evan plans on a down payment of $1000 and to extend the payments to 18 months.

So that you do not lose the information on the first model, you will create a copy of the worksheet and enter the information for the second espresso machine in the new worksheet. Since you are finished creating the button, you will close the Forms toolbar first.

1

- **Close the Forms toolbar.**
- **Rename the sheet tab E91 Ambassador.**
- **Copy the worksheet and name the new worksheet tab ES1500 Royal.**

Having Trouble?

Choose **M**ove or Copy from the sheet tab shortcut menu, select **C**reate a Copy and click OK.

- **Enter the information for the ES1500 described above in the worksheet. Use the same 7.5 percent interest rate.**

Your screen should be similar to Figure 5.24

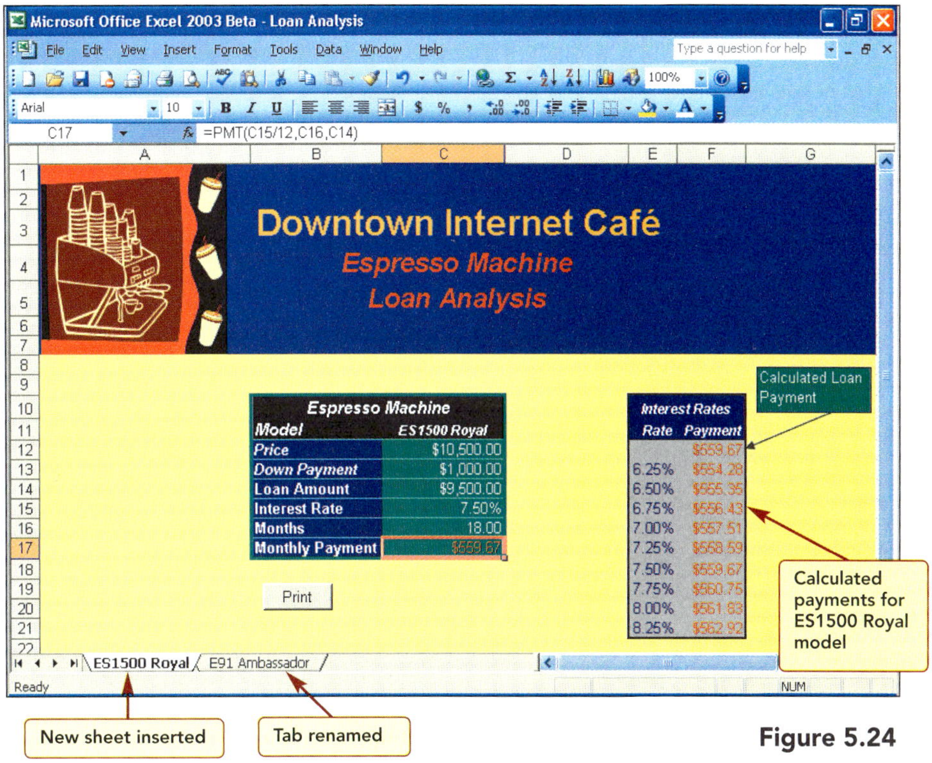

Figure 5.24

Now, you will use the Print button to print the worksheet. Before testing the new macro, it is a good idea to save the workbook first in case the macro performs some unexpected actions.

2 Move to cell A8 and save the workbook.

- If necessary, click OK to close the Privacy warning message box.

Additional Information

Throughout the lab, whenever a privacy warning appears, click OK to continue.

- Click Print.

Additional Information

The worksheet blinks while the macro is in progress.

- Close the workbook.

Another Method

You could also use Tools/Macro/Macros/Print Landscape/Run to run the macro to print the worksheet.

The macro was executed and the worksheet containing the new loan information is printed.

Creating a Form

Your second project is to create a spreadsheet that records customer monthly connection times and calculates Bonus Dollars earned by each customer. Bonus Dollars are awarded to customers based on their monthly connection time use and can be applied toward any other purchases at the Café. You will create a form to record and calculate this information.

Concept 5

Form

5 A **form** is a formatted worksheet with blank spaces that can be filled in online on an individual computer or on a network, or printed and completed on paper. The steps in creating a form are the same for both purposes. However, certain elements are more appropriate for one than for the other. For example, color and shading are more effective on online forms, while simplicity of design and layout is very important in printed forms. In addition, online forms can contain formulas that immediately calculate results such as totals, whereas printed forms would need to include blank spaces where the calculations would be entered manually.

The first step when creating a form is to decide what should appear on the form and what information will be entered into the form. When customers sign on to the computers, they enter their names, and the system tracks the time between sign-on and sign-off. Obtaining connection times for each customer is just a matter of checking the computers' logs. The Bonus Dollar form needs to be designed to accept input of customer connection times and to calculate Bonus Dollars earned. Although Evan wants the form to be electronic, he also wants to be able to print it out for reference.

You have already started designing the form by entering much of the text, many of the formulas, some formatting to improve the appearance, and some sample data. To see what has been done so far,

1

- **Open the workbook file** ex05_Bonus Dollars.
- **If necessary, maximize the worksheet.**

Your screen should be similar to Figure 5.25

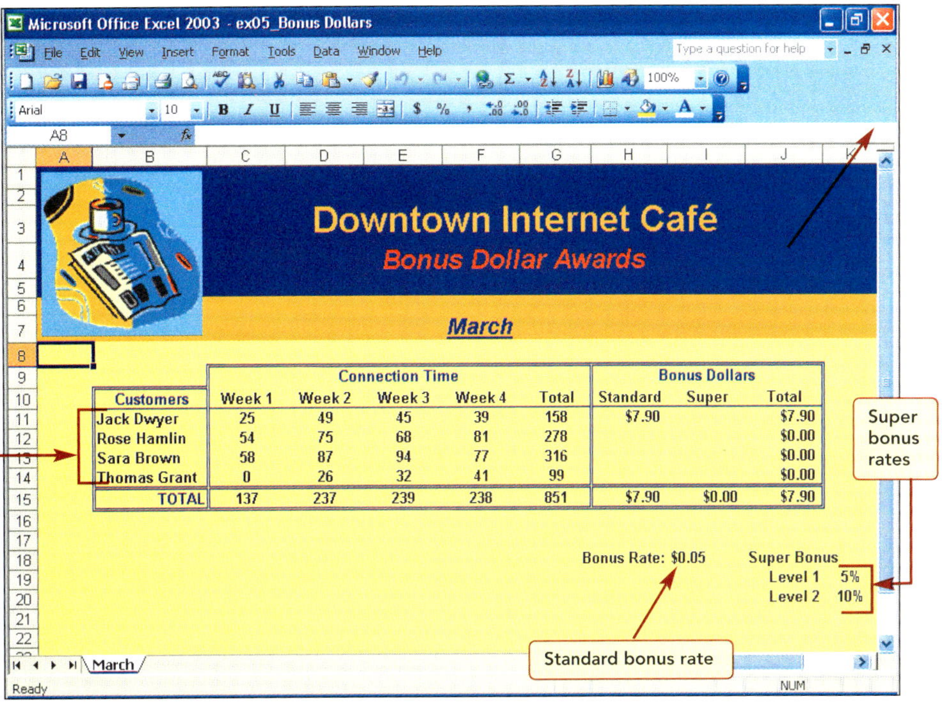

Figure 5.25

The worksheet displays the names of four customers and their connection time in minutes for each week in columns C through F.

The last three columns will be used to calculate and display customer Bonus Dollars. The Downtown Internet Café awards Bonus Dollars based on total connection time. A Standard Bonus is applied to every customer at a rate of $.05 per minute of connection time. An additional Super Bonus is awarded at two different levels for those customers who stay connected more than 100 minutes. The bonus awards are explained in the following table.

Bonus	Award
Standard Bonus	Total connection time in minutes multiplied by $.05
Super Bonus Level 1	If total connection time is greater than 100 minutes but less than or equal to 200 minutes, Standard Bonus + 5%
Super Bonus Level 2	If total connection time is greater than 200 minutes, Standard Bonus + 10%

Naming Cell References

The formula to calculate the Standard Bonus for Jack Dwyer has already been entered.

1 **Move to H11.**

Your screen should be similar to Figure 5.26

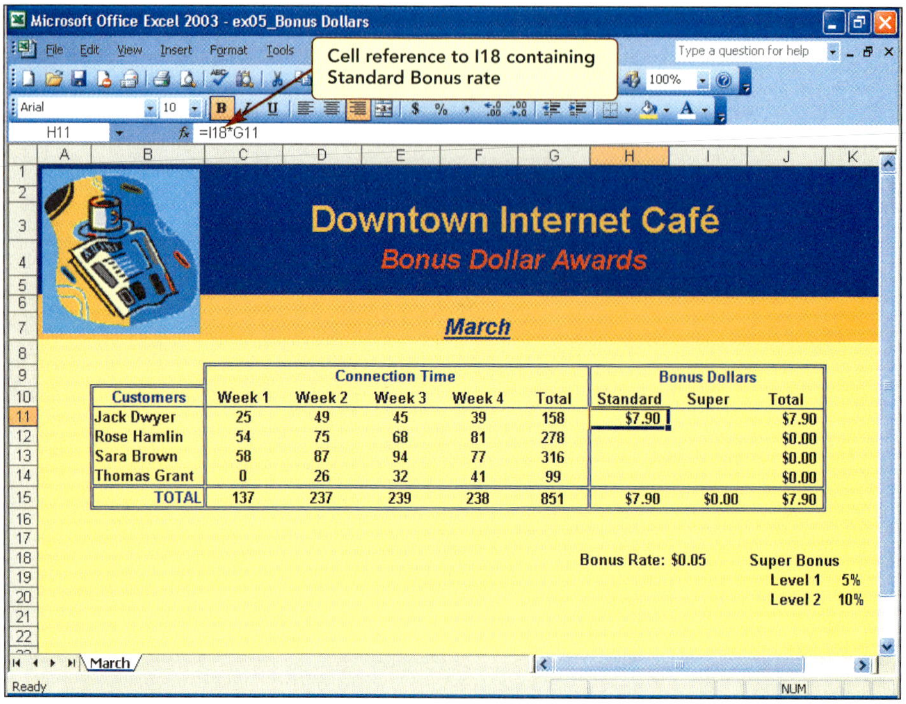

Figure 5.26

The formula references cell I18. This cell contains the Standard Bonus rate amount of $.05 per minute. To make the formula easier to read and understand, you will assign a name to this cell. A **name** is a description of a cell or range of cells that can be used in place of cell references. The name can be used any time a cell or range is requested as part of a command or in a formula or function.

2 **Move to I18.**

Choose Insert/Name/Define.

Your screen should be similar to Figure 5.27

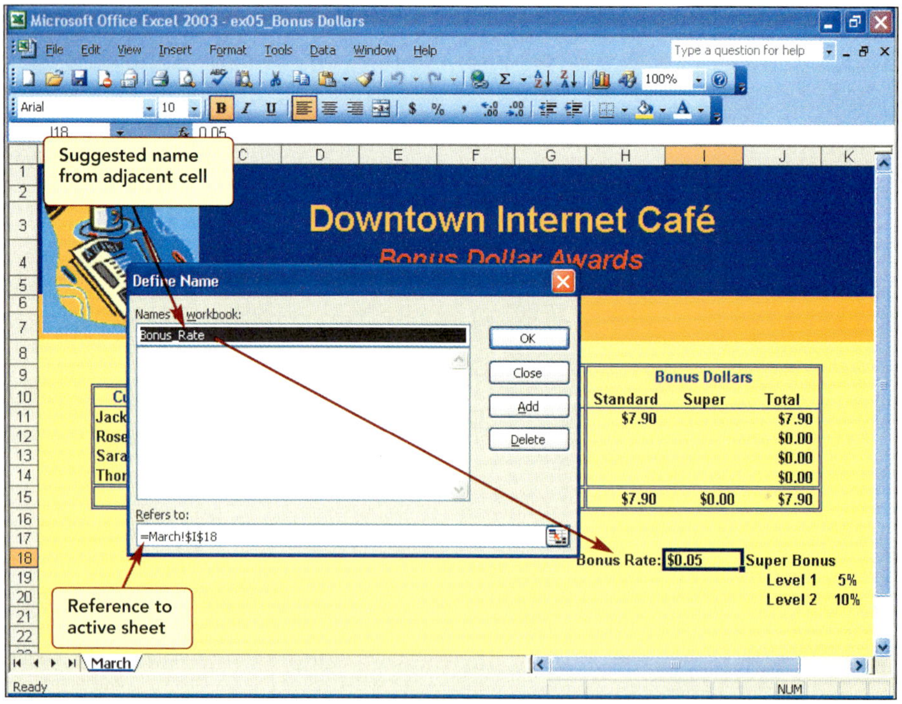

Figure 5.27

Additional Information

A name must begin with a letter, underline, or backslash and can be up to 255 characters long. It can include letters, numbers, underlines, periods, backslashes, and question marks. It cannot contain spaces. A name that resembles a cell reference is not allowed.

The Define Name dialog box is used to name, modify, and delete cell names. In the Names in Workbook text box, Excel has proposed the name Bonus_Rate. Excel automatically proposes a name for the cell or range using the contents of the active cell if it contains text, or the cell above or to the left of the active cell if the active cell does not contain text. If none of the proposed names is appropriate, you can type the name in the text box. In this case, the proposed name is the contents of the cell to the left of the active cell. Excel replaced the blank space between the words with an underline character.

The Refers To text box displays the reference for the active cell. The reference includes the sheet name and cell reference. By default Excel makes named cell references absolute. The Names in Workbook list box is empty because this worksheet does not contain any names yet. In this case, both the name and the cell reference are acceptable.

3 Click OK.

Your screen should be similar to Figure 5.28

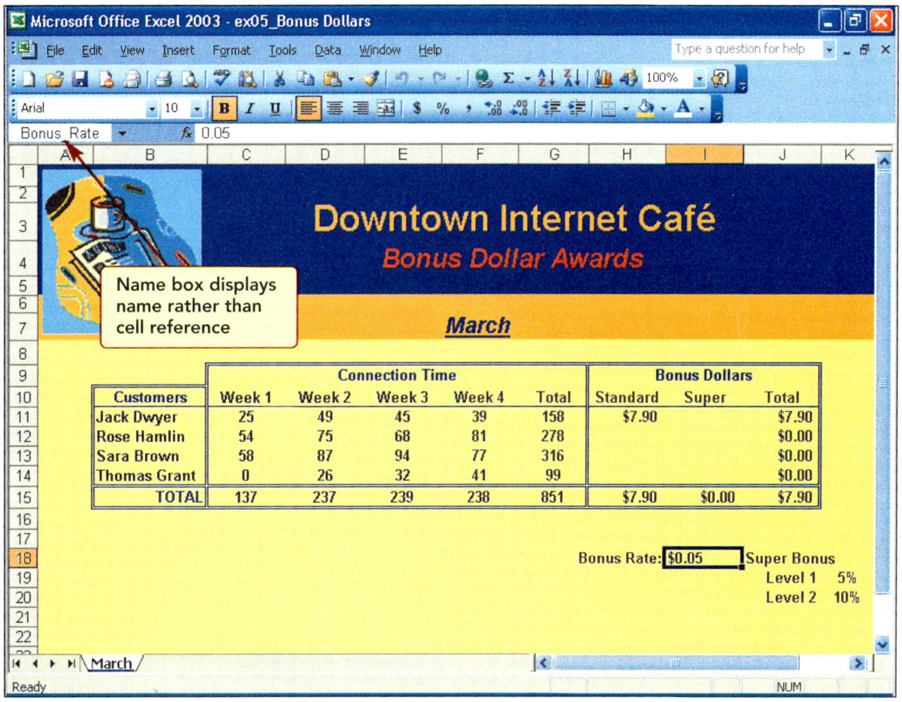

Figure 5.28

Additional Information

You can toggle between temporarily displaying the cell reference and the name by holding down the mouse button on the cell to display the cell reference and releasing it to display the name.

In place of the cell reference in the Name box of the formula bar, the name is displayed.

Now you need to replace the cell reference in the formula in cell H11 with the name.

4 Move to H11.

Change to Edit mode.

Select (highlight) the cell reference I18 in the formula.

Choose **I**nsert/**N**ame/**P**aste.

Your screen should be similar to Figure 5.29

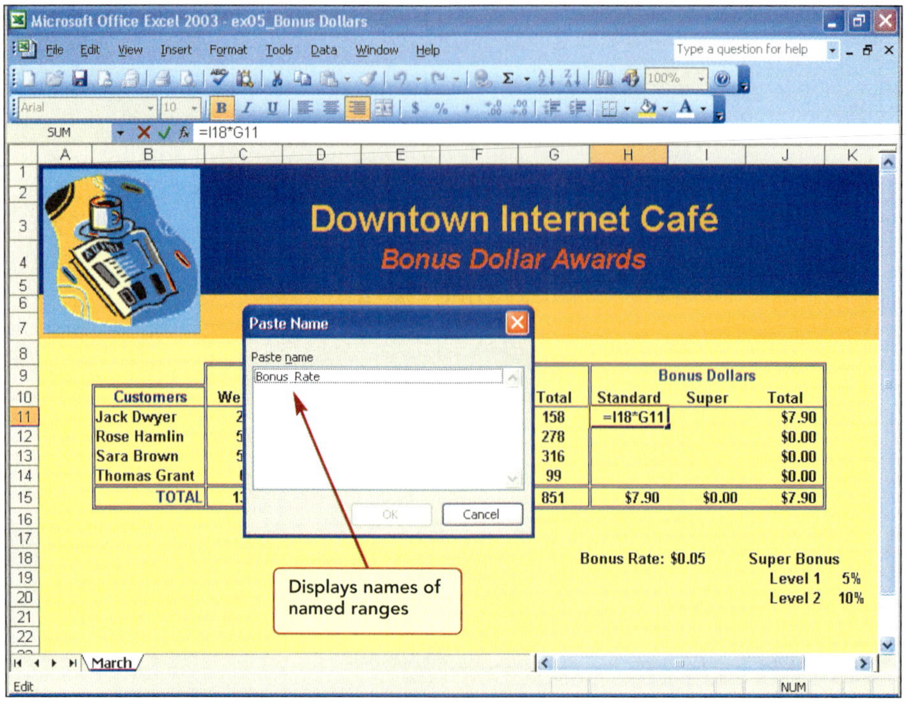

Figure 5.29

From the Paste Name dialog box, you select the name you want to use in place of the selected cell reference.

5 Select Bonus_Rate.

Click OK.

Click ✓ Enter.

Your screen should be similar to Figure 5.30

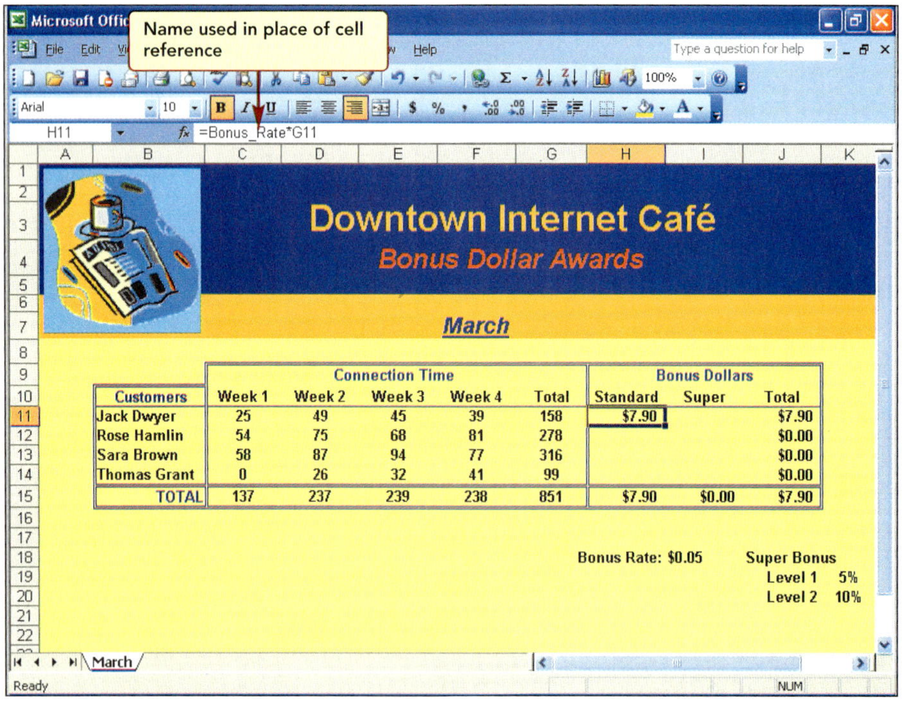

Figure 5.30

The selected name has replaced the reference to cell I18 in the formula. Using a name makes the formula easier to understand.

Next, you will name the Super Bonus levels in cells K19 and K20 that will be used in the formula to calculate the Super Bonus. You will name both cells at the same time using the labels in J19 and J20 as the names.

6 • **Select J19 through K20.**

• **Choose Insert/Name/Create.**

Your screen should be similar to Figure 5.31

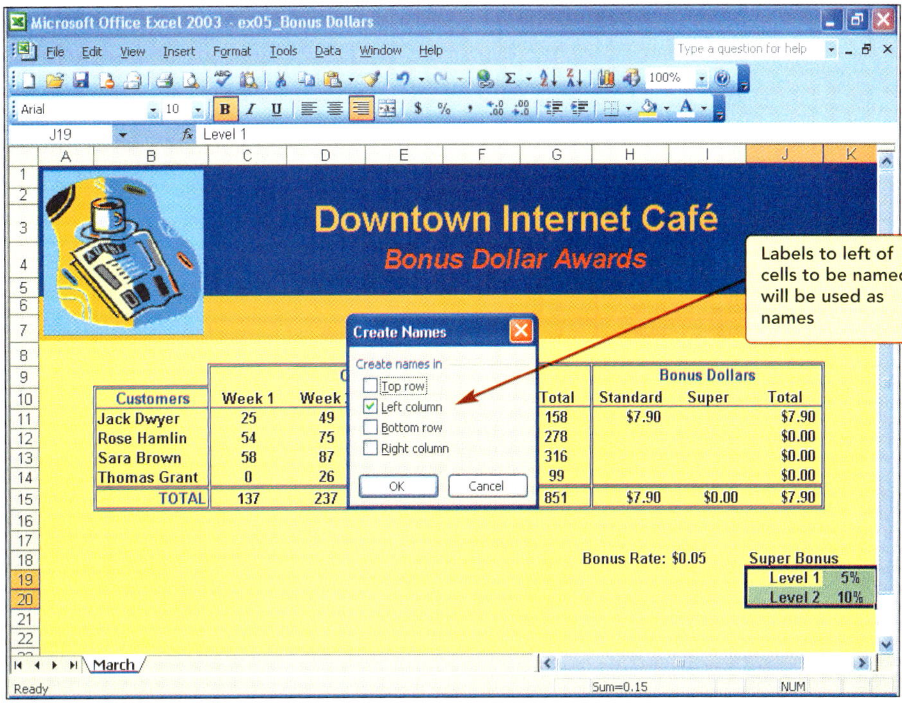

Figure 5.31

The Create Names dialog box lets you specify the location of the labels you want to use for names in relation to the cells to be named. In this case, you want to use the labels in the column to the left (J), which is the default. You will accept the default and then move to the cells to verify that the names have been created.

7 • **Click OK.**

• **Move to K19 and note that Level_1 is displayed in the Name box.**

• **Move to K20 and note that Level_2 is displayed in the Name box.**

• **Save the workbook as** Bonus Dollars.

Your screen should be similar to Figure 5.32

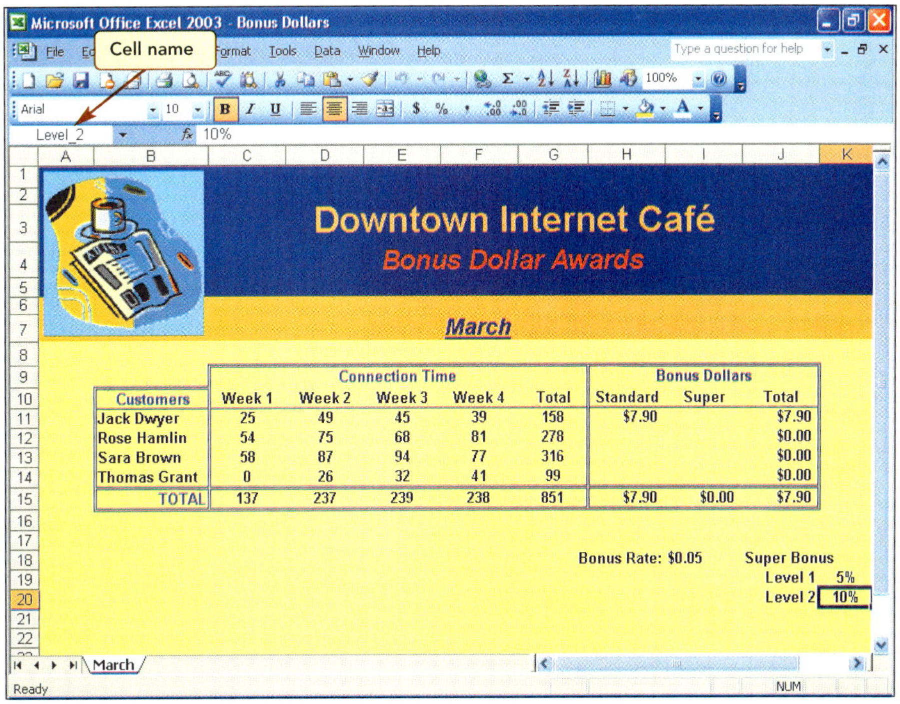

Figure 5.32

Using the IF Function

Now you are ready to enter a formula in cell I11 to calculate the Super Bonus. For any customer with more than 100 minutes of connection time, the Super Bonus is calculated using one of two levels. The highest level is for those with more than 200 minutes. Those customers receive a Super Bonus equal to 10 percent of their Standard Bonus. The other level is for those with less than or equal to 200 minutes. Those customers receive a Super Bonus equal to 5 percent of their Standard Bonus. You will use the IF function to calculate the Super Bonus.

Concept 6

IF Function

6 The **IF function** checks to see if certain conditions are met and then takes action based on the results of the check. The syntax for this function is:

IF(logical_test,value_if_true,value_if_false)

This function contains three arguments: logical_test, value_if_true, and value_if_false. The logical_test argument is an expression that makes a comparison using logical operators. **Logical operators** are symbols used in formulas that compare numbers in two or more cells or to a constant. The result of the comparison is either true (the conditions are met) or false (the conditions are not met). The logical operators are:

Symbol	Meaning
=	Equal to
<	Less than
>	Greater than
<=	Less than or equal to
>=	Greater than or equal to
<>	Not equal to
NOT	Logical NOT
AND	Logical AND
OR	Logical OR

The logical_test argument asks the question, "Does the entry in this cell meet the stated conditions?" The answer is either True (Yes) or False (No). The second argument, value_if_true, provides directions for the function to follow if the logical test result is true. The third argument, value_if_false, provides directions for the function to follow if the logical test result is false.

First you will enter the formula to calculate the bonus earned for a connection time of 200 minutes or more. Then you will modify the function to include the other conditions.

1

- Move to cell I11.
- Open the Σ AutoSum drop-down menu and choose More Functions.
- Select IF from the Most Recently Used or Logical Function categories.
- Click OK.

Your screen should be similar to Figure 5.33

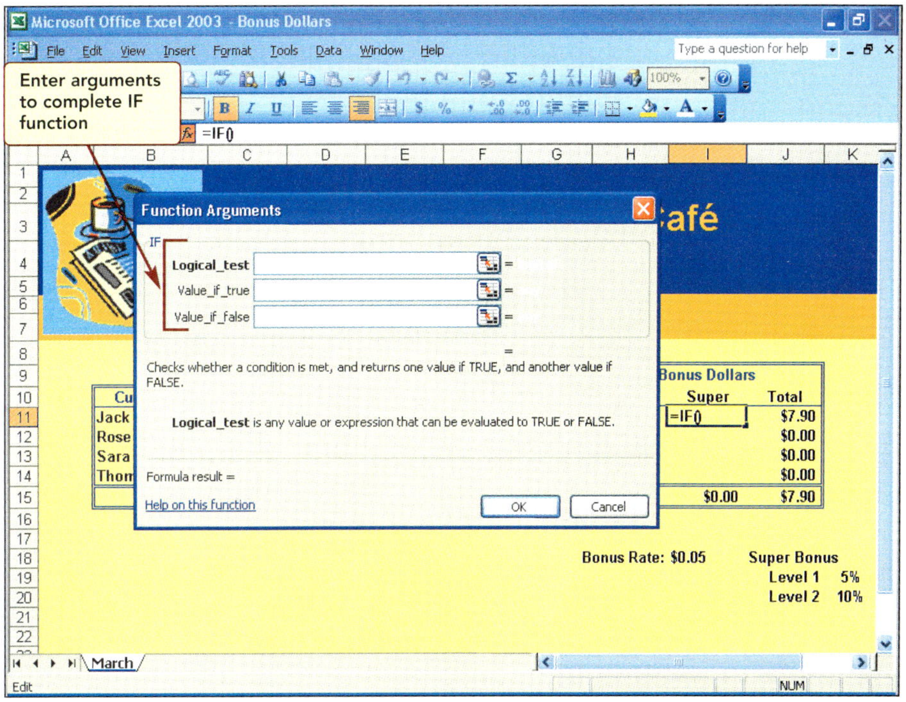

Figure 5.33

The Insert Function feature starts automatically to help you enter the parts of the function. The upper section of the Function Arguments dialog box contains three text boxes, one for each IF statement argument. The lower section provides information about the selected argument. The logical test is whether the total connection time for a customer is greater than 200, and the value_if_true argument provides directions for what to do if the logical test is true. In this case, the value_if_true directions are to multiply the value in cell H11 times the value in the cell named Level_2.

2

- In the Logical_test text box, type **G11>200**.
- Press Tab.
- In the Value_if_true text box, type **Level_2*H11**.

Your screen should be similar to Figure 5.34

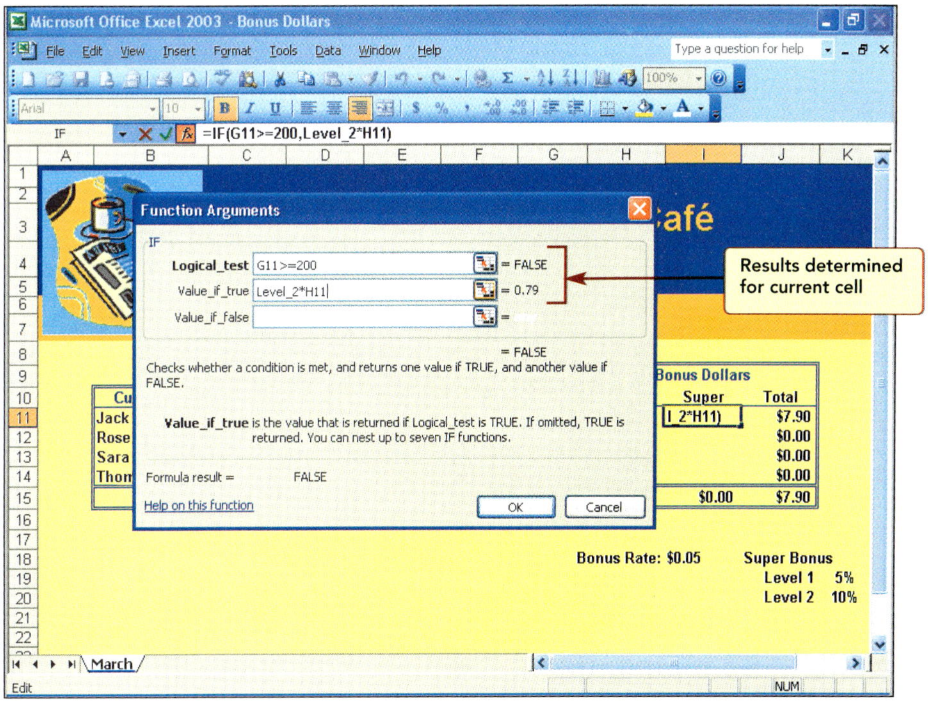

Figure 5.34

As you specify the arguments, to the right of the argument text box Excel has already determined whether the conditions are true or false for the current customer based on the values in the referenced cells. In this case, because the value in G11 is less than 200, the logical test result is False and a Level 2 bonus would be 0.79 if True.

Next, you need to enter the value_if_false argument. It contains instructions that are executed if connection time is less than or equal to 200 minutes. If the connection time is greater than 100, then the Level_1 amount is used to calculate the Super Bonus; otherwise, connection time is less than or equal to 100 and the Super Bonus is 0. To enter this condition, you include a second IF statement that will apply the Level 1 bonus. The arguments for the second IF statement are enclosed in their own set of parentheses. This is called a **nested function**.

3 ● **In the Value_if_false text box, type IF(G11>100,Level_1*H11,0).**

Your screen should be similar to Figure 5.35

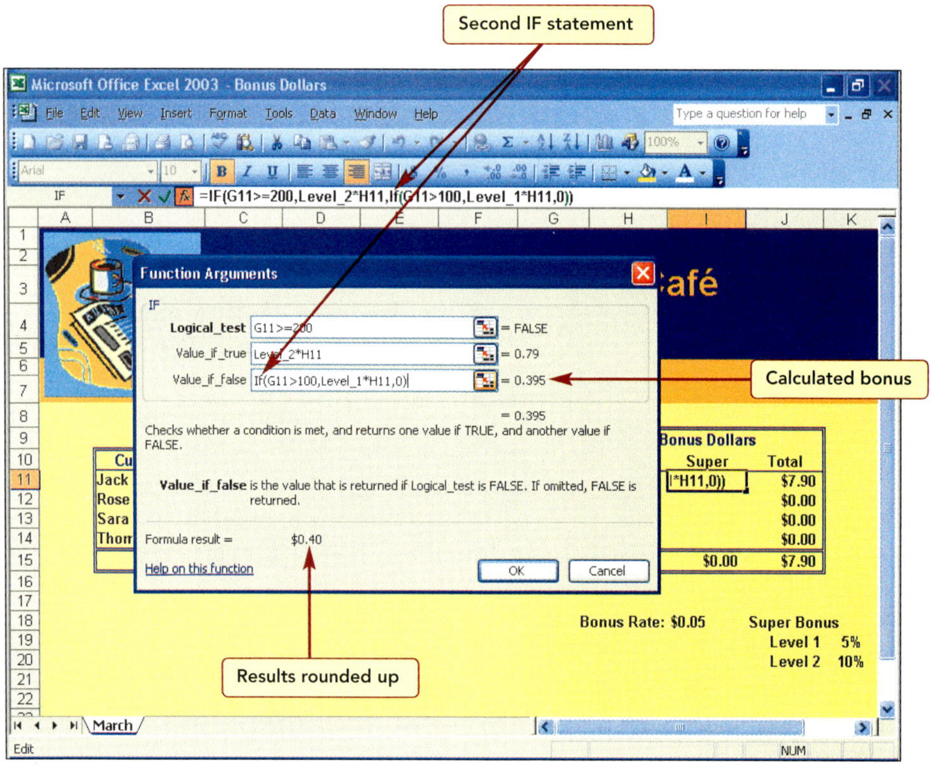

Figure 5.35

Now the calculated result is .395 for the current customer. The formula result will be rounded up to $.40.

4 Click OK.

Your screen should be similar to Figure 5.36

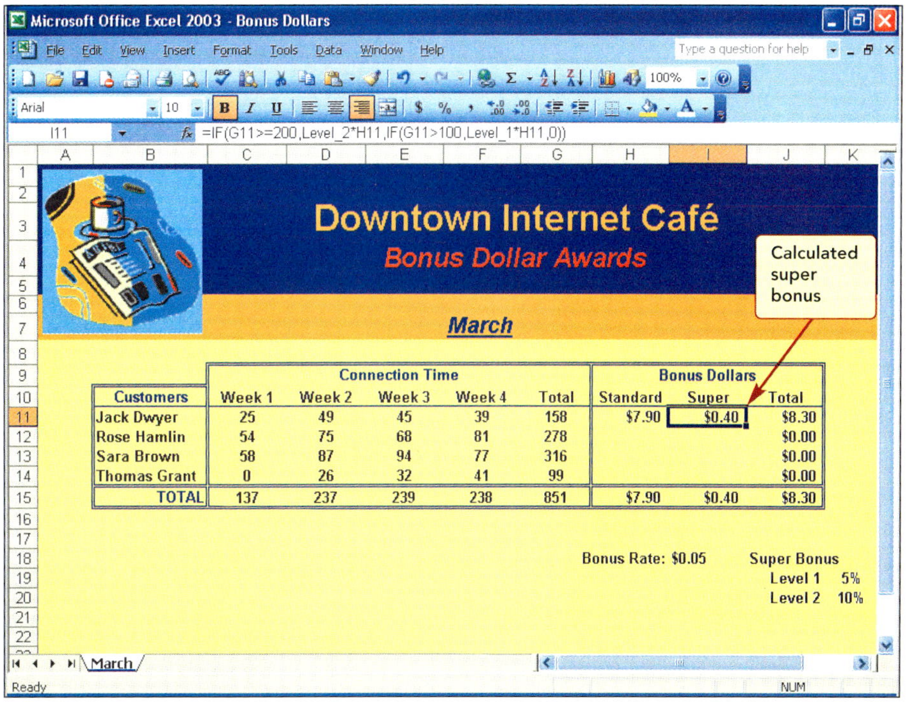

Figure 5.36

The Super Bonus for Jack Dwyer is $.40. The IF function determined that the number in cell G11 was less than 200 but greater than 100. Therefore, the Super Bonus was calculated using Level_1, or 5 percent. Next, you will enter formulas to make these same calculations for the other three customers.

5
- **Using the fill handle, copy cells H11 through I11 to the range H12 through I14.**
- **Click cell H12 to deselect the range.**
- **From the AutoFill Option button menu, choose Fill Without Formatting.**
- **Increase the width of column H slightly to display the border lines fully.**

Your screen should be similar to Figure 5.37

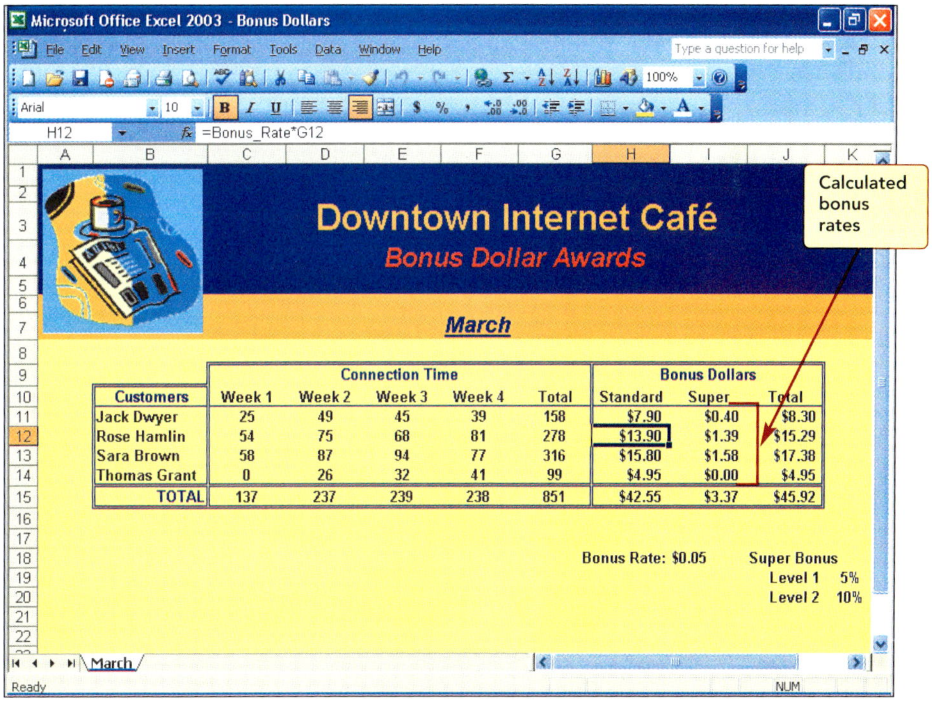

Figure 5.37

Because the named references in the copied formulas are absolute, they copied correctly. Both Rose and Sara earned Super Bonus awards of 10 percent because the values in cells G12 and G13 are greater than 200. Thomas did not earn a Super Bonus because the value in cell G14 is less than 100.

Adding a Combo Box Control

Evan really likes the layout of the form. A change needs to be made, however, to the Standard Bonus rate. During some months the bonus rate may be raised to $.10 or $.15 per minute. The formulas to calculate the bonuses will need to be adjusted to use the other two bonus rates during those months. You could create two additional forms that would each have a different bonus rate in cell I18. This would require that the correct form used for that month's input be based on the bonus rate for that month. A simpler way to deal with this problem is to add a combo box control to the form.

Adding controls to forms makes it easier to fill out a form and increases the accuracy of the information entered in it. This is because many of the controls can include a list of options from which the user selects. Although controls are most effectively used in online forms, they can also be used in printed forms. For example, controls such as buttons and check boxes can be printed blank and then filled in by the user.

A combo box control displays a text box and button that will display a drop-down list with the items that can be selected. The first step in creating a combo box control is to enter the items you want to appear in the combo box drop-down list in a columnar range. You will enter the three bonus amounts as items to be used.

1 **In cells H19 through H21, enter .05, .10, and .15.**

Additional Information

Cells H19:H21 were preformatted to Currency.

- **Display the Control Toolbox toolbar.**
- **If necessary, move the toolbar to the left side of your screen.**

Your screen should be similar to Figure 5.38

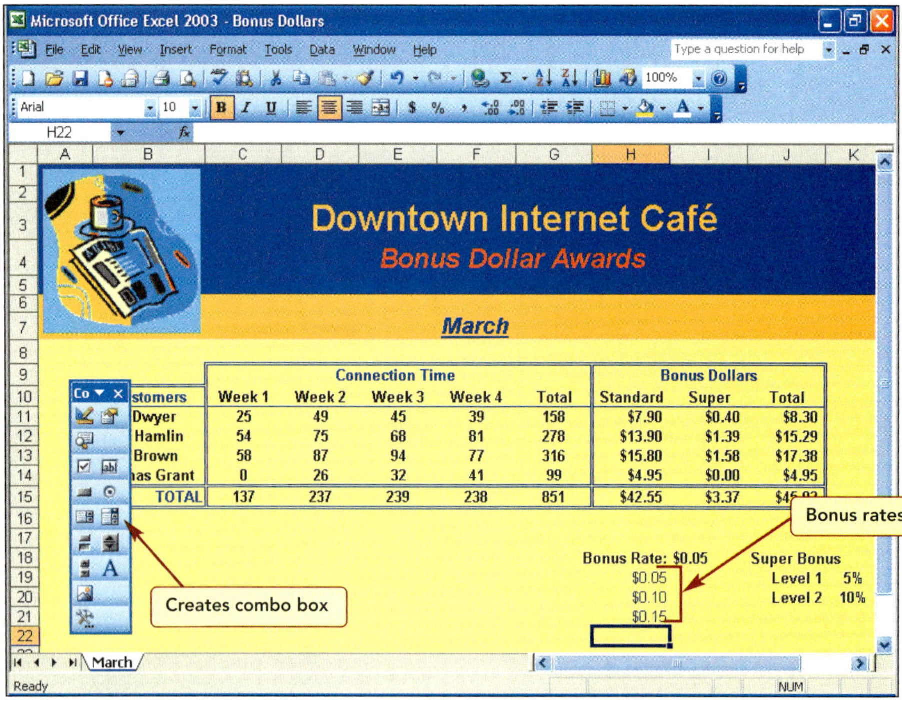

Figure 5.38

The Control Toolbox toolbar has many of the same buttons as the Forms toolbar. However, the buttons created using this toolbar are ActiveX controls that do not need to be associated with a macro and can be customized to your needs. They can be used with most online forms and are appropriate for most situations. You will add a combo box control to the form.

2 **Click Combo Box on the Control Toolbox toolbar.**

Click and drag over cell C17 to create a combo box.

Additional Information

The combo box is a selected object that can be sized or moved like any other object.

Your screen should be similar to Figure 5.39

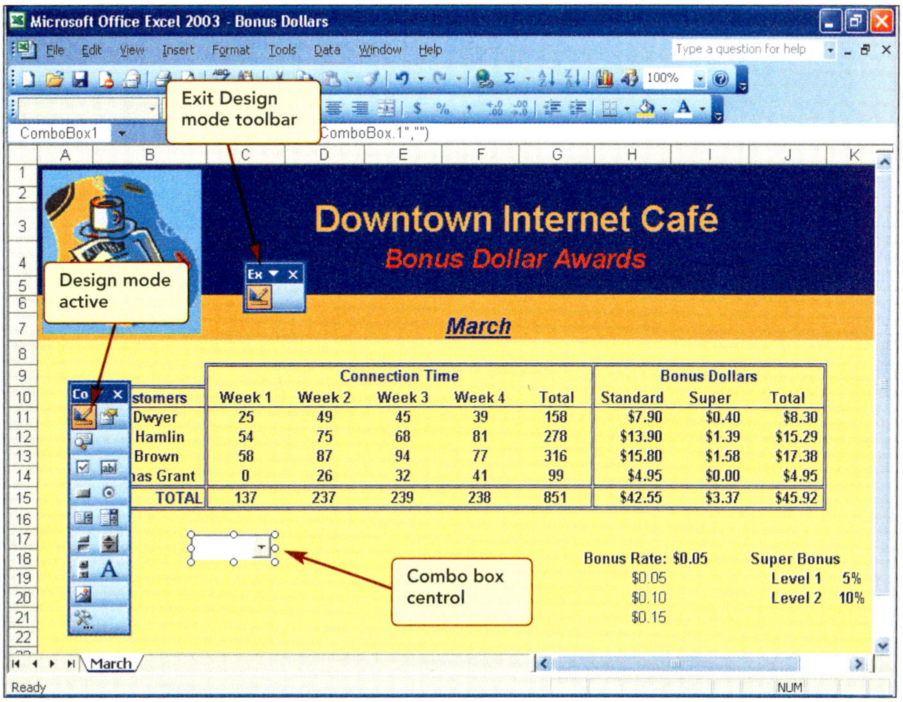

Figure 5.39

Additional Information

The Design Mode button appears highlighted when Design mode is active.

When you first create an ActiveX control, Excel automatically turns on Design mode so that you can modify the control. The Exit Design mode toolbar is automatically displayed. You need to specify the information to be displayed in the combo box drop-down list and the location of the link cell where the selection will be entered. You do this by setting the properties of the combo box.

3 Click Properties.

- If necessary, open the Alphabetic tab.

Your screen should be similar to Figure 5.40

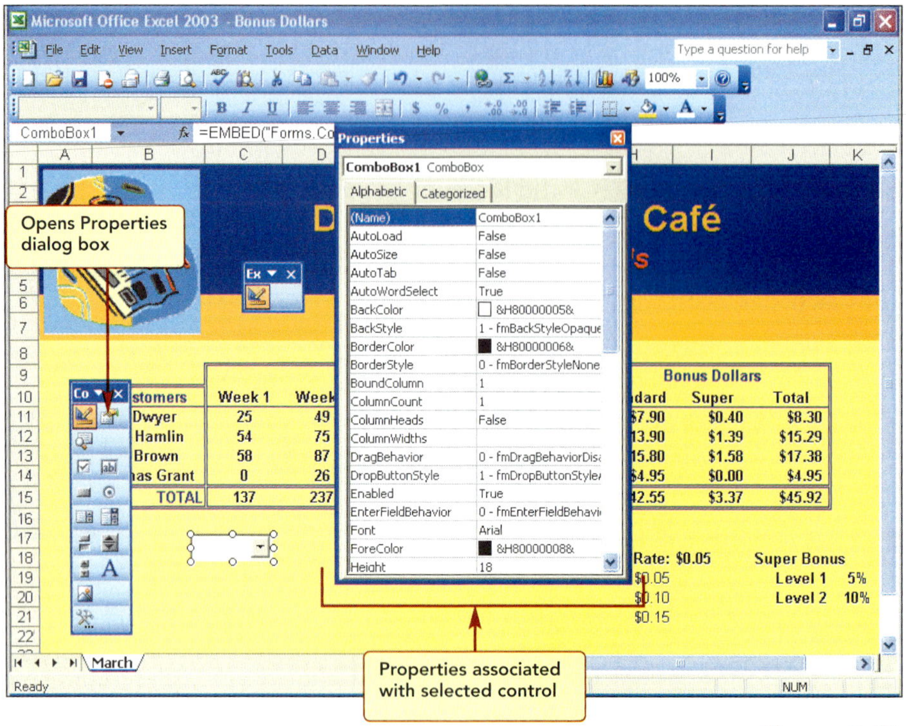

Figure 5.40

Additional Information

You can also change a command button's font attributes by selecting Properties from the button's shortcut menu and selecting font and color settings.

The Alphabetic tab displays the properties for the selected control in alphabetical order. The ListFillRange option is used to specify the location of the cells containing the information to be displayed in the combo box drop-down list, and the LinkedCell option is used to specify the cell to receive the selection.

4

- Scroll the list to locate the ListFillRange property box.
- Enter the range H19:H21 as the ListFillRange.
- Enter cell I18 as the LinkedCell.

Your screen should be similar to Figure 5.41

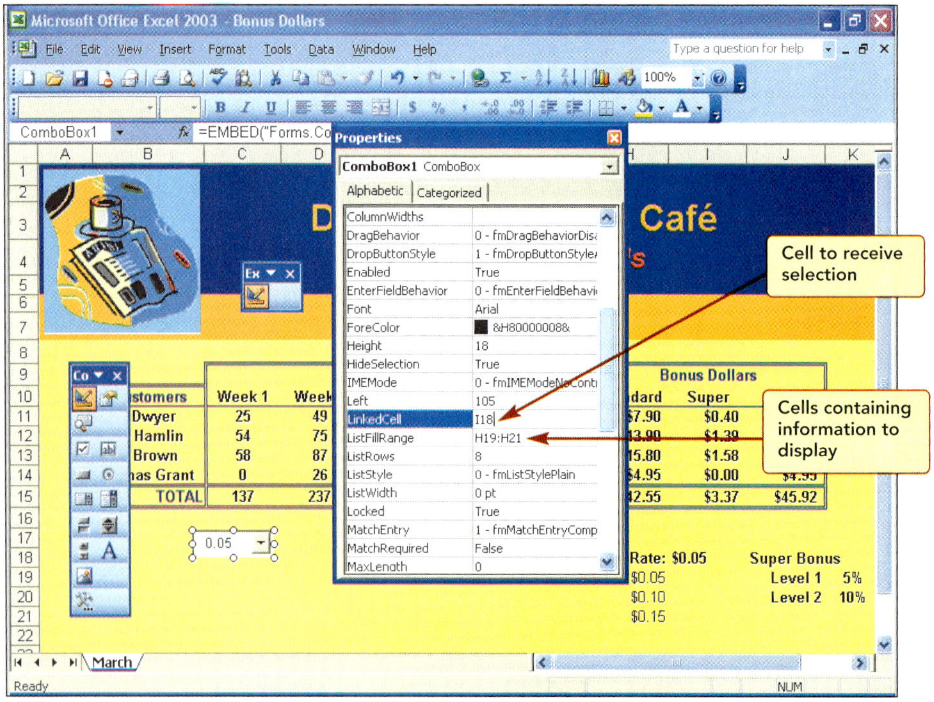

Figure 5.41

You are finished defining the properties and want to add a label next to the combo box. Then you will try it out.

5 Click to close the Properties dialog box.

- Enter the label **Select Bonus Rate** in cell B17 to identify the combo box.

> **Additional Information**
> Cell B17 was preformatted to be right-aligned.

- Reposition and size the combo box control as needed to align with the label (see Figure 5.42).
- Click Exit Design Mode.
- Close the Control Toolbox toolbar.
- Open the combo box drop-down list.
- Select $0.15.
- Save the workbook.

Your screen should be similar to Figure 5.42

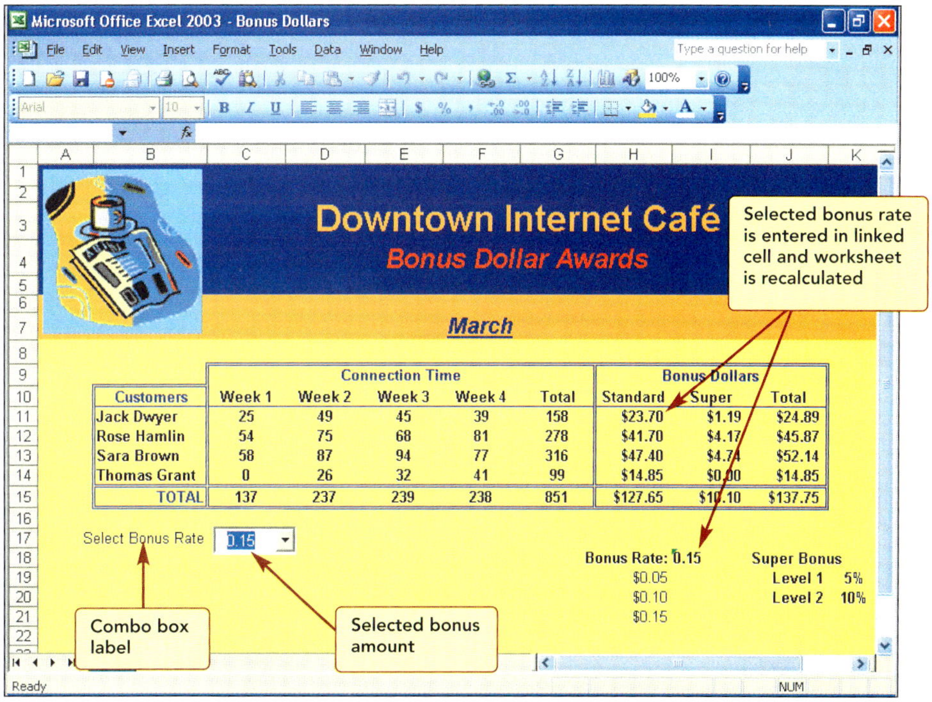

Figure 5.42

The selection you made from the combo box is entered in the Bonus Rate cell, I18, and the worksheet is recalculated using the new bonus rate.

Finalizing the Form

Now you will prepare the form to be used for entry of the same information for other months. A well-designed form is simple to use and uncluttered in design. To make the form easy to use, you will add comments and a command button to print the output. To simplify the design, you will hide nonessential items. Then you will prepare the workbook to be saved as a template to be used each month to record the customer's Bonus Dollar earnings. You will clear the sample data, unlock all data entry areas, and protect the worksheet. You will also add documentation to the workbook to clarify the purpose of the template.

Adding Comments

Since someone else will most likely use the form, it is a good idea to include instructions on how to use it. Typically, these instructions are a combination of text entries and comments.

Concept 7

Comment

7 A **comment** is a note attached to a cell that can be used to help clarify the meaning of the data, provide documentation, or ask a question. Using comments is a good method of adding instructions that do not interfere with the appearance of the worksheet.

A cell containing a comment displays a red indicator triangle in the upper-right corner. Pointing to a cell containing a comment displays the comment text in a comment box. You can move and resize a comment box just as you would any other type of graphic object. If you move the cell that contains a comment, the associated comment box moves with it.

You will add one text entry and three cell comments that will provide the instructions for this form.

1 **Move to cell A8.**

- **Enter** For help on how to complete this form, point to the red triangles..
- **Format cell A8 using a font color of red and bold.**
- **Insert a blank row below row 8.**

Your screen should be similar to Figure 5.43

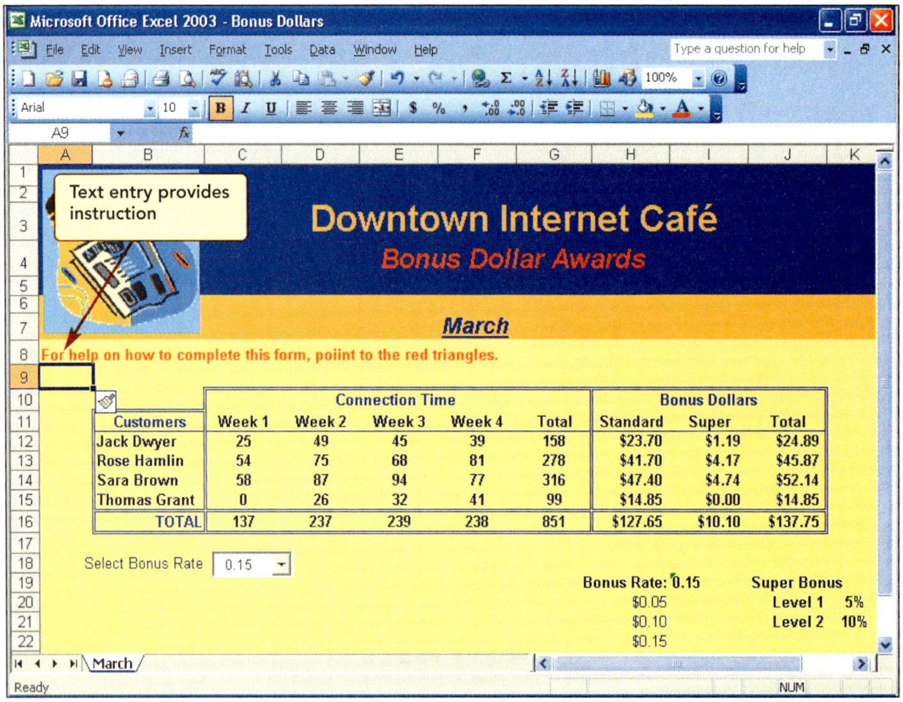

Figure 5.43

Next, you will add the cell comments using the Reviewing toolbar. The first comment will appear in cell F7 and will direct users to update the month.

2

- Display the Reviewing toolbar.
- If necessary, move the toolbar to the lower-right corner of the worksheet.
- Move to F7.
- Click New Comment in the Reviewing toolbar.

Another Method

The menu equivalent is Insert/Comment.

Your screen should be similar to Figure 5.44

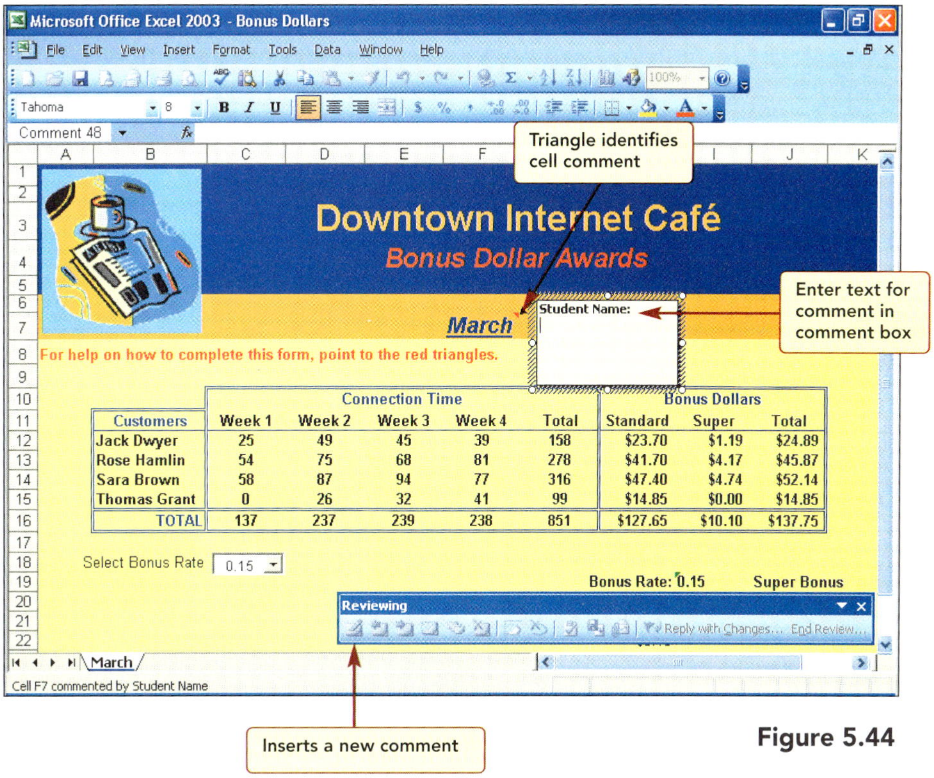

Figure 5.44

By default, the comment box includes the user name. You will delete the text for the comment.

3

- Select the user name and press Delete.
- Type **Enter the month.**
- Size the comment box to fit the text.
- Click on any cell to complete the comment.
- Point to cell F7.

Your screen should be similar to Figure 5.45

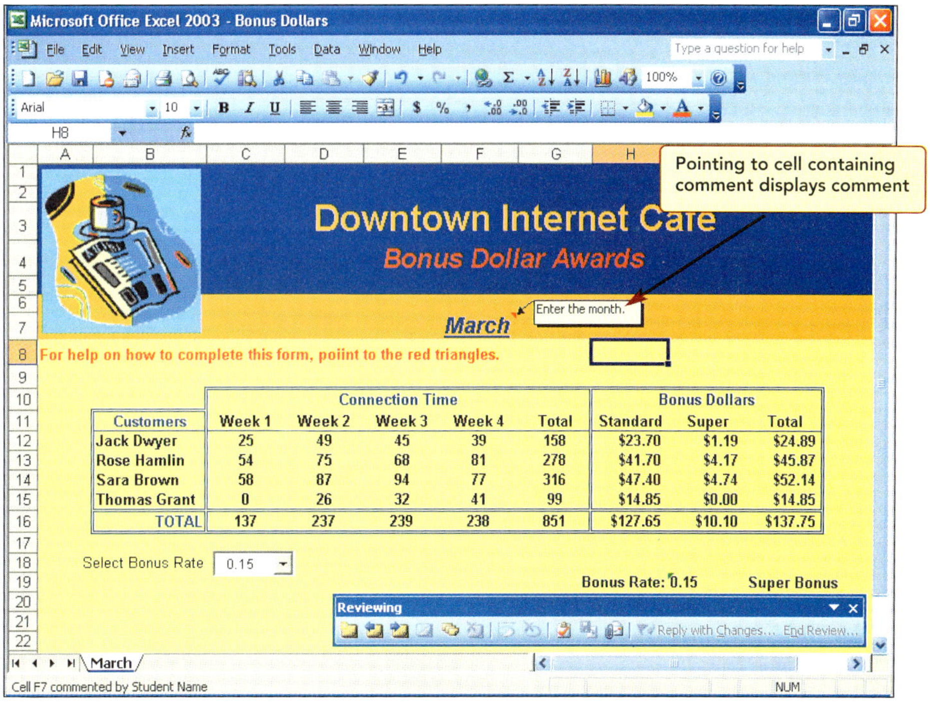

Figure 5.45

A red triangle appears in the upper-right corner of the cell containing the comment. When you point to a cell containing a comment, the comment text is displayed in a comment box. An arrow from the comment box points to the cell to which the comment is attached.

The second comment will be entered in cell C12.

Having Trouble?

If the red triangle is not displayed, choose Tools/Options/View and select Comment indicator only.

1

- **Add a comment to C12 containing the text Enter weekly times here. and size the comment box to fit the text.**
- **Click on any cell to complete the comment.**
- **Point to cell C12 to display the comment.**

Another Method

You can also move to a cell containing a comment and click Show/Hide Comments to display and then hide the comment. The comment remains displayed until you hide it again.

Your screen should be similar to Figure 5.46

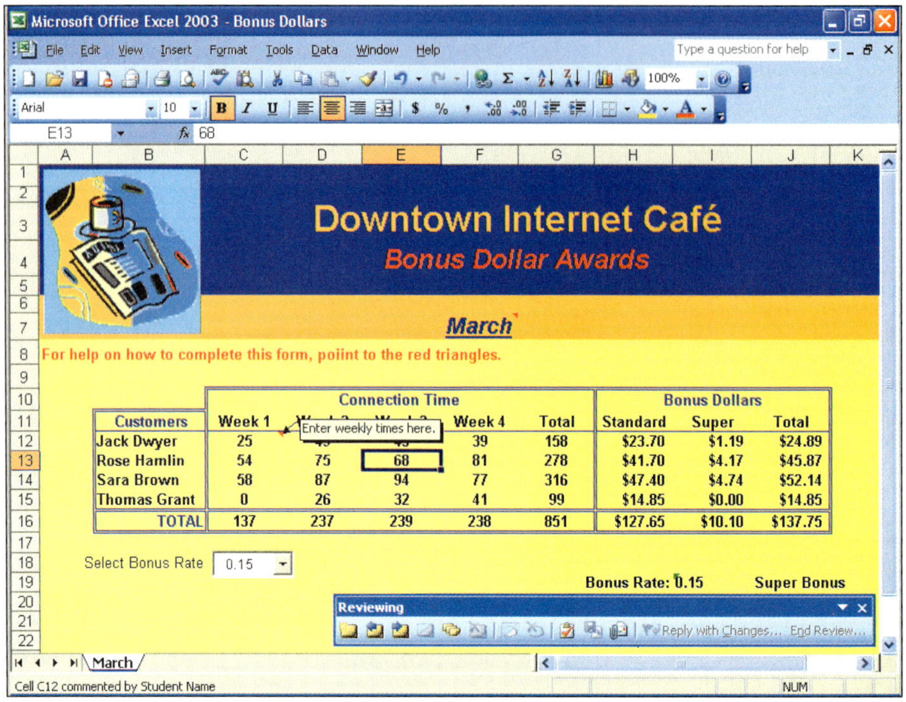

Figure 5.46

Editing comments

You decide the comment is not descriptive enough and will edit the comment text.

2 Move to cell C12 and click ![] Edit Comment.

Another Method

You can also edit a comment using Insert/Edit Comment or choose Edit Comment from the shortcut menu.

- Move the insertion point before the word "times" and type the word **connection** followed by a space.
- Size the comment box to fit the text.

Your screen should be similar to Figure 5.47

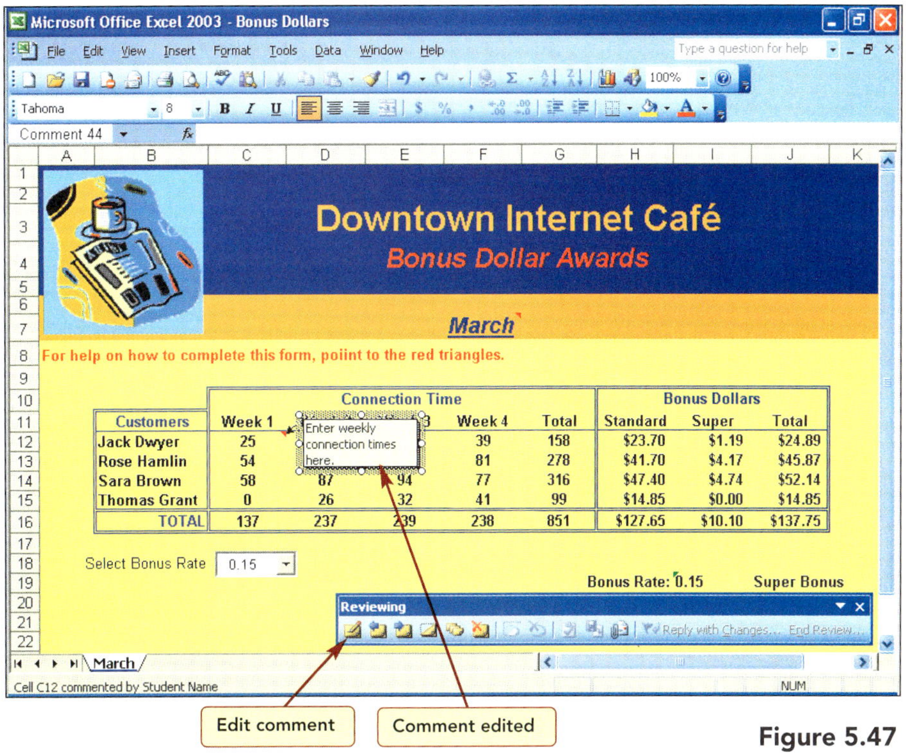

Figure 5.47

Additional Information

You can delete a comment using Edit/Clear/Comments or Delete Comment from the shortcut menu or by clicking ![] Delete Comment.

The comment text now appears as you want it.

3 Click on any cell to complete the comment.

- Display the comment.
- Add a comment to B18 containing the text **Select this month's bonus rate.** and size the comment box to fit the text.
- Click on any cell to complete the comment.
- Display the comment.

Your screen should be similar to Figure 5.48

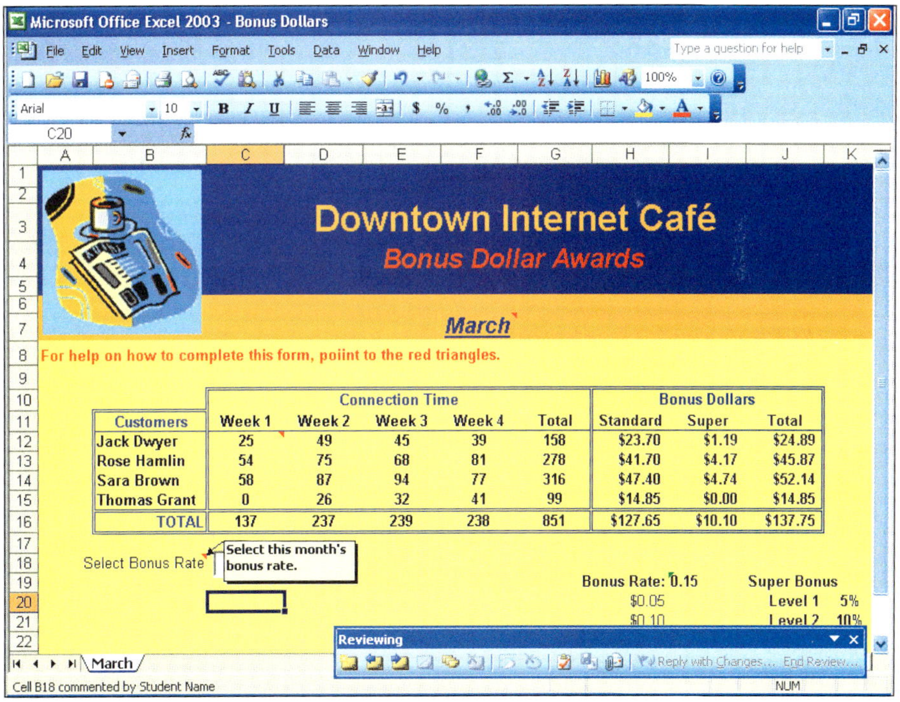

Figure 5.48

You have added three comments to the form to provide directions on how to use the form.

Viewing All Comments

To quickly check all comments, rather than displaying each comment individually, you can display all the comments at the same time.

1 Click Show All Comments.

Your screen should be similar to Figure 5.49

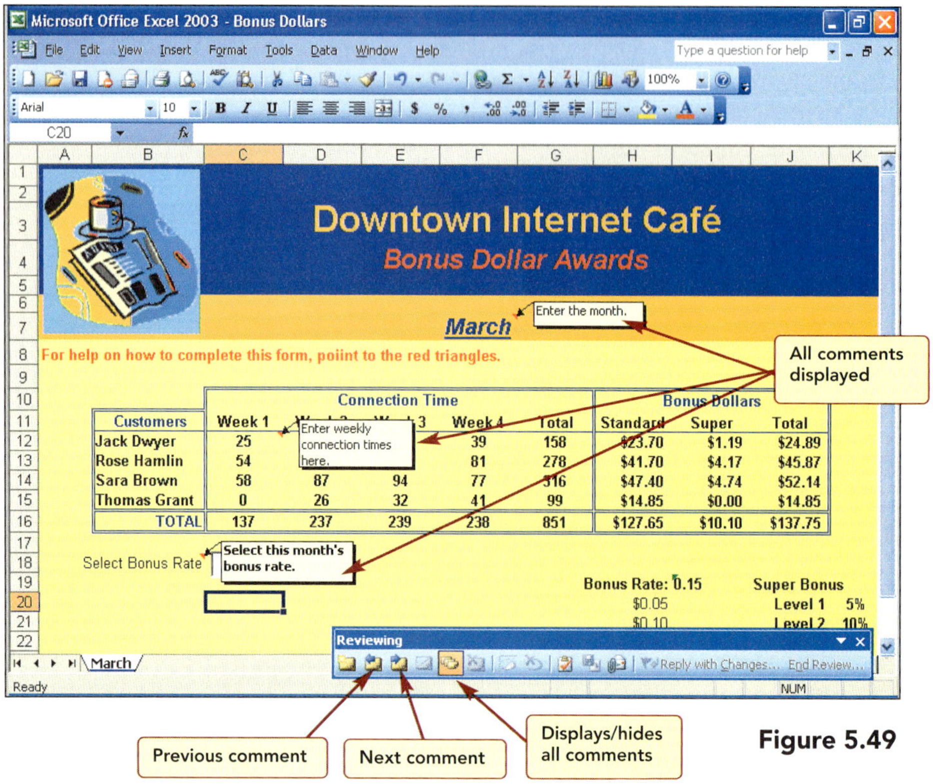

Figure 5.49

Another Method

You can also click Previous Comment or Next Comment to cycle from one comment to the next.

Additional Information

You can also print comments where they appear on the worksheet or in a list at the end of the worksheet by selecting the appropriate option from the Print dialog box.

The three comments you entered are displayed. If comments overlay one another, you can move them around just like any other graphic object. However, when you hide and redisplay the comments, they return to their original location.

2 Click Hide All Comments.

Another Method

The menu equivalent, View/Comments, will display all comments or hide all displayed comments.

- Close the Reviewing toolbar.
- Save the workbook.

Your screen should be similar to Figure 5.50

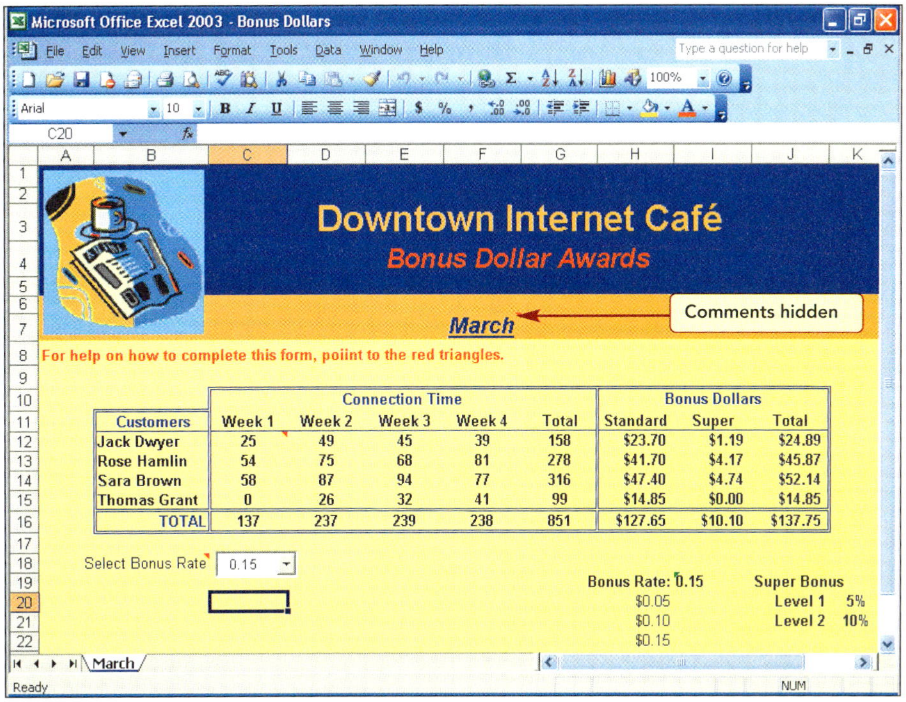

Figure 5.50

Hiding Rows

Next, you will add a command button to make it easy to print the output. Then you will hide any nonessential information in the form to simplify its appearance.

1 Open the Forms toolbar and add a command button over cell E18.

- Name the macro **PrintForm** and record a macro to print the worksheet in landscape orientation, centered horizontally on the page. Include a custom footer that displays your name and date only.
- Label the button **Print Form** and size it to fit the text.
- Close the Forms toolbar.

Your screen should be similar to Figure 5.51

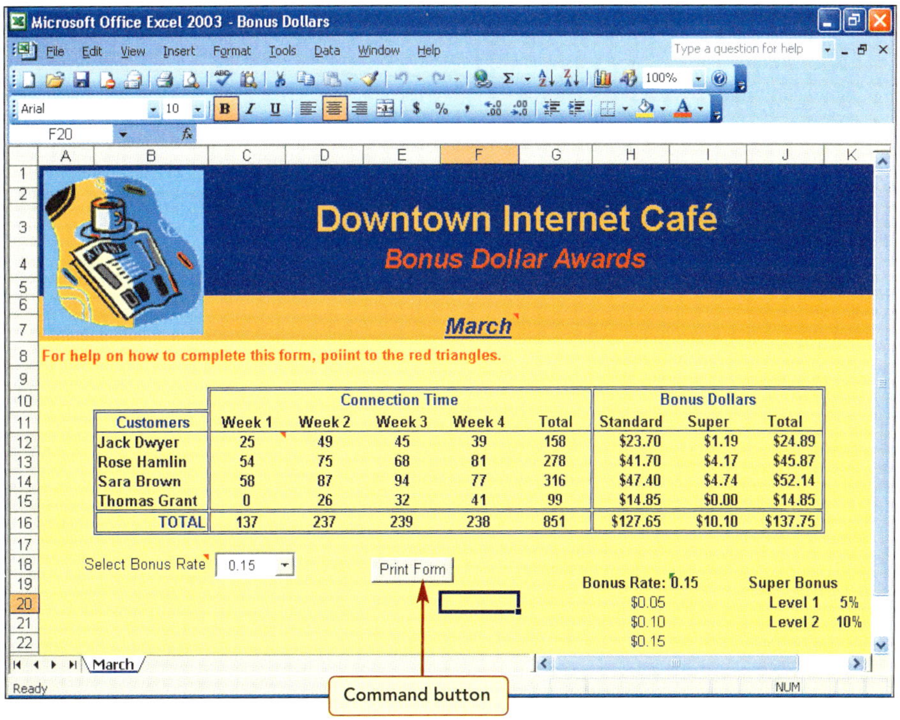

Figure 5.51

Users of this form do not need to see the list of rates and the two bonus levels. To simplify the form, you will hide this information.

2 **Select rows 19 through 22.**

Additional Information

Click the row number to quickly select an entire row.

- **Choose Format/Row/Hide.**

- **Save the workbook.**

Additional Information

To redisplay hidden rows, select the rows above and below the hidden rows and use Format/Row/Unhide.

Your screen should be similar to Figure 5.52

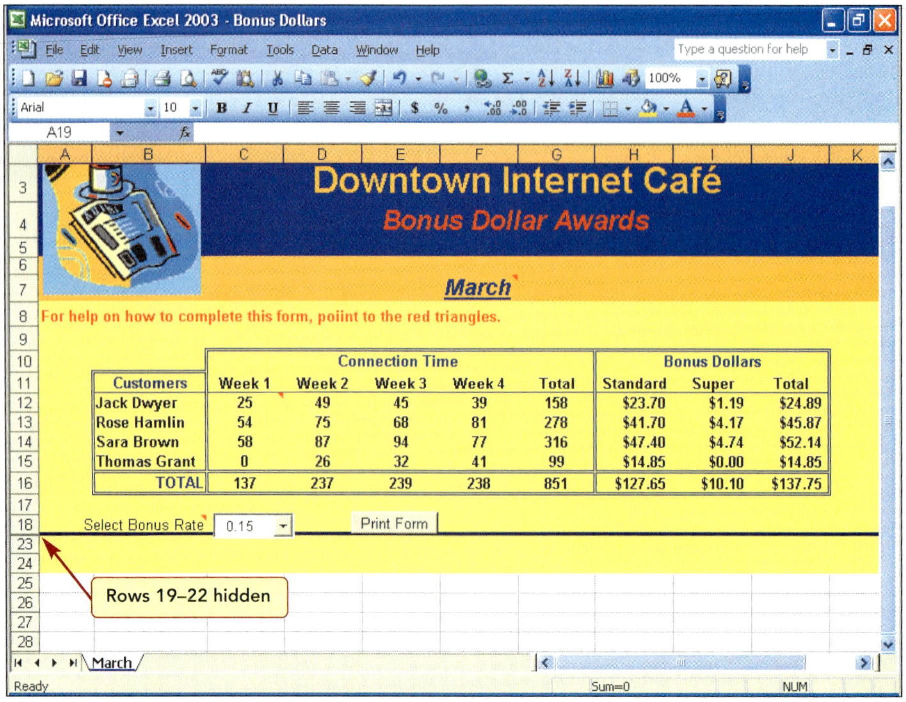

Figure 5.52

Now only the information that is necessary to complete the form is displayed.

Preparing the Form Template

Each month the form will be used to record the customer's Bonus Dollar earnings. You need to clear the sample data and protect the worksheet. Finally, you will save it as a template file. You also want to include the file documentation so that users of the template will understand the purpose of the file.

First, you will clear the contents of the entry areas and unlock these cells for editing. Then you will protect the worksheet.

1. Clear the contents of cell F7 and cells C12 through F15.
   - Unlock cell F7.
   - Unlock the cells for weekly connection times (cells C12 through F15).
   - Use Edit/Go To to move to cell I19 that displays the selected bonus rate.
   - Unlock cell I19.
   - Protect the worksheet.

Your screen should be similar to Figure 5.53

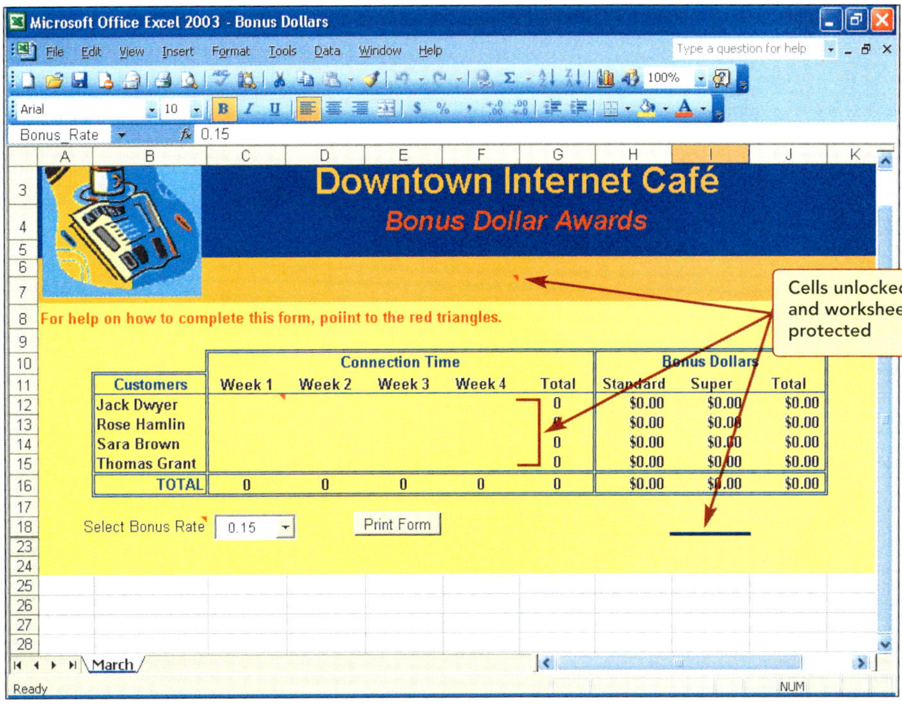

Figure 5.53

Next, you will enter basic documentation regarding the worksheet file.

2. Choose File/Properties.
   - If necessary, open the Summary tab.
   - In the Subject text box, type **Monthly record of connection times and bonuses**.
   - Enter **your name** in the Author text box.
   - In the Comments text box, type **Point to the red triangles for instructions. Select the bonus amount for the month from the Bonus Rate drop-down list.**.

Your screen should be similar to Figure 5.54

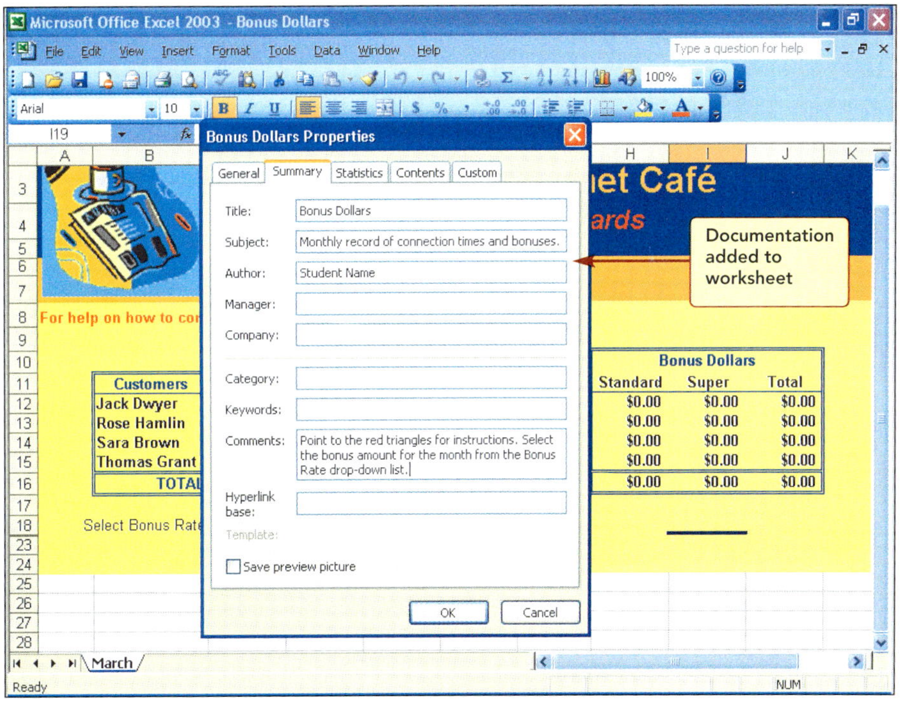

Figure 5.54

You are now ready to save the form as a workbook template.

3. - Click OK to close the Properties dialog box.
   - Move to cell A9.
   - Save the workbook as a template to your data file location using the file name Monthly Bonus Form.
   - Click OK in response to the privacy warning.
   - Click Print Form to print the template.
   - Close and save the workbook and exit Excel.

Focus on Careers

EXPLORE YOUR CAREER OPTIONS

Payroll Clerk

Have you ever wondered who makes sure you get your paycheck? Have you ever had to address inaccuracies on your paycheck with someone in payroll? Payroll clerks track employee hours and compute employee pay after making subtractions for taxes and insurance. Payroll clerks also add new employees to the system and prepare earnings statements employees use for filing taxes. They must have excellent math skills and good communication skills. Some offices use automated payroll systems, but in these situations payroll clerks are typically responsible for doing analysis and looking at trends using spreadsheet programs. Salary range is typically between $30,000 and $40,000 depending on experience. The demand for payroll clerks is expected to decrease slightly as many companies move towards automation.

LAB 5

Using Data Tables, Creating Macros, and Designing Onscreen Forms

Data Table (EX5.9)

A data table is a range of cells that is used to quickly calculate multiple what-if versions in one operation and to show the results of all variations in the worksheet.

Macro (EX5.17)

A macro is a series of keystrokes and commands that are stored as instructions in a unit or module of Microsoft Visual Basic, a programming language.

Control (EX5.19)

A control is a graphic object that is designed to help the user interact with the worksheet.

Macro Recorder (EX5.20)

The Macro Recorder automatically creates a macro by recording a series of actions as macro commands.

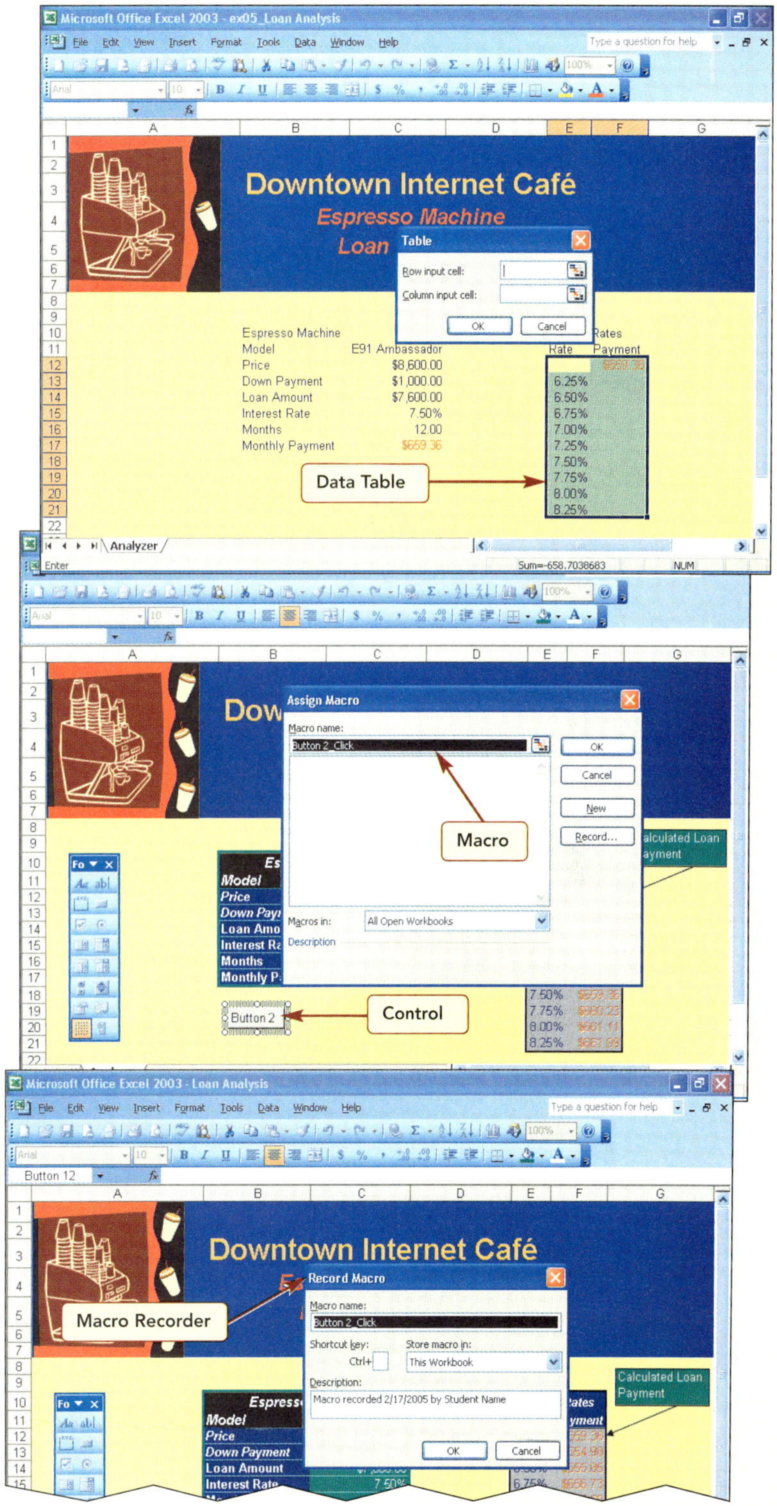

concept summary

Form (EX5.26)

A form is a formatted worksheet with blank spaces that can be filled in online on an individual computer or on a network, or printed and completed on paper.

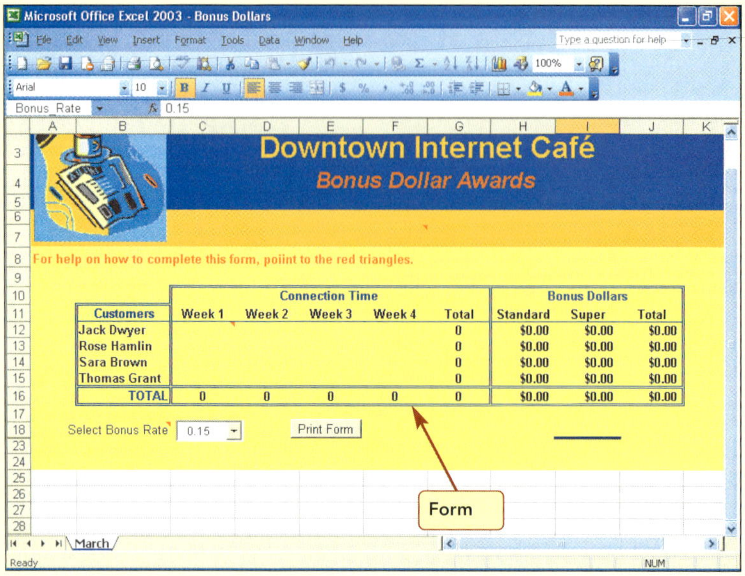

IF Function (EX5.32)

The IF function checks to see if certain conditions are met and then takes action based on the results of the check.

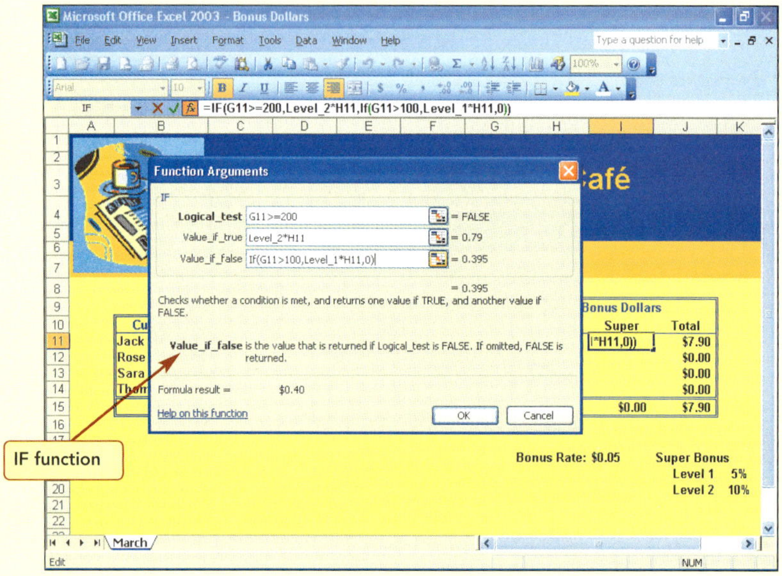

Comment (EX5.40)

A comment is a note attached to a cell that can be used to clarify the meaning of the cell contents, provide documentation, or ask a question.

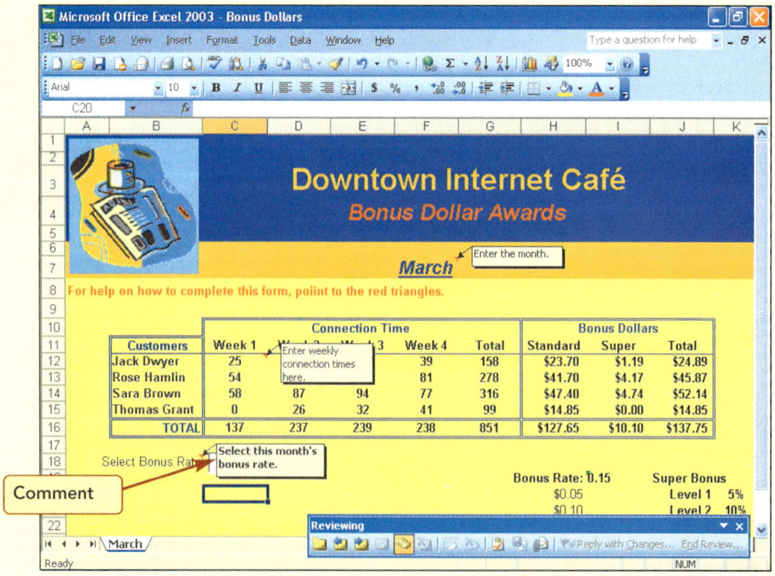

lab review

LAB 5

Using Data Tables, Creating Macros, and Designing Onscreen Forms

key terms

column-oriented EX5.9
comment EX5.40
control EX5.19
data table EX5.9
digital signature EX5.18
form EX5.26
IF function EX5.32
input cell EX5.11
logical operator EX5.32
macro EX5.17
Macro Recorder EX5.20
module EX5.17
name EX5.28
nested function EX5.34
one-variable data table EX5.9
PMT function EX5.6
principal EX5.6
property EX5.19
row-oriented EX5.9
text box EX5.14
two-variable data table EX5.9

microsoft office specialist skills

The Microsoft Office Specialist certification program is designed to measure your proficiency in performing basic tasks using the Office 2003 applications. Certification demonstrates that you have the skills and provides a valuable industry credential for employment. After completing this lab, you have learned the following Microsoft Office Excel Specialist skills:

Skill	Description	Page
Creating Data and Content	Locate, select and insert supporting information	EX5.7
Analyzing Data	Use statistical, date and time, financial, and logical functions in formulas	EX5.32
Formatting Data and Content	Apply and modify cell formats	EX5.12
	Modify row and column formats	EX5.45
Collaboration	Insert, view and edit comments	EX5.40
Managing Workbooks	Set up pages for printing	EX5.22,5.45

command summary

Command	Shortcut Key	Button	Action
File/Properties			Displays information about a file
Edit/Clear/Comments			Deletes comment in selected cell
Edit/Go To			Goes to the specified place in the document
View/Comments			Displays all comments
Insert/Name/Define			Assigns a name you specify to a cell or range of cells
Insert/Name/Paste			Places selected range name in formula bar or lists names in worksheet
Insert/Name/Create			Creates a range name using text in cells
Insert/Comment			Inserts a new comment in selected cell
Insert/Edit Comment			Edits comment in selected cell
Format/Row/Hide			Hides selected rows
Format/Row/Unhide			Displays rows that were previously hidden
Format/AutoFormat			Applies selected format to range
Tools/Macro/Macros	Alt + F8		Runs, edits, or deletes selected macro
Tools/Macro/Record New Macro			Records a series of actions as a macro
Tools/Macro/Stop Recording			Stops the recording of a macro
Tools/Macro/ Security			Sets security level associated with macros in a workbook
Tools/Options/View/ Comment Indicator only			Displays comment indicators
Data/Table			Creates a data table based on specified input values and formulas

lab exercises

matching

Match the letter on the right to the item in the numbered list on the left.

1. data table	______	**a.** a stored series of keystrokes and commands
2. AutoFormat	______	**b.** a note attached to a cell
3. IF function	______	**c.** a built-in combination of formats
4. controls	______	**d.** a range of cells that is used to quickly calculate multiple what-if versions
5. macro	______	**e.** a function that checks to see if a condition is met and takes action based on that condition
6. form	______	**f.** authentication that confirms a macro
7. Macro Recorder	______	**g.** a description of a cell or range that can be used in place of the cell or range reference
8. digital signature	______	**h.** graphic objects that help users interact with the worksheet
9. logical operators	______	**i.** compares numbers in two or more cells or to a constant
10. comment	______	**j.** a tool used to create a macro
11. name		

multiple choice

Circle the correct response to the questions below.

1. A ________________ is a note attached to a cell.
   a. comment
   b. text box
   c. command button
   d. macro

2. The ___________ automatically creates a macro by recording a series of actions.
   a. Macro Recorder
   b. nested function
   c. Macro Reader
   d. none of the above

3. A(n) ____________ is a formatted worksheet with blank spaces that can be filled in online.
   a. template
   b. form
   c. object
   d. cell

4. When a macro is _____________, the actions within it are performed automatically.
   a. displayed
   b. run
   c. created
   d. opened

5. A _____________ data table can be row- or column-oriented.
   a. multi-variable
   b. two-variable
   c. single-variable
   d. one-variable

6. An Excel form can contain _____________.
   a. text
   b. graphics
   c. cell comments
   d. all of the above

7. A(n) _________________ is a built-in combination of formats that can be applied to a range of cells.
   a. object
   b. diagram
   c. AutoFormat
   d. font

8. A name assigned to a cell must start with _____________.
   a. a letter
   b. a number
   c. a backslash
   d. any of the above

9. A(n) ______________ argument is an expression that makes a comparison using logical operators.
   a. if_then
   b. logical_test
   c. and_or
   d. logical_if

10. ____________________ are used in formulas and functions that compare numbers in two or more cells.
   a. Logical operators
   b. Function arguments
   c. Relational operators
   d. Command buttons

true/false

Circle the correct answer to the following questions.

1.	When a macro is executed, the stored actions are performed automatically.	True	False
2.	A control's properties can be changed or customized.	True	False
3.	Comments are attached to cells.	True	False
4.	A form created in Excel cannot be used online.	True	False
5.	The result of an IF argument is either true or false.	True	False
6.	Low security automatically disables macros if they are not digitally signed.	True	False
7.	A range name can only include letters.	True	False
8.	An apostrophe identifies a macro instruction as a remark.	True	False
9.	The IF function requires three arguments.	True	False
10.	A text box can be use to display graphics.	True	False

fill-in

Complete the following statements by filling in the blanks with the correct key terms.

1. A ______________ can consist of any combination of 255 characters.
2. ______________ are used in formulas and functions that compare values in two or more cells.
3. A(n) ______________ appears as a note box attached to a cell.
4. The __________ function checks to see if certain conditions are met and takes actions based on the results.
5. A built-in combination of formats that can be applied to a selected range is called a(n) ________________.
6. A(n) ____________ is a stored set of keystrokes and commands.
7. In a data table, when the data is ______________, the data is displayed across a row instead of down a column.
8. The PMT function contains three arguments: __________, nper, and pv.
9. A(n) ______________ is a formatted worksheet that is intended to be filled in by the user.
10. A graphical object that is placed on a worksheet that can be used to execute a recorded macro is a ________________.

rating system
★ Easy
★★ Moderate
★★★ Difficult

step-by-step

Animal Rescue Foundation Volunteer Rewards ★

1. After viewing the revenue analysis you provided, Samuel Johnson and the other Animal Rescue Foundation board members have begun the budget planning for the next year. They have realized that daily operation of the agency depends on the volunteers. To repay them for their time, the board has decided to implement a rewards program with some of the budget surpluses you have anticipated. You have been asked to create a worksheet to track the number of hours people have worked and determine their award level. Your completed worksheets should be similar to the one shown here.

a. Open the workbook file ex05_ARF Volunteers.

b. Enter formulas to calculate the average and total hours for the year in columns F and G. Copy the formulas down the columns.

c. Enter the labels **Star Level 1**, **Star Level 2**, and **Star Level 3** right-aligned in cells I40 through I42. In cells J40 through J42, enter **300**, **200**, and **100** as the award levels.

d. Apply an AutoFormat to enhance cells I40 through J42. Adjust the column widths and layout as necessary.

e. Use the Name Range command to name the values for the star levels.

f. In cell H5 enter the following formula to calculate the award level for the volunteers: **=IF(G5>=Star_Level_1,1,IF(G5>=Star_Level_2,2,IF(G5>=Star_Level_3,3,0)))**.

g. Change the value in cell B5 to **450** and then to **0** to check the formula. Return the value to **45**. Copy the formula down the column.

h. Add cell comments to the worksheet that explain the Star System.

i. Select the entire worksheet excluding the star values. Enter **your name** and the **current date** in a header, then center the worksheet horizontally.

j. Print the selection. Save the workbook as Volunteers.

Student Name [Current Date]

ANIMAL ANGELS VOLUNTEERS

	1st Qtr	2nd Qtr	3rd Qtr	4th Qtr	Average	Total	Level
Bell, Patricia	45	34	102	35	54	216	2
Carey, Ronnie	105	42	50	102	74.75	299	2
Carver, Kathi	30	83	3	3	29.75	119	3
Chorley, Besty	68	2	235	96	100.25	401	1
Clark, Jamel	51	30	28	58	41.75	167	3
Cody, Martin	28	66	6	45	36.25	145	3
Dickson, Diane	70	18	88	27	50.75	203	2
Edwards, Mike	12	20	61	28	30.25	121	3
Ferguson, Robby	99	12	0	43	38.5	154	3
Forester, Kimberly	30	63	34	44	42.75	171	3
Franklin, Stacey	57	98	93	80	82	328	1
Fulton, Anne	12	18	68	122	55	220	2
Garcia, Maria	5	23	61	36	31.25	125	3
Gatens, Chris	0	100	58	85	60.75	243	2
Henderson, James	9	76	51	60	49	196	3
Ingram, Helen	29	12	33	12	21.5	86	0
Isbell, Sonya	46	65	47	3	40.25	161	3
Johnson, Thaman	3	30	20	6	14.75	59	0
Jones, April	70	83	38	79	67.5	270	2
Kelly, William	12	76	63	94	61.25	245	2
Kettonhoeffer, Bill	4	59	57	8	32	128	3
Kullman, Rodney	28	30	35	16	27.25	109	3
La Paglia, Sally	39	10	12	134	48.75	195	3
Lee, Su	56	6	5	0	16.75	67	0
Legge, Cristan	3	81	73	34	47.75	191	3
Lopez, Andrew	86	34	5	156	70.25	281	2
Marcus, Danielle	3	19	24	2	12	48	0
Merwin, Michael	44	9	95	37	46.25	185	3
Nelson, Faith	9	112	6	0	31.75	127	3
Pennington, Neil	75	62	8	79	56	224	2
Peterson, Tracey	83	3	165	0	62.75	251	2
Pierce, Kai	6	98	4	75	45.75	183	3
Tranthom, Ellie	27	35	19	12	23.25	93	0

Wilson Electronics Financial Analysis ★ ★

2. You have been hired as a salesperson for the Wilson Electronics Company. You want to be able to give your customers up-to-date and accurate information on the cost of high-end electronics you sell. To automate the process, you plan to use a data table containing the model information and a table to calculate the different payments. The completed worksheet will be similar to the one shown here.

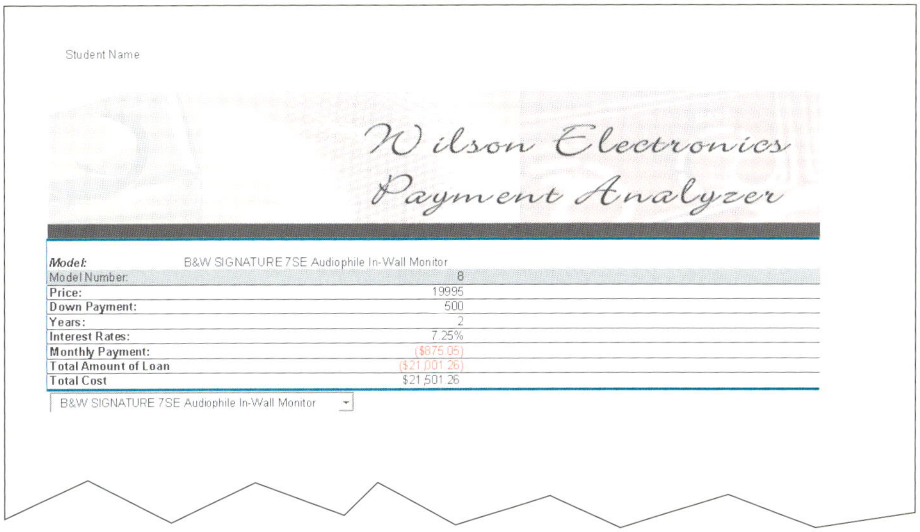

   a. Open the file ex05_Electronics Analyzer.

   b. Instead of typing in the model and price of the item each time, you want to be able to choose it from a drop-down list that links to a data table. The information for the data table has already been created in cells D23 through E36. Enter the number **1** in cell B13. You will use the Choose function. In cell B12 enter: **=CHOOSE(B13,D23,D24,D25,D26,D27,D28,D29,D30,D31,D32,D33,D34,D35,D36)** to select the items in the data table based on the number entered in cell B13.

   c. Create a similar Choose function in cell B14 to display the price associated with each item.

   d. Enter the following sample data: **$500** for the down payment in cell B15, **2** for the years in cell B16, and **.0725** for the interest rate in cell B17.

   e. Enter the PMT function **=PMT(B17/12,B16*12,B14-B15)** in cell B18. To calculate the total amount of the loan, enter the formula **= B18*(B16*12)** in cell B19. To calculate the total cost, enter the formula **=B15-B19** in cell B20.

   f. To see how the calculator works, enter **8** in cell B13.

   g. Since each customer orders a different item, you would like to create a combo box that will allow you to quickly select the item rather than have to type the reference number in the cell.

   h. Enter the numbers 1 to 14 in cells C23 to C36. (These will correspond to the model numbers.)

   i. Open the Control Toolbox toolbar and create a combo box control below cell D13. Specify the Input Range as D23 through D36 and the Cell Link as B12.

   j. Adjust the size and placement of the combo box and display it below the form data. Close the Control Toolbox toolbar. Select an item from the combo box list to test it.

   k. Hide rows 23 through 36.

   l. Select cells A11:E20 and apply the List 1 AutoFormat. Adjust the column widths and layout as necessary.

   m. Include cell comments to inform the user how to use the form.

n. To see how the worksheet works, enter the following for changing variable values: **Sonance DR7001 DR Series In-Ceiling**

Model Number: **6**

Down payment: **2,500**

Years: **5**

Interest Rate: **.085**

o. Record a macro that prints the worksheet.

p. Unlock cells B13 through B17. Protect the worksheet without a password.

q. Include a text box with an arrow pointing to the combo box. Enter directions on how to use the form.

r. Include your name and the current date in a header and print the worksheet in landscape orientation. Save the worksheet as Electronics Analyzer.

Adventure Travel Tours Package Analysis ★ ★

3. Adventure Travel Tours agents work hard to sell travel packages. To give their customers the best possible fares, ATT agents make reservations based on group rates. Because the rates are calculated as a percentage of the previous year's sales, you would like to create a worksheet that will show the effects of a change in sales from –5 percent to 10 percent. The completed Adventure Travel Sales worksheet will be similar to the one shown here.

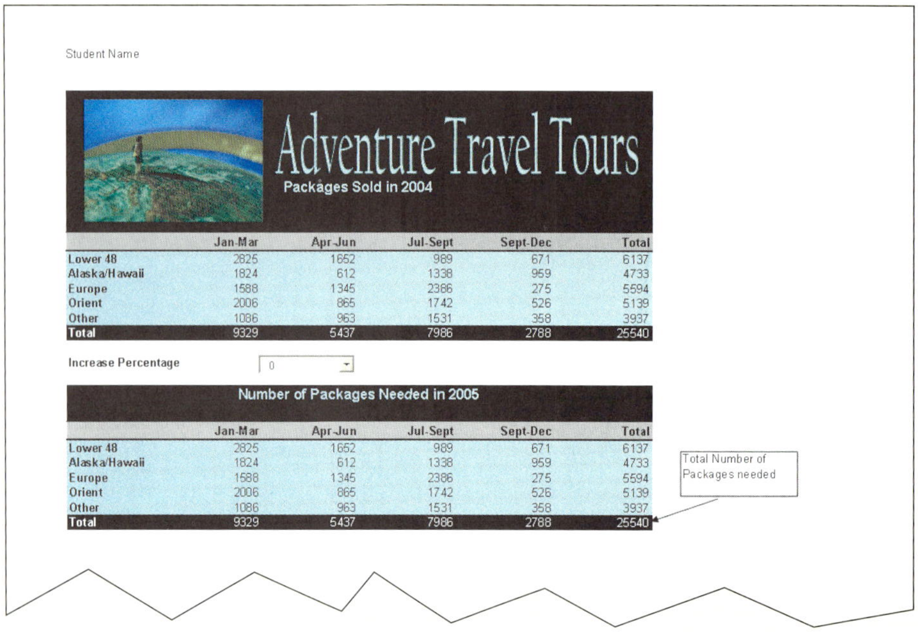

Student Name

Adventure Travel Tours

Packages Sold in 2004

	Jan-Mar	Apr-Jun	Jul-Sept	Sept-Dec	Total
Lower 48	2825	1652	989	671	6137
Alaska/Hawaii	1824	612	1338	959	4733
Europe	1588	1345	2386	275	5594
Orient	2006	865	1742	526	5139
Other	1086	963	1531	358	3937
Total	9329	5437	7986	2788	25540

Increase Percentage 0

Number of Packages Needed in 2005

	Jan-Mar	Apr-Jun	Jul-Sept	Sept-Dec	Total
Lower 48	2825	1652	989	671	6137
Alaska/Hawaii	1824	612	1338	959	4733
Europe	1588	1345	2386	275	5594
Orient	2006	865	1742	526	5139
Other	1086	963	1531	358	3937
Total	9329	5437	7986	2788	25540

Total Number of Packages needed

a. Open the file ex05_ATT Sales.

b. Enter functions to calculate the totals.

c. Starting in cell K5, enter the values –5% to 10% at 1% increments. These will be used for the values in a combo box.

d. Using the Control Toolbox toolbar, create a combo box that contains these values and display the combo box over cell C13. Link the combo box to cell J5. Enter the label **Increase Percentage** in cell A13.

e. Copy cells A3 through F11 to cell A15. Change the title in row 15 to **Number of Packages Needed in 2005**.

f. In cell B18 enter the formula **=B6*(1+$J$5)**. Copy the formula through the cell range B18:E22.

g. Enter comments to tell the user how to use the worksheet.

h. Hide columns J and K. Set the percentage increase to 3%.

i. Record a macro that prints the worksheet.

j. Add a text box that points to the total number of packages needed.

k. Enter your name and the current date in a header, center the worksheet horizontally, and print the worksheet in landscape orientation.

l. Save the workbook as ATT Sales2.

Hayes Furniture Sales Form ★ ★ ★

4. The sales staff at Hayes Furniture needs a quick way to let customers know how much they need to pay for optional delivery. Your boss would like the form to be easy to modify if the tax rate and delivery charges change. You will finish the form that your boss started. The completed sales form will be similar to the one shown here.

a. Open the workbook file ex05_ Furniture Sales.

b. Name the values in H5 through H10 using the labels in column G. Name the value in cell H12 using the label in G12.

c. In cell C8 enter the If function that calculates the delivery charge using the named range based on the number entered in cell C6. (Hint the first IF is: =IF(C6<=5,0_to_5,IF...)).

d. In cell C7 enter the formula to calculate the tax due on the order total. In cell C9 enter the formula to calculate the total due on delivery.

e. Enter the following cell comments:

Cell	Comment
C4	**Enter the amount of the total order before taxes**
C5	**Enter the down payment**
C6	**Enter the delivery distance in whole miles**

f. Test the worksheet by entering the following values.

Price: **100.00**

Down Payment: **25.00**

Delivery Distance: **8**

The amount due on delivery should be $93.50.

g. Unlock the cell contents of cells C4 through C6. Hide columns G and H.

h. Add a text box and arrow to the sheet to identify the order total.

i. Entering the following values.

Order Total: **500.50**

Down Payment: **300.00**

Delivery Distance: **25**

j. Enter your name and the current date in a header, center the worksheet horizontally, and print the worksheet.

k. Record a macro that prints the worksheet.

l. Protect the worksheet without a password.

m. Save the workbook as **Furniture Sales Form**.

Grade Book Maintenance ★★★

5. You are a graduate assistant and have been assigned to work for a university professor. You are responsible for maintaining the grade book and have decided to create a worksheet that will calculate the students' final grades. You started the workbook by entering the row and column labels and the points earned for a sample set of students in four categories. You need to add formulas that will total the students' points on a summary worksheet and then use this new total to calculate the grade for the course. Your completed workbook should be similar to that shown here.

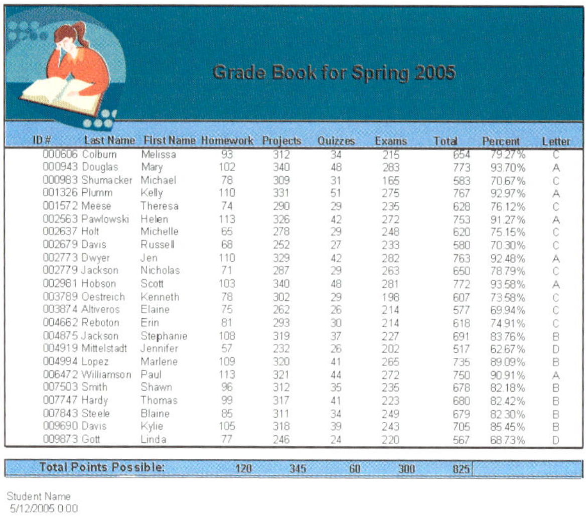

Grade Book for Spring 2005

ID #	Last Name	First Name	Homework	Projects	Quizzes	Exams	Total	Percent	Letter
000606	Colburn	Melissa	93	312	34	215	654	79.27%	C
000943	Douglas	Mary	102	340	48	283	773	93.70%	A
000983	Shumacker	Michael	78	309	31	165	583	70.67%	C
001326	Plumm	Kelly	110	331	51	275	767	92.97%	A
001572	Meese	Theresa	74	290	29	235	628	76.12%	C
002563	Pawlowski	Helen	113	326	42	272	753	91.27%	A
002637	Holt	Michelle	65	278	29	248	620	75.15%	C
002679	Davis	Russell	68	252	27	233	580	70.30%	C
002773	Dwyer	Jen	110	329	42	282	763	92.48%	A
002779	Jackson	Nicholas	71	287	29	263	650	78.79%	C
002981	Hobson	Scott	103	340	48	281	772	93.58%	A
003789	Oestreich	Kenneth	78	302	29	198	607	73.58%	C
003874	Altiveros	Elaine	75	262	26	214	577	69.94%	C
004662	Reboton	Erin	81	293	30	214	618	74.91%	C
004875	Jackson	Stephanie	108	319	37	227	691	83.76%	B
004919	Mittelstadt	Jennifer	57	232	26	202	517	62.67%	D
004994	Lopez	Marlene	109	320	41	265	735	89.09%	B
006472	Williamson	Paul	113	321	44	272	750	90.91%	A
007503	Smith	Shawn	96	312	35	235	678	82.18%	B
007747	Hardy	Thomas	99	317	41	223	680	82.42%	B
007843	Steele	Blaine	85	311	34	249	679	82.30%	B
009690	Davis	Kylie	105	318	39	243	705	85.45%	B
009873	Gott	Linda	77	246	24	220	567	68.73%	D
Total Points Possible:			120	345	60	300	825		

Student Name
5/12/2005 0:00

a. Start Excel 2003 and open the file ex05_Grades.

b. Set cell D6 of the Summary sheet equal to the total on the Homework sheet (H6). Copy the formula down the column to insert the total homework points for all the students in the Summary sheet.

c. Repeat this step for the Projects, Quizzes, and Exams columns.

d. Enter a formula in column H of the Summary sheet to calculate the students' total points for the four categories.

e. Name cell H30 **PossiblePoints**. Enter the formula **=H6/ PossiblePoints** in cell I6. Copy the formula down the column for the other students. Apply the percentage format with two decimal places.

f. Enter the following IF statement in cell J6: **=IF(I6>0.899,“A”,IF(I6>0.799,“B”,IF(I6>0.699,“C”,IF(I6>0.599,“D”,“E”))))**. You can use the Insert Function feature or type the IF statement directly into the cell. Copy the IF statement down the column for the other students.

g. Enter your name and the current date using the NOW function below the worksheet data.

h. Preview the Summary worksheet. Make any necessary formatting changes. Remove the header from the worksheet.

i. Save the workbook as Gradebook and print the worksheet.

j. Add comments to explain the formula that obtains the letter grade.

k. Record a macro that prints the worksheet.

l. Save the file as Gradebook.

on your own

Macro Library ★

1. In a blank new worksheet, use the Macro Recorder to record five macros for procedures that you use frequently and for which using a macro would save you time. For example, you may want to create a macro to modify the font, color, and style in a cell. You should also add comments and a text box and arrow. Make sure that the macros are available to other open worksheets by using the Tools/Macros/Macros command. Enter your name and the current date in the worksheet. Test the macros and save the file as My Macros. Print both the macro and new worksheet.

401K Analysis ★

2. The company you work for will contribute 3 percent of your gross pay to an individual retirement account (IRA). You can add up to another 15 percent of your gross pay to the same IRA. Create a worksheet with the following columns: Gross Wages, Employer Contribution, My Contribution, and Total Contribution. Enter your gross wages and create a formula to calculate the company contribution. In a column to the right, enter the numbers 0 to 10. Format them as percentages. Create a combo box that uses the percentages and calculates your contribution for the My Contribution column. Total the contributions. Use the combo box to see how much of your gross pay you can contribute to the IRA. Select the value you think is most appropriate for you. Enter your name and the current date in the worksheet. Save the file as My 401K and print the worksheet.

Furniture Purchase Analysis ★ ★

3. You have been furniture shopping for family room furniture and have your decision down to three groupings from different stores. Part of your decision depends on what the monthly payments will be, based on the terms offered at the stores. The three stores offer different interest rates over a 3-year payment period. Using the information shown below and the features you learned in this lab, create a workbook to calculate the monthly payments for different interest rates. Use an AutoFormat to enhance the appearance of the worksheet. Save it as Furniture Loan Analysis. Print the analysis for the furniture grouping you want to purchase. Include your name and the current date in a header.

	Store 1	Store 2	Store 3
Purchase Total	$14,975	$12,320	$8,470
Down payment	$2,500	$2,000	$1,000
Interest rate	7.5%	6.5%	15%

Speeding Fine Calculator ★ ★

4. You have been hired to work for a local traffic court. Create a worksheet that the clerks can use to calculate the amount of speeding tickets. The worksheet should contain the following information: actual speed limit, speed the offender was traveling, and number of tickets the offender has received. The worksheet should calculate miles above speed limit, cost of ticket ($10.00 for each mile), and court cost ($53.50). Create a combo box to calculate additional charges of $20.00 for each offense after the first offense. Calculate the amount due the court. Enter your name and the current date centered in a header of the worksheet. Save the file as Speeding Fines and print the worksheet.

Personal Computer Comparison Shopping ★ ★ ★

5. You are interested in buying a new laptop computer. Use the Internet or newspaper advertisements to find prices for computers with similar features manufactured by different companies. Using the features you learned in this lab, create a worksheet that allows you to compare multiple computers on the same worksheet. Use a combo box to change the loan interest rate you have to pay for financing the purchase. Link the down payment, number of years, and interest rates to cells that can vary. Format the worksheet in an attractive manner. Enter your name and the current date in a header and print the worksheet. Save the worksheet as Laptop Computers.

Creating Lists and Web Pages

LAB 6

Objectives

After you have read this chapter, you should be able to:

1. Create a list.
2. Use a data form to add and modify records.
3. Create, edit, and use hyperlinks.
4. Sort data.
5. Filter records.
6. Calculate list values.
7. Save a workbook as a Web page.

Case Study

Downtown Internet Café

The form you created to track the Downtown Internet Café's customer Internet connection times and Bonus Dollar awards is working quite well. Evan would now like to have a separate worksheet that contains the café customers' contact information so that he can use it to send out the Bonus Dollars discount coupons. This type of information can be entered into a worksheet as a list. While using Excel to create the list, you will learn about locating, modifying, sorting, and filtering records in the list. You will also learn how to analyze information in a list using totals and subtotals.

Now you have two workbooks containing data pertaining to the Downtown Internet Café customers. To make it easier to work with the two workbooks, you will create a hyperlink in one workbook to open the other workbook.

The second project Evan has asked you to look into is to make the Bonus Dollars worksheet available to customers on the Web site to check their award status. To do this you will convert it to a Web page.

A printout of a filtered list and the Bonus Dollars Web page are shown here.

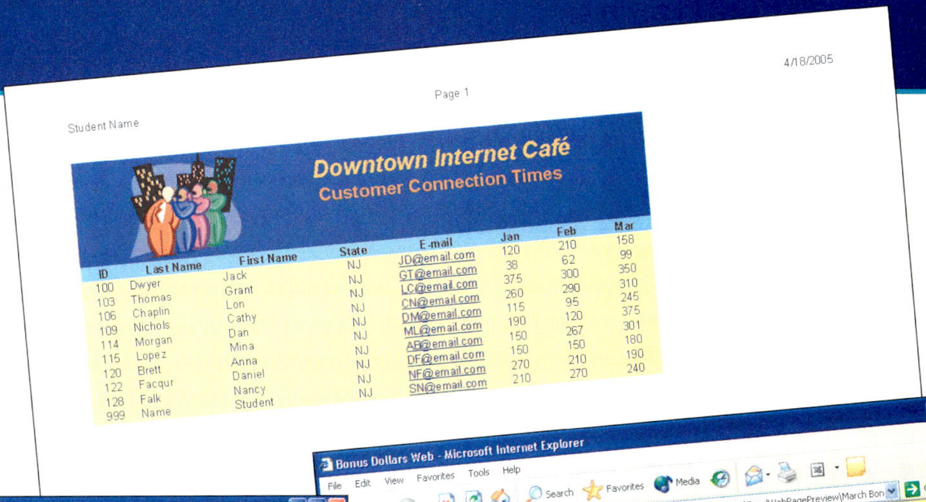

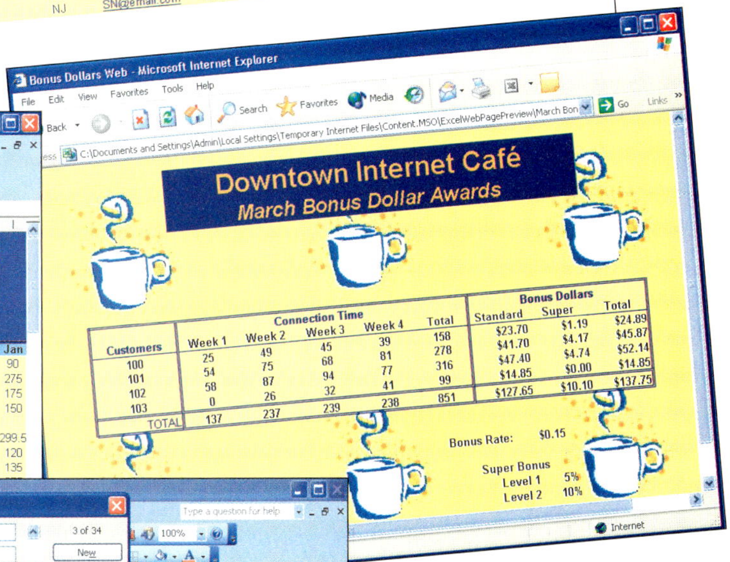

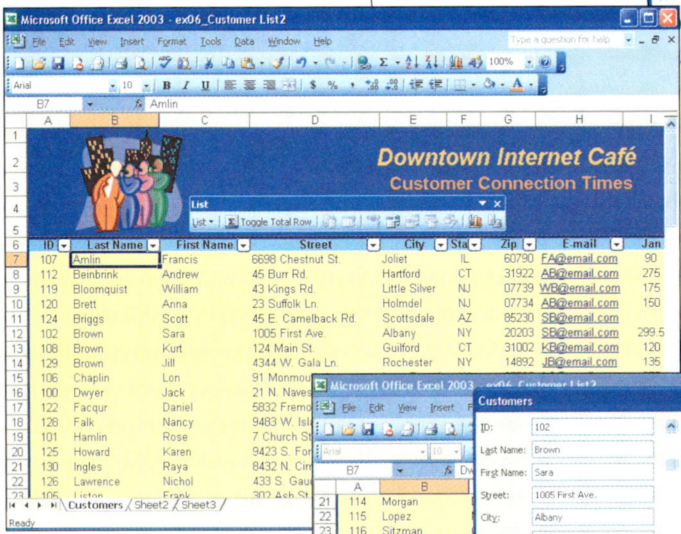

Creating a list is useful for organizing related information.

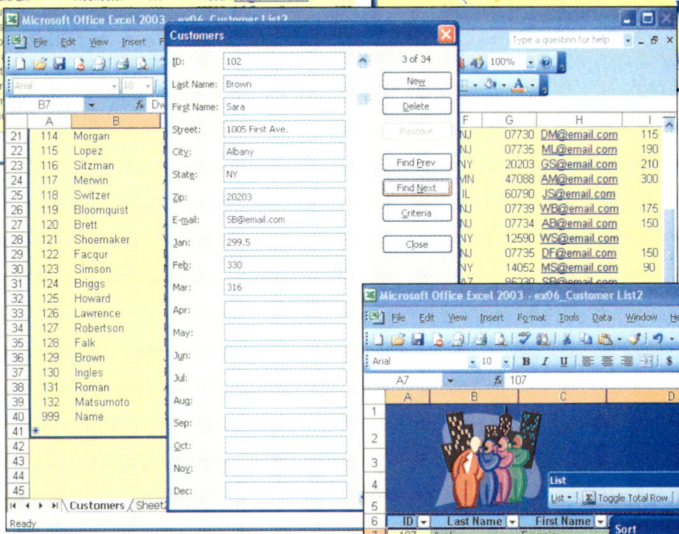

Using a data form speeds up entering and locating records in a list.

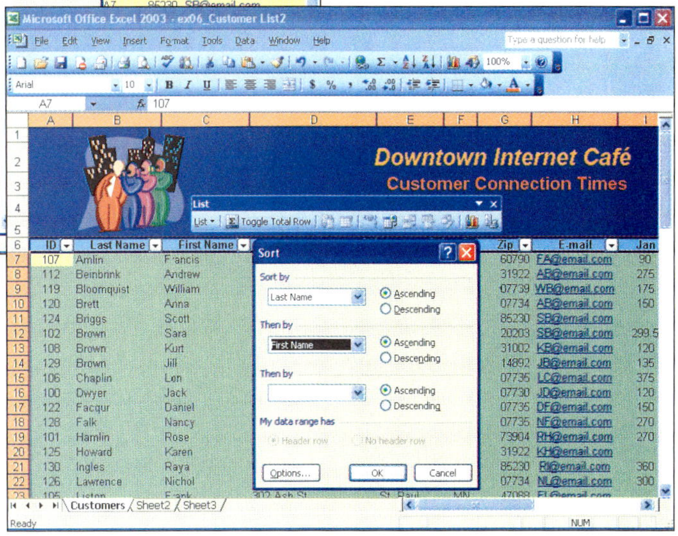

Sorting the information in a list displays the information you need in the specified order—alphabetically, numerically or by date.

Concept Preview

The following concepts will be introduced in this lab:

1. **List** A list, also called a database, is an organized collection of related information that is entered into a series of worksheet rows and columns.
2. **Hyperlink** A hyperlink is a connection or link to a destination location. The destination can be a location in the current file, in another file, a Web page, or an e-mail address.
3. **Sort** You can sort or arrange data in a specified sequence: alphabetically, numerically, or by date.
4. **Filter** A filter is a restriction you place on records in a list to quickly isolate and display a subset of records.
5. **Web Page** A Web page is a document that can be used on the World Wide Web (WWW) and displayed in a browser.

Creating a List

You want to create an Excel worksheet that will contain the café's customer contact information and Internet connection times. So that you can manipulate the data the way you want, you decide to format this worksheet as a list.

Concept 1

List

1 A **list**, also called a **database**, is an organized collection of related information that is entered into a series of worksheet rows and columns. Each row contains a **record**, which is all the information about one person, thing, or place. Each column is a **field**, which is the smallest unit of information about a record.

The first row in a list must contain column labels that serve as field names. A **field name** is a descriptive label used to identify the data stored in the field. The field names are used to create reports and find and organize data stored in the list. All rows below the field names contain the records. The area containing the records is called the **list range**.

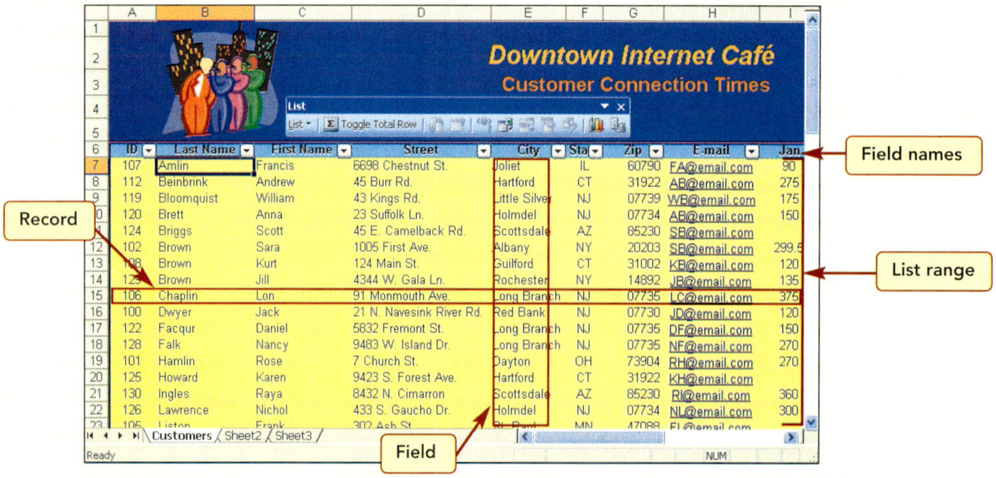

You have already entered many of the field names to create the structure for the list and have saved it in a workbook file named Customer List.

1 **Start Excel and open the workbook file** ex06_Customer List**.**

Your screen should be similar to Figure 6.1

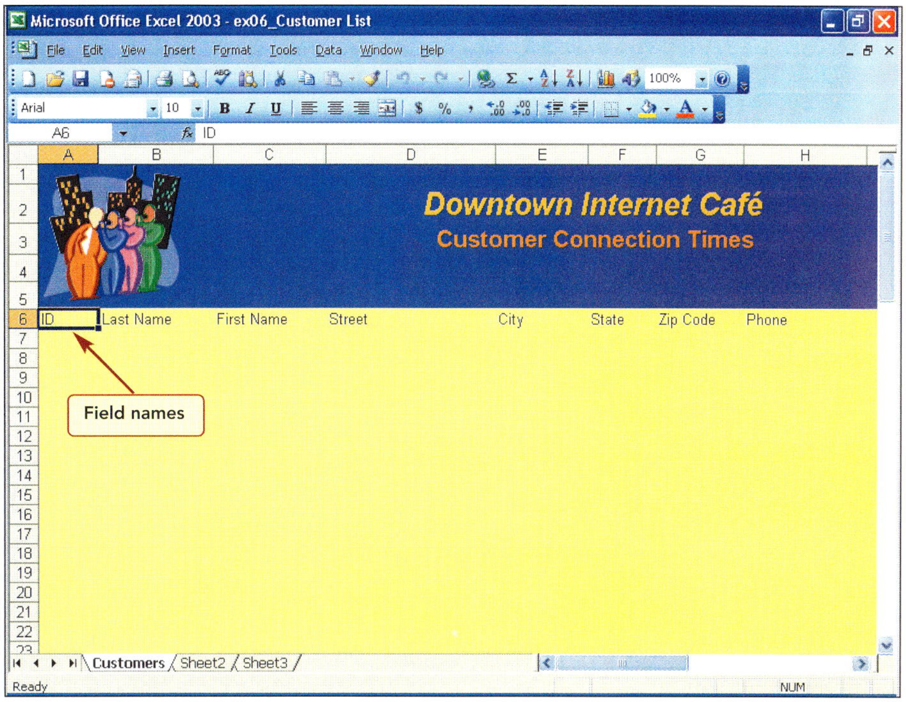

Figure 6.1

Row 6 contains the field names for the customer information that will be entered in the list.

Adding and Formatting Field Names

You decide to change the phone field to a field for each customer's e-mail address. Additionally, you still need to add field names for the months, which will be used to record the monthly connection times for each customer. In addition, it is a good idea to use formatted column labels for field names to help differentiate the labels from the data in the list. You will center, bold, and add a blue fill color to all the field name labels.

1 Replace the entry in H6 with **E-mail**.

Additional Information
Field names must be text entries.

- Enter **Jan** in cell I6.
- Drag the fill handle of cell I6 to extend the range through December (cell T6).
- Center, bold, and add the Pale Blue fill to the entire range A6 through T6.
- Move to A6.
- Save the worksheet as Customer List.

Your screen should be similar to Figure 6.2

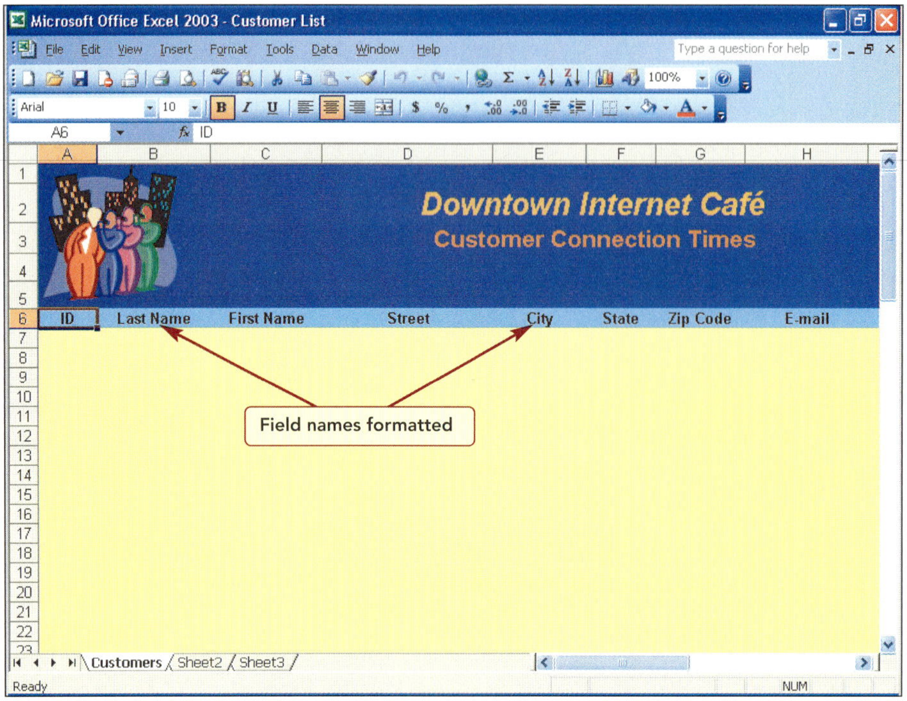

Figure 6.2

Defining the List Range

Next, you define the row containing the field names as the list range, the area where the records will be entered. Designating a range as a list lets you manage and analyze the data in the list independently of other data in the worksheet.

1 Select the range A6 through T6.

- Choose Data/List/Create List.

Another Method
The keyboard shortcut is Ctrl + L.

- Select My list has headers.
- Click OK.
- Click on cell A7.

Your screen should be similar to Figure 6.3

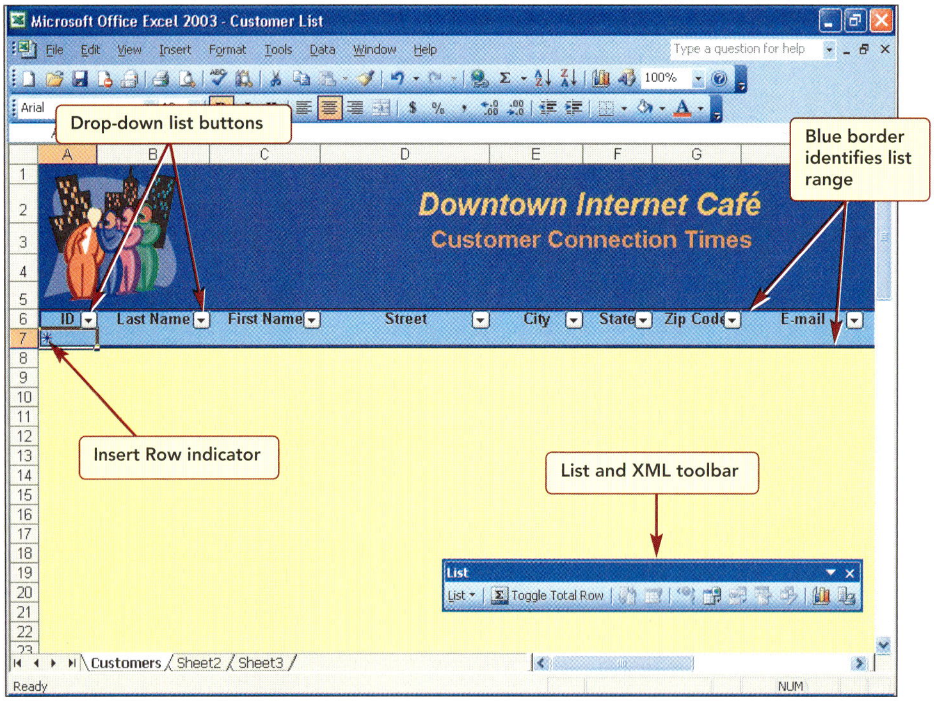

Figure 6.3

Additional Information

You could also define the list range after records have been entered by including the field name row and all rows containing records in the range.

The list range area is identified by a blue border and includes a blank row below the field names where the first record can be entered. The ✱ symbol in the blank row is an Insert Row indicator that identifies where data for a new record can be entered.

The List and XML toolbar is also displayed. In addition, drop-down list buttons appear next to each field name. These buttons indicate the AutoFilter feature is on. The AutoFilter feature is used to filter and sort the data in the list. You will learn about these features shortly.

When you select a cell outside the list, the list becomes inactive. It continues to display the blue border, but the AutoFilter buttons and the Insert Row indicator are not available.

You are now ready to begin entering the information for the first record.

Entering Records

You have the customer information and connection time data for the first two months of the year and want to enter this information into the list range. The first record in the list must begin in the row immediately below the row of field names. Although you can enter the record information by typing it directly in the cells of the insert row, Excel includes a special form, called a **data form**, that makes it easy to enter database records. Excel generates the data form from the field labels. When using the data form, the cell selector must be on any cell in the row containing the field labels in order to identify the location of the labels.

1 **Choose Data/Form.**

Your screen should be similar to Figure 6.4

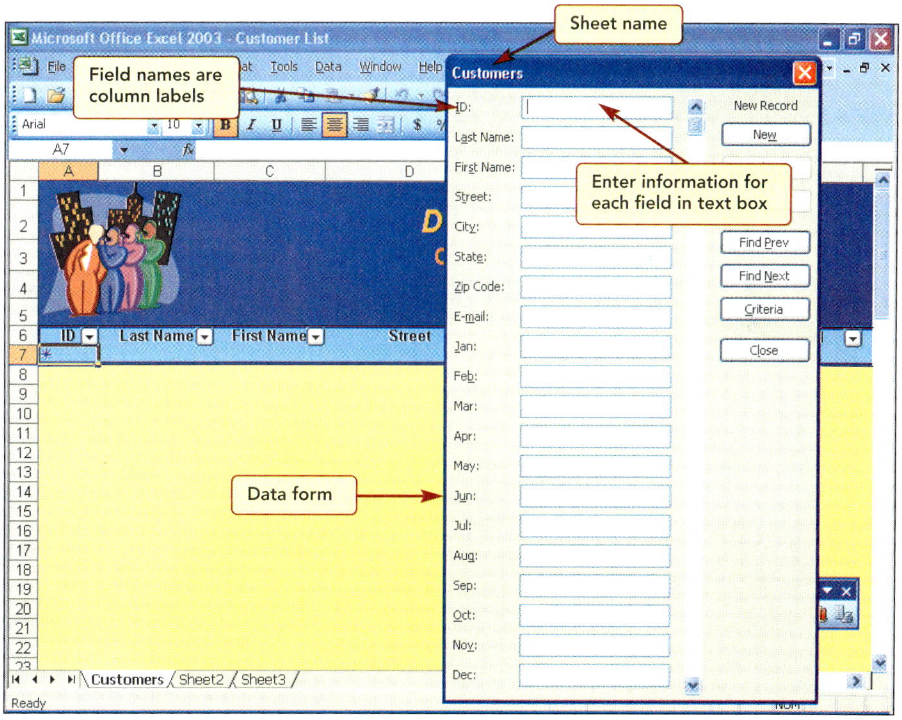

Figure 6.4

Additional Information

A data form can display a maximum of 32 fields.

Notice that the Data Form dialog box has the name of the worksheet as its title and the column labels as its field names. In the text box to the right of each label, you enter the record information for that field.

Having Trouble?

If you press ↓ a new record form is displayed. Press ↑ or Find Prev to return to the previous record.

When entering the data in a list, it is important that you enter it consistently. For example, if you abbreviate the word "Street" as "St.", it should be abbreviated in the same way for each record where it appears. Also, be careful not to include blank spaces before or after an entry as this can cause problems when trying to locate information in the list. When a field entry is complete, use Tab to move to the next field entry box or click on the box you want to move to. Use ⇧Shift + Tab to move to a previous box. Do not use the ↓ and ↑ keys to move within the data form as this will display the next or previous record or a blank new form.

2 • Enter the information shown here for the first record.

ID	**100**
Last Name	**Dwyer**
First Name	**Jack**
Street	**21 N. Navesink River Dr.**
City	**Red Bank**
State	**NJ**
Zip	**07730**
E-mail	**JD@email.com**
Jan	**120**
Feb	**210**

Additional Information

Connection time is recorded in minutes.

Your screen should be similar to Figure 6.5

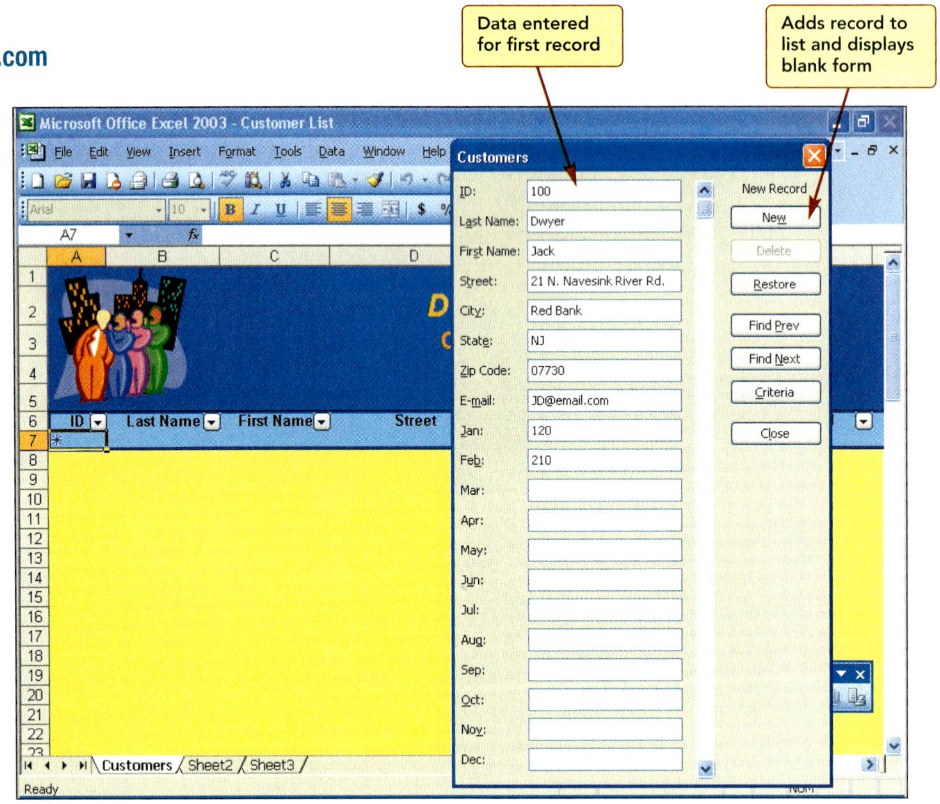

Figure 6.5

The data for the first record is complete. You will add it to the list and display another blank entry form to add the information for another record. You will add three more records and then you will close the data form.

3 • Click New.

Another Method

You can also press ←Enter or ↓ to move to a new entry form if you are on the last record.

• **If necessary, click OK in response to the inserted rows advisory message.**

• **Enter the information shown to the right for the next three records.**

	Record 2	Record 3	Record 4
ID	101	102	103
Last Name	Hamlin	Brown	Thomas
First Name	Rose	Sara	Grant
Street	7 Church St.	1005 First Ave.	159 Branch Ave.
City	Dayton	Albany	Red Bank
State	OH	NY	NJ
Zip	73094	20203	07730
E-mail	RH@email.com	SB@email.com	GT@email.com
Jan	270	299.5	38
Feb		330	62

Additional Information

While you are adding a record, you can make changes and correct mistakes. You can also undo all changes by clicking Restore, as long as you do it before moving to another record or closing the data form.

• **Click Close.**

• **AutoFit the Street column width so that the entire entry is visible.**

• **Move to G7.**

Your screen should look similar to Figure 6.6

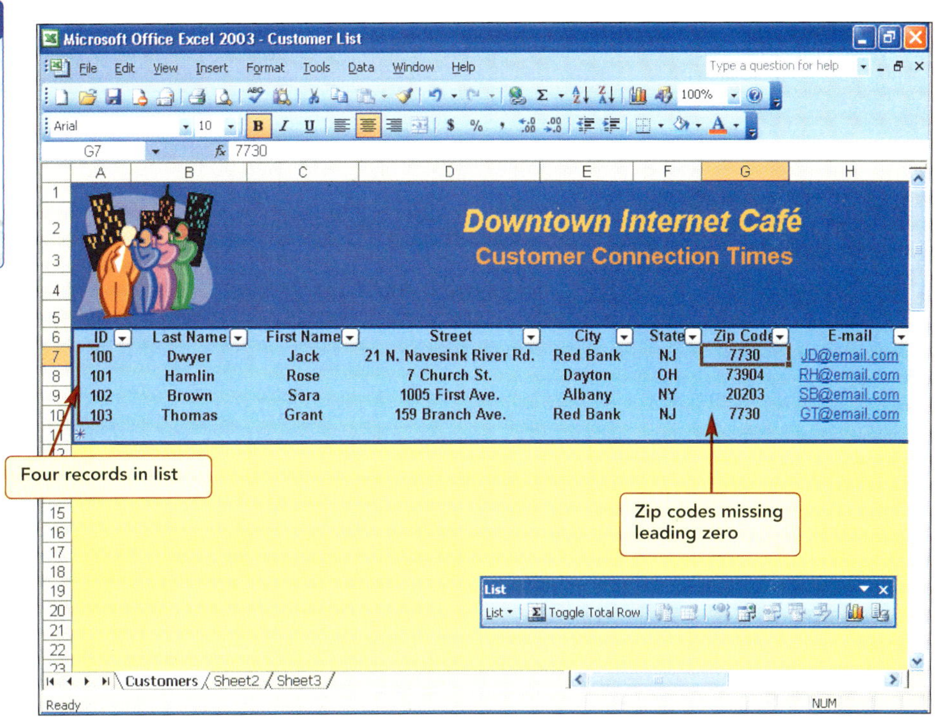

Figure 6.6

The field information for the first four records is displayed in the list range. The list range area has expanded to include the new records.

Formatting Zip Codes

Notice that the zip codes for the first and last records do not display the leading zero (07730). This is because Excel drops leading zeros for numeric data. Since this field will not be used in calculations, you can change the format for the field so that numeric entries will appear as entered. Since you will be adding many more records to the database, you will extend the format for this field beyond the records that are currently entered.

1 Select the range G7 through G30.

- Choose Format/Cells.
- Open the Number tab.
- Select Special from the Category list.

Your screen should look similar to Figure 6.7

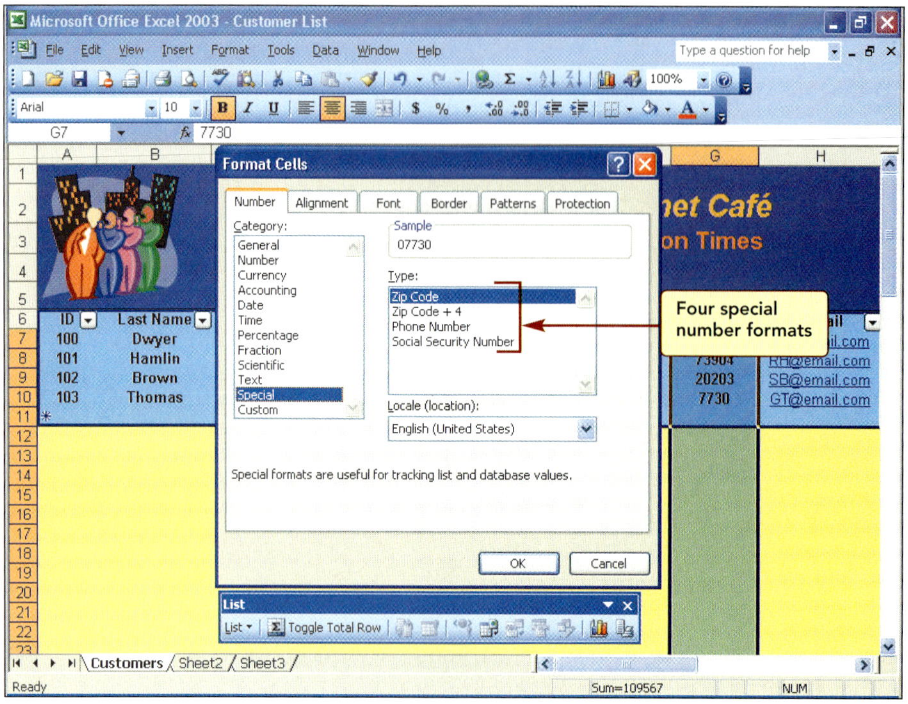

Figure 6.7

There are four special formats that are designed particularly for use in lists where numeric data is frequently entered but not used for calculations. You want to format the selection to the standard zip code format.

2 From the Type list box, select Zip Code.

- Click OK.

Your screen should look similar to Figure 6.8

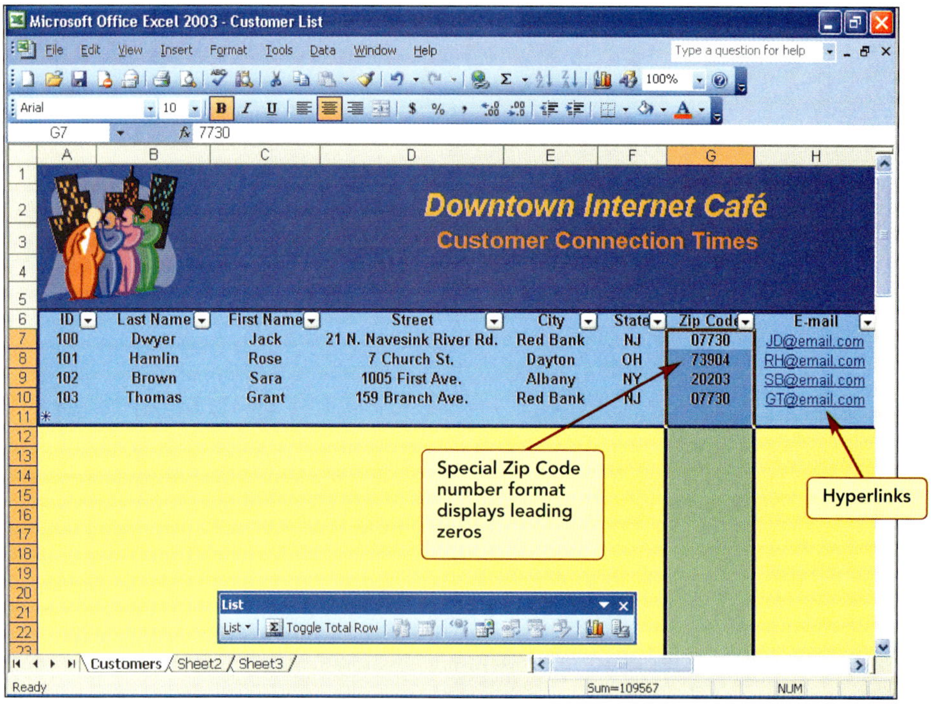

Figure 6.8

The number entries appear as they were entered because they are formatted as a special number entry. However, the entries are stored as numbers without the zero.

Working with Hyperlinks

Notice the addresses in the E-mail column are underlined and in blue. This is because they were automatically identified as an e-mail address and formatted as a hyperlink.

Concept 2

Hyperlink

2 A **hyperlink** is a connection or link to a destination location. The destination can be a location in the current file, in another file, a Web page, or an e-mail address. The hyperlink itself can be text or a picture. Clicking a hyperlink allows the user to quickly navigate or jump to the destination location when viewing the document on the screen. The action that occurs when you click a hyperlink depends on the type of destination. For example, if the hyperlink destination is a Web page, clicking the hyperlink starts a browser program and displays the specified Web page. If it is to an e-mail address, an e-mail program is started and a new message window that is preaddressed to the e-mail address hyperlink is opened.

When a hyperlink is created, it stores the information about the location of the destination as a **Uniform Resource Locator** (URL). A URL is an address that specifies the location of the destination document.

The automatic identification of Internet or network paths and the conversion to hyperlinks is a feature common to all Office programs. Sometimes you may not want the item to be automatically formatted as a hyperlink. You can turn off this feature using **T**ools/**A**utoCorrect Options and clearing the "Internet and network paths with hyperlinks" option in the AutoFormat As You Type tab. You can also remove the hyperlink autoformatting from an individual cell by selecting Remove Hyperlink from the shortcut menu.

Using a Hyperlink

In this case, clicking on the hyperlink opens a new e-mail message window to allow you to send a message to the address. You think this would be a convenient method of notifying customers of special sales as well as their Bonus Dollar status.

1 Click on the e-mail hyperlink for the first record.

Additional Information

The mouse pointer appears as a hand when pointing to a hyperlink.

Your screen should be similar to Figure 6.9

Having Trouble?

Your new message window may be different than shown depending on the e-mail program on your system.

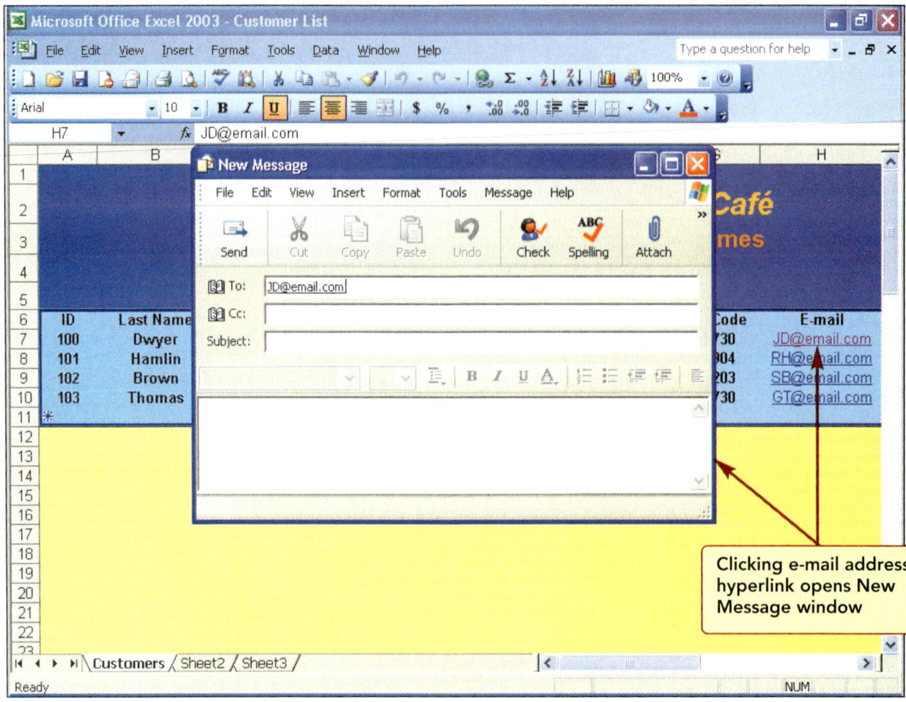

Figure 6.9

The new message window for the e-mail application on your system opens and is already addressed to the selected address. You will learn more about e-mailing later in this lab.

To select a cell containing a hyperlink without activating the hyperlink, click and hold on the cell until the mouse pointer changes to a cross. This indicates it will select the cell rather than jumping to the hyperlink destination.

2 Click Close to close the New Message window.

- If necessary, click No to discard the message.
- Point to cell H8.

Additional Information

A ScreenTip appears when you point to a hyperlink with instructions on how to follow a link or select the cell.

- Click and hold on cell H8.
- Release the mouse button when the mouse pointer changes to a cross.

Your screen should look similar to Figure 6.10

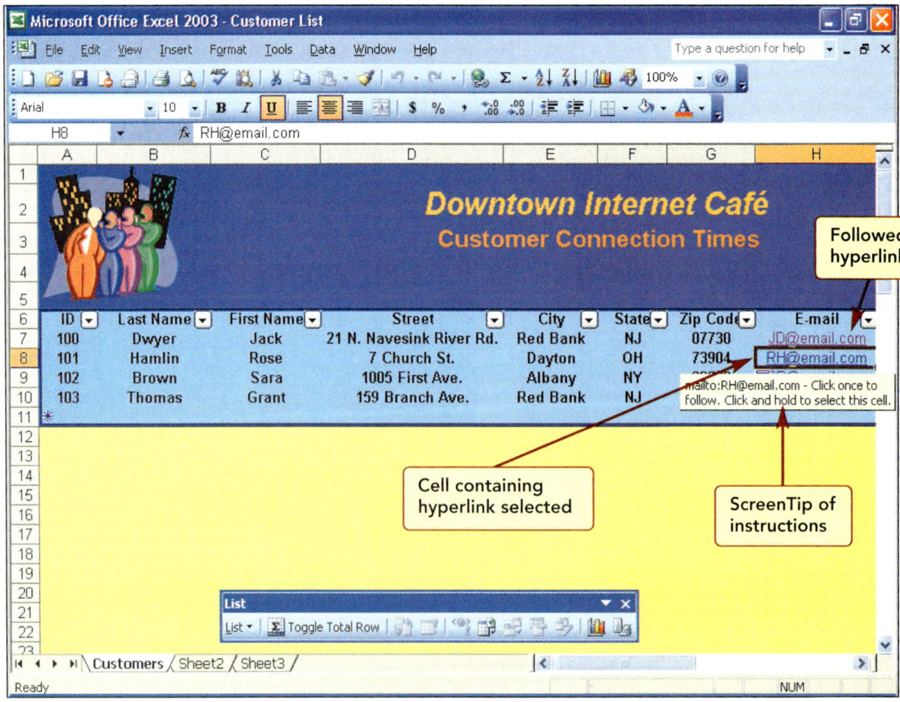

Figure 6.10

The cell containing the hyperlink is now selected and can be edited as needed. Notice that the color of the hyperlink that you clicked in cell H7 is purple, while the color of the hyperlinks in the other cells is the default color of blue. The change in color indicates the link has been followed.

Creating a Hyperlink Between Workbooks

Now that you see how convenient hyperlinks can be, you decide to add a hyperlink from the Customer List workbook to the Bonus Dollars workbook (created in Lab 5). Adding this hyperlink will make it easy to switch to the appropriate sheet in the Bonus Dollars workbook and copy the customers' total monthly connection times into the list. You will link to the Bonus Dollars workbook file and will display the hyperlink in cell K5, above the March column of data.

1 **Move to K5.**

Click Insert Hyperlink

Another Method

The menu equivalent is Insert/Hyperlink and the keyboard shortcut is Ctrl + K. You can also select Hyperlink from a cell's shortcut menu.

Your screen should be similar to Figure 6.11

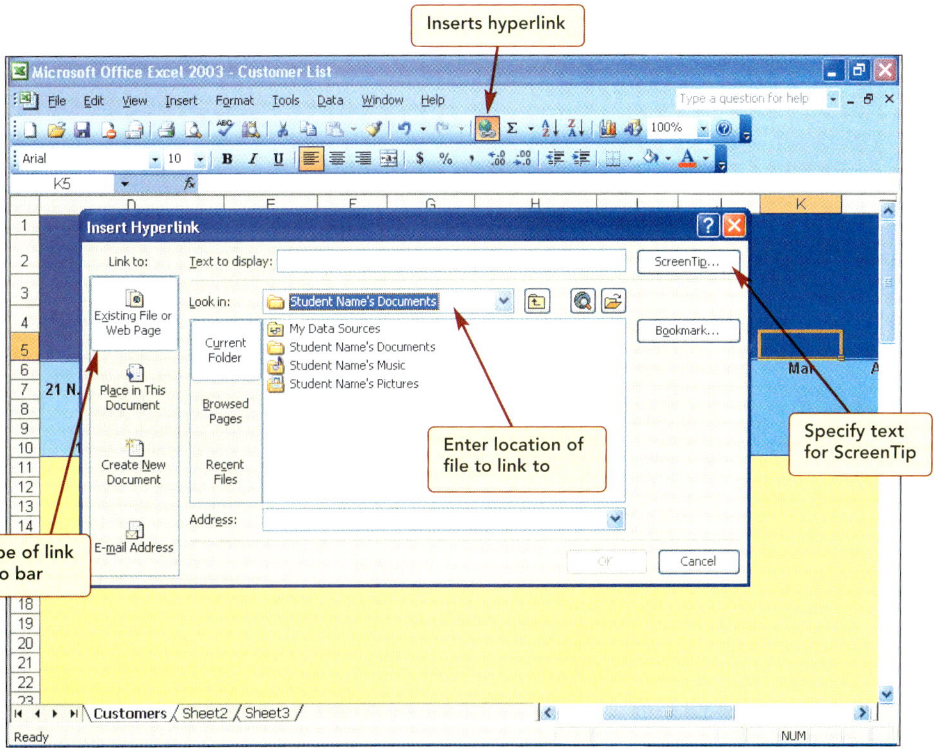

Figure 6.11

From the Insert Hyperlink dialog box, you first need to specify the type of link from the Link To bar. The four options are described below.

Option	Effect
Existing File or Web Page	Creates a link in an existing Web page or file.
Place in This Document	Creates a link to a place in the active file.
Create New Document	Creates a link to a file that you have not created yet.
E-mail Address	Creates a link that allows users to create an e-mail message with the correct address in the To line.

You want to create a link to a location in another workbook file. You also need to enter the text that the hyperlink will display in the worksheet. If you do not enter anything in the Text to Display box, the hyperlink automatically displays the path of the linked file. Finally, you will add instructions that will appear in the hyperlink ScreenTip.

2

- **If necessary, select Existing File or Web Page from the Link To bar.**
- **Specify the location of your Excel solution files in the Look In location.**
- **Select Bonus Dollars from the file list.**
- **Replace the entry in the Text to Display text box with March.**
- **Click [ScreenTip...].**
- **Type Click to open the worksheet.**
- **Click [OK]**

Your screen should be similar to Figure 6.12

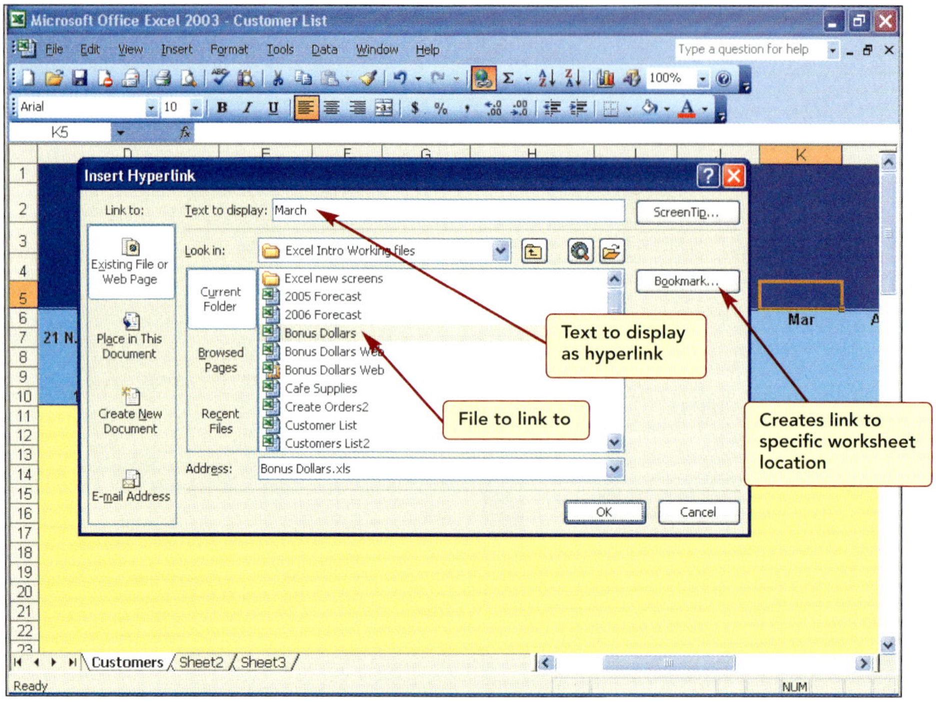

Figure 6.12

In the future, as you record each month's Bonus Dollar awards using the Monthly Bonus Form template, you plan to maintain the completed monthly worksheets in a single workbook file. When the workbook contains many worksheets, you will want to make sure that the user is taken directly to the worksheet containing the data for the appropriate month. To do this, you create a bookmark to that location in the linked workbook file. A **bookmark** establishes a link to a specific worksheet location.

4. Click **Bookmark...**.
   - If necessary, click **Enable Macros**.

Your screen should be similar to Figure 6.13

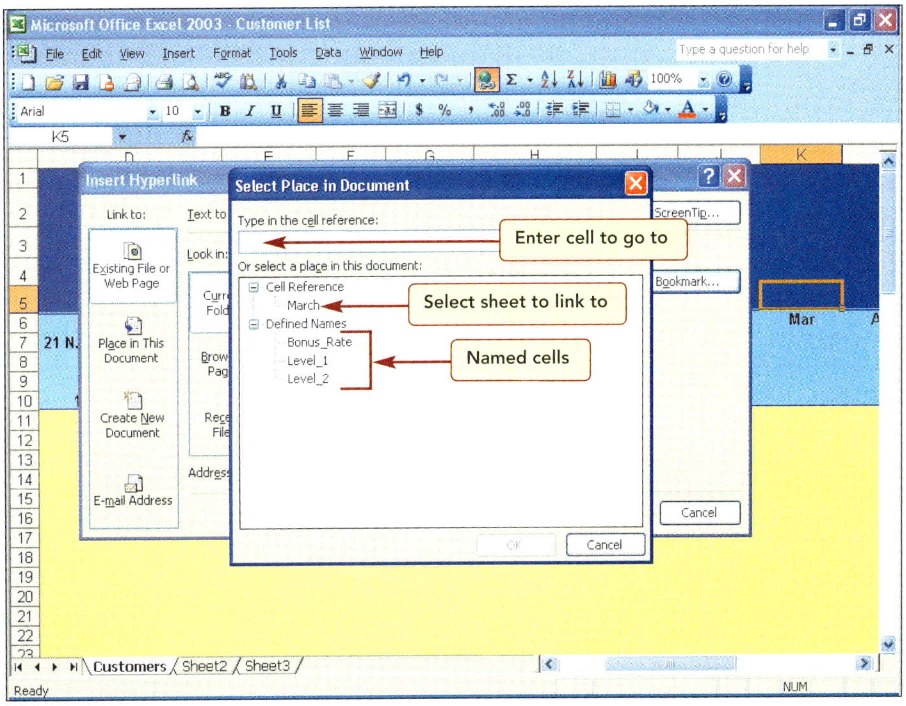

Figure 6.13

In the Select Place in Document dialog box, you select a specific location to which you want the user to be taken in the linked document. The list box displays a tree diagram showing the outline of the information in the workbook and named ranges. From the outline, you select the location to which you want to link. In this case, you want the cell pointer positioned on the first customer's total connection time data (G12).

5. Select March in the Cell Reference list.
   - In the Type in the cell reference text box, enter G12.
   - Click **OK** to close the Select Place in Document dialog box.
   - Click **OK** to close the Insert Hyperlink dialog box.
   - Point to cell K5.

Your screen should be similar to Figure 6.14

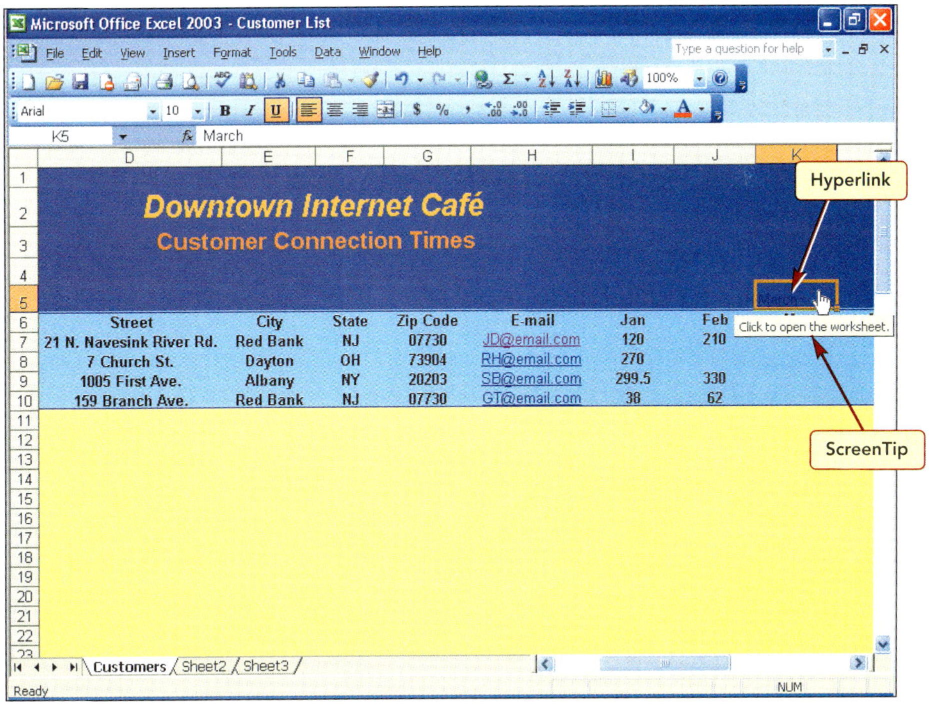

Figure 6.14

The text you entered for the hyperlink is displayed in the cell. It appears underlined and in the default hyperlink colors. The ScreenTip displays the text you entered.

Editing a Hyperlink

As you read the ScreenTip you realize it does not provide enough information. You decide to change the ScreenTip text to include the worksheet name. Also, because the default color of the hyperlink text is difficult to see against the blue background, you will change the text color and bold the entry. Then you will use the hyperlink to open the worksheet.

First you will change the color of the hyperlink text and then you will edit the ScreenTip text.

1 Click and hold to select cell K5.

Having Trouble?

Remember to select the cell, not the hyperlink.

- Change the font color to light orange and bold.

Additional Information

You can edit the text of the hyperlink just like any other cell entry.

- Right-click on the hyperlink and choose Edit Hyperlink from the shortcut menu.

Another Method

When the cell containing a hyperlink is selected, you can also use Insert/Hyperlink to edit the hyperlink.

Your screen should be similar to Figure 6.15

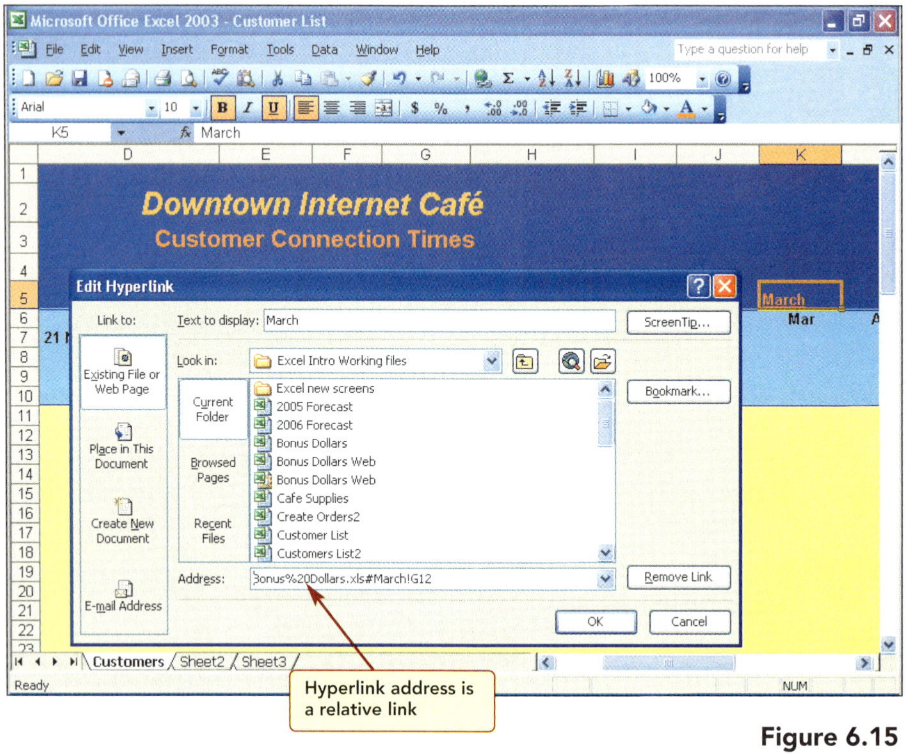

Figure 6.15

The Edit Hyperlink dialog box displays the hyperlink destination. The Look In location identifies the location of the current workbook file. The Address box displays the destination workbook file name and cell location the link will follow. Notice the Address box does not include the drive and folder location of the destination workbook file as part of the address. This is because it is a **relative link**, which means it will locate the destination workbook file relative to the location of the current workbook file. If you move both files to the same location, the link will continue to operate correctly because the relative positions of the files remains unchanged. If you move one of the files to another location, the link would not work. You would then need to edit the address to include the complete destination path location, making the address an **absolute link**.

Additional Information

You can remove a hyperlink using Remove Hyperlink on the shortcut menu or by clicking Remove Link in the Edit Hyperlink dialog box.

You will edit the ScreenTip text to include the destination workbook file name.

2 Click ScreenTip... .

- In the Set Hyperlink ScreenTip dialog box, add the text March Bonus Dollars before the word "worksheet".
- Click OK .
- Click OK .
- Reapply the light orange font color and bold.
- Point to the hyperlink cell to see the ScreenTip.

Your screen should be similar to Figure 6.16

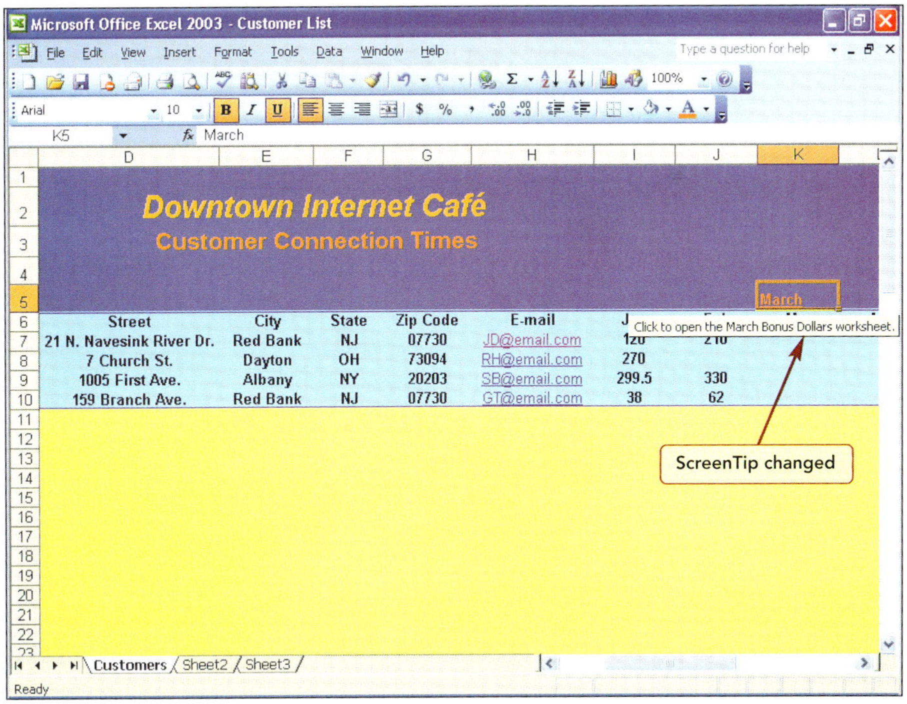

Figure 6.16

The revised ScreenTip is now much more descriptive of the purpose of the hyperlink. Now you will use the hyperlink.

3 Click on the hyperlink.

- If necessary, click Enable Macros .

Your screen should be similar to Figure 6.17

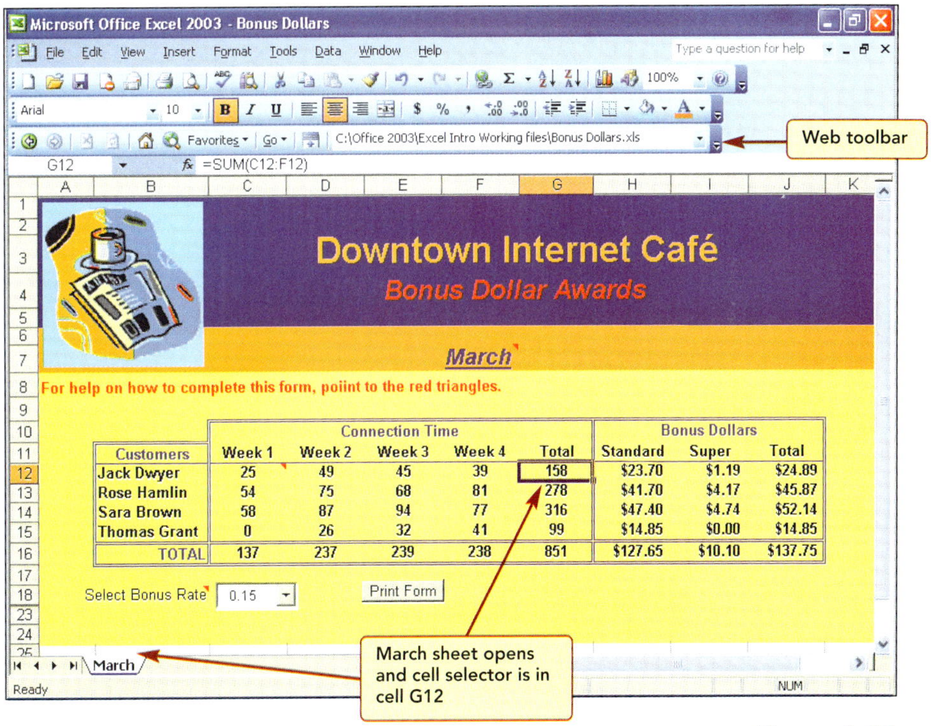

Figure 6.17

Additional Information

The Web toolbar is displayed automatically whenever you use a hyperlink.

The Bonus Dollars workbook is open and the cell selector is in the location you specified as the bookmark. The user can now copy the customer monthly Internet connection totals from the March Bonus Dollars form to the Customer List worksheet.

Copying Between Workbooks

Once both workbooks are open, you can switch back and forth between them or tile the two workbooks so that you can see them both simultaneously. You will tile the windows and copy the March total values into the list.

1

- **Choose <u>W</u>indow/<u>A</u>rrange/<u>T</u>iled/ OK.**
- **Scroll the Bonus Dollars sheet to display column G.**
- **Copy the total values in cells G12 through G15.**
- **Scroll the Customer List worksheet to see column K.**
- **Paste the copied values into cells K7 through K10.**
- **From the Paste Options button, select <u>V</u>alues only.**

Your screen should be similar to Figure 6.18

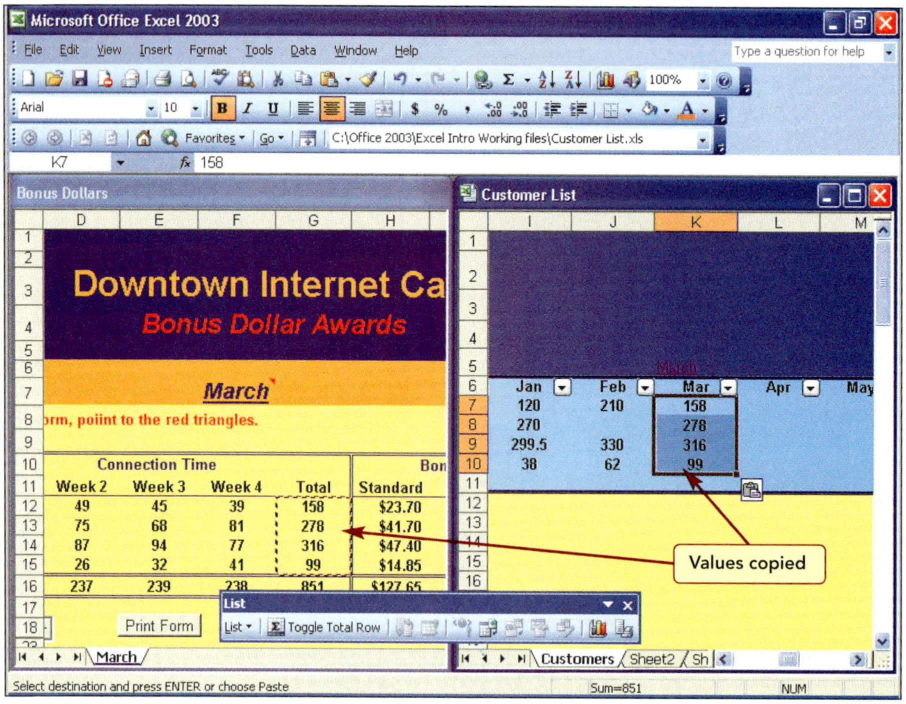

Figure 6.18

You have continued to work on the café customer list by adding additional records. You will open the workbook file and continue working on the list.

2

- Maximize and close the file Bonus Dollars workbook.
- Save and close the Customer List workbook file.
- Close the Web toolbar.
- Open the workbook file ex06_Customer List2.
- Move to any cell within the list.
- Choose **D**ata/F**o**rm and click New.
- Enter data for yourself using ID number 999. Enter connection times of 210, 270, and 240 for the Jan, Feb, and Mar fields. All other information can be fictitious.
- Close the data form.
- Scroll to see your record in row 40.

Your screen should be similar to Figure 6.19

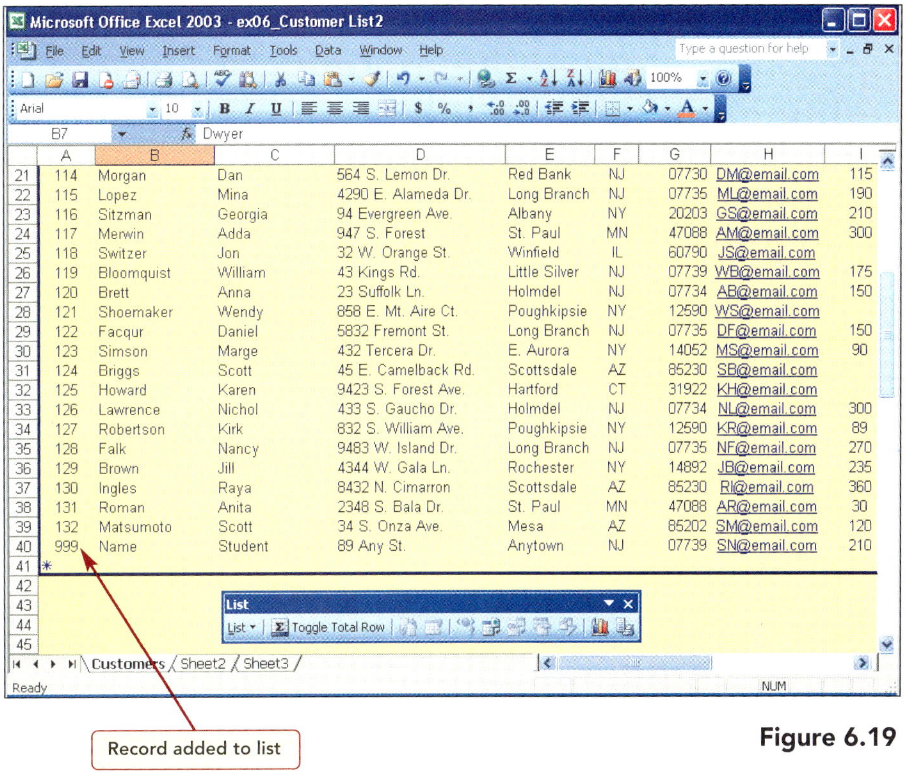

Figure 6.19

Finding and Modifying Records

You realize you entered the wrong data for one customer. You can also use the Data Form to find and modify existing records. You will use this method to make the final change to your data, correcting the connection time for Jill Brown.

1 Choose **Data/Form.**

Click **Criteria**.

Your screen should be similar to Figure 6.20

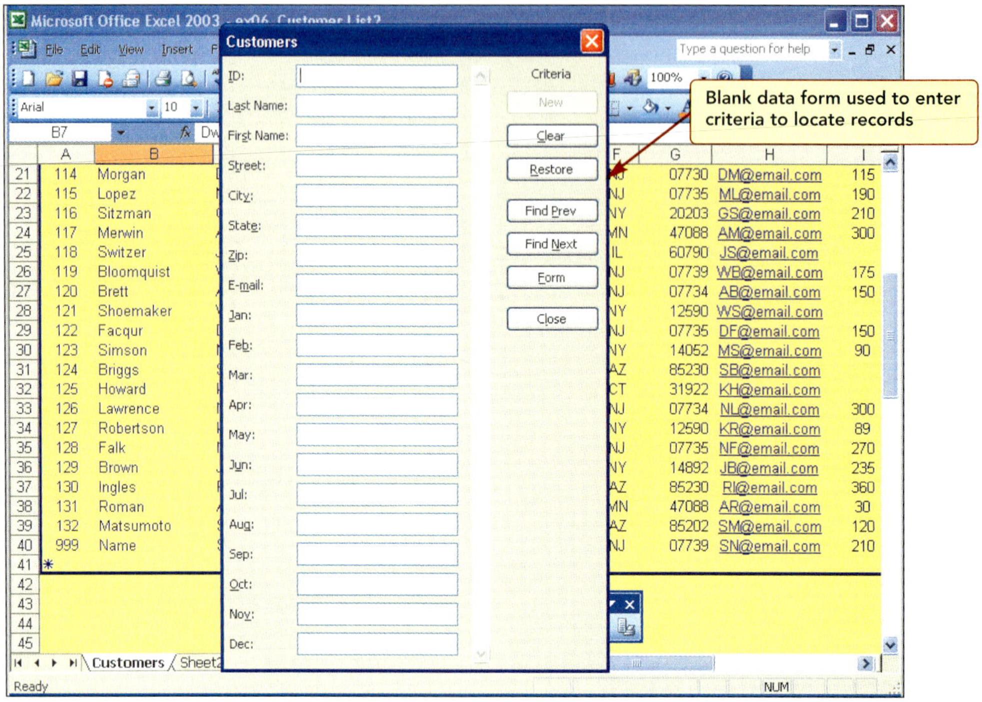

Figure 6.20

Additional Information

The criteria is not case sensitive.

A blank data form is displayed in which you can enter the **criteria** or conditions for the record to meet in order to be located. The more precise and unique the criteria you enter, the fewer matches will be located. In this case, you will enter the customer's last name, Brown, to locate and display the record for Jill Brown.

2 Type **Brown** in the Last Name field text box.

Click **Find Next**.

Your screen should be similar to Figure 6.21

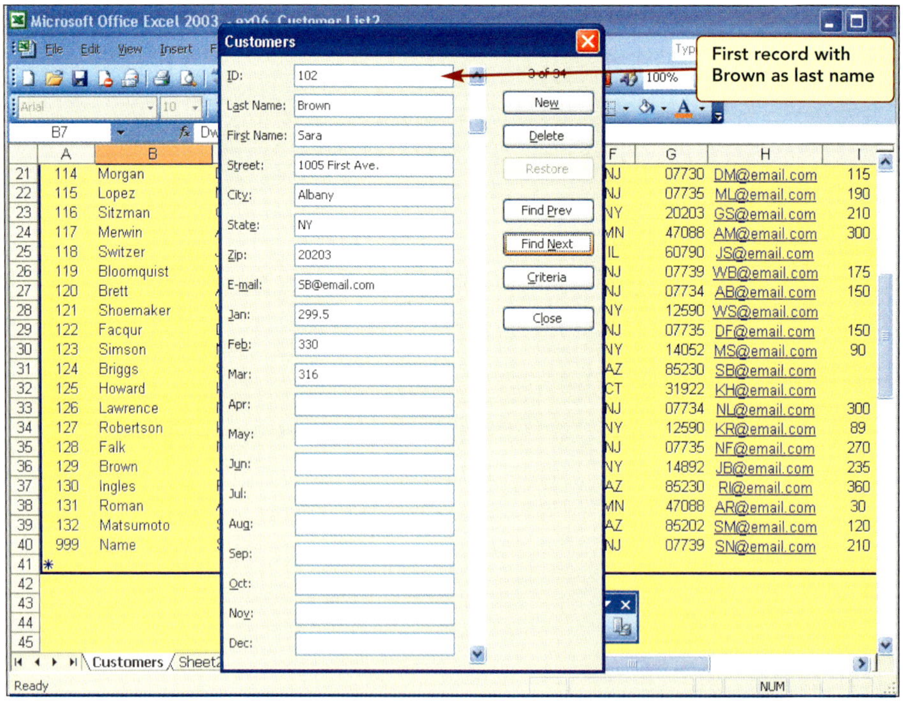

Figure 6.21

Additional Information

You could refine the search by entering criteria in other fields, such as Jill in the First Name field; then only records meeting all criteria will be located.

The first located record with a last name of Brown, Sara Brown, is displayed in the data form. Because there are several records with a last name of Brown, the located record is not the record you want to edit. You want to find the record for Jill Brown.

3

- **Click Find Next two more times until Jill Brown's record is displayed.**
- **Double-click the Jan field text box to highlight the current value, 235.**
- **Type 135.**
- **Click Close.**
- **Scroll the list to see Jill Brown's record in row 36.**

Your screen should be similar to Figure 6.22

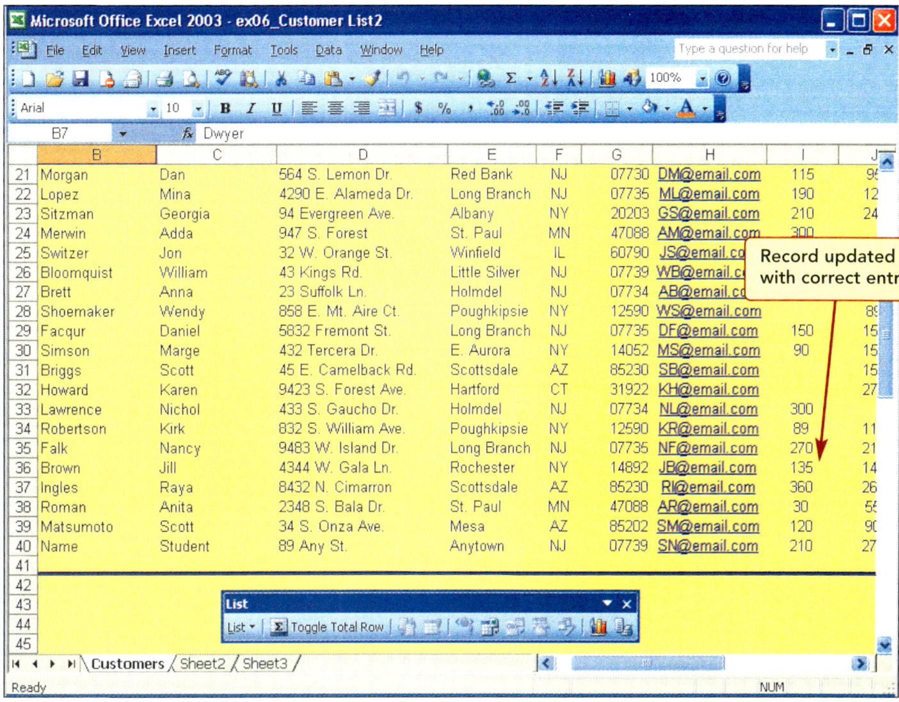

Figure 6.22

The record for Jill Brown is updated and now contains the correct value, 135, in the January connection time field.

Now that your data entries are error-free, you are ready to move on to sorting the data in a logical order.

Sorting Data

Currently, the records in the list are in the order in which you entered them. However, you feel that they would be easier to work with if they were displayed in alphabetical order by last name. To do this, you can sort the records in the list.

Concept 3

Sort

3 You can **sort** or arrange data in a specified sequence: alphabetically, numerically, or by date. Sorting data often helps you find specific information quickly. The data in a worksheet can be sorted into ascending (A to Z, 1 to 9, earliest date to most recent date) or descending (Z to A, 9 to 1, most recent date to earliest date) order. When you sort, Excel rearranges the rows, columns, fields, or individual cells according to the sort order you specify.

A single sort operation can be based on up to three columns or fields of data. When a sort is done on more than one column or field, it is called a **multilevel sort**. For example, if you wanted to rearrange a list of employee data to begin with those who have worked for the company the longest, you could sort it in ascending order by date and then by name.

Sorting on a Single Field

For the first sort, you want the records arranged in ascending alphabetical order by last name. The cell selector needs to be in any cell in the field to be sorted.

1 **Move to cell B7.**

Click Sort Ascending on the Standard toolbar.

Another Method

You can also select Sort Ascending from the field name's AutoFilter drop-down menu.

Your screen should be similar to Figure 6.23

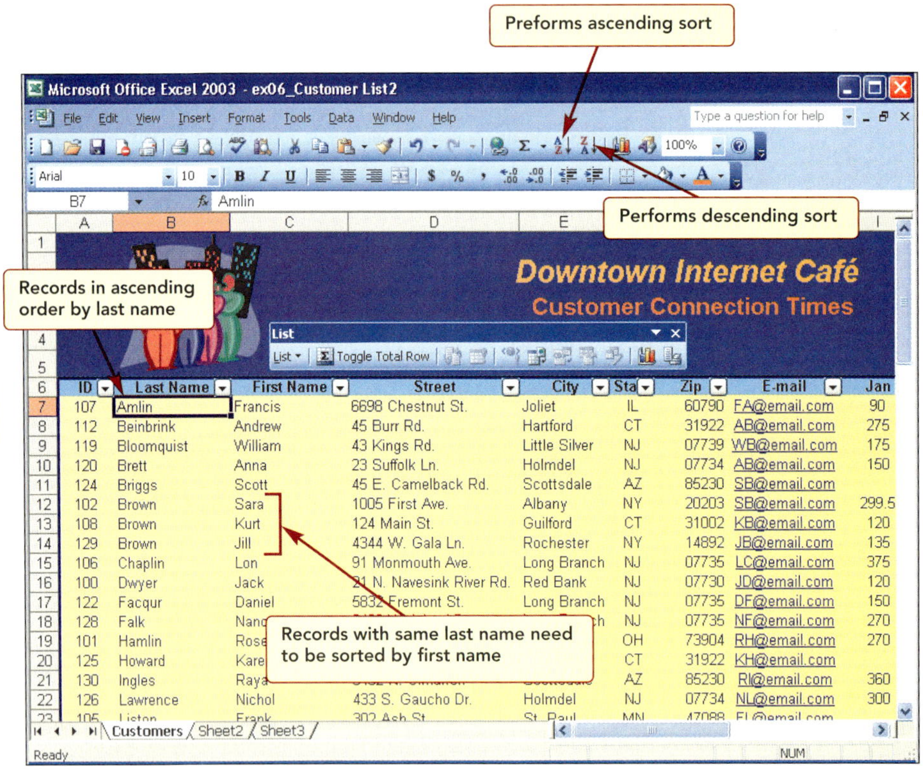

Figure 6.23

The records in the list range are rearranged to display in ascending alphabetical order by last name. However, notice that although the records for Sara, Kurt, and Jill Brown are sorted correctly by last name, they are not sorted correctly by first name.

Sorting on Multiple Fields

You want records that have the same last name to be further sorted by first name. To do this, you will perform a multilevel sort.

1 Open the List drop-down menu (on the List toolbar) and select Sort.

Another Method

The menu equivalent is **D**ata/**S**ort.

Your screen should be similar to Figure 6.24

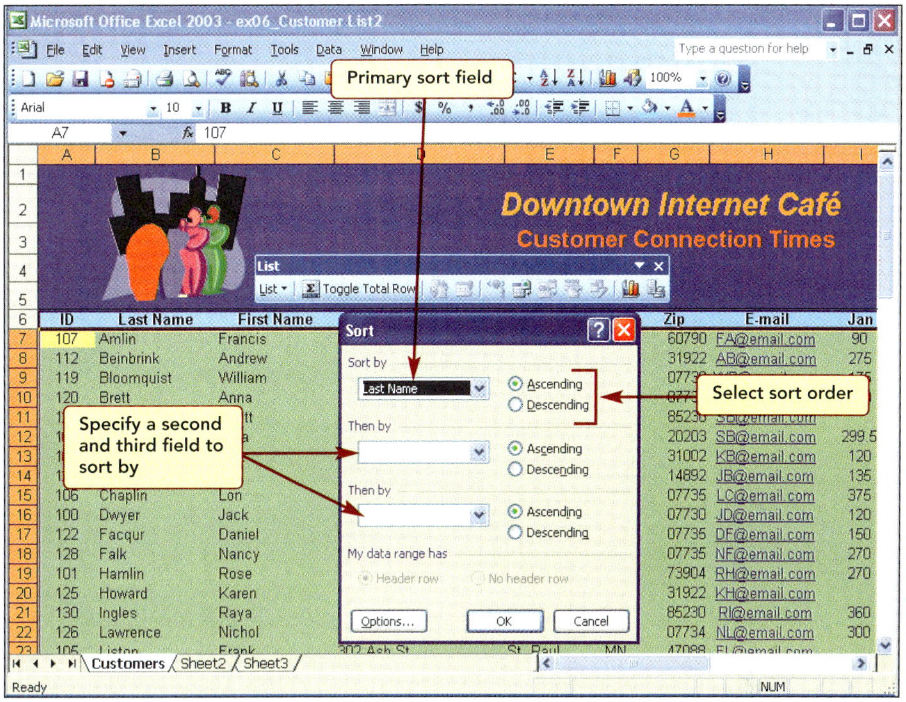

Figure 6.24

A multilevel sort uses the first field name selected in the Sort By section of the dialog box as the primary sort field; all other fields are sorted in order after the primary sort is performed. The Sort By text box correctly displays the name of the field on which the primary sort will be performed. Additionally, because the default setting is Ascending sort order, this option does not need to be changed. You need to specify the secondary sort field as the First Name field.

2 **Select First Name from the first Then By drop-down list.**

Your screen should be similar to Figure 6.25

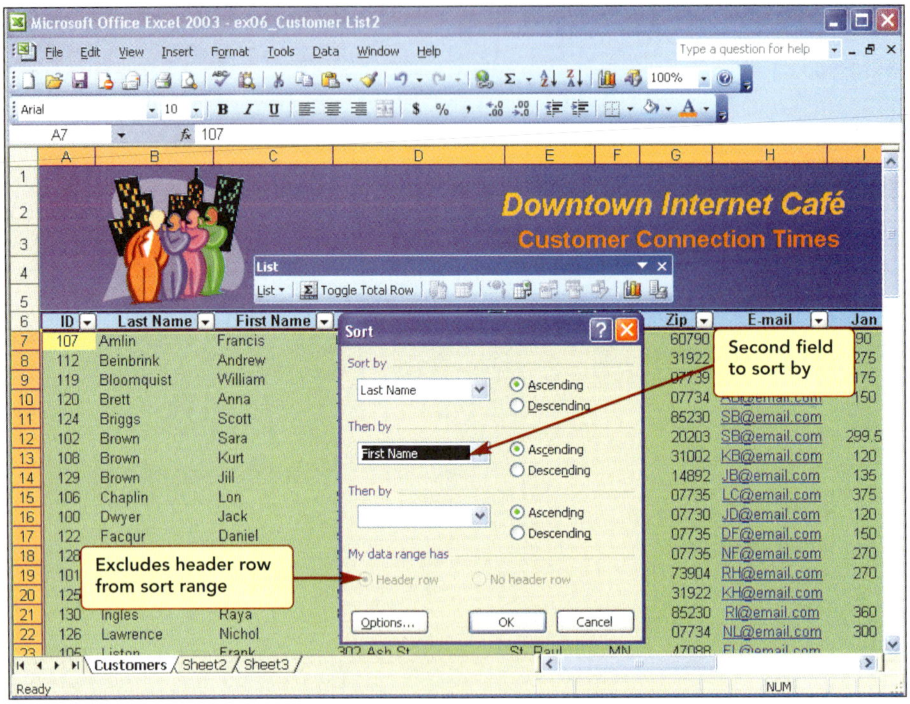

Figure 6.25

When a sort is performed, Excel assumes that you want all data except the uppermost row contained in contiguous rows and columns surrounding the selected cell to be sorted. The first row is not included in the sort range because the default setting assumes that the first row contains column labels or field names that you do not want included in the sort. If your data did not include a column label or field name as the first row in the range, you would need to choose the No Header Row option to change the setting to include this row in the sort. Since this worksheet includes field names in the first row, the Header Row option is correctly specified already.

3 **Click** OK.

Save the changes you have made to this workbook as Customer List2.

Your screen should be similar to Figure 6.26

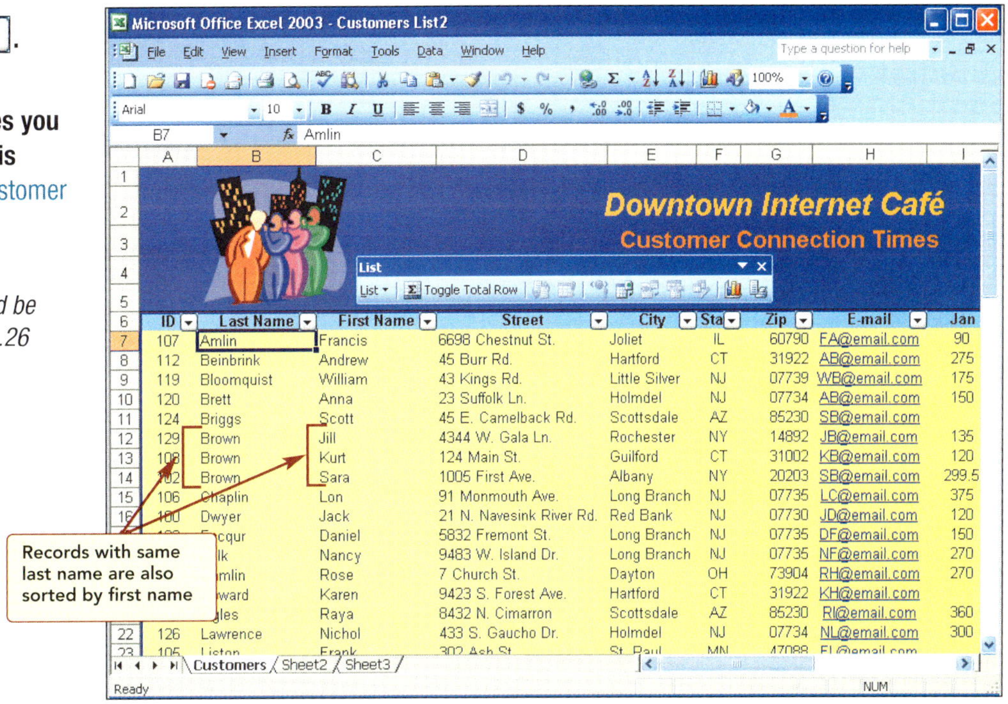

Figure 6.26

The records are now in sorted order first by last name and second by first name within the same last names. As you can see, sorting is a fast, useful tool. The sort order remains in effect until you replace it with a new sort order. If the order in which you enter records in a list is important, include a field for a unique record number, such as the ID field in this list that identifies each customer. Then you can return to the entry order by sorting on the number field.

Filtering Data

Evan has informed you that he is sending out "valued customer" e-mail notes to the in-state customers who have been connecting at the café since the beginning of the year. He has asked you for a printout of the connection times and e-mail address information for those customers. To locate this information, you can filter the database list to show only the requested records.

Concept 4

Filter

4 A **filter** is a restriction you place on records in the list to quickly isolate and display a subset of records. A filter is created by specifying criteria that you want records to meet in order to be displayed. A filter is ideal when you want to display the subset for only a brief time and then return immediately to the full set of records. You can print the filtered records as you would any worksheet. A filter is only temporary, however, and all records are redisplayed when you remove the filter.

Unlike the Sort feature, the Filter feature does not rearrange a list but temporarily hides rows that do not meet the specified criteria. Data in a filtered list can be edited, formatted, charted, or printed.

Additional Information

Only the first 1,000 unique entries appear in the AutoFilter list.

Filtering on a Single Criterion

You will filter the list to display only New Jersey residents first. To specify the criteria, you select the field value from the AutoFilter drop-down menu which displays a list of the unique entries in the field.

1 **Click on the State field's AutoFilter button.**

Another Method

The menu equivalent is Data/Filter/AutoFilter.

Your screen should be similar to Figure 6.27

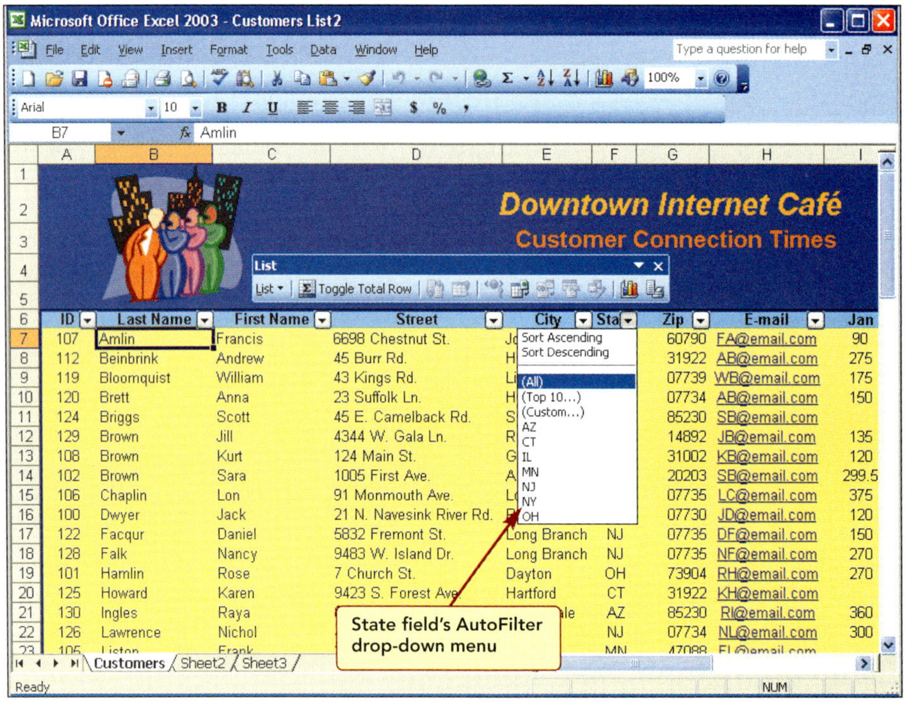

Figure 6.27

The drop-down list contains the current values in the field. In addition, you can select from these options:

Option	Effect
Sort Ascending	Changes record order to ascending.
Sort Descending	Changes record order to descending.
(All)	Displays all records regardless of the value in this field.
(Top 10)	Displays the records with the highest values in this field.
(Custom)	Used to specify ranges of values that a record must meet to be displayed.
(Blanks)	Displays only those records that do not contain a value in this field.
(NonBlanks)	Displays only those records that contain a value in this field.

You want to specify that only records that have a state value of NJ are displayed.

2 **Choose NJ from the drop-down list.**

Your screen should be similar to Figure 6.28

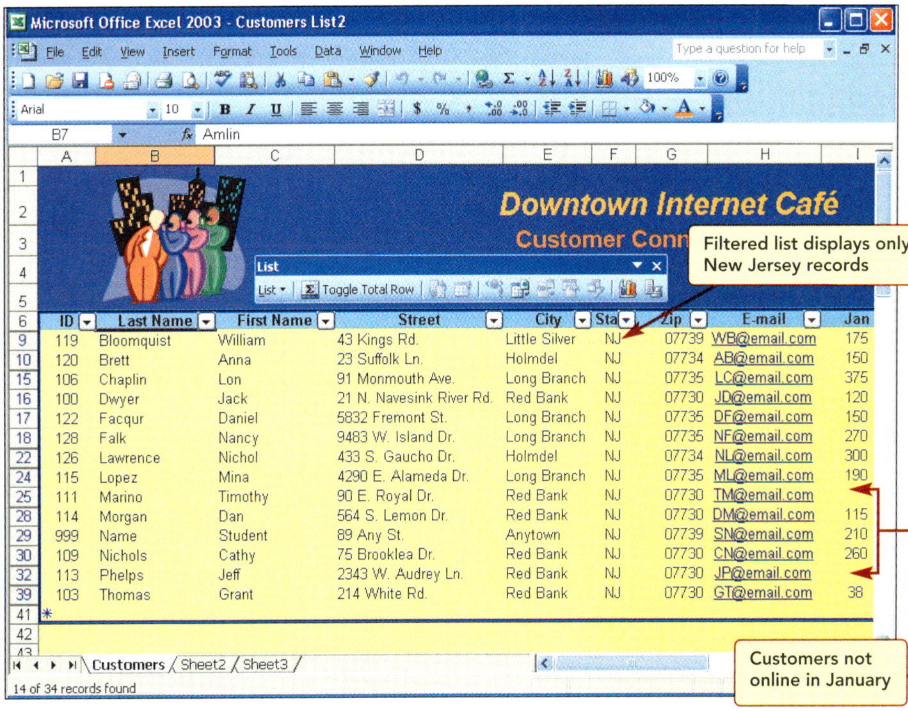

Figure 6.28

Filtering on Multiple Criteria

Only those records for customers in New Jersey are displayed. However, not all of these customers have been online at the café all three months. Therefore, you want to specify further criteria to accept only "nonblanks" in the month fields.

1. Open the Mar AutoFilter drop-down list.
   - Choose (NonBlanks).
   - In a similar manner, choose (NonBlanks) for January and February.

Your screen should be similar to Figure 6.29

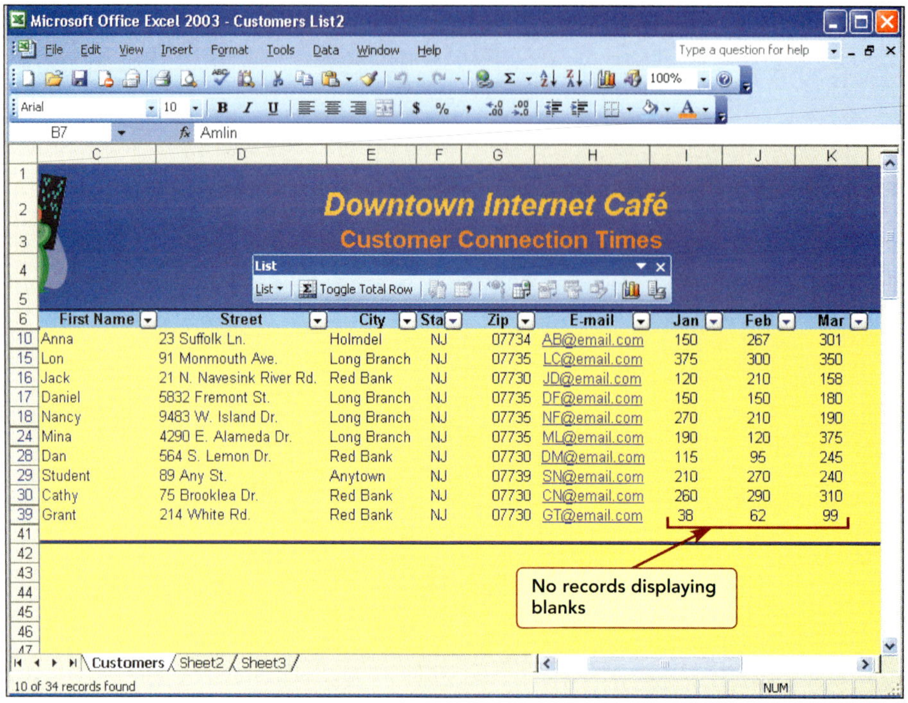

Figure 6.29

Only the records that meet the specified criteria are displayed.

Creating a Custom Filter

You would also like to see the same information for the out-of-state customers. To do this, you could change the State criteria and print each filter result. However, a faster way is to create a custom filter for the State field.

1. From the State drop-down list, select (Custom...).

Your screen should be similar to Figure 6.30

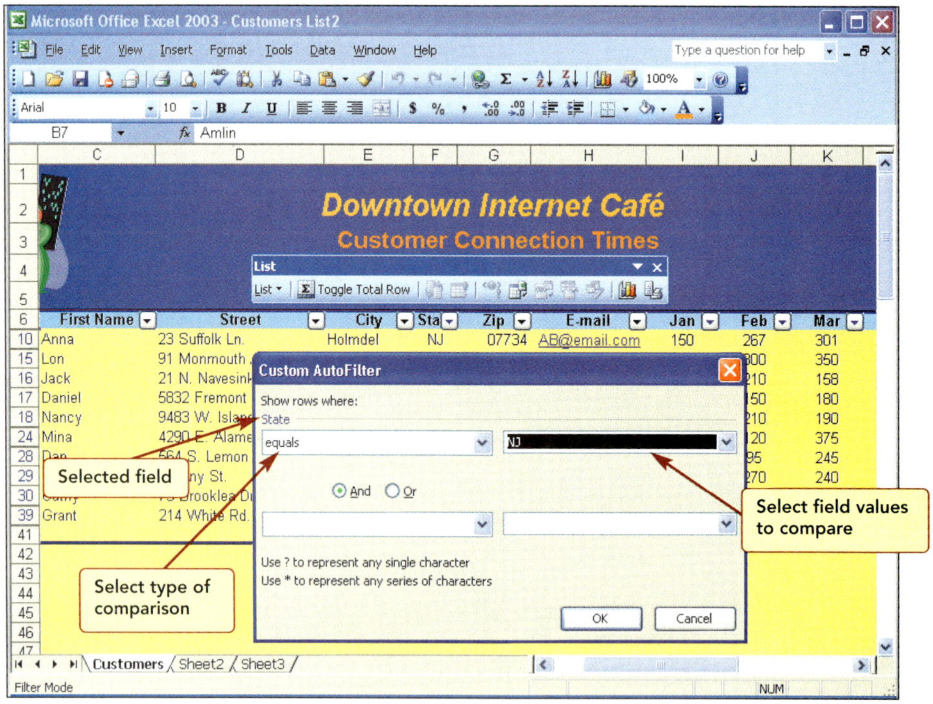

Figure 6.30

The Custom AutoFilter dialog box is used to specify a filtering operation that makes comparisons between two values. The type of comparison to make is specified in the box on the left, and the value to compare to is specified in the box on the right. You can include a second set of criteria by selecting the And or Or options and specifying the settings in the lower row of boxes. The AND and OR operators are used to specify multiple conditions that must be met for the records to display in the filtered list. The AND operator narrows the search, because a record must meet both conditions to be included. The OR operator broadens the search, because any record meeting either condition is included in the output.

You want to display records for all states except New Jersey.

2 **From the box on the left, select "does not equal" from the drop-down list of operations.**

Click OK.

Additional Information

Your record may appear in the filtered list if your state field entry is not NJ.

Your screen should be similar to Figure 6.31

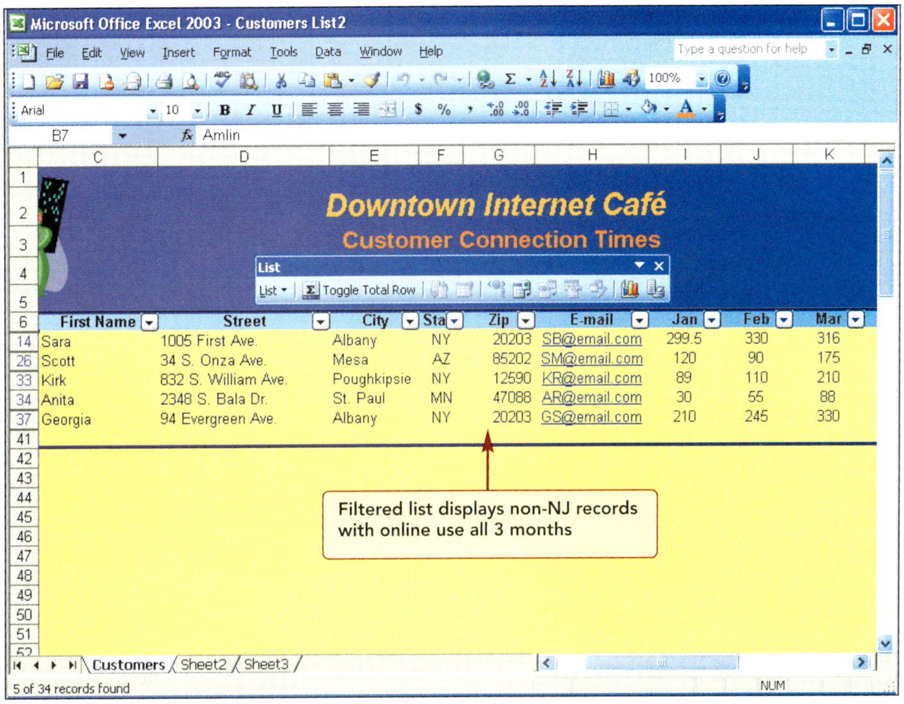

Figure 6.31

Now the filtered list displays records for all states except New Jersey that have connection time usage in all three months. As expected, only a few out-of-state customers meet this requirement.

Calculating List Values

The next item Evan has requested is a total for the number of connection minutes for each state for the three months and a grand total of each month's connection times. Additionally, he wants to see a count of the number of records in the list. You can get this information easily by displaying a total row and inserting subtotals.

Displaying a Total Row

To calculate statistics for all records in the list, you can display a total row and select the type of calculation you want performed on the data in a field. You will use this feature to display a count of records in the list. First, you will display all the records again.

1 Choose **Data/Filter/Show All.**

Another Method

You could also select All from the State, Jan, Feb, and Mar AutoFilter drop-down lists to display all the records.

Click **Toggle Total Row** in the List toolbar.

Your screen should be similar to Figure 6.32

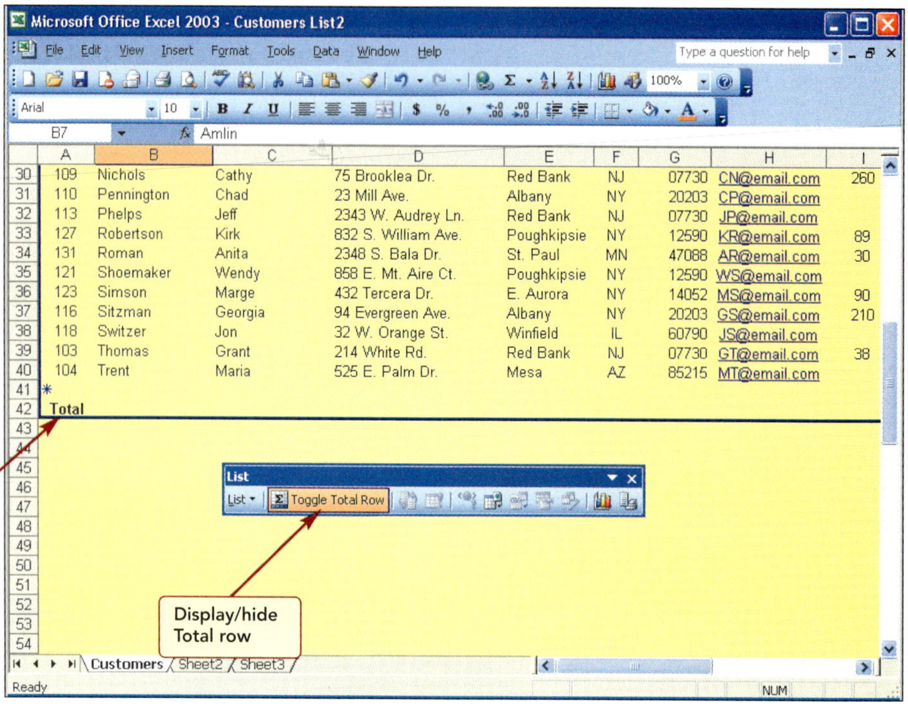

Figure 6.32

A new row is displayed below the Insert Row indicator. It displays the word "Total" in the left-most cell and an appropriate calculation in the right-most cell of the list. Selecting any cell in the Total row displays a drop-down list arrow that when clicked displays a list of function names from which you can select. You will use the Count function to display the number of records below the Last Name field column.

2 Click in the Total row for the Last Name field.

Open the drop-down list and select Count.

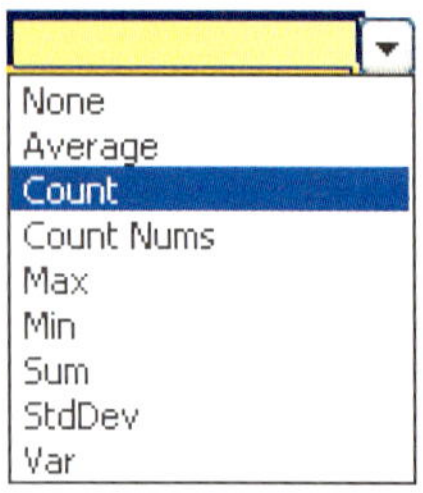

Your screen should be similar to Figure 6.33

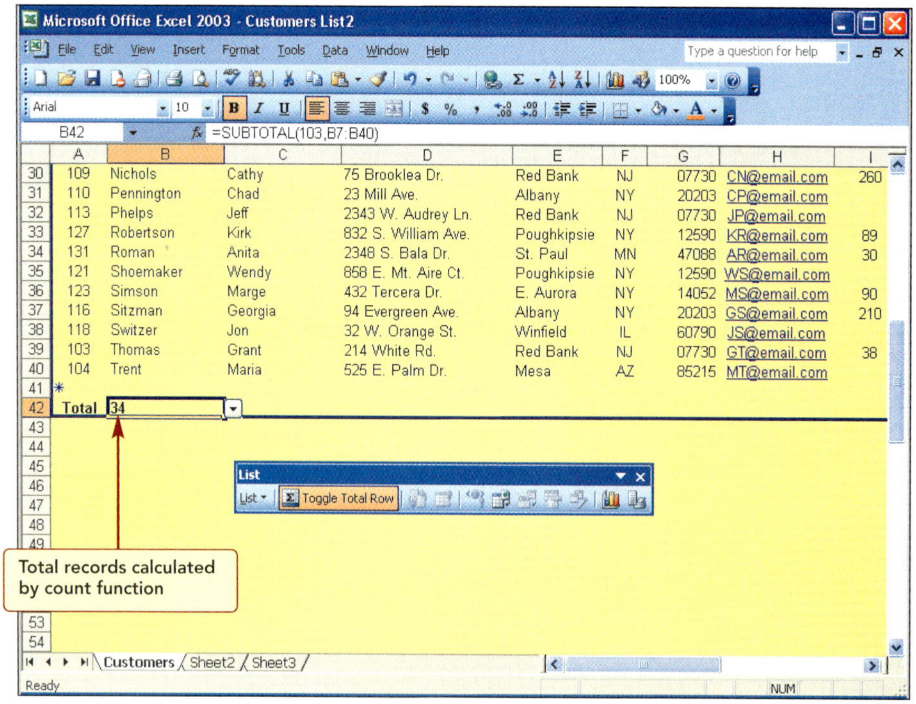

Figure 6.33

A count of all entries in the Last Name field column is displayed. If a filter were applied to the list, the value would reflect a count of displayed records only.

Calculating Subtotals

Next you will calculate subtotals for the connection time data. When using subtotals, you first need to sort the list so that the rows you want to subtotal are grouped together. Then you can calculate subtotals on any column containing numbers.

1

- **Click Toggle Total Row to hide the total row.**
- **Sort the data by state and then by city.**
- **Click on any cell in the row immediately below the last record in the list range (row 41).**
- **Choose Data/Subtotals.**

Your screen should be similar to Figure 6.34

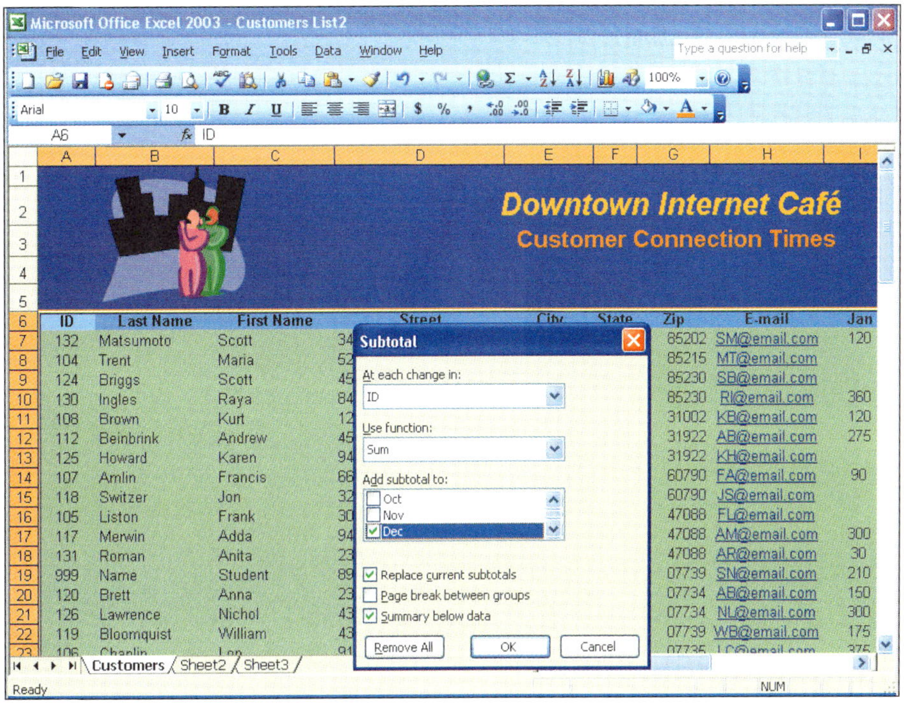

Figure 6.34

From the Subtotal dialog box, you first specify the field you want to display subtotals after each change in data. In this case, you want subtotals calculated after each change in state. Then you select the type of function you want to use to calculate the subtotals, such as Sum, Count, or Average. You want to calculate a sum. Finally, you select the fields that contain the values you want to subtotal. You will display subtotals for the three months of connection time values. You can also have an automatic page break after each subtotal and can have the subtotals displayed above the subtotaled rows instead of below.

2 Choose State from the **At Each Change In** drop-down list.

- Click on Dec in the **Add Subtotal To** list to remove the checkmark.
- Select Jan, Feb, and Mar in the **Add Subtotal To** list.
- Click OK.
- Scroll to see the bottom of the list range and the monthly usage data.

Your screen should be similar to figure 6.35

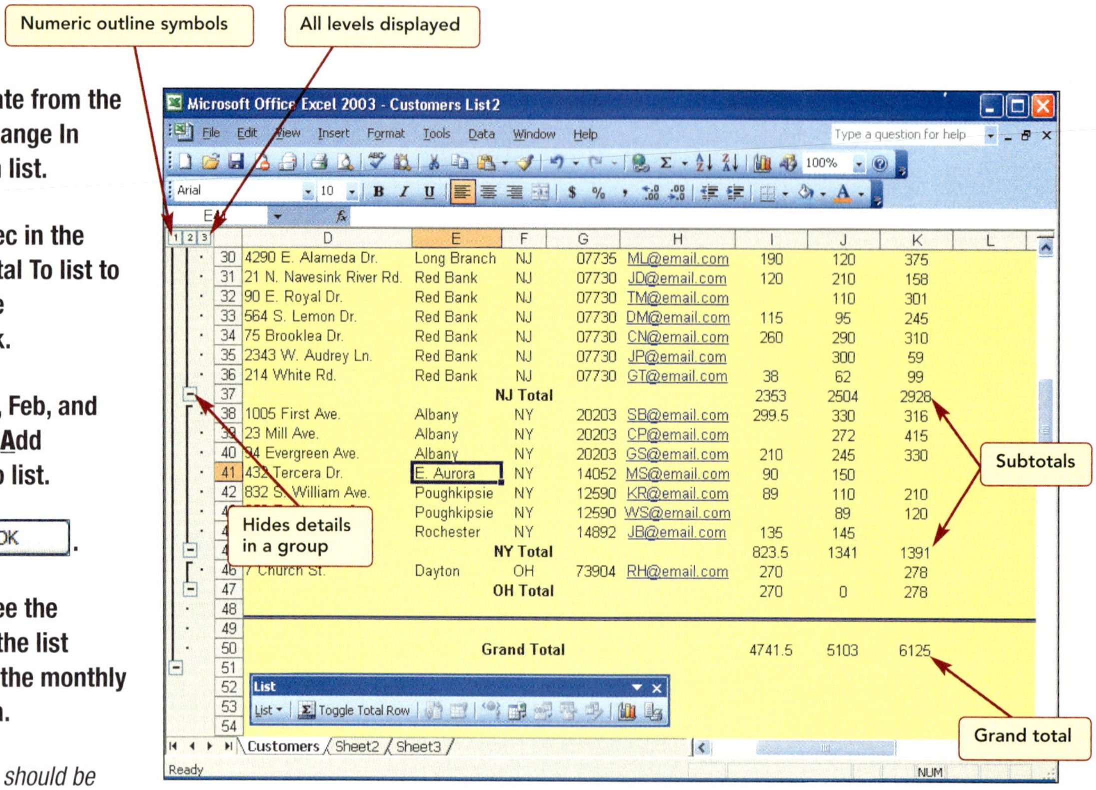

Figure 6.35

The worksheet now contains a subtotal for each change in state and a grand total for each month. Additionally, along the left side of the row numbers, the list is outlined so you can see its structure. You can create a summary report by clicking the numeric outline symbols 1, 2, 3 to display different levels of detail. Clicking 1 displays the grand total only, 2 the subtotals, and 3 all levels. You can also use + to display and − to hide the details within a group.

3 Click 2.

- Scroll the worksheet to see the state and month columns.
- AutoFit the State column.

Your screen should be similar to figure 6.36

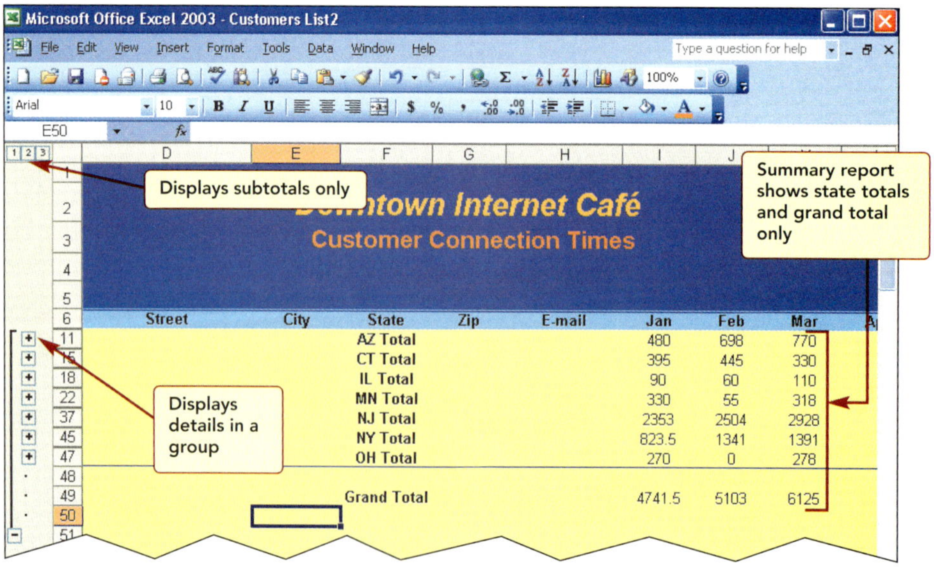

Figure 6.36

Additional Information

You can also create a chart of the visible data in a list that contains subtotals.

The list displays the subtotals and grand total values only.

Printing the Summary Report

Next you will print the summary report for Evan showing the State and the three month columns only. To do this, you will hide the Zip and E-mail columns. Then you will select the range of cells containing the data that you want printed.

1

- **Hide columns G and H.**
- **Select the range containing the field names and summary statistics (F6:K50).**
- **Choose File/Print/Selection.**
- **If necessary, select the printer.**
- **Click Preview.**
- **In the left section of a custom header, enter Connection Time on the first line and Summary Statistics on the second.**
- **In the right section of a custom header, enter your name on the first line and the current date on the second.**

Your screen should be similar to figure 6.37

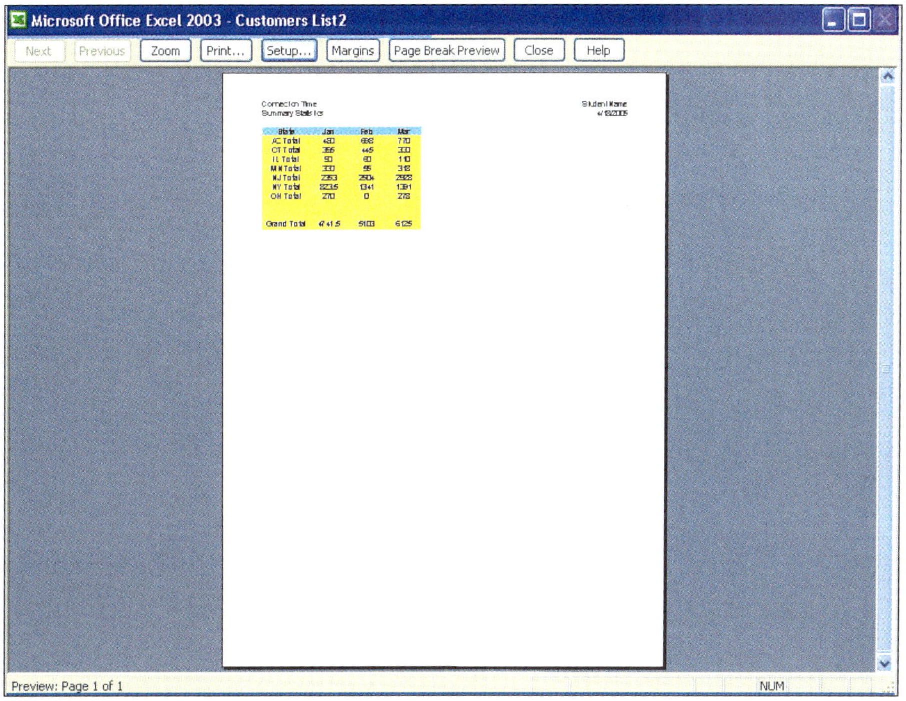

Figure 6.37

Only the selected range of the worksheet is displayed in the preview window.

2 Click [Print...] to print the selection.

- Unhide the two columns.
- Click [3] to show all details.
- Click outside the list range.
- Choose Data/Subtotals and click [Remove All].
- Sort the list in ascending order by ID.
- Move to cell A5 and save the workbook.

Your screen should be similar to figure 6.38

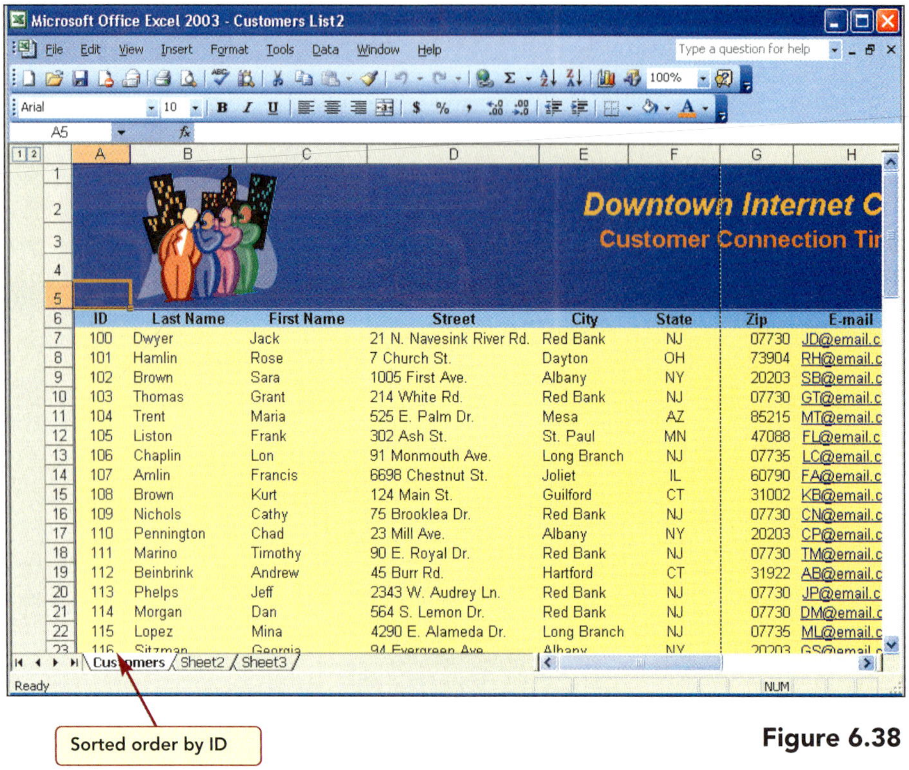

Figure 6.38

The list is in sorted order by ID number.

Creating a Web Page

The second project Evan has asked you to look into is to make the Bonus Dollars worksheet available to customers on the Café's Web site so they can check their award status. To do this, you will convert the Excel worksheet to a Web page.

Concept 5

Web Page

5 A **Web page** is a document that can be used on the World Wide Web (WWW) and displayed in a browser. A **browser** is a program that connects to remote computers and displays the Web pages you request. The browser interprets the HTML commands that are included in the Web page in order to know how to display the page contents. **HTML (Hypertext Markup Language)** is a programming language used to create Web pages. HTML commands control the display of information on a page, such as font colors and sizes, and how an item will be processed. HTML also allows users to click on hyperlinks and jump to other locations on the same page, other pages in the same site, or to other sites and locations on the WWW.

Previewing the Web Page

Note: This section of the lab assumes that a Web browser is installed on your computer.

You made several changes to the worksheet that were needed before it could be used on the Web. First, you replaced the Customer name with the ID number and removed the Select Bonus Rate combo box and the Print command button from the form. Then you removed the graphic and cell comments. Finally, you removed and modified fill colors and text colors to match other pages on the Web site.

1 **Open the workbook file** ex06_Bonus Dollars Web**.**

Your screen should be similar to Figure 6.39

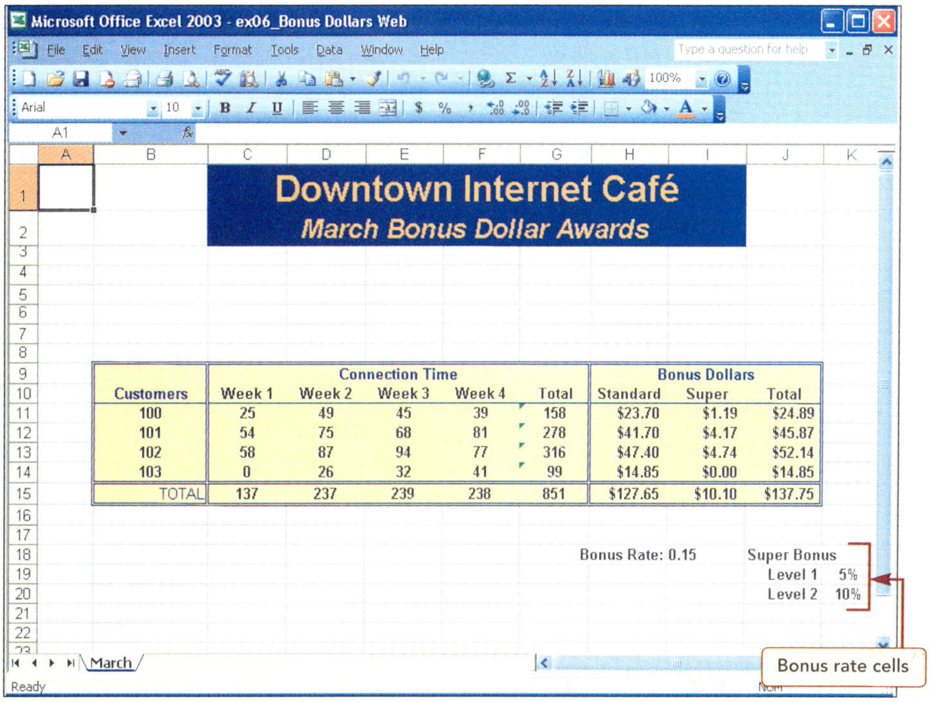

Figure 6.39

The only information remaining below the form are the Bonus Rate cells used to calculate the Bonus Dollars. Before you convert the worksheet, you want to preview how it will look as a Web page first.

2 Choose **File/Web Page Preview.**

If necessary, click OK **in response to the privacy warning.**

Maximize the browser window.

Your screen should be similar to Figure 6.40

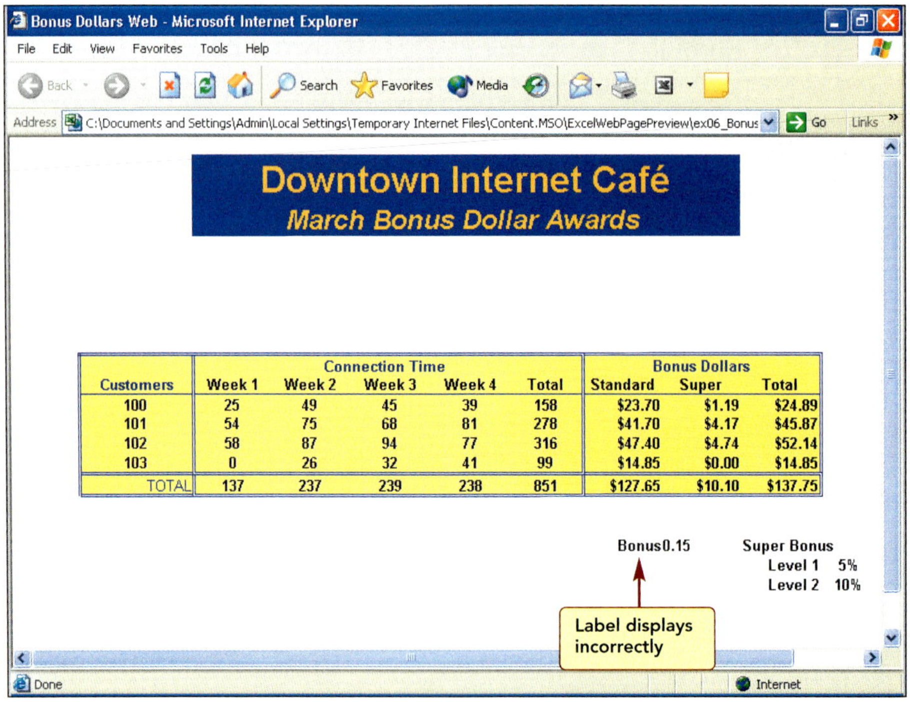

Figure 6.40

The browser on your system opens and displays the worksheet as it would appear when converted to a Web page. The name of the worksheet appears in the browser window title bar. Although most of the information looks good, the Bonus Rate label is not completely displayed. You will correct that shortly. Before converting the worksheet to a Web page, you decide to add a background image to make it more interesting.

Adding a Worksheet Background

A background is a graphic that is repeated to fill the viewing area of the sheet. You will add a graphic of a blue coffee cup with a yellow background behind the worksheet content. Adding a graphic to the background is similar to inserting a picture or clip art to the worksheet.

1. **Close the browser application.**

   Choose F̲ormat/Sh̲eet/B̲ackground.

   Select ex06_Cup **from your data file location.**

   Click Insert.

   Your screen should be similar to Figure 6.41

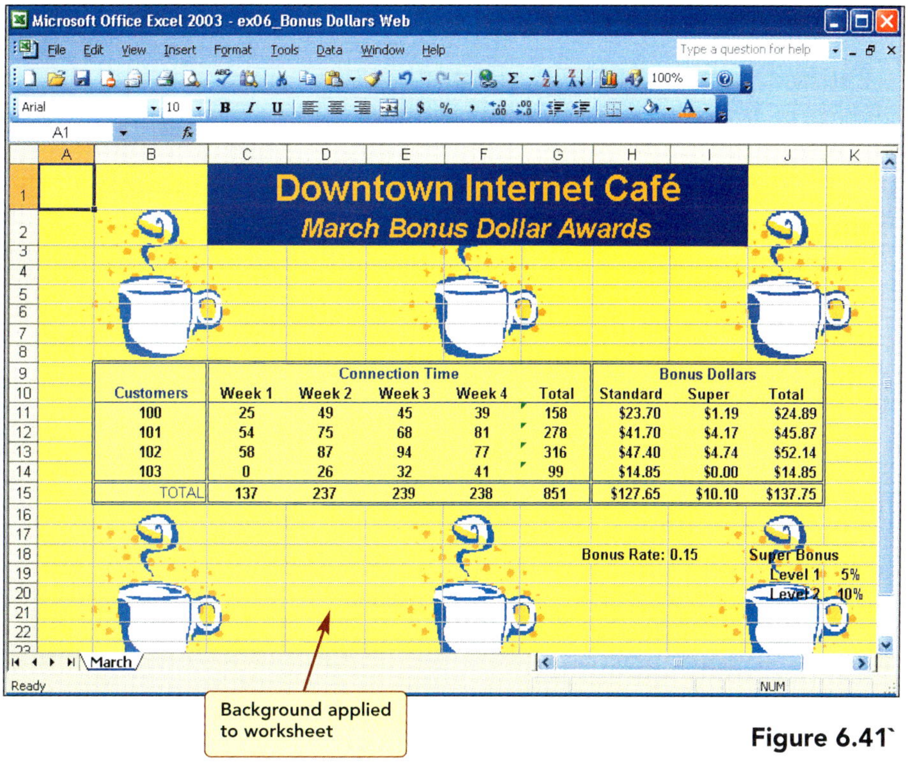

Figure 6.41

Additional Information

Background patterns do not print when you print the worksheet data.

A repeated pattern of coffee cups appears behind the worksheet data.

Saving the Worksheet as a Web Page

You think the background makes the worksheet more interesting and decide to go ahead and save the worksheet as a Web page. You can save the entire workbook, a worksheet, or selected portions of a worksheet as a Web page. Additionally, the worksheet can be saved with or without interactivity. When it is saved with interactivity, users can manipulate data and formatting, switch between sheets, and change formulas while viewing the worksheet in the browser. When saved without interactivity, the data appears as it would in Excel, but users cannot change or interact with the data in the browser.

1 **Choose File/Save as Web Page.**

Your screen should be similar to Figure 6.42

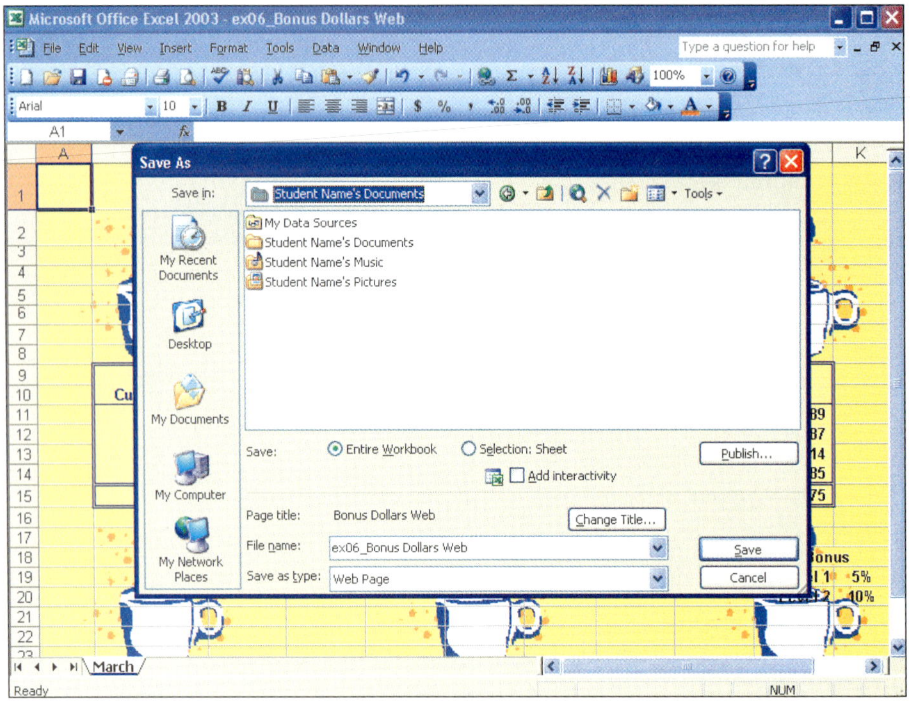

Figure 6.42

In the Save As dialog box, you enter a name for the Web page file, choose the location where you want the file saved, and specify whether you want the entire workbook or the current selection saved as your Web page contents. To retain the background image, you need to save the entire workbook as a Web page. You can also add a title that will appear centered over the selection and add interactivity to your Web page. You will save the entire workbook without interactivity as the contents for the Web page. Because the worksheet already contains its own title, you will not add a title.

Additional Information

You can also preselect a range to use as the area to save as a Web page.

2

- If necessary, select the location where you save your files.
- Select Entire Workbook.
- Change the file name to March Bonus Dollars.
- Click Save.
- Click OK in response to the privacy warning.
- Preview the Web page in your browser.

Your screen should be similar to Figure 6.43

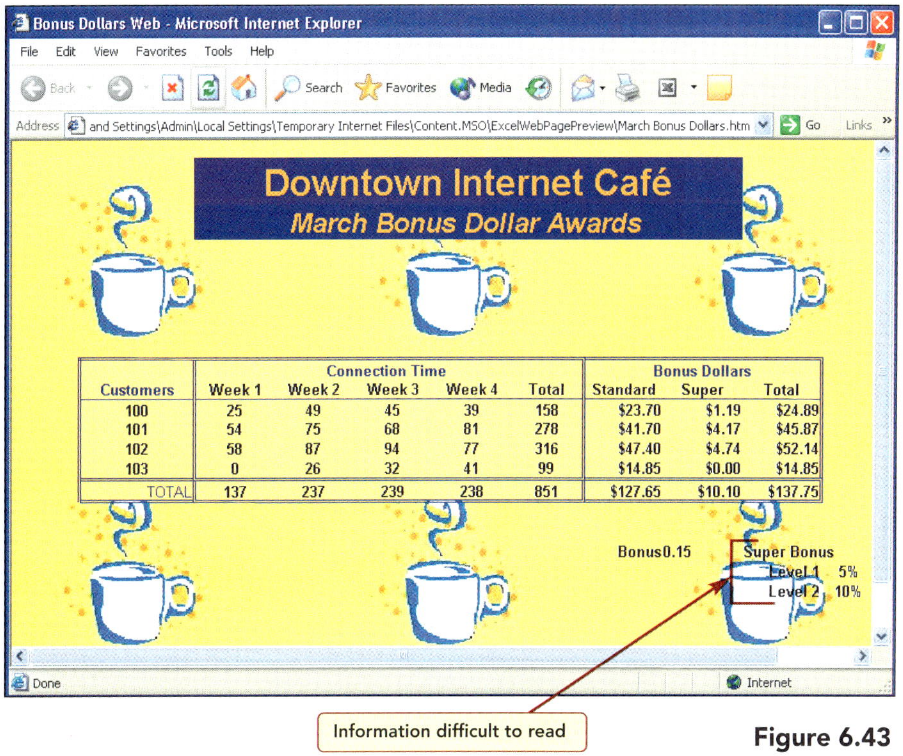

Figure 6.43

The background image looks good; however, it makes the Super Bonus information difficult to read. You will return to the worksheet to correct that and the Bonus Rate label. Then you will preview the Web page to check how it looks again.

3

- Switch to the Excel March Bonus Dollars worksheet window.
- Select cells G18 through H18 and click Merge and Center.
- Format cell I18 as Currency with two decimal places.
- Move the contents of J18 through K20 to H20.
- Preview the Web page in your browser again.

Your screen should be similar to Figure 6.44

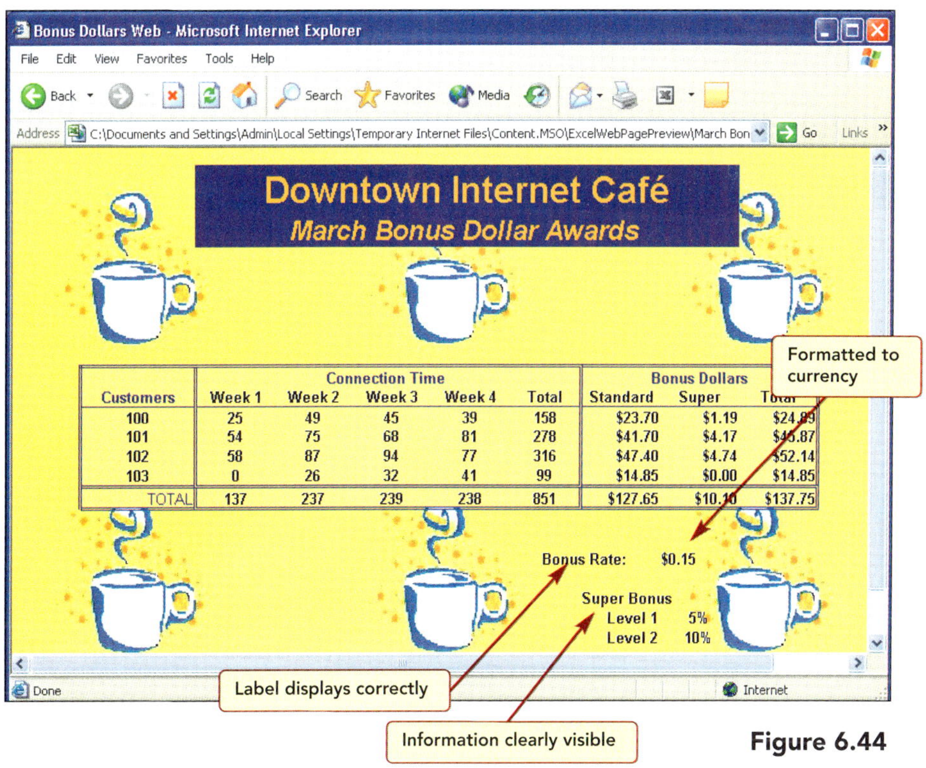

Figure 6.44

The revised worksheet is displayed in the browser window. You like the way this looks and need to save the changes you made to the worksheet to update the Web page file.

4

- **Close the browser application.**
- **Save the worksheet.**
- **Click OK in response to the privacy warning.**
- **Print preview the worksheet.**
- **Change the orientation to landscape and add a header that includes your name, the current date, and page number.**

Your screen should be similar to Figure 6.45

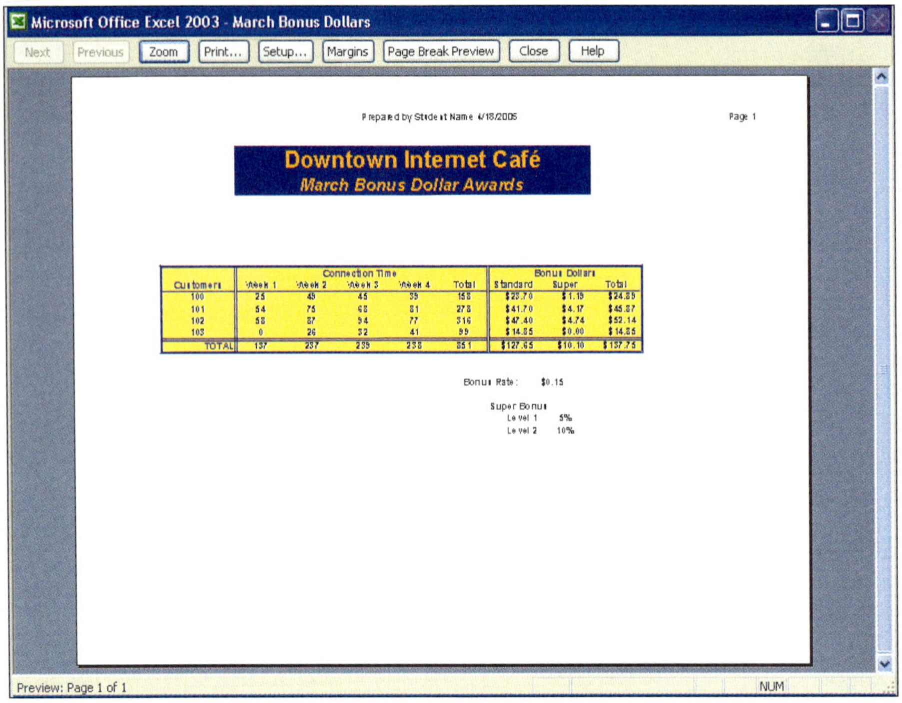

Figure 6.45

Notice the preview of the March Bonus Dollars worksheet does not include the background image. This is because background images are designed for viewing only.

5

- **Print the worksheet.**
- **Close all open workbooks and exit Excel.**

Making a Web Page Public

Now that you have created a Web page, in order for others to see it you need to make it available on the Internet. The steps that you take to make your pages public depend on how you want to share them. There are two main avenues: on your local network or intranet for limited access by people within an organization, or on the Internet for access by anyone using the WWW. To make pages available to other people on your network, save your Web pages to a network location. To make your Web pages available on the WWW, you need to either install Web server software on your computer or locate an Internet service provider that allocates space for Web pages.

Focus on Careers

EXPLORE YOUR CAREER OPTIONS

Lodging Manager

Have you ever wondered who ensures you get excellent customer service and enjoy your stay at a hotel? Have you ever attended a convention in a hotel and wondered who made sure the equipment and resources the group needed were attended to? Lodging managers are responsible for making sure customers are satisfied and the establishment is profitable. Managers must use guidelines to allocate and disperse funds for needed improvements and maintenance. They must track income and manage overhead. Many use spreadsheet programs to handle these tasks. The salary range for lodging managers is typically between $25,000 and $40,000. College graduates with experience in the lodging industry will have a competitive advantage in this industry.

LAB 6

Creating Lists and Web Pages

List (EX6.4)

A list, also called database, is an organized collection of related information entered in sequential rows and columns.

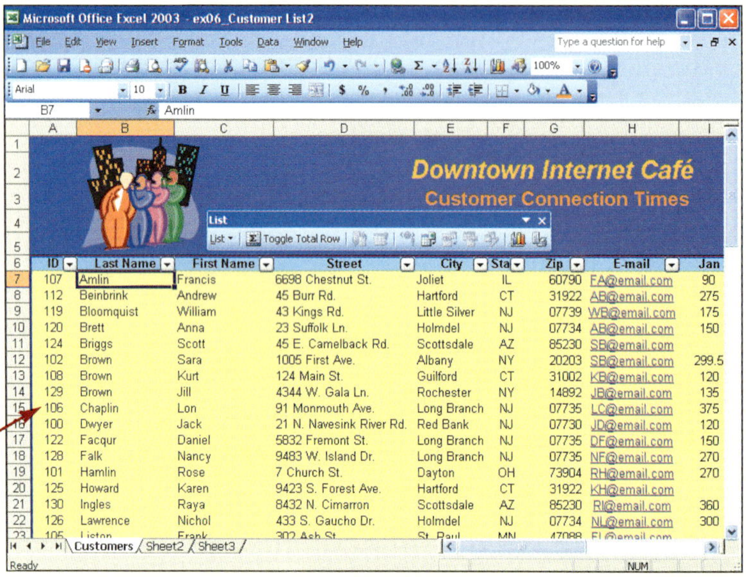

Hyperlink (EX6.5)

A hyperlink is a connection or link to a destination location. The destination can be a location in the current file, in another file, a Web page, or an e-mail address.

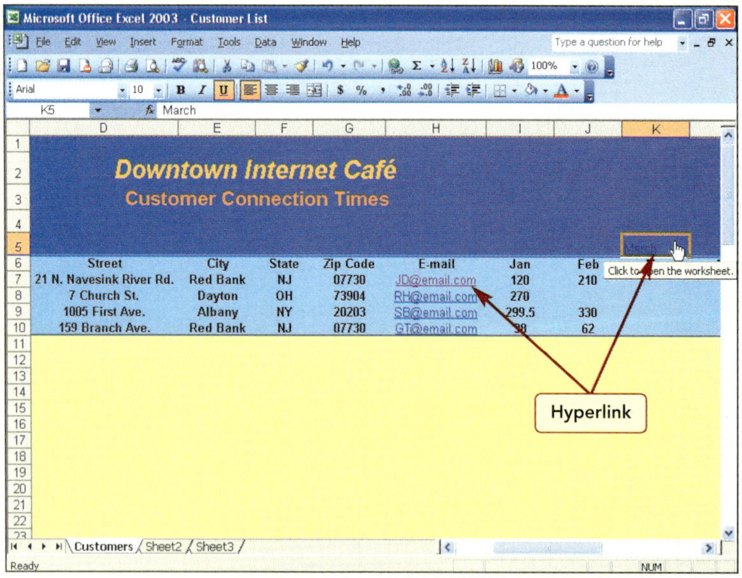

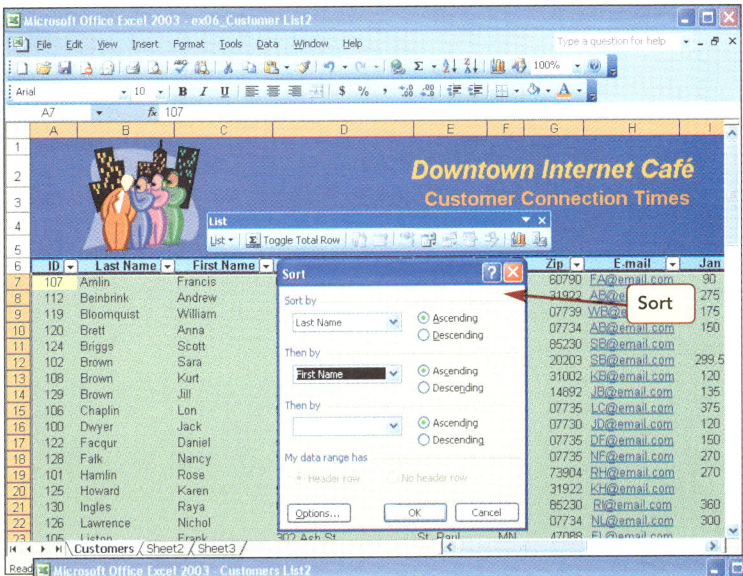

Sort (EX6.22)

You can sort or arrange data in a specified sequence: alphabetically, numerically, or by date.

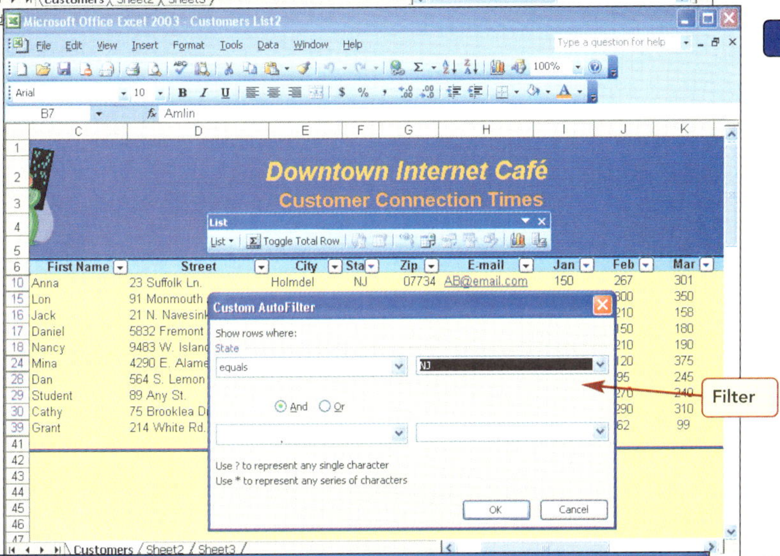

Filter (EX6.26)

A filter is a restriction you place on records in a list to quickly isolate and display a subset of records.

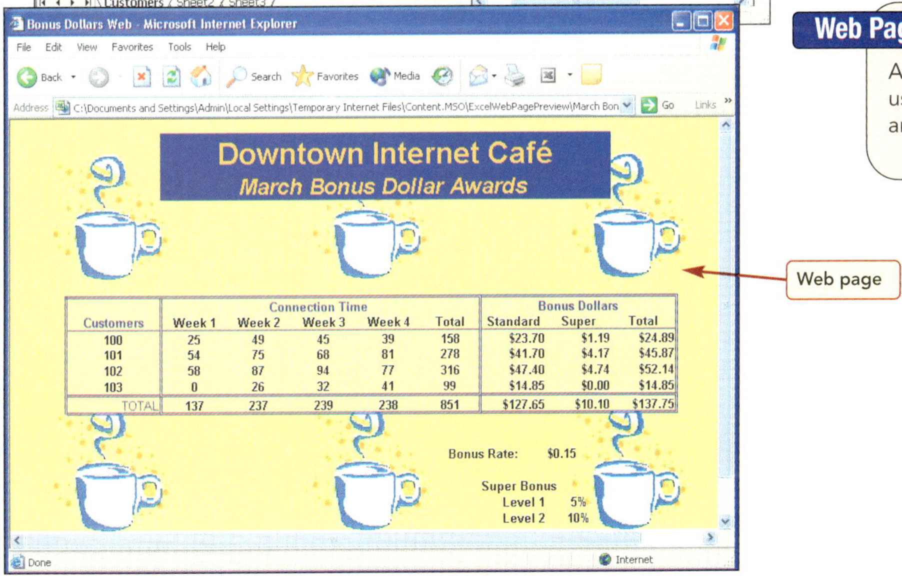

Web Page (EX6.34)

A Web page is a document that can be used on the World Wide Web (WWW) and displayed in a browser.

LAB 6

Creating Lists and Web Pages

key terms

absolute link EX6.16
bookmark EX6.14
browser EX6.342
critera EX6.0
database EX6.7
data form EX6.7
field EX6.4
field name EX6.4
filter EX6.26
HTML (Hypertext Markup Language) EX6.34
hyperlink EX6.11
list EX6.4
list range EX6.4
multilevel sort EX6.22
record EX6.4
relative link EX6.16
sort EX6.22
Uniform Resource Locator (URL) EX6.11
Web page EX6.34

microsoft office specialist skills

The Microsoft Office Specialist certification program is designed to measure your proficiency in performing basic tasks using the Office 2003 applications. Certification demonstrates that you have the skills and provides a valuable industry credential for employment. After completing this lab, you have learned the following Microsoft Office Excel Specialist skills:

Skill Set	Skill Standard	Page
Analyzing Data	Filter lists using AutoFilter	EX6.26
	Sort lists	EX6.21
Formatting Data and Content	Format worksheets	EX6.36
Managing Workbooks	Create and modify hyperlinks	EX6.11
	Preview data in other views	EX6.35
	Save data in appropriate formats for different uses	EX6.34

command summary

Command	Shortcut Key	Button	Action
File/Save as Web Page			Saves worksheet as a Web page
File/Web Page Preview			Previews workbook as a Web page in browser
Insert/Hyperlink	Ctrl + K		Inserts a new hyperlink or modifies selected hyperlink
Insert/Hyperlink/Remove Link			Removes hyperlink settings from selected cell
Format/Cells/Number/Category/Special			Applies selected special format to number entries
Format/Sheet/Background			Adds background to worksheet
Tools/Autocorrect Options			Turns on/off AutoCorrect features
Data/Sort			Arranges data alphabetically, numerically, or by date
Data/Filter/AutoFilter			Displays records based on specified criteria
Data/Filter/Show All			Redisplays all records
Data/Form			Displays a data form for record entry and modification
Data/Subtotals			Displays totals for each change in a category
Data/List/Create List	Ctrl + L		Converts a range of data into a list

matching

Match the letter on the right to the item in the numbered list on the left.

1. hyperlink	_____	**a.** an organized collection of related information
2. Web page	_____	**b.** displays a subset of records according to specified criteria
3. data form	_____	**c.** a connection to a location in another file
4. sort	_____	**d.** Z to A order
5. filter	_____	**e.** a row of a list or database that contains a group of related fields
6. field name	_____	**f.** used to enter information in a list
7. field	_____	**g.** a document that can be displayed in a browser
8. descending	_____	**h.** the smallest unit of information about a record
9. list	_____	**i.** organizes data in a specified sequence
10. record	_____	**j.** the label used to identify the data stored in a field
11. multilevel sort		

multiple choice

Circle the correct response to the questions below.

1. A _______________ is one group of information in a list.
- **a.** field
- **b.** record
- **c.** sort
- **d.** database

2. The _______________ from the list appear as the column labels in a data form.
- **a.** record names
- **b.** column letters
- **c.** field names
- **d.** cell references

3. The single-level sort feature lets you sort _______________ field(s) in a list at a time.
- **a.** 1
- **b.** 2
- **c.** 3
- **d.** 4

4. The ________________ option in a filter field drop-down list enables you to specify ranges of values that the record must meet to be displayed.
   a. Criteria
   b. Range
   c. Values
   d. Custom

5. The area containing the records in a list is called the:
   a. data field
   b. criteria range
   c. list range
   d. list data

6. ______________ can be used to summarize numbers in a list.
   a. Filters
   b. Subtotals
   c. Graphics
   d. Sorts

7. Use a _____________ to quickly jump to another location in a file.
   a. Web page
   b. hyperlink
   c. browser
   d. filter

8. The programming language used in Web pages is:
   a. HTLM
   b. HTXT
   c. HTML
   d. HXLS

9. A ________________ is a hyperlink to a specific location in a file.
   a. marker
   b. absolute link
   c. relative link
   d. bookmark

10. A _____________ is a document that can be used on the World Wide Web (WWW) and displayed in a browser.
   a. browser page
   b. Web document
   c. Web page
   d. none of the above

lab exercises

true/false

Circle the correct answer to the following questions.

1. You can erase any changes you made to a record in the data form after proceeding to the next record or by closing the dialog box.	True	False
2. Each column is a field, which is the smallest unit of information about a record.	True	False
3. A hyperlink is a connection to a location in the current file, in another file, or to a Web site.	True	False
4. A data form can be used to locate records.	True	False
5. A multilevel sort displays a subset of the records.	True	False
6. A filter rearranges data according to the criteria you specify.	True	False
7. An absolute link includes the complete destination path location.	True	False
8. Field names are entered in the first row of a list.	True	False
9. A browser is used to display Web pages.	True	False
10. Subtotals can be added above each category in the list.	True	False

fill-in

Complete the following statements by filling in the blanks with the correct key terms.

1. A ________________ is used to enter records into a list.
2. ____________ a list to display records in a specified order.
3. Apply a __________ to a list to display a subset of records.
4. A __________ is a descriptive label used to identify the data stored in the field.
5. A ____________ jumps you to a new location in a worksheet, workbook, a document, or Web page.
6. The area containing the records is called the _____________________.
7. A ____________ is a program that connects you to a remote computer and displays Web pages.
8. An organized collection of related information is called a _________ or __________________.
9. The group of related fields in a database is called a ______________.
10. A ________________________ does not include the drive and folder location of the destination file as part of the address.

rating system

★ Easy

★★ Moderate

★★★ Difficult

step-by-step

Lifestyle Fitness Club Employee Database ★

1. You work in Human Resources at the Lifestyle Fitness Club. One of your duties includes maintaining an Excel database of employee information. Your supervisor requested some payroll information that will be used to determine pay raises. You have been asked to provide an analysis of jobs and pay rates. Your completed analysis will be similar to the one shown here.

Student Name 10/26/2005

Lifestyle Fitness Club
Employee Database

ID #	Hire Date	Last Name	First Name	Job Title	Pay Rate	Hours	Weekly Pay
0427	02/01/95	Schiff	Marc	Greeter	$6.00	25	$150.00
5341	04/15/00	Lembi	Damon	Child Care Provider	$6.75	20	$135.00
6211	10/19/00	Schneider	Paul	Child Care Provider	$6.75	20	$135.00
5300	01/29/00	Reilly	Erin	Child Care Provider	$8.25	40	$330.00
5330	03/10/00	Jensen	Chris	Maintenance	$8.25	32	$264.00
3631	04/12/98	Delano	Gordon	Instructor	$8.50	25	$212.50
4421	03/02/99	West	Jeff	Instructor	$9.00	25	$225.00
6210	10/17/00	Vaccaro	Louis	Program Coordinator	$9.75	40	$390.00
2341	05/01/96	Morgan	Dan	Sales Associate	$10.00	35	$350.00
0873	12/12/95	Pennington	Chad	Sales Associate	$10.50	35	$367.50
2987	01/10/96	Spehr	Timothy	Sales Associate	$10.75	35	$376.25
5349	06/19/00	Steele	Jeff	Program Coordinator	$11.25	40	$450.00
5329	03/08/00	Delucchi	Bill	Aerobics Director	Salary		
0632	07/08/95	Smith	Cathy	Office Manager	Salary		

a. Open the file ex06_LFC Database.

b. Using the data form, enter a new record into the database. Use **your name** as the employee. Enter **9999** as your employee number, the **current date** as the hire date, **Sales Associate** as your job title, **10.00** as your pay rate, and **20** as your hours.

c. Use the data form to edit the entry for Kimberly Kieken. Her last name is now **Beinbrink**.

d. Sort the list to display the records by pay rate first, job title second, and hire date third. Filter the list to exclude records with a pay rate of salary. Add your name and the current date to the header. Print the sorted list in landscape orientation.

e. Filter the complete list again to display only those records with a hire date before November 2000. Print the filtered sheet.

f. Remove the filter.

g. Save your completed workbook as LFC Analysis.

Kodiak Construction Database ★★

2. The Kodiak Construction Company uses an Excel list to keep track of jobs for the year and the permit fees paid on them. They have asked you to do some analysis on the data so they can better see trends and make any needed adjustments. Your completed analysis of the list will be similar to the one shown here.

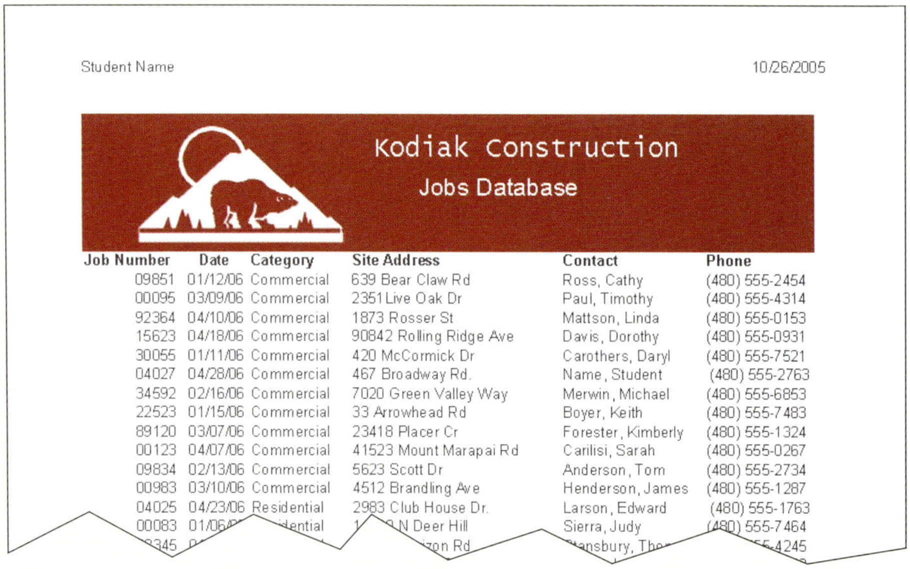

Student Name 10/26/2005

Kodiak Construction
Jobs Database

Job Number	Date	Category	Site Address	Contact	Phone
09851	01/12/06	Commercial	639 Bear Claw Rd	Ross, Cathy	(480) 555-2454
00095	03/09/06	Commercial	2351 Live Oak Dr	Paul, Timothy	(480) 555-4314
92364	04/10/06	Commercial	1873 Rosser St	Mattson, Linda	(480) 555-0153
15623	04/18/06	Commercial	90842 Rolling Ridge Ave	Davis, Dorothy	(480) 555-0931
30055	01/11/06	Commercial	420 McCormick Dr	Carothers, Daryl	(480) 555-7521
04027	04/28/06	Commercial	467 Broadway Rd.	Name, Student	(480) 555-2763
34592	02/16/06	Commercial	7020 Green Valley Way	Merwin, Michael	(480) 555-6853
22523	01/15/06	Commercial	33 Arrowhead Rd	Boyer, Keith	(480) 555-7483
89120	03/07/06	Commercial	23418 Placer Cr	Forester, Kimberly	(480) 555-1324
00123	04/07/06	Commercial	41523 Mount Marapai Rd	Carilisi, Sarah	(480) 555-0267
09834	02/13/06	Commercial	5623 Scott Dr	Anderson, Tom	(480) 555-2734
00983	03/10/06	Commercial	4512 Brandling Ave	Henderson, James	(480) 555-1287
04025	04/23/06	Residential	2983 Club House Dr.	Larson, Edward	(480) 555-1763
00083	01/06/…	…idential	… N Deer Hill	Sierra, Judy	…80) 555-7464

a. Open the workbook file ex06_Kodiak Database.

b. Format the Phone field using the special phone number format.

c. You have been given invoices for three new jobs. Using the data form, enter the following three new records into the database.

Job Number	Date	Category	Site Address	Contact	Phone	Permit Fees
04025	04/23/06	Residential	2983 Club House Dr	Larson, Edward	(480) 555-1763	$58.50
04026	04/26/06	Residential	20234 Midway Ave	Wilson, Gary	(480) 555-0031	$400.00
04027	04/28/06	Commercial	467 Broadway Rd	Name, Student	(480) 555-2763	$1,275.50

d. Close the data form and scroll to the end of the list.

e. The Accounting department has requested a list of jobs whose permit fees were more than $1,000. Filter the database to display these records only. Print the filtered list in landscape orientation, centered horizontally.

f. Marketing has also requested a copy of the job list sorted by category. Sort the list on Category. Change the layout to portrait and include your name and the current date in the header. Print all the fields except the Permit Fees field.

g. Save the workbook as Kodiak Database Update.

Wilson Electronics Employee Database ★★

3. Part of your job in the Personnel department at Wilson Electronics is to maintain the employee sales database. Recently, in order to boost sales, the company has been running a rewards program for the employees based on sales performance. In addition to the standard database maintenance, you have been asked to examine the employee database and determine the appropriate rewards. Your completed analysis and update of the database should be similar to that shown here.

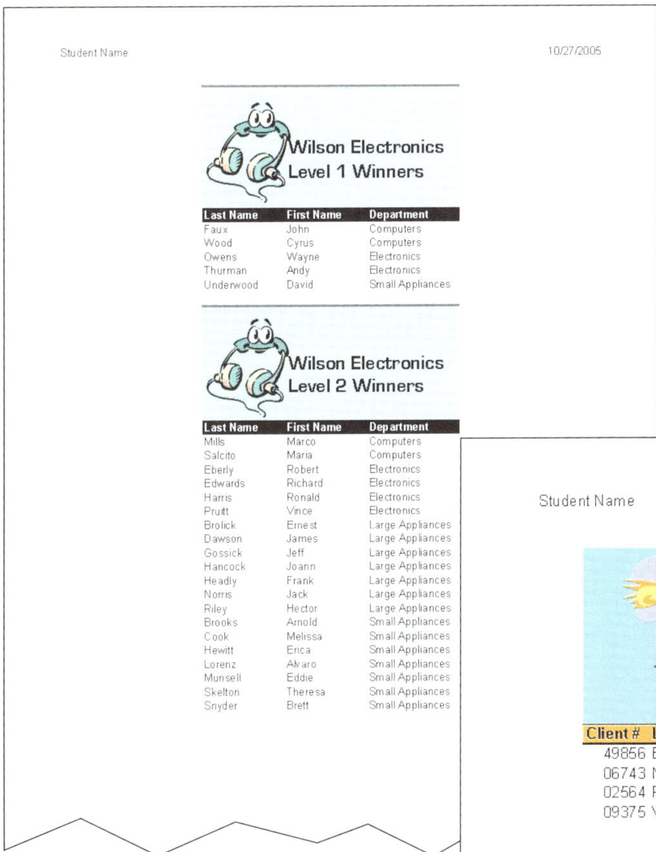

Student Name 10/27/2005

Wilson Electronics
Level 1 Winners

Last Name	First Name	Department
Faux	John	Computers
Wood	Cyrus	Computers
Owens	Wayne	Electronics
Thurman	Andy	Electronics
Underwood	David	Small Appliances

Wilson Electronics
Level 2 Winners

Last Name	First Name	Department
Mills	Marco	Computers
Salcito	Maria	Computers
Eberly	Robert	Electronics
Edwards	Richard	Electronics
Harris	Ronald	Electronics
Pruitt	Vince	Electronics
Brolick	Ernest	Large Appliances
Dawson	James	Large Appliances
Gossick	Jeff	Large Appliances
Hancock	Joann	Large Appliances
Headly	Frank	Large Appliances
Norris	Jack	Large Appliances
Riley	Hector	Large Appliances
Brooks	Arnold	Small Appliances
Cook	Melissa	Small Appliances
Hewitt	Erica	Small Appliances
Lorenz	Alvaro	Small Appliances
Munsell	Eddie	Small Appliances
Skelton	Theresa	Small Appliances
Snyder	Brett	Small Appliances

Student Name

Mediterranean Tour

Student Name Client List

Client #	Last Name	First Name	Phone	E-mail Address	Europe	Lower 48	Alaska/H
49856	Berdahl	Tara	555-3874	kt874@mail.com	Yes	Yes	No
06743	Nelson	Shane	555-8374	nelson_shane@mail.com	Yes	No	Yes
02564	Reyes	Michelle	555-9833	michelle_reyes@mail.com	Yes	Yes	No
09375	Valdez	Terri	555-0686	terri@mail.com	Yes	No	Yes

a. Open the file ex06_Wilson Employees.

b. The employee data for several new employees has not been included in the database. Use the data form to enter the records shown below.

Employee #	Last Name	First Name	Department	Total Sales
45925	Phillips	Jennifer	Audio	$752.98
08420	Schwartz	Grant	Small Appliances	$1,230.79
64301	Thurman	Andy	Electronics	$2,951.50
00345	Wood	Cyrus	Computers	$3,450.97

c. Apply an ascending sort to the Last Name column to alphabetize your list.

d. There have been some personnel changes since the last database update. Eugene Radden and Tony Patel are no longer with the company. Use the Data Form to find and remove their records from the database. Joann Keifer recently got married. Find her record and change her last name to **Hancock**.

e. You have finished making the necessary changes to the database and can now begin your analysis. Use a multilevel sort to display the records first by department and then by last name.

f. Now that you have the data organized, you need to filter the records to determine which employees have earned rewards. There are two awards levels. Those who have sales of at least $2,000 receive $75, and those with sales of at least $4,000 receive $150. Use AutoFilter and apply a custom filter to determine those employees whose sales are greater than or equal to $2,000 but less than $4000. Copy this filtered sheet to a new sheet and name it **Bonus Winners**. Adjust the formatting as needed.

g. Redisplay all the records on the Employee Sales sheet and apply a custom filter to determine those employees whose sales are greater than or equal to $4,000. Copy this information including the column labels to the Bonus Winners sheet below the other information, separated by a blank row.

h. Change the subtitle to **Level 1 Winners**. Insert a new row above the second set of column labels and enter the subtitle **Level 2 Winners**.

i. You need to print the list of winners to post in the break room, but some of the information included in your new sheet is confidential. Hide column E. Define a print area to include only the employees' last and first names, their department, and the department total.

j. Adjust the formatting so the printout will include the title information and graphic. Center the worksheet horizontally and fit to one page. Print the Bonus Winners worksheet with your name and the current date centered on a separate line in a header.

k. Remove the filter from the sales worksheet. Save your completed workbook as Wilson Employee Rewards.

Adventure Travel Tours Client Database ★★★

4. As a travel agent at Adventure Travel Tours, you maintain an Excel database of your clients. You have recently created several new tour packages and would like to inform your clients about them. Your database includes information about where customers have traveled in the six areas your new packages cover. You would like to target those who have already traveled in the new areas of your packages. Some of your completed worksheets will be similar to those shown here.

Student Name 10/27/2005

ADVENTURE TRAVEL TOURS

Mediterranean Tour

Client #	Last Name	First Name	Phone	E-mail Address	Europe	Lower 48	Alaska/Hawaii	Asia	Africa	Indonesia
49856	Berdahl	Tara	555-3874	kt874@mail.com	Yes	Yes	No	No	Yes	No
06743	Nelson	Shane	555-8374	nelson_shane@mail.com	Yes	No	Yes	No	Yes	No
02564	Reyes	Michelle	555-9833	michelle_reyes@mail.com	Yes	Yes	No	No	Yes	Yes
09375	Valdez	Terri	555-0686	terri@mail.com	Yes	No	Yes	No	Yes	No

a. Open the file ex06_ATT Client List.

b. Merge and center **your name** and the words **Client List** under the company name at the top of the worksheet. Increase the font size to 14.

c. The data for one of your clients has changed since you last worked with the workbook. Use the data form to locate the record for Debby Shaw. Change her e-mail address to **debby_shaw@mail.com**.

d. One of your new packages is a tour of Indonesia. Filter the list to display those clients who have traveled to Indonesia in the past. Insert a new sheet and name it **Indonesia**. Copy the filter results (including the title) to the new sheet. AutoFit the columns. Change the subtitle to **Indonesia Tour**.

e. Insert your name and the current date in a header. Print the Indonesia Tour sheet centered horizontally in landscape orientation.

f. You have another tour package that explores the Mediterranean and then ventures into Africa. You need to display a list of clients who have traveled to Africa and Europe. In the Client List sheet, display all the records. First filter for those who have traveled to Europe. Then filter the list to determine which of those clients have traveled to Africa.

g. Insert a new sheet titled **Mediterranean**. Copy the filtered Client List sheet to the new sheet. AutoFit the columns. Change the title to **Mediterranean Tour**. Insert your name and the current date in a header. Print the Mediterranean Tour sheet centered horizontally in landscape orientation.

h. Right-click the e-mail link for Shane Nelson replace the e-mail address with your or your instructor's e-mail address. Click the link to open a new e-mail message. Complete the e-mail:

Subject: **Mediterranean Tour**

Message: **We are planning a new tour so I wanted to test the email function in Excel ... call me about dinner this week.**

i. Send the e-mail message.

j. Return to the Client List sheet and remove the filter. Save your completed worksheet as ATT Client List2.

Animal Rescue Foundation Donation Inventory ★ ★ ★

5. The Animal Rescue Foundation relies on donations to furnish foster homes with the supplies they need. They have started to record the donation information in an Excel workbook so they can keep an inventory of goods. You have been asked to update and maintain this inventory and furnish the board of directors with an inventory that calls attention to supply shortages. The directors have also asked you to create a Web page of inventories so foundation members can make donations accordingly. Your completed worksheets should be similar to those shown here.

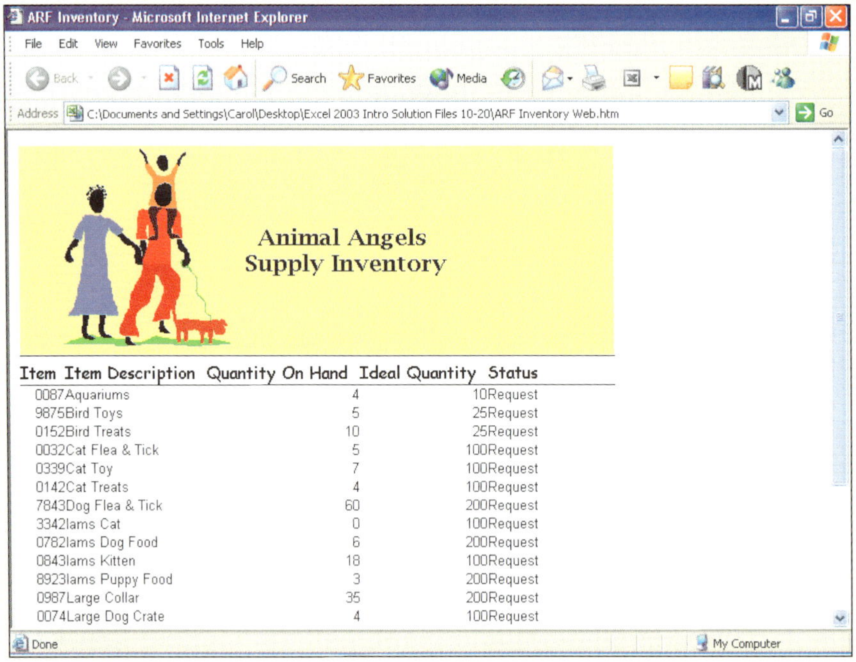

a. Open the file ex06_ARF Inventory.

b. The inventory consists of a list of items showing the quantity on hand and the desired quantity. You need to add a column that will identify the need status of each item. Add the label **Status** in cell E9. Adjust the formatting as needed.

c. In order to indicate a need for an item, you will enter a formula that will calculate when an item's on-hand amount is less than half of the ideal amount, and display either "Stocked" or "Request" based on the determination. Enter the formula **=IF(C10<(D10/2), "Request","Stocked")** in cell E10. Copy the formula to the rest of the cells in that column.

d. You now have a list that displays which items need to be restocked. Now you need to provide a list of low-stock items to the board. Display only those items with "Request" status.

e. The board does not need most of the information in the sheet. They would like a list showing only the item description and the status. Hide columns A, C, and D. Add the titles **Inventory** in cell E2 and **Shortages** in E3. Apply formatting of your choice. Preview the sheet. Add **your name** and the **current date** to a custom header and print the sheet centered horizontally.

f. Unhide the columns. Delete the titles in cells E2 and E3. Remove the AutoFilter. Save your completed workbook as ARF Inventory2.

g. You have been asked to create a Web page with the inventory information. Preview the Web page. Fix and enhance the formatting of the sheet as needed.

h. Save the Inventory worksheet as a Web page called ARF Inventory Web.

i. Print the Web page.

on your own

Bradford Suppliers Database ★

1. Bradford Building Supply needs you to create a database to hold supplier information such as company name, location, sales representative, and product category (such as wood, hardware, hand tools, electric tools, and so on). Enter a list of at least 20 records in an Excel worksheet with the appropriate fields. Format the worksheet in an attractive manner. Sort the list by the supplier's state. Filter the list to display suppliers of the same category of product. Enter a subtotal to count the number of records. Print the filter results with your name and the current date as a header. Save the workbook as Bradford Suppliers.

Kids Express Inventory Analysis ★ ★

2. The Kids Express Toy Company needs help with its inventory. Create a worksheet that has 20 inventory records. The records should contain a product identification number, description, wholesale distributor, wholesale price, retail price, and quantity on hand. Format the worksheet in an attractive manner. Sort the records by distributor. Filter the records to display a selected distributor and total the quantity on hand for that distributor. Enter your name and the current date as a header to the filter results and print them. Filter the list next to find all items with a retail price higher than a selected value. Enter your name and the current date as a header to the filter results and print them. Save the workbook as Toy Inventory.

Baseball League Roster ★ ★

3. You have a summer internship working in your town's community activities department. You have been asked to create a database of players enrolled in the summer baseball program in order to divide them into the various teams. Create a database that lists the players' names, addresses, phone numbers, ages, and positions. Format the worksheet in an attractive manner. Enter 30 records in the list. Include your name as one of the records and a position of pitcher. Sort the database by player name, position, and age. Filter the list to show only pitchers. Enter your name and the current date as a header to the worksheets. Print the filter results. Save the workbook as Summer Baseball League.

Cleaning Service Customer List ★ ★ ★

4. Desert Rescue Cleaning wants to keep track of its customers with an Excel worksheet database. Create a worksheet database that includes customer ID number, cleaning address with suite or apartment number, contact name, phone number, and square footage. Format the worksheet in an attractive manner. Enter 15 records into the database. Enter your name as the contact for the first record. Sort the database by contact name. Filter the list to display only those records with a square footage larger than a specified value. Enter functions to display the minimum and maximum square footage values. Include appropriate labels. Enter your name and the current date as a header to the worksheets. Print the filter results. Save the workbook as Cleaning Company Customers.

Spring Break Budget Planning ★ ★ ★

5. After analyzing your budget to see if you will have enough money to take a trip over spring break, you tell your friends about the results. They would also like to analyze their budgets. To make the worksheet available to your friends, you decide to create a template of the worksheet and make it available on your Web site for them to use. Clear out your personal data to create the template and preview it as a Web page. Make any necessary adjustments to the worksheet and then save it as an interactive Web page with the file name Budget Analysis. Try out the worksheet to make sure it works in the browser and modify again as needed. Print the blank worksheet in the browser.

Working Together 2: Importing Access Data and Using the Visual Basic Editor

Case Study

Downtown Internet Café

On a weekly basis you need to check the inventory on hand of certain items. If some items are overstocked, such as a certain type of coffee beans, you run a special on them to lower inventory. On the other hand, if certain items are low, you reorder the item with the vendor. The inventory information is maintained in an Access database table. You plan to import the table into Office Excel 2003 to quickly analyze the inventory numbers.

The second project you are working on is a macro to automate the input for an inventory order workbook. You will use the Visual Basic Editor to create the macro. You plan to have a clerk enter the data, so you want to make sure it is easy to use.

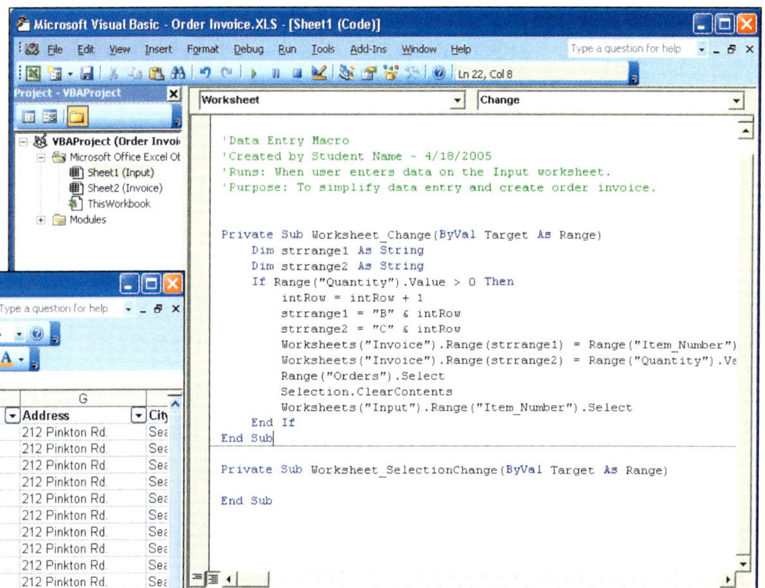

Many worksheet actions can be stored as a macro using the Visual Basic Editor program.

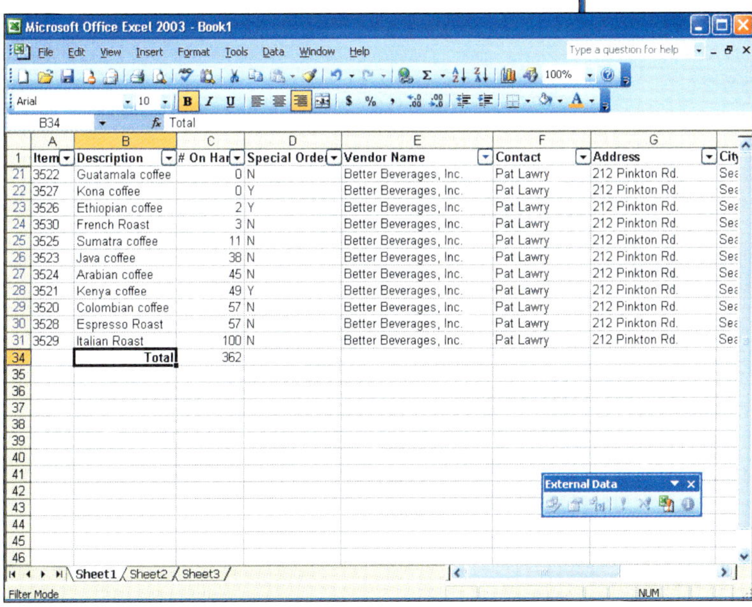

Importing data from Access allows you to analyze the list information using Excel.

Importing Data

Additional Information

Exporting saves data in another format so that it can be used in an application other than the application in which it was created.

The inventory information is maintained in an Access database table. You have found however, that it is easier to use Excel to analyze the inventory numbers. To do this, you will import the information in the Access database table into Office Excel 2003. **Importing** converts external data that has been saved in another format into a format that can be used by the application. **External data** is data, such as a database or text file, that is stored outside the application, in this case Excel.

Importing Access Table Data to Excel

You want to import the data from the Vendors table of the Café Supplies Access database to an Excel workbook so you can more easily analyze the inventory on hand data.

1

- **Start Office Excel 2003.**
- **Close the Getting Started task pane.**
- **Choose Data/Import External Data/Import Data.**
- **Select** exwt2_Café Supplies.mdb **from your data file location.**
- **Click** Open.
- **Select the Vendors table from the Select Table dialog box.**
- **Click** OK.

Your screen should be similar to Figure 1

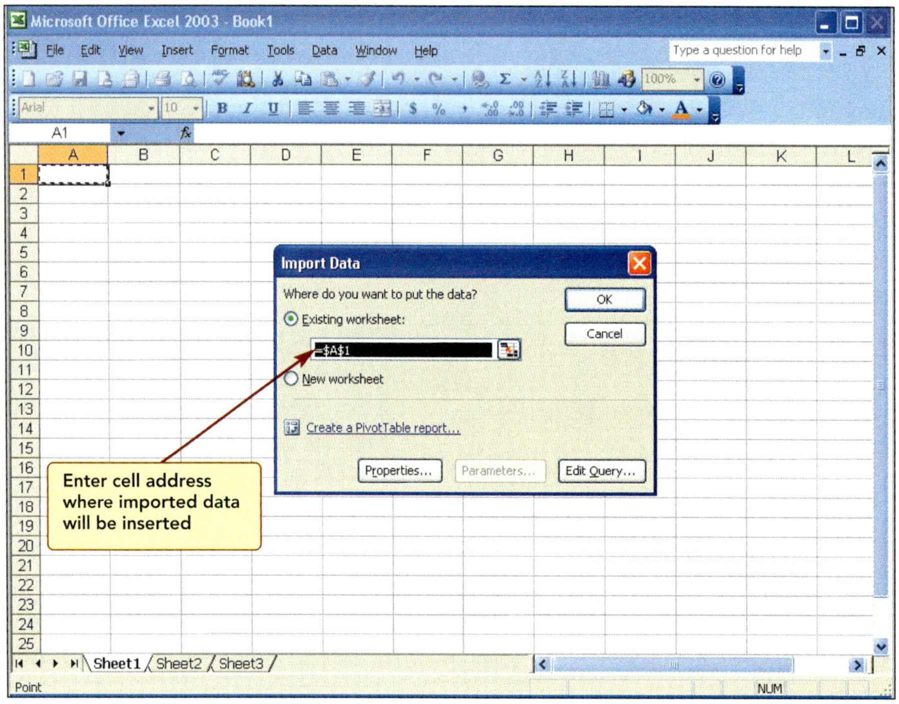

Figure 1

In the Import Data dialog box, you need to specify where you want the data inserted. The default selection, cell A1, in the worksheet is appropriate. When specifying the location, be careful to select an area that is empty below and to the right of the selected cell so that any existing data in the worksheet is not overwritten.

2 **Click** OK.

Your screen should be similar to Figure 2

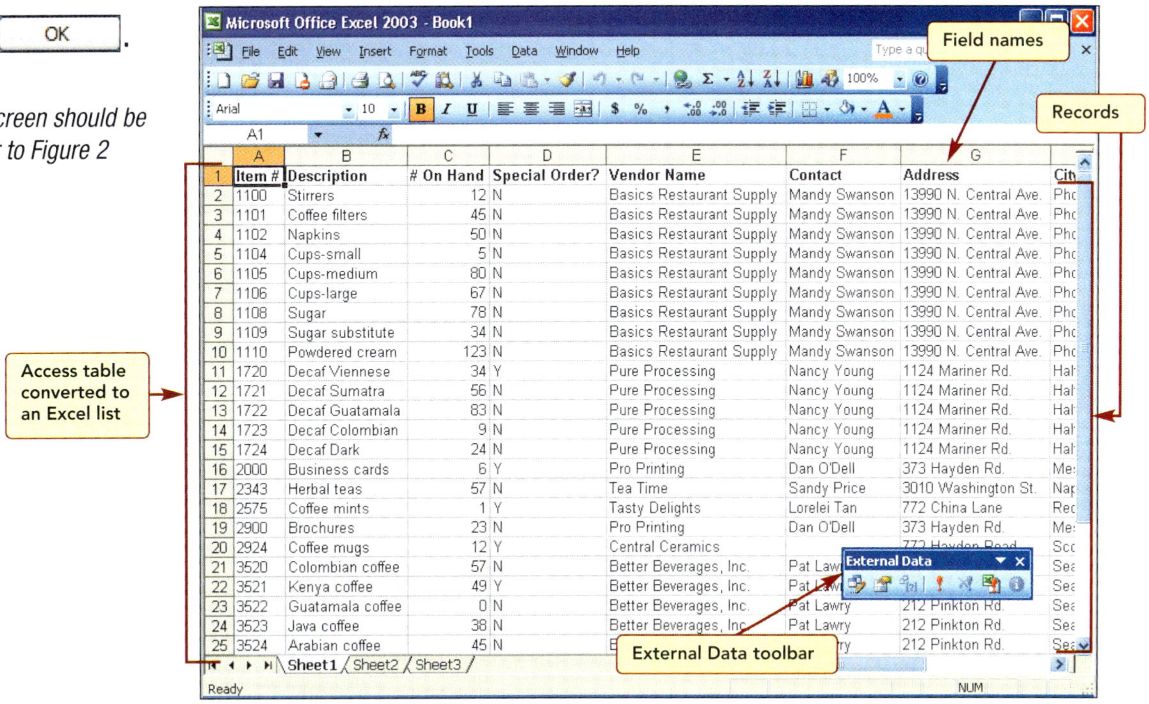

Figure 2

The database table is converted to an Excel list with the field names in the first row of the worksheet and the records beginning in row 2. The column heads and column widths are formatted as they appeared in the Access table. The External Data toolbar may be automatically displayed.

Analyzing the List

Now the data can be manipulated using Excel commands and features. You want to find out how much coffee is on hand to determine what coffee specials to offer next week. Because you only plan to use this worksheet temporarily to analyze the on-hand stock, you decide to not bother defining a list range. Because the data is set up as a list, you can still filter the data and use Excel functions to calculate values. Some list features, such as the total row, are not available, however.

1. Choose **Data/Filter/AutoFilter**.
   - From the Vendor Name field select Better Beverages, Inc.
   - Sort the # On Hand field in ascending sort order.
   - Use the SUM function in cell C34 to calculate the total coffee on hand.
   - Enter, bold, and right-align the label **Total** in cell B34.

Your screen should be similar to Figure 3

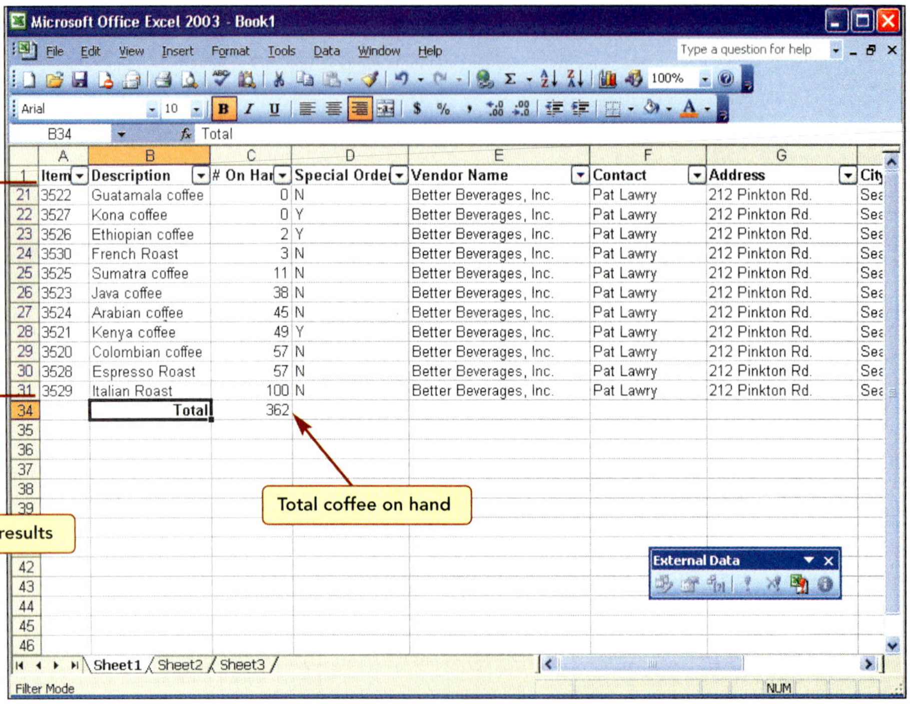

Figure 3

You can now easily see that the Italian Roast coffee quantity on hand is very high and decide to offer a special on that item. At the same time, you need to order several coffees whose quantity is very low. You will print out the filtered list for Evan to confirm your ordering decisions.

2. Select the range A1 through C34.
   - Specify this range as the selection to print and then preview the worksheet.
   - Center the worksheet horizontally.
   - Enter your name and the current date right-aligned on separate lines in a custom header.
   - Print the worksheet.

Your printed output should be similar to that shown here.

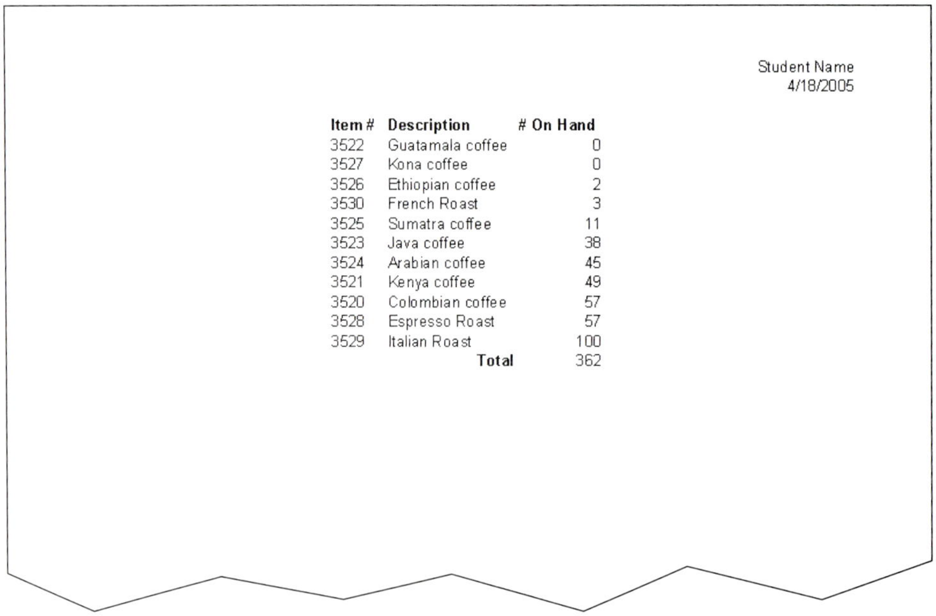

Student Name
4/18/2005

Item #	Description	# On Hand
3522	Guatamala coffee	0
3527	Kona coffee	0
3526	Ethiopian coffee	2
3530	French Roast	3
3525	Sumatra coffee	11
3523	Java coffee	38
3524	Arabian coffee	45
3521	Kenya coffee	49
3520	Colombian coffee	57
3528	Espresso Roast	57
3529	Italian Roast	100
	Total	362

Now that you have the information you need, you will remove the filter and save the workbook.

3 Remove the filter.

- If necessary, close the External Data toolbar.
- Save the workbook as Café Supplies.
- Close the workbook.

After Evan reviewed the printout you gave him of the coffee inventory status, he returned the document with the coffees he wants to order and an order quantity written next to the On Hand column.

Creating an Order Invoice

Now you need to place the order with the vendor. To do this, you need to create an order invoice for the vendor containing the item number and amount. You decide to simplify the process of creating the order invoice by creating a form that can be used to input the order information. Then you will write a macro to copy the order information to the order invoice automatically for you.

You have already started a worksheet that will be used to create the order invoice.

1 Open the file exwt2_Order.

- Click Enable Macros.

Your screen should be similar to Figure 4

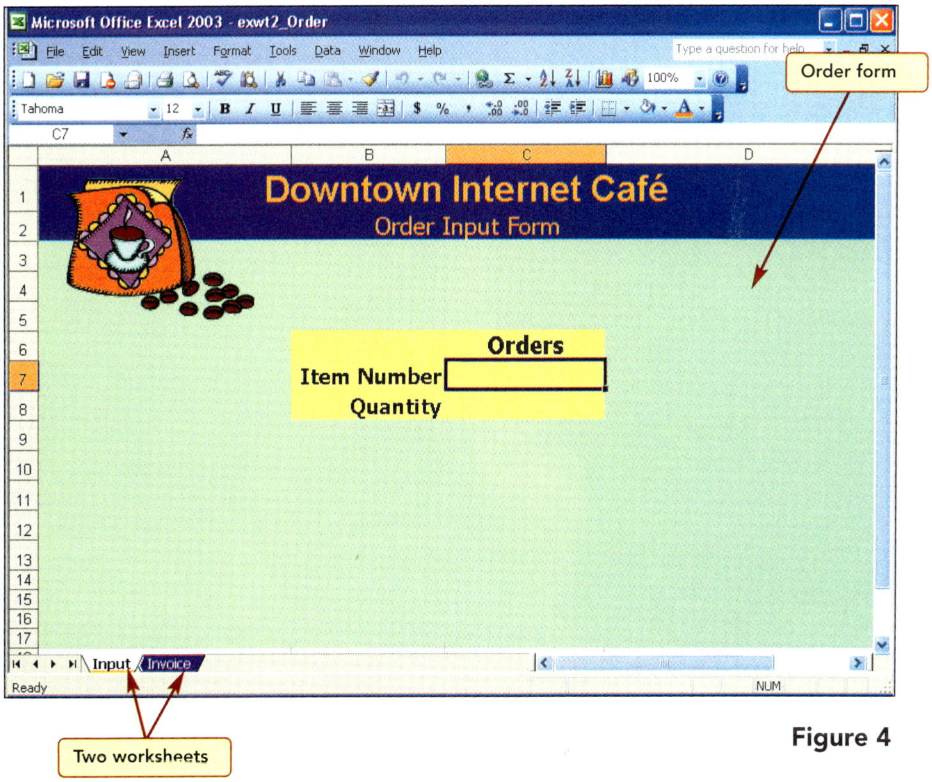

Figure 4

The workbook contains two worksheets, the Input sheet and the Invoice sheet. The Input sheet will be used to enter the order data. The order invoice will be generated automatically in the Invoice sheet as the order data is entered in the form.

Setting Data Validation

First you want to ensure that the data entered in the input form is acceptable or valid by restricting the entry in cells C7 and C8 to number entries within certain limits. First you will limit the Item Number entry to a number in the range 0 to 5000.

1

- **Move to C7.**
- **Choose Data/Validation.**
- **From the Settings tab, set the following limits:**

  Allow: Whole Number

  Data: Between

  Minimum: 0

  Maximum: 5000

  Clear the Ignore Blank check box

Your screen should be similar to Figure 5

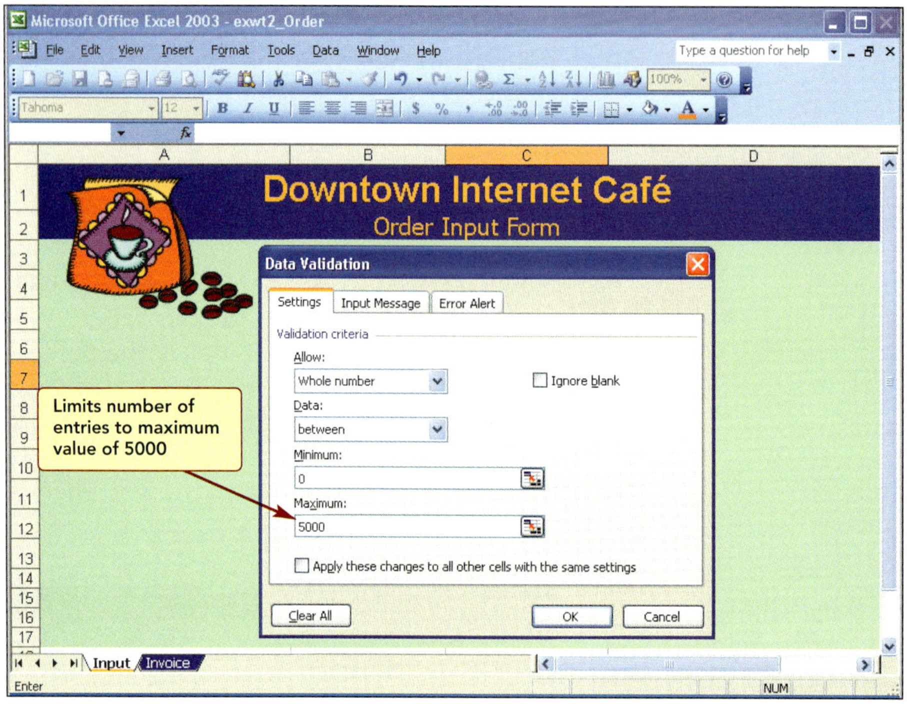

Figure 5

You would also like the cell to display a message, similar to a comment, when it is selected. The message will help the user know what data to enter.

2 **Open the Input Message tab.**

- **Type** Enter item number **in the Title text box.**
- **Type** Valid entries are 0 to 5000. **in the Input Message text box.**

Your screen should be similar to Figure 6

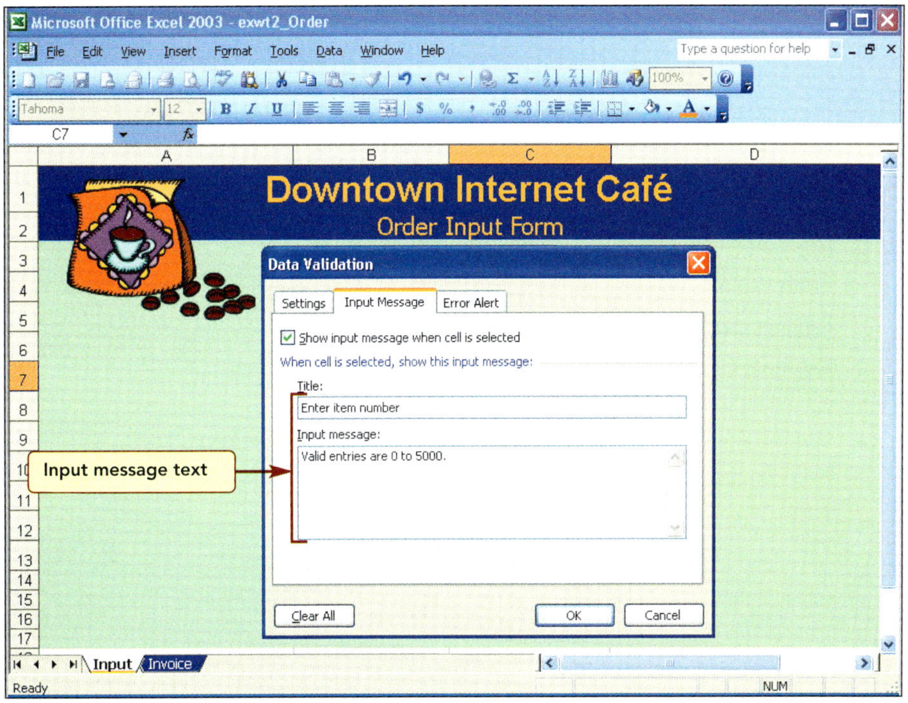

Figure 6

Finally, you want to enter a message that will display if incorrect data is entered in the cell.

3 **Open the Error Alert tab.**

- **Type** Numeric entry required **in the Title text box.**
- **Type** Valid entries are 0 to 5000. **in the Error Message text box.**
- **Click** OK.

Your screen should be similar to Figure 7

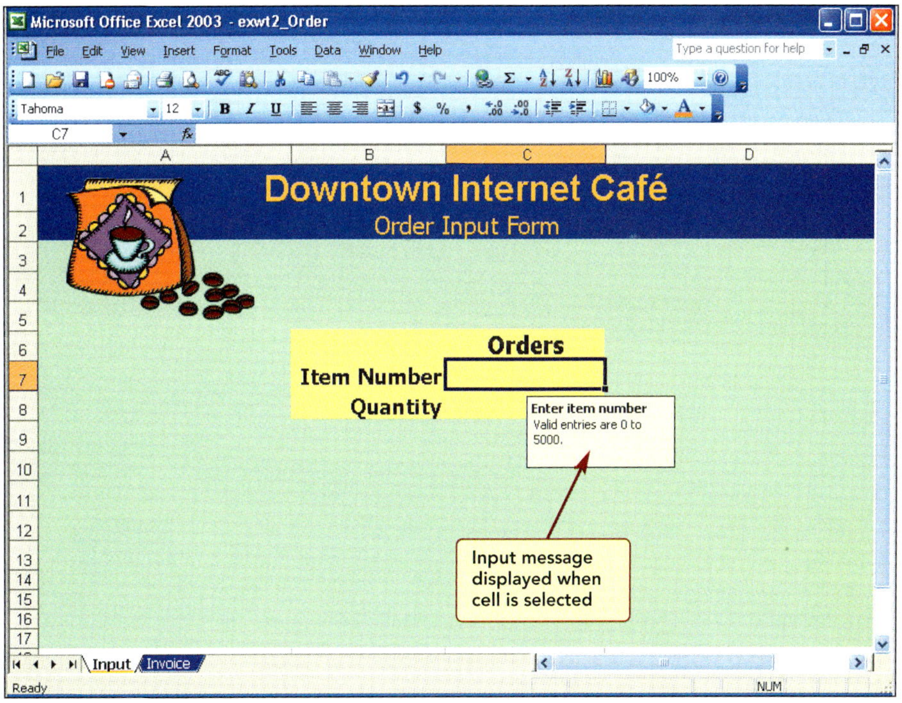

Figure 7

The input message you entered is displayed when the cell is selected. Next, you will add the data validation information for the Quantity cell.

4 Move to cell C8.

- Change the data validation settings to:

  Allow: Whole number

  Data: Greater than

  Minimum: 0

  Clear the Ignore Blank check box

- Add the input message **Enter quantity to order** in the Title text box.

- Enter **Numeric entries only** in the Input Message text box.

- Enter **Positive numbers only** in the Error Message text box.

- Click OK.

Your screen should be similar to Figure 8

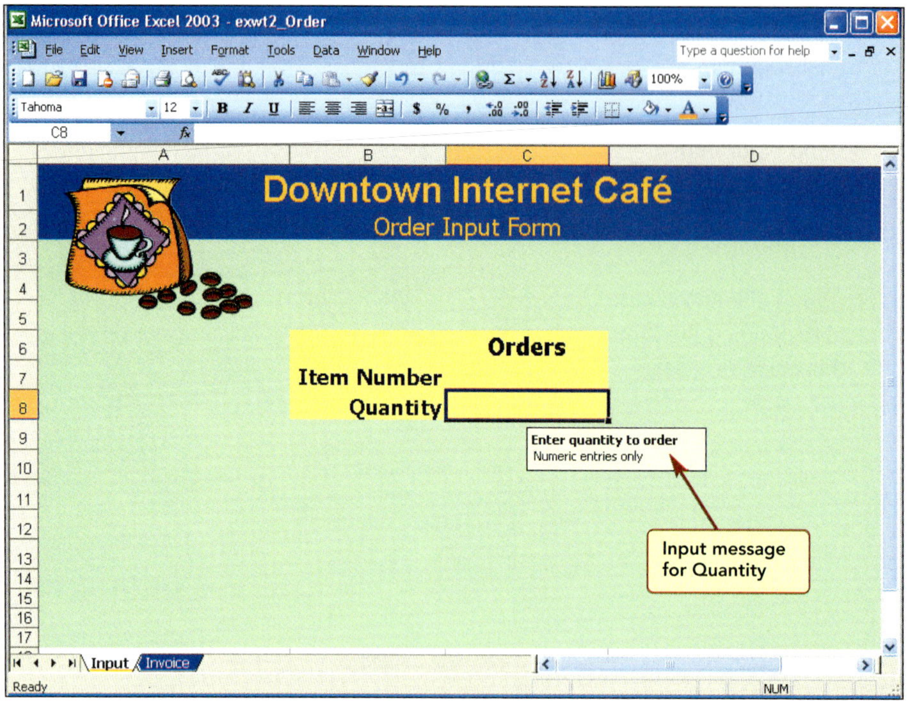

Figure 8

Testing Data Validation

Now you will test the data validation settings by entering some incorrect data.

1 **Type 6000 in cell C7 and press ←Enter.**

Your screen should be similar to Figure 9

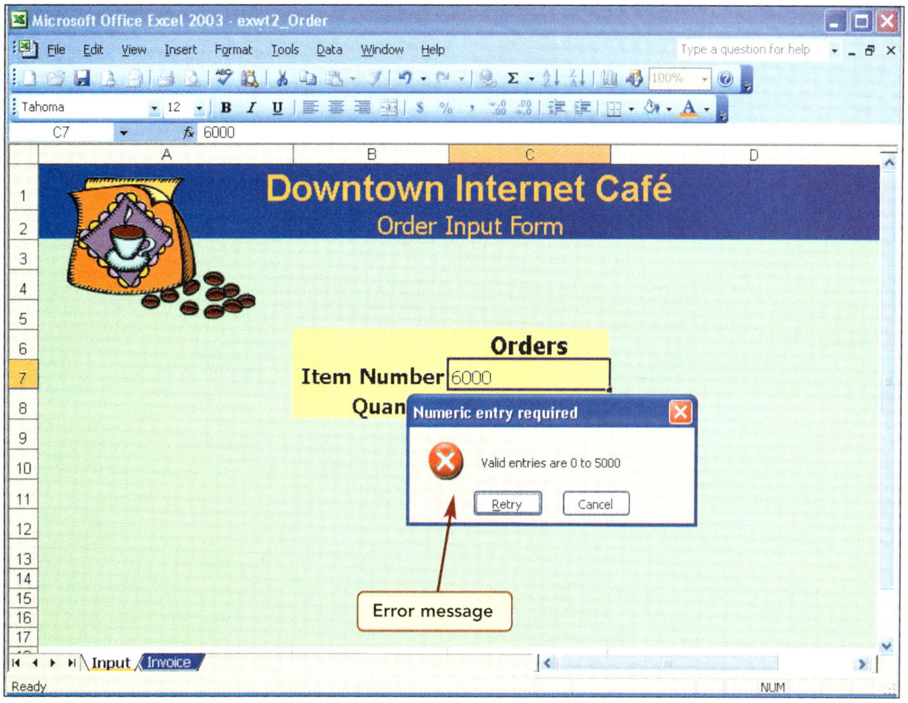

Figure 9

Because the value you entered was greater than 5000, the error message is displayed. You will enter an alphabetic entry next and finally a correct entry.

2 **Click Retry.**

- **Type cocoa and press ←Enter.**
- **Click Retry.**
- **Type 4000 and press ←Enter.**

Your screen should be similar to Figure 10

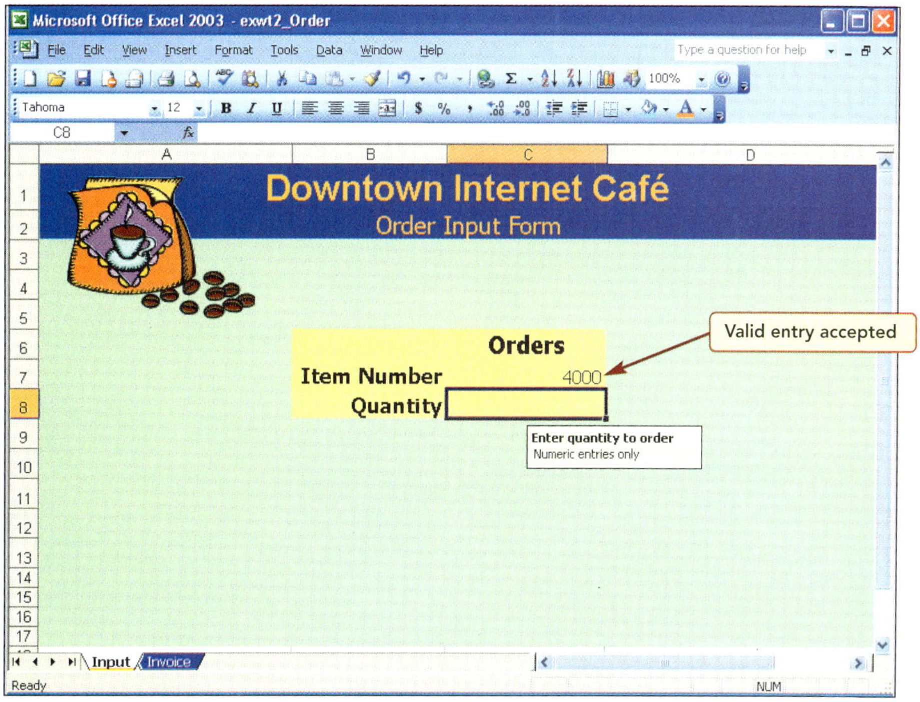

Figure 10

The entry of 4000 is accepted. Next, you will try out the Quantity field validation settings.

3 Type **0** in cell C8 and press ←Enter.

Click Retry.

Type **-10** and press ←Enter.

Click Retry.

Type **10** and press ←Enter.

Your screen should be similar to Figure 11

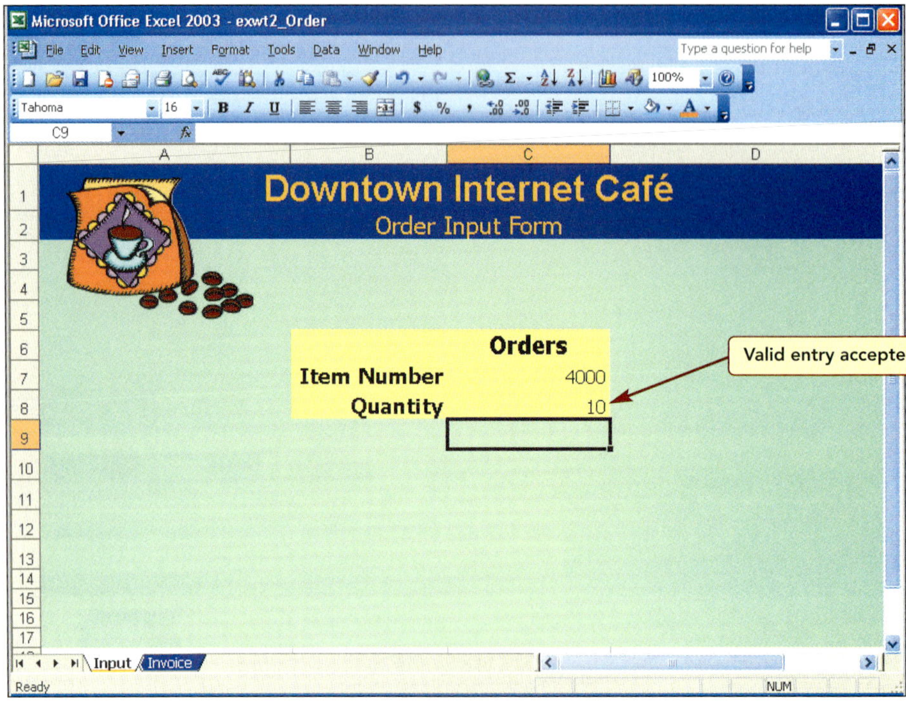

Figure 11

Each time you entered an invalid entry, the error message was displayed.

Naming Cells and Protecting the Sheet

Next, you will name the input cells so that you can use the names instead of the cell references in the macro code you will write.

1 Select B7 through C8.

Choose Insert/Name/Create/ OK.

Select C7 through C8 and name the range **Orders**.

Move to cell C7.

Your screen should be similar to Figure 12

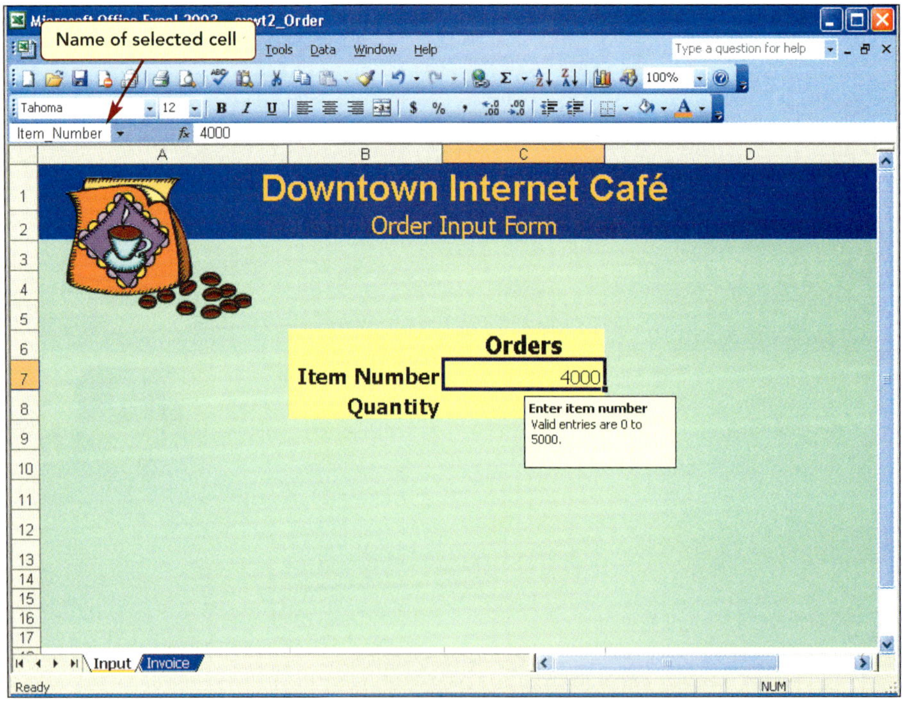

Figure 12

The cell name appears in the Name box instead of the cell address. The last thing you want to do before writing the macro is to restrict data entry to only cells C7 and C8 by unlocking these cells, and protecting all other cells in the worksheet.

2

- **Select C7 through C8 and unlock them.**
- **Protect the worksheet.**

Having Trouble?

Use Format/Cells/Protection/Locked to unlock the cells and Tools/Protection/Protect Sheet to protect the worksheet.

- **Delete the values in cells C7 and C8.**
- **Save the workbook as Order Invoice.**

Additional Information

If you enter a password, you will need to remember it to make any changes to the worksheet.

All cells except cells C7 and C8 are locked and the entire worksheet is protected.

Creating a Macro Using the Visual Basic Editor

Now you are ready to create a macro to copy the input data to the Invoice worksheet. When you want a worksheet to do something that cannot be recorded using the Macro Recorder, you enter the macro statements directly using the Visual Basic Editor window.

The **Visual Basic Editor** is an application used to write and edit macros attached to Excel workbooks. Although Visual Basic is a programming language, you can enter information into the Visual Basic Editor just as you would in a word processor—by typing to enter text, pressing ←Enter to end a line, using the arrow keys to move around the screen, and pressing Delete and Backspace to remove and correct text.

The types of information you enter into the Visual Basic Editor are called statements. A **statement** is a complete instruction that tells Excel to execute a specific task. A series of statements is a **Sub procedure**. A Sub procedure begins with a statement that starts the macro (such as when a command button is pressed) and ends with one that closes the macro (an End Sub statement). Sub procedures can also include remarks about the macro (such as its name and purpose) and functions (such as returning values to the procedure).

The syntax of a Sub procedure statement is as follows:

Object ("x").Property

The **object** is the item that the statement will affect (such as a cell, cell range, worksheet, or workbook). The object is enclosed in parentheses and surrounded by quotes. The **property** is the action you want to perform on the object. The property consists of words that have special meaning, called **reserved words**, that direct Excel to perform the specified action.

The object is separated from the property by a period. For example, the statement to tell Excel to select the range C2 through C10 is:

```
Range("C2:C10").Select
```

Planning the Macro

It is very important to plan a macro before creating it to ensure that the Visual Basic statements are in the exact order in which you want them to be executed. It is often helpful to write out the macro steps and then try them out manually in Excel before entering them in the Visual Basic Editor. The steps you want this macro to perform and the macro statements that will perform these actions are shown in the following table:

Step	Action	Macro Statement
1	Create variables.	**Dim strRange1 As String** **Dim strRange2 As String**
2	Check to see if the Quantity is greater than zero.	**If Range ("Quantity").Value > 0 Then**
3	Increase the row number by one in the Invoice worksheet where the data will be copied.	**intRow = intRow + 1**
4	Assign values to the two variables to hold the next available cell in column B and C.	**strRange1 = "B" & intRow** **strRange2 = "C" & intRow**
5	Take the data from cell C7 (Item Number) and place it in the next available row in column B of the Invoice sheet.	**Worksheets("Invoice").Range(strRange 1) = Range("Item_Number").Value**
6	Take the data from cell C8 (Quantity) and place it in the next available row in column C of the Invoice sheet.	**Worksheets("Invoice").Range(strRange 2) = Range("Quantity").Value**
7	Select cells C7 and C8 (Orders range) of the Input worksheet.	**Range("Orders").Select**
8	Delete the data from the Orders range.	**Selection.ClearContents**
9	Move back to cell C7 (Item Number range)	**Worksheets("Input").Range ("Item_Number").Select**

Entering the Macro Statements

Now you are ready to start the Visual Basic Editor and create the macro.

1 • **Choose Tools/Macro/Visual Basic Editor.**

Another Method

The keyboard shortcut is Alt + F11.

• **If necessary, click Project Explorer to display the Project Explorer task pane.**

• **Double-click on the Sheet1 (Input) item in the Project task pane.**

Another Method

The menu equivalent is View/Project Explorer.

Your screen should be similar to Figure 13

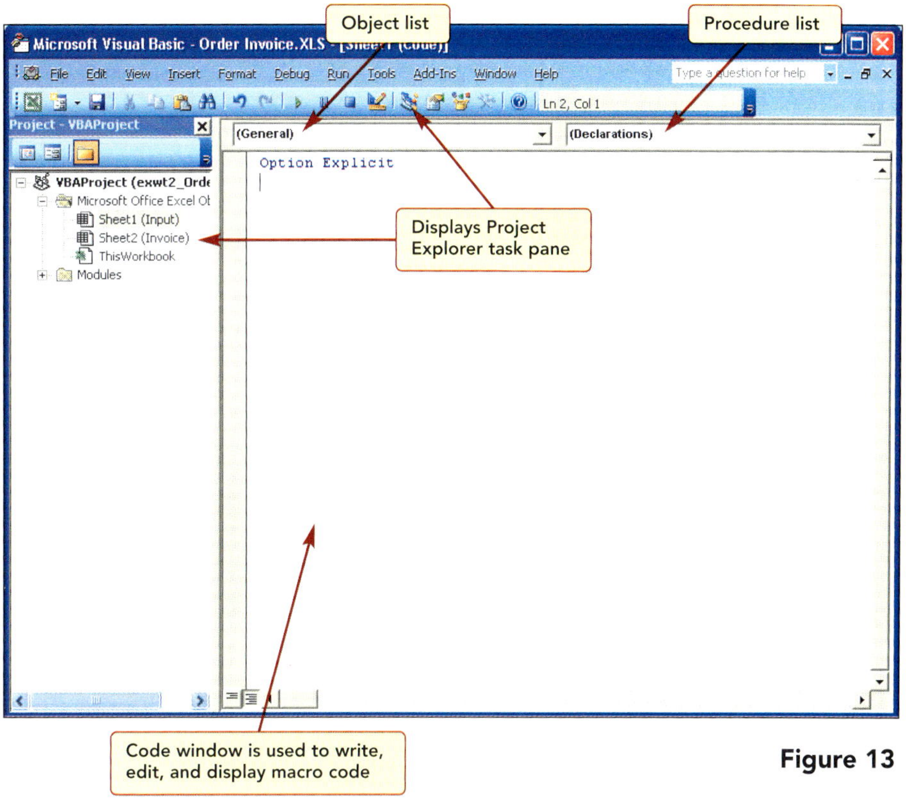

Figure 13

Having Trouble?

If Option Explicit is not displayed, choose Tools/Options and open the Editor tab. If necessary, select Require Variable Declaration to turn on this feature.

The Code window is used to write, display, and edit the macro statements or code. The Project Explorer task pane is used to select objects, such as the different worksheets, in order to see the macro code that has been written for that object. In this case, the Sheet1 object is selected and the Code window is blank, except for the words Option Explicit, because you have not written any macro statements yet in that worksheet. Option Explicit indicates that a feature that advises you of errors as you specify variables is on. At the top of the Code window are two drop-down lists that are used to create Sub procedures. The left is the Object list and the right is the Procedure list.

Statements in a macro are written inside a Sub procedure. To open the Sub procedure, you first select the object or element of an application from the Object drop-down list box, which by default displays "(General)." In this case, the object will be a worksheet. Then you select the procedure that will trigger the macro from the Procedure drop-down list box, which by default displays "(Declarations)." A **procedure** is a named sequence of statements that are executed as a unit and tell the macro how to perform a task. All macro code must be contained in a procedure. You will use the Change procedure, which is used to change data in the selected object.

2 Choose Worksheet from the Object drop-down list.

Choose Change from the Procedure drop down list.

Your screen should be similar to Figure 14

Additional Information

Do not be concerned about the extra procedure for the Selection Change procedure. When you save the macro, this extra procedure will be deleted.

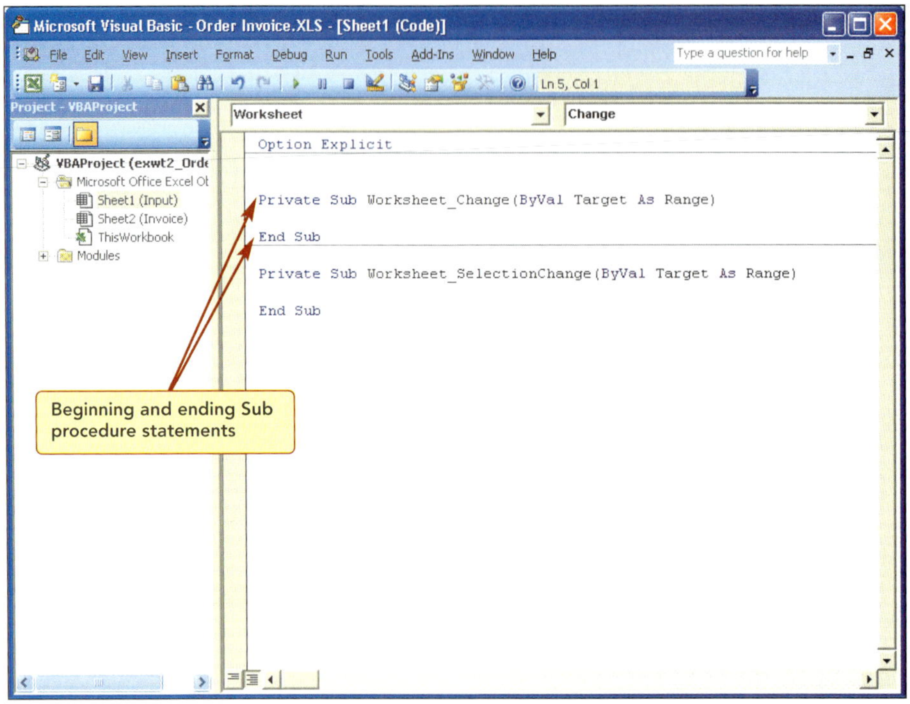

Figure 14

Additional Information

"Sub" is an abbreviation for "Sub procedure."

The Sub and End Sub statements for the Change procedure are entered automatically. You will enter the macro statements between the Sub statements. First, however, you want to include several remark statements that describe the macro and include overall procedural documentation. Remark statements always begin with an apostrophe, which tells Excel to ignore the information on that line.

3 Enter a blank line above the first Private Sub line in the window.

Type **'Data Entry Macro** on the newly inserted blank line.

Press ←Enter.

Having Trouble?

If you forgot to enter the apostrophe, a Compile error message is displayed. Click OK to clear the message and edit the line.

Your screen should be similar to Figure 15

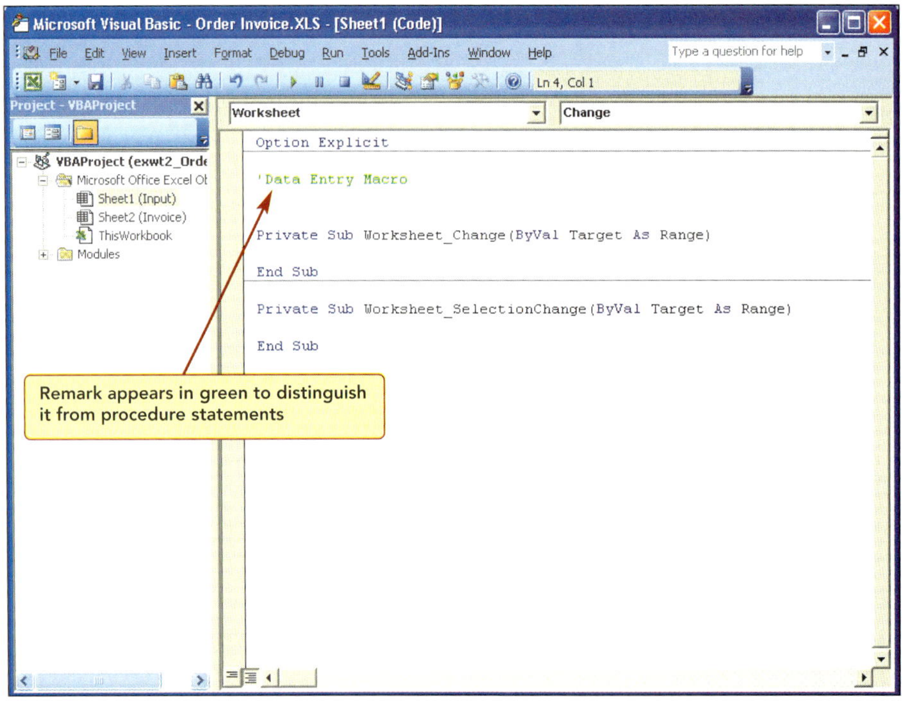

Figure 15

Remark lines generally appear in green type to distinguish them from the procedure statements.

4 **In the same manner, enter the following three additional remarks:**

'Created by your name - today's date

'Runs: When user enters data on the Input worksheet.

'Purpose: To simplify data entry and create order invoice.

Having Trouble?

Remember to begin each remark statement with an apostrophe and press ←Enter to move to the next line.

Your screen should be similar to Figure 16

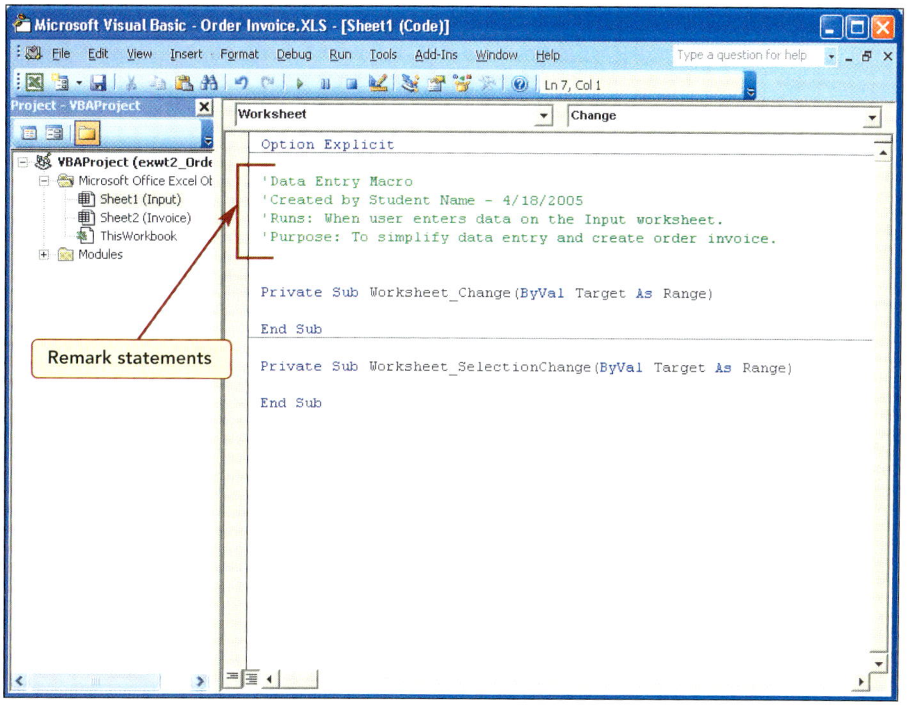

Figure 16

Next, you will enter the Sub procedure statements. To differentiate the Sub statements from the rest of the code, you should indent them using Tab. Once you indent the first Sub statement line, the subsequent lines are automatically indented the same number of spaces. As you are typing, the Visual Basic Editor displays a list of acceptable statement properties. You can select the property you want from the list or continue typing it yourself. The first two statements will create the variable. **Variables** are storage locations in memory that hold information. In this case, the variables will hold the current cell references in the second worksheet. They are called a **string**, which means they consist of both letters and numbers.

5 **Move the insertion point to the blank line between the Private Sub and End Sub statements of the Worksheet_Change procedure.**

- **Press** Tab.
- **Type Dim strRange1 As String.**
- **Press** ←Enter.

Having Trouble?

If a Visual Basic statement is not entered using the correct syntax, an error message box is displayed and the error is identified in red. You must correct the error before you can move to the next line.

Your screen should be similar to Figure 17

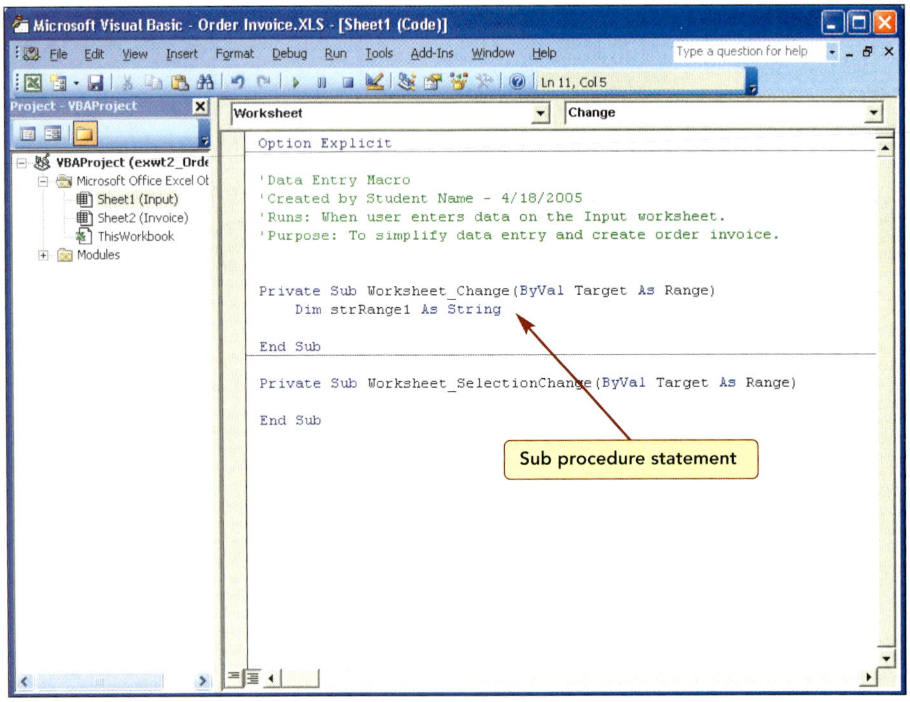

Figure 17

You will continue entering the Visual Basic statements. To save time, you can copy statements with common elements and then edit them. You can also type cell references and reserved words in lowercase and they will be automatically capitalized. In addition, any extra spaces will be removed.

6 **In the same manner, enter the following Sub statements, each on separate lines:**

Dim strRange2 As String

If Range ("Quantity").Value > 0 Then

Press Tab.

intRow = intRow + 1

strRange1 = "B" & intRow

strRange2 = "C" & intRow

Worksheets("Invoice").Range(strRange1) = Range("Item_Number").Value

Worksheets("Invoice").Range(strRange2) = Range("Quantity").Value

Range("Orders").Select

Selection.ClearContents

Worksheets("Input").Range("Item_Number").Select

End If

Your screen should be similar to Figure 18

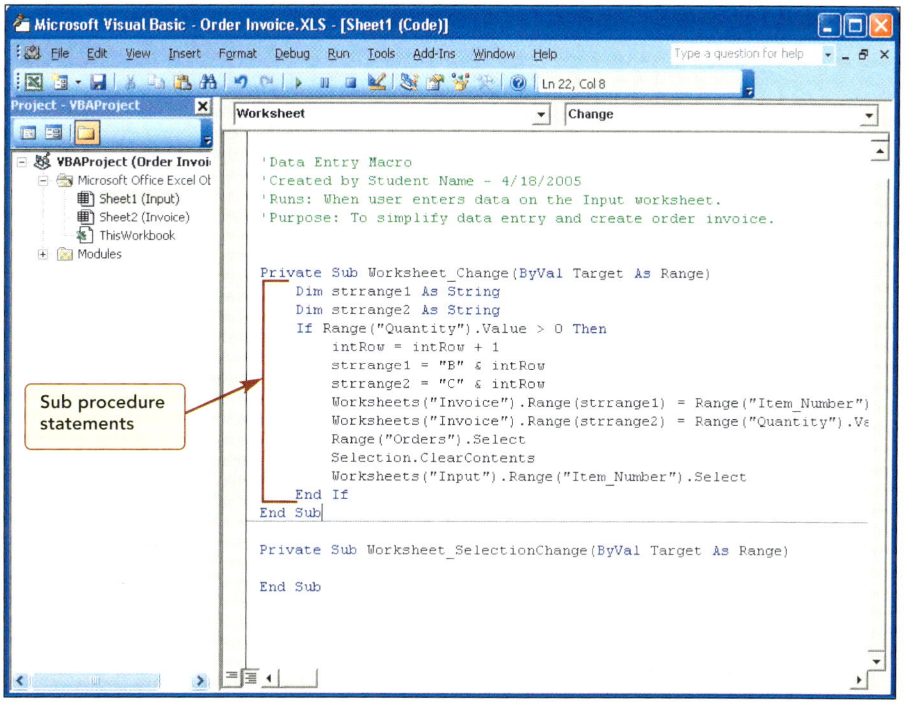

Figure 18

You are finished creating the macro. You will print the code, then close the Visual Basic window and return to the worksheet to try out the macro. Before testing a new macro, it is a good idea to save the workbook file first in case the macro performs some unexpected actions.

7 Print the code.

- Click Close in the title bar of the Visual Basic window.

Another Method

The menu equivalent is File/Close and Return to Microsoft Excel. The keyboard shortcut is Alt + Q.

- If necessary, maximize the Excel window.
- Save the workbook.

Your screen should be similar to Figure 19

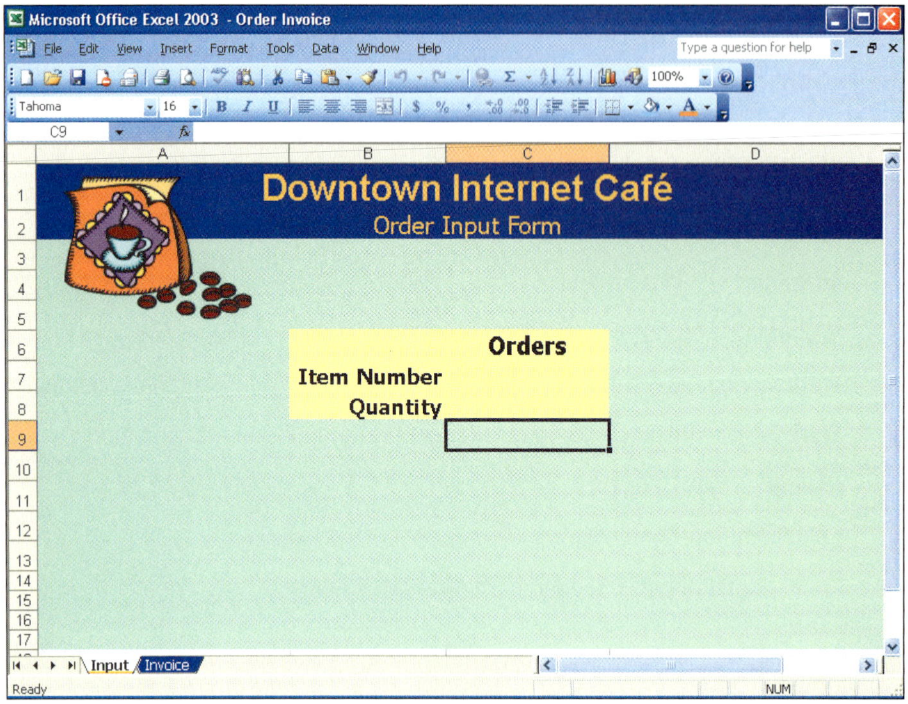

Figure 19

Testing the Macro

The next step is to test the macro by entering some data to run it. You will enter orders for Guatemala coffee and Kona coffee.

1 Type **3522** in cell C7.

- Press ←Enter.
- Enter **25** in cell C8.
- Enter **3527** in cell C7.
- Enter **12** in cell C8.

Additional Information

You can interrupt the execution of a macro at any time by pressing Esc.

Your screen should be similar to Figure 20

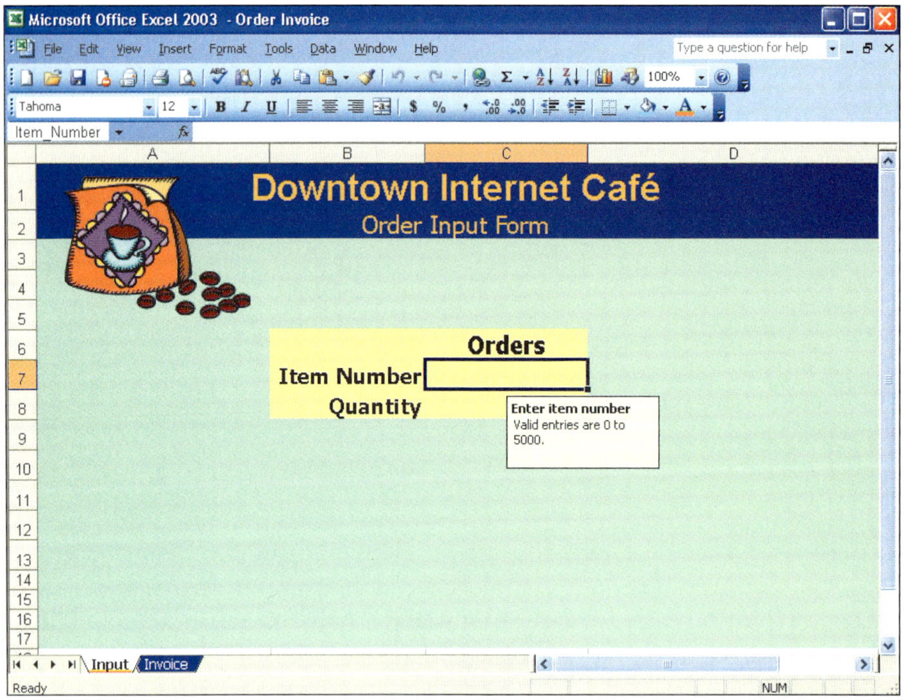

Figure 20

Having Trouble?

If your macro did not run correctly, you will need to correct any statement errors.

As you complete the Item Number entry, it is displayed in the appropriate worksheet cell. But as soon as you complete the data in the Quantity cell, the data in both cells is cleared. Now, you want to see what is happening on the Invoice worksheet.

2 **Display the Invoice sheet.**

Your screen should be similar to Figure 21

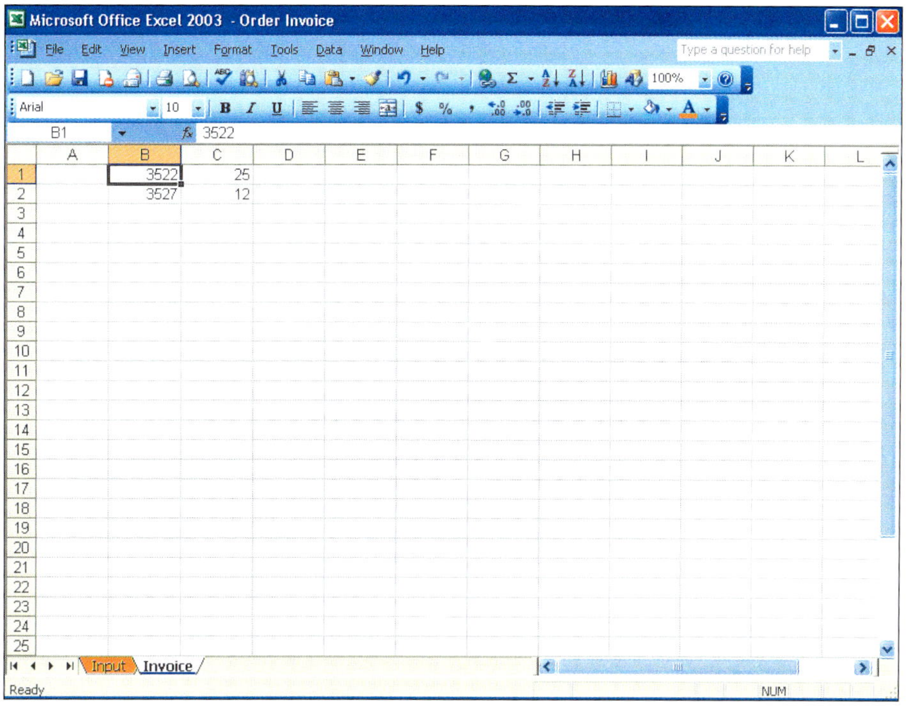

Figure 21

Additional Information

You will create another macro to improve the appearance of the invoice in Step-by-Step exercise 3.

The Invoice worksheet displays the data you entered in one column on the Input worksheet as two columns of data. As you continue to enter the order, the Invoice worksheet will expand to display each item ordered as it is entered.

3 **Save the worksheet again.**

Close Excel.

lab review

WORKING TOGETHER 2

Importing Access Data and Using the Visual Basic Editor

key terms

export EXWT2.2
external data EXWT2.2
import EXWT2.2
object EXWT2.11
property EXWT2.11
reserved word EXWT2.11
statement EXWT2.11
string EXWT2.15
Sub procedure EXWT2.11
variable EXWT2.15
Visual Basic Editor EXWT2.11

command summary

Command	Shortcut Keys	Button	Action
Tools/Macro/Visual Basic Editor	Alt + F11		Opens the Visual Basic Editor window
Data/Import External Data/ Import Data			Imports data from an external source into a worksheet
Data/Validation			Sets limits for data entered in a cell
Visual Basic Editor			
File/Close and Return	Alt + Q		Closes the Visual Basic Editor window and returns to active Excel worksheet
View/Project Explorer			Opens the Project task pane

rating system

★ Easy

★★ Moderate

★★★ Difficult

step-by-step

Decorator's Resource Gallery ★

1. Alice works at the Decorator's Resource Gallery. An invoice for a garden-themed office has arrived. The decorator has requested the prints all be by the same artist. Alice believes Williams prints will be ideal. She needs to find out the number of prints by Williams in stock. To do this, she plans to use the information in the Access Gallery Database file and analyze it using Excel.

Student Name 12/14/2005

Decorator's Resource Gallery: Artist Inventory				
ID	Artist	Title	Vendor	Stock
2	Bassett	Meadow Walk	Art Galore	22
7	Bassett	Botanical	Apple Farms Print Co.	9
10	Bassett	Hudson River	Concord Gallery Catalogue	24
15	Bassett	English Garden	Augusta Prints	5
16	Bassett	Quiet Respite	Art Galore	16
20	Bassett	Wild Flower	Art Galore	9
23	Bassett	Botanical II	Concord Gallery Catalogue	56
			Total in Stock	141

a. Open a blank workbook in Excel.

b. Import the Vendor table from the exwt2_Decorator's Resource Gallery file.

c. Filter the list to display the artist Bassett only.

d. Total the Stock column. Include a label for the total value. Add the title **Decorator's Resource Gallery: Artist Inventory** above the data. Apply formatting of your choice.

e. Save the workbook as Artist Inventory.

f. Include your name and the date in a header. Print the filtered list.

g. Remove the filter and close the file.

Currency Exchange Calculator ★★

2. You work for Johnson & Scannell, an investment company that handles a lot of foreign accounts. As a result, the company does a lot of currency exchanging and you would like to create a worksheet that will help employees quickly calculate the conversion. You have already created a worksheet that has the calculations for U.S. dollars to Canadian dollars. So that the worksheet works for any type of foreign currency, you will create a command button to ask the user to input the country's currency, the current exchange rate, and the U.S. dollar amount. The completed Exchange Rate worksheet and Visual Basic code window will be similar to the ones shown here.

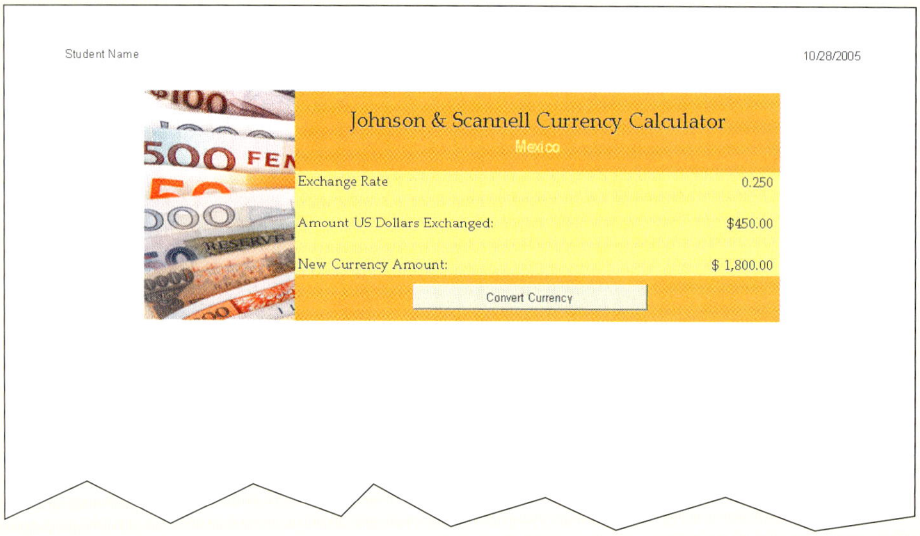

   a. Open the Excel workbook file exwt2_Currency Exchange. Open the Control Toolbox toolbar and create a command button positioned as shown in the example. Edit the command button to display the words **Convert Currency**.

   b. Start the Visual Basic Editor to create the Command Button macro.

   c. Enter the following remarks above the Sub procedure header:

      'Used to calculate US dollars to a different currency

      'Written by [Student Name]

      'Last Modified [Current Date]

      'Run from Currency worksheet by clicking the Convert Currency button

      'User enters the country, exchange rate from US dollars, and the amount of US currency to change

   d. Inside the Sub and End Sub statements enter the following:

      Sheets("Currency").Select

      Range("B3,C5,C7").Select

      Selection.ClearContents

      Range("B3").Value = InputBox("What country's currency?", "Enter")

      Range("C5").Value = InputBox("What is today's exchange rate from dollars?", "Enter")

      Range("C7").Value = InputBox("How much US money do you want to exchange?", "Enter")

      Range("B1").Select

e. Print the text in the Code window and close the Visual Basic window. Exit Design mode and close the Control Toolbox toolbar.

f. If necessary, change your macro security level to medium.

g. Click the command button and enter the following to check the accuracy of your command button. (The calculator should return $803.57.)

Country:	**Australia**
Rate:	**$0.56**
US Money:	**$450.00**

h. Enter your name and the current date in a header and print the worksheet showing the exchange of Mexican pesos.

j. Save the workbook as Currency Converter.

Downtown Internet Café ★ ★ ★

3. You have completed the macro to enter the orders, and would like to count the number of records and total the quantities so that when you print the invoices, you can be sure everything was ordered correctly.

a. Start Excel and open the workbook file Order Invoice that you created in Working Together 2. Be sure to enable the macro if prompted.

b. Enter the following orders using the macro you created.

Item No.	Quantity
1104	55
2000	100
3522	25
3527	45
3520	50

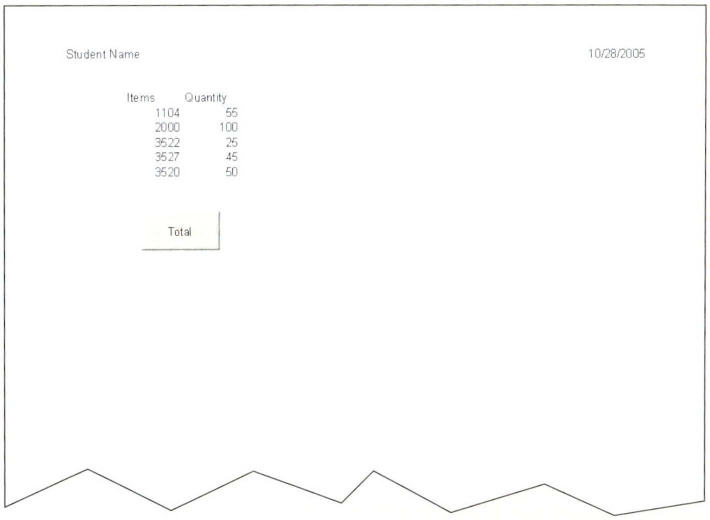

c. Create a command button on the Invoice sheet. Change the button's caption to **Total**.

d. Doubleclick on the button to open the Visual Basic Editor window. You would like the macro to do the following:

- Insert a new row as row 1
- Enter the title "Items" in B1 and "Quantity" in B2
- Name the ranges using the titles
- Ask the user to enter the cell that will contain the Count formula
- Calculate the count
- Ask the user to enter the cell that will contain the Total formula
- Sum the quantities column

e. Enter the following code in the Click Sub procedure:

```
'Used to count and total orders
'Written by [Student Name]
'Last Modified [Current Date]
'Run from Report worksheet by clicking the Total button

'Insert a new row and labels the columns
Selection.EntireRow.Insert
Range("B1").Select
ActiveCell.FormulaR1C1 = "Items"
Range("C1").Select
ActiveCell.FormulaR1C1 = "Quantity"

'Names the ranges using the labels
Range("B1").Select
Range(Selection, Selection.End(xlDown)).Select
Range(Selection, Selection.End(xlToRight)).Select
Selection.CreateNames Top:=True, Left:=False, Bottom:=False, Right:= False

'Asks user for cells to use for formulas and enters the formulas
strTotalRow = InputBox("Please enter the Items count cell", "Count Rows")
Range(strTotalRow).Select
ActiveCell.FormulaR1C1 = "=COUNT(Items)"
strTotalRow = InputBox("Please enter the Quantity total cell", "Total Rows")
Range(strTotalRow).Select
ActiveCell.FormulaR1C1 = "=SUM(Quantity)"
```

f. Save and print the code.

g. Close the Visual Basic Editor.

h. Run the macro by clicking on the command button. Correct any errors.

i. Save the workbook as Order Invoice2 and print the Invoice worksheet with your name and the date in the header.

Command Summary

Command	Shortcut Key	Button	Voice	Action
File/**N**ew	Ctrl + N		New File	Opens a new workbook
File/**O**pen <file name>	Ctrl + O		Open	Opens an existing workbook file
File/**C**lose			Close	Closes open workbook file
File/**S**ave	Ctrl + S		Save	Saves file while using same file name
File/Save **A**s <file name>				Saves current file on disk using a new file name
File/Sen**d** to/**M**ail Recipient				Sends active document to e-mail recipient
File/Page Set**u**p/Margins/**H**orizontally				Centers worksheet horizontally on the page
File/Page Set**u**p/Margins/**V**ertically				Centers worksheet vertically on the page
File/Page Set**u**p/Page/**L**andscape				Changes page orientation to landscape
File/Page Set**u**p/Header/Footer				Adds header and/or footer
File/Page Set**u**p/Sheet/Gridline				Displays/hides gridlines
File/Page Set**u**p/Margins/Horizontal				Horizontally centers contents between margins
File/Page Set**u**p/Page/Fit To				Sizes print area to fit on a specified number of pages
File/Print Pre**v**iew			Print Preview	Displays worksheet as it will appear when printed
File/**P**rint	Ctrl + P		Print	Prints a worksheet
File/**P**rint/**E**ntire Workbook				Prints all sheets in a workbook
File/Propert**i**es				Displays information about a file
File/Propert**i**es/Summary				Specifies information to document a file
File/Save as Web Pa**g**e				Saves worksheet as a Web page
File/We**b** Page Preview				Previews workbook as a Web page in browser

Command	Shortcut Key	Button	Voice	Action
File/E**x**it				Exits the file
Edit/**U**ndo	Ctrl + Z		Undo	Undoes last editing or formatting change
Edit/**R**edo	Ctrl + Y		Redo	Restores changes after using Undo
Edit/Cu**t**	Ctrl + X		Cut	Cuts selected data from document
Edit/**C**opy	Ctrl + C		Copy	Copies selected data to System Clipboard
Edit/Office Clip**b**oard				Displays Office Clipboard task pane
Edit/**P**aste	Ctrl + V		Paste	Pastes selections stored in System Clipboard
Edit/Paste **S**pecial				Inserts object as an embedded object
Edit/Lin**k**s				Modifies selected link
Edit/F**i**ll				Fills selected cells with contents of source cell
Edit/Cle**a**r/Co**m**ments	Delete		Delete	Deletes comment in selected cell
Edit/De**l**ete Sheet				Deletes the entire sheet
Edit/**D**elete Cells/Shift Cells Left				Deletes selected cells and shifts remaining cells to left
Edit/**D**elete Cells/Shift Cells Up				Deletes selected cells and shifts remaining cells up
Edit/**M**ove or Copy Sheet				Moves or copies selected sheet
Edit/**F**ind	Ctrl + F			Searches entire worksheet for specified text, numbers, and/or formats
Edit/R**e**place	Ctrl + H			Finds specified characters or formats and replaces them with the specified replacement characters or format
Edit/**G**o To	Ctrl + G			Goes to a specified cell location in worksheet
View/**N**ormal		Normal View		Changes view of window back to Normal
View/**P**age Break Preview				Displays worksheet in page break preview
View/Tas**k** Pane	Ctrl + F1		Task Pane	Displays or hides task pane
View/**Z**oom		100%	Zoom	Changes magnification of window

Command	Shortcut Key	Button	Voice	Action
Insert/C**e**lls/Shift Cells Ri**g**ht				Moves existing cells to right when new cells are inserted
Insert/C**e**lls/Shift Cells **D**own				Moves existing cells down when new cells are inserted
Insert/Cut C**e**lls				Inserts cut cells into a table
Insert/Copied C**e**lls				Inserts row and copies text from Clipboard
Insert/**N**ame/**D**efine				Assigns a name you specify to a cell or range of cells
Insert/**N**ame/**P**aste				Places selected range name in formula bar or lists names in worksheet
Insert/**N**ame/**C**reate				Creates a range name using text in cells
Insert/Co**m**ment				Inserts a new comment in selected cell
Insert/**E**dit Comment				Edits comment in selected cell
Insert/**R**ows				Inserts a blank row
Insert/**C**olumns				Inserts a blank column
Insert/**C**hart			Chart Wizard	Starts the Chart Wizard
Insert/Remove Page **B**reak				Removes page break
Insert/**P**icture/**C**lip Art			Insert clip art	Inserts a selected graphic from Clip Organizer and Microsoft's Clip Art and Media Web site
Insert/**P**icture/**F**rom File				Inserts a picture from a file
Insert/**O**bject				Inserts objects of different types
Insert/**W**orksheet				Inserts a new worksheet into the workbook
Insert/**F**unction				Inserts a function into a cell
Insert/Dia**g**ram				Inserts a diagram in worksheet
Insert/Hyperl**i**nk	Ctrl + K			Inserts a new hyperlink or modifies selected hyperlink
Insert/Hyperl**i**nk/**R**emove Link				Removes hyperlink settings from selected cell
F**o**rmat/C**e**lls/Number/**C**ategory/Special				Applies selected special format to number entries
F**o**rmat/C**e**lls/Number/Accounting	Ctrl + 1		Currency Style	Applies Accounting format to selection

Command	Shortcut Key	Button	Voice	Action
Format/Cells/Number/Date	Ctrl + 1			Applies Date format to selection
Format/Cells/Number/Percent	Ctrl + 1		Percent Style	Applies Percent format to selection
Format/Cells/Number/Decimal	Ctrl + 1		Increase Decimal Decrease Decimal	Increases or decreases number of decimal places associated with a number value
Format/Cells/Protection/Locked				Toggles between locking and unlocking a cell
Format/Cells/Alignment/Horizontal/Left (Indent)			Left	Left-aligns entry in cell
Format/Cells/Alignment/Horizontal/Center			Center	Center-aligns entry in cell
Format/Cells/Alignment/Horizontal/Right			Right	Right-aligns entry in cell
Format/Cells/Alignment/Indent				Indents cell entry
Format/Cells/Alignment/Horizontal/Center Across Selection/Merge Cells				Centers cell contents across selected cells and combines cells
Format/Cells/Font/Font			Font	Changes text font
Format/Cells/Font/Size			Font Size	Changes text size
Format/Cells/Font/Font Style/Bold	Ctrl + B		Bold	Bolds selected text
Format/Cells/Font/Font Style/Italic	Ctrl + I		Italic	Italicizes selected text
Format/Cells/Font/Underline/Single	Ctrl + U		Underline	Underlines selected text
Format/Cells/Font/Color			Font Color	Adds color to text
Format/Cells/Patterns/Color			Fill Color	Adds color to cell background
Format/Row/Height				Changes height of selected row
Format/Row/Hide				Hides selected rows
Format/Row/Unhide				Displays rows that were previously hidden
Format/AutoFormat				Applies selected format to range
Format/Column/Width				Changes width of column
Format/Column/AutoFit Selection				Changes column width to match widest cell entry
Format/Sheet/Background				Adds background to worksheet
Format/Sheet/Hide				Hides selected sheets

Command	Shortcut Key	Button	Voice	Action
Format/Sheet/Unhide				Unhides selected sheet
Format/Sheet/Rename				Renames sheet
Format/Sheet/Tab Color				Changes color of sheet tabs
Format/Style				Applies selected style to selection
Format/Style/Percent			Percent Style	Changes number to percentage
Format/Selected Chart Title	Ctrl + 1			Changes format of selected chart title
Format/Selected Data Series	Ctrl + 1			Changes format of selected data series
Tools/Spelling	F7		Spelling	Spell-checks worksheet
Tools/Error Checking				Checks worksheet for formula errors
Tools/Goal Seek				Adjusts value in specified cell until a formula dependent on that cell reaches specified result
Tools/Macro/Macros	Alt + F8			Runs, edits, or deletes selected macro
Tools/Macro/Record New Macro				Records a series of actions as a macro
Tools/Macro/Stop Recording				Stops the recording of a macro
Tools/Macro/ Security				Sets security level associated with macros in a workbook
Tools/Macro/Visual Basic Editor	Alt + F11			Opens the Visual Basic Editor window
Tools/Protection/Protect Sheet				Prevents unauthorized users from changing a worksheet's contents
Tools/Protection/ Unprotect Sheet				Unprotects worksheet and allows modification of contents
Tools/Scenarios				Starts scenario manager tool to create sets of data for what-if analysis
Tools/Solver				Starts Solver tool to perform what-if-analysis
Tools/Autocorrect Options				Turns on/off AutoCorrect features entered in a cell
Tools/Add-Ins/Solver Add-In				Adds Solver tool to menu
Tools/Formula Auditing/ Show Watch Window				Opens Watch Window toolbar

Command	Shortcut Key	Button	Voice	Action
Tools/Options/View/ Comment Indicator only				Displays comment indicators
Tools/Customize/Options				Changes settings associated with toolbars and menus
Tools/Customize/Options/Show Standard and Formatting Toolbars on two Rows				Shows Standard Toolbar and Formatting Toolbar in two rows
Chart/Chart Type				Chart typeChanges type of chart
Chart/Chart Options				Changes title, legend, and other chart options
Chart/Location				Places chart in selected worksheet or chart sheet
Data/Table				Creates a data table based on specified input values and formulas
Data/Sort				Arranges data alphabetically, numerically, or by date
Data/Filter/AutoFilter				Displays records based on specified criteria
Data/Filter/Show All				Redisplays all records
Data/Form				Displays a data form for record entry and modification
Data/Subtotals				Displays totals for each change in a category
Data/List/Create List	Ctrl + L			Converts a range of data into a list
Data/Import External Data/ Import Data				Imports data from an external source into a worksheet
Data/Validation				Sets limits for data
Window/New Window				Displays a new window
Window/Arrange				Arranges open windows vertically, horizontally, tiled, or cascaded
Window/Hide				Hides current workbook
Window/Unhide				Unhides selected workbook
Window/Freeze Panes				Freezes top and/or leftmost panes
Window/Unfreeze Panes				Unfreezes window panes

Command	Shortcut Key	Button	Voice	Action
Window/Split				Divides window into four panes at active cell
Window/Remove Split				Removes split from active worksheet
File/Exit	Alt + F4			Exits Office Program
View/Comments				Displays all comments
View/Toolbars			View	Hides or displays toolbars
View/Task Pane	Ctrl + F1		Task pane Show task pane View task pane Hide task pane	Hides or displays task pane
Tools/Customize/Options				Changes settings associated with toolbars and menus
Visual Basic Editor				
File/Close and Return	Alt + Q			Closes the Visual Basic Editor window and returns to active Excel worksheet
Tools/Macro/Visual Basic Editor	Alt + F11			Opens the Visual Basic Editor window
View/Project Explorer				

Glossary of Key Terms

3-D reference A reference to the same cell or range on multiple sheets in the same workbook.

absolute link An address with the complete destination path location.

absolute reference A cell or range reference in a formula whose location remains the same (absolute) when copied. Indicated by a $ character entered before the column letter and row number or both.

active cell The cell displaying the cell selector that will be affected by the next entry or procedure.

active sheet A sheet that contains the cell selector and that will be affected by the next action.

active workbook The workbook that contains the cell selector and that will be affected by the next action.

adjacent range A rectangular block of adjoining cells.

adjustable cell In Solver, the cell or cells whose values will be changed in order to attain the value set in the target cell.

alignment The vertical or horizontal placement and orientation of an entry in a cell.

antonym Words with opposite meaning, such as "cheerful" and "sad."

area chart A chart that shows trends by emphasizing the area under the curve.

argument The data used in a function on which the calculation is performed.

attachment A copy of a file that is included with an e-mail message.

AutoCorrect Makes some basic assumptions about the text you are typing and, based on these assumptions, automatically corrects the entry.

AutoFill Feature that logically repeats and extends a series.

AutoFit Used to automatically adjust the width of a column to fit the contents.

AutoFormat A preset design scheme that can be applied to a range of cells or to a diagram.

bar chart Displays data as evenly spaced bars.

bookmark Establishes a link to a specific worksheet location.

browser A program that connects you to remote computers and displays the Web pages you request.

cascade The window arrangement that displays one workbook window on top of another, cascading down from the top of the screen.

category axis Another name for the X axis of a chart.

category-axis title A label that describes the X-axis.

category name A label displayed along the X axis in a chart to identify the data being plotted.

cell The space created by the intersection of a vertical column and a horizontal row.

cell reference The column letter and row number of a cell.

cell selector The heavy border surrounding a cell in the worksheet that identifies the active cell.

character effect A modification to the characters, such as bold or italics, that enhances the appearance of text

chart A visual representation of data in a worksheet.

chart gridlines Lines extending from the axis lines across the plot area that make it easier to read and evaluate the chart data.

chart object One type of graphic object that is created using charting features included in Excel 2003. A chart object can be inserted into a worksheet or into a special chart sheet.

chart title Appears at the top of a chart and is used to describe the contents of the chart.

clip art A collection of graphics that is usually bundled with a software application.

column A vertical block of cells one cell wide in the worksheet.

column chart A chart that represents data as evenly spaced bars.

column letters The border of letters across the top of the worksheet that identifies the columns in the worksheet.

column-oriented In a data table, the orientation of the data in a table down a column as opposed to across a row (row-oriented).

comment Notes attached to cells that can be used to clarify the meaning of the cell contents, provide documention, or ask a question.

constant A value that does not change unless you change it directly by typing in another entry.

control A graphic object that is designed to automate the process of completing information in a worksheet.

copy area The cell or cells containing the data to be copied; also called the source.

criteria A set of limiting conditions that you want records to meet in order to be displayed.

custom dictionary An additional dictionary you create to supplement the main dictionary.

data form A special form that makes it easy to enter records in a list.

data labels A label for a data point or bar that shows the values being plotted on a chart.

data marker Represents a data series on a chart. It can be a symbol, color, or pattern, depending upon the type of chart.

data series The numbers to be charted.

data table A range of cells that is used to quickly calculate multiple what-if versions in one operation and to show the results of all variations together in the worksheet.

database An organized collection of related information consisting of fields and records. Also called a list in Excel.

default Initial program settings.

destination The cell or range of cells that receives the data from the copy area or source; also called the paste area.

destination cell The cell that receives the linked data.

destination file A document in which a linked object is inserted.

destination workbook The linked workbook that receives the data.

diagram A graphic object that can be used to illustrate concepts and to enhance your workbook.

digital signature An electronic encryption-based stamp of authentication.

docked toolbar A toolbar fixed to an edge of the window that displays a vertical bar called the move handle, on the left edge of the toolbar.

Document Map Displays the headings in the document in a separate pane.

document window Large center area of the program window where open application files are displayed.

drawing canvas The area that surrounds an entire diagram and keeps all pieces of the diagram together as a unit.

drawing object An object consisting of shapes such as lines and boxes that can be created using features on the Drawing toolbar.

embed Information inserted into a destination file of another application that becomes part of this file but can be edited within the destination file using the server application.

embedded chart A chart that is inserted into another file.

embedded object Information inserted into a destination file of another application that becomes part of this file but can be edited within the destination file using the server application.

explode To separate a slice of a pie chart slightly from the other slices in the pie.

export To save data in another format so that it can be used in an application other than the application in which it was created.

external data Data that is created in another application.

external reference formula A formula that creates a link between workbooks.

field A single category of data in a list, the values of which appear in a column of a worksheet.

field name A label used to identify the data stored in a field.

file property A setting that is associated with a file, such as the date or author.

fill handle A small black square located in the lower-right corner of the selection that is used to create a series or copy to adjacent cells with a mouse.

filter A restriction placed on records in a database to temporarily isolate a subset of records.

Find and Replace Feature that quickly finds and automatically replaces specific information with new information.

floating toolbar A toolbar that appears in a separate window and can be moved anywhere on the desktop.

font A set of characters with a specific design; also called a typeface.

footer A line (or several lines) of text that appears at the bottom of each page just above the bottom margin.

form A formatted worksheet that is designed to be completed by filling in data in the blank spaces.

format Settings such as font, color, patterns, etc. that affect the display of entries in a worksheet.

Format Painter A feature that applies the formats associated with the current selection to new selections.

Formatting toolbar A toolbar that contains buttons used to change the format of a worksheet.

formula An entry that performs a calculation.

formula bar The bar near the top of the Excel window that displays the cell contents.

freeze panes To fix in place on the screen specified rows or columns or both when scrolling.

function A prewritten formula that performs certain types of calculations automatically.

Goal Seek Tool used to find the value needed in one cell to attain a result you want in another cell.

graphic A non-text element or object, such as a drawing or picture, that can be added to a document.

group Two or more objects that behave as a single object when moved or sized.

header A line (or several lines) of text that appears at the top of each page just below the top margin.

heading Row and column entries that are used to create the structure of the worksheet and describe other worksheet entries.

horizontal The window arrangement that displays one open workbook window above the other.

HTML (Hypertext Markup Language) A programming language whose commands are interpreted by the browser software you are using and which controls how the information on a Web page is displayed.

hyperlink A special type of link that provides a shortcut or jump to another location in the same or a different workbook, to a document in a different application, to a Web site, or to an e-mail address.

IF function A function that checks that certain conditions are met and takes action based on the check.

import To bring in external data for use in a worksheet.

input cell A cell in which a list of values is substituted to see the resulting effect on the related formulas. Input values can be listed down a row or across a column.

keyword A word or phrase descriptive of a type of graphic.

landscape The orientation of the printed document so that it prints sideways across the length of the page.

legend A brief description of the symbols that represent the data ranges in a chart.

line chart A chart that represents data as a set of points along a line.

link A relationship created between files that allows data in the destination file to be updated automatically when changes occur in the source file.

linked object Information created in a source file from one application and inserted into a destination file of another application while maintaining a link between files.

list An organized collection of related information consisting of files and records. Also called a database.

list range The area of the worksheet containing the records in a list.

live link A linked object that automatically reflects in the destination document any changes made in the source document when the destination document is opened.

logical operator A symbol used in formulas that compares values in two or more cells.

macro A stored series of keystrokes and commands. When the macro is executed or run, the stored actions are performed automatically.

Macro Recorder A tool used to create a macro by recording a series of actions as macro statements as they are performed.

main dictionary The dictionary included with Office 2003.

margin The blank space around the edge of the paper.

menu bar Located below the title bar, this bar displays the application's program menu.

merged cell A cell made up of several selected cells combined into one.

mixed reference A cell address that is part absolute and part relative.

module A series of macro commands stored in Microsoft Visual Basic.

multilevel sort A sort on more than one column or field.

name A description of a cell or range that can be used in place of cell or range references.

Name box The area located on the left side of the formula bar that provides information about the selected item such as the reference of the active cell.

nested function A second argument in a function that is enclosed within its own set of parentheses.

nonadjacent range Cells or ranges that are not adjacent but are included in the same selection.

NOW Function Automatically updates the date and time when a workbook is opened.

nper The argument in the PMT function that is the total number of payments.

number A cell entry that contains any of the digits 0 to 9 and any of the special characters + = ( ) , . / $ % ? =.

number format Affects how numbers look onscreen and when printed.

object An element such as a text box that can be added to a workbook and that can be selected, sized, and moved. In Visual Basic Editor, the object is the item that the statement will affect (such as a cell, cell range, worksheet, or workbook). The object is enclosed in parentheses and surrounded by quotes.

one-variable data table A data table that contains one or more formulas, with each formula referring to one input cell.

operand A value on which a numeric formula performs a calculation.

operator Specifies the type of calculation to be performed.

order of precedence Order in which calculations are performed; can be overridden by the use of parentheses.

page break The location where one printed page ends and another starts.

pane A division of the worksheet window, either horizontal or vertical, through which different areas of the worksheet can be viewed at the same time.

paste area The cells or range of cells that receive the data from the copy area or source; also called the destination.

password A secret code that prevents unauthorized users from turning off protection in a workbook.

picture An illustration such as a scanned photograph.

pie chart A chart that compares parts of the whole. Each value in the data range is a slice of the pie (circle).

plot area The area of the chart bounded by the axes.

PMT function Calculates a periodic function on a loan.

point Measure used for height of type; one point equals 1/72 inch.

portrait The orientation of the printed document so that it prints across the width of the page.

principal The amount of a loan.

print area The area that is highlighted and where a page break shows where the selected range will print on a page.

property In Visual Basic Editor, the property is the action you want to perform on the object. It consists of reserved words that have special meaning and direct Excel to perform the specified action.

protection A worksheet feature that prevents users from making changes to data and formats.

pv The argument in the PMT function that is the amount of the loan, also called the principal.

range A selection consisting of two or more cells in a worksheet.

range reference Identifies the cells in a range.

rate The argument that is the interest rate of the loan in the PMT function.

recalculation A feature that, when a number in a referenced cell in a formula changes, automatically recomputes all formulas that are dependent on the changed value.

record A row of a database or list consisting of a group of related fields.

relative link Workbook link that will locate the destination workbook file relative to the location of the current workbook file.

relative reference A cell or range reference that automatically adjusts to the new location in the worksheet when the formula is copied.

reserved word Words stored in macro properties that direct Excel to perform specified actions.

row A horizontal block of cells one cell high in the worksheet.

row numbers The border of numbers along the left side of the worksheet that identifies the rows in the worksheet.

row-oriented In a data table, the orientation of the data in a table across a row as opposed to down a column (column-oriented).

sans serif A font, such as Arial or Helvetica, that does not have a flair at the base of each letter.

scenario A named set of input values that you can substitute in a worksheet to see the effects of a possible alternative course of action.

scroll bar Used with a mouse to bring additional lines of information into view in a window.

selection cursor A colored highlight bar that appears over the selected command.

serial value The way Excel stores dates, with each day numbered from the beginning of the century.

series formula A formula that links a chart object to the source worksheet.

serif A font, such as Times New Roman, that has a flair at the base of each letter.

sheet Used to display different types of information in Excel, including charts. The primary sheets are worksheets and chart sheets.

sheet name A descriptive name that you create to help identify the contents of the sheet.

sheet reference Used in references to other worksheets. Consists of the name of the sheet enclosed in quotes and separated from the cell reference by an exclamation point.

sheet tab On the bottom of the workbook window, the tabs where the sheet names appear.

shortcut menu By right clicking on an item, this menu displays only the options pertaining to that item.

size The height and width of a character in a font, commonly measured in points, abbreviated pt.

sizing handle Box used to size a selected object.

Solver A tool that is used to perform what-if analysis to determine the effect of changing values in two or more cells, called the adjustable cells, on another cell, called the target cell.

sort To rearrange the records in a list in a specified sequence.

source The cell or range of cells containing the data to be copied.

source cell The cell or range of cells containing the data you want to copy.

source file The document that stores the data for the linked object.

source program The program in which an object was created.

source workbook The workbook file that supplies linked data.

spelling checker Feature that locates misspelled words and proposes corrections.

split window A feature that allows you to divide a worksheet window into sections.

spreadsheet A rectangular grid of rows and columns used to enter data.

stack The order in which objects are added in layers to the worksheet.

stacked column chart A chart that displays the data values as columns stacked upon each other.

Standard toolbar A toolbar that contains buttons used to complete the most frequently used menu commands.

statement A Visual Basic instruction that tells Excel to execute a specific task.

status bar A bar displayed at the bottom of the document window that advises you of the status of different program conditions and features as you use the program.

style A named combination of formats that can be applied to a selection.

Sub procedure A series of statements in Visual Basic Editor.

synonyms Words with similar meanings, such as "cheerful" and "happy."

syntax Rules of structure for entering functions.

tab scroll buttons Located to the left of the sheet tabs, they are used to scroll sheet tabs right or left.

target cell In Solver, the cell you can set to the value that you want to attain.

task pane A pane that provides quick access to features as you are using them.

template A workbook file that contains predesigned worksheets that can be used as a pattern for creating other similar sheets in new workbooks. It has the .xlt file extension.

text A cell entry that contains text, numbers, or any other special characters.

text box A rectangular object in which you type text.

Thesaurus A reference tool that provides synonyms, antonyms, and related words for a selected word or phrase.

thumbnail A miniature image displayed in the Clip Organizer.

tiled A window arrangement in which open workbook windows are displayed one after the other in succession, across and down the screen.

toolbar Buttons that are mouse shortcuts for many of the menu items.

two-variable data table A data table that uses only one formula that refers to two different input cells, one column-oriented and one row-oriented. The purpose of this table is to show the resulting effect on the formula when the values in both of these cells are changed.

typeface A set of characters with a specific design; also called a font.

Uniform Resource Locator (URL) An address that specifies the location of the destination document.

value axis Y axis of a chart that usually contains numerical values.

value-axis title A label that describes the values on the Y axis.

variable The resulting value of a formula that changes if the data it depends on changes.

vertical The window arrangement in which open workbook windows are displayed side-by-side.

Visual Basic Editor A programming application used to write and edit macros attached to Excel workbooks.

Web page A document that can be used on the World Wide Web (WWW) and is displayed in a browser.

what-if analysis A technique used to evaluate what effect changing one or more values in formulas has on other values in the worksheet.

window arrangement A feature that displays open workbook files in separate windows on the screen, to make it easy to view and work with information in different workbooks.

Wizard An interactive program that guides you through the steps to help you quickly perform many complicated tasks.

workbook The file in which you work and store sheets created in Office Excel 2003.

workbook window A window that displays an open workbook file.

worksheet Similar to a financial spreadsheet in that it is a rectangular grid of rows and columns used to enter data.

X axis The bottom boundary line of a chart.

XML (Extensible Markup Language) Converts a structured file, such as a worksheet, into a text file that follows standard guidelines and can be read by a variety of applications.

Y axis The left boundary line of a chart.

Z axis The left boundary line of a 3-D chart.

Reference 1

Data File List

Supplied/Used	Created/Saved As
Lab 1	
ex01_Forecast1	Forecast
	Forecast1
Step-by-Step	
1. ex01_Animal Housing	Animal Housing Analysis
2. ex01_Activity by Age	Activity by Age2
3. ex01_Poverty Level	Poverty Level2
4. ex01_Entertainment Salaries	Entertainment Salaries2
5. ex01_Pecan Groves Budget	Pecan Groves Budget2
On Your Own	
1.	Class Grades
2.	Personal Budget
3.	Weekly Hours
4.	Phone Analysis
5.	Home Sales Analysis
Lab 2	
Ex02_Cafe Sales	Café Sales Forecast
Ex02_Computer	
Step-by-Step	
1. ex02_Money Data	Teens and Money
ex02_Money	
2. ex02_Email Professors	Email Analysis
ex02_Email	
3. ex02_Adoptions	Adoption Tracking
ex02_Pets	
4. ex02_Soccer	Youth Sports Data
ex02_Volleyball	
5. ex02_Man	Internet Use Comparison
ex02_Woman	
On Your Own	
1. ex02_Job Market	Seminar
2.	Grades
3.	Stocks
4. ex02_Graduate School	Graduate School2
5.	Insurance
Lab 3	
ex03_First Quarter Forecast	Forecast3
ex03_Annual Forecast	Forecast/Annual Forecast

Supplied/Used	Created/Saved As
Step-by-Step	
1. ex03_Ice Cream Shop	Ice Cream Shop2
2. ex03_Animal Angels	Animal Angels2
3. ex03_Thai Tour	Tour Analysis/Thai Tour2
4. ex03_Grade Report	Grade Analysis/Grade Report2
5. ex03_DVD Direct	DVD Direct2
On Your Own	
1. Personal Budget (from Lab 1)	Personal Budget2
2.	College Programs/Art Expenses
3.	Stocks/Stock Analysis
4.	Inventory Tracking
5.	My Business
Working Together 1	
exwt1_Sales Forecast Memo.doc	Sales Forecast Memo.doc
exwt1_Sales Charts	Sales Forecast Linked
exwt1_Second Quarter Memo.doc	Second Quarter Memo.doc
exwt1_Second Quarter	Second Quarter.xml
Step-by-Step	
1. exwt1_Rescue Memo	Rescue Memo Linked
exwt1_Contributions	Contributions2.XML
2. exwt1_Tour Status Report	March Status Report
exwt1_Adventure Travel Status	Adventure Travel Status2.XML
3. exwt1_Home Price Memo	Home Price Memo2
exwt1_Real Estate Prices	
Lab 4	
ex04_Revised Annual Forecast	2005 Forecast
	2006 Forecast
Step-by-Step	
1. ex04_IronWorks Income	IronWorks Income1
	IronWorks Income (template)
2. ex04_Art Department	Art Department
3. ex04_Travel Analysis	Air Revenue Analysis
	ATT Projected Income (template)
4. ex04_Book Ends	Book Ends 2005
ex04_Book Ends 2004	Book Ends Analysis Template
5. ex04_ARF Contributions	ARF Contributions Reviewed
	ARF Analysis Template
On Your Own	
1.	Video Game Projections
2.	Spring Break Analysis
3.	Expansion Projections
4.	Stock Analysis
5.	New Car Loan
	Loan Analysis Template
Lab 5	
ex05_Loan Analysis	Loan Analysis
ex05_Bonus Dollars	Bonus Dollars
	Monthly Bonus Form

Supplied/Used	Created/Saved As
Step-by-Step	
1. ex05_ARF Volunteers	Volunteers
2. ex05_Electronics Analyzer	Electronics Analyzer
3. ex05_ATT Sales	ATT Sales2
4. ex05_Furniture Sales	Furniture Sales Form
5. ex05_Grades	Gradebook
On Your Own	
1.	My Macros
2.	My 401K
3.	Furniture Loan Analysis
4.	Speeding Fines
5.	Laptop Computers
Lab 6	
ex06_Customer List	
ex06_CustomerList2	Customer List2
ex06_Bonus Dollars Web	March Bonus Dollars
ex06_Cup	
Step-by-Step	
1. ex06_LFC Database	LFC Analysis
2. ex06_Kodiak Database	Kodiak Database Update
3. ex06_Wilson Employees	Wilson Employee Rewards
4. ex06_ATT Client List	ATT Client List2
5. ex06_ARF Inventory	ARF Inventory2
	ARF Inventory Web
On Your Own	
1.	Bradford Suppliers
2.	Toy Inventory
3.	Summer Baseball League
4.	Cleaning Company Customers
5.	Budget Analysis
Working Together 2	
exwt2_Café Supplies.mdb	Café Supplies
exwt2_Order	Order Invoice
Step-by-Step	
1. exwt2_Decorator's Resource Gallery	Artist Inventory
2. exwt2_Currency Exchange	Currency Converter
3. Order Invoice (from EXWT2)	Order Invoice2

Reference 2

Microsoft Office Specialist Skills

Office Excel 2003 Specialist Certification

Reference Number	Skill Sets and Skill Standards	Lab Exercises			
		Lab	Page	Step-By-Step	On Your Own
XL03S-1	**Creating Data and Content**				
XL03S-1-1	Enter and edit cell content	1	1.14	1,2,3,4,5	1,2,3,4,5
		3	3.11,3.20	1,2,3,4,5	1,2,3,4,5
XL03S-1-2	Navigate to specific cell content	3	3.29,3.37	4,5	
XL03S-1-3	Locate, select and insert supporting information	1	1.35	5	
XL03S-1-4	Insert, position and size graphics	2	2.7	1,2,3,4,5	1,2,3,4,5
XL03S-2	**Analyzing Data**				
XL03S-2-1	Filter lists using AutoFilter	6	6.26	1,2,3,4,5	1,2,3,4,5
XL03S-2-2	Sort lists	6	6.21	1,2,3,4,5	1,2,3,4,5
XL03S-2-3	Insert and modify formulas	1	1.47	1,2,3,4,5	1,2,3,4,5
		3	3.6,3.10,3.12	1,2,3,4,5	1,2,3,4,5
XL03S-2-4	Use statistical, date and time, financial, and logical functions	1	1.73	1,2,3,4,5	1,2,3,4,5
		3	3.7	1,2,3,4,5	1,2,3,4,5
XL03S-2-5	Create, modify, and position diagrams and charts based on worksheet data	2	2.15	1,2,3,4,5	1,2,3,4,5
XL03S-3	**Formatting Data and Contents**				
XL03S-3-1	Apply and modify cell formats	1	1.68	1,2,3,4,5	1,2,3,4,5
		3	3.16	1,2,3,4,5	1,2,3,4,5
XL03S-3-2	Apply and modify cell styles	2			
XL03S-3-3	Modify row and column formats	1	1.34,1.58	1,2,3,4,5	1,2,3,4,5
XL03S-3-4	Format worksheets	3	3.18	1,2,3,4,5	1,2,3,4,5
		6	6.36	1,2,3,4,5	1,2,3,4,5
XL03S-4	**Collaborating**				
XL03S-4-1	Insert, view and edit comments				
XL03S-5	**Managing Workbooks**				
XL03S-5-1	Create new workbooks from templates	4	4.18	1,2,3,4,5	1,2,3,4,5
XL03S-5-2	Insert, delete, and move cells	1	1.45,1.57	1,2,3,4,5	1,2,3,4,5
		WT1	1.5,1.10	1,2,3	
XL03S-5-3	Create and modify hyperlinks	6	6.11		1,2,3,4,5
XL03S-5-4	Organize worksheets	3	3.26	1,2,3,4,5	1,2,3,4
XL03S-5-5	Preview data in other views	1	1.74	1,2,3,4,5	1,2,3,4,5
		3	3.52	1,2,3,4,5	1,2,3,4,5
		6	6.35	1,2,3,4,5	1,2,3,4,5
XL03S-5-6	Customize Window layout	3	3.38	1,3,4,5,6	2,3,4
XL03S-5-7	Setup pages for printing	2	2.53	1,3,4,5	2,3,4
		3	3.52	1,2,3,4,5	1,2,3,4,5
XL03S-5-8	Print data	1	1.76	1,2,3,4,5	1,2,3,4,5
		2	2.51	1,2,3,4,5	1,2,3,4,5
		3	3.60	1,2,3,4,5	1,2,3,4,5

Reference Number	Skill Sets and Skill Standards	Lab Exercises			
		Lab	Page	Step-By-Step	On Your Own
XL03S-5-9	Organize worksheets using file folders	3	3.35	3,4	2,3
XL03S-5-10	Save data in appropriate formats for different uses	WT1	1.12	1,2,3	
		6	6.34	4,5	

Index

http://www.unlv.edu/faculty/wrewar/

Section 002